Volume I: Cliffs
How and Why America's Billionaires and the Republican/Libertarian/Tea Party Are Pushing Us Over

CURTIS A. MOORE

DEDICATION

To My Kids, Sarah and Travis, Who Started All This; My Helpmate of 20 Years, Lorraine Giovinazzo; And, Most of All, My Wife, Judith

ACKNOWLEDGMENTS

There are simply too many people to thank by name.
So many helped, and thank you all.

CONTENTS

i

1
INTRODUCTION

This book, *Cliffs I*, is the first of a two volume-set. It asks, but does not answer, the most important question facing my generation of Americans: can democracy survive in this nation?

Mine is the first generation in United States history to leave to its sons and daughters a nation that is poorer than that we received. Over a span of three years, Americans watched the economic progress of almost a generation evaporate.[a] America's middle class is disappearing, dropping from 61 percent of all adults 40 years ago to a bare majority now.[b] For some Americans—white women without a high school diploma—life expectancy dropped by five years between 1990 and 2008.[c]

The United States remains the world's largest economy and its mightiest military force. It is still home to the intellectual forces that gave the world mini-computers, passenger jets, solar electricity, electric vehicles able to out-accelerate Porsche sportsters and arguably the world's best highway system. Yet those are the fruits of decisions made decades ago, before America's rich and its corporations decided to wrest control of the government and society.

---

[a] Jesse Bricker, Arthur B. Kennickell, Kevin B. Moore, and John Sabelhaus "Changes in U.S. Family Finances from 2007 to 2010: Evidence from the Survey of Consumer Finances," *Federal Reserve Bulletin*, June, 2012.

[b] Rebecca Trounson, "Eroding middle class falls to 51%, survey finds," *Los Angeles Times*,, Aug. 23, 2012.

[c] Sabrina Tavernise, "Life Spans Shrink for Least-Educated Whites in the U.S.," *New York Times*, Sept. 20, 2012.

We are now beginning to witness the results of decisions made starting with Ronald Reagan's presidency and the rich who made it possible. In the words of *Time* magazine–

> According to the Organisation for Economic Co-operation and Development (OECD), our 15-year-olds rank 17th in the world in science and 25th in math. We rank 12th among developed countries in college graduation (down from No. 1 for decades). We come in 79th in elementary-school enrollment. Our infrastructure is ranked 23rd in the world, well behind that of every other major advanced economy. American health numbers are stunning for a rich country: based on studies by the OECD and the World Health Organization, we're 27th in life expectancy, 18th in diabetes and first in obesity. Only a few decades ago, the U.S. stood tall in such rankings. No more. There are some areas in which we are still clearly No. 1, but they're not ones we usually brag about. We have the most guns. We have the most crime among rich countries. And, of course, we have by far the largest amount of debt in the world.[d]

This book and its companion volume, *Cliffs II*, started as an attempt to answer questions posed by readers of *Green Gold: Japan, Germany the United States and the Race for Environmental Technology*, which my good friend Alan S. Miller and I wrote nearly twenty years ago. In it, we described technologies that could ignite an American-led technological revolution, ranging from 100 mile-per-gallon cars to zero-polluting ways of generating electricity.

Almost unfailingly we would be asked why, if these and other technological wonders existed, they were not being used. Our explanations, while accurate enough, seemed hollow, like an incompletely told story. The short answer was money. It turns out that the long answer, provided by *Cliffs I*, is also money.

The story is longer and more complicated than I ever expected twenty years ago when the search for answers began. What I found is that there are two societies in America: the one most of us know, and a second, darker one. Its beginning can be traced to the Presidential election of 1964 and the ensuing 16 years during which America's billionaires and corporations quietly but very effectively seized control of history's oldest democracy, America. This required killing the Republican Party,

---

[d] Fareed Zakaria, "Are America's Best Days Behind Us?" *Time*, Mar. 3, 201.

keeping its name alive but replacing it with a political instrument forged to protect property and those who own it.

Americans have had this argument before. Protection of property was consciously excluded from the Declaration of Independence and its protection accorded only a secondary role in the U.S. Constitution. We fought a great Civil War over whether Americans had a right to own one specific kind of property—human slaves—and the result was clear. They do not.

Yet the rich and monied have re-fought this battle time and again, and are doing so again. This time, they may win. They have a powerful political instrument on their side: today's Republican Party and money, immense amounts of it. With these, they quietly killed the Party of Lincoln, placing in its stead the party of Reagan or, more accurately, the party of Koch and Adelson and Scaife and other billionaires.

The death of the Republican Party began on June 18, 1964. Sen. Barry Goldwater, soon to be the Republican nominee for President, announced on the floor of the U.S. Senate that he would oppose the Civil Rights Act of 1964. It would, he said, lead to an "informer" society and a "federal police force of mammoth proportions." These, he said, were the "hallmarks of the police state and landmarks in the destruction of a free society." The next day, June 19th, he and five other Republicans voted against the bill. Thus, racism became the first leg of the modern Republican Party, one that bears no resemblance to the Party founded 160 years ago.

The second leg of the modern Republican party was added at the urging of a then little-known Richmond, Virginia attorney, Lewis F. Powell, Jr. He would be nominated to the U.S. Supreme Court two months later by President Nixon. A very good case can be made, however, that he changed the future of America more with a memo dated August 23, 1971 than with all his Supreme Court decisions combined.

(Although, once on the court, he continued to pursue advancement of the Manifesto in cases. He secured, for example, a 5–4 decision in *First National Bank of Boston V. Bellotti* that led directly and almost inevitably to the 2010 *Citizens United* case allowing Super PACs and unlimited corporate spending on campaigns.)

Powell, then a corporate lawyer and member of the boards of 11 corporations, wrote a memo at the request of his friend Eugene Sydnor, Jr., of the U.S. Chamber of Commerce. Few now recall that this was a time when students had seized college buildings in protest of the Viet Nam war, which America was losing to disciplined and diminutive men clad in black and wearing sandals cut from used tires. Streets of cities afire were filled with rioting blacks—Nixon rallies, they were wryly called, because of the support they built for him. And the Congress was responding to public demands by enacting new laws to protect blacks, women, workers and the environment.

Powell inventoried all these, concluding that the "American economic system is under broad attack" by "New Leftists and other revolutionaries." Never mind that rivers were catching fire from pollution, young men were being drafted to die in a war that seemed increasingly pointless and Richard Nixon, a *Republican* for heaven's sake, had imposed wage and price controls to save a teetering economy. Powell was correct, of course, the American economic system was under attack—not by leftists and revolutionaries, but American citizens and democracy.

Business, wrote Powell "including the boards of directors' and the top executives of corporations great and small and business organizations at all levels, often have responded—if at all—by appeasement, ineptitude and ignoring the problem." What corporations had to do, he counseled, was open their checkbooks and executive suites to the funding of efforts to solidify their grip on the Republican Party. They did.

Powell's manifesto was distributed to 100,000 members of the U.S. Chamber of Commerce. Corporations quickly ramped up their lobbying and campaign giving, started the Business Roundtable, created executive vice presidents for governmental affairs, and formed political action committees and Washington, D.C.-based, self-styled think tanks. Thus was added not only the second leg of the Republican Party, protection of the rich and the corporations they owned and controlled, but money, massive amounts of it, to fuel the engine of change that the Party was becoming.

One of the checks was written by Colorado beer magnate Joseph Coors to allow Republican operative Paul Weyrich to found what later became known as the Heritage Foundation. He used it as a platform to reach out to religious fundamentalists of all religions, first intervening in a school textbook dispute in Kanawha County, West Virginia.

The man knew how to fan flames. By the time Weyrich finished, one school had been dynamited and two firebombed. Others were damaged by gunfire and vandalism. Two men were wounded by gunfire, and a CBS news crew was roughed up. The houses of children who went to school despite boycotts were stoned and car windows broken. Shots were fired into the car of the president of the Classroom Teachers Association. Minutes after a School Board meeting adjourned, 15 sticks of dynamite were detonated beneath the building's gas meter. One school, Midway Elementary, was hit by a Molotov cocktail and a dynamite bomb.

West Virginia was Weyrich's spring board into the religious movement. Soon, he met in Lynchburg, Virginia where he told Rev. Jerry Falwell that outside the walls was a "moral majority" desperate for leadership. By the year of Regan's election in 1980, conservative Protestants, Jews, and Mormons were firmly wed to support of the Republican Party. Thus was the third leg of the modern Republican Party added.

Still, it was a quarter century later before one of the most important relationships was concreted, and the seeds that Falwell planted came into full bloom. It was June 2004, U.S. President George Bush, on an official trip to the Vatican, met with Vatican Secretary of State Angelo Soldano. He complained that in his re-election campaign push for "values," especially opposition to gay marriage and abortion, "not all American bishops are with me."

Within a week, the president of the bishops conference of the United States, William Gregory, had sent a letter to all American bishops urging them to pressure their respective senators on the issue of gay marriage. This letter was coupled with a memorandum to "offer guidance to U.S. bishops," from the head of the Vatican's Congregation for the Doctrine of the Faith, laying out the principles for denying communion to politicians who "promote legal abortion." The prelate who signed the letter, Cardinal Joseph Ratzinger, is now Pope Benedict XVI.

Bush won the Presidential election and Democrats lost seven of eight Senate seats that had been deemed tossups. In every case, messages from the pulpit, by Catholic priests or bishops and archbishops in their newsletters, that voting for a candidate who supported women's right to choose whether to have an abortion was a "mortal sin," played a pivotal role. Looking closely at all those elections demonstrates that the margin of victory was provided by Catholics, many voting under instruction from the Roman Catholic Church's hierarchy.

Barry Goldwater and what would later become the Republican/ Libertarian/Tea Party had consciously rejected a campaign of moderation. In doing so, he also rejected the moderate wing of the Republican Party—at the time, about 40 percent of its membership. Today, of course, the very term "Republican moderate" is an oxymoron, a species as extinct as the dodo bird or as rare as the prairie chicken.

Yet it was these moderates—men like Abraham Lincoln, Teddy Roosevelt and Dwight Eisenhower—who founded the Republican Party and led it to greatness. This was not only the party that freed the slaves and preserved the union, but busted trusts, opened the West, and protected national parks.

One of the finest moments of the Republican Party was in 1964, when 27 Republican Senators cast their votes with Minority Leader Everett Dirksen of Illinois, overcoming for the first time in history a Southern filibuster of civil rights legislation. Majority Leader Mike Mansfield of Montana said it was Dirksen's "finest hour." Dirksen himself declared that "equality of opportunity must prevail if we are to complete the covenant that we have made with the people."

Had there not been a Republican Party, America would not exist today. The United States would have become at least two nations, possibly more. But Lincoln and other Republicans would not allow that to happen, nor would they suffer the enduring evil of slavery. The Republican Party was founded for the express purpose of eliminating slavery altogether if possible and halting its spread at a bare minimum. It turned out that to do this, America had to be preserved as a single nation, so they did. This was not a commitment on the part of one president or even a few individuals, but millions of men and women.

Yes, it was the greatest Republican President, Abraham Lincoln, who freed the slaves. But after his death, other Republicans enshrined the protection of blacks in the 13th, 14th and 15th amendments to the Constitution. A Republican Chief Justice of the U.S. Supreme Court, Earl Warren, oversaw the unanimous 1954 decision 9–0 in *Brown v. Board of Education* desegregating America's schools. Another Republican President, Dwight Eisenhower, dispatched federal troops to Little Rock, Arkansas to assure that black children could walk through the schoolhouse door.

Yet after the enactment of the Civil Rights Act and the nomination of Barry Goldwater, all of that was to change.

Two days after the Senate vote, on June 21, 1964, three civil rights workers, sped through the Mississippi night in their blue Ford station wagon, pursued by Neshoba County Deputy Sheriff Cecil Price. He arrested the three, released them a few hours later into the waiting hands of fellow Ku Klux Klansmen, who beat and shot the three, then bulldozed their bodies into an earthen dam.[e]

---

[e] The Federal Bureau of Investigation arrested 18 men in October 1964 in connection with the murders. Mississippi prosecutors refused to try the killers for the state

(continued...)

Later that year, Goldwater lost in a landslide. He carried only his home state of Arizona and the five Deep South states of Alabama, Georgia, Louisiana, Mississippi and South Carolina, thus creating one of the three legs of the modern Republican Party, racism.

Richard Nixon was no fool. He recognized that if a candidate who advocated battlefield nuclear weapons for generals and sending the Marines into Cuba could carry five states, a candidate who appeared reasonable and moderate could sweep the nation by quietly appealing to racism, using code words. In 1968, having been assured the Republican presidential nomination by the efforts of South Carolina Sen. Strom Thurmond, Nixon ran on racism in the South. It worked so well that in 1972 Nixon emulated Alabama governor George Wallace, and ran on racism everywhere. He won handily.

The move away from democracy accelerated in the mid- to late-1970s under the quiet leadership of Nixon's Secretary of the Treasury William Simon, who guided millions of dollars from the Olin and other foundations into the creation of a "counterintelligensia."[f] His rivers of money combined with others from the Koch brothers, owners of Koch Petroleum and two of the twenty richest individuals in the world; the Coors family of brewing wealth; the Lynde and Harry Bradley Foundation, funded with proceeds from the sale of a family company in 1985 to the Rockwell Corporation for $1.6 billion; the Scaife Foundation, with riches from Gulf Oil and Alcoa Aluminum (and which funded "the Arkansas Project," an aggressive and ultimately fruitless attempt to discredit and unseat President Bill Clinton), to name but a few.

---

[e] (...continued)
crime of murder, claiming lack of evidence.

The federal government nevertheless filed conspiracy charges. Seven men were convicted and sentenced to three to ten years imprisonment, though none served more than six. One man, said to have been the principal organizer of the murders, Edgard Ray "Preacher" Killen was acquitted. The presiding federal judge, William Cox, said, "They killed one nigger, one Jew, and a white man. I gave them all what I thought they deserved." It was 41 years to the day after the murders of James Chaney, Andrew Goodman, and Michael Schwerner, on June 21, 2005, before a Mississippi jury of nine whites and three blacks, that Edgar Ray Killen was found guilty of three counts of manslaughter. The evidence used to convict him was largely what the U.S. government had collected for the federal charges of conspiracy. Had it not been for federal law, it is unlikely that any of the murderers would have been tried for the crime of murder, much less sentenced to jail.

[f] Counterintelligensia can be found to be spelled in different ways. For consistency purposes in this book, we will use the spelling that William E. Simon preferred to use.

With literally billions in cash flowing out of such foundations, Republican operatives established hundreds of organizations that like to call themselves "market oriented" or "free market" or "libertarian" think tanks modeled on university and university-like scholarly centers, but with one crucial difference: the new breed of "scholars" at such organizations is in single-minded pursuit of policies favored by corporations and the rich. They are "front tanks"—neither pure corporate front groups nor legitimate think tanks, but a combination of the two.

Some are general in nature, but many cater to specific elements of the elite. The American Legislative Exchange Council (ALEC) seeks out state legislators and drafts "model" bills to help them. Well, in truth, the bills are drafted by the corporations and foundations that support ALEC.

The Federalist Society caters to lawyers and judges, including justices of the U.S. Supreme Court. The Foundation for Research on Economics and the Environment invites federal judges to spend time at a dude ranch in Montana, listening to presentations from current or former corporate executives, with plenty of free time for horseback riding or mountain biking. There are even events for conservative politicians, though the public is not supposed to know of them. For example, Florida Gov. Rick Scott admitted in June 2011 that he snuck away to a Koch brothers' invitation-only retreat for conservative politicians in Vail, Colorado—a trip that wasn't on his public schedule.

There are hundreds of these "front tanks." They operate nationally, regionally and at the state level. Their purpose is to carry a single message to multiple audiences: the market is good, government is bad.

The front tanks recruit, train, then spin off into Congress, the executive branch, and universities operatives whose reputations are made by being quoted with approval by other Republicans. The result is a sort of an echo chamber with an amplifier, with the message becoming louder and louder, faster and faster from more and more places. Like over-dubbing a record, a single song can seem to have dozens of instruments and voices when, in reality, there is only one or two.

The massive influx of money professionalized Republican campaigns, attracting a string of career managers ranging from "bad boy" Lee Atwater to "Bush's brain" Karl Rove.

The Republican reign was interrupted by Watergate and a southern Democrat, Jimmy Carter. But it reasserted itself in 1980. After Ronald Reagan secured the Republican presidential nomination, his first speech in Philadelphia,

Mississippi was at the Neshoba County Fairgrounds a few miles from where the civil rights workers had been murdered. The words "state's rights," code words for racism, did not appear in the prepared text of Reagan's speech that day. But he inserted them, and when he uttered them, the crowd roared its approval.

Reagan's 1980 campaign in the South was run by Lee Atwater, who also managed the entire Presidential campaign of George H.W. Bush in 1988. Strom Thurmond, a Senator from South Carolina and the racist Dixiecrat candidate for President in 1952, ran the Nixon southern campaigns in 1968 and 1972.

After Reagan's victory, Atwater moved into the White House as an aide to the new President. During the first year of Reagan's presidency, Atwater (who died in 1991) granted an interview to a political science professor from Case Western Reserve University. Believing, incorrectly, that he was off the record, Atwater explained what had become known as the Southern Strategy.

> You start out in 1954 by saying, "Nigger, nigger, nigger." By 1968, you can't say "nigger"—that hurts you. Backfires. So you say stuff like forced busing, states' rights, and all that stuff. You're getting so abstract now [that] you're talking about cutting taxes, and all these things you're talking about are totally economic things, and a byproduct of them is [that] blacks get hurt worse than whites.

Handed down from generation to generation, from Goldwater to Nixon, thence to Reagan and the two Bush presidents, the southern strategy has reshaped the Republican Party. It, in turn, has reshaped the South.

Goldwater's characterization of what would happen under the 1964 Civil Rights Act proved utterly wrong. Some would agree that what Goldwater had predicted has come to pass—a "federal police force of mammoth proportions" one of the "hallmarks of the police state and landmarks in the destruction of a free society." But, if so, it has resulted from the policies of Reagan, George H.W. Bush and, especially, George W. Bush.

Today the "homeland" is fenced across its southern border and patrolled by uniformed federal guards. Across the northern border, entry into or from Canada is permitted only with a passport. Every traveler, including children and barely-able-to-walk elderly are searched at airports, shoes and belts removed and sometimes even clothing. These are not creations as a result of the "new Leftists and other revolutionaries" reviled by Richmond lawyer Lewis F. Powell, Jr? No, of the men and women that he helped bring to power.

Indeed, a strong case can be made that today's Republican Party is, in fact, the "Liberty Party" (as in libertarian) that William Simon believed it should become. Today, it is once more moving further in the direction of protection of the rich and corporations under pressure from Tea Party groups, supported by the Koch brothers and other billionaires.

Today, rather than protect blacks and other minorities, the Party and its candidates demonize them as welfare cheats, murderers, and rapists. Today, rather than a party with candidates ranging from the likes of Nelson Rockefeller and Jacob Javits to Norris Cotton, or more recently Robert T. Stafford and John Chafee to Orin Hatch, it is ideologically pure, cleansed in a political Kristallnacht.

The Republican Party has benefitted immensely by another innovation used in the 1964 elections for the first time: political marketing. That is, winning not by appealing to the values of a majority, but just the reverse—identifying what positions will construct a majority, then developing appeals to them using polls, focus groups and other tools.

The first, and certainly most infamous, television advertisement of 1964—perhaps forever—was the "Daisy" ad in which a 4-year-old girl stands in a meadow with chirping birds, picking the petals of a daisy flower, counting each petal slowly. As her count reaches nine, a male voice overrides hers, and begins the downward sequence for a nuclear launch. The screen fills with a closeup of her eyes. They disappear in the harsh flash of a nuclear explosion and mushroom cloud.

Created by legendary New York advertising agent Tony Schwartz, the Daisy ad became, in the words of contemporary Republican political consultant Frank Luntz, "the single most devastating political spot of all time." Schwartz employed, for the first time in a modern political campaign, personalized communication in which the target audience participates, often responding to a rhetorical question: "Where's the beef?" or "Are you better off today than four years ago?"

Schwartz was good, but the modern Republican party has raised such communication to high science, using people like Luntz and George W. Bush's handler, Karl Rove. They work for Republicans during the campaign season, and for companies—Philip Morris, in the case of Rove; Ameriquest Mortgages, Merrill Lynch and Bear Stearns, in the case of Frank Luntz—during the other 18 months. Appeals can be targeted to specific audiences using mailings or select radio stations, church pulpits, evangelicals and dozens of other mechanisms. Sometimes the roles are confused, as in the case of Rove persuading Gov. George Bush to propose the lawsuit "reform" ardently sought by Rove's employer, the maker of Marlboro cigarettes.

While the Republican Party and its strategists initially developed these marketing stratagems to make coded appeals to racism, modern American politics requires more. Political marketing has morphed into appeals to "values," especially those embraced by religious fundamentalists. The Party is now, like Marlboro cigarettes and Bud Light beer, a brand, associated by the public with specific qualities.

Indeed, in July 2011 when the Congress was edging toward a default by the federal government because House Republicans refused to approve a rise in the debt ceiling, the Republican leader in the Senate, Mitch McConnell of Kentucky, quietly intervened. His concern was not that troops deployed in Iraq, Afghanistan and elsewhere would not be paid, or that Social Security checks would be halted, but that the Republican "brand" might suffer. Speaking on a radio talk show, he explained that "the reason that default is no better an idea today than when Newt Gingrich tried it in 1995 is it destroys your brand."

What makes appeals to "values" possible, creates a rigid "Tea Party" element in the GOP, and imbues it with a slavish devotion to the invisible hand of the market, however, is the flood of money from corporations and the rich. Chief among these are the Koch brothers, the Wichita, Kansas billionaires, who have by themselves created a parallel universe in which children are identified almost literally at birth for advancement into the societal elite.

It is not surprising that the Koch brothers have an affinity for the libertarian philosophy. Charles was the vice presidential candidate for the Libertarian Party in 1980. Their father, Fred, was one of the John Birch Society founders while Charles and brother David started the self-described libertarian Cato Institute and free-market advocacy group Citizens for a Sound Economy (now called FreedomWorks, which funds much of the Tea Party). The FreedomWorks website says of the Occupy Wall Street protestors that Communism is "their preferred ideology."

The Koch money is seemingly everywhere, shaping ideology and grooming elites from an early age. House Majority Leader Eric Cantor of Virginia, who helped coin the characterization of rigid ideologues like himself as "young guns," was born into a family whose father, Eddie, was Virginia finance chairman for Ronald Reagan in 1980.

Michelle Bachman, the Minnesota Republican Representative who sought the nomination for President was a product of the Koch-funded American Legislative Exchange Council. So is Ken Cuccinelli, the Republican attorney general of Virginia, who intends to run for governor. Peel away the veneer of virtually any rising star of the Republican Party in the United States and beneath will lie a Koch clone, a boy or girl from Wichita, not unlike the Hitler clones in the book and movie, *Boys from Brazil.*

As time has passed, so too have the initial donors like Joe Coors, operatives like Paul Weyrich and campaign strategists like Lee Atwater. Now in its third, or perhaps fourth, generation, money is being provided not only by the likes of the Koch brothers, tied at 17th place, according to *Forbes* magazine's list of the richest people in the world. Tens of millions flow from other billionaires, including casino mogul Sheldon Adelson, America's 11th richest billionaire, according to *Forbes* magazine.

Today, the Moral Majority is now off the front pages, replaced by the Tea Party. The candidates are no longer Goldwater, Nixon, Reagan and the two Bushs, but emerging stars such as Paul Ryan, chair of the House Budget Committee, and Virginia Attorney General Ken Cuccinelli.

These and other candidates, working with pollsters and strategists, have perfected the approach of running campaigns on "values" such as opposition to abortion and gay rights and support of prayer in public schools. Once elected, however, candidates deliver on the corporate agenda, creating a series of crises, ranging from the savings and loan crisis of the late-1980s to early-1990s, in which failed S&Ls were bailed out with $160.1 billion in general taxes and another $124.6 billion from charges on savings and loan accounts. White evangelicals and Catholics are being played for suckers, but as in any good con, they just keep coming back for more.

In 1990, for example, the United States went to war. Why? To protect the flow of oil from the Persian Gulf, keeping the price of United States gasoline low enough to sustain sales of gas-guzzling sports utility vehicles, which protected the profits of both Detroit automakers and oil companies such as ExxonMobil. Lower oil prices, in turn, increased the profits from U.S. coal, helping not only the owners of coal mines, but railroads (coal is the number one commodity shipped on U.S. rails), electricity-generating utilities (coal is the number one fuel) and some ports (it is the largest export through Norfolk).

At the federal level, and in many states, electricity suppliers were "degregulated," allowing them to convert billions, possibly trillions, of dollars in assets built with payments from families and small businesses, to their own private property. The global buying spree—some might say orgy is not too strong a term—that followed, together with freedom from oversight after three-quarters of a century, squandered tens of billions and pushed some companies into bankruptcy, only to once again be bailed out by taxpayers.

Powell's manifesto and Simon's counterintelligensia targeted government spending while pressing for a succession of tax cuts that have lowered payments by corporations and the wealthy, increasing the burden on America's middle class and swelling the national deficit. Powell and Simon were focused on more than just money, however: they wanted to put government out of the business of protection, whether of civil rights, public health, food and drug purity, worker safety or the environment. Increasingly, government was ridiculed, rejected and treated as the enemy.

"Government," famously proclaimed Ronald Reagan, "is not the solution to our problem; government IS the problem." Under that banner Reagan and his successors have profitized America—my word, not theirs. The nation has become a series of profit streams for billionaires and their corporations. Pensions to enable people to work 40 years, knowing that at retirement they will be provided for, are a thing of the past. Now people save for retirement in 401(k) or similar investment plans, generating $150,000 or more in management fees. They risk losing everything in one of the stock market's periodic gut wrenching drops.

Companies that pocket the profits now run U.S. prisons, fight U.S. wars, and collect our garbage. The American taxpayer has become the source of bailouts, whether of savings and loan companies or auto manufacturers. Meanwhile, the rich gamble. If they bet right, they pocket the profits; if they guess wrong, taxpayers pick up the tab. It is a "heads I win, tails you lose," system that enriches those who created it.

But the worst is yet to come. That will be covered in greater detail in *Cliffs II*.

For the oil and gas, coal, electricity and motor vehicle industries that funded Powell's Manifesto, Simon's Counterintelligensia and Reagan's Revolution, there is no greater threat to profit than environmental protection generally and, specifically, controls on air pollution, especially those that cause global warming.

During the eight years of Reagan's presidency, a virtual war was waged between his Administration and those in the Congress seeking to protect the nation's flagship environmental law, one that had been copied in whole or part by virtually every nation in the world, the Clean Air Act of 1970. Reagan's presidency ended in a virtual tie: almost nothing had been done to weaken the statute itself, but political appointees had weakened it in every way possible that required no Congressional assent.

At the same time, Reagan had quietly, almost invisibly, created and adopted a U.S. energy policy aimed at increasing U.S. reliance on imported oil.

Earlier efforts by Presidents Nixon, Ford and Carter at establishing energy independence were, according to Reagan's first director of the Office of Management and Budget, David Stockman, "cramped, inward looking" strategies based on "Chicken Little logic." The world's cheapest energy was Persian Gulf oil at 25 cents a barrel, and the United States should fuel its entire economy on it. To guard against interruptions, all that was required were "strategic reserves and strategic forces," wrote Stockman.

Thus, Marines, sailors, soldiers and airmen became not merely instruments of U.S. foreign policy, but agents of protection for the interests of ExxonMobil oil, Southern Company electricity, Arch Coal, the Burlington Northern Railroad and General Motors, to name but a few. Our young men and women are today being killed and crippled to keep a broken system running, fueling America's engines with their blood.

Thus, what had been a wholly Presidential charge for over two centuries—the conduct of foreign policy to protect the national security of the United States— became intermingled with and corrupted by domestic decision-making as well. And beginning to emerge at the end of Reagan's second term as the largest single threat to his energy policy and his environmental desires was a threat of unprecedented dimensions, global warming.

Reducing air pollution to cope with global warming—especially carbon dioxide, the chief cause of warming, released when coal, oil and other carbon-rich fuels are burned—would be a direct threat to the profits or, indeed, perhaps the very survival of firms that mined, pumped, refined, shipped, burned coal or oil, as well as others that manufacturered cars and other machines that consumed coal or oil.

By the time of George H.W. Bush's accession to the Presidency in 1989, the executives, lobbyists and strategists of American business had become not merely well practiced, but downright adept at manipulating the Presidency, appointees, members of Congress and their staffs—not to mention the public. They could play the Congress and Executive Branch like a fiddle. The tactics and strategies employed to implement the Powell Manifesto and establish the Simon Counterintelligensia worked equally well outside the United States.

Which companies launched the global campaign to monkey-wrench international efforts to curb global warming will likely never be known. Those who know aren't telling. Probably the Southern Company was one, because its chief executive attended the international "Conferences of the Parties" (COPs), or meetings. Probably ExxonMobil participated as well, because as the strategies were implemented they involved oil producing nations such as Saudi Arabia, Nigeria and Kuwait, where it has a substantial presence. In addition, ExxonMobil representatives worked the subject on both sides of the Atlantic, regularly attended international meetings and successfully sought to have a number of scientist federal employees fired by President George W. Bush.

The key victory for American business came in 1997, as the international community adopted an agreement, the Kyoto Protocol, to reduce emissions of pollutants that cause global warming—an agreement that was doomed before it was ever entered into.

Since the very first COP, and at many other associated assemblies, a handful of veteran American lobbyists, seasoned by as many as four decades in the trenches defending the interests of coal, oil, auto, cement and other companies, have been a fixture. For many years, their coordinator was Donald Pearlman, a silver-haired Washington lawyer who had worked in the Reagan Administration for Secretary of Energy Don Hodel (where he proposed that the public wear hats and sunglasses instead of eliminating emissions of CFCs, the industrial chemicals that heighten the risk of skin cancer by destroying the stratospheric ozone layer that filters out radiation).

In 1997, it became clear that some sort of global agreement would be reached to curb global warming and, more likely than not, the United States would be a party. Pearlman, however, concocted a strategy for preventing this.

First, he recruited Sen. Robert C. Byrd of West Virginia, now dead. A former coal miner, Byrd was a pit bull when it came to protecting or advancing the interests of the state or its miners. Joined by freshman Republican Chuck Hagel of Nebraska, the two did not oppose an international agreement outright, but instead objected to mandating emission reductions in the United States and other industrialized nations unless "new specific scheduled commitments" were imposed on developing nations as well. Without this, the ratification by the Senate of any proposed treaty, a prerequisite to becoming effective, would be rejected. The resolution zipped through the Senate 95–0.

Next, Pearlman simply instructed the delegations from oil-rich developing nations like Nigeria—with which he had openly dealt with for several years—to object in Kyoto to the imposition of new commitments. Viola! The Protocol was dead before it was even adopted. After the Nigerian announcement, one observer insisted that in Kyoto he overheard Pearlman cackling gleefully while huddled with a Nigerian delegate, exalting over the victory, saying "we've done it, we've done it, we've killed it."

There now have been over two decades of not only massive disinformation, but outright lies and fraud by so-called scientists. Many of them are the very same individuals who in the early 1990s also dismissed fears of passive tobacco smoking, or secondhand smoke, as "junk science," saying the U.S. Environmental Protection Agency "cooked the data." Their campaign, The Advancement of Sound Science Coalition (TASSC), is run by APCO Associates, a public relations firm owned by Arnold & Porter, the Washington, D.C. law firm.

In 2011, Republicans have so effectively sterilized the soil of Washington and the state capitals that nothing can grow without their assent. Money is tilled into soil of politics just as farmers fold in fertilizers and pesticides, killing what they consider weeds and spurring the health and growth of what they consider crops.

Virtually no policy can advance in Washington or its 50-state counterparts without the consent of corporations and the rich who own them. They, after all, control one of the two political parties, the Republicans, absolutely, and maintain vast sway over the rival Democrats. Tax cuts do not expire, unless they wish it. Global warming legislation does not advance unless they approve it. Health insurance reform can be enacted only if corporations are fragmented.

Today's Republicans bear no resemblance to those who founded the Party in pursuit of free soil, free labor and free men. It has rejected the conservation and trust-busting of one great Republican President, Teddy Roosevelt. It has, heedless to the warnings of Dwight Eisenhower, embraced enthusiastically the corporations that form the military-industrial complex. It has turned its back on history's greatest Republican President, Abraham Lincoln.

To many, the Obama health reforms are a step forward. But if they had failed, the result would have been merely more untreated illnesses among the poor and higher bills for others.

Perhaps the tax cuts for multi-millionaires should have been allowed to expire. But their continuation means only that today's rich will have even more money to spend today, and our children less tomorrow.

Perhaps wars in Iraq and Afghanistan should end this year, not the next or the one after. But the fighting will assure the continued flow of oil at the relatively modest price of several thousand lives and tens of thousands of injuries to men and women who could have chosen not to place themselves in harm's way.

Harsh realities, but realities nonetheless.

Global warming is a different reality, however. It is indisputably real, and it is indisputably occurring and the survival of humanity is indisputably at risk.

Yet even though the corporations that are preventing action to address global warming are sentient, intelligent beings, they are not human beings. They do not laugh or cry, grow hungry or thirsty, sleepy or tired. They have neither children nor parents, morals nor ethics. They speak one language and only one: money. They exist for one reason and only one: to make money, as much as possible, without regard to the consequences.

Humanity has become the second sentient race on Earth. We are competing against corporations and those who control them. To date, corporations have demonstrated an energy, ingenuity and tenacity exceeding that of humans. They have successfully employed their one tool, money, to create a supportive and nurturing environment for themselves by manipulating humanity. Yet corporations exist only because they were created by human beings as a tool to implement our collective will in a productive and efficient way. What remains to be seen is whether we humans have the will to win.

2
THE GREATEST REDISTRIBUTION OF WEALTH IN HISTORY

If a man proposes to redistribute wealth, he means explicitly and necessarily that the wealth is his to distribute. If he proposes it in the name of the government, then the wealth belongs to the government; if in the name of society, then it belongs to society. No one, to my knowledge, did or could define a difference between that proposal and the basic principle of communism.

"The Dead End,"
The Ayn Rand Letter, I, 20, 2

America stands at the brink of the greatest redistribution of wealth in world history. The balance of wealth in America has already changed profoundly since the Republican/Libertarian/Tea Party was launched forty years ago by Powell, Simon and Weyrich. The rich have captured control of it, increasing their income and slashing their taxes, so the burden would be shifted to ordinary working class Americans.

Now the Republican/Libertarian/Tea Party proposes to once again increase spending for tanks, airplanes and troops in uniform, slash spending for everything else by 89.3 percent and raise the taxes on everybody making less than $200,000 per year, all to—

- Cut taxes on those making between $500,000 and $1 million by $35,000.

- Cut taxes on those making over a million dollars. "The average redistribution of wealth comes to an unbelievable $285,000," writes *U.S. News & World Report*.

Old America was a nation where, in the words of President John F. Kennedy, "a rising tide lifts all boats."[1] But in today's America, the rich are robbing Peter—that's you and me and other ordinary Americans—to pay Paul—that's themselves. In other words, the rich are getting richer, the rest of us are getting poorer, and America's middle class is disappearing.

This results from two changed trends:

- First, the rich and corporations are making more money, while the rest of us earn less and less.

- Second, taxes on the rich and corporations have fallen to record lows, while the burden of paying for the government has shifted to working class Americans and, through the deficit, future generations.

It makes no difference how the onion is sliced. The results are always the same, and they are a direct result of the Libertarian revolution launched by Powell, Simon and Weyrich. These are conclusions reached not just by liberal economists, but the likes of Bruce Bartlett, who was a senior policy analyst in the Reagan White House, and deputy assistant secretary for economic policy at the Treasury Department during the George H.W. Bush administration.

THE UNITED STATES TAX BURDEN IS LOW

Writing in the *New York Times* in May 2012, Bartlett said federal taxes are now at their lowest level in more than 60 years. "The Congressional Budget Office estimated that federal taxes would consume just 14.8 percent of the G.D.P. this year," he wrote, then continued "The last year in which revenues were lower was 1950, according to the Office of Management and Budget."[2]

The United States actually has the lowest corporate tax burden of any of the member nations of the Organization for Economic Cooperation and Development (OECD). The corporate rates as a percentage of the gross domestic product in OECD member countries ranges from a high of 12.5 percent in Norway to 1.8 percent in Turkey and the United States. [3]

Despite the reality that U.S. taxes are low, whether compared to the past or to other industrialized economies, the common impression is the reverse. Why? Sleight of hand. Republicans, wrote Bartlett, persuade people otherwise "by ignoring the effective tax rate and concentrating solely on the statutory tax rate, which is often manipulated to make it appear that rates are much higher than they really are."[4]

TODAY'S RICH ARE CORPORATE EXECUTIVES

The sources of wealth that defines "rich" have changed in the past several decades. Before World War Two, the richest Americans were people who made their money from corporate dividends—in other words, those who owned corporations.[5]

Today, however, the rich are the presidents and other senior executives who work for the corporations. They are, in other words, the people who decide to which candidates and what campaigns corporate funds will flow. Not surprisingly, their salaries have soared. American governments are more protective of these executives and their corporations, and less concerned with the welfare of ordinary working Americans.

The rich are making more and more money but paying less and less of the cost of running America, and so are the corporations they run. In contrast, ordinary wage earners—men and women who draw their salary in pay envelopes or checks issued based on the number of hours they work—are making less, but paying more and more of the tax burden required to finance the government. Today, according to an Associated Press study of the salaries of chief executives in 2011, the typical American worker would have to labor for 244 years to make what the typical boss of a big public company makes in one.[6]

The AP study, which used data from executive pay research firm Equilar, found that the head of a typical public company in the United States made $9.6 million in 2011. That was up more than 6 percent from the previous year, and is the second year in a row of increases. The figure is also the highest since the AP began tracking executive compensation in 2006.[7, a]

At the same time, ordinary working Americans are falling further and further behind. According to the AP, the median pay for U.S. workers in 2011 was about $39,300. That was up 1 percent from the year before, not enough to keep pace with inflation.[8]

---

[a] Two in three CEOs got raises. For 16 CEOs in the sample, their pay more than doubled from a year earlier, including Bank of America's Brian Moynihan (from $1.3 million to $7.5 million), Marathon Oil's Clarence Cazalot Jr. (from $8.8 million to $29.9 million) and Motorola Mobility's Sanjay Jha (from $13 million to $47.2 million).

NET WORTH OF ORDINARY AMERICANS LOWEST IN 21 YEARS

The impact of these income and tax burden disparities is taking its toll on the wealth of ordinary Americans. A report in June 2012 by the Federal Reserve report found that the typical American family's net worth had fallen 39 percent. Similar figures were released by the U.S. Census Bureau, showing a 35 percent decline in net worth between 2005 and 2010. For people between the ages of 35 and 44, the drop was what *Time* magazine termed "a staggering 59 percent."[9]

The magazine added that "for middle-class Americans, losses have fully offset the gains for more than two decades," adding that—

> But a *Bloomberg Businessweek* analysis of Fed data concluded that the real net worth of a typical family in 1989 was 3% greater ($79,600 after adjustment for inflation) than it was in 2010. That means there was a 21-year stretch—or half a working life—during which the typical family's growth in net worth averaged out to less than nothing. There's no way most people will ever be able to make up financially for so much lost time.[10]

The wage structure in the United States is grossly misshapen.[11] The share of national income going to the top 1 percent of wage earners has more than doubled, and now stands at about 21 percent.[12]

The share of national income going to the top 0.1 percent has increased nearly four-fold.[13] Canada and the United Kingdom's top 0.1 percent follow a similar, though less pronounced, trend. Japan and France do not; there, the top 0.1 percent received about the same proportion of national income, about 2 percent, as the wealthiest Americans did in all five countries prior to Republican/Libertarian /Tea Party launch.[14] In a 2009 paper, Saez and Piketty surveyed several other industrialized nations; in none of them did the wealthy come anywhere near the 7.7 percent share of national income found in the United States.[15]

POVERTY HAS INCREASED

Simultaneously, the number of Americans living in poverty has risen inexorably since the Libertarian revolution began.[b]

---

[b] Since 1965, there have been two slightly different versions of the federal poverty

(continued...)

The number of Americans living in poverty is now the highest since we started counting in 1973, when it was 11.1 percent. Today, 46 million Americans—15 percent of the population—live below the property level. Poverty among families with children headed by single mothers exceeds 40 percent. If the federal government had failed to enact programs to keep people out of poverty—Social Security, food stamps, the earned-income tax credit and so on—another 40 million Americans would be living in poverty. According to the Center on Budget and Policy Priorities, poverty would nearly double were it not for these safety nets.[16]

As noted above, it's not that the whole economy stagnated. There's been growth, a lot of it, but it has stuck at the top: 99 percent of Americans have been left in the dust by the 1 percent at the top.

THE REPUBLICAN/LIBERTARIAN/TEA PARTY PLAN

In the face of this, what does the Republican/Libertarian/Tea Party propose? There are few better places to find the answer to that question than the budget proposed by House Budget Committee Chairman and Mitt Romney's Vice Presidential pick Rep. Paul Ryan R. Wisc.). Ryan's budget has been endorsed by House Republicans, most Senate Republicans and Republican Presidential nominee Romney. It also has been called "an election-year blueprint for the GOP."[17] So, what would Paul Ryan and the Republican/Libertarian/Tea Party do?

U.S. News and World Report says that the Ryan Budget, which he calls the "Path to Prosperity," is "truly class warfare, Robin Hood in reverse, stick it to the middle class."[18] That said, the Romney-Ryan Republican Plan is difficult to assess. Essentially, it addresses two parts of the budget: taxes and spending.

The tax provisions are fairly straightforward, so the results are predictable. The Romney-Ryan Republican Budget continues the Republican embrace of reducing taxes for the rich.

---

[b] (...continued)
measure: (1) the poverty thresholds, and (2) the poverty guidelines. The poverty *guidelines* are sometimes loosely referred to as the "federal poverty level" or "poverty line." The *thresholds* are used mainly for statistical purposes—for instance, preparing the estimates of the number of Americans in poverty for each year's report. Two are extremely similar. For example, for 2010, the poverty threshold for two persons under the age of 65 was $14,676, while the guideline for the 48 continental states was $14,710. Source: "What are Poverty Thresholds and Poverty Guidelines?" Institute for Research on Poverty, University of Wisconsin, http://www.irp.wisc.edu/faqs/faq1.htm, accessed Aug. 7, 2012.

UN-TAX THE RICH, TAX EVERYBODY ELSE

Peter Fenn, writing in *U.S. News and World Report* magazine concluded that the "Romney-Ryan plan" would—

- *Increase taxes* on those making $50,000 to $100,000 by $1,300;

- *Increase* taxes on those making between $100,000 to $200,000 by $2,600.

- *Cut taxes* on those making between $500,000 and $1 million by $35,000.

- *Cut taxes* on those making over a million dollars. "The average redistribution of wealth comes to an unbelievable $285,000," writes *U.S. News & World Report*.

What would happen under the spending proposals is unclear. Yes, there has been an assessment by the non-partisan Congressional Budget Office (CBO), but under rules laid down by Ryan. In its first paragraph, the CBO analysis states explicitly that—

> (C)alculations do not represent a cost estimate for legislation or an analysis of the effects of any given policies. In particular, CBO has not considered whether the specified paths are consistent with the policy proposals or budget figures released today by Chairman Ryan as part of his proposed budget resolution.[19]

That is CBO double speak for saying, we don't know whether the proposed budget will achieve what Ryan says it will because we didn't look at that. CBO continues, saying that, "The amounts of revenues and spending to be used in these calculations for 2012 through 2022 were provided by Chairman Ryan and his staff, adding that "The amounts for 2023 through 2050 were calculated by CBO on the basis of growth rates, percentages of gross domestic product (GDP), or other formulas specified by Chairman Ryan and his staff."[20]

This is not unlike being forced to bet on a football game based on what a bookie says—how many yards each team will gain, how many fumbles and interceptions there will be and the final score. Then, after your bet is placed, the real game is played to determine whether you win or lose and by how much. It is simply not possible to say with confidence, except in the most general terms, what effect the Romney-Ryan Republican budget will have on spending, because so much is left unsaid.

A PROFOUNDLY RADICAL DOCUMENT

The Romney-Ryan Republican budget, which the *New Yorker* magazine calls "a profoundly radical document,"[21] would dramatically cut food stamps, Medicaid and other safety net programs, converting them to so-called "block grants" run at the discretion of individual states. Medicaid would lose $770 billion compared to Obama's budget, according to Ryan's documents.

But even this prediction could prove incorrect, because it depends on how many states will choose the options provided by Ryan or in other cases, how many taxpayers will do so.

Ryan instructs CBO to *assume* his tax plan will raise revenues to 19 percent of the gross domestic product (GDP) and then hold them there. He instructs analysts to *assume* his Medicare plan will hold cost growth in Medicare to GDP +0.5 percentage points. He instructs them to *assume* that spending on Medicaid and the Children's Health Insurance Program won't grow any faster than inflation. He instructs them to *assume* that all federal spending aside from Medicare, Medicaid and Social Security will fall from 12.5 percent of GDP in 2011 to 3.75 percent of GDP in 2050. [22]

But there are some certainties. One of these is the defense budget. Annual defense spending has risen more than a hundred percent since 2001, and it now is more than half of all discretionary government spending.

Since the wars in Iraq and Afghanistan are both winding down, the next few years should be an opportune time to cut spending on tanks, ships, bombers and troops in uniform. After the Korean War, President Eisenhower cut defense spending by twenty-seven percent; after Vietnam, Nixon cut it by twenty-nine percent; and, after the end of the Cold War, the defense budget was cut by twenty percent.

Yet the Romney-Ryan Republican Plan would cut not one penny of defense spending. Just the opposite, in fact: it would prevent nearly $500 billion in automatic cuts and roll back some of the $487 billion reduction that has already been approved. The Republican/Libertarian/Tea Party plan actually *increases* national defense spending to $554 billion in 2013, which boosts it by $8 billion over the $546 billion already agreed to under the Budget Control Act.[23]

That would reverse some of the $487 billion in cuts that the Pentagon has already planned for the next decade. Over 10 years, the Republican/Libertarian/Tea

Party budget would spend $6.2 trillion on defense, which is $500 billion higher than the $5.97 trillion level set under the Budget Control Act.[24]

INCREASED SPENDING FOR WEAPONS STARVES ALL ELSE

Increases in defense spending will automatically trigger cuts in everything else. The Romney-Ryan Republican Plan would, by 2050, reduce federal spending to its lowest point, as a percentage of GDP, since 1951. The CBO analysis of the Romney-Ryan Republican Plan finds that by 2050, all the government's discretionary spending, including defense, would represent just 3.75 percent of the GDP. However, defense spending in the postwar era has never been less than 3 percent of GDP, so the rest of the government's discretionary spending would have to be squeezed out of that remaining 0.75 percent.

This hammer-and-tong approach would effectively starve the rest of government. Non-defense discretionary spending has never been less than 8 percent. So, in practical terms, virtually all of what the federal government does would be eliminated because spending would be cut 89.3 percent. Interstate highways would disappear, as would air traffic controllers and FBI agents. There would be zero or near zero money for clean air and water, cutting American dependence on foreign oil, and putting out forest fires.

Because other areas of the Republican/Libertarian/Tea Party budget could cut Medicare, Medicaid and Social Security to supplement cuts in highways and the like, there would be plenty of money for tax cuts. Again, just to make sure you understand this fundamental point: these safety net programs would virtually disappear and taxes would be increased on everybody making less than $200,000 per year to:

- Cut taxes on those making between $500,000 and $1 million by $35,000.
- Cut taxes on those making over a million dollars.

This almost certainly would be the greatest redistribution of wealth in history.

Some economists see these changes as a result of factors external to the United States or, for that matter, human control. Writing in the *New York Times* and citing a recent book, *The Great Divergence*, economist Benjamin Friedman said the causes of income inequality could be due to—

the failure of America's schools to keep pace with the step-up in skills that advancing technology demands from our labor force; America's skewed immigration policy, which inadvertently brings in more unskilled than skilled immigrants and thereby subjects already lower-income workers to greater competition for jobs; rising competition with China, India and other low-wage countries, as changing technology enables Americans to buy ever more goods and even services produced overseas; the failure of the federally mandated minimum wage to keep up with inflation; (or) the decline of labor unions, especially among employees of private-sector firms …[25]

IS THIS REALLY COINCIDENCE?

Can it be merely coincidence that all these changes have occurred since the launch of the Libertarian revolution? Is it happenstance that this occurred at the very time that the foundations of the rich have poured millions into re-shaping America? Or at the at the same moment in time that corporations and the wealthy have flooded the halls of Congress and legislatures with their money? Is it an accident that the United States has moved in precisely the same direction that the rich and corporations have sought to direct it?

The law assumes that people intend the natural consequences of their actions. Should we not assume the same with respect to Powell, Simon, Weyrich and the many others who have followed in their footsteps. They said the objective was to remake America, and it has been remade.

3
HIGHJACKING HISTORY

> Tyranny, like hell, is not easily conquered; yet we have this
> consolation with us, that the harder the conflict, the more glorious
> the triumph.
>
> Thomas Paine,
> *The American Crisis No. 1*
> 1776

Today, as in 1776, 1859, 1914, 1933, 1963, 1958, and 1964, Americans are fighting over which is more important, property or people. On the property side are businesses, those who own them and the people they hire. On the other side, is everybody else (you and me).

America had this argument in 1776 and the "everybody else" side won. We have also had the argument many times since, and the "everybody else" side has always won. It is good to have the likes of Thomas Jefferson, Benjamin Franklin, Abraham Lincoln, Teddy Roosevelt and Franklin Delano Roosevelt on your side.

Today, "everybody else" is in danger of losing. Indeed, in the Supreme Court, the rest of us have already lost, with the Justices saying that money, another word for property, is speech and that a corporation is a "citizen," so they can run as many campaign advertisements as they want. If I were a betting man, I would bet against you and me.

In the past, business attempts to impose what Lincoln termed the "tyrannical principle" that exalts property over freedom have failed. They were, as often as not, ham-handed and often transparent efforts to control the nation, the products of paranoid mentality. In 1933, businesses and the rich even attempted a violent overthrow of the United States, if you can believe it, but made the serious mistake of approaching a two-time Medal of Honor winner, a Marine who was, of all things, a Quaker. He ratted them out in sworn testimony before a committee of the U.S. House of Representatives.

To place today's numerous tea parties in perspective, it helps to review the many instances in which these two forces have previously collided, sometimes violently.

1776: THE DECLARATION OF INDEPENDENCE

The first was in 1776, in the drafting of the Declaration of Independence.

This was a time when more of the colonists themselves were becoming convinced of the inevitability of independence. Thomas Paine's *Common Sense*, published in January 1776, was sold by the thousands. By the middle of May 1776, eight colonies had decided that they would support independence. On May 15, 1776, the Virginia Convention passed a resolution that "the delegates appointed to represent this colony in General Congress be instructed to propose to that respectable body to declare the United Colonies free and independent states."[1]

On June 7, in what was then the Pennsylvania State House but later to be named Independence Hall, Richard Henry Lee of Virginia read the resolution of independence—"Resolved: That these United Colonies are, and of right ought to be, free and independent States, that they are absolved from all allegiance to the British Crown, and that all political connection between them and the State of Great Britain is, and ought to be, totally dissolved."[2]

There were still some delegates to the Continental Congress, including those bound by earlier instructions from their respective colonies, who hoped for reconciliation with Britain. On June 11, Congress voted seven to five, with New York abstaining, to delay a vote on Lee's resolution. Congress then recessed for three weeks, appointing a "Committee of Five" to draft a statement presenting to the world the colonies' case for independence.

The Committee of Five

The committee consisted of two New Englanders, John Adams of Massachusetts and Roger Sherman of Connecticut; two from the Middle Colonies, Benjamin Franklin of Pennsylvania and Robert R. Livingston of New York;[a] and, one southerner, Thomas Jefferson of Virginia.[3]

---

[a] Livingston believed the Declaration was premature, and never signed it.

The task of creating a first draft was given to Jefferson. Much later, in 1823, he recalled that the other members of the committee—

"unanimously pressed on myself alone to undertake the draught [*sic*]. I consented; I drew it; but before I reported it to the committee I communicated it separately to Dr. Franklin and Mr. Adams requesting their corrections … I then wrote a fair copy, reported it to the committee, and from them, unaltered to the Congress."[4]

(Jefferson's original draft, including the changes suggested by Adams and Franklin, is now held by the Library of Congress.)

Jefferson chose as a model for the Declaration of the thirteen colonies, the Virginia Declaration of Rights.[5, 6] Although the Declarations are quite similar in wording, they differ in one crucial detail, one that has produced 235 years of nearly unrelenting conflict.

Virginia's Declaration of Rights provided that "all men are by nature equally free and independent and have certain inherent rights, of which, when they enter into a state of society, they cannot, by any compact, deprive or divest their posterity; namely, the enjoyment of life and liberty, *with the means of acquiring and possessing property*,[7] and pursuing and obtaining happiness and safety." (Emphasis added.)[8]

Jefferson and the drafters the Declaration of Independence, however, took a contrary view. Their draft—and this cannot have been an accident of drafting—held that "that all men are created equal, that they are endowed by their Creator with certain unalienable Rights, that among these are Life, Liberty and the pursuit of Happiness."[9] Thus, the drafters of the American Declaration self-consciously and knowingly eliminated from the draft any reference to protecting "property," instead embracing "Life, Liberty and the pursuit of Happiness."

Jefferson's original draft of the Declaration contained no reference to protecting property, nor did the draft forwarded by the Committee of Five, nor did that debated and adopted by the delegates. Thus, Jefferson, Franklin and the other delegates—the "Founding Fathers" as some prefer to call them today—placed themselves squarely on the side of protecting human rights, not property.

The Declaration of Independence triggered outright warfare between the colonies and Great Britain, which ended in 1781. General George Washington's army besieged and defeated General Cornwallis' army at Yorktown, Virginia, and in 1783, the Treaty of Paris brought the Revolution to a close. Peace, however, did not come to the state of Massachusetts.

1786–1787: SHAYS' REBELLION

During the War, Massachusetts had issued $50 notes that depreciated to 1/40th of their face value. Having been paid for the service to the Revolution in such paper notes, former Revolutionary soldiers, besieged by creditors and jailed by the courts in Debtors' Prisons, had no choice but to redeem them at a fraction of their face value. The Massachusetts legislature, yielding to the Boston merchants and bankers who had bought the notes at steep discounts, required that they be redeemed at face value, paying for the costs through a new tax that, not surprisingly, fell most heavily on those who had fought in the war.

The former soldiers fought back, forcing courts to close, thus preventing debt collection and imprisonment. The government, supplied with money by Boston merchants and bankers, hired a private army. In the ensuing violence, which included Shays' Rebellion, Massachusetts officials committed acts that would later lead to specific prohibitions in the Bill of Rights to the Constitution. The Massachusetts' legislature adopted a Riot Act, which forbad gatherings of more than 12 armed persons. It authorized sheriffs to kill rioters with impunity. The law required the Riot Act to be read aloud at every church in the Commonwealth. Rioters were imprisoned without bail and the right of habeas corpus was suspended.

It can be said fairly that Shays' Rebellion marked a triumph of property over individual rights. Men were imprisoned, the right of habeas corpus suspended, and manifestly unjust taxes were imposed for the purpose of supporting those of property. It demonstrated the evils that government, unconstrained by explicit rules of law, would be willing to adopt at the behest of the rich and propertied.

1787–1789: THE CONSTITUTION OF THE UNITED STATES AND THE BILL OF RIGHTS

Shays' Rebellion, like similar uprisings in other states, so alarmed George Washington and other Revolutionary leaders that they assembled in Philadelphia to revise the nation's governing document, the Articles of Confederation. Once more, tension between those with property and those favoring individual liberties, rose.

After struggling to agree on amendments to the Articles of Confederation, delegates to the Constitutional Convention finally decided to write a fresh document. The result was a Constitution that paid little attention to individual liberties. The framers were primarily focused on establishing the machinery for an effective federal government.[b]

The absence of protections for individual liberties proved to be a flaw that was nearly fatal. During the debate over the Constitution, two factions emerged: the Federalists, who supported adoption, and the Anti-Federalists, who opposed it.[10] Federalists, who supported a strong central government, were fundamentally comfortable with the Constitution as drafted. Not so with Anti-Federalists, however. They feared that the new system would threaten liberties.

Expressing these fears, Thomas Jefferson (who did not attend the Constitutional Convention) wrote in a December 1787 letter to James Madison, a Virginian and one of the Constitution's principal drafters, that the omission of a bill of rights was a major mistake: "A bill of rights is what the people are entitled to against every government on earth."[11]

With ratification in serious doubt, Federalists announced a willingness to take up the matter of a series of amendments, to be called the Bill of Rights,[c] soon after ratification and the First Congress came into session. The concession was undoubtedly necessary to secure the Constitution's hard-fought ratification.

---

[b] As adopted, the Constitution included only a few specific rights guarantees: protection against states impairing the obligation of contracts (Art. I, Section 10), provisions that prohibit both the federal and state governments from enforcing ex post facto laws (laws that allow punishment for an action that was not criminal at the time it was undertaken) and provisions barring bills of attainder (legislative determinations of guilt and punishment) (Art. I, Sections 9 and 10). The framers, and notably James Madison, its principal architect, believed that the Constitution protected liberty primarily through its division of powers that made it difficult for an oppressive majorities to form and capture power to be used against minorities. Delegates also probably feared that a debate over liberty guarantees might prolong or even threaten the fiercely-debated compromises that had been made over the long hot summer of 1787.

[c] The Bill of Rights protects freedom of speech, freedom of religion, the right to keep and bear arms, freedom of assembly and freedom to petition. It also prohibits unreasonable search and seizure, cruel and unusual punishment and compelled self-incrimination. Among the legal protections it affords, the Bill of Rights prohibits Congress from making any law respecting establishment of religion and prohibits the federal government from depriving any person of life, liberty or property without due process of law. In federal criminal cases it requires indictment by a grand jury for any capital offense, or infamous crime, guarantees a speedy public trial with an impartial jury in the district in which the crime occurred, and prohibits double jeopardy.

It is fair to say that with the inclusion of the Bill of Rights, the Constitution represented a re-affirmation of the importance of the protection of individual liberties. It was the glue with which Federalists and Anti-Federalists could be bound to one another, making possible a national union.

Seeking to quell the fears of Americans over the Constitution, James Madison, Alexander Hamilton and John Jay wrote a series of essays in its support. "The Federalist" (later called the "the Federalist Papers") explained the Constitution's provisions and the reasoning for them. In Federalist No. 43, Madison was confronted with the difficult question of explaining why the Articles of Confederation should be set aside in favor of the Constitution. His explanation struck at the very heart of why there should be a government at all.

To explain why those who drafted and approved the Constitution believed that the Articles of Confederation should be displaced, Madison asked, then answered, a question "of a very delicate nature."[12]

"On what principle the Confederation, which stands in the solemn form of a compact among the States," Madison asked, "can be superseded without the unanimous consent of the parties to it?"[13]

The answer, he responded , was that "*safety and happiness of society are the objects at which all political institutions aim,* and to which all such institutions must be sacrificed." (Emphasis added.) The Articles of Confederation had failed at assuring these and, thus, had to be set aside.[14]

The Articles, Madison explained, had been "a compact between independent sovereigns" that had been repeatedly violated. This authorizes the individual sovereigns "if they please, to pronounce the compact violated and void." The individual states had done this and drafted a proposed Constitution that would be binding on all states.[15] There was no mention of property or its protection in the essay.

One paper in particular, Number 10, has been cited as saying the protection of private property is "the first object of government."[16] This is false. What Number 10 actually says is—

The diversity in the faculties of men, from which the rights of property originate, is not less an insuperable obstacle to a uniformity of interests. The protection of these faculties is the first object of government.[17]

Thus Madison, the author of Federalist 10, describes the Constitution as protecting "faculties," not "property." This is a characterization of government's proper role being the protection of humans and human qualities such as "faculties."

For example, after adoption of the Constitution, George Washington was elected President. At his inaugural address, delivered on April 30, 1789, Washington focused on the importance of assuring "the liberties and happiness of the People of the United States."[18] There was no mention of property or its protection.

There remained in the nation one kind of property that was afforded special treatment by the Constitution: slaves. Not only was the practice of keeping slaves ratified by the Constitution, it was rewarded. For purposes of calculating representation in Congress, one slave was valued at three-fifths of a non-slave. The Constitution's drafters danced around not only the issue of slavery, but the very term itself.

Instead of using the term "slave" they used phrases like "importation of Persons"[19] or "other persons"[20] and "person held to service or labor."[21] Euphemisms, however, were used in vain. Despite them, the nation went to war with itself, and the issue that divided America was property rights; specifically, whether a slave was to be property or a human.

APRIL 12, 1861: THE CIVIL WAR

The Civil War was fought for many reasons, but chief among them was slavery. The subject had nearly brought the two great regions of the nation to war on several occasions, but armed conflict had been avoided by one last minute compromise or another. The stage was set for the Civil War, however, when the Whig Party, which had been founded in opposition to the regime of "Jacksonian" democracy that prevailed following Andrew Jackson's election, was divided.

Members of the Whig Party fell into two camps: anti-slavery "conscience" Whigs of the north; and, pro-slavery "cotton" Whigs of the south.[22] This division over slavery was the Whig Party's death sentence. By 1856, it had imploded. Pro-slavery Whigs fled to the Democratic Party or the American ("Know-Nothing") Party, neither of which would take a definitive stand on slavery. Conscience Whigs joined the staunchly anti-slavery Republican Party.[23]

The newly-formed Republican Party was created expressly to halt the spread of slavery and, if possible, eliminate it altogether. Republicans viewed slavery as an intrinsic evil. The best expression of this proposition was likely that of Abraham Lincoln during the legendary Lincoln-Douglas debates:

> It is the eternal struggle between these two principles—right and wrong—throughout the world. They are the two principles that have stood face to face from the beginning of time; and will ever continue to struggle. The one is the common right of humanity, and the other the divine right of kings. It is the same principle in whatever shape it develops itself. It is the same spirit that says, "You toil and work and earn bread, and I'll eat it." No matter in what shape it comes, whether from the mouth of a king who seeks to bestride the people of his own nation and live by the fruit of their labor, or from one race of men as an apology for enslaving another race, it is the same tyrannical principle.[24]

Had there ever been doubt as to the status of slaves, it was eliminated entirely by the U.S. Supreme Court in 1857. In *Dred Scott v. Sandford*, 60 U.S. 393 (1857), the court confirmed the status of slaves as property, not citizens.[25] Chief Justice Roger Taney of the slave state of Maryland, declared that an African American could not be entitled to rights as a U.S. citizen, such as the right to sue in federal courts. In fact, Taney wrote, African Americans had "no rights which any white man was bound to respect."[d]

Less than three years later, Abraham Lincoln was elected as President of the United States and forced to contend with the question of slavery. It was another great confrontation of property rightsversus those of humans. Once again human rights prevailed.

When Lincoln was elected President in 1860, much of the South was galvanized into action. In South Carolina, Ft. Sumpter was fired upon and seized, triggering the Civil War. No single cause can be assigned to the development of something as complex and lengthy in the making as a war. Nevertheless, even if slavery was not the sole cause, it was a major contributor to the Civil War. As Lincoln said in his Second Inaugural Address on March 4, 1865—

---

[d] The decision applied to all blacks—slaves, as well as free. By the terms of the decision, they were not and could never become citizens of the United States.

One-eighth of the whole population were colored slaves, not distributed generally over the Union, but localized in the southern part of it. These slaves constituted a peculiar and powerful interest. All knew that this interest was somehow the cause of the war. To strengthen, perpetuate, and extend this interest was the object for which the insurgents would rend the Union even by war, while the Government claimed no right to do more than to restrict the territorial enlargement of it.[26]

At the War's conclusion, the nation adopted four amendments to the Constitution emphatically affirming the status of slaves as humans. But the end of the Civil War brought no peace on this subject.

Blacks—as well as American Indians, the Chinese and others—continued to be denied human rights, as a matter of fact, without regard to what the law might say. For a century, race riots or massacres erupted regularly throughout the nation—Memphis, Tennessee; Meridian, Mississippi; Colfax, Louisiana; Vicksburg, Mississippi; Washington, D.C.; and, dozens of other places. In the Wilmington Massacre of 1898, white supremacists in North Carolina illegally seized power from an elected government, running officials out of the city, and killing many blacks in widespread attacks. Among their weapons, they used a Gatling gun mounted on a wagon.[27]

On October 24, 1871, a mob of over 500 white men entered Los Angeles' Chinatown to attack, rob and brutally murder Chinese residents of the city. In San Francisco, on July 24, 1877, the city's whites waged a two-day pogrom against Chinese immigrants, killing four and destroying more than $100,000 in property. On September 2, 1885, white miners in Rock Springs, Wyoming, killed 28 Chinese miners, injured 15 and burned 75 homes. In Seattle, one Chinese immigrant was killed and four wounded in a riot in February 1886.[28]

The violence continued unabated to the mid-20th century. Only with the enactment of the Civil Rights Act of 1964 did it effectively abate. But there was more.

1933: THE AMERICAN LIBERTY LEAGUE

In language that is strikingly evocative of the claims of today's tea partiers, something called the American Liberty League burst onto the national scene in 1933. It was only part of a wide-ranging embrace by American business of Fascism.

The businessmen who founded it made no secret of the League and their ambitions for it. Its creation was announced in Washington, D.C., on August 22, 1934, by a group of businessmen. The League's purpose was to combat radicalism, preserve property rights, and uphold and preserve the Constitution.[29]

Preserve property rights? What rights?

The Constitution does not establish property rights.

Yes, it acknowledges the existence of property in the Fifth Amendment, declaring that "No person shall be … deprived of life, liberty, or property, without due process of law; nor shall private property be taken for public use, without just compensation." In other amendments, the Constitution speaks of "freedom of speech, or of the press" and certain very specific "rights."

Amendment 1, for example, protects "the *right* of the people peaceably to assemble, and to petition the Government for a redress of grievances." The Forth Amendment guarantees the *"right* of the people to be secure in their persons, houses, papers, and effects." (Emphasis added.)

Amendment 6 assures "the *right* to a speedy and public trial, by an impartial jury of the State and district wherein the crime shall have been committed, which district shall have been previously ascertained by law, and to be informed of the nature and cause of the accusation; to be confronted with the witnesses against him; to have compulsory process for obtaining witnesses in his favor, and to have the Assistance of Counsel for his defense (*sic)*." (Emphasis added.)

And, Amendment 9 explicitly protects some rights, saying, "The enumeration in the Constitution, of certain *rights*, shall not be construed to deny or disparage others retained by the people."(Emphasis added.)

Yes, property may be one of those "rights … retained by the people." But the Constitution neither creates nor explicitly affirms the existence of a property right, and to suggest that it does is hogwash—a lame excuse to gull people into believing that something is there when it isn't.

To the extent that the Constitution should be read in the context of the Declaration of Independence, owning property is different than having life or liberty or pursuing happiness. Those rights are "inalienable," which mean they cannot be "alienated," or transferred to another person. They cannot be taken by force, nor can they be sold. They are "inalienable." Period. The end. No more discussion.

Property, however, is a different story. It can be alienated. It can be sold, or it can be taken by government. That puts property in an entirely different category than "life, liberty and the pursuit of happiness."

Property can be taken. Yes, the taking must be with "due process" and "just compensation" must be provided. But it can be taken. And, what, exactly, do the terms "due process" and "just compensation" mean? Abraham Lincoln took property—slaves—throughout the South by issuing the Emancipation Proclamation. Individuals that on one day had been the property of another, ceased to be their property, or anyone else's, on the next. The Emancipation Proclamation is possibly the greatest taking of "property" in human history. Yet it was not even an act of law, but a mere "proclamation."

Those who founded the American Liberty League, like those who today fund the tea partiers, would have Americans believe that they possess their vast wealth because the Constitution gave them a "right" to it. Nonsense.

Still, we can understand why billionaires want to maintain that status. So, they founded the American Liberty League. Much of the money came from the DuPont company and family.

According to Gerard Colby, author of *DuPont Dynasty*, full-time organizers established League chapters at twenty-six colleges and universities. About 100 pamphlets were written and printed, and several million copies distributed. A speakers' bureau was established and the League sponsored many nationwide radio addresses, all echoing Lammot DuPont's demand that "all government regulation of business ... should be abolished."[30]

From a 31-room office manned by fifty people, press releases constantly attacked New Deal programs. Payment of the bonus promised to veterans of World War I was decried as an "extravagance," as was the Social Security Act and "burdensome taxes imposed upon industry for unemployment insurance and old age pension."[31]

Most of the major newspapers of the country fell in line, printing releases or carrying favorable news articles on the League's positions. The *New York Times* gave the League front-page billing 35 times between August 1934 and November 1936.[32]

Another major supporter of the League was Andrew Mellon, an heir to the Mellon banking and oil fortunes, and U.S. Secretary of the Treasury under Presidents Harding, Coolidge and Hoover (1921–1923, 1923–1929, 1929–1932).[33]

Mellon reduced taxes for the rich and cut government spending on social programs. In 1921, the excess profits tax was eliminated, saving corporate stockholders about $1.5 billion: U.S. Steel got $27 million and the Mellon Bank got $91,472. The biggest beneficiary was John D. Rockefeller, who received $457,000. Mellon himself got the second biggest rebate, $404,000.

In 1923, the "Mellon Plan" proposed that taxes paid by the country's rich be reduced from 50 percent to 25 percent, while taxes paid by those with the lowest incomes would be cut from 4 percent to 3 percent. By 1926, Mellon finally succeeded in slashing taxes on the rich, and another law cut corporate taxes even more. At that time, the top 10 percent received 50 percent of the country's total income, while the top 1 percent received 24 percent. Under Mellon, corporations got tax rebates of $6 billion, and those with incomes over $300,000 had taxes reduced by 60 percent.

If what happened then bears an eerie resemblance to the events of the past decade, that is no accident, because the same family—the Mellons—that influenced three Presidents and helped finance the American Liberty League then, is doing the same today through family foundations that all trace their money back to the Mellons.[e]

The foundations are run by Richard Mellon Scaife, son of Andrew Mellon's niece, Sarah, and heir to much of the Mellon fortune. Together with the Kochs, Bradleys and a handful of other billionaire Americans, Scaife has financed many of the organizations that are part of or laid the foundations for, the tea parties.

According to the on-line encyclopedia, Wikipedia, Scaife's money has supported American Enterprise Institute, Atlas Economic Research Foundation, David Horowitz Freedom Center, Committee for a Constructive Tomorrow (which advocates for free-market solutions to environmental issues and denies global warming), Commonwealth Foundation for Public Policy Alternatives, the Federalist Society, Foundation for Economic Education, Free Congress Foundation, Freedom House, GOPAC (once headed by Newt Gingrich), Heritage Foundation,

---

[e] The Sarah Scaife Foundation, Carthage Foundation, Allegheny Foundation, and the Scaife Family Foundation.

Independent Women's Forum, Intercollegiate Studies Institute (which operates the Collegiate Network), Judicial Watch, Landmark Legal Foundation, Media Research Center (headed by Brent Bozell), Pacific Legal Foundation, World Affairs Council of Pittsburgh, and the Reason Foundation, to name but a few. [Author's note: giving by the Scaife-controlled foundations to these entities was independently confirmed by random searches using the Foundation Directory on-line, a fee-for-service subscription that tracks the giving on non-profit 501(c)(3) corporations.)

Those who support the tea parties of today have enjoyed such success at manipulating the public and press over the past three decades, that going beyond the widespread application of money has been unnecessary. Not so with the American Liberty League, however. Despite lavishing vast amounts of money, it was still failing to gain traction with the public. So, in due time, they approached the most decorated Marine in history and asked him to lead their revolution.

During his 34-year career as a Marine, Smedley Butler participated in military actions in the Philippines, China, Central America and the Caribbean during the Banana Wars, and France in World War I. By the end of his career, he had received 16 medals, five of which were for heroism. He is one of 19 men to twice receive the Medal of Honor, one of three to be awarded both the Marine Corps Brevet Medal and the Medal of Honor, and the only man to be awarded the Brevet Medal and two Medals of Honor, all for separate actions. He was, of all things, a Quaker.[34, f]

Smedley Butler not only rejected the League's offer, but carefully gathered the evidence, took it to Congress and testified against the plotters.

Butler alleged the existence of a political conspiracy of Wall Street interests to overthrow President Roosevelt, a series of allegations that came to be known in the media as the Business Plot. A special committee of the House of Representatives headed by Representatives John W. McCormack of Massachusetts and Samuel Dickstein of New York heard his testimony in secret. (The McCormack-Dickstein committee was a precursor to the House Committee on Un-American Activities.)

---

[f] Butler faced gunfire 120 times. Columnist Will Rogers wrote of him: "He is what I would call a natural born warrior. He will fight anybody, any time. ... He carries every medal we ever gave out. He has two Congressional Medals of Honor. ... You give him another war and he will get him another one. ... I do admire him."

Butler told the committee that a group of businessmen, saying they were backed by a private army of 500,000 ex-soldiers and others, intended to establish a fascist dictatorship. Butler had been asked to lead it.

The parties that Butler said were involved, said there was no truth in the story, calling it a joke and a fantasy. But when the committee's final report was released, it sided with Butler. According to the *New York* Times, the committee said "a two-month investigation had convinced it that General Butler's story of a Fascist march on Washington was alarmingly true." Continuing, "Definite proof had been found," it reported, "that the much publicized Fascist march on Washington ... was actually contemplated."

The McCormack-Dickstein Committee's report said that, "In the last few weeks of the committee's official life it received evidence showing that certain persons had made an attempt to establish a fascist organization in this country.

"There is no question," it continued, "that these attempts were discussed, were planned, and might have been placed in execution when and if the financial backers deemed it expedient."

Franklin Roosevelt, for one, took the League seriously.

On January 3, 1936, in an unprecedented joint session of Congress, when President Roosevelt announced a ban on military exports to fascist Italy, he blasted the American Liberty League:

> They steal the livery of great national ideals to serve discredited special interests ... This minority in business and industry ... engage in vast propaganda to spread fear and discord among the people. They would gang up against the people's liberties ... They seek the restoration of their selfish power ... Give them their way and they will take the course of every aristocracy of the past—power for themselves, enslavement for the public.[35]

Like the rich and their foundations today, however, the DuPonts and Mellons of the 1930s did not put their eggs all in one basket. The League was by no means the only initiative. There were many others.

One, for example, was "The Crusaders," headed by Fred G. Clark as "national commander." It had started in the late 1920s to campaign for repeal of Prohibition, receiving help from various interested manufacturers. (Repealing

Prohibition would make taxes on alcohol once again a major source of revenue, thus relieving reliance on the income tax.) In 1933, with big business apprehensive of the incoming Franklin Delano Roosevelt Administration, Clark saw wider fields for crusades. The organization was revised "to oppose all forces destructive to sound government."

Some months later, a lunch meeting was held in Chicago attended by about fifty business leaders at which the Commander broached the idea about a radio voice of the Crusaders to implement the opposition to destructive forces. A radio fund of $160,000 was quickly raised, subscribed largely at the lunch. Contributions came from Kenneth G. Smith of Pepsodent; Lester Armour of Armour & Co.; and John Stuart and R. Douglas Stuart of Quaker Oats.

Others who contributed included top-tier executives of DuPont, General Mills, National Biscuit Co., Corn Products, Heinz, Wrigley, Swift & Co., Sun Oil Company, Standard Oil Company of Indiana, A.B. Dick Company and Montgomery Ward. The Columbia Broadcasting System agreed to provide free network time.

The Crusaders set up a New York office and the weekly broadcasts began in 1934 at 79 CBS stations, with Commander Clark at the microphone. Now and then he got suggestions from the donors as to what to attack—the Agricultural Adjustment Act, the Tennessee Valley Authority, the Banking Bill—and he usually complied promptly. At a Senate study of lobbying activities, the Commander denied that he had been trying to influence public opinion; but seeking "merely to clarify public thinking."[36]

There were still other groups. A partial list includes the American Federation of Utility Investors, American Taxpayers League, Economists National Committee, Farmers Independence Council, League for Industrial Rights, Minute Men and Women of Today, National Economy League, New York State Economic Council, Sentinels of the Republic, Southern Committee to Uphold the Constitution and Women Investors in America, Inc.[37]

Despite immense amounts of money, the American Liberty League and other groups failed, then the nation was swept up into World War II, the Atomic Era and the Korean Conflict. Once again, those who, like Jefferson, Franklin, Lincoln and Roosevelt believed the nation was committed to the protection of individual liberties such as speech, assembly and trial by jury had prevailed over those of property.

But as America settled into the post-war era, new and frightening trends began to once again emerge. Fear of Communists[g] was an underlying current in virtually all discussions in the era and some began to see many developments with which they disagreed as the product of a Communist conspiracy.

1958: THE JOHN BIRCH SOCIETY

For example, *Brown v. Board of Education*, the 9–0 decision of the US. Supreme Court to overturn "separate but equal" schools in the United States, leading to racial desegregation, was attacked as the product of a Communist conspiracy by the New York chapter of the Sons of the American Revolution. An official of the chapter attributed the impetus behind the Court's action to "the worldwide Communist conspiracy" and claimed that the NAACP had been financed by "a Communist front."[38]

Into this political climate, millionaire candy-maker Robert Welch introduced the idea of the "John Birch Society"[h] at an Indianapolis, Indiana meeting he convened on December 9, 1958. Twelve "patriotic and public-spirited" men attended.[39] One of them was Fred Koch, father of David and Charles.[40] The identities of several others have been obscured by history.[i]

---

[g] Sometimes the word begins with a lower case, sometimes with an upper case. The difference seems to be where the source lies on the political spectrum. See e.g., http://www.conservapedia.com/Communism *and* http://www.forbes.com/sites/billfrezza/2011/07/19/give-greece-what-it-deserves-communism/versus ("Communism") versus http://www.britannica.com/EBchecked/topic/129104/communism ("communism").

[h] According to *Time* magazine Birch was a slender, 27-year-old captain in the Army Air Forces. On Aug. 25, 1945, ten days after the end of World War II, he was killed in China by a band of Communists. "Nation: Who was John Birch?" *Time*, April 14, 1961 http://www.time.com/time/magazine/article/0,9171,872243,00.html, accessed May 16, 2012.

[i] Other earlier members of the Society, perhaps as Founders, included the following: **Willis Carto**, Founder of Liberty Lobby, Institute for Historical Studies (an organization denying the occurrence of the Holocaust, according to Phyllis B. Gerstenfeld and Diana R. Grant, *Crimes of Hate*, Sage Publications, 2004); **Joseph Coors, Sr.**, who according to his obituary in the *New York Times*, "helped make his family's beer a nationwide brand and who used his fortune to support conservative causes, notably the Heritage Foundation;" **Kent H. Courtney**, identified by NNDB only as a "ultraconservative activist;" **William J. Grede**, described by the *New York Times* as "militantly anti-union," and said by the *Times* to have once referred to the progressive income tax as "the very foundation of all socialistic programs, the most socializing agency in the country;" **Edgar W. Hiestand**, a staunch Anti-Communist who served ten years in the United States

(continued...)

The first chapter was founded a few months later in February1959. The core thesis of the society was contained in Welch's initial Indianapolis presentation, transcribed almost verbatim in *The Blue Book of the John Birch Society*, and subsequently given to each new member.[41]

ⁱ (...continued)

Congress; *H. L. (Haroldson Lafayette) Hunt*, an oil tycoon who turned an oil well win in a game of five-card stud into a global oil empire that made him one of the world's half-dozen wealthiest men, he funded two right-wing radio shows, Facts Forum and Life Line; his son, *Nelson Bunker Hunt*, funder of conservative religious causes, who filed for bankruptcy after plans to corner the silver market collapsed; *Fred C. Koch*, the billionaire founder of Koch Industries and ardent anti-Communist, even though it was Soviet Russia that launched his path of immense wealth; *Alfred Kohlberg*, a wealthy New York businessman and fanatical anticommunist and supporter of Chiang Kai-shek against Mao Tse Tung's communist government; *Tim LaHaye*, author of the "Left Behind" series of books; *Pat Manion*, dean of the Notre Dame Law School from 1941 to 1952 and host of the popular weekly radio program, *The Manion Forum*, from the mid-1950s until his death in 1979 (his true place in Republican history, however, is from persuading Barry Goldwater to author a book whose name Manion chose: *The Conscience of a Conservative*); *Robert Mathews*, who became a criminal and murderer, who was killed on Dec. 8, in a shootout with FBI agents; *Larry McDonald*, the second president of the John Birch Society and a Democratic member of the U. S. House of Representatives from Georgia who was a passenger on Korean Air Lines Flight 007, believed killed when it was shot down by Soviet interceptors on Sep. 1, 1983; *Evan Mecham*, governor of Arizona, 1987–88, and the first U.S. governor to simultaneously face removal from office through impeachment, a scheduled recall election, and felony indictment. (Ronald J. Watkins, *High Crimes and Misdemeanors: The Terms and Trials of Former Governor Evan Meacham);* Tom Metzger, activist and white supremacist ; *Revilo P. Oliver*, a University of Illinois professor forced to resign from the Birch Society after saying at a rally that "vaporizing" Jews was a "beatific vision"; *Westbrook Pegler*, a popular columnist for the Hearst newspaper chain who wrote in November 1963 at the height of the civil rights movement, that it is "clearly the bounden duty of all intelligent Americans to proclaim and practice bigotry" and said the label racist, "a common but false synonym for Nazi, used by the bigots of New York;" *William Pierce*, author of *The Turner Diaries*, a "future history" of a white revolution in America that leads to the overthrow of the government and the extermination of minorities; *Archie Roosevelt*, the third son of President Theodore Roosevelt and a former executive of Sinclair Oil, who publicly accused President Harry S. Truman of shielding Communists; *Rep. John H. Rousselot*, a former Member of Congress who staunchly opposed spending and tax increases, proposed cuts in the food stamp program, and worked for deregulation of the savings and loan industry; *John G. Schmitz*, later expelled for extremist statements—in 1982 his staff issued a press release entitled "Senator Schmitz and His Committee Survive 'Attack of the Bulldykes'" after a contentious public hearing on abortion rights)—who as a Member of Congress, opposed sex education in public schools, believed citizens should be able to carry loaded guns, and called the Watts race riots of 1965 "a Communist operation;" *Eric Show*, a major league baseball pitcher; *Kevin Strom*, a white supremacist and founder of National Vanguard; *Edwin A. Walker*, ended his 30-year Army career as a major general saying he "could no longer serve in uniform and be a collaborator with the release of United States sovereignty to the United Nations."

According to Welch, both the United States' and Soviet governments were controlled by the same furtive conspiratorial cabal of internationalists, greedy bankers, and corrupt politicians. If left unexposed, the traitors inside the U.S. government would betray the country's sovereignty to the United Nations for a collectivist new world order managed by a "one-world socialist government." The Birch Society incorporated many themes from the Liberty League and other pre-WWII groups opposed to the New Deal, and had its base in the business sector.[42]

In January 1960 the Birch Society had 75 chapters and 1,500 members, and by September 1960 there were 324 chapters and some 5,300 members. In March of 1961, according to Welch, there was "a staff of twenty-eight people in the Home Office; about thirty Coordinators (or Major Coordinators) in the field, who are fully-paid as to salary and expenses; and about one hundred Coordinators (or Section Leaders as they are called in some areas), who work on a volunteer basis as to all or part of their salary, or expenses, or both." Estimates of Society membership by the end of 1961 ranged from 60,000 to 100,000.[43]

The Birch Society pioneered the approach of combining grassroots lobbying with educational meetings, petition drives, and letter writing campaigns that would in 1980s and later be used with vast success by groups funded by the rich and corporations. One early campaign against the second Summit Conference between the U.S. and the Soviet Union generated over 600,000 postcards and letters, according to the Society. A June1964 Birch campaign to oppose Xerox Corporation sponsorship of TV programs favorable to the UN produced 51,279 letters from 12,785 individuals.[44]

The John Birch Society also began the practice of pigeon-holing both its campaigns and those of its opponents. It brought advertising into politics, together with all of its baggage. It sought to restore prayer in school, repeal the graduated personal income tax, stop "Communist influences within our communications media," and stop the "trend of legislation by judicial fiat." It mounted a campaign to "Impeach Earl Warren," the Chief Justice of the U.S. Supreme Court who presided over the *Brown* and other decisions. Highway billboards throughout the nation generated a reported 500 letters per day to members of Congress.[45]

The Society brought lasting changes to the American political culture. As one organization that has followed the group closely wrote—

> In a sense, the Birch society pioneered the encoding of
> implicit cultural forms of ethnocentric White racism and Christian
> nationalist antisemitism rather than relying on the White supremacist

biological determinism and open loathing of Jews that had typified the old right prior to WWII. Throughout its existence, however, the Society has promoted open homophobia and sexism.[46]

Unlike the American Liberty League and the many other organizations that preceded it, the John Birch Society has not gone quietly into the night, even though institutional Communism and the Soviet Union have long since ceased to exist. Most recently, it has revived the Civil War-era and civil rights opposition concept of "nullification," in which a state interposes itself between its citizens and the federal government. The Birch Society wants to halt so-called "ObamaCare" national health insurance by persuading state legislatures to enact prohibitions on its implementation. "Nullification," said its current director of marketing, Larry Greenley, "for the JBS goes along with our emphasis on returning to the Constitution."[47]

Returning to the Constitution? Exactly where in the original Constitution does the word "nullification" appear? Or the Declaration of Independence? Or any of the amendments to the Constitution? Nowhere.

Once again, those who would sacrifice human rights for the sake of the rich and propertied are attempting to revive a long-dead doctrine. Nullification was first formally invoked when South Carolina declared the tariff acts of 1828 and 1832 "unauthorized by the constitution of the United States, and violate the true meaning and intent thereof and are null, void, and no law, nor binding upon this State."[48]

In response, on December 10, 1832, President Andrew Jackson issued a proclamation to the people of South Carolina that disputed a state's right to nullify a federal law. Congress passed the Force Act that authorized the use of military force against any state that resisted the tariff acts.[49] That ended the matter, for the time being.

Thirty years later, however, South Carolina was again attempting to invoke nullification. Joined by other slave-holding states in the Deep South, it attempted to secede from the Union, triggering the Civil War. After four years of bloodshed, the doctrine was buried, a stake through its heart. Yet today, the descendants of those who considered men and women to be property are attempting to revive a dead and divisive doctrine and, with that, eviscerate the government of the United States.

With the passage of time, the John Birch Society was joined by others seeking to establish a rule of property in the United States.

September 20, 1964—the date of the last concert of the Beatles' 1964 tour of the United States, the number one song was Roy Orbison's *Pretty Woman*, and the front page headline of the *New York Times* announced what any fool knows today—"Aid to Right Wing Laid to Big Firms."

In 1964, after three years of investigation, the Anti Defamation League charged that many of the same families and firms that had supported past attempts to remake America—and would support future ones as well—were at it again: Gulf Oil (the Mellons), Pew, United States Steel, the Sloan Foundation, Armco Steel Foundation, Republic Steel, Olin-Mathieson and many others.

Today, many of those same interests are once again seeking the same outcome—a change in the nation's direction—through different means. Today, so called "tea parties" nurtured by new forces like the Koch brothers, and some of the same old ones—Mellon banking and oil money, Olin Mathieson firearms and chemicals wealth and the Allen-Bradley electronics fortunes—have become household words.

However, businesses and the rich have learned from past mistakes.

No longer are efforts backed by the rich and businesses thinly disguised. Roosevelt advisor James Farley said of the American Liberty League and its 1933 cabal backed by DuPont, Sun and Gulf Oil, Mellon Bank and dozens of other corporations and families, it "ought to be called the 'American Cellophane League' because first it's a DuPont product and second, you can see right through it.'"[50] The connections are carefully hidden and uniformly denied.

In the case of the Koch brothers and the Tea Parties, for example, money made by Koch Industries is distributed to the Kochs or one of their employees, then transferred to one of the foundations that they control (Fred C. and Mary R. Koch; Charles G. Koch; David H. Koch; and, the Claude R. Lambe Foundations). From there, funds are handed out to any one of dozens of front groups with innocent-sounding names (Americans for Prosperity [AFP], for example), which are run by hired hands (Dick Armey, in the case of AFP or perhaps one of the other groups that specializes in writing "policy" papers, such as the Heritage Foundation).

They will, in turn, provide services, such as training or printing of placards, to groups that seem to spontaneously appear. The faces on the evening news will not be those of the Kochs, but tea partiers from, say, Seattle, who were trained with Koch money at a facility bought by Koch money by employees paid by Koch money after they were flown to Washington, D.C. by Koch money, housed at a place paid for by Koch money and fed by food bought with Koch money.

As this was described by AlterNet—

> In a darkened hotel ballroom, on the eve of Glenn Beck's burlesque of self-righteousness at the Lincoln Memorial, some 2,500 activists listened politely to the tall, impeccably dressed elder at the podium as he stumbled through his introduction of the evening's guest of honor, the conservative columnist George Will. The speaker was introduced simply as chairman of the board of the Americans For Prosperity Foundation, the organization that sponsored the event.
>
> Few among the rank-and-file recognized the billionaire David Koch—heir to the fortunes of Koch Industries—or knew him as the man who bankrolls their activism, whose largess subsidized many of their trips to the nation's capital to take part in AFP's organizing conference, and the Beck rally the following day.[51]

Yet the Koch brothers, themselves, provide no money "directly" for tea party rallies. They give money to one or more of the foundations they control, which gives it to Americans for Prosperity, which passes it on to AFP chapters, which organize tea party rallies and report to the beaming Chairman, David Koch—who, after all, gave them no money "directly."

Is there a connection between the Kochs and tea parties? Of course.

Then it is denied, takes a long time to explain, even longer to prove, then it is denied, and for those of a paranoid disposition, the connection will be disbelieved. Besides, it's all perfectly legal. (After all where do the people who write the laws get their campaign contributions?)

As a result, when Koch Industries receives a query about connections between the billionaire brothers and the tea parties, this is the reply:

> Koch companies value free speech and believe it is good to have more Americans engaged in key policy issues. That said, Koch companies, the Koch foundations, Charles Koch and David Koch have no ties to and have never given money to FreedomWorks. In addition, no funding has been provided by Koch companies, the Koch foundations, Charles Koch or David Koch specifically to support the tea parties. Thanks for your consideration.[52]

Well, that's true.

The Kochs are not currently giving money to FreedomWorks, even if they did found and support for roughly two decades the organization that morphed into FreedomWorks, Citizens for a Sound Economy. No, today, FreedomWorks has been cut loose from the Kochs and instead bankrolled by other foundation fronts with which they collaborate, such as the Scaife (Mellon) foundations.

Instead, the Kochs are giving their dough to another foundation front, Americans for Prosperity. The effect is the same.

Those demanding change are not billionaires in four-button suits, because that doesn't work with brainwashing the public. Instead, overweight, aging men and women faced with the prospect of living their last years, if not in poverty, at least in reduced circumstances, demand change. They are angry and should be. The United States government has gifted immensely rich corporations with hundreds of billions of dollars, but cast ordinary Americans adrift. The irony is that the government has done this because of money (principally in the form of campaign contributions) from the very same rich people and corporations that are fueling their anger.

The Lynde and Harry Bradley Foundation, for example, has given one of the prime coordinators of tea party protests, Americans for Prosperity, $740,000. Others who support AFP include the Anschutz, Armstrong, Bechtel, Brauer, Briggs and Stratton, Castle Rock, Challenge, Ciocca, Community, Craig, Friedman, Houston, Humphreys, JM, Keiser, Kern, Kirby, Koch, Lambe, Lattner, Marshall Heritage, McKenna, Moeller, Morris, Nagel, Nichols, Peters, Pope, Scaife, Searle Freedom, Susquehanna, Templeton, Tykeson Family, Wiegund and Wisconsin Energy Foundation or Trust.[53]

The odds now appear to favor the rich folks, like the Koch brothers and their allies, who are funding the tea parties and their thousands of overweight, aging members. In the past, the other guys, the little ones have won.

Today, however, the rich have the upper hand. They control the Supreme Court as well as one house of Congress, and make it impossible for the other house, the Senate, to legislate. Although a Democrat was elected President after eight disastrous years under the George W. Bush White House, he began to be hounded by partisans demanding his scalp before he had been in office for 90 days, blaming him for the trouble that his predecessor had created. The Kochs and their country club buddies control universities, newspapers, radio and television stations—indeed entire networks of both. They have hundreds of front groups, legislators and judges.

This time, they seem likely to win, and for "everybody else," this is a single elimination tournament. One loss and you're out.

4

AN IDEA IS BORN:
GO HUNTING WHERE THE DUCKS ARE

You start out in 1954 by saying "Nigger, nigger, nigger." By 1968 you can't say "nigger"—that hurts you. Backfires. So you say stuff like forced busing, states' rights, and all that stuff. You're getting so abstract now [that] you're talking about cutting taxes, and all these things you're talking about are totally economic things and a by-product of them is [that] blacks get hurt worse than whites. And subconsciously maybe that is part of it. I'm not saying that. But I'm saying that if it is getting that abstract, and that coded, that we are doing away with the racial problem one way or the other. You follow me—because obviously sitting around saying, "we want to cut this," is much more abstract than even the busing thing and a hell of a lot more abstract than "Nigger, nigger."

Lee Atwater
Republican Campaign Strategist

It was June of 1964, and in motion 750 miles apart were two chains of events. One was in Washington, D.C. and destined to change America, perhaps irrevocably. The other was in Mississippi. It would leave three young civil rights workers murdered and bull dozed into an earthen dam, also changing America irrevocably.

In Washington, D.C., the United States Senate was debating the Civil Rights Act of 1964. Southern Democrats were staging a filibuster in an attempt to talk the bill to death, a tactic that had always worked in the past. To halt a filibuster required a vote of 60 and never had opponents been able to collect that many on civil rights legislation.

As usual, Southerners were citing "state's rights" as the principle for which they were fighting, just as they had almost exactly 42 years earlier when anti-lynching legislation was brought to the Senate floor. Then, Sen. William Borah, an

Idaho Republican, joined in the filibuster to kill the proposal, citing "states rights" as the reason, though a majority of GOP Senators supported the bill.[1] He did the same in 1935. Then seeking the Republican nomination for President at the age of 71, Borah bluntly asserted that were he to receive the "unexpected and great honor" of being elected, he would veto anti-lynching legislation.[2] And yet again in 1938, he helped southern Democrats kill a proposal to outlaw lynching, once more citing states rights.[3]

In 1964, Senate southern Democrats once again had the support of only a handful of Republicans, with the rest opposing the filibuster and seeking enactment of the landmark legislation. Chief among the filibuster's supporters was Barry Goldwater of Arizona who, as Borah had in 1936, was seeking the GOP Presidential nomination and citing his stand in support of states rights as a primary reason.

Unlike Borah, however, Goldwater would receive the nomination, run a campaign seeking votes, especially in the South, citing his opposition to civil rights legislation. He would win five Deep South States and by so doing establish a "southern strategy" as the hallmark of the Republican Party and shift it from one committed to liberty and equal rights for blacks to one seeking power through covert and overt appeals to whites, not just in the South, but throughout the nation, and their racial resentments. It would mark the beginning of a time of sharp division in America, not just over race, but on a wide range of other "values."

As debate raged in Washington, events were unfolding in Mississippi that starkly demonstrated the need for the proposed civil rights legislation.

On the night of June 18, 1964 "the Jew boy with the beard," hurtled through the Mississippi night in his blue1963 Ford station wagon, fleeing Deputy Neshoba County Sheriff David Price. Finally forced to the shoulder of Highway 19, Michael Schwerner, a 24-year-old "Freedom Rider" being paid $9.80 a week to help blacks register to vote, was dragged from his car and shoved into the back seat of the cruiser. So, too, were another Freedom Rider, Andrew Goodman, and their black co-worker, James Chaney.[a]

Price guided the cruiser down Highway 19, then turned right onto unpaved Rock Cut Road and stopped where a knot of Ku Klux Klansmen stood waiting.

---

[a] Except where otherwise noted, the description of the Mississippi murders and the events surrounding them are based on Howard Ball, *Murder in Mississippi:* United States v. Price *and The Struggle for Civil Rights*, University Press of Kansas (Lawrence, Kansas, 2004).

THERE IS A BLOODY HISTORY TO STATES' RIGHTS

In the minds of many Southerners, the Civil War was fought over whether southern states had the inherent right to manage their own affairs as a matter of "states' rights." As it turns out, the specific subject that triggered the conflict between north and south was slavery, but many historians believe had slavery not triggered the war, something else would have. As one Texas textbook taught students, "The North based its cause on loyalty to the Union; the South on loyalty to the principle of States' rights. ... Slavery was the issue that set this sectional feeling on fire. It was but the occasion of the war, not its cause."

Horrific wrongs by and within states were justified in the name of states' rights. Some of the worst were brutal lynchings, which increased sharply after federal troops withdrew from the south at the end of Reconstruction. From 1880 to 1930, about 723 whites and nearly 5,000 blacks were lynched. Lynching peaked in 1892 with 155 black and 71 white victims that year, but between 1917 and 1918, the rate doubled.

In 1920, Rep. Leonidas Dyer, a St. Louis, Missouri Republican from a largely black district, introduced an anti-lynching bill, endorsed by the new Republican president, Warren Harding. Southern Democrats in the House opposed it for openly racist reasons, saying the lynching of "niggers" was a necessary check on the propensity of black men to rape white women. The House passed it 231 to 199, with only 17 Republicans opposing and eight Northern or border-state Democrats in support. In the Senate, however, the bill ground to a halt, with a rift in the Republican Party that presaged the schism nearly 40 years later.

Majority Leader Henry Cabot Lodge of Massachusetts supported the bill, just as Everett Dirksen did the 1964 Civil Rights Act. And just as some Republicans would later claim they were not racists, but opposed the proposed Civil Rights Act on principle, so, too, did Sen. William Borah of Idaho, who chaired the Judiciary Committee subcommittee to which the bill was referred, express reservations about intruding on states' rights. With Borah's vote, the bill was defeated in subcommittee, but was nonetheless brought to the floor by the Republican leadership. Predictably, Southern Democrats mounted a filibuster, but it, unlike its counterpart in 1964, succeeded, as it did on three later instances when Congress sought to ban lynchings under U.S. law.

The repeated invocations of states' rights by candidates must be viewed in the context of what that term has been used to justify: the bloodiest war in American history and murder in the most brutal fashion of thousands of men, women and children because they were of a subordinate race.

(Source: Oscar H. Cooper, Henry F. Estill and Leonard Lemmon, *From the Southern Point of View: History of Our Country.* A Textbook for Schools, Ginn & Co., Boston, 1895 quoted in the *New York Times*, Oct. 5, 1895.)

One of the Klansmen, Wayne Roberts, a 26-year-old who had been dishonorably discharged from the U.S. Marine Corps, walked to the cruiser, dragged Schwerner from the rear seat to a narrow roadside ditch.

"Are you that nigger lover?" he asked softly. Schwerner started to reply, but spoke only four words, before Roberts shoved a pistol against Schwerner's chest and fired point blank, killing the Freedom Rider instantly. Roberts returned to the cruiser, dragged Goodman out, and shot him point blank in the chest as well, also killing him instantly. Joined by another Klansman, James Jordan, the two pulled Chaney from the car and shot him, but the wound was not instantly fatal. As Chaney lay dying, Jordan, a 38-year-old mobile home salesman, shot him in the head. "Well," he said to the ex-Marine, "You didn't leave me nothing but a nigger, but at least I killed me a nigger." Their bodies were stuffed into the dirt of an earthen dam a few miles away and not found for a month.

In Washington, Goldwater was accumulating the votes required to capture the Republican nomination for President at the convention in July. Standing on the Senate floor, he announced that he would vote against the Civil Rights Act of 1964. Reading rapidly and tonelessly, Goldwater declared that he had always been "unalterably opposed to discrimination." But this proposal, if enacted, Goldwater warned, would create "a federal police force of mammoth proportions," turning neighbor against neighbor and worker against worker.[4] "The Federal police force and an 'informer' psychology," he said, "are the hallmarks of the police state, and the landmarks in the destruction of a free society."[5]

On June 19, 1964, the Civil Rights Act passed the Senate. The remainder of the GOP Senators provided the votes to defeat, after 73 days of debate and for the first time in history, a filibuster of civil rights legislation by white southern Senators.[6] Without those Republican votes, civil rights legislation would never have become law.[7, b] In Mississippi, the Freedom Riders were still missing.

The stand by Goldwater and five other Senate Republicans in favor of the filibuster, and their subsequent success at transforming the Party, was a stunning reversal of a century of support by the GOP for enlarging the rights and privileges of blacks, Indians and other minorities. The Party had been created for the express purpose of preventing the spread of slavery and, if at all possible, eliminating it where it already existed.

Before the Great Depression, from Reconstruction onward, blacks had cast their political lot with the Republican party. Even after the collapse of the

---

[b] The bill outlawed discrimination in places of public accommodation, publicly owned facilities, employment and union membership and Federally-aided programs. It gave the Attorney General new powers to speed school desegregation and enforce the right to vote.

American economy in 1929, when whites were delivering to Franklin Roosevelt a landslide victory, black Americans voted overwhelmingly for Hoover. As late as 1932, voting Democratic was still viewed within many black communities as "the equivalent of a traitorous act."[8]

While Roosevelt's election signaled the beginning of the end of black Republicanism,[9] the Party continued to receive a significant share of the vote. Indeed, in the Presidential election of 1960, many black leaders, including Martin Luther King, Sr., and Jackie Robinson, initially supported Nixon's bid for the presidency.[10, c]

With the election of John F. Kennedy in 1960, Democrats began to be seen as friends of civil rights. In 1956, for example, only about 10 percent of voters believed the Democratic Party to be more liberal on matters of race. That number dropped to less than 5 percent in 1958, but jumped to 50 percent in 1962 and has held steady at about 45 percent since.[11] This dramatic shift presented Republicans generally, and Goldwater specifically, with an unprecedented and historic opportunity to shift loyalties of southern whites from Democrats to Republicans.[12]

Goldwater won the nomination with remarkable ease, winning with 883 votes versus the combined total of 425 for his rivals.[13] This was in large measure due to support from the South.[14] His prospects in Dixie were buoyed further by the enthusiastic assistance of Sen. Strom Thurmond of South Carolina, who had run for President in 1948 as a segregationist Dixiecrat candidate. Thurmond had been elected to the Senate as a Democrat, but on September 16, 1964 he switched to the GOP. In the Senate, Goldwater and Thurmond were, in the words of Harry Dent, Thurmond's principal aide "like the goldust twins" because of their close mutual friendship and collaboration on legislation.[15]

In his remarks on and off the Senate floor, Goldwater articulated a forceful defense of states' rights, denounced "forced integration," and attacked the Supreme

---

[c] This changed in October 1960 when Rev. Martin Luther King, Jr. was jailed in Atlanta for participating in a sit-in. Nixon's opponent, Sen. John F. Kennedy, phoned the minister's wife, Coretta Scott King, to convey his sympathy. Nixon, unwilling to make such a call, sat on the sidelines. King and Nixon had enjoyed a warm relationship, but "when this moment came, it was like he had never heard of me," King later said. He later criticized the former Vice President: the inaction made Nixon appear to be "a moral coward and one who was really unwilling to take a courageous step and take a risk," Nixon's refusal to act may have cost him the election, because Kennedy's phone call gained him the support of many black voters, and he later defeated Nixon by less than one percent of the popular vote. *King Encyclopedia*, Stanford University.

Court. Then he began using racial code wording, condemning "wave after wave of crime in our streets and in our homes," and the "riot and disorder in our cities." He expressed contempt for political leaders who had sought "political advantages by turning their eyes from riots and violence."[16]

His Vice Presidential nominee, Rep. William Miller of New York, at an October speech in Philadelphia, Pennsylvania drew perhaps the crudest connection between civil rights and civil unrest:

> It's all right to send hundreds of FBI agents and U.S. Marshals into Philadelphia, Mississippi, to protect the civil rights of a few people there; but no White House effort is made to protect the property and civil rights of thousands of people in Philadelphia, Pennsylvania.[17]

What Goldwater and those who inherited his mantle achieved was a triumph of the pursuit of power for its own sake over the pursuit of principle. Goldwater said on the Senate floor and in his speeches throughout the South—his first and last campaign speeches were both in South Carolina—that his opposition to the Civil Rights legislation was a matter of principle. But he first described the southern strategy three years earlier at a 1961 meeting in Atlanta, Georgia:

> Republicans, said Goldwater were "not going to get the Negro vote as a bloc in 1964 and 1968," adding that "so we ought to go hunting where the ducks are"—white southerners. School integration, he contended was "the responsibility of the states.[18]

Throughout his life, Goldwater insisted that he was no racist, claims that are echoed by candidates of the Republican Party for themselves since 1964 to the present day. That may very well be true.[d] But in 1961, when he proposed hunting

---

[d] That Goldwater was a man of genuine conviction and principle is demonstrated by an episode shortly before the election. Goldwater was trailing badly by this time, and virtually certain to lose. The organizer in October 1961 of the draft Goldwater movement, F. Clifton White, reasoned that Goldwater was running against fear—fear of the bomb, fear of the ending of Social Security and others as well. Goldwater had to strike back with a counter-fear. American emotions had to be galvanized by fear of domestic violence. White produced a documentary-like advertisement, *Choice*, supposedly under the aegis of Mothers for a Moral America. It showed bare-breasted women protesters, blacks rioting and looting and other scenes depicting a national moral decay. The nation seemed to be engulfed in violence and hatred, as blacks took to the streets. When Goldwater was shown

(continued...)

"where the ducks are," there was no civil rights bill to oppose on the basis of principle or anything else. It simply did not exist. President John F. Kennedy did not propose such legislation until June 11, 1963. Addressing the nation after National Guardsmen had been mobilized to assure the peaceful admission of two black students at the University of Alabama, Kennedy said—

> It ought to be possible for American consumers of any color to receive equal service in places of public accommodation, such as hotels and restaurants and theaters and retail stores, without being forced to resort to demonstrations in the street, and it ought to be possible for American citizens of any color to register to vote in a free election without interference or fear of reprisal.

> It ought to be possible, in short, for every American to enjoy the privileges of being American without regard to his race or his color. In short, every American ought to have the right to be treated as he would wish to be treated, as one would wish his children to be treated. But this is not the case.

> The Negro baby born in America today, regardless of the section of the Nation in which he is born, has about one-half as much chance of completing high school as a white baby born in the same place on the same day, one-third as much chance of completing college, one-third as much chance of becoming a professional man, twice as much chance of becoming unemployed, about one-seventh as much chance of earning $10,000 a year, a life expectancy which is 7 years shorter, and the prospects of earning only half as much.[19]

Perhaps Goldwater was not a racist. If so, he was something much worse: a politician willing to abandon his personal moral convictions in favor of cynical and conscious appeals to the worst instincts of voters—activating hatred and animosity— for the express purpose of getting their votes. Goldwater's campaign

---

[d] (...continued)
the film, he flatly refused to authorize it, declaring it to be an inflammation of racism and ordered it suppressed. It is a remarkable contrast with the willingness of Bush-the-Father 24 years later to run the overtly racist Willie Horton television ad. Theodore H. White, *The Making of the President 1964*, pp. 349–50, Atheneum Publishers, New York, 1965. White remained active in Republican politics, working for Sen. Jesse Helms and Ronald Reagan, as well as major corporations.

was overtly racist, a transparent appeal to the basest instincts of white southerners in an attempt to recruit them to the GOP.

Goldwater closed his campaign for the presidency in Columbia, South Carolina, delivering a televised speech carried over the entire South. Surrounded at the podium by famous heroes of southern resistance (including Thurmond), Goldwater chose the moment to repeat his attack on the Civil Rights Act of 1964. Of this episode, Southern historians Earl and Merle Black wrote, "Goldwater was pitching his anti-civil rights message so low to the ground that even the least astute of his audience would get the point."[20]

The race question was an ever-present concern in the lower South.

One historian has said of Louisiana, that it "seemed engulfed by a wave of pro-segregationist and anti-Johnson feelings that fall."[21] According to the novelist Walker Percy's interpretation of the vote in Mississippi, "it would not have mattered if Goldwater had advocated the collectivization of the plantations and open saloons in Jackson; he voted against the Civil Rights bill and that was that."[22]

"By coming south," the journalist Richard H. Rovere wrote, "Barry Goldwater had made it possible for great numbers of unapologetic white supremacists to hold great carnivals of white supremacy."[23] Surveys of white voters outside the South showed that Johnson received 91 percent of the vote cast by Democrats, 69 percent of that by independents, and 27 percent of that by Republicans—an overwhelming Democratic victory.

In the South, however, Goldwater carried an estimated 55 percent of the region's white voters, and a startling 71 percent in the Deep South. For the first time in American history, the Republican party had won a larger percentage of the popular vote in the ex-Confederate states than in any other region.[24] For the first time in U.S. history, the GOP played the role of the "traditional" party of the South, one opposed to integration and equality for blacks.[25]

This was no accident, but the result of a calculated electoral strategy. At Goldwater campaign headquarters were maps displaying the manner in which the strategy had to be executed: start with the 11 southern states; add to them Oklahoma, Kentucky and Arizona; then the traditionally Republican states of Nebraska, Kansas, Wyoming, Colorado and the Dakotas. That left three states—Ohio, Illinois and California—that if won would assure victory, without a single vote from the Eastern seaboard, which Goldwater had once advocated sawing off and letting it drift out to sea.[26]

What's wrong with this picture? Exactly how did Goldwater and his strategists expect to capture all eleven southern states, a region where Republicans had lost for nearly a century, especially in year when the opponent was a Texan, Lyndon Johnson. There could be one, and only one way of accomplishing that: run a race-based campaign with code-worded appeals to white southerners. Implicit in the map in the Goldwater headquarters was a statement that Goldwater and his advisers had made the decision to embrace Satan for the sake of winning.

Goldwater lost the election, but his southern strategy succeeded. He won the five Deep South States—Alabama, Georgia, Louisiana, Mississippi and South Carolina—by wide margins. In Mississippi, for example, Goldwater won 87 percent of the popular vote. Goldwater might have lost the Presidency, but he nearly doubled the number of southern white votes bestowed on Nixon four years earlier,[27] and his coattails swept Republicans into office throughout the Deep South.

In 1958, Republicans in the South held two seats in the Senate, eight in the House, zero governorships and fewer than 100 state legislators. Goldwater's run in 1964 laid the groundwork for the solid south that the GOP enjoys today. Not since Reconstruction had Georgia, Alabama or Mississippi sent a Republican to Capitol Hill. But in 1964, the only Republican on Mississippi's congressional ballot scored the state's greatest political upset in memory: Prentiss Walker, a hard-shell poultry farmer, ousted William Arthur Winstead, who had been in the House for 22 years. In rural Georgia, Republican Howard ("Bo") Callaway, a slick-campaigning textile millionaire, topped former Lieutenant Governor Garland T. Byrd, while in Alabama's eight districts, the G.O.P. put up candidates in six races and won five. The victors included W. Jack ("Thank God for Goldwater") Edwards. All were opposed to civil rights laws.[28]

By 1968, a party that had been unable to boast a presence in the South for almost one century had six members in the U.S. Senate, 29 in the House, four governorships and almost 300 state legislators in Dixie.[29]

These results also had the effect of beginning the GOP transformation in a different way: Republican moderates in states as distant and different as Colorado, Texas and Connecticut, were swept out of office. The initial shrinkage in the presence of moderates was largely a result of President Lyndon Johnson's overwhelming victory over Goldwater: his coattails outside the South carried Democrats to victory and swept out Republicans. Later, however, Republicans would begin to eat their own, launching efforts to rid the party of liberal to moderate voices such as Sens. Clifford Case of New Jersey, Hugh Scott of Pennsylvania and Jacob Javits of New York.[30] In the Senate of the 85th Congress,

1957 to 1959, two-thirds of all racial liberals were Republicans. In the wake of the Goldwater loss, the 89th Congress, 1965 to 1967, that number had dropped to 18 percent.[31]

Much of the Republican success in the South could be attributed to the efforts of Sen. Strom Thurmond. Using a vehicle called "Thurmond Speaks for Goldwater Committee" and operating with funds that it raised, and none from either the Arizonan's campaign or the Republican National Committee, Thurmond stumped the south. The region was blanketed with television and radio ads. The principal coordinator of the campaign was Harry Dent, a Thurmond Senate aide who took a leave of absence to manage the campaign.[32]

Buoyed by the warm welcomes—and the prospect for a quick ascendance to office in the fledgling southern GOP organizations as opposed to long periods of service in established Democratic hierarchy—Republican ranks began to swell. As they did, early appeals in the South were blatantly racist as avowed segregationists ran for statewide offices under the Republican banner. For example, the GOP's 1963 candidate for Governor of Mississippi, Rubell Philips, declared himself a "staunch segregationist" who if elected would "fight for genuine racial harmony in keeping with Mississippi traditions."[33]

Racism began to ripple through the party, well beyond the confines of the South. At a 1963 meeting of State Republican party chairman in Denver, Colorado, two of the southern representatives carried on a loud and boisterous conversation about "niggers" and "nigger-lovers." An eastern chairman later recalled that "nobody criticized them for doing it, and only a few of us were uncomfortable." It became increasingly clear that a large number of the Republican Party's leaders were quite comfortable with racism and bigotry if it brought them electoral victory. "Remember this is not South Africa," one observed at breakfast. "The white man outnumbers the Negro nine to one in this country."[34]

That number—one black for every nine whites—made the transformation that followed Goldwater's defeat almost inevitable. Goldwater's appeals to racist whites had been so blatant that blacks were left with little choice but to embrace the Democratic Party. Revisionist Republicans like to contend that it was northern Democrats who created a racial divide by appealing to blacks. If so, Democratic appeals were of an entirely different sort: the party proposed and enacted laws aimed at assuring blacks the opportunity to vote, and not be lynched for it; a seat at the same lunch counter as whites; and, the chance to provide their children with a decent education. Those scarcely count as appeals to black racism.

In Goldwater's defeat, some strategists saw the possibility of a bright political future for Republicans, based on splitting white voters from their loyalty to Democrats. There were two lessons to be drawn from Goldwater's defeat:

Today is not 1964 when those tensions existed because of four centuries of slavery[e] and another 100 years of Jim Crow laws and violence. For them to exist and be exploited in the 21st century requires that they be sustained and nurtured, and therein lies perhaps the most evil and pernicious consequence of the southern strategy. Racial appeals exist at the expense of black progress and they perpetuate racial conflict for the sake of electoral gain.

Despite all of this, Goldwater not only carried the Deep South, but did so with massive majorities. If racial politics could draw white voters to a candidate as extreme and unelectable as Barry Goldwater, then it was among the most potent forces in American politics—perhaps even the most powerful. What might happen if it were exploited with greater subtlety by a more attractive candidate?

"Southern Strategy" is a benignly inoffensive name for an intrinsically evil and racially divisive calculus aimed at acquiring and maintaining power by indefinitely extending racial animosity. By definition, there cannot be a southern strategy without racially resentful whites. This means that the Republican Party must keep the nation in a state of, if not constant then periodic, racial tension. It is as if every two to four years the scabs of racial healing are torn away, reopening, time and again, wounds that had begun to heal.

White support for the principles of racial equality and integration has increased almost boundlessly over the last half-century. At the same time, however, support for policies designed to remedy the consequences of two centuries of slavery and one more of segregation—that is to actually integrate blacks and others of color into society, thus creating a single, seamless and unified America—has increased scarcely at all. Indeed, in some cases, white support has actually declined.[35] This has resulted in two distinctly different views of America: while most white Americans believe that prejudice and discrimination are problems of the past, black Americans see prejudice and discrimination everywhere.[36]

---

[e] Slavery was the legal order in the United States for four centuries, starting as early as 1663 when the British crown granted the Company of Royal Adventurers to Africa a monopoly of the African slave trade to what were then the colonies. Richard B. Morris, *Encyclopedia of American History*, p. 44, Harper & Row, New York, 1965.

As a result, there is in America a tragic dichotomy. Because of civil rights laws and other changes in American culture, racial segregation and white supremacy have disappeared even from mention and even in the deepest parts of the South. Today, racial conflicts and suspicions are, or at least can be, expressed in more subtle and socially acceptable ways. Because of this, political debate on matters of race now takes place in a code that communicates a well-understood but implicit meaning while preserving the deniability of that meaning, a sort of rhetorical wink, if you will.[37]

This has created a political opportunity for those willing to exploit it, and Republicans have been willing. Instead of appeals that explicitly refer to race, messages employ proxy terms.

As explained by Kinder and Sanders—

At the core of this new resentment was not whether blacks possessed the inborn ability to succeed, but rather whether they would try.[38]

A new form of prejudice has come to prominence, one that is preoccupied with matters of moral character, informed by the virtues associated with the traditions of individualism. At its center are the contentions that blacks do not try hard enough to overcome the difficulties they face and that they take what they have not earned. Today, we say, prejudice is expressed in the language of American individualism.[39]

At the conclusion of Goldwater's 1964 campaign, what the Republican Party required was a core of political strategists and consultants who could craft a campaign with a mixture of code-worded appeals to resentful whites, all while maintaining a patina of racial equality. This would draw backlash votes without alarming the rest of the electorate. As even more time passed and support for allowing blacks to eat at the same restaurants, attend the same schools and otherwise be treated as equals to whites, tolerance for overt racism virtually disappeared. Republican overtures became increasingly subtle.

The Southern Strategy was once explained by Republican strategist Lee Atwater, who ran Ronald Reagan's campaigns for the Presidency in the South and George Bush-the-father's nationally. Atwater was a peer of Karl Rove, who has run all the Bush-the-son's campaigns (except for an unsuccessful run for Congress in 1978). And, in 1988, when Bush-the-son was assigned by the Bush family to be

Atwater's watcher, the South Carolinian no doubt schooled Bush-the-son on politics and campaigning. Raised in Aiken County, South Carolina, Atwater's knowledge and understanding of racial politics, particularly in the South, were quite simply unrivaled.

Atwater has since died, but while a member of Reagan's White House staff, he was interviewed by an academic who later made the transcript public.[f]

> **Atwater:** As to the whole southern strategy that Harry Dent and others put together in 1968, opposition to the Voting Rights Act would have been a central part of keeping the South. Now [the new Southern strategy of Ronald Reagan] doesn't have to do that. All you have to do to keep the South is for Reagan to run in place on the issues he's campaigned on since 1964 ... and that's fiscal conservation, balancing the budget, cut taxes, you know, the whole cluster. ...

> **Questioner:** But the fact is, isn't it, that Reagan does get to the Wallace voter and to the racist side of the Wallace voter by doing away with Legal Services, by cutting down on food stamps ... ?

> **Atwater:** You start out in 1954 by saying "Nigger, nigger, nigger." By 1968 you can't say "nigger"—that hurts you. Backfires. So you say stuff like forced busing, states' rights, and all that stuff. You're getting so abstract now [that] you're talking about cutting taxes, and all these things you're talking about are totally economic things and a by-product of them is [that] blacks get hurt worse than whites. And subconsciously maybe that is part of it. I'm not saying that. But I'm saying that if it is getting that abstract, and that coded, that we are doing away with the racial problem one way or the other. You follow me—because obviously sitting around saying, "we want to cut this," is much more abstract than even the busing thing and a hell of a lot more abstract than "Nigger, nigger."[40]

---

[f] Atwater interned in the Washington office of Thurmond, where he was schooled by Harry Dent, who ran Nixon's 1968 Presidential campaign in the South as he had for Goldwater in 1964. After Nixon's victory, Dent joined the White House staff where another promising young Republican strategist, Karl Rove, worked for the "ratfuckers," the cadre of Nixon aides that launched dirty tricks against potential Presidential rivals, whether real or imagined. Some believe the true architect of the southern strategy was Dent.

A half century ago appeals to racism were not so implicit. They were overt, plain spoken and unmistakable. Consider Strom Thurmond's unvarnished, and today repulsive speech to a crowd of 6,000 States' Rights Democrats gathered in Birmingham, Alabama to select a nominee for president in 1948:

> "There's not enough troops in the Army to force the southern people to break down segregation and admit the nigger race into our theaters, into our swimming pools, into our homes and into our churches," The crowd roared.[41]

When the statement was read back to him 41 years later, Thurmond was initially incredulous that it was accurate, but after finally conceding its correctness, he said, "If I had to run that race again, some of the wording I used would not be used. I would word it differently."[42]

Of course he would word it differently. If he or any other politician in the United States used those words today, the public would , as they say in the South, pounce on him like a duck on a June bug. But in 1948, overt and open appeals to racism were not only perfectly acceptable in the South, but they worked: the fact that Thurmond carried Alabama, Louisiana, Mississippi and South Carolina, garnering 39 electoral votes and 7.3 percent of the popular vote that year,[43] leaves no doubt that even the vilest sort of racist remarks were embraced by southern voters then.

But in 1989, when Thurmond said he would use different words to convey the message, he was admitting that such overt appeals to racist impulses not only don't work anymore, they trigger a backlash. Implicit or indirect appeals, however, do work, which is why they are so widely used by Republicans.

Because of this, a candidate perceived as being racist, or overtly appealing to racism, has virtually zero chance of being elected. Proof of one-half of this statement—that explicit appeals to racism can blow up in a candidate's face—were provided in 2006 when a potential candidate for the Republican presidential race, Sen. George Allen of Virginia, suffered a swift fall and a humiliating defeat with his encounter with "macaca," a racial slur.

In 2006, Allen was running for reelection, and a lot more. His return to the Senate was considered such a sure thing, that he was looking beyond that to a possible run for the Presidency in 2008. At a rally in western Virginia, a college student, S.R. Sidarth, was videotaping Allen's remarks for the Democratic opponent, James Webb. Shadowing a candidate to assure that he says the same thing on Tuesday in one part of the state as on Thursday in a different area, is a common practice.

Without warning and with a smirk on his face, Allen pointed to Sidarth, and called out "This fellow here, over here with the yellow shirt, macaca, or whatever his name is. He's with my opponent. He's following us around everywhere. And it's just great," as his supporters began to laugh. Allen continuing, saying that his opponent was raising money in California with a "bunch of Hollywood movie moguls."[44]

He then added, "Let's give a welcome to macaca, here. Welcome to America and the real world of Virginia." Allen then began talking about the "war on terror."[45]

Sidarth was every bit as American as Allen, and more Virginian. He had been born in Fairfax County, Virginia and was a student at the University of Virginia. Allen had been born and raised in California.

When Allen's campaign manager, Dick Wadhams, was called by reporters, he initially dismissed the issue with an expletive and insisted the senator had "nothing to apologize for." Hours later, however, the campaign issued an apology, and in the following weeks it imploded. Allen started the campaign with a 16-point lead in the polls and had been, in the words of the *Washington Post*, "a wildly popular governor" and "considered a shoo-in for reelection."[46] Yet when the polls closed, the Senator-elect was James Webb.

Allen's rapid decline and ultimate defeat were due in part to the "macaca" slur. But more damaging than macaca was the string of revelations triggered by the publicity it attracted. Allen, son of a Hall of Fame football coach who guided the Washington Redskins to a Super Bowl appearance, was born and raised in California. Once in Virginia, however, he demonstrated a fondness for things Southern: he wore a Confederate flag lapel pin and displayed a Confederate flag and a noose—yes, a noose, as in lynchings—in his home and office. A former football teammate said Allen had routinely used an ugly racial slur and once stuffed a severed deer head into a black family's mailbox in the 1970s.

If macaca and the rebel flags weren't enough, they were followed by the ultimate *coups de grace*. At a televised debate with Webb, a reporter asked Allen the following: "It has been reported," said Peggy Fox, that "your grandfather Felix, for whom you were given your middle name, was Jewish. Could you please tell us whether your forebearers include Jews and, if so, at which point Jewish identity might have ended?"[47] Allen's mother, it turned out, who was born in Tunisia, (where "macaca" is a racial epithet)[48] was from a well known Sephardic Jewish Lumbroso family.[49]

What left some observers dumbfounded, however, was the intensity of Allen's reaction. A card-carrying Presbyterian who wears cowboy boots and chews tobacco, Allen "recoiled as if he had been struck," in the words of the *Washington Post*. Visibly furious, he admonished the questioner to stop "making aspersions."[50] He was, on the one hand, contending that his religious ancestry was irrelevant[51]—"To be getting into what religion my mother is, I don't think is relevant," Allen said—but on the other, viewing a reference to his Jewish forebearers as an "aspersion."

Allen sank in the polls—both public opinion and in the voting booth—like a rock. Webb's win was razor thin, 49.59 percent of the vote compared to 49.20 percent for Allen, but it was nevertheless a stunning upset. He suffered the political death of a thousand cuts, most self-inflicted, causing voters to conclude he was a racist.[52]

But a closer examination of the election results reveals how powerful racial appeals remain: of voters that considered "values," a code word for appeals to resentful whites and religious fundamentalists, "extremely important," Allen garnered 63 percent of the vote. In the Webb-Allen race, these voters accounted for 46 percent of the electorate,[53] so had Allen not stumbled so badly and so often, he almost certainly would have prevailed. In many ways, the contest reflected the deep divisions between the world views of white and black Americans.

Despite backfires like that of Allen, Republican candidates remain willing to play the race card because it is such a powerful weapon. Another 2006 Senate election demonstrated this.

In 2006, Rep. Harold Ford, Jr. a black Democrat, and Bob Corker, a white Republican, were vying for the Tennessee Senate seat being vacated by Sen. Bill Frist, a two-term Republican. The Democratic candidate posed a thorny problem for Republicans. Harold Ford was not merely black and experienced, but a hawkish Democrat, opposed to amnesty for illegal immigrants and a supporter of banning gay marriage. His race with the Republican Candidate, former Chattanooga mayor Bob Corker, was a dead heat. Corker switched campaign managers, "rolling out the big guns," in the words of one political blogger.[54] He hired Tom Ingram, chief of staff for the other Tennessee Senator, Lamar Alexander. He also hired Hollywood media consultant Fred Davis, whose previous clients had included California

Gov. Arnold Schwarzenegger and Bush-the-Son. Within days, a 30-second television ad paid for by the Republican National Committee began to air in Tennessee. It has deeply racist, but extremely subtle, overtones. The Republican Party played the race card: the ad featured a scantily clad white woman winking and inviting Ford—whom she met at a Playboy Club, the ad informs viewers—to "call me," followed by a broad wink.

"It is a powerful innuendo that plays to pre-existing prejudices about African American men and white women," said Hilary Shelton, head of the Washington office of the National Association for the Advancement of Colored People, the country's oldest civil rights organization. Former Republican Sen. William S. Cohen of Maine, was more blunt. Cohen said on CNN that the ad was "a very serious appeal to a racist sentiment."[55]

John Geer, a Vanderbilt University political scientist who published a book that year on attack ads, "*In Defense of Negativity*," said he had watched the anti-Ford spot repeatedly in recent days. "I just couldn't believe what I was seeing," he said. "I don't see how you can think it's not playing a racial card. It's making references to interracial sex. It's an ad that is in some sense breaking new lows."[56]

In a later review of race-baiting ads, the University of California at Berkeley school of law and public administration, wrote of the ad—

> That race-baiting is still regarded as an effective strategy is clear from the 2006 Tennessee Senate race, the first case reviewed in this report. Two weeks before that election, Democrat Harold Ford, an African-American, was in a statistical dead heat with his GOP opponent, Bob Corker. The National Republican Senatorial Committee produced a TV commercial that made hay of the unproven claim that Ford had attended a party at a Playboy mansion. The ad ended with a scantily clad Playboy bunny saying, enticingly: "Call me, Harold." That message played directly on the old taboo of a black man having sex with a white woman. And the ad's punch-line, "He's just not right," might as well have read "just not white." Did the ad turn the tide? Despite howls of protest, it ran for more than a week—until the polls began turning against Ford, who ultimately lost.[57]

The ad, (view at http://www.youtube.com/watch?v=cWkrwENN5CQ), has many deeply racist, but extremely subtle, overtones. Can you spot them?

"He's just not right." (Meaning, Ford is black and should stay in his place, and not be so uppity.)

"So he took money from porn movies. Doesn't everybody?"

"Canada can take care of North Korea." (Believe it or not, "Canada" has become a code word for blacks.[g])

"I'd love to pay higher marriage taxes." (Another cue racialized by Reagan, because the taxes support welfare, and all the people on welfare are black— actually whites are the largest recipients of support.)

"I met Harold at the Playboy party." (This is a trigger for the fears of black southern men raping the white southern women; and, white women who have relationships with black men are sexually loose or tainted.)

"When I die, Harold Ford will let me pay taxes again." (Ronald Reagan was such an effective communicator that he racialized certain phrases, "taxes," being one of them. Merely say that word or others such as "big government spending" or "special interests" and it pulls the trigger on racial animosities.)

"Too many guns." (This triggers fears of black violence, and the era in the South when whites were allowed to own guns, but not blacks.)

"Terrorists need their privacy." (What color are terrorists?)

The first woman in the ad is an apparently light-skinned black, mentioning Ford's name, a reminder that he is black as well.

Racial tags:

The Ad: As it plays, there is music in the background—a "bouncy" multiple notes, repeated time and again like jungle drums.

Screen text at the end of the Ad: Against a black background, "Harold Ford" fades up, followed after about a ½ second pause by "He's just not right." in somewhat smaller type.

---

[g] Here is the definition offered at Urban Dictionary: Expression for black people used by whites as "code" when they want to refer to blacks in a semi-derogatory manner without being detected in a group of people. "Jeezus, look at all the Canadians out tonight." http://www.urbandictionary.com/define.php?term=canadian

Unknown: "Harold. Call me." (White bimbo-looking woman with a broad smile, and at "Call me," winks her right eye)

Unknown: So he took money from porn movie producers? I mean, who hasn't? (Sleazy looking white guy, black hair, sunglasses, black Polo shirt, mid-30s who smirks after laughing following "who hasn't.")

Unknown: Canada can take care of North Korea. They're not busy. (A couple—a Wilford Brimly-type older man on the left wearing overalls and a gray-haired older woman to his right.)

Unknown: I'd love to pay higher marriage taxes. (White woman, with short cropped dark hair, late 30s, early 40s.)

Unknown: I met Harold at the Playboy party. (White "bimbo" blonde, shown from just above her breasts up, wearing only a small gold locket or similar necklace.)

Unknown: Ford's right. I do have too many guns. (White man in hunting camouflage, wearing a billed cap, cloths, appears to be early 30s.)

Unknown: When I die, Harold Ford will let me pay taxes again. (White man, in about his 60s, standing next to a somewhat younger white woman, whose head is turned looking at him in profile.)

Unknown: Terrorists need their privacy. (Young white woman, black hair, black sweater.)

Unknown: Harold Ford looks nice, isn't that enough? (Young woman, darker skinned, but not obviously African American, wearing pink T shirt, with wisps of hair, escaping.)

Unknown: The Republican National Committee is responsible for the content of this advertising.

America will never be able to free itself of its heaviest burden and fulfill its potential as a democracy until the country rids itself of racism. That cannot happen until Americans squarely confront and reject perpetuation of the racist spirit by the Republican Party and its candidates.

5

THE THREE WHO STARTED A REVOLUTION

It is enough that the people know there was an election. The
people who cast the votes decide nothing. The people who count the
votes decide everything.

Joseph Stalin, Undated[a]

It is impossible to tell the story of America's re-making without crediting
three utterly un-alike men. Two are towering figures within their own fields. One is
relatively unknown, in large part because he chose to remain in the background.

These three lent flesh to the skeleton of what came to be called the "Reagan
Revolution." In truth, Ronald Reagan was merely the beneficiary of the revolution.
It was these three, and, of course, others, who built and manned the ramparts. A
case can be made, and it is one in which I believe, that without all of these three,
there would have been no revolution. Each brought unique and irreplaceable skills
and drive to the task.

The three are—

- *Lewis F. Powell, Jr.,* best known to most Americans as a member of the
  U.S. Supreme Court;

- *William E. Simon,* most often remembered as Secretary of the Treasury and
  energy "czar" under Presidents Nixon and Ford; and,

---

[a] "Biography of Joseph Stalin," National Cold War Exhibition,
http://www.nationalcoldwarexhibition.org/explore/biography.cfm?name=Stalin,%20Joseph,
accessed Sept. 18, 2012

- **Paul Weyrich,** a Republican operative described by one commentator as of "no influential family; no real wealth, even at his death."[1]

Powell was invariably described as courtly. In the words of former Justice Sandra Day O'Connor, "For those who seek a model of human kindness, decency, exemplary behavior, and integrity, there will never be a better man."[2]

In contrast, investment banker Simon was in the words of the *Washington Post*, "legendarily mean." Simon's old friend Edwin Feulner, president of the Heritage Foundation, said he was "a mean, nasty, tough bond trader who took no BS from anyone." Feulner said Simon was known to awaken his children on weekend mornings by dousing their heads with buckets of cold water.

Weyrich was once called "a little-known political mechanic" by *New Republic* magazine.[3] It is true that in his later years (he died in 2008) Weyrich's influence was diminished. But for a quarter-century, before there was such a creature as the "new right," Weyrich was a visionary. He melded the Republican Party with the religious right. That not only created a political instrument of extraordinary influence, but imbued campaigns with "values," ranging from opposition to abortion to resistance to gay marriage.

As importantly, Weyrich created institutions that had immense impacts: the Heritage Foundation, which was the first of the modern self-styled "free market" think tanks, which revolutionized the way that Congress could be influenced by quickly-written and widely distributed "issue briefs" to influence legislation. Weyrich also founded the American Legislative Exchange Council, the portal through which corporations dictate the content and wording of state laws.

However these three might have differed in their personal attributes, they were peas in a pod on the subject of politics. Each was intensely driven, though Powell hid this behind an air of southern gentility. Powell's influence can be seen in two ways: first, the opinions that he shaped while a member of the U.S. Supreme Court, delivering immense power to corporations; and, as the author of the "Powell Manifesto," which became the blueprint for delivering control of America to corporations and the rich.

In August 1971, just before his appointment to the U.S. Supreme Court by Richard Nixon and at the request of a neighbor, Powell wrote what became known to many as the "Powell Manifesto." The previous few years had seen America's transition from the Ozzie and Harriet-Dwight Eisenhower era to a nation wracked by violent protest against the war in Viet Nam, race riots in major cities and, for the first time in history, legally-mandated protections for blacks, women and other minorities, the environment and workers. The economy was sliding and wage and price controls had been imposed to halt inflation.

Powell's "confidential" memo was sent by the U.S. Chamber of Commerce, for which his friend worked, to its 100,000 members. Titled "Attack on[b] the American Free Enterprise System." Leading the assault, wrote Powell, were "disquieting voices" joined in criticism "from perfectly respectable elements of society: from the college campus, the pulpit, the media, the intellectual and literary journals, the arts and sciences, and from politicians."

Powell advocated "constant surveillance" of textbook and television content, as well as a purge of left-wing elements and a wide range of other actions with one overarching goal: changing how individuals and society think about the corporation, the government, the law, the culture, and the individual.

Corporations responded immediately, creating new vice president positions for governmental affairs or public relations, hiring lobbyists, starting or reviving Washington, D.C.-based trade groups and, perhaps most importantly, starting the search for a new, louder and more effective voice.

The first of these organizations was started with $250,000 from arch-conservative Colorado beer magnate, Joseph Coors.[c] He was so moved by the Powell Manifesto that he approached his U.S. Senator, Gordon Allott, saying that he wanted to assure that it was implemented. Did Allot know who might take on the task?

Allot suggested his press secretary, Paul Weyrich. Coors gave him the money and Weyrich started what later became known as the Heritage Foundation. Today, this may seem a modest achievement. At the time, however, Heritage was revolutionary, because it was a different breed of think tank. Its predecessors avoided "advocacy" for fear of losing their tax-exempt status.[4]

---

[b] Some on-line reproductions of the Manifesto say "on" while others say "of."

[c] According to Lee Edwards, official historian of the Heritage Foundation, beer magnate Joseph Coors said the memorandum convinced Coors that American business was "ignoring a crisis," which led him in 1971 to invest the first $250,000 to fund what later became the Heritage Foundation. John C. Jefferies, Jr., Justice Lewis F. Powell, Jr.: A Biography (Fordham Univ Press, 2001).

In contrast, Heritage explicitly devoted itself to "formulate and promote conservative public policies." Heritage used direct-mail fund-raising, a tactic borrowed from political campaigns. It considered itself as much an organ of the conservative movement as of the Washington intellectual world—perhaps more.[5]

Weyrich was a dynamo who seemed to be everywhere at once. Aside from creating a number of influential organizations, he relentlessly pushed Republicans to demand limited government, tax cuts and his version of individual responsibility. He seemed to have a steel backbone and a willingness to speak what he saw as the truth to power, no matter how unpleasant it might be.[6]

When Weyrich came to power, he was cherubic, a smiling face with a sharp tongue. Weyrich constantly drank Pellegrino bottled water. In his last years, diabetes forced him to have both legs amputated. Photos taken shortly before his death show a thin, sharp-faced man with an aquiline nose.[7]

Weyrich started as a reporter in Milwaukee, moved to Denver, then came to Washington in 1967 as press secretary to United States Senator Gordon Allott, a Republican from Colorado. After the Powell Manifesto, he started what would eventually become the Heritage Foundation, then the Free Congress Foundation and later the American Legislative Exchange Council (ALEC). All three became immensely influential.[8]

Weyrich also founded the Free Congress Foundation, an influential organization patronized at its weekly lunches by Republican political operatives. For a time, an essay by Eric Heubeck was posted at the Free Congress website, but has since been removed. Fortunately, the Yurica Report was able to retain and post a copy, which can be found at http://www.yuricareport.com/Dominionism/FreeCongressEssay.html.

Titled "The Integration of Theory and Practice: A Program for the New Traditionalist Movement," the essay is a matter-of-fact overview of the exact tactics that libertarians (they call themselves "conservative," but will reluctantly agree that this is a misnomer) use to keep moderates and liberals out of office and off the media radar.

Heubeck writes, in part, "We must, as Mr. Weyrich has suggested, develop a network of parallel cultural institutions existing side-by-side with the dominant leftist cultural institutions. The building and promotion of these institutions will require the development of a movement that will not merely reform the existing post-war conservative movement, but will in fact be forced to supersede it—if it is to succeed at all—because it will pursue a very different strategy and be premised on a very different view of its role in society … "

The process includes three stages: developing a "highly motivated elite able to coordinate future activities;" developing "institutions designed to make an impact on the wider elite and a relatively small minority of the masses;" and, transforming "the overall character of American popular culture ... " Heubeck describes the movement as "entirely destructive, and entirely constructive. We will not try to reform the existing institutions. We only intend to weaken them, and eventually destroy them."

Weyrich and his colleagues might have abandoned a public embrace of the tactics described by Heurich, but they pursued their implementation single-mindedly. When Ronald Reagan was elected in 1980, for example, Heritage was ready. It issued a *Mandate for Leadership*, a compendium of more than 2,000 specific policy recommendations. By the end of Reagan's second term, more than 60 percent had been adopted by the administration, including, most famously, the Roth-Kemp across-the-board tax cuts.[9]

Using Heritage as a springboard, Weyrich launched an effort to recruit fundamentalist Protestant and evangelicals to what he termed the "Moral Majority." The rest became history.

But it might not have become history had it not been for William Simon,[d] who turned a handful of "voices"—self-styled "free market" or "enterprise" think tanks that use money from corporations and the rich to sing the praises of competition. He established the means to oversee. coordinate and mobilize them.

Simon's term as Secretary of the Treasury ended with the defeat in 1976 of Republican incumbent Jerry Ford by peanut farmer, former Georgia governor and evangelical Jimmy Carter. Before that, however, Simon witnessed first hand the ignominious resignation of Richard M. Nixon in the wake of the Watergate scandal.

According to Edwin Feulner, Simon came away from Watergate "with a disgust for the partisan character of the affair. The experience of the Nixon impeachment convinced him that partisanship was necessarily poisonous, but that his opponents were far better at partisanship than his side was."[10]

---

[d] After graduating from Lafayette College in 1952, Simon traded municipal bonds at a $75-a-week job. By 1964 he was working at Salomon Brothers and by the early 1970s he was earning $2 million a year.

Leaving Washington, Simon became rich.[11] He later boasted "Just give me a handful of dimes and a working phone, and I'll make money.'"[12] He certainly did.

Broke when he left government, within ten years Simon had amassed a fortune estimated by *Forbes Magazine* at more than $400 million. Simon became famous among traders from making $70 million from an initial investment of $330,000 to buy the Gibson greeting card company.[e]

Simon was not only rich, but controversial. "There are few tepid opinions when the subject of Simon's character is raised," wrote the *New York Times*.[13]

The description of Simon's tactics then are hauntingly comparable to those of the Republican Presidential candidate of 2012, Mitt Romney, former governor of Massachusetts, and retired from a venture capital firm, Bain Capital. As described by the *Times*—

> Simon's touch proved almost magical; he cleared $70 million in the legendary Gibson Greeting Card deal alone. But his tactics were clear: Buy low, sell high—in his case, take a company private, picking it up for a song; load it up with debt, take it public again at the right moment, and make a bundle, always moving with the speed and decisiveness that were his hallmarks.[14]

Simon took these skills, but most importantly, his vision and intensity, to the Olin Foundation, where he became the chief executive in 1977. From then into the late 1970s and through the 1980s and 1990s, he focused, in the words of the Philanthropy Roundtable (which Simon helped found) on "the grant programs of the John M. Olin Foundation on building the intellectual basis of conservative thought and on buttressing the intellectual underpinnings of the free enterprise system."[15]

---

[e] Simon and a partner created Wesray, a company that bought Gibson for $80 million—but only $1 million of it in cash. Simon's share of the initial payment was about $330,000. Some fourteen months later, Gibson was sold in a public offering that netted $290 million. Wesray used the offering proceeds to pay off the debt, pocketed $48 million from selling some of their own stock in the offering and were left owning stock worth about $190 million and rising. When all was said and done, Simon's $330,000 was worth close to $70 million. Brian Trumbore, "William Simon," http://www.buyandhold.com/bh/en/education/history/2000/william_simon.html, accessed July 7, 2012.

Simon was a bitter critic of conventional foundations, describing applying for a grant from the MacArthur Foundation as "the most frustrating experience of my life."[16] What Simon ran at the Olin Foundation, however, was decidedly different. According to the Roundtable, Simon worked "100-hour weeks."[17]

Probably, Weyrich worked 100 hours a week as well, and perhaps Powell, too. However much they worked, there can be no doubt that each made an immense contribution. Sadly, it was to a revolution in support of corporations and the rich.

6

LEWIS F. POWELL, JR.: THE CORPORATE LAWYER WHO CHANGED HISTORY[a]

I fell into a Supreme Court time warp the other day. Preparing to teach a seminar this fall on the court under Chief Justice Warren E. Burger—the court of the 1970s to mid-1980s—I picked up for the first time in many years a decision from 1978, *First National Bank of Boston v. Bellotti*. The case is not well-known today, although it should be. It was the decision that really opened the door to corporate money in politics, leading 32 years later to a very well-known case: *Citizens United*.

Linda Greenhouse
"Over the Cliff"
New York Times
Aug. 24, 2011

Lewis Powell was a former corporate lawyer, a member of the board of directors of the company that made Marlboro cigarettes and very single-minded man. He described what corporate America should to do to wrest control of the nation in his *Manifesto*, then set about implementing it once he was appointed to the U.S. Supreme Court.

Powell almost single-handedly re-shaped the American legal system into a business-friendly institution, and crafted majorities that ultimately and inevitably led to *Citizens United v. Federal Election Commission*.[b] The ruling in *Citizens*

---

[a] This chapter focuses on Powell's role as a Justice of the Supreme Court. The Manifesto is discussed elsewhere, as are the contributions of Simon and Weyrich.

[b] In a 5–4 decision, the U.S. Supreme Court ruled that corporations and unions

(continued...)

United shifted the campaign finance landscape of the United States, opening the door to the massive political expenditures that helped shape the 2012 presidential race and, perhaps more importantly, the contests for the U.S. Senate and House of Representatives. The *Citizens United* decision was 5–4, split along ideological lines, with Republican justices voting in the majority and Democrats in the minority.

Two years later, the Court reaffirmed the right of corporations to make independent political expenditures, summarily overturning a 100-year-old Montana state law—and, by implication, all other state laws as well—that barred corporations from such political activity.[1] In *American Tradition Partnership, Inc. v. Bullock*,[2] the Court struck down Montana's Corrupt Practices Act, which had been passed by voter referendum in 1912 in response to a history of business-driven corruption. The Act had decreed that a "corporation may not make … an expenditure in connection with a candidate or a political party that supports or opposes a candidate or a political party."[3]

One of the friend-of-the-court briefs filed in support of overturning the Montana law was written by National Chamber Litigation Center, Inc., a legal arm of the U.S. Chamber of Commerce, created in direct response to the recommendations in Powell's Manifesto.[4]

More importantly, Powell wrote the decision, and lobbied for the five votes to adopt it that led directly to *Citizen's United*. The case was *First National Bank of Boston v. Bellotti*.[5] Had the decision in *Bellotti* been different, there would never have been a *Citizens United* ruling, and there would still be limits on corporate financing of campaigns. Taken together, the two cases have

Anti-smoking warnings invalidated by the D.C. Court of Appeals.

---

[b] (…continued)
have the same political speech rights as individuals under the First Amendment. It found no compelling government interest for prohibiting corporations and unions from using their general treasury funds to make election-related independent expenditures. Thus, it struck down a federal law banning this practice and also overruled two of its prior decisions. Additionally, in an 8–1 decision, the Court ruled that the disclaimer and disclosure requirements associated with electioneering communications are constitutional.

delivered what Powell—recall that he was a member of the Board of Directors of the tobacco company that makes Marlboro cigarettes—would have believed was justice. It is not surprising that in quick order the mandates of graphic anti-smoking warning on cigarette packages were overturned.[c]

Powell was, in the words of the *New York Times* "a patrician son of the Old South." Born into an old Virginia family descended from original Jamestown colony settlers, he became president of the American Bar Association and a partner in one the nation's most influential law firms, Richmond-based Hunton & Williams (which included Powell's name as well until his departure for the Supreme Court).[6]

Most dominant in Powell's professional experience was his work as a highly successful corporate attorney, including membership on the boards of eleven corporations. "Powell's nearly forty years of experience in corporate boardrooms led him to trust the character of the average American businessman," declared law professor A.C. Pritchard.[7]

"In Powell's world, free enterprise and the businessmen who made it work were the foundation of strong communities," added Pritchard. His decisions were "colored by his experience in corporate boardrooms," he added.[8] The boards of directors of which Powell was a member included Philip Morris.[9]

Powell began his fifteen years on the Supreme Court in 1972 as part of a wave of new faces and ideologies. Between mid-1969 and the beginning of 1972, Nixon appointed four new justices, including Harry Blackmun, Warren E. Burger as chief justice following the retirement of Earl Warren, and William H. Rehnquist.

By some measures, Justice Powell would prove a consistent centrist, siding with the majority in ninety percent of the cases—more than any other justice—and casting fewer dissenting votes during his time on the bench.[10] Craig Evan Klafter wrote that "[a]s a pragmatist, Powell had a distinct advantage. … There was nothing but his own sense of justice to keep him from building a majority with justices on either side of the ideological spectrum."[11]

Powell's strident tone in the Manifesto cannot and should not be taken as posturing. There is no doubt that he believed what he wrote then, and set out to

---

[c] *R.J. Reynolds Tobacco Co. V. Food and Drug Administration*, U.S. Court of Appeals for the District of Columbia, opinion unpublished, but available at http://www.cadc.uscourts.gov/internet/opinions.nsf/4C0311C78EB11C5785257A64004EBF B5/$file/11-5332-1391191.pdf.

himself implement its recommendations once appointed to the Supreme Court. If there might have been any doubt as to Powell's seriousness, he eliminated it by repeating the message public at least three times.

Although Powell's Manifesto has attracted the most attention, it was by no means the first time that he voiced his criticisms of what he called the "New Left." On November 11, 1968, Powell spoke to the American Association of State Colleges and Universities, saying that "The goals of the New Left are first to disrupt and then to destroy our system of higher education and our representative form of government."[12]

Powell warned the educators that academic freedom was at threat unless "current trends toward license, discord, even anarchy on campus and in the streets are not checked. The sooner New Leftists and their faculty allied are expelled, the sooner our campuses will resume their historic roles as centers of reason and intellectual pursuit."[13]

Calling some students "radicals," Powell said it would be impossible to mollify them. "Their objective is revolution; not reform." The fault, counseled Powell, lay with "academic freedom and academic tenure," which he said were "defended blindly and ferociously" by faculty.[14] Worse, radicalism was spreading to society as a whole:

> It is important to under-stand *(sic)* that there is a close relationship between the discord on the campus and lawlessness in the streets. There is abroad in this country an escalating unrest which has led to un-precedented crime, civil disobedience and disrespect for law and due process. As others have noted, we are also witnessing a pervasive permissiveness—on the campus, in the churches, the homes and in our political institutions. Ancient standards of morality, decency and good taste have crumbled; concepts of duty, patriotism and responsibility are often subordinated. Even the most respected values of western civilization are under virulent attack.[15]

Two years earlier, Powell had also taken aim at "a heresy which could weaken the foundations of our system of government and make impossible the existence of the human freedoms it strives to protect."[16] The source of this evil? Civil disobedience—Rosa Parks refusing to move to the back of the bus, where blacks were supposed to be; students "sitting in" at the Greensboro, North Carolina, F.W. Woolworth's lunch counter that refused to serve blacks; peaceful demonstrations to protest laws mandating racial segregation, greeted by savage and bloody beatings, as in Birmingham, Alabama.

Powell viewed such actions as "heresy" that threatened "the foundations of our system of government." Such a view might be understandable in the former Soviet Union or Persian Gulf dictatorships, but never in the United States. The fundamental premise of the American Revolution—which was far from non-violent—was that citizens have at least a right and perhaps even a moral duty—to disobey unjust laws. In contrast, Powell took the view that the law, right or wrong, had to be obeyed. Civil disobedience, he wrote, was putting the "old wine of revolution into the new wineskin of constitutional government."[17]

The report on Powell's background by the Federal Bureau of Investigation listed a number of speeches given or articles written by him, including "The Attack on American Institutions," an article in *U.S. News & World Report*, "Civil Disobedience: Prelude to Revolution," a pamphlet, "Alienation of the Campus from National Defense," another pamphlet, "Anarchy on the Campus," and, a speech, "The Ideological Assault on America."[d]

In addition, the report listed a number of articles in the local newspapers, the *Richmond Times-Dispatch* and The *Richmond News Leader*. These included, "Powell Says Law and Order Suffer," "Powell Urges Action to Stop Defiance of the Law," "Powell Voices Concern on 'New Left'," "U.S. Faces Internal Destruction," "A Lawyer Rebukes the Court," and "Anti-Militarism Called Threat."[e]

Once on the Court, Powell bent the law to fit his pre-conceived concepts of morality. Yes, he was undoubtedly a courtly man of even temper. As a reporter for the Associated Press in Raleigh, North Carolina, I once interviewed a legislator with a reputation for being spiteful and mean. After I wrote up the interview, I said in an aside to the bureau chief, Noel Yancy, that the legislator had seemed like a nice guy.

Noel, squinting through his thick-lensed glasses peered up and said, "Nice? Yeah he's nice. He smiles while he squeezes your balls."

---

[d] Federal Bureau of Investigation, Subject: Lewis F. Powell, Jr. File # 77-HQ-121928, (undated), vault.fbi.gov/lewis-f.-powell-jr/lewis-f.-powell-jr.-part-02.../file, accessed July 18, 2012.

[e] Federal Bureau of Investigation, Subject: Lewis F. Powell, Jr. File # 77-HQ-121928, (undated), vault.fbi.gov/lewis-f.-powell-jr/lewis-f.-powell-jr.-part-02.../file, accessed July 18, 2012.

As a Justice, Powell was positioned to judge the arguments echoing his sentiments, made by the organizations whose creation he had urged. In response to Powell's suggestion in the Manifesto, corporations and corporate executives funded a wave of new "legal foundations" in the 1970s. These legal foundations carried into every court the same radical message Powell had made. Using the echo chamber created by Simon, the message was repeated time and again, until it became a mantra of sorts: corporations are persons with constitutional rights, including the right of speech.

The Chamber of Commerce created the National Chamber Litigation Center. Other "legal" foundations quickly multiplied: the Pacific Legal Foundation, the Mid-Atlantic Legal Foundation, the Mid-America Legal Foundation, the Great Plains Legal Foundation (Landmark Legal Foundation), the Washington Legal Foundation, the Northeastern Legal Foundation, the New England Legal Foundation, the Southeastern Legal Foundation, the Capital Legal Center, the National Legal Center for the Public Interest, and many others.[18]

One critic later wrote—

These foundations began filing brief after brief challenging state and federal laws across the country, pounding away at the themes of corporations as "persons," "speakers" and holders of constitutional rights. Reading their briefs, one might think that the most powerful, richest corporations in the history of the world were some beleaguered minority fighting to overcome oppression. The foundations and the corporate lawyers argued that "corporations are persons" with the "liberty secured to all persons." They used new phrases like "corporate speech," the "rights of corporate speakers," and "the corporate character of the speaker." They demanded, as if to end an unjust silence, "the right of corporations to be heard" and "the rights of corporations to speak out."[19]

The first major victory for the corporate rights advocates came in 1978, with a corporate attack on a Massachusetts law in *First National Bank of Boston v. Bellotti*.[20] For the first time in history, the Court held that a state criminal statute barring certain expenditures by banks and corporations aimed at influencing votes on referendum proposals violated the First Amendment rights of those entities. Who wrote that 5–4 opinion? Lewis Powell.[f]

Massachusetts had prohibited banks and other business corporations from making contributions or expenditures "for the purpose of … influencing or affecting the vote on any question submitted to the voters, other than one materially affecting any of the property, business or assets of the corporation." Companies wanted to publicize their views on a proposed constitutional amendment to allow the legislature to impose a graduated tax on the income of individuals. The Attorney General of Massachusetts, informed them that he would seek to fine them, so the banks sued to have the statute declared unconstitutional.

The Massachusetts Supreme Judicial Court sided with the state. The U.S. Supreme Court, however, rejected the Massachusetts courts' reasoning saying that—

> If the speakers here were not corporations, no one would suggest that the State could silence their proposed speech. It is the type of speech indispensable to decision making in a democracy, and this is no less true because the speech comes from a corporation rather than an individual.[21]

Although the vote was 5–4, it required months of persuasion and cajoling for Powell to create a majority. To achieve it, Powell deftly cast the issue differently from litigants and other Justices. They all focused on the source of the communication: namely, the corporations.

Powell, however, couched the case in terms of the nature of the message, not the speaker. The issue was not who was speaking, but instead what was being said. In this way, he was able to protect corporations because they were engaged in "the type of speech indispensable to decision making in a democracy, and this is no less true because the speech comes from a corporation rather than an individual. "[22] It took a long time and a great deal of effort to reach this result, however.

Two days after the oral arguments, the Justices met to discuss the case. Eight of them preferred not to address the question of corporate First Amendment

---

[f] Much of the discussion describing development of the *Belotti* opinion is drawn from Robert L. Kerr, "The 'Attack' Memorandum and the First Amendment," *Journal of Media Law & Ethics, Volume 2, Numbers 3/4* (Summer/Fall 2010), a masterful article.

rights. Justice William J. Brennan, Jr., was assigned to write the majority opinion. Then a few days later, he told the others that he had concluded the Court must address the broader question—and if it did he would uphold the constitutionality of the Massachusetts regulation. He reminded others that "[c]orporate spending as a corrupting influence in the political process ... has produced numerous corrupt practice acts."[23]

Chief Justice Burger expressed similar "misgivings about the case, particularly on its potential for undermining the well established Corrupt Practices Act's limitations." Powell then expressing his interest in drafting an opinion grounded in his view that "circumscribing speech on the basis of its source, in the absence of a compelling interest that could not be attained otherwise, would be a most serious infringement of First Amendment rights."[24]

After working on the draft for more than two months, Powell garnered support from Justice Potter Stewart. However, he lost Brennan and Justice Thurgood Marshall, each of whom agreed to join the dissent written by White.[25] It was growing clear how deeply divided the Court would be in *Bellotti*.

Powell wrote Blackmun, Rehnquist, Stevens, and Chief Justice Burger. In an effort to win them over, he narrowed the opinion. Chief Justice Burger agreed to join, but still voiced concern over the potential to undermine corrupt practices laws.[26, g]

Justice John Paul Stevens, asked for additional changes in the opinion. Powell made them and had a majority.[27]

Powell continued his attempts to win over Rehnquist, but in vain. When the ruling was handed down April 26, five months after oral arguments, Rehnquist remained bitterly opposed—

> "It cannot be so readily concluded that the right of political
> expression is equally necessary to carry out the functions of a
> corporation organized for commercial purposes," he would write. "A

---

[g] Burger's fears were eventually realized in June 2012 when the Court overturned a Montana corrupt practices law that had been adopted by voters a century earlier in the wake of political corruption scandals. Mike Sacks, "Supreme Court Reverses Anti-Citizens United Ruling From Montana," *Huffington Post*, http://www.huffingtonpost.com/2012/06/25/supremecourt-reversed-citzens-united-montana_n_1605355.html, accessed July 12, 2012.

State grants to a business corporation the blessings of potentially perpetual life and limited liability to enhance its efficiency as an economic entity. It might reasonably be concluded that those properties, so beneficial in the economic sphere, pose special dangers in the political sphere.[28]

Corporate spending on public referendums lay "at the heart of the First Amendment's protection" wrote Powell. He was, however, faced with two withering dissents, one written by Justice White, the other by Justice Rehnquist, who was scornful of the majority's decision:

(T)he Congress of the United States, and the legislatures of 30 other States of this Republic have considered the matter, and have concluded that restrictions upon the political activity of business corporations are both politically desirable and constitutionally permissible. The judgment of such a broad consensus of governmental bodies expressed over a period of many decades is entitled to considerable deference from this Court.[29]

White described the impact of the majority decision almost prophetically—

It has long been recognized, however, that the special status of corporations has placed them in a position to control vast amounts of economic power which may, if not regulated, dominate not only the economy but also the very heart of our democracy, the electoral process . ... The State need not permit its own creation to consume it.[30]

What White presumably did not know was that Powell's objective was to achieve precisely what White most feared: corporations that could "dominate not only the economy but also the very heart of our democracy, the electoral process." In the Manifesto, Powell called for an aggressive expansion of corporate legal and political power and, specifically, greater spending by corporate interests to influence political outcomes. In *Belotti*, he achieved it.

For the first time in history, the Court held that a state criminal statute barring certain expenditures by banks and corporations aimed at influencing votes on referendum proposals violated the First Amendment rights of those entities. To accomplish this, Powell relied on a crucial decision cited in a footnote: "It has been settled for almost a century that corporations are persons within the meaning of the

Fourteenth Amendment. *Santa Clara County v. Southern Pacific R. Co.*, 118 U.S. 394 (1886)."[31]

But nowhere did Powell acknowledge that Santa Clara was revolutionary. The "person" contemplated by the Amendment—adopted in 1868, soon after the end of the Civil War—was the newly-freed slave. The Amendment's first words speak of "All persons born or naturalized in the United States."[32]

Powell had succeeded Justice Hugo L. Black who had said in 1938, in *Connecticut General Life Insurance Co. v. Johnson*, that the Amendment's history "proves that the people were told that its purpose was to protect weak and helpless human beings and were not told that it was intended to remove corporations in any fashion from the control of state governments."[33]

Robert Kerr, associate professor in the Gaylord College of Journalism and Mass Communication at the University of Oklahoma. reviewed Powell's notes, Powell's communications with his law clerks and interviewed some of the clerks. He concluded that—

> This analysis of Justice Powell's work in the corporate political media spending cases finds that most of it suggests a determined effort to advance interests basically consistent with the theme of his "Attack on American Free Enterprise System" memorandum. His files on those cases document that even though his efforts often conflicted with the views of other justices, Justice Powell was able to prevail over considerable opposition in key cases, particularly *Bellotti* ...[34]

Powell protected corporations and created new and unprecedented rights for them so they could implement the vision he had defined in the Manifesto. It is not an overstatement to say that Powell's Manifesto foreshadowed the legal decisions that ultimately led to unbridled corporate spending in political campaigns under the 2010 decision in *Citizens United*.

Today's court, however, has gone even further. Not only has is expressly allowed unlimited corporate spending in *Citizens United*, it has invalidated efforts by a state to eliminate the influence of money in campaigns.

In June 2011, in *Arizona Free Enterprise Club's Freedom Club PAC v. Bennett*,[h] the court struck down a voluntary public financing system for political campaigns, adopted by Arizona voters in a public referendum 13 years earlier in response to corruption scandals. As an incentive to accept public financing, without fear of being outspent by a wealthy, privately financed candidate, the system offered a publicly financed candidate an extra dollar for every dollar that the opponent spent above the law's cap on public money.

The court determined that Arizona's dollar-for-dollar match violated the rights of rich persons, saying that such matches "inhibit robust and wide-open political debate." The *New York Times* observed, correctly, that "Not only in commercial speech, but in the area of pure political speech as well, the current majority threatens to drive the First Amendment off a cliff."[35]

A judge, whether on the Supreme Court or elsewhere, is obliged to determine what the law is and apply it. Powell's papers, once private but now public, reveal a Justice in single-minded pursuit of a desired outcome, not one dispassionately making a judgment on legality. Courtly? Yes. Determined, as well? Definitely yes.

As a Justice, Powell shaped the law to respond to threats that he perceived, arming corporations with weapons he believed they required. In the end, Powell demonstrated that he was a modest success as a Justice of the Supreme Court, but a damned fine corporate lawyer. Probably the best that money could buy.

---

[h] 131 S.Ct. 1672 (2011).

APPENDIX
THE POWELL MANIFESTO:
THE ORIGINAL TEXT OF THE POWELL
ATTACK MEMO

ATTACK ON AMERICAN FREE ENTERPRISE SYSTEM

Background

The Powell Memorandum: When National Chamber Director Eugene B. Sydnor, Jr., became chairman of our Education Committee, he discussed with his neighbor and long-time friend, Lewis F. Powell, Richmond attorney, ways to provide the public a more balanced view of the country's economic system.

At Mr. Sydnor's request, Mr. Powell, based on his broad experience as chairman of the Richmond City School Board, as well as the Virginia State Board of Education, prepared a memorandum in which he incorporated a number of possible approaches. The memorandum covered a broad range of educational and other activities for study and consideration by the National Chamber.

The memorandum was dated August 23, 1971, two months before Mr. Powell was nominated to become a member justice of the Supreme Court of the United States. It has been under study and evaluation by Chamber officers and staff members. Several of its approaches have been put into practice. Others would require substantial new resources to carry out.

Recently, Jack Anderson, the syndicated columnist, wrote several columns discussing the memorandum. Mr. Anderson obtained a copy of the memorandum without the knowledge or permission of the National Chamber. Anyone reading the Powell memorandum will easily conclude that it objectively and fairly deals with a very real problem facing the free enterprise system.

To give all members of the National Chamber an opportunity to read the memorandum and to allow each to evaluate all the points raised, *Washington Report* presents the document in its entirety.

Confidential Memorandum:
Attack of American Free Enterprise System
DATE: August 23, 1971
TO: Mr. Eugene B. Sydnor, Jr., Chairman, Education Committee, U.S. Chamber of Commerce
FROM: Lewis F. Powell, Jr.

This memorandum is submitted at your request as a basis for the discussion on August 24 with Mr. Booth (executive vice president) and others at the U.S. Chamber of Commerce. The purpose is to identify the problem, and suggest possible avenues of action for further consideration.

Dimensions of the Attack
No thoughtful person can question that the American economic system is under broad attack.[1] This varies in scope, intensity, in the techniques employed, and in the level of visibility.

There always have been some who opposed the American system, and preferred socialism or some form of statism (communism or fascism). Also, there always have been critics of the system, whose criticism has been wholesome and constructive so long as the objective was to improve rather than to subvert or destroy.

But what now concerns us is quite new in the history of America. We are not dealing with sporadic or isolated attacks from a relatively few extremists or even from the minority socialist cadre. Rather, the assault on the enterprise system is broadly based and consistently pursued. It is gaining momentum and converts.

Sources of the Attack
The sources are varied and diffused. They include, not unexpectedly, the Communists, New Leftists and other revolutionaries who would destroy the entire system, both political and economic. These extremists of the left are far more numerous, better financed, and increasingly are more welcomed and encouraged by other elements of society, than ever before in our history. But they remain a small minority, and are not yet the principal cause for concern.

The most disquieting voices joining the chorus of criticism come from perfectly respectable elements of society: from the college campus, the pulpit, the media, the intellectual and literary journals, the arts and sciences, and from politicians. In most of these groups the movement against the system is participated in only by minorities. Yet, these often are the most articulate, the most vocal, the most prolific in their writing and speaking.

Moreover, much of the media—for varying motives and in varying degrees—either voluntarily accords unique publicity to these "attackers," or at least allows them to exploit the media for their purposes. This is especially true of television, which now plays such a predominant role in shaping the thinking, attitudes and emotions of our people.

One of the bewildering paradoxes of our time is the extent to which the enterprise system tolerates, if not participates in, its own destruction.

The campuses from which much of the criticism emanates are supported by (i) tax funds generated largely from American business, and (ii) contributions from capital funds controlled or generated by American business. The boards of trustees of our universities overwhelmingly are composed of men and women who are leaders in the system.

Most of the media, including the national TV systems, are owned and theoretically controlled by corporations which depend upon profits, and the enterprise system to survive.

Tone of the Attack
This memorandum is not the place to document in detail the tone, character, or intensity of the attack. The following quotations will suffice to give one a general idea:

William Kunstler, warmly welcomed on campuses and listed in a recent student poll as the "American lawyer most admired," incites audiences as follows:

> "You must learn to fight in the streets, to revolt, to shoot guns. We will learn to do all of the things that property owners fear."[2] The New Leftists who heed Kunstler's advice increasingly are beginning to act —not just against military recruiting offices and manufacturers of munitions, but against a variety of businesses: "Since February 1970, branches (of Bank of America) have been attacked 39 times, 22 times with explosive devices and 17 times with fire bombs or by

arsonists."[3] Although New Leftist spokesmen are succeeding in radicalizing thousands of the young, the greater cause for concern is the hostility of respectable liberals and social reformers. It is the sum total of their views and influence which could indeed fatally weaken or destroy the system.

A chilling description of what is being taught on many of our campuses was written by Stewart Alsop:

"Yale, like every other major college, is graduating scores of bright young men who are practitioners of 'the politics of despair.' These young men despise the American political and economic system ... (their) minds seem to be wholly closed. They live, not by rational discussion, but by mindless slogans.[4] A recent poll of students on 12 representative campuses reported that: "Almost half the students favored socialization of basic U.S. industries."[5]

A visiting professor from England at Rockford College gave a series of lectures entitled "The Ideological War Against Western Society," in which he documents the extent to which members of the intellectual community are waging ideological warfare against the enterprise system and the values of western society. In a foreword to these lectures, famed Dr. Milton Friedman of Chicago warned: "It (is) crystal clear that the foundations of our free society are under wide-ranging and powerful attack—not by Communist or any other conspiracy but by misguided individuals parroting one another and unwittingly serving ends they would never intentionally promote."[6]

Perhaps the single most effective antagonist of American business is Ralph Nader, who—thanks largely to the media—has become a legend in his own time and an idol of millions of Americans. A recent article in Fortune speaks of Nader as follows:

"The passion that rules in him—and he is a passionate man—is aimed at smashing utterly the target of his hatred, which is corporate power. He thinks, and says quite bluntly, that a great many corporate executives belong in prison—for defrauding the consumer with shoddy merchandise, poisoning the food supply with chemical additives, and willfully manufacturing unsafe products that will maim or kill the buyer. He emphasizes that he is not talking just about 'fly-by-night hucksters' but the top management of blue chip business."[7]

A frontal assault was made on our government, our system of justice, and the free enterprise system by Yale Professor Charles Reich in his widely publicized book: "The Greening of America," published last winter.

The foregoing references illustrate the broad, shotgun attack on the system itself. There are countless examples of rifle shots which undermine confidence and confuse the public. Favorite current targets are proposals for tax incentives through changes in depreciation rates and investment credits. These are usually described in the media as "tax breaks," "loop holes" or "tax benefits" for the benefit of business.[a] As viewed by a columnist in the Post, such tax measures would benefit "only the rich, the owners of big companies."[8]

It is dismaying that many politicians make the same argument that tax measures of this kind benefit only "business," without benefit to "the poor." The fact that this is either political demagoguery or economic illiteracy is of slight comfort. This setting of the "rich" against the "poor," of business against the people, is the cheapest and most dangerous kind of politics.

The Apathy and Default of Business
What has been the response of business to this massive assault upon its fundamental economics, upon its philosophy, upon its right to continue to manage its own affairs, and indeed upon its integrity?

The painfully sad truth is that business, including the boards of directors' and the top executives of corporations great and small and business organizations at all levels, often have responded—if at all—by appeasement, ineptitude and ignoring the problem. There are, of course, many exceptions to this sweeping generalization. But the net effect of such response as has been made is scarcely visible.

In all fairness, it must be recognized that businessmen have not been trained or equipped to conduct guerrilla warfare with those who propagandize against the system, seeking insidiously and constantly to sabotage it. The traditional role of business executives has been to manage, to produce, to sell, to create jobs, to make profits, to improve the standard of living, to be community leaders, to serve on charitable and educational boards, and generally to be good citizens. They have performed these tasks very well indeed.

---

[a] Italic emphasis added by Mr. Powell.

But they have shown little stomach for hard-nose contest with their critics, and little skill in effective intellectual and philosophical debate.

A column recently carried by the Wall Street Journal was entitled: "Memo to GM: Why Not Fight Back?"[9] Although addressed to GM by name, the article was a warning to all American business. Columnist St. John said:

> "General Motors, like American business in general, is 'plainly in trouble' because intellectual bromides have been substituted for a sound intellectual exposition of its point of view." Mr. St. John then commented on the tendency of business leaders to compromise with and appease critics. He cited the concessions which Nader wins from management, and spoke of "the fallacious view many businessmen take toward their critics." He drew a parallel to the mistaken tactics of many college administrators: "College administrators learned too late that such appeasement serves to destroy free speech, academic freedom and genuine scholarship. One campus radical demand was conceded by university heads only to be followed by a fresh crop which soon escalated to what amounted to a demand for outright surrender."

One need not agree entirely with Mr. St. John's analysis. But most observers of the American scene will agree that the essence of his message is sound. American business "plainly in trouble;" the response to the wide range of critics has been ineffective, and has included appeasement; the time has come—indeed, it is long overdue—for the wisdom, ingenuity and resources of American business to be marshalled against those who would destroy it.

Responsibility of Business Executives

What specifically should be done? The first essential—a prerequisite to any effective action—is for businessmen to confront this problem as a primary responsibility of corporate management.

The overriding first need is for businessmen to recognize that the ultimate issue may be survival—survival of what we call the free enterprise system, and all that this means for the strength and prosperity of America and the freedom of our people.

The day is long past when the chief executive officer of a major corporation discharges his responsibility by maintaining a satisfactory growth of profits, with due regard to the corporation's public and social responsibilities. If our system is to survive, top management must be equally concerned with protecting and preserving the system itself. This involves far more than an increased emphasis on "public relations" or "governmental affairs"—two areas in which corporations long have invested substantial sums.

A significant first step by individual corporations could well be the designation of an executive vice president (ranking with other executive VP's) whose responsibility is to counter—on the broadest front—the attack on the enterprise system. The public relations department could be one of the foundations assigned to this executive, but his responsibilities should encompass some of the types of activities referred to subsequently in this memorandum. His budget and staff should be adequate to the task.

Possible Role of the Chamber of Commerce

But independent and uncoordinated activity by individual corporations, as important as this is, will not be sufficient. Strength lies in organization, in careful long-range planning and implementation, in consistency of action over an indefinite period of years, in the scale of financing available only through joint effort, and in the political power available only through united action and national organizations.

Moreover, there is the quite understandable reluctance on the part of any one corporation to get too far out in front and to make itself too visible a target.

The role of the National Chamber of Commerce is therefore vital. Other national organizations (especially those of various industrial and commercial groups) should join in the effort, but no other organizations appear to be as well situated as the Chamber. It enjoys a strategic position, with a fine reputation and a broad base of support. Also—and this is of immeasurable merit—there are hundreds of local Chambers of Commerce which can play a vital supportive role.

It hardly need be said that before embarking upon any program, the Chamber should study and analyze possible courses of action and activities, weighing risks against probable effectiveness and feasibility of each. Considerations of cost, the assurance of financial and other support from members, adequacy of staffing and similar problems will all require the most thoughtful consideration.

The Campus

The assault on the enterprise system was not mounted in a few months. It has gradually evolved over the past two decades, barely perceptible in its origins and benefiting (sic) from a gradualism that provoked little awareness much less any real reaction.

Although origins, sources and causes are complex and interrelated, and obviously difficult to identify without careful qualification, there is reason to believe that the campus is the single most dynamic source. The social science faculties usually include members who are unsympathetic to the enterprise system. They may range from a Herbert Marcuse, Marxist faculty member at the University of California at San Diego, and convinced socialists, to the ambivalent liberal critic who finds more to condemn than to commend. Such faculty members need not be in a majority. They are often personally attractive and magnetic; they are stimulating teachers, and their controversy attracts student following; they are prolific writers and lecturers; they author many of the textbooks, and they exert enormous influence—far out of proportion to their numbers—on their colleagues and in the academic world.

Social science faculties (the political scientist, economist, sociologist and many of the historians) tend to be liberally oriented, even when leftists are not present. This is not a criticism per se, as the need for liberal thought is essential to a balanced viewpoint. The difficulty is that "balance" is conspicuous by its absence on many campuses, with relatively few members being of conservatives or moderate persuasion and even the relatively few often being less articulate and aggressive than their crusading colleagues.

This situation extending back many years and with the imbalance gradually worsening, has had an enormous impact on millions of young American students. In an article in Barron's Weekly, seeking an answer to why so many young people are disaffected even to the point of being revolutionaries, it was said: "Because they were taught that way."[10] Or, as noted by columnist Stewart Alsop, writing about his alma mater: "Yale, like every other major college, is graduating scores' of bright young men … who despise the American political and economic system."

As these "bright young men," from campuses across the country, seek opportunities to change a system which they have been taught to distrust—if not, indeed "despise"—they seek employment in the centers of the real power and influence in our country, namely: (i) with the news media, especially television; (ii) in government, as "staffers" and consultants at various levels; (iii) in elective politics; (iv) as lecturers and writers, and (v) on the faculties at various levels of education.

Many do enter the enterprise system—in business and the professions—and for the most part they quickly discover the fallacies of what they have been taught. But those who eschew the mainstream of the system often remain in key positions of influence where they mold public opinion and often shape governmental action. In many instances, these "intellectuals" end up in regulatory agencies or governmental departments with large authority over the business system they do not believe in.

If the foregoing analysis is approximately sound, a priority task of business—and organizations such as the Chamber—is to address the campus origin of this hostility. Few things are more sanctified in American life than academic freedom. It would be fatal to attack this as a principle. But if academic freedom is to retain the qualities of "openness," "fairness" and "balance"—which are essential to its intellectual significance—there is a great opportunity for constructive action. The thrust of such action must be to restore the qualities just mentioned to the academic communities.

What Can Be Done About the Campus

The ultimate responsibility for intellectual integrity on the campus must remain on the administrations and faculties of our colleges and universities. But organizations such as the Chamber can assist and activate constructive change in many ways, including the following:

Staff of Scholars

The Chamber should consider establishing a staff of highly qualified scholars in the social sciences who do believe in the system. It should include several of national reputation whose authorship would be widely respected—even when disagreed with.

Staff of Speakers

There also should be a staff of speakers of the highest competency. These might include the scholars, and certainly those who speak for the Chamber would have to articulate the product of the scholars.

Speaker's Bureau

In addition to full-time staff personnel, the Chamber should have a Speaker's Bureau which should include the ablest and most effective advocates from the top echelons of American business.

Evaluation of Textbooks

The staff of scholars (or preferably a panel of independent scholars) should evaluate social science textbooks, especially in economics, political science and sociology. This should be a continuing program.

The objective of such evaluation should be oriented toward restoring the balance essential to genuine academic freedom. This would include assurance of fair and factual treatment of our system of government and our enterprise system, its accomplishments, its basic relationship to individual rights and freedoms, and comparisons with the systems of socialism, fascism and communism. Most of the existing textbooks have some sort of comparisons, but many are superficial, biased and unfair.

We have seen the civil rights movement insist on re-writing many of the textbooks in our universities and schools. The labor unions likewise insist that textbooks be fair to the viewpoints of organized labor. Other interested citizens groups have not hesitated to review, analyze and criticize textbooks and teaching materials. In a democratic society, this can be a constructive process and should be regarded as an aid to genuine academic freedom and not as an intrusion upon it.

If the authors, publishers and users of textbooks know that they will be subjected—honestly, fairly and thoroughly—to review and critique by eminent scholars who believe in the American system, a return to a more rational balance can be expected.

Equal Time on the Campus

The Chamber should insist upon equal time on the college speaking circuit. The FBI publishes each year a list of speeches made on college campuses by avowed Communists. The number in 1970 exceeded 100. There were, of course, many hundreds of appearances by leftists and ultra liberals who urge the types of viewpoints indicated earlier in this memorandum. There was no corresponding representation of American business, or indeed by individuals or organizations who appeared in support of the American system of government and business.

Every campus has its formal and informal groups which invite speakers. Each law school does the same thing. Many universities and colleges officially sponsor lecture and speaking programs. We all know the inadequacy of the representation of business in the programs.

It will be said that few invitations would be extended to Chamber speakers.[11] This undoubtedly would be true unless the Chamber aggressively insisted upon the right to be heard—in effect, insisted upon "equal time." University administrators and the great majority of student groups and committees would not welcome being put in the position publicly of refusing a forum to diverse views, indeed, this is the classic excuse for allowing Communists to speak.

The two essential ingredients are (i) to have attractive, articulate and well-informed speakers; and (ii) to exert whatever degree of pressure—publicly and privately—may be necessary to assure opportunities to speak. The objective always must be to inform and enlighten, and not merely to propagandize.

Balancing of Faculties

Perhaps the most fundamental problem is the imbalance of many faculties. Correcting this is indeed a long-range and difficult project. Yet, it should be undertaken as a part of an overall program. This would mean the urging of the need for faculty balance upon university administrators and boards of trustees.

The methods to be employed require careful thought, and the obvious pitfalls must be avoided. Improper pressure would be counterproductive. But the basic concepts of balance, fairness and truth are difficult to resist, if properly presented to boards of trustees, by writing and speaking, and by appeals to alumni associations and groups.

This is a long road and not one for the fainthearted. But if pursued with integrity and conviction it could lead to a strengthening of both academic freedom on the campus and of the values which have made America the most productive of all societies.

Graduate Schools of Business

The Chamber should enjoy a particular rapport with the increasingly influential graduate schools of business. Much that has been suggested above applies to such schools.

Should not the Chamber also request specific courses in such schools dealing with the entire scope of the problem addressed by this memorandum? This is now essential training for the executives of the future.

Secondary Education

While the first priority should be at the college level, the trends mentioned above are increasingly evidenced in the high schools. Action programs, tailored to the high schools and similar to those mentioned, should be considered. The implementation thereof could become a major program for local chambers of commerce, although the control and direction—especially the quality control—should be retained by the National Chamber.

What Can Be Done About the Public?

Reaching the campus and the secondary schools is vital for the long-term. Reaching the public generally may be more important for the shorter term. The first essential is to establish the staffs of eminent scholars, writers and speakers, who will do the thinking, the analysis, the writing and the speaking. It will also be essential to have staff personnel who are thoroughly familiar with the media, and how most effectively to communicate with the public. Among the more obvious means are the following:

Television

The national television networks should be monitored in the same way that textbooks should be kept under constant surveillance. This applies not merely to so-called educational programs (such as "Selling of the Pentagon"), but to the daily "news analysis" which so often includes the most insidious type of criticism of the enterprise system.[12] Whether this criticism results from hostility or economic ignorance, the result is the gradual erosion of confidence in "business" and free enterprise.

This monitoring, to be effective, would require constant examination of the texts of adequate samples of programs. Complaints—to the media and to the Federal Communications Commission—should be made promptly and strongly when programs are unfair or inaccurate.

Equal time should be demanded when appropriate. Effort should be made to see that the forum-type programs (the Today Show, Meet the Press, etc.) afford at least as much opportunity for supporters of the American system to participate as these programs do for those who attack it.

Other Media

Radio and the press are also important, and every available means should be employed to challenge and refute unfair attacks, as well as to present the affirmative case through these media.

The Scholarly Journals

It is especially important for the Chamber's "faculty of scholars" to publish. One of the keys to the success of the liberal and leftist faculty members has been their passion for "publication" and "lecturing." A similar passion must exist among the Chamber's scholars.

Incentives might be devised to induce more "publishing" by independent scholars who do believe in the system.

There should be a fairly steady flow of scholarly articles presented to a broad spectrum of magazines and periodicals—ranging from the popular magazines (Life, Look, Reader's Digest, etc.) to the more intellectual ones (Atlantic, Harper's, Saturday Review, New York, etc.)[13] and to the various professional journals.

Books, Paperbacks and Pamphlets

The news stands—at airports, drugstores, and elsewhere—are filled with paperbacks and pamphlets advocating everything from revolution to erotic free love. One finds almost no attractive, well-written paperbacks or pamphlets on "our side." It will be difficult to compete with an Eldridge Cleaver or even a Charles Reich for reader attention, but unless the effort is made—on a large enough scale and with appropriate imagination to assure some success—this opportunity for educating the public will be irretrievably lost.

Paid Advertisements

Business pays hundreds of millions of dollars to the media for advertisements. Most of this supports specific products; much of it supports institutional image making; and some fraction of it does support the system. But the latter has been more or less tangential, and rarely part of a sustained, major effort to inform and enlighten the American people.

If American business devoted only 10% of its total annual advertising budget to this overall purpose, it would be a statesman-like expenditure.

The Neglected Political Arena

In the final analysis, the payoff—short-of revolution—is what government does. Business has been the favorite whipping-boy of many politicians for many years. But the measure of how far this has gone is perhaps best found in the anti-business views now being expressed by several leading candidates for President of the United States.

It is still Marxist doctrine that the "capitalist" countries are controlled by big business. This doctrine, consistently a part of leftist propaganda all over the world, has a wide public following among Americans.

Yet, as every business executive knows, few elements of American society today have as little influence in government as the American businessman, the corporation, or even the millions of corporate stockholders. If one doubts this, let him undertake the role of "lobbyist" for the business point of view before Congressional committees. The same situation obtains in the legislative halls of most states and major cities. One does not exaggerate to say that, in terms of political influence with respect to the course of legislation and government action, the American business executive is truly the "forgotten man."

Current examples of the impotency of business, and of the near-contempt with which businessmen's views are held, are the stampedes by politicians to support almost any legislation related to "consumerism" or to the "environment."

Politicians reflect what they believe to be majority views of their constituents. It is thus evident that most politicians are making the judgment that the public has little sympathy for the businessman or his viewpoint.

The educational programs suggested above would be designed to enlighten public thinking—not so much about the businessman and his individual role as about the system which he administers, and which provides the goods, services and jobs on which our country depends.

But one should not postpone more direct political action, while awaiting the gradual change in public opinion to be effected through education and information. Business must learn the lesson, long ago learned by labor and other self-interest groups. This is the lesson that political power is necessary; that such power must be assidously (sic) cultivated; and that when necessary, it must be used aggressively and with determination—without embarrassment and without the reluctance which has been so characteristic of American business.

As unwelcome as it may be to the Chamber, it should consider assuming a broader and more vigorous role in the political arena.

Neglected Opportunity in the Courts
American business and the enterprise system have been affected as much by the courts as by the executive and legislative branches of government. Under our constitutional system, especially with an activist-minded Supreme Court, the judiciary may be the most important instrument for social, economic and political change.

Other organizations and groups, recognizing this, have been far more astute in exploiting judicial action than American business. Perhaps the most active exploiters of the judicial system have been groups ranging in political orientation from "liberal" to the far left.

The American Civil Liberties Union is one example. It initiates or intervenes in scores of cases each year, and it files briefs amicus curiae in the Supreme Court in a number of cases during each term of that court. Labor unions, civil rights groups and now the public interest law firms are extremely active in the judicial arena. Their success, often at business' expense, has not been inconsequential.

This is a vast area of opportunity for the Chamber, if it is willing to undertake the role of spokesman for American business and if, in turn, business is willing to provide the funds.

As with respect to scholars and speakers, the Chamber would need a highly competent staff of lawyers. In special situations it should be authorized to engage, to appear as counsel amicus in the Supreme Court, lawyers of national standing and reputation. The greatest care should be exercised in selecting the cases in which to participate, or the suits to institute. But the opportunity merits the necessary effort.

Neglected Stockholder Power

The average member of the public thinks of "business" as an impersonal corporate entity, owned by the very rich and managed by over-paid executives. There is an almost total failure to appreciate that "business" actually embraces—in one way or another— most Americans. Those for whom business provides jobs, constitute a fairly obvious class. But the 20 million stockholders— most of whom are of modest means—are the real owners, the real entrepreneurs, the real capitalists under our system. They provide the capital which fuels the economic system which has produced the highest standard of living in all history. Yet, stockholders have been as ineffectual as business executives in promoting a genuine understanding of our system or in exercising political influence.

The question which merits the most thorough examination is how can the weight and influence of stockholders—20 million voters—be mobilized to support (i) an educational program and (ii) a political action program.

Individual corporations are now required to make numerous reports to shareholders. Many corporations also have expensive "news" magazines which go to employees and stockholders. These opportunities to communicate can be used far more effectively as educational media.

The corporation itself must exercise restraint in undertaking political action and must, of course, comply with applicable laws. But is it not feasible—through an affiliate of the Chamber or otherwise—to establish a national organization of American stockholders and give it enough muscle to be influential?

A More Aggressive Attitude

Business interests—especially big business and their national trade organizations—have tried to maintain low profiles, especially with respect to political action.

As suggested in the Wall Street Journal article, it has been fairly characteristic of the average business executive to be tolerant—at least in public—of those who attack his corporation and the system. Very few businessmen or business organizations respond in kind. There has been a disposition to appease; to regard the opposition as willing to compromise, or as likely to fade away in due time.

Business has shunted confrontation politics. Business, quite understandably, has been repelled by the multiplicity of non-negotiable "demands" made constantly by self-interest groups of all kinds.

While neither responsible business interests, nor the United States Chamber of Commerce, would engage in the irresponsible tactics of some pressure groups, it is essential that spokesmen for the enterprise system—at all levels and at every opportunity—be far more aggressive than in the past.

There should be no hesitation to attack the Naders, the Marcuses and others who openly seek destruction of the system. There should not be the slightest hesitation to press vigorously in all political arenas for support of the enterprise system. Nor should there be reluctance to penalize politically those who oppose it.

Lessons can be learned from organized labor in this respect. The head of the AFL-CIO may not appeal to businessmen as the most endearing or public-minded of citizens. Yet, over many years the heads of national labor organizations have done what they were paid to do very effectively. They may not have been beloved, but they have been respected—where it counts the most—by politicians, on the campus, and among the media.

It is time for American business—which has demonstrated the greatest capacity in all history to produce and to influence consumer decisions—to apply their great talents vigorously to the preservation of the system itself.

The Cost
The type of program described above (which includes a broadly based combination of education and political action), if undertaken long term and adequately staffed, would require far more generous financial support from American corporations than the Chamber has ever received in the past. High level management participation in Chamber affairs also would be required.

The staff of the Chamber would have to be significantly increased, with the highest quality established and maintained. Salaries would have to be at levels fully comparable to those paid key business executives and the most prestigious faculty members. Professionals of the great skill in advertising and in working with the media, speakers, lawyers and other specialists would have to be recruited.

It is possible that the organization of the Chamber itself would benefit from restructuring. For example, as suggested by union experience, the office of President of the Chamber might well be a full-time career position. To assure maximum effectiveness and continuity, the chief executive officer of the Chamber should not be changed each year. The functions now largely performed by the President could be transferred to a Chairman of the Board, annually elected by the membership. The Board, of course, would continue to exercise policy control.

Quality Control is Essential

Essential ingredients of the entire program must be responsibility and "quality control." The publications, the articles, the speeches, the media programs, the advertising, the briefs filed in courts, and the appearances before legislative committees—all must meet the most exacting standards of accuracy and professional excellence. They must merit respect for their level of public responsibility and scholarship, whether one agrees with the viewpoints expressed or not.

Relationship to Freedom

The threat to the enterprise system is not merely a matter of economics. It also is a threat to individual freedom.

It is this great truth—now so submerged by the rhetoric of the New Left and of many liberals—that must be re-affirmed if this program is to be meaningful.

There seems to be little awareness that the only alternatives to free enterprise are varying degrees of bureaucratic regulation of individual freedom—ranging from that under moderate socialism to the iron heel of the leftist or rightist dictatorship.

We in America already have moved very far indeed toward some aspects of state socialism, as the needs and complexities of a vast urban society require types of regulation and control that were quite unnecessary in earlier times. In some areas, such regulation and control already have seriously impaired the freedom of both business and labor, and indeed of the public generally. But most of the essential freedoms remain: private ownership, private profit, labor unions, collective bargaining, consumer choice, and a market economy in which competition largely determines price, quality and variety of the goods and services provided the consumer.

In addition to the ideological attack on the system itself (discussed in this memorandum), its essentials also are threatened by inequitable taxation, and—more recently—by an inflation which has seemed uncontrollable.[14] But whatever the causes of diminishing economic freedom may be, the truth is that freedom as a concept is indivisible. As the experience of the socialist and totalitarian states demonstrates, the contraction and denial of economic freedom is followed inevitably by governmental restrictions on other cherished rights. It is this message, above all others, that must be carried home to the American people.

Conclusion

It hardly need be said that the views expressed above are tentative and suggestive. The first step should be a thorough study. But this would be an exercise in futility unless the Board of Directors of the Chamber accepts the fundamental premise of this paper, namely, that business and the enterprise system are in deep trouble, and the hour is late.

ABOUT THIS DOCUMENT:

On August 23, 1971, the U.S. Chamber of Commerce distributed the Powell Memorandum to its national membership of leading executives, businesses, and trade associations. The memo, published here in its entirety, constituted the entire contents of the issue of its regular publication WASHINGTON REPORT to members.

7

THE COUNTERINTELLIGENSIA
AND THE LIBERTY PARTY

I know of nothing more crucial than to come to the aid of the intellectuals and writers who are fighting on my side. And I strongly recommend that any businessman with the slightest impulse for survival go and do likewise. The alliance between the theorists and men of action in the capitalist world is long overdue in America, It must become a veritable crusade if we are to survive in freedom.

William E. Simon,
A Time for Truth[a]
1976

If Lewis Powell was the architect of the strategy for corporations and the rich to quietly seize control of America, a relatively little known Wall Street banker, Bill Simon, was the carpenter (also the roofer, electrician, plumber, grounds keeper, painter and virtually everything else as well). It is Simon who almost singlehandedly—and most certainly single-mindedly—created the intellectual underpinnings for the modern Republican—he preferred to call it "Liberty"—Party.

Simon was a radical, not a conservative. So were—are, really, since most of them are still alive—his allies. Not conservatives. Radicals.

The very first organization created in direct response to the Powell Manifesto was the Heritage Foundation with $250,000 from Joseph Coors. It became one of the foundation stones of the Simon counterintelligensia. Its founder, Paul Weyrich, would tell anybody who would listen "We are no longer working to preserve the status quo. We are radicals, working to overturn the present power structure of this country."[1]

---

[a] Reader's Digest Press, 1978.

Weyrich also once wrote in a 1987 *Washington Post* article that "If we are going to be a serious nation, we need a serious system for selecting our leaders and advisors. We need some type of shadow government, in which leaders and top advisors can be identified and developed ..."[2] That shadow government was provided by Simon's counterintelligensia.

Simon became a self-made millionaire because of the opportunities afforded by this nation.[b] The son of an insurance executive, he attended Lafayette College on the G.I. Bill.[3] After graduation, he became a bond trader, rising to chief of government bond trading at Salomon Brothers. He was made an assistant Secretary of the Treasury by Richard Nixon, then promoted to full job and appointed to be the nation's energy czar after the first Arab oil boycott. He left government broke, but within a few years was again rich, worth an estimated $400 million. Not exactly a Horatio Alger rags-to-riches story, but pretty close.[4]

Curiously, Simon shared a quality often found in the nation's wealthy: he seemed to hate the America that made him both rich and famous. He set out to destroy it. He very largely succeeded.

Simon was a demon obsessed, one who seemingly loathed every aspect of America in the 1970s. The intensity of his vitriol almost boils off the pages of his first book, *A Time to Choose*. He, and eventually others who joined him, were animated by a fierce animosity, a visceral hatred of government and ordinary Americans. He viewed them with extraordinary contempt and hostility. Seldom have words expressed such loathing and detest so strongly as in his 1978 book:

> There has never been such freedom before in America to speak freely, indeed, to wag one's tongue in the hearing of an entire nation; to publish anything and everything, including the most scurrilous gossip; to take drugs and to prate to children about their alleged pleasures; to propagandize for bizarre sexual practices; to watch bloody and obscene entertainment. ... Americans today are left free by the state to engage in activities that could, for the most part, be carried just as readily in prisons, insane asylums, and zoos.[5]

Simon's greatest and most enduring accomplishment was the creation of a massive echo chamber, which he termed a "counterintelligensia."[6] It applauds the merits of the "free market" and wars against government, whether the subject is health

---

[b] After graduating from Lafayette College in 1952, Simon traded municipal bonds at a $75-a-week job. By 1964 he was working at Salomon Brothers and by the early 1970s he was earning $2 million a year.

care, tobacco, global warming or any of dozens of other issues. Most importantly, the counterintelligensia has helped kill the Republican Party of Abraham Lincoln, Teddy Roosevelt and Dwight Eisenhower. In its place—still calling itself the Republican Party—is something entirely new: a libertarian party. For convenience, let's call it the Liberty Party, since that's the name Simon himself chose for it.

His contempt extended to the American people themselves. The Preamble to the U.S. Constitution begins "We the people." The Declaration of Independence explains that it had become "necessary for one people to dissolve the political bands which have connected them with another." Politicians and statesmen from Benjamin Franklin[c] to Ronald Reagan[d] have talked of the "American people." Simon would have none of it. "There is no such thing as the People: it is a collectivist myth," he wrote angrily, adding that—

> There are only individual citizens with individual wills and individual purposes. There is only one social system that reflects this sovereignty of the individual: the free market, or capitalist system, which means the sovereignty of the individual …

What Simon sought, and achieved, was a massive, unprecedented remaking of America from a nation founded on protection of individuals to one dedicated to protecting property and those who own it.

Simon was master of the leveraged buyout. He once bought a greeting card company, Gibson, with $330,000 of his own money. He sold it for a $70 million profit.[7] The messages from members of the counterintelligensia, like those from the greeting card company, are simple.

Slash taxes. Distrust government—*all* government. Put churches, not the government, in charge of caring for the poor. Support private schools with public money. Use corporations to collect the trash, run the prisons, feed soldiers at war—indeed, go even further and profitize the military itself. Eliminate the

---

[c] "The Constitution only guarantees the American people the right to pursue happiness. You have to catch it yourself." Benjamin Franklin, http://www.goodreads.com/quotes/show/40251, accessed July 9, 2012.

[d] "Government growing beyond our consent had become a lumbering giant, slamming shut the gates of opportunity, threatening to crush the very roots of our freedom. What brought America back? The American people brought us back—with quiet courage and common sense; with undying faith that in this nation under God the future will be ours, for the future belongs to the free." Ronald Reagan, http://www.pbs.org/wgbh/americanexperience/features/general-article/reagan-quotes/, accessed July 9, 2012.

minimum wage and curtail unions' powers. Convert Social Security to a voluntary program.

Simon's counterintelligensia claims that "environmental conservation requires a commonsense approach that limits the scope of government," acid rain is a "so-called threat [that] is largely nonexistent," and global warming is "a verdict in search of evidence." The message is always the same, always designed to benefit corporations and the rich—precisely as Simon intended.

What Simon delivered to the Republican Party as well as the corporations and the rich who now control it, was a veneer of intellectual respectability, together with tools that could be used in concert with political contributions, advertising blitzes, public relations campaigns and other instruments, to not only fundamentally remake American attitudes toward government, but develop a shadow society.

THE LIBERTY PARTY

The only party with a philosophical heritage which might permit it to be the Liberty Party in the United States is the Republican Party. ... The only thing that can save the Republican Party, in fact, is a counterintelligensia. Without such a reservoir of antiauthoritarian scholarship on which to draw, it is destined to remain the Stupid Party and to die. It may even deserve to die.

William E. Simon
A Time for Truth, 1978

There are two principal components of the counterlligensia. One consists of self-styled "think tanks," (which bear about as much of a relationship to thinking as military music does to music). The think tanks were originally based principally in Washington, D.C., but have expanded to include every region and virtually every state.

The university arm includes a variety of parts, such as endowed professorships and "chairs" at dozens of schools,[e] as well as heavily funded "centers" and "institutes"[f] at a number of well-known and highly-respected institutions. These include Harvard, Stanford, Washington of St. Louis, Chicago, and Berkeley, for example.

---

[e] For example, Michael J. Cima is the David H. Koch Professor of Engineering at the David H. Koch Institute at the Massachusetts Institute of Technology. See http://ki.mit.edu/.

[f] For example, the Institute for Humane Studies and the Mercatus Institute, both located at George Mason University and both heavily supported by Koch Industries.

There are profession-specific groups such as the Federalist Society, with 25,000 lawyer-members. It started in 1982, when a small group of law students sought support from Olin for a conference at Yale University. According to John J. Miller, author of *A Gift of Freedom: How the John M. Olin Foundation Changed America*, the Olin Foundation paid for that meeting, and ultimately gave $5.5 million over 20 years to the Federalist Society.[8]

There also are crosscutting organizations, such as the National Association of Scholars, an innocent enough name for a radical organization.[g] Despite that name, NAS is unquestionably radical. It was founded by radicals (if you consider Bill Simon to have been one). It supports radicals. What Simon and the counterintelligensia, including NAS, oppose is the current social order. They seek to overturn it. In my book, and by every reasonable definition, that makes them "radical."

(Does that make them wrong? Not necessarily. Those who sought to break with Great Britain and establish a new nation, were radicals of their time. So were those who sought to eliminate slavery, root and stem. As were women who sought the vote, blacks who fought Jim Crow and students who resisted the war in Viet Nam. All were radical, but some were correct. Was Bill Simon?)

NAS clearly believes the radical label works. It relentlessly attacks and demonizes others as "radical": a professor hired by Brown University;[9] college students protesting tuition increases;[10] University of California professors;[11] and, feminists,[12] to name but a few.

The point to be taken here is that Simon and his ilk were, and are, perfectly willing to embrace and enforce radical notions, if they are *their* radical notions. Say what they will, their's is not an attempt to establish a more just and perfect society,

---

[g] Its former board members include sociologist Irving Louis Horowitz, who worried that "left-wing fascists" and "professional savages" were subverting objective, empirical approaches to the social sciences. Another former member was Irving Kristol, termed the "Godfather of Modern Conservatism" by the *New York Times*. A current member is Eugene Genovese. His profile by the Bradley Foundation (one of the 11 Keystone Foundations) describes him as a one-time Marxist who "became intellectually, politically, and morally disillusioned ... (and) joined his wife in converting to Roman Catholicism (and) helped to found The Historical Society to resist the encroachment of ideology in historical studies." Another current member, Christina Hoff Sommers, wrote *Who Stole Feminism? How Women Have Betrayed Women*, and *The War Against Boys*. Another advisor, Shelby Steele, wrote in the *Wall Street Journal* after black teenager Trayvon Martin was shot to death by an armed Neighborhood Watch patrol that "Trayvon's sad fate clearly sent a quiver of perverse happiness all across America's civil rights establishment." Common to all of these Advisor's comments are attacks—on liberals, academics, civil rights leaders, and, of all things, women for being ... well, women.

except insofar as it protects them and their interests. What motivates them is greed, pure and simple. The best expression of this proposition was likely that of Abraham Lincoln during the legendary Lincoln-Douglas debates:

> It is the eternal struggle between these two principles—right and wrong—throughout the world. They are the two principles that have stood face to face from the beginning of time; and will ever continue to struggle. The one is the common right of humanity, and the other the divine right of kings. It is the same principle in whatever shape it develops itself. It is the same spirit that says, "You toil and work and earn bread, and I'll eat it." No matter in what shape it comes, whether from the mouth of a king who seeks to bestride the people of his own nation and live by the fruit of their labor, or from one race of men as an apology for enslaving another race, it is the same tyrannical principle.[13]

Simon had plenty of vitriol to spread around. "America's universities are today churning out young collectivists by legions"[14] and "bureaucracies themselves should be assumed noxious, authoritarian parasites on society."[15] Simon, like Powell, had a clear vision of what had to be done: create a counterintelligensia with "a massive and unprecedented mobilization of the moral, intellectual financial resources" by businessmen using "the immense corporate funds presently earmarked for education, 'public relations,' and 'institutional advertising' into the organizations needed to sustain and expand the counterintelligensia."[16]

"It must," Simon concluded, "become a veritable crusade if we are to survive in freedom,"[17] adding—

> Funds generated by business … must rush by the multimillions to the aid of liberty … to funnel desperately needed funds to scholars, social scientists, writers, and journalists who understand the relationship between political and economic liberty. [Business must] cease the mindless subsidizing of colleges and universities whose departments of economy, government, politics, and history are hostile to capitalism.

The depth, breadth and sophistication of the counterintelligensia is vast. Simon understood that the task at hand was Herculean and, of necessity, had to start with universities. "Ideas are weapons," he wrote, "indeed, the only weapons with which other ideas can be fought."

Although rich in his own right, Simon's impact on America was due principally to the wealth of the John M. Olin Foundation which he was chosen to run. He dispensed its money at will and utterly at his own discretion. "The best way to think of the John M. Olin Foundation," the *National Review* once wrote, "is not as a charitable foundation, but as a source of venture capital for the vast right-wing conspiracy."[18]

With it, Simon not only provided seed money to dozens of so-called think tanks, but recruited other wealthy donors, rich individuals and corporations alike, to the cause. But Simon's true stroke of genius was to create the Philanthropy Roundtable. Initially it was an informal group of about one dozen foundations devoted to advancing the interests of corporations and the rich (or, as the Roundtable states euphemistically "to promote greater respect for private, voluntary approaches to individual and community betterment."[19]).

Today, the Roundtable boasts an annual budget of nearly $4.5 million, a staff of 18, and a membership of over 550 philanthropic organizations and families.[20]

In a 1997 study, Sally Covington of the National Committee on Responsive Philanthropy examined the spending of the 12 core foundations for three years, 1992–94. In that period alone and from only those 12 foundations, $210 million was funneled into the corporate cause, though they are always careful to describe themselves as "conservative" or "free market" or "libertarian." It bears repeating that these foundations are committed not so much to the causes of the "right wing" or conservatism, but instead to advancing the interests of those who own property. Their cause has little to do with principle and everything to do with principal.

The core foundations include the following:

- Lynde and Harry Bradley Foundation, money originally from Allen-Bradley Company, a major manufacturer of electronic and radio components.[21]

- Smith Richardson Foundation, money from the Vicks Vaporrub fortune.[22]

- Sarah Scaife Foundation and Carthage Foundation (other Scaife foundations include Allegheny and Scaife Family foundations, money originally from the Mellon family fortune, whose holdings included Gulf Oil, Alcoa and Mellon Bank.)[23]

- Philip McKenna Foundation, money from Kennametal, a leading global supplier of tooling, engineered components and advanced materials.[24]

- John M. Olin Foundation (now defunct), money from Olin Industries chemical and munitions manufacturing.[25]

- Henry Salvatori Foundation, money from Western Geophysical, now the oil exploration arm of Litton industries.[26]

- Charles G. Koch, David H. Koch, Claude R. Lambe Foundations, sustained by profits from Koch Industries, the largest privately-owned company in the United States.

- Earhart Foundation, money from White Star Oil.[27]

- J.M. Foundation, money from Borden Milk.[28]

Today, literally hundreds of millions are invested each year in an immense echo chamber in which politically and economically inspired messages are honed by the think tanks, then beamed into homes and business by messengers also funded by corporations and the rich: the cable TV network, National Empowerment Television (which, thankfully, entered bankruptcy in 2000); magazines like *National Interest/Public Interest* (which received $1.9 million in Covington's study), as well as the *American Spectator* and the *New Criterion* ($1.7 million each); over the airwaves by the likes of Rush Limbaugh, Oliver North and G. Gordon Liddy, and scores of sound-alikes that dominate the local AM dials. To assure a patina of respectability, the voices, and faces, of the late William F. Buckley and Ben Wattenberg were kept in front of the viewers of public television by donations ($3.2 million).

At the same time, money keeps alive efforts to purge all traces of "liberal" bias from public stations ($3.3 million to the Center for the Study of Popular Culture, which wants to "change the leftist, anti-American, elitist culture that is dominant in the entertainment industry [and to expose] the idiocies and the viciousness of the radical leftism in universities, the media, mainstream churches, and everywhere else this modern plague is found" in part through its Committee on Media Integrity (COMINT), the leader in the de-funding attacks on public television; $1.2 million to the Center for Media and Public Affairs; and, $365,000 to Accuracy in Media (funded in part also by the Adolph Coors Foundation, the Texaco Philanthropic Foundation Inc. and Texaco itself), which once attacked Walter Cronkite as a "Soviet dupe."

Simon remained fixed on more fundamental changes, so the Olin Foundation devoted more of its resources to studying how laws influence economic behavior than any other project. The law schools at Chicago, Harvard, Stanford, Virginia, and Yale all have law-and-economics programs named in honor of Olin.[29]

Harvard has the John M. Olin Institute for Strategic Studies.[30] The John M. Olin Institute of Employment Practice and Policy is based at George Mason University in Virginia near Washington, D.C.

Which grant made by the John M. Olin Foundation has mattered the most is hard to say, but surely its support for a 1982 conference of law students and professors that served as a springboard for the creation of the Federalist Society is at or close to the top of the list.

With 45,000 members,[31] chapters at 218 law schools,[32] scores of close affiliates nationwide and the top tier of America's judges, including Supreme Court Chief Justice John Roberts,[33] Justices Clarence Thomas, Antonin Scalia,[34] as well as Samuel Alito,[35] a wide range of current and former Senators, U.S. Attorneys General and Solicitors General and many lower court judges, the Federalist Society is in the words of the *Washington Monthly*, "quite simply the best-organized, best-funded, and most effective legal network operating in this country."[36] And it would not exist had it not been for Bill Simon and the Olin Foundation.

Over time, other self-styled "conservative" foundations joined Olin. Under federal law, the identity of funders must be provided to the IRS, but not necessarily to the public. However, the Society's secretary inadvertently gave my research assistant its complete 1988 IRS 990 tax return, including the list of funders. That year, according to its IRS Form 990, the Society received exactly zero of its money from membership dues. That's right, *zero*. Instead, of the roughly $12 million in income, every penny came from the 11 core foundations.

It is little wonder that Federalist Society members have ascended the legal and corporate ladders of America with such ease. Monica Goodling, the principal deputy director of public affairs at Bush-the-Son's Justice Department was responsible for vetting the power to appoint or dismiss department appointees. The job exploded in her face in 2007, when the Bush Administration abruptly fired seven United States Attorneys on December 7, 2006. In the subsequent Congressional investigation, it was revealed that Goodling had illegally applied a political litmus test not only to possible political appointees, but to applicants for career positions as well.

For nearly two years Goodling sought to cultivate a "farm system" for Republicans at the Justice Department, hiring scores of prosecutors and immigration judges who espoused conservative priorities and Christian lifestyle choices. Exercising what amounted to veto power over a wide range of critical jobs, Goodling was asking candidates for their views on abortion and same-sex marriage, maneuvering around senior officials who outranked her, including the department's second-in-command. This was revealed in an investigation by the Department's Office of the Inspector General and Office of Professional Responsibility, which interviewed 85 witnesses and scoured documents and computer hard drives.[37, h]

Papers handed over during the investigation included Goodling's spreadsheet for qualifications of job applicants. There along with experience and other factors was membership in the Federalist Society, a column labeled "FedSoc."[38]

It is little wonder that Federalist Society has served as a gateway for judges and lawyers during the 24 years that Republicans have controlled the White House since it was created. It's existence has vastly simplified the task of determining who will serve the wills of corporations and the rich and who will not. What matters most is neither the law nor justice, but property and those who own it.

Simon's willingness to provide seed money for the Federalist Society typified his approach to creating the counterintelligensia. He applied the same principles to the creation of the university-based centers.

---

[h] The Goodling episode also illustrates how the core foundations and their allies have created a network for moving their own up the career ladder.

She majored in communications at Messiah College, a Christian school in Grantham, Pa., that does not have co-ed dorms or allow alcohol on campus. She enrolled in law school at American University but transferred to Regent University, founded by one-time candidate for the Republican nomination and televangelist Pat Robertson "to produce Christian leaders who will make a difference, who will change the world."

After graduating in 1999, Goodling worked in the opposition research war room for the Bush campaign, then moved to the Justice Department's press office. She spent six months with the U.S. attorney's office in the Eastern District of Virginia, then returned to Washington where her former co-workers from the opposition research guided her up the ranks.

Goodling helped recruit new office managers who included John Nowacki, another Regent University graduate, who had little experience as a prosecutor, but had previously served as the director of legal policy at the Free Congress Foundation, the research arm of the Free Congress political action committee. She was but one of Regent University spin-offs to land in the Bush Administration.

When Bush-the-Son took office, the former dean of Regent's Robertson School of Government, Kay Coles James, was promptly installed as the Director of the Office of Personnel Management. What Goodling did at Justice, James did government-wide, hiring up to 150 graduates of Regent, ranked a "tier four" school by *US News & World Report* and tied for 136th place, with little or no experience. Jim David, the assistant dean for administration in the Robertson School of Government, was deputy director of the Justice Department's Task Force for the Faith-Based & Community Initiative.

Typical of the intellectual products of these centers was Allan Bloom's book *Closing of the American Mind: How Higher Education Has Failed Democracy and Impoverished the Souls of Today's Students*, published in 1987. In it, Bloom, who was at the University of Chicago's Olin School, examines—

> the students in our prestige universities, and he finds them deficient in moral formation, in reading of serious books, in musical tastes, and above all in love. They are shallow. They have no longing in their souls for anything high or great. Their minds are empty, their characters weak, and their bodies sated with rock and roll and easy sex—or at least with the belief that sex is "no big deal."[39]

The Olin Foundation supplied Bloom with a grant that helped him write an article for *National Review* that became the basis of *The Closing of the American Mind*, and also backed the John M. Olin Center for Inquiry into the Theory and Practice of Democracy for Bloom at the University of Chicago.[40]

Bloom's work served a dual purpose: one was to advance the ideas espoused by Simon; the other was to launch a frontal assault on the credibility and integrity of true scholars at mainstream universities. Soon, he was joined by others whom Simon had groomed, all aimed to damage the credibility and reputations of main stream scholars, painting them as "political correctness" tyrants who impose their views on innocent and helpless students. One of them, Dinesh D'Souza, wrote in *Illiberal Education* that—

> Traditionally liberal professors are retiring and making way for a new generation weaned on the assorted ideologies of the late 1960s, such as the movement for black separatism and the burgeoning causes of feminism and gay rights.

AND THIS IS JUST A PARTIAL LIST

A partial list of Federalist Society Members in the Bush Administration includes former Attorney General John Ashcroft, former Secretary of the Department of Energy Spencer Abraham, Secretary of the Department of Interior Gale Norton, former Solicitor of Labor Eugene Scalia (Supreme Court Justice Antonin Scalia's son), former General Counsel of the Department of Education Brian Jones, former Deputy Attorney General Larry Thompson, former Solicitor General Ted Olson, former Assistant Attorney General for Legal Policy Viet Dinh, Inspector General of Department of Defense Joseph E. Schmitz, former Asst. Attorney General for Environment and Natural Resources Thomas L. Sansonetti, former Principal Deputy Solicitor General Paul Clement [Currently Solicitor General], former Associate Deputy Attorney General and former Director of the Federal Trade Commission's Office of Policy Planning R. Ted Cruz, former Director of National Institute of Justice Sarah V. Hart, former Associate White House Counsel Bradford Berenson, former Associate White House Counsel Noel Francisco, Federal Judicial Nominees, Samuel Alito, confirmed to the U.S. Supreme Court, John Roberts, confirmed to the U.S. Supreme Court, Janice Rogers Brown, confirmed to the U.S. Court of Appeals for the DC Circuit, Miguel Estrada, nominated to the U.S. Court of Appeals for the DC Circuit [withdrawn], Brett Kavanaugh, confirmed to the U.S. Court of Appeals for the DC Circuit, D. Brooks Smith, confirmed to the U.S. Court of Appeals for the Third Circuit, Michael Chertoff, confirmed to the U.S. Court of Appeals for the Third Circuit, currently Secretary of the Department of Homeland Security, William Haynes, nominated to the U.S. Court of Appeals for the Fourth Circuit, Edith Brown Clement, confirmed to the U.S. Court of Appeals for the Fifth Circuit, Priscilla R. Owen, confirmed to the U.S. Court of Appeals for the Fifth Circuit, Henry Saad, nominated to the U.S. Court of Appeals for the Sixth Circuit [withdrawn], Susan Neilson, confirmed to the U.S. Court of Appeals for the Sixth Circuit, Deborah Cook, confirmed to the U.S. Court of Appeals for the Sixth Circuit, Jeffrey Sutton, confirmed to the U.S. Court of Appeals for the Sixth Circuit, David W. McKeague, confirmed to the U.S. Court of Appeals for the Sixth Circuit, Diane Sykes, confirmed to the U.S. Court of Appeals for the Seventh Circuit, Steven Collonton, confirmed to the U.S. Court of Appeals for the Eighth Circuit, Raymond Gruender, confirmed to the U.S. Court of Appeals for the Eighth Circuit, Carlos Bea, confirmed to the U.S. Court of Appeals for the Ninth Circuit, Carolyn B. Kuhl, nominated to the U.S. Court of Appeals for the Ninth Circuit [withdrawn], Jay Bybee, confirmed to the U.S. Court of Appeals for the Ninth Circuit, Harris L. Hartz, confirmed to the U.S. Court of Appeals for the Tenth Circuit, Michael McConnell, confirmed to the U.S. Court of Appeals for the Tenth Circuit, Timothy M. Tymkovich, confirmed to the U.S. Court of Appeals for the Tenth Circuit, William Pryor, confirmed to the U.S. Court of Appeals for the Eleventh Circuit, Thomas B. Griffith, confirmed to the U.S. Court of Appeals for the DC Circuit, Other High-Profile Federalist Society Members [partial list], Justice Antonin Scalia, U.S. Supreme Court, Senator Orrin Hatch (R-Utah), Kenneth Starr, former White House Independent Counsel whose investigation led to President Clinton's impeachment, Judge Robert Bork, failed Supreme Court nominee, Linda Chavez, President of the Center for Equal Opportunity, Charles Murray, controversial author who asserted that some races are inherently less intelligent than others, Don Hodel, former Christian Coalition president, Michigan Governor John Engler, Justice Maura Corrigan, Michigan Supreme Court Chief Justice (4 other justices on the state supreme court are also members of the FS), former Attorney General Don Stenberg, Nebraska, former Attorney General Alan Lance, Idaho.

Source: RightWingWatch, http://www.rightwingwatch.org/content/federalist-society

D'Souza is a perfect illustration of Simon's success. At Dartmouth, he helped found the infamous ultra-conservative *Dartmouth Review* as an undergraduate student, made possible by funding from the Collegiate Network,[i, j] which receives money from the Intercollegiate Studies Institute, that is supported by the core foundations.[k]

The Collegiate Network, a consortium of conservative college newspapers got its start in 1980, with a small grant to a student publication at the University of Chicago by the Institute for Educational Affairs, a group supported by the John M. Olin Foundation.

The paper was started to combat what it has called "the twisted idealism of the 60's, a bastard brand of liberalism" that supports co-education, affirmative action, and a weakening of Dartmouth's old image as a hard-drinking, all-male school.[41]

---

[i] The *Review* is part of the Collegiate Network (CN), a Delaware-based conduit of core foundation money that pays for similar newspapers at 109 campuses. These would never come into being without CN money, nor would they continue to exist. Posted on the CN website are expressions of gratitude from the University of Michigan and Claremont:

"Through its 20 years of existence, the *Review* has received more support from the Collegiate Network than any other organization or individual, in terms of financial and educational support. The financial backing of CN operating grants is what keeps the papers operating."

"Thank you for all the support the CN has provided over the years. Without your help, the *Claremont Independent* would not exist."

[j] Many of its alumni have gone on to prominence in the major media and in politics, including *National Review* editor Rich Lowry, CNN correspondent Jonathan Karl and conservative pundit Ann Coulter. Collegiate Network alumni have gone on to work for both right-wing and mainstream media, including CNN, the *Washington Post*, the *Wall Street Journal*, *Time*, *Newsweek*, Fox News, *National Review*, the *Weekly Standard*, *Detroit News*, *New York Post*, *Commentary*, the *Charlotte Observer*, and the *Atlantic Monthly*, leaving their imprint on the main stream media.

[k] Aside from CN's financial support for corporate student newspapers, it also provides other support services including:
- an annual training conference for student newspaper editors concentrating on practical skills;
- sponsoring nine paid internships "at national publications in New York City and Washington, D.C. available to editors and reporters of CN member papers;"
- establishing a "Geostrategic Correspondent Course" in June 2001 to cater to international reporting. The course has been developed in close collaboration with Heritage Foundation with one part of its program undertaken at the Prague Security Studies Institute in the Czech Republic;
- visits by CN staff to participating publications, including 'troubleshooting' support if necessary.

In its first year, the *Review* sponsored a free lobster-and-champagne feast to coincide with a campus fast for the world's hungry. In 1981 it published a list of members of the school's Gay Students Association. Then in 1982, it ran a column in "black English" suggesting that black students were illiterate. As an editor, D'Souza once wrote, "The question is not whether women should be educated at Dartmouth, but whether they should be educated at all."[42]

D'Souza was hired as the editor of *Prospect*, a magazine published by Concerned Alumni of Princeton (CAP), a group formed in 1972 to oppose the admission of women and other changes to make admissions based more on merit and less on gentility.[43] The group, and the magazine, propounded "offensive views about women, minorities and AIDS victims," in the words of the *New York Times*.[44] Under D'Souza, *Prospect* was "outwardly destructive and irresponsible" in the words of Robert Durkee, Princeton's vice president for public affairs.[45] Among other things, D'Souza wrote a cover story identifying a freshman who had begun a sexual relationship, offering details of the woman's sex life.

How D'Souza got the job is unclear, but CAP was founded by William Rusher, editor of the *National Review*, which describes itself as "America's most widely read and influential magazine and web site for Republican/conservative news, commentary, and opinion."[46]

D'Souza's next stop was the Heritage Foundation, heavily funded by the core foundations, where he was named managing editor of its journal, *Policy Review*, when he was only 24. He was joined at Heritage by another of the Simon babies, Laura Ingram, who had worked with D'Souza, at the *Dartmouth Review*, also succeeding him as editor of *Prospect*.[47]

From Heritage, D'Souza and Ingram leapt to the Reagan White House to work on abortion and school prayer.[48] When Reagan left office, D'Souza began receiving annual grants from the Olin Foundation. D'Souza wrote *Illiberal Education* as a John M. Olin Fellow at the American Enterprise Institute—and sparked the debate that helped turn the term "political correctness" into a familiar pejorative.

Then, again with support from Olin and the other core foundations, he wrote *The End of Racism: Principles for a Multiracial Society,* a vile, racist tract on African-Americans and all aspects of African-American culture. D'Souza blamed "black cultural defects" for what he predicts will be the ultimate failure of affirmative action. He creates a laundry list of the "dysfunctional" aspects of

African-American culture: "high rates of criminal activity ... the normalization of illegitimacy ... the predominance of single-parent families ... high levels of addiction to alcohol and drugs ... a parasitic reliance on government provision ... a hostility to academic achievement ... and ... a scarcity of independent enterprises."[49] In describing the book for the *Washington Post*, D'Souza employed a different title: *The End of Racism: The White Man's Burden.*[50]

What is truly extraordinary is that D'Souza was not born in the United States, but Bombay, India.

In D'Souza's book, *The Enemy at Home: The Cultural Left and its Responsibility for 9/11*,[51] he asserts that Americans who criticize the war do so because military defeat is an acceptable price for defeating Bush. Terrorists hate America not for its foreign policy but for its moral depravity, declaring that the cultural left is responsible for 9/11.

> What disgusts [Muslims] is not free elections but the sights of hundreds of homosexuals kissing one another and taking marriage vows. The person that horrifies them the most is not John Locke but Hillary Clinton.

D'Souza remains at the American Enterprise Institute, but is also a fellow at the Hoover Institution at Stanford University, which is heavily supported by the core foundations.

[Not to allow her thread to lapse, Ingram went to law school at the University of Virginia School of Law in 1991, and she served as a law clerk for Judge Ralph K. Winter, Jr., who was appointed by Ronald Reagan, of the U.S. Court of Appeals for the Second Circuit in New York.[52] Later, she clerked for U.S. Supreme Court Justice Clarence Thomas.[53] Ingram did not abandon her writing career, however, writing a book *The Hillary Trap*, then *Shut Up & Sing: How the Elites in Hollywood, Politics ... and the UN are Subverting America* and *Power to the People*, which focuses on what she calls the "pornification" of America.[54]]

[Gary Bauer became president of the Family Research Council, which "champions marriage and family as the foundation of civilization, the seedbed of virtue, and the wellspring of society," from 1988–1999. He resigned from this position to run for the Republican nomination for President of the United States, but dropped out of the race after the primaries in February 2000. He then became president of American Values, which describes itself as "deeply committed to the defense of all human life against the assaults of the culture of death."][55]

D'Souza, Ingram and Bauer are only three of thousands who, to use Simon's words, are "churned out" by modern universities. The model for many of them is the Hoover Institution on War, Revolution, and Peace, founded in 1919 at Stanford University as the Hoover War Library when the alumnus Herbert Hoover donated $50,000 to assemble and maintain documents about World War I, the League of Nations and the Bolshevik revolution.[56] For decades, it collected documents, producing bibliographies and anthologies. But during the anti-Communist era of the 1950s, it became an independent institution operating outside normal university government, accounting to Stanford's trustees, not its faculty.[57]

After W. Glen Campbell arrived at Hoover from six years at the American Enterprise Institute, one of the original corporate think tanks, its size and influence began to expand rapidly. From 1960 to 1990, the number of its "scholars" jumped from 6 to 85,[58] and 167 in 2008.[59]

Because a primary focus of *Cliffs I* is the propagation of half-truths and even outright lies by corporate fronts like Hoover, examining its record on that account is revealing.

"Gifts" are nothing of the sort, for their transfer is for a *quid pro quo*—literally a thing for a thing. Since global warming is a primary focus of *Cliffs II*, the companion to this book, consider the money that Hoover has received from just one oil company, ExxonMobil: $135,000 in 1998, $50,000 in 1990, $20,000 in 2002, $20,000 in 2003, and $20,000 in 2005.[60]

Having received one thing, Hoover delivered the other. A partial list of Hoover articles includes the following: The Pseudoscience of Global Warming, The Politics behind Global Warming, Global Warming and Globaloney, The Science behind Global Warming, Bootleggers, Baptists, and Global Warming, Happiness Is a Warm Planet, Cooling the Global-Warming Debate, Who Says the Globe Is Warming?, An Economist Looks at Global Warming and Global Chill.

One of Hoover's fellows, Thomas Gale Moore, author of *Climate of Fear: Why We Shouldn't Worry About Global Warming*, is the most prominent global warming science skeptic associated with the Hoover Institution, but by no means the only one. Another, Tom Bethell, warns to "prepare for a new wave of lies, dressed up as science" from "enviro-fanatics."[61] Global warming? According to

Bruce Berkowitz, "There is probably no other issue today about which so many hold such strong views with so little firsthand knowledge."[62]

Hoover's pitching for market solutions to threats that the market itself produced does not stop with global warming. Richard A. Epstein says "health care reform may be bad for your health."[63] Annelise Anderson agrees that "Our system of financing political campaigns is indeed in need of reform," but the solution is not to limit the amount that candidates can receive or corporations can give, but to "abolish campaign spending limits." Limits would, of course, lessen the ability of corporations and the rich to impose their wills on candidates. And David R. Henderson's view of the level at which the minimum wage should be set? Zero.[64]

Hoover's board, like most, is a virtual *Who's Who* of corporate executives, core foundation officials and officers or trustees from other fronts. For example, Richard Mellon Scaife, head of two of the core foundations, is on Hoover's large Board of Overseers. The Sarah Scaife foundation, overseen by Richard, gave the Hoover Institution a $450,000 grant in 2001, $370,000 in 2000, and $635,00 in 1999. In 2003, Olin gave it $35,000 for a "Fellowship for D. D'Souza," and in 2001, it gave $100,000 for "the Robert and Karen Rishwain Fellowship for Dinesh D'Souza" followed in 2002 by another $65,000. All of the core foundations have given money for general support: $175,000 in 2005 from Olin, for example, and $725,000 in 2004 from Sarah Scaife Foundation.[65]

Hoover's Board includes many with direct connections to a variety of industries. Jack R. Anderson, for example, has been President of Calver Corporation, a health care consulting and investing firm.[66] Joy A. Timken, is an heir to a fortune accumulated by the company that is one of the world's largest maker of bearings.[67] Thomas J. Tierney of Boston is the former chief executive of Bain & Company, an international management consulting firm with 25 offices worldwide (and former home to Mitt Romney).[68]

Typical of the university-based think tanks is that only a small fraction of their budget is devoted to teaching. The Hoover Institution, for example, spent 60 percent of its budget on research and publications, 33 percent on libraries (the reason it was created in the first place) and 7 percent on administration. Of the nearly $4 million that Harvard University's Center for International Affairs received in 1991, only $33,040, or less than 1 percent, was spent on student programs. When money does go to students, it is often in the form of grants or scholarships to select students: those who have demonstrated an affection for the "free market" values that their institutes espouse.[69]

One of the beneficiaries of the Koch Foundation and family support is the Mercatus Center at George Mason University in Fairfax, Virginia a few miles south of Washington, D.C. In 2006, for example, one Koch grant alone was $3.9 million.[70] The general director of the Center is Tyler Cohen, an economist who occupies the Holbert C. Harris Chair of Economics. Cohen does a great deal: A recent book, for example, is *Discover Your Inner Economist: Use Incentives to Fall in Love, Survive Your Next Meeting, and Motivate Your Dentist*. He is also director of both the James Buchanan Center, and writes a blog, The Marginal Revolution. He has written a ton of articles: "Does the Welfare State Help the Poor?" for example, and "Terrorism and Theater: Analysis and Policy Recommendations."

But, wow, a lot of them are in *Public Choice*, which is published by the very same institution he heads, the James Buchanan Center. Others are in *Social Philosophy and Policy*, published by the Center of the same name located at Bowling Green State University in Ohio. Where does that Center and, hence its journal, get its money? From the usual suspects: the Sarah Scaife Foundation ($625,000 in each of 2003–05, and more earlier); Earhart Foundation ($325,000 in 2005, $60,000 in each of 2002–04); and, comparable sums from Olin and Carthage Foundations.[71]

But does Cohen teach? No.

In St. Louis, the Center for the Study of American Business at Washington University has also prospered thanks to funding from the core foundations. The Lynde and Harry Bradley Foundation support the Bradley Graduate and Post Graduate Fellowship Program, while Olin created the John M. Olin Visiting Professor of Labor Economics and Public Policy, not to mention $2,000,000 for a distinguished professorship in the John M. Olin School of Business and $97,450 for the John M. Olin Visiting Professor of Labor Economics and Public Policy.[72]

And what do the Foundations—or, more accurately, those who funded them and are themselves rich—get in return for their money?

- A conclusion, supposedly by Washington University, that complying with federal regulations costs small businesses billions of dollars and millions of worker hours each year.[73]

- And, another conclusion that "budget outlays are only the beginning of the true economic burden of federal regulations. The Center for the Study of American Business estimates that each dollar Congress appropriates gives rise to an additional $20 of compliance costs borne by the private sector, either by requiring more costly ways of doing business, or in paperwork costs for filling out the torrent of regulatory forms and questionnaires. So we are talking about an aggregate economic burden of about $210 billion from federal regulations, nearly 5 percent of GNP."[74]

- Yet another conclusion: Airline safety regulations that increase costs may make air travel less safe.[75]

In sum, Simon's plan was incredibly successful. In the space of less than 20 years, he not only established a counterintelligensia, but it fundamentally recast American attitudes toward government, taxes, and regulations. Some believe, including this writer, that he laid the groundwork for the savings and loan disaster, the meltdown of the American banking system, the decline of the U.S. auto and other industries, the increasing dependence of America on Persian Gulf Oil, which, in turn, has led to three wars. And, of course, America and the world are going over the climate cliff, as global warming becomes irreversible.

But Simon did not accomplish all this single-handedly. He had help, especially from the echo chamber that was created to spread the messages of the counterintelligensia.

"COUNTERINTELLIGENSIA" ORGANIZATIONS SUPPORTED BY THE JOHN M. OLIN FOUNDATION

Name	Total $$
Harvard University	26,016,819
University of Chicago	21,216,891
Washington University	20,767,686
Yale University	17,282,509
University of Rochester	9,725,230
Stanford University	8,944,835
Heritage Foundation, The	8,620,835
American Enterprise Institute for Public Policy Research	7,507,124
George Mason University	6,890,824
Manhattan Institute for Policy Research, Inc	5,699,500
Harvard Law School	5,545,345
Hoover Institution on War, Revolution and Peace	5,190,660
Federalist Society for Law and Public Policy Studies	4,790,000
New York University	4,323,105
University of Virginia	4,199,066
Columbia University	4,064,000
National Bureau of Economic Research, Inc	3,876,400
Intercollegiate Studies Institute, Inc	3,502,600
Hudson Institute, Inc	3,034,840
Georgetown University	2,759,082
Princeton University	2,744,759
Cornell University	2,642,725
Foundation for Cultural Review, Inc	2,618,000
Washington Legal Foundation	2,585,000
California, University of, Los Angeles (UCLA)	2,478,761
Boston University (Boston)	2,464,321
Association of Graduates of the United States Military Academy	2,437,500
Academy Research and Development Institute	2,328,704
National Association of Scholars, Inc	2,285,000

Name	Total $$
David Horowitz Freedom Center	2,285,000
Ethics and Public Policy Center, Inc	2,183,500
Center for Strategic and International Studies	2,112,318
Producers Incorporated for Television	2,100,000
Johns Hopkins University — SAIS	2,075,652
California, University of, Berkeley	2,050,823
National Right to Work Legal Defense Foundation	1,985,000
Center for Individual Rights	1,965,000
University of Southern California	1,879,908
Institute on Religion and Public Life, Inc	840,000
University of Toronto	1,818,703
National Affairs, Inc	1,793,500
Claremont McKenna College	693,000
Duke University	679,260
Pacific Legal Foundation	665,000
University of South Carolina	652,500
Project Hope	650,000
Madison Center for Educational Affairs	642,600
Property and Environment Research Center (PERC)	640,775
Capital Research Center	617,500
Education & Research Institute	615,000
Rockefeller University	600,000
Student Sponsor Partners	600,000
National Humanities Center	584,945
California Institute of Technology	578,500
Fordham University	571,400
Empire Foundation for Policy Research The	570,000
East Hampton Library Society	550,000
Institute for Educational Affairs	547,389
Emory University	534,813

Name	Total $$
Americans for Tax Reform Foundation.	525,000
Vanderbilt University.	524,000
American Spectator Foundation, Inc..	510,000
Clark University.	506,430
National Humanities Center.	584,945
California Institute of Technology.	578,500
Fordham University..	571,400
Empire Foundation for Policy Research, The..	570,000
East Hampton Library Society.	550,000
Institute for Educational Affairs..	547,389
Emory University.	534,813
Americans for Tax Reform Foundation.	525,000
Vanderbilt University.	524,000
American Spectator Foundation, Inc..	510,000
Clark University.	506,430
Media Research Center, Inc..	495,000
Institute on Religion and Democracy, Inc..	489,000
Smith College.	488,000
American Council of Trustees and Alumni.	485,000
Foundation for Research on Economics and the Environment (FREE).	484,250
Boston College.	470,930
Hillsdale College..	452,600
Statistical Assessment Service.	450,000
Whidbey Island Films.	450,000
Hugh O'Brian Youth Leadership..	440,000
Gilder Lehrman Institute of American History, The.	421,200
National Taxpayers Union Foundation.	405,000
Institute for Advanced Studies in Culture..	400,000
Landmark Legal Foundation.	395,000
Michigan State University..	394,490
Acton Institute For The Study of Religion and Liberty.	390,500

Name	Total $$
Becket Fund, Inc., The.	380,000
Northcote Parkinson Fund..	365,000
Alexis de Tocqueville Institution.	362,500
Employment Policy Foundation.	360,000
National Strategy Information Center, Inc..	354,920
George C. Marshall Institute.	350,000
University of Dallas..	346,998
New Citizenship Project, Inc..	345,000
Educational Reviewer, Inc., The..	343,000
Oxford University.	336,644
Children's Educational Opportunity (CEO) Foundation America.	325,000
University of London.	324,402
University of California, Berkeley.	316,417
American Law and Economics Association.	316,398
Institute for Policy Innovation..	305,000
Eagle Forum Education and Legal Defense Fund.	303,500
Mount Sinai Hospital, The.	300,000
Rockford Institute.	300,000
University of Kansas..	300,000
Judicial Watch..	300,000
National Alumni Forum.	300,000
American Foundation for Resistance International.	295,000
Wisconsin Policy Research Institute, Inc..	292,500
Radio Free Europe/Radio Liberty Fund.	292,000
University of Miami.	291,000
American Studies Center, The..	290,000
Michigan, University of..	286,000
Corporation for Educational Radio and Television.	285,000
Center for Education Reform.	285,000
Northwestern University..	284,378
University of Michigan, Ann Arbor.	282,000
Historical Society (Boston, MA)..	280,000
Naval War College Foundation, Inc.	280,000
Reason Foundation.	276,500

Name	Total $$	Name	Total $$
New York City Public/Private Initiatives, Inc.	275,000	Kenyon College.	193,123
Lafayette College.	261,100	University of Arizona.	180,000
Center for Security Policy, Inc.	261,000	Corporation for Maintaining Editorial Diversity in America.	178,500
Research Foundation of the City University of New York.	251,261	KCET Television.	175,000
Princeton University - James Madison Center.	250,000	Center for Neighborhood Enterprise.	175,000
George Mason University Foundation, Inc.	250,000	U.S. Term Limits Foundation.	175,000
Thomas Aquinas College.	250,000	University of Maryland at College Park, The.	175,000
Institute for Research on the Economics of Taxation.	250,000	State University of New York at Stony Brook.	173,000
Core Knowledge Foundation.	250,000	Criminal Justice Legal Foundation.	165,000
James Madison Foundation, The.	236,195	Women's Freedom Network.	160,000
Yale University Press.	231,270	Donors Trust.	156,000
Competitive Enterprise Institute.	230,300	State Policy Network.	155,000
Center for Educational Studies, Inc.	230,000	University of Michigan, Regents of the.	154,000
Brownson Institute, Inc., The.	230,000	Center for Judicial Studies.	151,250
George Washington University.	227,575	WNET/Thirteen Educational Broadcasting Network.	150,000
Committee for the Free World, Inc.	225,000	Trust for the Bicentennial of the US Constitution.	150,000
Palmer R. Chitester Fund.	225,000	Capital Legal Foundation.	150,000
University of Oxford.	224,400	Library of America Literary Classics of the United States.	150,000
American Legislative Exchange Council.	215,000	School Choice Scholarships Foundation.	150,000
St. John's College (Annapolis).	214,791	Environmental Literacy Council.	150,000
Atlantic Legal Foundation.	210,000	Historical Society (Cambridge, MA)	150,000
Loyola University of Chicago.	210,000	Hanover Review, The.	150,000
Rutgers University.	209,500	Alliance for School Choice, Inc.	150,000
Oxford Institute for American Studies.	202,124	Media Institute.	148,750
University of Washington.	201,207	Progress & Freedom Foundation, The.	145,000
Association of American Educators Foundation.	200,000	Southeastern Legal Foundation, Inc.	145,000
City Innovation.	200,000	Clare Boothe Luce Policy Institute.	145,000
School Choice Alliance.	200,000	Morley Publishing Group, Inc.	145,000
Teacher Education Accreditation Council.	200,000	National Legal and Policy Center.	140,000
Institute for International Economics.	200,000	Colgate University.	138,287
Convent of the Sacred Heart, The.	200,000	Ohio State University.	138,078
Colorado School of Mines Foundation.	200,000	Rand Corporation, The.	137,500
		James Madison Education Fund.	135,000
		University of Houston.	134,401

Name	Total $$	Name	Total $$
Williams College	131,255	United States Olympic Committee Foundation	100,000
Foundation for the United States Constitution	130,000	Richard Nixon Library and Birthplace Foundation	100,000
Foundation for Student Communication	130,000	University of Pittsburgh	97,690
Fund For American Studies, The	129,570	National Endowment for the Humanities	92,500
Education Policy Institute	127,500	Dartmouth College	90,161
Florida State University	125,150	Claremont Graduate University	88,660
Philadelphia Society, The	125,000	Catholic University of America	86,856
Frontiers of Freedom Institute	125,000	International Parliamentary Group for Human Rights in the Soviet Union	85,150
Institute of Public Affairs	119,000	Issues and Views Open Forum Foundation, Inc.	85,000
Clemson University	115,709	Legislative Studies Institute, The	85,000
Utah State University	111,416	Mont Pelerin Society, The	83,000
Center for Immigration Studies	110,000	Pro Demca	80,000
California Association of Scholars	105,000	Puebla Institute, Inc.	80,000
Executive Council on Foreign Diplomats	105,000	International Rescue Committee, Inc.	80,000
University of Vermont	103,150	Encounter for Culture and Education, Inc.	80,000
Hispanic Council for Reform and Educational Options	100,000	Foundation for Community and Faith Centered Enterprise	79,000
Drew Pearson Foundation, The	100,000	Syracuse University	76,872
Institute for Liberty and Community	100,000	New England Legal Foundation	75,200
National Development Council	100,000	Brigham Young University	75,000
National Center for Public Policy Research, Inc.	100,000	Jobs for America's Graduates	75,000
Children First America (Bentonville, AR)	100,000	Empower.org	75,000
Center for New Black Leadership	100,000	American Alliance for Better Schools Foundation	75,000
Black Alliance for Educational Options	100,000	Goldwater Institute	75,000
Center for the Community Interest	100,000	Baruch College	75,000
New York University Medical Center	100,000	Louisiana State University	74,880
Foundation for Individual Rights in Education, Inc.	100,000	Kansas Cultural Trust	74,750
Buffalo Bill Historical Center	100,000	United States Military Academy	74,129
American Council for Capital Formation	100,000	Marquette University	73,000
Institute of World Politics	100,000	Carthage College	72,062
Jesse Helms Center Foundation	100,000	East Carolina University	71,995
National Academy for the Advancement of the Liberal Arts	100,000	National Endowment for Democracy	71,500
		University of Michigan, Dearborn	71,450
		University of Maryland, The	71,400
		Young America's Foundation	70,000
		Ernest Martin Hopkins Institute	70,000

Name.................... Total $$	Name.................... Total $$
Princeton Alumni Viewpoints...... 70,000	Common Good.................. 50,000
Character Education Partnership.... 70,000	Project HOPE (Millwood, VA)..... 50,000
Center for The Community	Renew International............. 50,000
Interest, The................ 70,000	Inner-City Scholarship Fund. 50,000
Wesleyan University............ 69,317	Rampant Lion Foundation......... 50,000
Business Foundation of North Carolina/	Per Scholas.................. 50,000
Kenan Institute of Private	Americans Back In Charge. 50,000
Enterprise. 67,000	James Madison Memorial Fellowship
Trinity College (CT). 66,826	Foundation................. 50,000
John M. Ashbrook Center for	Concord Coalition. 50,000
Public Affairs. 65,000	Nathan Hale Institute............ 50,000
Independent Institute............ 65,000	Committee in Support of Solidarity.. 50,000
Concord College. 64,763	American Cinema Foundation...... 50,000
Boise State University............ 64,640	Regulation Foundation, The. 50,000
California, University of, San Diego. 64,200	Campus Coalition for Democracy... 50,000
California, University of, Davis..... 63,790	American Institute for Strategic
Brandeis University............. 63,250	Cooperation................ 50,000
National Legal Center for The Public	Foundation for American
Interest.................... 63,000	Communications. 50,000
Washington Strategy Seminar...... 62,000	Atlantic Council of the
Center for Military Readiness...... 60,000	United States, The............ 50,000
Institute for Advanced Study....... 60,000	Institute for International Studies. .. 50,000
Galen Institute, Inc................ 60,000	Davidson College............... 49,840
Ripon College. 60,000	Franklin and Marshall College. 49,630
East-West Roundtable........... 60,000	Norwich University.............. 49,573
Committee for Economic Development 60,000	University of Illinois at
Center for the New West......... 55,300	Urbana-Champaign........... 47,250
Freedom's Foundation at Valley	Cambridge University. 46,700
Forge..................... 55,000	Clemson University Foundation. ... 46,555
Citizens Against Government Waste. 55,000	Northern Illinois University........ 46,411
Eisenhower World Affairs Institute.. 55,000	University of Oklahoma, The. 46,259
Ashland University. 55,000	Project for the New American
Mary Institute and St. Louis Country Day	Century. 46,000
School..................... 55,000	Donors Forum on International
University of Wisconsin, Madison. . 51,550	Affairs..................... 45,000
Southwest Texas State University... 50,474	Institute for European Defence and
International Swimming Hall	Strategic Studies. 45,000
of Fame.................... 50,000	International Society for New Institutional
Bill of Rights Institute............ 50,000	Economics.................. 45,000
Sea Research Foundation, The...... 50,000	Howard University................ 45,000
Chapman University. 50,000	University of Tulsa. 44,584
University of California,	Washington Institute Foundation.... 44,000
Los Angeles................ 50,000	National Institute for Public Policy.. 43,500

Name	Total $$
Santa Clara University	43,173
Opportunities Industrialization Centers of America	42,500
University of North Texas	42,437
University of Georgia	40,199
University of Maine	40,180
Historical Society (Philadelphia, PA)	40,000
Heartland Institute	40,000
Christian Rescue Effort for the Emancipation of Dissidents	40,000
Bowling Green State University	40,000
Center for Science, Technology and Media, Inc.	40,000
Small Business Survival Foundation	38,000
Oglethorpe University	37,700
University of Nevada	37,494
Council of Chief State School Officers	36,750
Colorado College	36,250
Mars Hill Audio	35,000
Center for International Relations	35,000
Video Information Network	35,000
Tax Foundation	35,000
Institute for Democracy in Eastern Europe	35,000
Center for Livable Cities	35,000
American Alliance for Rights and Responsibilities	35,000
Criminal Policy Justice Foundation	34,500
Hampden-Sydney College	32,500
Bowdoin College	30,930
Association of Literary Scholars and Critics	30,000
Americas Society	30,000
America's Future, Inc.	30,000
Federation for American Immigration Reform	30,000
Phelps Memorial Hospital Center, The	30,000
East West Foundation for International Affairs	30,000
Potomac Foundation, The	30,000

Name	Total $$
East Hampton Beach Preservation Society	30,000
Russell Sage Foundation	30,000
New York Academy of Sciences	30,000
Institute for Research on Public Policy	30,000
American Council on Economics and Society	30,000
Village of Sleepy Hollow	29,000
Consumer Alert	28,000
John Jay College of Criminal Justice	26,500
American Public Philosophy Institute, Inc.	26,200
City College of New York	26,024
National Humanities Institute	26,000
Council for Basic Education	25,600
Friends University	25,278
University of Illinois at Chicago	25,150
Global Foundation, Inc.	25,000
Inter-University Seminar on Armed Forces and Society	25,000
George Bush Presidential Library Foundation	25,000
International Republican Institute	25,000
Midwest Research Institute	25,000
Residential Living Services, Inc.	25,000
Bryce Harlow Foundation	25,000
California, University of, Irvine	25,000
Institute for Liberty and Democracy	25,000
Interlochen Center for the Arts	25,000
Boys Harbor	25,000
Greater Washington Educational Television Association, Inc.	25,000
New York Civil Rights Coalition	25,000
Morristown Memorial Health Foundation, Inc.	25,000
Roman Catholic Archdiocese of Newark	25,000
George Washington's Mount Vernon Estate and Gardens	25,000
Boys Club of New York	25,000
Southwest Missouri State University	25,000
Focus on the Family	25,000

Name	Total $$
Center for the New Europe.	25,000
Center for Educational Innovation.	25,000
St. John's College (Santa Fe).	25,000
Pacific Forum, CSIS.	25,000
Business Enterprise Trust.	25,000
High Frontier.	25,000
National Wilderness Institute.	25,000
Committee to Rethink Vietnam.	25,000
University of The South.	25,000
National Federation of State High School Associations.	25,000
Forum for International Policy.	25,000
Charles Edison Memorial Youth Fund	25,000
National Radio Theatre of Chicago.	25,000
Atlantic Salmon Federation.	25,000
Colorado Council on Economic Education.	25,000
National Intelligence Study Center.	25,000
Afghanistan Documentary Movie Project Company, Inc.	25,000
Educate America.	25,000
London School of Economics and Political Science, The.	25,000
Metroconomy, Inc.	24,025
Research Foundation of State University of New York.	23,828
Foundation for Economic Education.	22,500
People-To-People Health Foundation, Inc.	22,209
Progressive Foundation, The.	22,000
University of Calgary.	21,500
Institute for Democracy in Vietnam.	21,200
Free Africa Foundation.	21,000
National Communications Institute.	20,000
Simon Bolivar Foundation, Inc.	20,000
American Catholic Conference.	20,000
Quodlibetal Publications, Inc.	20,000
Better Government Association, Inc.	20,000
Magellan Productions, Inc.	20,000
International Institute for Economic Research	20,000
Institute for Policy and Management Research.	20,000

Name	Total $$
Fairfield University.	20,000
Freedom of Expression Foundation.	20,000
Washington Institute for Policy Studies.	20,000
Foundation for Classic Studies in Statecraft and Jurisprudence.	20,000
Pennsylvania Right-To-Work Defense and Education Foundation.	20,000
Historical Research Foundation.	20,000
Pioneer Institute for Public Policy Research.	20,000
California, University of, Santa Cruz.	20,000
Center for International Management Education.	20,000
Accuracy in Academia.	20,000
University Centers for Rational Alternatives, Inc.	20,000
Cuban American National Foundation, The.	20,000
Arthur F. Burns Fellowship Program, Inc.	20,000
Center of the American Experiment.	20,000
Iona College.	20,000
Warren Historical Society.	20,000
Nichols College.	19,500
Lehigh University.	19,000
National Review Institute.	19,000
Harvard College.	18,015
Center for Advanced Studies of the Americas.	18,000
Center for Security Studies.	18,000
University of North Carolina Press.	17,837
Shavano Institute for National Leadership, The.	16,000
Salzburg Seminar In American Studies, Inc.	15,000
Manhattanville College, Economic Freedom Institute.	15,000
Aurora Foundation.	15,000
Security Conference on Asia and the Pacific.	15,000
New York Foundation For The Arts, Inc.	15,000

Name	Total $$	Name	Total $$
Public Research, Syndicated.	15,000	International Academy for Philosophy.	10,000
United States Space Foundation.	15,000	University of Connecticut, The.	10,000
Christian Renewal Effort for Emerging Democracies.	15,000	Harvard Journal of Law and Public Policy.	10,000
National Committee on American Foreign Policy.	15,000	Congressional Human Rights Foundation, The.	10,000
Washington Campus, The.	15,000	International Academy of Philosophy.	10,000
Center for Communication, Inc..	15,000	Hermitage Performing Arts Co., Inc..	10,000
National Endowment for the Humanities.	15,000	Independent Educational Services.	10,000
National History Day, Inc...	15,000	National Archives Trust Fund Board.	10,000
Wellesley College.	14,850	Students in Free Enterprise.	10,000
Pacific Lutheran University..	14,375	America's Future Foundation.	10,000
American Institute for Public Service.	12,500	American Opportunity Foundation.	10,000
American Economic Association.	12,500	Cities In Schools, Inc..	10,000
Universities Field Staff International.	12,000	United States Global Strategy Council.	10,000
Le Moyne College.	12,000	International Foundation for Human Sciences, Inc..	10,000
Texas A&M University.	11,900	Persephone Productions, Inc..	10,000
Hackley School, The.	11,000	Academy of Political Science, The.	10,000
Research Center for Religion & Human Rights.	10,000	Civic Institute.	9,160
Partners Advancing Values in Education, Inc..	10,000	International House.	9,000
Libertarian Review Foundation.	10,000	G K Chesterton Society USA Inc..	8,000
American Council on Germany.	10,000	American Federation of Teachers Educational Foundation.	6,700
University of Chicago Press, The.	10,000	Varied Directions International.	6,000
George C. Marshall Foundation.	10,000	Procurement Roundtable.	5,000
Midtown Pregnancy Support Center.	10,000	Centre for Policy Studies..	5,000
Munson Healthcare Regional Foundation.	10,000	Teach for America, Inc...	5,000
Public Agenda.	10,000	Treasury Historical Association.	5,000
Fraser Institute, The..	10,000	International Foundation for Electoral Systems, Inc..	5,000
First Freedom Coalition Educational Fund.	10,000	Atlas Economic Research Foundation.	5,000
Empowerment Network Foundation, The.	10,000	Riverworks Creative Arts Center.	5,000
South Bronx Educational Foundation.	10,000	Hank Aaron Chasing the Dream Foundation, Inc..	5,000
League of Women Voters Education Fund.	10,000	Middle East Media & Research Institute.	5,000
American Literary Society.	10,000	Link Institute.	5,000
Freedom Federation, Inc...	10,000	Vocational Foundation, Inc..	5,000
Democracy for China Fund, Inc..	10,000	Chamber Dance Project, The..	5,000
		City University of New York.	5,000

Name	Total $$	Name	Total $$
Catholic League for Religious and Civil Rights.	5,000	Institute for American Values.	3,000
National Executive Service Corps.	5,000	Junior Achievement, Inc.	2,500
Amherst College.	5,000	New York Historical Society.	2,500
Vietnam Veterans Memorial Fund, Inc.	5,000	Leukemia Society of America.	2,500
		National Bible Association.	2,500
Defense Forum Foundation, Inc.	5,000	Tarrytown/Sleepy Hollow Pop Warner Football and Cheerleaders, The.	2,500
Springfield College.	4,900	Best Friends Foundation.	2,000
Carleton University.	4,500	Francis Marion University.	2,000
Carnegie Hall Society, The.	4,000	Manpower Education Institute.	2,000
Textbook League.	4,000	Young People's Leadership Foundation.	1,500
American Catholic Committee.	3,500	Association for the Study of Nationalities of the U.S.S.R. and Eastern Europe.	1,000
Central Westchester Humane Society, The.	3,000	College Student of the Year.	1,000
Evans Scholars Foundation.	3,000	Illinois State University.	1,000
Hudson Valley Writer's Center, The.	3,000	Founders' Association, The.	1,000
		National Council for Adoption.	1,000

(Source: MediaTransparency)

8
MOVING DOWN BALLOT
WITH THE KOCH BROTHERS

> Karl Rove has lately been broadcasting the importance of down
> ballot elections in places with names like Brushy Creek. This is not a
> lesson in civics. It is a lesson in power. And he's right.
>
> Justin Levitt,
> Roll Call,[a]
> March 23, 2010

"You know us better than you think," boast the ads of Koch Industries, a
conglomerate owned by reclusive billionaire brothers Charles and David Koch
(pronounced "coke"). And it's true: Most of us have unknowingly wolfed a burger
ground from Koch beef, ridden on tires made from Koch's Trevira polyester,
escaped the rain beneath a roof covered with Koch asphalt, drunk water from Dixie
cups or scrubbed a counter with Brawny paper towels. And that's not even
mentioning Flint Hills Resources, which operates refineries in Alaska, Minnesota
and Texas, the pipelines they own or the tar sands oil, the world's dirtiest, that they
important from Canada.

When I first profiled the two brothers in the summer of 2002,[1] very few
people had ever heard of them. They were reclusive and kept most of their
activities hidden from public view. Since then, they've become much more open,
but what we see is merely the tip of an immense iceberg. The brothers are richer
than many nations. They are responsible for many of the profound changes in
America since 1980, when David was the Libertarian Party's candidate for vice
president.[b]

---

[a] http://www.rollcall.com/issues/55_108/-44522-1.html, accessed Oct. 2, 2012

[b] David's candidacy made it possible for them to dodge the campaign finance laws
of the time because he was able to spend unlimited amounts of his own money.

One of the ways that David and Charles Koch launder their money is through the many foundations they control. Although these foundations are, in theory, charities under 501(c)(3) of the Internal Revenue Code, they can be and are used for overtly political purposes. The table on page 147 lists contributions of only one year from only one of the foundations they control, the Claude R. Lambe Charitable Foundation. Often, giving from the foundations is coordinated both with each other and with political contributions from the brothers, the company's political action committee and its executives.

That is the dark side of their boast that "You know us better than you think." Through their foundations, the Kochs propagate their messages. Turn on National Public Radio most any afternoon, leaf through a newspaper or news magazine, watch a congressional hearing, or surf the Internet, and you will likely encounter the thoughts of Charles and David Koch. The views will seem to be coming from an independent think tank—the Cato Institute or Americans for Prosperity, for example.

The foundations through which the Koch brothers funnel their money include—

- Fred C. and Mary R. Koch Foundation
- Charles G. Koch Charitable Foundation
- David H. Koch Foundation
- Koch Cultural Trust (founded 1986 as Kansas Cultural Trust, renamed in 2008
- Claude R. Lambe Charitable Foundation
- Charles Koch Institute (founded 2011)

Yet behind these groups stands the brothers' vast fortune: Koch Industries is either the largest or second largest privately-owned company in the United States (it plays tag with Cargill) with annual revenues of $110 billion. If Koch Industries had been a public company in 2007, it would have ranked about 16 in the Fortune 500[2] keeping company with Home Depot, Morgan Stanley and IBM.[3]

Charles co-founded the libertarian Cato Institute in 1977; in 1986 David helped launch Citzens for a Sound Economy, which has since morphed into Americans for Prosperity. The brothers are following in dad's footsteps: Fred Koch was a charter member of the ultraconservative John Birch Society in 1958.

Today, Koch money—and cash infusions from corporate allies such as Exxon, Philip Morris, General Motors, and General Electric—funds industry-friendly messages that fill our airwaves and editorial pages, and influence outcomes in the halls of Congress and courtrooms across the country.

Consider, for example, Citizens for a Sound Economy (CSE). It was a Washington, D.C.–based organization bolstered by periodic bursts of funding from both co-founder David Koch and brother Charles. CSE was often described as a "consumer group," but according to internal documents leaked to the *Washington Post*, 85 percent of CSE's 1998 revenues of $16.2 million came not from its 250,000 members, but from contributions of $250,000 and up from Koch Industries, as well as other corporations, including U.S. West and Philip Morris.

What kind of exposure can such money buy? In 1995, for instance, CSE's $17 million budget (made possible that year with grants from the Kochs, Archer Daniels Midland, DaimlerChrysler, and General Electric, among others) was spent producing more than 130 policy papers, delivering them to every single congressional office, sending out thousands of pieces of mail, and getting coverage of its viewpoints in more than 4,000 news articles around the nation. CSE's representatives have appeared on hundreds of radio and television shows and published 235 op-ed articles.

What do they tell us? Among other things, that "environmental conservation requires a commonsense approach that limits the scope of government," acid rain is a "so-called threat [that] is largely nonexistent," and global warming is "a verdict in search of evidence."

These opinions were echoed on MSNBC, C-SPAN, PBS's NewsHour With Jim Lehrer, and elsewhere by representatives from the libertarian Cato Institute. Cato "experts" are working hard to pound home a variety of anti-environmental points. They have argued that the global ban on chlorofluorocarbons—the chemicals that destroy stratospheric ozone—is a case of science being "distorted, even subverted."

They've suggested that concerns over lead paint, asbestos, radon, and similar in-home poisons amount to "hysteria." And they've maintained that federally-funded research at Harvard and other universities—used, for example, in the regulation of air pollution—"has frequently been tainted by poor methodology … and even borderline cases of fraud."

CSE has since been reconstituted as Americans for Prosperity (see Box next page).

Moving Down Ballot
With AFP and the Koch Brothers

Americans for Prosperity (AFP), the libertarian group backed by billionaire brothers Charles and David Koch, has pledged to spend nearly $1 million in Arkansas in 2012. The prize? Both houses of the Arkansas legislature, because every seat is up for reelection for the first time in a decade.

By the time this is read, that election will have been held. Regardless of whether the Kochs prevail, however, Arkansas illustrates the immense influence that the brothers and their fellow billionaires can have. With $1 billion equaling 1,000 times $1 million, each of the brothers could sway votes 17,000 times in an entire state. Little wonder that in 2010, campaigns funded by such cash vaulted Republican/Libertarian/Tea Party (RLTP) candidates into control of the U.S. House of Representatives.

Among those wearing Koch-embroidered bullseyes is state Sen. Robert Thompson who was unopposed in his last election and faced only a primary opponent four years earlier. Thompson noted that a little money goes a long way in a state legislative race: "If any outside group comes in and spends $10,000, that's a big chunk of what the candidates are going to spend."

The Kochs need to flip just a handful of seats to win to control of the legislature by the RLTP for the first time since the end of the Civil War. Using a bus tour across the state, Koch money makes its case for smaller government. It fights tax increases and curbs development and is leading the charge against the creation of a state health insurance exchange, a key part of President Obama's health-care law.

Voters are drawn to Koch-funded rallies by robo-calls and a promise of free barbecue. Once there, they find a large green bus with two-foot-high lettering: "Obama's Failing Agenda Tour."

Created in 2004, AFP was, according to the *Washington Post,* "fully engaged in more local issues and races in 35 states, with a $100 million budget*"* tripling what it spent in 2010. No longer content to dictate to the President and his Administration, the United States Senate, House of Representatives and Supreme Court, the Koch brothers are moving their influence down ballot, targeting even small-potatoes local issues and candidates

In Virginia, for example, the Kochs fought the expansion of the Metrorail subway transit service into Loudoun County, one of Washington, D.C.'s sprawling ex-urbs. In Detroit, they opposed construction of a new bridge to Canada, saying it is a poor use of taxpayer money. In their home state of Kansas, the Kochs—working through AFP—helped defeat eight moderate Republican state senators. And the brothers countered labor with door-to-door campaigning in Wisconsin to help Gov. Scott Walker (RLTP)—whose original campaign they had funded—survive a recall attempt, while at the same time advocating for a large new iron mine.

Source: T.W. Farnam, "Americans for Prosperity puts big money on legislative races in Arkansas," *Washington Post*, Oct. 2, 2012.

Fashioning themselves after the very university research centers they deplore (or old-style "think tanks" that are only a step removed from universities), these groups have neither the neutrality nor the expertise of their academic counterparts. They are simply self-described as "libertarian" or "market liberals," as if this explains why their conclusions differ so sharply from those of academic or government researchers. No mention is made of the corporate money that is lavished on them—or the corporate agenda, which is, at heart, their raison d'être.

Indeed, if the voices denying the existence of global warming or decrying tighter fuel-economy standards were obviously those of the oil, coal, auto, and similar industries, the messages would be seen for what they are—half-truths at best, and outright lies at worst—and ignored. But when the voices appear to be those of disinterested, public-spirited organizations advocating "economic freedom" or "sound science," the messages are often accepted uncritically by journalists—and then by the public at large.

John Stossel, the former ABC correspondent, has become notorious for blurring the line between industry spin and science. On June 29, 2001 while still with ABC, in a one-hour special called "Tampering With Nature," Stossel interviewed a scientist identified as "Pat Michaels of the University of Virginia" who not only discounted the dangers of global warming, but said, "Maybe a little warming is better." It is true that Michaels is a professor at the University of Virginia—but he is also a senior fellow at the Cato Institute and has been on a personal retainer from the Western Fuels Association, a group of coal-owning, coal-burning electricity generators located in the West and upper Midwest.

Doubtless, at least a few of ABC's 9 million viewers that evening believed Michaels's assertion that "maybe a little warming is better"—but would they have believed it had they known that they were hearing the voice of the coal industry, speaking through a scientist on its dole?

Stossel is by no means alone in failing to adequately identify his sources. Michael Dolny, a senior research associate at the Center for Criminal Justice Research at California State University, San Bernardino, has used the LexisNexis database to study article citations in major newspapers as well as transcripts from major radio and television outlets. Dolny found that none of the four most-cited think tanks—the Brookings Institution, Heritage Foundation, American Enterprise Institute, and Cato Institute—was described as "corporate-backed" or anything similar, even though big-business money supplied a third of their support. The business-backed centers not only outspent their "liberal" counterparts such as the Economic Policy Institute, the Urban Institute, and the Freedom Forum four to one, but were also quoted more often.

141

Cato and Heritage are only two of roughly 400 industry-funded groups that are helping businesses and the wealthy convert their vast economic and market power into political might. Their messages are invariably the same: Government regulation—most especially environmental protection—is bad, and any science that justifies it is "junk." Usually these messages are reinforced by money deployed to campaign coffers.

Take the Clinton administration's ill-fated 1993 proposal for an energy tax. It was killed using techniques and strategies stitched together and established as the "law killer." Used for the first time against the Clinton Energy campaign, the model has since successfully been deployed by industry to kill a wide range of laws. The law killer techniques were used against "Obamacare," as well, but the President and his Congressional allies managed to prevail by splitting corporations.

Designed to curb the nation's appetite for imported oil and gasoline, Clinton's legislation was defeated with the help of a massive press and public-relations campaign mounted by Citizens for a Sound Economy, the predecessor of Americans for Prosperity and, like AFP, founded and funded by the Koch brothers. It targeted Senator David Boren (D-Okla.), the swing vote on two key committees. After being hammered on radio and television as well as in print, Boren, who later headed the University of Oklahoma, agreed to oppose the Clinton tax, thus effectively killing it.

Within days of his decision, Boren was being supported by the same Koch interests that were funding CSE. In the three-month period from April 22 to July 8, 1993, in fact, Boren received at least $22,500 from the oil industry.

Koch financed influence extends even into the branch of government designed to be immune to it: the judiciary.

The Kochs and their puppet, Americans for Prosperity, have discovered that the Dollar Store of political influences is not just down ballot races generally, but especially judges. It doesn't cost a lot to knock off a judge and replace him or her with a more sympathetic ear. Even better, once a friendly judge is on the bench, it will be years and years before there's another election. Replacing a few judges every few years is a lot cheaper than hundreds of legislators every two years. Moreover, if more than one justice is targeted, there's the possibility of winning three elections for the price of one—after all it just requires adding two more names to the target list.

Take the example of the Florida Supreme Court, where the Kochs are asking voters to oust three state Supreme Court justices; and give the Legislature greater power over both Supreme Court appointments and judicial rules of procedure.[4] The campaign against the justices is similar to the successful 2010 push in Iowa to defeat three Iowa Supreme Court justices over a ruling that allowed same-sex marriage. (A fourth Iowa justice who also ruled in the case was to be targeted in 2012.)

In Florida, the issue is not same-sex marriage or even another politically divisive matter, but rather the attempt by the justices to assure that a ballot initiative was accurately described to voters. In 2010, a non-binding amendment allowing Floridians to refuse to buy mandatory health insurance had been placed on the ballot. The Florida Supreme Court removed it, because its summary contained "misleading and ambiguous language." The Legislature fixed the wording and the initiative was back on the ballot in 2012.

Florida Supreme Court justices appear on the ballot every six years as part of a system of "merit retention" adopted in the 1970s after a series of scandals involving popularly elected partisan judges. Justices are appointed, and after six years Floridians vote yes or no on whether they should remain on the bench. Until the Kochs intervened, Florida's process was "widely praised and largely free of politicking," according to the *New York Times*.[5]

The three targeted were Justices R. Fred Lewis and Barbara J. Pariente, both initially named by Gov. Lawton Chiles, a Democrat; and, Justice Peggy A. Quince, chosen by both Chiles and his successor, Republican Jeb Bush, during the 1998 transition. All three were returned to the bench in 2000 and again in 2006. No justice has ever lost a retention battle.

In 2012, retention of the three was opposed by the state's Republican Party because of their "judicial activism," exactly the same phrase for their conduct used by Americans for Prosperity, the Koch-funded attack group. It broadcast television advertisements in several cities highlighting the health care amendment ruling, saying "The Florida Supreme Court removed the amendment from the ballot, denying us a voice and a vote on a historically important issue," and continuing, "Shouldn't our courts be above politics and protect our rights to choose? You be the judge."

Justice Lewis condemned the campaign to remove them as "a full-frontal attack" on what he termed "a fair and impartial judicial system, which is the cornerstone and bedrock of our democracy."

The three have found that defending themselves isn't easy. The judges are forced to raise a combined total of about $1 million. Fund raising is not the strong suit of judges and can also lead to the perception of being beholden to donors. They also could be accused of ruling on politically sensitive cases for the wrong reasons. Judicial rules also restrict what they can say in a campaign.

Justice Pariente compared it to fighting with both hands and one leg tied behind your back, but "we are trying to keep the high road."

Retired U.S. Supreme Court Justice Sandra Day O'Connor made a video for the Florida Bar Association's Web site about the retention battle's significance (http://www.floridabar.org/thevotesinyourcourt), saying "Judicial independence is very hard to create and establish, and easier than most people imagine to damage and destroy." Those supporting retention include the fire and police unions and 23 past presidents of the Florida Bar Association.

Even victory could spell defeat, however. What if merely firing a shot across the bow of justice is enough, never mind that it misses?

"It's a really good question," said Florida Sen. Paula Dockery, a Lakeland Republican and one of the few members of her party to oppose the campaign. "Just the thought that this can happen could have a chilling effect," she told the *Tampa Bay Times*.[6]

"What I'm hoping is that not only does this backfire, but it sends a message that you can spend a lot of money and still lose this battle," she said. "Because it's not just Florida. This is becoming a national issue. Florida is like a test case. And we need to send the message that we don't like the idea of blurring the lines between politics and the judiciary," she added.[7]

American justice, whether at the national or state levels, is predicated on fair, open- minded and even-handed judges. Those who wear robes are supposed to be immune to politics. But the Kochs and their allies are not interested in a system that delivers for the American people. They simply want to win—every time in every place.

Much of that influence is exerted by intervention in lawsuits to make arguments that favor industry to exploit the "vast area of opportunity" seen by Powell and since exploited. In 1999, for example, the Citizens for a Sound Economy Foundation (CSEF) paid for "friend of the court" briefs that sought to declare the Clean Air Act unconstitutional.

Where might a nonprofit charity like CSEF come up on short notice with the money required to pay lawyers who can charge $5,000 an hour? Answer: the Claude Lambe Foundation, also controlled by the Kochs, which gave CSEF $600,000 for "general operating support;" the DaimlerChrysler Corporation Fund, which kicked in another $250,000; and General Electric, which matched the DaimlerChrysler Fund's donation. There's no way of knowing whether that $1.1 million paid for the legal briefs, but that amount buys a lot of lawyers, even at Washington prices.

Influence is also exercised less directly. For example, the same Claude Lambe Foundation that gave to CSEF also donated $150,000 to the Foundation for Research on Economics and the Environment (FREE), based in Bozeman, Montana. FREE conducts seminars for federal judges—including those at the D.C. Circuit Court of Appeals, where CSEF's briefs were filed.

FREE is in ideological lockstep with organizations like CSEF: While the foundation works the legal angle, FREE "educates" the judges who will hear the cases. Indeed, the two judges, Douglas Ginsburg and Stephen Williams, who held the Clean Air Act unconstitutional (a ruling that was later overturned by the Supreme Court), based their decision largely on the arguments advanced by CSEF. And both judges had enjoyed the all-expenses-paid FREE seminars. (Ginsburg attended them each year from 1993 to 1998; Williams went in 1993 and 1998.)

The Montana seminars feature horseback riding and hiking at FREE's dude ranch near Big Sky. In each of two years, 1999 and 2000, 6 percent of the federal judiciary took in these junkets. A typical day includes morning presentations, free time in the afternoon, an evening cocktail hour, and then dinner with a speech by, say, Alfred DeCrane Jr., retired head of Texaco, called "The Environment—A CEO's Perspective."

FREE says its seminars focus on "economic implications of science, risk, and environmental issues." Sounds innocent enough, until you peruse some of the reading material. One seminar handout discusses the "bureaucratic pathologies of … agencies like the EPA" and the "irresponsible efforts [of] … environmentalists hostile toward industrial civilization." FREE defends its seminars and its reliance on quasi-corporate funding on the grounds that "federal judges are smart, mature, sophisticated men and women …. disposed by training to be discerning, critical, and alert to shoddy arguments."

It appears that FREE seminars have been successful at winning over these discerning judges. According to the Community Rights Counsel, a public-interest law firm based in Washington, D.C., that has gathered and analyzed an immense amount of data on FREE, in one case, "the judge ruled in favor of a litigant that [was] funded by the same special interests that helped fund his seminar."

That judge, Stephen Williams (the same one who ruled the Clean Air Act unconstitutional), reversed himself in a highly publicized suit brought by the timber industry to gut the Endangered Species Act. At issue in *Sweet Home v. Babbitt* was the power of the government to protect endangered species by regulating habitat. In a two-to-one opinion issued on July 23, 1993, Williams and another judge upheld that power. Two weeks later, Williams attended his first FREE seminar. When he returned to Washington, he granted a rehearing to the timber industry, switched his vote, then wrote an opinion (later overturned by the Supreme Court) striking down the habitat regulations.

Central to the functioning of American democracy is a judicial system that dispenses justice with an even hand. Yet CSEF, FREE, and other like-minded groups seem intent on reshaping the judiciary in their own image. Chief among these groups is the shadowy but powerful Federalist Society.

Another regular recipient of Koch largesse, the Federalist Society is described by the *Washington Monthly* as "the best-organized, best-funded, and most effective legal network operating in this country." (See "Lay of the Land," March/April 2002.) Lawyers who belong to or are active in the society include at least two Supreme Court justices—Antonin Scalia and Clarence Thomas—as well as dozens of other federal judges, former Attorney General John Ashcroft, former Solicitor General Ted Olson, and former Secretary of Energy Spencer Abraham.

The society boasts a total membership of "20,000 legal professionals [and] active chapters in 60 cities." Yet, according to its 1998 federal tax return (which was provided to me when researching this story and which mistakenly included its list of donors), the Federalist Society's income that year included $4,934,325 in grants from the Kochs' and other such foundations but zero—yes, zero—in membership dues.

The full extent of industry funding for these myriad front groups is impossible to determine with certainty. Although information on donors is provided to the Internal Revenue Service, this is not (for the most part) available to the public. However, bits and pieces gleaned from searching a variety of databases—the Foundation Directory Online, for example—can be stitched together to provide a rough idea of the scope of special-interest spending. According to one such tally, the Kochs gave more than $21 million to the Cato Institute alone between 1977 and

1994. And in 1999, at least $1.4 million came to CSEF from just two of the several foundations controlled by the Kochs.

For Koch Industries, the amounts of money it can save by sabotaging environmental rules make the sums diverted to the think tanks that do the dirty work pale in comparison. The year 2000 was particularly rough for the Kochs. In January, Koch Industries agreed to pay about $35 million for violations of the Clean Water Act related to 310 oil spills in six states. Two months later, Koch admitted to environmental violations at its oil refinery in Rosemount, Minnesota, and was forced to cough up another $8 million in penalties. Then in July, it agreed not only to spend about $80 million to cut emissions from its Rosemount facility and from two other refineries in Texas, but was also accessed to pay a $1 million fine for air pollution violations.

THE KEYSTONE XL PIPELINE: INCREASING GASOLINE PRICES TO BOOST KOCH PROFITS

Most recently, the Koch brothers and their allies have mounted a massive campaign to assure approval of the Keystone XL Pipeline, which would transport an oil-like substance called bitumen from the tar sands of Ontario, Canada to refineries along the Gulf of Mexico in Canada.

Charles and David Koch are already among the largest importers of tar sands oil. Reuters, citing a SolveClimate News analysis, reports that Koch imports close to 25 percent of the oil sands crude already brought into the United States and "is well-positioned to benefit from increasing Canadian oil imports."

Although the pipeline's advocates say it would provide the United States with a source of "friendly" oil from Canada and help curb gasoline prices, its boosters must have hired a modern Franz Kafka for their analysis. TransCanada, developer of the Keystone XL Pipeline, estimates that the price of tar sands oil would increase about $3 per barrel as a result of the pipeline, and that is far and away the smallest rise in prices predicted.

In truth, rising tar sands prices would likely lift all oil prices in the United States. The oil already makes it way into the U.S., but gets only as far as Cushing, Oklahoma. There, it becomes a glut on the market, depressing U.S. prices of gasoline, diesel and other petroleum products, regardless of the source of the oil being refined. Building Keystone would allow the oil to flow from Cushing to Texas, eliminating the glut and allowing gasoline, diesel fuel and other prices to jump.

According to an analysis by Canadian economist and consultant Philip Verleger the Keystone XL pipeline would increase gas prices by 10 to 20 cents per gallon across the United States. The greatest price increase would occur in 15 mostly central states: between Illinois west to North and South Dakota where prices would increase by an estimated $6.55 per barrel of crude oil in the Midwest and $3 average per barrel across the United States.

For the Koch brothers, whose oil company already imports 400,000 barrels of tar sands bitumin daily, the jump in profits would be a minimum of about $1.2 million per day, or $438 million per year.[8] That's big money even for billionaires.

The Koch brothers' fortune is generated a dollar at a time from its complex web of industries. Like drops of water falling from a swollen cloud, the profit stream forms trickles, rivulets, then rivers, finally flowing to industrial impoundments, where a small fraction is released in controlled, coordinated flows. Some of that money goes to pay fines and operate machinery. But a nice pool of it is directed toward Cato, the Federalist Society, the Foundation for Research on Economics and the Environment and other foundations.

All so you can know them better.

2009: ONE YEAR OF GIVING BY THE KOCH-CONTROLLED CLAUDE LAMBE FOUNDATION

Organization Name	Organization Location	Amount of Money	My Take
American Council for Capital Formation	Washington, DC	$100,000	Slowing global warming would cost too much.
American Spectator	Arlington, VA	$4,500	Corporate yellow journalism, calling Obama a "stealth socialist"
American Legislative Exchange Council	Washington, DC	$125,000	Promote pro-corporation laws and rules at state legislature
Americans for Prosperity Foundation	Washington, DC	$366,725	Trainer and organizer for tea parties
Ayn Rand Institute	Irvine, CA	$25,000	Government caused the on-going economic crisis; and, the solution is full laissez-faire capitalism.
Cato Institute Public	Washington, DC	$250,000	Libertarian think tank promoting "limited government, individual liberty, and peace."
Center for Independent Thought	New York, NY	$35,000	Libertarian group that promotes "Stossel in the Classroom" and similar efforts
Competitive Enterprise Institute Public	Washington, DC	$10,000	A global warming denier and supporter of "market" solutions
ConSource Inc. Public	Washington, DC	$4000	Provides access to source materials for the Constitution, Declaration of Independence and similar documents

Organization Name	Organization Location	Amount of Money	My Take
Federalist Society	Washington, DC	$175,000	Libertarian, pro-"market" lawyers and students funded by 11 major corporate-front foundations
Foundation for Research on Economics & Public	Bozeman, MT	$65,000	"Dude ranch" seminars for federal judges paid for by corporations; The Environment (FREE)
George Marshall Institute Public	Arlington, VA	$70,000	A shameless appropriation of the name of one of America's great soldiers and diplomats to cynically deny global warming
George Mason University Foundation	Fairfax, VA	$20,000	George Mason is the university that the Koch brothers have showered with millions to build libertarian, pro-market classes and forces.
The Heritage Foundation	Washington, DC	$618,571	Among the earliest and most consistently Republican, pro-market self-styled think tanks that specializes in producing succinct but mis-leading briefing papers for politicians and staff
Independent Women's Forum	Washington, DC	$150,000	An anti-feminist group that favors traditional rolls for women, and whose board includes some Koch-nurtured members

Organization Name	Organization Location	Amount of Money	My Take
Manhattan Institute for Policy Research	New York, NY	$200,000	Founded by William J. Casey, who later became President Ronald Reagan's CIA director, as part of an Anglo-American circle of "free market" self-styled "think tanks." The Manhattan Institute is committed to developing a pro-business message, then marketing it.
National Center for Policy Analysis	Dallas, TX	$25,000	A Dallas, Texas-Washington, D.C.-based group dedicated to profitizing virtually every function of government, from Social Security to global warming. The Center's expression of science is absurd.
Pacific Research Institute Public	San Francisco, CA	$100,000	One of four (Manhattan, Atlas, and the National Center for Policy Analysis) "free market" groups founded in the 1970s, PRI specializes in "man-bites-dog" fairy tale claims that rain forests are growing not shrinking and that Prince William Sound in Alaska is just fine after the *Amoco Cadiz* disaster.

Organization Name	Organization Location	Amount of Money	My Take
Reason Foundation	Los Angeles, CA	$50,000	The stated goal of the Atlas Research Foundation "is to litter the world with free-market think-tanks," and one of them is the Reason Foundation.
Tax Foundation	Washington, DC	$50,000	The Tax Foundation's bread-and-butter issue is announcing a "tax freedom" day—after which Americans owe no more taxes—within nano-seconds of April 15, and arguing that U.S. corporations are overtaxed.
Texas Public Policy Foundation Public	Austin, TX	$100,000	Yet another clone of the national self-styled "free market" corporate fronts, TPPF essentially repeats the half-truths and outright lies of national groups, especially on global warming.
Washington Legal Foundation Public	Washington, DC	$200,000	Unlike the so-called "free market" groups fighting in Congress and the streets, WLF assaults are staged in courtrooms and rule-making proceedings.

9

THEIR GOD IS ON THEIR SIDE

One of the reasons I have written books and given speeches warning Christian leaders not to be seduced by the wiles and the attractiveness of power in the White House, and to keep our distance and never mix the gospel with politics, is that I saw how well I exploited religious leaders when I was in that job. But that's what politicians do.

Chuck Colson, Aide to Richard M. Nixon and Convicted felon,
With God On Our Side, 1996

How is it that the rich, corporations and the Republican/Libertarian/Tea Party (RLTP) are able to manipulate America's governments with such impunity?

Faith. Organized religion. Specifically, white Protestant evangelicals and, increasingly, the Roman Catholic hierarchy as well. Without them the Party would wither and die. With them, it can be confident of near-certain victory.

Yet an examination of RLTP positions suggests that white Protestant evangelicals are being snookered. They have been played like violins. The rich and corporations are getting what they want. But are white evangelicals? No.

I was raised a Baptist and went to many a revival. Church services during my time in South Carolina were Pentecostal. I am not now a man of those faiths, but I know people who are very well, and they are—or at least were—of the finest stock, the backbone of America, the men who would go to war for the nation and the women who would tend to the house and children, all while working in a textile mill for as many hours as the men.

In the past half-century, these men and women have been scooped out of America, like seeds and pulp from a pumpkin, and thrown away. In my judgment, one of the reasons for this has been their unwavering support of candidates, principally Republicans, who pander to them but seldom deliver. Jobs have been shipped to China, India, Viet Nam and dozens of other places to boost the profits of American corporations. U.S. factories have been shuttered. Women have been forced into the workplace so the extra money could help the family make ends meet. Their children were conscripted for a war in Viet Nam, and their grandchildren have been forced to enter the military or reserves or national guard because other jobs didn't exist. Then they have been shipped to Iraq, twice, and Afghanistan.

Frankly, I do not understand why they continue to vote against their own interests, but they do. As a result, the United States is on the verge of becoming a one-party nation. It has already become one in which, despite the fears and precautions of the founding fathers, the relationship between a political party and its most faithful constituency has become seamless. The idea that there is a true separation between church and state today is laughable.

White evangelical Protestants have been one of the most faithful Republican constituencies in recent years. In 2004, for example, 79 percent of white evangelicals voted for George Bush, while just 21 percent supported his Democratic opponent, John Kerry. White evangelicals accounted for a third of Bush's total votes that year.[1]

Most recently, the Tea Party has emerged as a supposedly spontaneous grassroots organization, a characterization that is widely accepted despite the huge sums that have been contributed by the billionaire brothers, Charles and David Koch. At the heart of this movement are what David Brody, White House Correspondent for Christian Broadcasting News, calls "Teavangelicals?"[2]

"They are," he writes "conservative Christians (typically evangelical) who strongly support the Tea Party agenda or are active in the Tea Party movement. I coined the term after the 2010 Midterm Elections when I noticed that the Tea Party was filled with evangelical Christians" adding that " Without them, Tea Party Libertarians would be lucky to fill half a teacup."

According to Brody, whose analysis is consistent with public opinion polls, Teavangelicals see the movement "as a way to reclaim this country's Judeo-Christian heritage, reduce taxes along with the size and scope of the federal government, return to fiscal responsibility and restore free market principles."[3]

These values fit almost perfectly with the RLTP. It also wants to reduce taxes, though mostly for those making $500,000 or more per year.

Better yet, the Protestant evangelicals fit Republican policies like a hand in glove. That's because the RLTP has consciously molded itself to be a good fit with evangelicals, but also because the issues of greatest importance to the rich are of least importance to evangelicals.

Brody cites the example of Ralph Reed's Faith and Freedom Coalition, an influential group bursting with Teavangelicals that has the cell phone numbers and emails of thirteen million evangelicals. "They're using that information to electronically distribute voter guides and contact them directly with the firm belief that they can add three million new evangelical voters in 2012, possibly as high as seven million."

Brody notes that many of the new Teavangelical voters will cast their anti-Obama ballots in the key swing states of Florida, Virginia and Ohio. "If that happens, it's game, set, match," he predicts.[4]

Before Paul Weyrich set out to bring white evangelicals into the Republican/Libertarian/ Tea Party fold, they were courted by President Richard M. Nixon. He exemplified the fears that led James Madison and others to insist on a Constitutional prohibition against "any law respecting an establishment of religion."

Madison wasn't fearful of church taking control of the government, but exactly the opposite. Two centuries later, no president had ever made such conscious, calculating use of religion as a political instrument as did Richard Nixon.[5] Of, course his Republican successors have rivaled, and arguably exceeded, Nixon. They, however, had the benefit of Paul Weyrich's efforts, while Nixon was operating mostly on instinct.

The keystone of Nixon's effort to present himself as a man deeply concerned with religion and religious values was the White House church service, which he initiated on the first Sunday after his inauguration, with Billy Graham as the preacher. Throughout his presidency, an uncommon amount of his staff's time and attention went into the White House Sunday services.[6]

Documents from the Nixon archives make it clear that piety was not the only item on the president's agenda. An early "action memo" to Charles Colson instructed him to get moving on the "president's request that you develop a list of rich people with strong religious interest to be invited to the White House church services." Colson and his colleagues apparently performed quite admirably; the guest list for a subsequent service included the president or board chairmen of a dozen of the nation's largest corporations.[7]

Colson had been the most cynical of Nixon's aides but after being imprisoned on felony charges he experienced what appeared to be, at the time, a thoroughly genuine religious conversion. He spent the remainder of his life leading the Prison Fellowship ministry and helped unite the Catholic hierarchy with Protestant evangelicals in support of the Republican/ Libertarian/Tea Party.

Colson recalled that, "Nixon was a very shrewd politician. He knew how to use religious people to maximum advantage. He recognized that there were voting blocs that were enormously influenced by their religious leaders. He recognized that the blue-collar, white ethnic group in the North that had been a pivotal vote for Democratic majorities in the past was open to wooing by Republicans, that they were identifying with us on more social issues—the great 'Silent Majority.' "

"And he recognized that many of them were Roman Catholics. Early in 1969, he said, 'I want an executive order [saying that] we are going to begin to recognize aid to parochial schools. We want to do something for the Catholics.' We got Cardinal Krol in from Philadelphia and took him out on the Sequoia [the presidential yacht], and the Cardinal was just absolutely mesmerized by Nixon. Needless to say, we got a lot of help in some of the Catholic precincts around Philadelphia, because the Cardinal put the word out.

"At the same time, Nixon recognized that the evangelical vote was the key to the Southern strategy, so he began to invite evangelical leaders in. And one of my jobs in the White House was to romance religious leaders. We would bring [religious leaders] into the White House and they would be dazzled by the aura of the Oval Office, and I found them to be about the most pliable of any of the special interest groups that we worked with."

As for the church services in the East Room, Colson said, "We turned those events into wonderful quasi-social, quasi-spiritual, quasi-political events, and brought in a whole host of religious leaders to [hold] worship services for the president and his family—and three hundred guests carefully selected by me for political purposes."[8]

Later, Colson's condemnation of the role he played in attracting conservative Christians to the Republican side was direct and sobering: "One of the reasons I have written books and given speeches warning Christian leaders not to be seduced by the wiles and the attractiveness of power in the White House, and to keep our distance and never mix the gospel with politics, is that I saw how well I exploited religious leaders when I was in that job. But that's what politicians do."[9]

The impact that these white evangelical voters could have on elections was graphically demonstrated in 2010, when they swept RLTP candidates into control of the U.S. House of Representatives. Self-identified white evangelical Christians were the largest bloc of voters in the midterm elections, totaling nearly 30 percent of those who went to the polls. Once there, they voted almost as a bloc, casting 78 percent of their ballots for Republicans, according to a post-election survey by Public Opinion Strategies.[10]

That turnout continued in 2012. According to a CBS News survey of voters either entering or existing the polling places in Republican primaries or caucuses, 50 percent were white evangelical, or born again, Christians.[11] In another poll, this one conducted by the Public Religion Research Institute in partnership with the Religion News Service, it found that after Mitt Romney essentially wrapped up his party's nomination, his favorability among white evangelical Protestants increased to 67 percent.[12]

Weyrich's recruitment of white evangelical Christians to the RLTP cause starting in the 1970s has conferred an immense advantage over competitors. Using the seemingly rock-solid majority that the white evangelicals deliver like an instrument of war, moderates were driven from the party in the 1970s and 1980s by the likes of Utah Republican Orrin Hatch.[a] Yesterday's conservatives are today's moderates and they, too, are being driven from the party as it seeks to become ever purer.

Six-term Utah Senator Orrin Hatch, seeking his seventh six-year period in office, narrowly defeated the challenge of a Tea Party-backed primary opponent. His Utah colleague, Sen. Wallace Bennett, was not as fortunate two years earlier, when he lost to a Tea Party challenger. Sen. Richard Lugar, considered an institution in Indiana, lost to the Tea Party candidate, state Treasurer Richard Mourdock.[13] In Missouri, Republicans picked veteran Rep. Todd Akin, a social and fiscal conservative, to take on Sen. Claire McCaskill, a conservative Democrat, in the November general election. The key to Akin's victory, according to the *Christian Science Monitor*, was the support of evangelicals:

---

[a] In 1976 in his first run for public office, Hatch was elected to the United States Senate, defeating Democrat Frank Moss, a three-term incumbent. Among other issues, Hatch criticized Moss's 18-year tenure in the Senate, saying "What do you call a Senator who's served in office for 18 years? You call him home." Hatch, completing his sixth term in the U.S. Senate and seeking a seventh, was not heard to repeat this slogan. Anthony C. Faber, "Hatch's seniority argument," *Salt Lake City Tribune*, March 3, 2012.

With his strong antitax stance and opposition to abortion and stem-cell research, Akin won over evangelical voters after lagging behind the other candidates in the polls—a move he credited in part to the endorsement of former Arkansas Gov. Mike Huckabee, a staunch evangelical, who is currently a Fox News personality.[14]

The influence of white evangelicals within the RLTP is immense. In the spring, 2012 Republican primaries, exit polls showed that 45 percent of Ohio voters and 71 percent of Tennessee voters identified themselves as evangelical Christians—up 5 percent from 2008 in both states.[15]

These voters are so important to the RLTP that it cannot afford to offend them—or at least, it can't afford to be *caught* offending them. As a result, the party and its candidates hew very closely to the beliefs of white evangelicals. This helps explain some of the Party's more curious stances.

An April 2012 poll, conducted by the California-based Barna Group, a marketing research firm that primarily serves Christian ministries, non-profit organizations and various media and financial corporations, found that evangelicals were "notably distinct from other groups" in the election issues of greatest importance.[16]

Among all likely voters, abortion ranked last on the list of influential issues. Among evangelicals, though, it ranked as the third most influential issue. Only taxes and health care were deemed more important in their candidate selection. Similarly, gay marriage was ranked tenth among likely voters, but was fifth on the list among evangelicals who are likely to cast a ballot in November.[17]

People who read the Bible, attended a church service, and prayed during the past week were substantially more likely than voters who are less active in pursuing their faith to rate candidate positions on abortion, gay marriage, and America's dependence on foreign oil as significant in their candidate selection process. Likely voters who are less active spiritually were significantly more likely to list environmental policies as especially meaningful in their selection process.[18]

Other polls have consistently demonstrated that white evangelicals are much more likely to support Republican candidates, while infrequent churchgoers and other "skeptics," to use the Barna Group's terminology, are more likely to vote for Democrats. Comparing the positions of these two segments on issues provides extremely useful insights into what issues candidates should emphasize when seeking the support of either group.

Barna Group's Survey:
A candidate's position on this issue will influence my vote "a lot"

Issue	Importance to Evangelicals	Importance to "Skeptics"
*Health care**	79 (1)	64 (1)
Taxes	68 (2)	48 (6)
Abortion	59 (3)	39 (9)
Foreign oil	58 (4)	46 (8)
Gay marriage	55 (5)	52 (4)
Middle East wars	52 (6)	49 (5)
Jobs/employment	51 (7)	34 (11)
Terrorism	49 (8)	35 (10)
Immigration	45 (9)	32 (12)
Education	41 (10)	54 (Tie-2)
Domestic Violence	36 (11)	47 (7)
Environment	22 (12)	54 (Tie-2)

*Presumably, evangelicals are opposed to the Affordable Care Act, while "skeptics" support it. Such positions would be consistent with other public opinion polls. Source: Barma Group, "Election 2012 Priorities: How the Faith of Likely Voters Affects the Issues They Care About," http://www.barna.org/faith-spirituality/563-election-2012-priorities-how-the-faith-of-likely-voters-affects-the-issues-they-care-about, accessed Aug. 7, 2012.

Thus, based on the Barna Group survey, a candidate seeking support from the most religious evangelicals could appeal to them on the basis of opposing abortion, gay marriage and dependence on foreign oil, but could safely ignore environmental issues, such as global warming. Indeed, the report concluded that—

> Perhaps the biggest loser in the forthcoming contest will be environmental policies. While there is a passionate constituency related to those issues, it is a small segment of voters. A huge majority of the voting public is indifferent to such matters,

essentially rendering speeches and promises related to environmentalism irrelevant to the goals of the campaigns: to solidify the support of existing supporters and to win over the hearts of the undecided electorate.[19]

This is not happenstance. Most of the money for the pro-corporation, pro-rich RLTP and its candidates comes from oil-patch billionaires and companies, such as Charles and David Koch of Koch Industries, and ExxonMobil. The Party's leaders include those who have emerged from the oil patch, such as former House Majority Leader Rep. Dick Armey of Texas. He now runs FreedomWorks, one of the largest and richest of the Tea Party groups.

Using oil patch money, the Party and its candidates have relentlessly fought any attempt to address global warming or, indeed, to even concede its reality. They have savaged the credibility of environment science generally and some individuals specifically.[b]

But sometimes the RLTP is caught between a rock and a hard place. Examples of this are its "cheap oil" policy first formulated during the Reagan Administration, which calls for continued reliance by the United States on Persian Gulf oil, with "strategic reserves and strategic forces" to guard against supply interruptions.[c] Few people seem to know of the "cheap oil" policy probably because Reagan quietly, almost invisibly, created and adopted it as U.S. energy policy.[20]

In pursuit of this policy, the United States has fought two wars in Iraq and a third in Afghanistan.

---

[b] Ken Cuccinelli II, for example, used his post as Attorney General of Virginia (he is now running for governor and virtually certain to win) to hound climate scientist Michael Mann, who had once been at the University of Virginia before moving to Pennsylvania State University. Mann had developed a so-called "hockey stick" graph depicting the stark and astonishing increase in world temperatures caused by global warming. Cuccinelli's attempts to subpoena records—including e-mails, drafts and handwritten notes—were rejected by the state Supreme Court. Anita Kumar, "Va. Supreme Court: U-Va. doesn't have to give Cuccinelli global-warming documents," *Washington Post*, March 2, 2011.

[c] Efforts by Presidents Nixon, Ford and Carter to achieve energy independence were attacked by Reagan's first director of the Office of Management and Budget, David Stockman, as "cramped, inward looking" strategies based on "Chicken Little logic." The world's cheapest energy was Persian Gulf oil at 25 cents a barrel, and the United States should fuel its entire economy on it. To guard against interruptions, all that was required were "strategic reserves and strategic forces" wrote Stockman.

The nation's corporations also use cheap immigrant labor (at the behest of domestic corporations that rely on it to cut their costs). A measure of the importance of some of these issues was a January 2012 survey by the *Christian Post* of board members of the National Association of Evangelicals (NAE) for their views on election issues. The survey, admittedly non-scientific, nevertheless provided guidance. Not surprisingly, the leaders picked economic recovery as the most important issue facing the nation.

"Evangelicals care deeply about the health of our nation," NAE Vice President of Government Relations Galen Carey told the *Christian Post*. "We recognize that a strong moral foundation based on justice and righteousness in all areas of our national life is the essential prerequisite to a safe and prosperous future."

The emphasis on what, exactly, should be done to strengthen the economy—raising taxes or cutting spending—was, however, distinctly the RLTPs.

Greg Johnson, president of Standing Together, said, "First and foremost, we need to honor God as a nation. We need leaders who will protect life, defend marriage, and care for the least of these among us. Second, we need to tackle our debt as a nation, and yes, this means we need to cut our national spending significantly. Third, we must get Americans back to work. We need job creation efforts to succeed. Fourth, we need to fix our immigration issues, compassionately and fairly."[21]

Still, despite the position of white evangelicals Protestants and the Roman Catholic hierarchy, recent surveys by the Public Religion Research Institute (PRRI) show that Americans are aware of increasing income inequality—and that they want the government to do something about it.

- Nearly 8-in-10 Americans (79 percent) say that the gap between the rich and the poor has gotten larger over the past 20 years.

- Two-thirds (67 percent) of Americans say that the government should do more to reduce the gap between the rich and the poor.

- Almost 7-in-10 (68 percent) of Americans agree that in order to reduce the deficit, it's fair to ask wealthier Americans to pay a greater percentage in taxes than the middle class or those less well off.

The RLTP has delivered magnificently for the rich and corporations. They are making more and paying less in taxes than at any time in recent history. But for white evangelical Protestants, however, the RLTP has delivered little.

The Barna Group's Survey concludes that the following issues are most important to white Protestant evangelicals in the following order: health care, taxes, abortion, foreign oil, gay marriage, middle east wars, jobs/employment, terrorism, immigration, education, domestic violence and the environment.

Knowing that the RLTP now effectively controls both houses of Congress, the Supreme Court of the United States and a large majority of both state legislatures and governor's offices, and have essentially run the nation for the past 32 years, what exactly, has it delivered to its single most important constituency?

✔ = RLTP position or political outcome agrees with white evangelicals.
✘ = RLTP position or political outcome disagrees with white Protestant evangelicals.

✘ **Health care:** the Affordable Care Act was enacted into law and found Constitutional by the Supreme Court, a majority of whose members are Republican.

✔/✘ **Taxes:** Since Ronald Reagan's election, Republicans have favored lowering taxes. Most of the time, however, that has translated to lower taxes for the very rich, but higher levies for everybody else, which presumably includes the vast majority of white Protestant evangelicals. In addition, Republicans consistently favor a lower tax on capital gains—which is what most rich people pay—as opposed to wages, which the rest of us earn.

✘ **Abortion:** still legal in all 50 states. RLTP candidates consistently support restrictions on abortion, but restrictions, save the Hyde Amendment, have yet to be delivered at the federal level.

✘ **Foreign oil:** the United States is still dependent on it and vast sums are exported to outright enemies or uneasy allies to pay for it. American dependence on foreign oil has been and is increasing, not decreasing. Moreover, RLTP candidates consistently and uniformly oppose wind, solar and other forms of non-oil, non-coal energy.

✘ **Gay marriage:** it is increasingly legal and increasingly supported. There has been no ban at the federal level, nor is any likely.

✘ **Middle east wars:** the United States is still fighting, and its men and women are being killed and grievously wounded in large numbers, because the United States continues to rely on the Reagan energy policy of cheap oil, complemented by strategic reserves and strategic forces. It is no overstatement to say that Ronald Reagan and RLTP policies made the attacks on the United States, such as the 9/11 tragedy, more likely.

✖ **Jobs/employment:** under Democratic President, Barack Obama, jobs are increasing, though at a painfully slow rate. Under another Democratic President, Bill Clinton, the United States enjoyed its greatest prosperity in a generation.

✖ **Terrorism:** Americans are still vulnerable, and will remain so as long as the nation remains utterly dependent on foreign oil, which RLTP candidates have pledged to continue by, for example, approving the Keystone XL pipeline, which would move bitumen "oil" from the tar sands of Canada to the refineries in the Gulf of Mexico. That bitumen would increase U.S. gasoline prices by about $15 cents per gallon.[22]

✖ **Immigration:** the RLTP Presidential candidate, Mitt Romney, "took one of the most strident positions on immigration reform during the GOP primary, saying he would veto the DREAM Act," according to Fox News. He said he has favored tough crackdowns on illegal immigration that would prompt undocumented immigrants to "self-deport."[23]

✔ **Education:** Republicans have long advocated "charter" schools, because segregated "Christian Academies" that sprang up in the South to evade the integration mandate of *Brown v. Board of Education*, which was initially limited to public schools. In 2012, Romney advocated the complete profitization of education in the United States. Students would be free to use $25 billion in federal money to attend any school they choose.[24] This probably helps evangelical white Protestants.

A 2001 study found that 75 percent of private school parents support vouchers to find schools that teach "better values." A 2002 assessment of "Religious practice, in addition to racial background, made the biggest contribution to the distinction between those who applied for the vouchers and those who did not."[25]

✔ **Domestic violence:** It is impossible to find a politician who favors the beating of women by their husbands or partners (or vice versa). There are, however, cases where a party position on protecting—or not protecting—women can be teased out. One of these was the vote by House Republicans to significantly weaken the protection of women immigrants by the Violence Against Women Act. For no apparent reason, Republicans eliminated long-standing protections for abused immigrants.[26]

✔ **The environment/global warming:** RLTP candidates view global warming as a hoax, and say so without reservation.

There is really little left to say or do. As a practical matter, while white Protestant evangelicals continue to deliver, without reason, 30 percent or more of the votes to the Republican/Libertarian/Tea Party, there can be no true democracy in America. My personal expectation is that this pattern will continue, and the results, both for America and the world, will be grievous.

10
PUSHED OVER THE CLIFFS

(A)n American household of two median-income earners
will pay, on average, almost $155,000 in 401(k) fees over 40 years.
Yes, you read that right.

Consumer Reports,
July 2012

America has been profitized.

A huge variety of tasks that were performed wholly or mostly by
government before Ronald Reagan's election and the ascendancy of the
Republican/Libertarian/Tea Parties are now done by for-profit corporations. They
collect garbage, teach children, ticket us for speeding, running red lights and
overtime parking, and even fight our wars and staff our prisons.

They prefer to use terms such as "privatization" or "public-private
partnerships." The truth is that the arrangements are about the private half of the
arrangement making a buck off of the public half. We are all assured that there is
"nothing wrong with making a profit." Yet profit, except for corporations and the
rich, is not the real issue.

Money is only one way of measuring value, and sometimes it is the least
important way. The question that ought to be asked is whether the job is being
done and at what non-monetary cost. In the context of retirement, are people able
to retire when and how they should? In the case of 401(k)s, the answer is clearly
and resoundingly negative. Americans are being forced to work longer and harder
and live on less than they did one generation ago.

A careful examination shows that ordinary Americans are being squeezed
dry and the middle class is disappearing. Every day, and sometimes it seems like in
every way, working Americans are being pushed over yet another financial cliff by
the greed and influence of corporations and those that run and own them.

SKIMMING THE PROFITS OF RETIREMENT

Chances are that if you are below the age of, say, 50, you're are being ripped off by your retirement plan, thanks to the Republican/Libertarian/Tea Party (RLTP). Or, in the words of the *New York Times*, "The fact is, fund companies and other providers of 401(k)s are getting rich off these plans. And in this zero-sum game, future retirees are definitely the poorer for it."[1] Here's why.

In 1981, the Internal Revenue Service kicked off the era of skimming retirements to benefit banks, mutual funds and others when it issued regulations allowing 401(k) plans. This began the profitization of American retirement, which has since become a major source of income for the rich because it assures that a portion of every retirement dollar set aside by an employee will be skimmed for profit by securities dealers, trustees and others who administer and invest their money.

The major alternative to a 401(k) plan is the old-fashioned pension: you work for a company, it promises to let you retire at a certain age when it will pay you a set amount of money each month.[a] What the employer and employee bargain for is a "defined benefit"—how much you will get and when.

In some industries—accounting, stock brokerages, banking, etc.—the end of the year is the time for bonuses, often huge ones, equal to several months salary or more. Enter the "Cash or Deferred Arrangement," or CODA, which some companies developed to deal with the problem of year-end bonuses. A CODA allows taxes on a bonus to be delayed if part or all of it is deposited into a qualified profit-sharing or stock bonus plan.[2]

In the Revenue Act of 1978, Congress allowed CODA-like plans in a provision that became Internal Revenue Code (IRC) Sec. 401(k) (for which the plans are named). It allowed employees to set aside a portion of their income to be taxed later. It's specifically for salary reductions as a source of plan contributions. The law went into effect on January 1, 1980, but regulations were not issued until November 1981.[3]

---

[a] Sadly, it did not always work that way. When I was a child, my uncle worked for the Wabash Railroad as an engineer for 29 years and 11 months. One month short of retirement, he was laid off indefinitely. He died working on the river barges that plied the Mississippi.

In the years soon after, large companies typically offered 401(k) plans as supplements to their "defined benefit (DB)" retirements.[b] With time, however, corporations began requiring 401(k) plans as substitutes for, not supplements of stand-alone retirement plans, or pensions.[4]

By 1984, there were 17,303 401(k) plans with 7,540,000 active participants and total assets of $91.75 billion. By 1990, those had risen to 97,614 plans, 19,548,000 active participants and total assets of $384.85 billion.[5]

Every day about 10,000 of us are pushed over the 401(k) retirement cliff, and that will continue each and every day until 2030. That's how many Americans reach the traditional retirement age of 65. Most find there's not enough money. It's supposed to be in their 401(k) retirement accounts, but it isn't: 75 percent of what's needed is missing.[c] It either was never deposited or has been skimmed by "the market," because our retirements, like much of the rest of America, have been profitized.

Before Ronald Reagan, retirement plans offered workers the security of knowing far in advance at what age they could retire and what their monthly payments would be. Workers participated in "defined benefit" programs. Since 1981, however, increasing numbers of companies are instead using "defined contribution," or 401(k) plans, in which workers receive a set amount of money each month to invest as they please. What a worker retires with depends on how much has been invested and what the returns have been. Scarcely any U.S. employer still offers a defined benefit, or pension, plan. Why?

Elizabeth Warren, a professor at Harvard University's School of Law was the driving force behind the Consumer Financial Protection Bureau (CFPB) and a sharp critic of banking practices explains:

---

[b] Traditionally, retirement plans have offered workers the security of knowing far in advance at what age they could retire and what their monthly payments would be, because they were participating in programs with "defined benefits." Since 1981, increasing numbers of companies are instead using "defined contribution" plans, in which workers receive a set amount of money each month to invest as they please. A worker retires with income depending how much has been invested and what the returns have been.

[c] According to the *Wall Street Journal*, which based its findings on an analysis conducted for it by the Center for Retirement Research at Boston College, the average household headed by a person aged 60 to 62 with a 401(k) account has less than one-quarter of what is needed in that account to maintain its standard of living in retirement. E.S. Browning, Retiring Boomers Find 401(k) Plans Fall Short, the *Wall Street Journal*, Feb. 19, 2011.

Much of the law governing 401(k)s, and much of the push toward 401(k)s, was not driven by ordinary workers looking for a way to set a few dollars aside for their retirements. It was driven by CEOs looking for tax protection in order to maximize the value of their retirements. … If you read the legislative history … of the 401(k), it's clear this was a little tax break for the folks who made lots and lots of money. … That's the irony. What it was designed for and what it's being put to use for are totally different from each other …[d]

America's largest employer, Walmart, provides its workers with retirement through a 401(k) system.[6] Ditto for the nation's second-largest employer, Kelly Services.[7] McDonald's, the fast food giant, also relies on 401(k) plans for retirement,[8] as does the "Big Brown" delivery service, UPS.[9] Even IBM, long considered to have the best benefits package of any corporation in America no longer has a "defined benefit" retirement, opting instead for a 401(k).[10]

The sums involved are immense—about $3,000,000,000,000 (three trillion) is deposited in 401(k) plans now—so if only a tiny fraction sticks to the walls of the pipe through which the money flows, the potential profits are immense.

Nowhere have the rich and corporations profited so immensely as in taking over the retirements of working Americans. (Of course, the nation's chief retirement protection, Social Security, is still run by the federal government. They want to profit from that as well, which is why they want it to be privately—that is, profit-making—operated.)

Today, 401(k) plans are the most common employer-sponsored retirement plans in the United States. At the end of 2005, there were more active participants in 401(k) plans and about as many assets as all other private pension plans combined.[11]

But 401(k) programs are not managed for free. Individuals must pay fees just to maintain them. Fees, of course, can be an enormous drain on retirement savings—but they are often obscured, giving many Americans the impression that the accounts are somehow cost-free. A 2012 survey published by the American Association of Retired Persons (AARP), for example, found that 71 percent of

---

[d] Elizabeth Warren, Public Broadcasting Service, " 401(k)s: The New Retirement Plan, for Better or Worse," *Frontline*, http://www.pbs.org/wgbh/pages/frontline/retirement/world/401k.html, accessed Aug. 23, 2012.

those polled believed that they did not pay fees on their 401(k)s. Six percent said they did not know whether fees were levied.

Until the fall of 2012, those profiting from these fees were under no obligation to disclose how much they were charging. But according to a Deloitte/Investment Company Institute study the average charge was 0.78 percent, although the range was between 0.28 percent to 1.38 percent.

With $3 trillion[e] invested in 401(k)s, 0.78 percent amounts to real money: $23.4 billion in one year; and $94 trillion over a 40-year investment lifetime.

Americans are increasingly forced to rely on 401(k) accounts for their retirements, and from the perspective of corporations, that's a very good turn of events. The risk of loss is shifted from them to the employees. So is the burden on deciding how much money to invest and in what. So, too, are the costs of paying actuaries, accountants, stock brokers and the like shifted away from employers and onto the backs of individuals.

Who amongst you truly believes that you can do as good a job of predicting the ups and downs of the stock market as General Motors, General Electric or Microsoft? As Felix Salmon of Reuters concluded—

> (D)efined-contribution pensions ... place an onerous set of responsibilities onto individuals who are wholly unqualified to discharge them in a sensible manner.[12]

As they were originally designed, 401(k) plans were simply yet another way to give rich people who were already going to invest their year-end bonus or other money anyway, a tax break for doing so. They turned out to be a way for employers to cancel fixed benefit pensions, thus effectively cutting back on a form of pay to employees. In short, 401(k) accounts weren't designed for you and me, but for rich people.

The money that is supposed to be there has been taken by "the market" that is run by the rich and their corporations. Some of it has been skimmed by day-to-day transactions. Some of it has just disappeared in the periodic ups and downs of the stock market. Some that might have gone into retirement plans has been used

---

[e] In the U.S., one trillion is written as the number "1" followed by 12 zeros (1,000,000,000,000), according to the National Aeronautics and Space Administration.

instead to bail out banks, car companies, insurance firms and the many others who have enriched themselves from tax bailouts.

Again in the words of the *Wall Street Journal*, "In 30 years, the 401(k) went from a small program to a multi-trillion-dollar industry supporting thousands of financial planners and money managers." In 1980, IRAs and 401(k) plans didn't exist, but today they're used by about 60 percent of households. And what they contain is too small "because of the stock market's weak returns and uncertainty about the future of Social Security and Medicare."

"Facing shortfalls," reported the *Journal,* "many people are postponing retirement, moving to cheaper housing, buying less-expensive food, cutting back on travel, taking bigger risks with their investments and making other sacrifices they never imagined."[13]

Americans forced to live on the savings in 401(k) retirement accounts were increasingly stressed. Personal savings peaked at 10.9 percent in 1982, but by 1999 it had plummeted to 2.2 percent—an annual rate not seen since the Great Depression, according to a General Accounting Office. Economists estimated the personal savings rate to be zero or negative for 2000.[14]

During the same period, household wealth dropped $2.3 trillion, or 8 percent. For workers nearing retirement, the choice to build back their savings was to either save more or hope the market recovered. Some experts said immediate prospects for either are slim.[15]

Yet even as the plight of these older people becomes obvious and undeniable, the RLTP is seeking to squeeze even more money from Americans. Most recently, the Party's Platform calls for converting Medicare, which pays for health care for the elderly, into a 401(k)-like system. As the *Los Angeles Times* reported—

> a draft of the platform states that Medicare should "change from an unsustainable defined-benefit entitlement model" to the "defined contribution model." Anyone with a retirement plan will immediately recognize the difference: pensions offer a "defined benefit," while 401(k) plans only a "defined contribution." The former assures the recipient of a specific level of benefits in the future, regardless of how the economy fares between now and then. The latter assures the recipient of, well, nothing.[16]

Since they took control of both the White House and the U.S. Senate in the elections of 1980, the RLTP has been pushing the rest of us over one cliff after another, picking our pockets to enrich themselves as we were falling.

THE PERIODIC SPASMS THAT ROB ORDINARY AMERICANS

If it were not enough that the nation's wealth is transferred daily from those who work for a living to the rich and their corporations, they also periodically raid the savings of Americans in large and spectacular ways. For months, or even years, newspapers will be filled with headlines offering details of the latest crisis. When the dust settles, yet another immense sum of money has found its way into the accounts of the rich and their corporations.

The pockets of American workers are also picked by periodic collapses and crises—the savings and loan crisis, the dot com collapse, mortgage meltdown, the global financial crisis or whatever. Every time, it is the ordinary American (or, in Europe, the German) taxpayer, who bails out the fats cats. They walk away enriched.

First came the savings and loan crisis of the 1980s. It began in 1984 as savings and loans (S&Ls) began a downward spiral, triggered largely by shoddy oversight and regulations that had been relaxed by the Reagan Administration to allow the "free market" virtually free rein.

> During the 1980s, the savings and loan industry experienced severe financial losses (because) regulators reduced capital standards and allowed the use of alternative accounting procedures to increase reported capital levels. While these conditions were occurring, institutions were allowed to diversify their investments into potentially more profitable, but risky, activities. ... In many cases, diversification was accompanied by inadequate internal controls and noncompliance with laws and regulations, thus further increasing the risk of these activities.
>
> United States General Accounting Office
> July 2, 1996

Most recently, came the autumn of 2008. During eight blustery trading days beginning in late September, horrified investors watched the Dow Jones industrial average tumble nearly 2,400 points, including a sickening 18 percent drop in a single week.

These are but two of the several times America has been pushed over a financial cliff since Reagan took the oath of office in 1981. In every case, at the end the rich were better off. The rest of us weren't.

THE SAVINGS AND LOAN CRISIS

From January 1, 1986, through year-end 1995, the number of federally-insured thrift institutions in the United States declined from 3,234 to 1,645, or by approximately 50 percent.[17] The loss of 1,043 institutions holding $519 billion in assets contributed to a massive restructuring of the number of firms in the industry.

Perhaps the greatest importance of the savings and loan bailout was the precedent it set: the rich and corporations would make the gambles, but the taxpayers would bear the risk. Heads, they win. Tails, we lose.

Why did these S&L's fail? Certainly, the high and volatile interest rates of the late 1970s and early 1980s contributed, as did difficulties in some of the regional economies. The key turning point, however, came in 1980 when Ronald Reagan was elected President and Republicans won control of the U.S. Senate. Sen. Jake Garn of Utah became chairman of the Senate Committee on Banking. Not surprisingly, Reagan appointed to chair the Federal Home Loan Bank Board an educator and businessman from Utah, Richard Pratt. He quickly set about "freeing" the industry from regulatory restraint.[18]

But Pratt and his cooperative allies in the Congress took one more important step: they shifted the risk of loss to the taxpayers. Without debate and behind closed doors, members of the House and Senate working out the details of what became known later as the Garn-St. Germain Depository Institutions Act of 1982 increased the insurance on each S&L deposit from $40,000 to $100,000.[19] This shifted the risk of loss from those running S&Ls to the taxpayers of the United States.

And with the other hand, the Congress enacted the Kemp-Roth[f] programs, which moved the tax burden in the United States away from the rich and corporations, toward the lower and middle classes. Thus, the rich were being given more money to gamble with, but if they lost a roll of the dice, the losses were picked up not by them—which is the way the "market" should have worked—but to America's taxpayers. A nice deal: win the bet, you pocket the money; lose the bet, the taxpayers pick up the tab.

Experts—including the Federal Deposit Insurance Corporation, created during the Franklin D. Roosevelt era to safeguard depositor's funds—point to several changes, including the following:

---

[f] In the interest of full disclosure, the author worked for Sen. Roth 1976–78 and other periods, but not at the time in question.

- August 1981 - The Economic Recovery Tax Act of 1981 (Pub.L. 97-34), also known as the "Kemp-Roth Tax Cut," reduced individual income tax rates by 23 percent over three years. The top rate fell from 70 percent to 50 percent and the bottom from 14 percent to 11 percent. This act slashed estate taxes, cut corporate tax by $150 billion over a five-year period and provided powerful tax incentives for real estate investment by individuals. This legislation helps create a "boom" in real estate and contributes to over-building.[20]

- September 1981 - State and federal deregulation, allowing thrifts to enter new—but riskier—loan markets. Federal Home Loan Bank Board permits troubled S&Ls to issue "income capital certificates" that make an S&L appear solvent, when it isn't.[21]

- 1982–1985 - Deregulation of savings and loan, but with no corresponding increase in examiners (for some years examiner resources actually declined). Industry assets increase by 56 percent between 1982 and 1985, while 40 Texas S&Ls triple in size, many of them growing by 100 percent each year. California S&Ls follow a similar pattern.[22]

- January 1982 - Reduced money-on-hand requirements open the door to "alternative" accounting procedures for calculating capital levels. S&Ls are allowed to meet the lower net worth standard not in terms of generally accepted accounting principles (GAAP), but of even looser regulatory accounting principles (RAP).[23]

- April 1982 - An increase in new S&Ls increases competition and cuts profits. The Bank Board eliminates restrictions on minimum numbers of S&L stock holders, allowing a single owner instead of the previous requirement of at least 400 stock holders of which at least 125 had to be from "local community," with no individual owning more than 10 percent of stock and no "controlling group" more than 25 percent. Purchases of S&Ls were made easier by allowing buyers to put up land and other real estate, as opposed to cash.[24]

- December 1982 - Garn-St Germain Depository Institutions Act of 1982 was a Reagan Administration initiative to expand powers of federally chartered S&Ls and enable them to diversify their activities with the view of increasing profits. Major provisions include: elimination of deposit interest rate ceilings; elimination of the previous statutory limit on loan to value ratio; and expansion of the asset powers of federal S&Ls by permitting up to 40 percent of assets in commercial mortgages, 30 percent in consumer loans, 10 percent in commercial loans, and 10 percent in commercial leases.[25]

- 1986 - The laws enacted in 1981 encouraging real estate investment by allowing "passive" losses such as depreciation to be used to reduce income taxes are repealed.

- 1980s–90s - Delays in funding the thrift insurance fund during the 1980s and the Resolution Trust Corporation during the 1990s, which led to regulators' failure to close many insolvent institutions in a timely manner.[26]

- 1980s - The development during the 1980s of the "brokered deposit market." (See "Hot Money" box.)[27, 28]

"HOT MONEY"

For 45 years after the Great Depression, bankers collected deposits, then loaned that money out. Success depended on depositors being willing to accept a lower interest rate than what was charged borrowers for their loan.

This worked until 1979, when the spread between what money markets would pay on one hand and banks were allowed by the government to pay became so large that money started moving out of banks and into other places.

Banks, until then largely local, wanted to go outside their home cities and states in search of deposits. Congress and Reagan let them. As they did, local deposits declined, forcing some banks to pay higher rates to institutional investors, such as retirement programs. As brokers helped institutional investors shop for the highest available rates, "brokered deposits" became a major engine of growth. Between 1980 and 1983, they grew at a yearly average of 60 percent.

Brokered deposits—sometimes referred to as "hot money"—widen a bank's deposit base, allowing it to lend more. But brokered deposits, having been linked to a number of S&L and bank failures, can disappear quickly if another institution offers better rates.

Fearing over-reliance on brokered deposits, regulators and Congress alike cracked down on them. Their use fell until about 2000, after George W. Bush was elected, when brokered deposits exploded, more than doubling between 2000 and 2005.

Fast forward to 2009, when the largest recession since the Great Depression hits. The culprit, according to the *New York Times*: "Hot money is ... one of the primary factors in the accelerating wave of failures among small and regional banks nationwide."

Sources: *FDIC Banking Review* and the *New York Times*.

Edwin J. Gray, sometimes referred to derisively as a "re-regulator in a deregulatory Administration" became head of the Federal Home Loan Bank Board in June 1983. "When I came, the industry had just lost one half of its net worth, the minimum capital requirements had been reduced from 5 percent in 1981 to 3 percent in early 1983. The bank board had seen the industry deregulated, but it simply did not have the supervisory apparatus to cope with the problems that would produce," he recalled in an interview with the *New York Times*.[29]

Gray was confronted by anti-regulatory ideologues at the Office of Management and Budget, who knew that one of the most effective ways of preventing government oversight is to limit troops in the field. "Time and again," he said, "I begged and pleaded with the Office of Management and Budget to increase our field examination force. But they would not allow it. And out of sheer frustration, we finally decided to take them out of the bank board, out of civil service, and put them into the 12 regional Federal Home Loan Banks—out from under O.M.B." he told the *Times*.[30]

- 1989 - Newly-elected President George H.W. Bush unveils S&L bailout plan in February. In August, Financial Institutions Reform Recovery and Enforcement Act (FIRREA) abolishes the Federal Home Loan Bank Board and FSLIC, and switches S&L regulation to the newly created Office of Thrift Supervision. Deposit insurance function shifted to the FDIC. A new entity, the Resolution Trust Corporation, is created to resolve the insolvent S&Ls.

Other major provisions of the reform act included: $50 billion of new borrowing authority, with most from general revenues and the industry; funds to the Justice Department to help finance prosecution of S&L crimes. New bank crime legislation the next year (i.e., the Crime Control Act of 1990) mandated a study by the National Commission on Financial Institution Reform, Recovery and Enforcement to uncover the causes of the S&L crisis, and come up with recommendations to prevent future debacles.

Special government task forces referred 1,100 cases to prosecutors, resulting in more than 800 bank officials going to jail. Among the best-known: Charles H. Keating Jr., of Lincoln Savings and Loan in Arizona, and David Paul, of Centrust Bank in Florida.[31]

In all, 757 institutions failed with total assets of $390 billion. The cost to taxpayers was placed at $123.8 billion (although that excludes taxpayer losses because the industry contributions were deductible from federal and state taxes).[32]

THE BLACK MONDAY OF 1987

On October 19, 1987, the U.S. stock market lost $500 billion, or 22.6 percent of its value, the largest one-day percentage drop in history. The market later recovered, and investment counselor Mike Rowan concluded that "with all of the trading stops, curbs, and preventative measures in place today, it is unlikely that we would have a drop of that magnitude in a single day.

"More than likely," he advised "a prolonged crash is the new reality."

Truer words were never spoken. Welcome to the global collapse.

Beginnings

In 1986, the United States economy slowed and inflation dropped. The stock market advanced significantly. The Dow-Jones Industrial Average, which tracks stock market activity, peaked in August 1987 at 2722 points, 44 percent above the previous year's closing of 1895 points.

Then, without warning, the Dow dropped 95.46 points (a then record) on October 14, to 2412.70. The next day, it fell another 58 points, followed by a loss on Friday, October 16, of another 108.35 points.

That weekend many investors worried over their stock investments. They had good reason.

The index is influenced by not only corporate and economic reports, but by domestic and foreign political events such as war and terrorism, as well as by natural disasters. On Monday, the crash began in Far Eastern markets. Two U.S. warships shelled an Iranian oil platform in the Persian Gulf in response to Iran's Silkworm missile attack on the U.S. flagged ship *MV Sea Isle City*.[33]

In early 1987, there had been a rash of investigations into insider trading, which rattled investors. By October, investors began a mass exodus out of the stock market. Computer programs that automatically order buying and selling began to kick in, put a stop loss on stocks and sent a sell order to the New York Stock Exchange. The instantaneous transmission overwhelmed printers, leaving investors effectively blind.[34]

Global panic followed. But, unlike 1929's "Black Thursday" and "Black Tuesday," the United States did not go into a depression. "The day barely caused a blip in long-term economic growth," *U.S. News & World Report* later wrote.[35] But twenty years later, the words of Jason Hsu, director of research and investment management at Research Affiliates, seemed prescient: "If the Dow were to drop a similar percentage today, we would likely trigger a global flight to quality selling of equities. I would hazard to guess that a U.S. Black Monday now would lead to a global Black Tuesday."[36]

In 2007, on the twentieth anniversary of Black Monday, stock analysts were saying the chance of a repeat crash were slim. Liz Ann Sonders, chief investment strategist at Charles Schwab Corp., called the chances "infinitesimal."[37] As she uttered those words, the U.S. economy was beginning its largest decline since the Great Depression, one that would spread to Europe and Asia, threatening a global collapse.

Who lost money on Black Monday?

Those who bought stock before Black Monday, panicked, and sold their stocks were in trouble. By year's end, investments were down 17 percent. Those who bailed out of the stock market just after Black Monday locked in their losses irretrievably.[38] That would include, of course, any people who reached retirement age during that period.

Although Black Monday was spectacular, there have been other crashes that have periodically stripped workers of their savings.

The collapse of 1990: Although the Dow Jones and the S&P 500 dropped only 14.7 percent, there was a decline in the NASDAQ from October 1989 to October 1990 of 28.0 percent.

The decline of 2000–2001: Then, in August 2000, the market started a fall that reached 22.9 percent by December 2001, according to the S&P 500. The collapse was much more severe when measured by the NASDAQ, which fell 50.7 percent from its July 2000 peak to December 2001.

The dot com collapse: When the dot com bubble burst, the value of corporate equities owned by households went from $9 trillion in 1999 to $4.1 trillion in the third quarter of 2002.[39] "Sadly, but not unexpectedly, major players in the stock market bailed when speculating became too risky," wrote one observer. "They left behind millions of investors holding stock in companies worth next to nothing."[40]

THE GLOBAL FINANCIAL CRISIS AND TARP

Yet all of these pale in comparison to the crash that began in 2007, the worst since the Great Depression. The Troubled Asset Relief Program (TARP), which helped launch the funding movement that, in turn, led to the creation of the Tea Parties, was created in 2008 to prevent financial collapse by allowing the U.S. government to buy up troubled assets. But it ended up being used to bailout big banks.

The Federal Reserve's unprecedented effort to keep the economy from plunging into depression included lending banks and other companies as much as $1.2 trillion of public money. Borrowers included—

- Morgan Stanley: The largest borrower, Morgan Stanley, got as much as $107.3 billion.

- Citigroup: $99.5 billion.

- Bank of America: $91.4 billion.

- The Royal Bank of Scotland: $84.5 billion.

- UBS AG: Switzerland's biggest bank borrowed $77.2 billion.

- Societe Generale SA: France's second-biggest bank took $17.4 billion in May 2008.

Where did that massive amount of money come from? America's present and future taxpayers.

Where did that money go? According to Neil Barofsky, special inspector general to oversee TARP, that money went "in the executives' pockets, even though they drove these institutions into the ground."[41]

Officials the the Department of the Treasury, he said, "did things that harmed, actually harmed people and protected the banks, instead of what they were supposed to do."[42]

Barofsky, now a professor of law at New York University and author of *Bailout: An Inside Account of How Washington Abandoned Main Street While Bailing Out Wall Street*, "financial interests have captured the governmental institutions."[43] Barofsky was interviewed on the Public Broadcasting System's NewsHour when his book was published.

"The biggest disillusionment" he continued, " was seeing how our elected officials and our appointed officials would put the interests of the giant financial institutions, the banks, banks that they had previously worked for, or banks they hoped to return to go work for once again, over the interests of struggling homeowners and over the interests of the broader economy."[44]

   Barofsky's conclusions were ominous but, in the judgment of some, including myself, correct. He ended the interview with the following exchange:[45]

Paul Solman: So what's going to happen? Where are we now?

Neil Barofsky: If we don't change our ways, if we don't do something about the size of these banks, we're going to end up in another financial crisis.

And because we don't have as much powder in the keg because of how much money we have spent, and because the banks are bigger now, it's going to be a bigger, more devastating financial crisis.

Paul Solman: You actually think that's going to happen?

Neil Barofsky: I don't think it; I know it's going to happen, if we don't stop this. Risk is going to pile up in ways that we don't even imagine, and it will blow up again.

Paul Solman: Neil Barofsky, thank you very much.

Neil Barofsky: Thanks for having me.

11

DAISY VS. CHOICE: THE ADVENT OF GUTTER POLITICAL ADVERTISING

"'Choice' was ahead of its time. The film started off with a political
strategy, and the production flowed from the strategy. And that's
modern-day political advertising. As opposed to what you had
before 1964, having a politician sitting there for half an hour talking,
or telling a nice story about somebody's biography."

Ron Faucheux, Editor and Publisher,
Campaigns and Elections[a]

The Goldwater-Johnson race brought something else new to political
campaigning: the down-and-dirty political ad. The most famous of the two premier
television political commercials was almost certainly "Daisy,"
(http://www.youtube.com/watch?v=63h_v6uf0Ao) described by the *New York
Times* as "the most negative political ad in American history."[1]

Imagine this: it's a Monday evening in September of 1964.
You gather your family in the living room to catch NBC's broadcast
of the Gregory Peck film "David and Bathsheba," a historical epic
about King David's affair with the wife of one of his soldiers.

At a commercial break, a young girl in a field counting daisy
petals as she pulls them off, melds into a booming countdown that
reaches zero, a mushroom cloud and President Lyndon Johnson's
Texas twang. This was called the most revolutionary television ad in
history.[2]

While it may be true that "Daisy" was "revolutionary" and the "most
negative," it was by no means the most important, nor the commercial that would

---

[a] Samuel G. Freedman, "The First Days of the Loaded Political Image," *New York
Times*, Sept. 1, 1996.

be emulated for the next half-century. That credit belongs to a much more obscure ad, one that was run—or almost run—by the Goldwater campaign: "Choice." (http://www.youtube.com/watch?v=xniUoMiHm8g)

The two ads differed starkly. "Daisy" was short and focused on the sweetness of youth. "Choice" was dark and long, offering rioters, muggers and gamblers on the one hand and children saluting the flag and lumberjacks felling trees on the other.

In its visual language, "Choice" anticipated Ronald Reagan's 1984 convention film "Morning in America" (http://www.youtube.com/watch?v=EU-IBF8nwSY) and attacks such as the Willie Horton commercial (http://www.youtube.com/ watch?v=EC9j6Wfdq3o) used by George Bush against Michael S. Dukakis in 1988 and the Swift Boat Veterans for Truth (http://www.youtube.com/watch?v=phqOuEhg9yE) assaults on the patriotism of Silver Star and Purple Heart winner Sen. John Kerry in 2004. "Choice" made it possible for Republicans to employ social issues to splinter white-ethnic voters from the New Deal coalition and thus bring their party back into national power.

With time, those ads evolved into what is today accepted as a normal part of the electoral process: distortions, half-truths, even outright lies, employing covert appeals and "frames," that participants not only rely upon, but admire and applaud.

It was not always thus.

Yes, candidates assailed one another, each heaping scorn, ridicule and abuse on the other, engaging in vicious attacks. But modern practice is different. The creation of political advertisements, their specific phrases and audiences has been reduced to a science, a tool used to destroy an adversary, not on the basis of legitimate and real differences on policy matters, but hidden and base appeals to bigotry, prejudice, ignorance and, worst of all, racism. It all started in 1964.

Both campaigns prepared first-of-a-kind television advertisements that were devastating—so much so that Johnson's was shown only once and the Goldwater campaign's (the candidate himself repudiated it) only twice. The two ads changed political campaigning forever. They were, in the words of the *New York Times*, "The first days of the loaded political image."[3]

Of the two, the commercial that most older Americans might remember best is Johnson's *Daisy*, in which the screen shows a small freckle-faced girl with wind-tossed hair standing a field of flowers, as she stands in innocent solitude picking the petals from a daisy and counting them. At number nine, a male "mission control" voice overrides hers and begins a downward countdown. The camera tightens, first on her face, then her eye and finally its pupil, which dissolves into the searing whiteness of a nuclear explosion as "zero" is uttered. The unmistakable voice of President Lyndon Johnson intones somberly, "These are the stakes—to make a world in which all of God's children can live, or to go into the dark. We must either love each other, or we must die." (http://www.youtube.com/watch?v=63h_v6uf0Ao)

Daisy was screened for the first and only time on the evening of Monday, September 7, 1964 during an NBC showing of the 1951 biblical epic *David and Bathsheba* starring Gregory Peck and Susan Hayward . It was seen then by an estimated 50 million viewers, but *Daisy* was re-shown on news programs so many times that the Johnson campaign found future paid showings unnecessary. *Daisy* was retired to the film vaults after a single use.

Johnson's Daisy advertisement.

The impact of *Daisy* on the Goldwater campaign was devastating. Theodore H. White, author of *The Making of the President: 1964*, later wrote that "The shriek of Republican indignation fastened the bomb message on them more tightly than any calculation could have expected."[4]

Some have argued that *Daisy* inaugurated a seemingly endless onslaught of negative political advertising. Others believe that it was the pro-Goldwater advertisement *Choice* that played this role. Of the two, most, but by no means all, of those familiar with the two believe that *Daisy* had the most enduring impact.

One of *Daisy*'s creators, Tony Schwartz, theorized in his 1973 book *The Responsive Chord* that "the best political commercials are Rorschach patterns. They do not tell the viewer anything. They surface his feelings and provide a context for him to express these feelings." Schwartz argued that *Daisy* "evoked a deep feeling in many people that Goldwater might actually use nuclear weapons. This mistrust was not in the *Daisy* spot. It was in the people who viewed the commercial. The stimuli of the film and sound evoked these feelings and allowed people to express what they inherently believed."[5]

Unlike *Daisy*, the Goldwater campaign's *Choice* was not short. It was, however, certainly to the point, from the first scene to the last emotional appeal by actor John Wayne (http://www.youtube.com/watch?v=xniUoMiHm8g). Most importantly, in terms of its content and message, it laid the path that the Republican Party would follow for the next half-century. But in doing so, many of the Republican advertisements, indeed entire campaign strategies for offices as great as the Presidency or as seemingly trivial as the state legislature, would employ the techniques of *Daisy*. They would meld the message of *Choice* with the creative genius of *Daisy* to produce cynical candidates and scorched earth campaigns of the most vile and evil sort.

Choice differed from the advertisements that preceded it in important ways.

- First, *Choice* was the first campaign advertisement to expressly identify—and most importantly, divide—the electorate based on so-called "values." "*Choice*," wrote the *New York Times*, "pointed the way for Republicans to employ social issues to splinter white-ethnic voters from the New Deal coalition and thus bring their party back into national power."

- Second, *Choice* overtly appealed to white racial fears of blacks, showing them looting or rioting, usually at dark. Goldwater almost instantly disavowed *Choice* as "nothing but a racist film" and ordered it not to be shown (though two California stations did).

- Third, *Choice* was supposedly not a product of the campaign itself, but instead of an outside, third-party group, Mothers for a Moral America, a group that included future first lady Nancy Reagan and a host of other wives of conservative, white Republicans, many of them former mayors, governors or other party officials. The advertisement was not produced with money from the Goldwater campaign, but outsiders who funneled $65,000 through Mothers into the making of *Choice*.[b]

---

[b] Writing from the national headquarters in Michigan, Moral Mothers wrote to community leaders across the country, enclosing a brochure urging "respect for law and order so that our children may be reared in a proper environment." Without explaining what they would do about the problem or ever mentioning Goldwater, the Mothers explained that "Young people are the major targets of the $500 million yearly pornography business in the United

(continued...)

- Fourth, and most importantly, *Choice* presented a view of Goldwater's opponents that was at best grossly distorted and at worst not merely false, but knowingly and intentionally so.

With barely a week to produce *Choice*, creators relied almost entirely on news clips to juxtapose a nation of looters, vandals, strippers and bums against one of astronauts, construction workers and smiling children. Time after time, *Choice* returns to a Lincoln Continental roaring down a dirt road, apparently meant to evoke Johnson on his Texas ranch, who was notorious for high speed driving.

There can be little doubt that the crafters of each advertisement genuinely believed in the facts of the message they sought to convey. Indeed, William Bernbach of the agency Doyle, Dane and Bernbach which created *Daisy*, said in a 1965 interview that belief is essential:

> Well, I fundamentally believe that what you think about something affects your writing. You know we had the Johnson campaign because we believe; we would never have taken the opposite side. No matter how much money was involved, we would not have taken it. What you believe, if you believe in something deeply, and you know it, is going to come across even if you don't have the skills your competition has. Now if you can combine skill with a deep belief, you're way ahead of the game.[6]

For his part, the creator of *Choice*, Clifton White, apparently believed in its message, too. In a memo to Goldwater on October 12, 1964 he wrote that "The big issue … is the moral crisis in America today … crime, violence, riots (the backlash), juvenile delinquency, the breakdown of law and order, immorality and corruption in high places, the lack of moral leadership in government, narcotics, pornography—it all adds up to the picture of a society in decay."[7]

White proposed forming "Mothers for Moral America" as a front group It would sponsor a documentary "on the breakdown of law and order" that would be shown during the final week of October in the television markets of swing states.[8]

One day after receiving White's plan, Goldwater approved it and told him to launch it "immediately."[9] The result was *Choice*.

---

[b] (…continued)
States." Michelle M. Nickerson, *Mothers of Conservatism: Women,* forthcoming 2012.

Choice is instantly in the viewer's face, as a black Lincoln limousine speeds down a dirt road billowing dust in its wake, careening into a sharp turn, crossing two lanes of pavement, then returning to the shoulder, sending more dust clouds rising behind it. The screen dissolves to a mini-skirted go-go dancer on spike heels, swiveling her hips. She fades quickly, as the nighttime darkness grows, showing helmeted police clubbing a white protestor with batons. Abruptly, the white male becomes a screen filled with young blacks being clubbed.

Seconds later, after cuts of protests, a bare breasted woman, an apparently naked man (at what certainly appears to be a Mardi Gras celebration), an empty beer can is tossed to the edge of a road, the screen fills with white children reciting the pledge of allegiance, then the Capitol dome with the American flag in the foreground, followed by the White House, the Statue of Liberty and finally it zooms across misty mountains as the Battle Hymn of the Republic soars.

> **THIS IS A FILM YOU CAN NEVER FORGET**
>
> **"CHOICE"**
>
> **THE DREAM OR THE NIGHTMARE, WHICH DO YOU CHOOSE**
>
> This film is frank, as brutally frank as riots in the streets. Smut peddlers on the corners . . .
> Never before such an honest film on TV.
> If you are concerned about the moral decay which is grabbing at your children . . . see this film!
> If you worry about the fast life, the fast buck, the fast answer and the wheeler dealer—if you don't like what is happening to our country, see this film.
> Phone your friends and neighbors to see it too. It presents the problem "Choice."
> It offers the answer. It is narrated by Raymond Massey with guest star John Wayne. This is a film you can never forget.
>
> **NBC-TV CHANNEL 4**
> **12:30 to 1 p.m. Thursday, Oct. 22**
>
> MOTHERS FOR A MORAL AMERICA
> Ann Arbor, Mich.
>
> Frances Goodrich, San Mateo County Chairman

The image of the Constitution of the United States fills the screen, as the narrator, actor Raymond Massey, intones in the voice-over "Now there are two Americas."

"One," says Massey, "is words like 'allegiance' and 'republic.' This America is an ideal, a dream," he tells us, as uniformed police and other white men wearing hard hats club and kick blacks, "The other America is no longer a dream but a nightmare. Our streets are not safe. Immorality begins to flourish."

"*Choice* was ahead of its time," said Ron Faucheux, the editor and publisher of *Campaigns and Elections*, a trade magazine for the political-campaign industry. "The film started off with a political strategy, and the production flowed from the strategy. And that's modern-day political advertising. As opposed to what you had before 1964, having a politician sitting there for half an hour talking, or telling a nice story about somebody's biography."

Kathleen Watters, an associate professor of communication at the University of Dayton in Ohio, who specializes in political advertising, said: "What *Choice* really did was establish the power of television to communicate American myths, values and beliefs. Its use of visual symbols was unique at that time. Its power came visually. And that power was reinforced by positing two different images of America."

Choice presented a 27-minute vision of an America that many might not recognize, as a nation divided into two camps: one, white, peaceful and smiling, the other black, snarling and violent. This became the emerging Republican view of America. It relied on images of riots and looting.

Choice did not merely exceed the boundaries of acceptable political speech, it redefined them. *Choice* was the forerunner of powerful personal attacks, but it was more—much more. *Choice* made the gutter, racist campaigns of the South acceptable on the national level. In 1968, they were embraced by Richard Nixon in the South. In 1972, Nixon used them everywhere.

In political advertisements the effects of *Choice* rippled through the years. The Nixon campaign in 1968, for example, attacked Hubert Humphrey with a commercial that intercut shots of the Democrat with snippets of war in Vietnam, poverty in Appalachia and student riots in Chicago. In the South, however, there was no campaign run by Richard Nixon or his national staff: it was wholly operated by former segregationist candidate for President in 1948, the Dixiecrat-turned-Republican, Strom Thurmond.

Choice, and Goldwater's campaign, also marked the beginning of the Republican quest for the votes of white southern men. It has been extraordinarily successful. Typically, this is cast as a search for the support of white men. It is not. It is a campaign for the votes of *southern* white men, and the vivid gripping quality of television advertising that has made this possible.

In the 1952 presidential election 40 percent of non-Southern white men voted Democratic; in 2004, that figure was virtually unchanged, at 39 percent.[10]

Democrats decisively won the popular vote in the 2006 House elections. Southern whites voted Republican by almost two to one.

The GOP's own leaders admit that the great Southern white shift was the result of a deliberate political strategy. "Some Republicans gave up on winning the African-American vote, looking the other way or trying to benefit politically from racial polarization," declared Ken Mehlman, the former chairman of the Republican National Committee, in 2005.[11]

The defenders of Richard Nixon, Barry Goldwater and the two Bushs will deny that they were racists. That may be so.

If it is, then their strategies of using advertisements—this is a discussion of televisions ads, but the same racist appeals were being made through direct mail and other communications—is doubly contemptible. Unlike George Wallace and Strom Thurmond, they didn't appeal to racist instincts because they themselves were prejudiced against blacks, but as a calculated campaign tool, designed to polarize voters and capture their votes. Yes, personal beliefs are very relevant—and very revealing.

Why bother demonstrating this now? Because the Republican/Libertarian/Tea Party (RLTP) is appealing to a shrinking pool of aging white male voters. This means the RLTP must search for appeals other than racism to bring voters into its ranks. It is apparent from discussion elsewhere that religion is at least in part filling that void. So, however, is the support by multi-billionaires and other rich Americans for bogus "Tea" parties.

Choice started these appeals. In 1980, when there were no more riots, they were replaced by "welfare queens" driving Cadillacs—we know who they are—in the words of Ronald Reagan. They gave way to Willie Horton a convicted murderer, a black who had been set free on work release from which he escaped and killed again,

Willie Horton, used by George H.W. Bush to defeat Democratic nominee Michael Dukakis.

providing a campaign spot for George H.W. Bush. (The Willie Horton commercial of 1988 formed just one part of the Bush campaign's broader assault on Mr. Dukakis as soft on crime; a companion commercial depicted prisoners—*black* prisoners—leaving jail through a revolving door.)

The theme echoed again in 2000, when George W. Bush operatives spread telephoned rumors that the black girl standing beside John McCain, his opponent in the South Carolina Republican primary, was an illegitimate daughter, born of an affair with a prostitute. In fact, the girl was a daughter that McCain and his wife had adopted from Africa.

In 2004, false claims that Democratic nominee John Kerry, a Viet Nam veteran who had won the Silver Star, had lied about his combat experience attracted so much attention that another anti-Kerry ad slipped beneath the radar screen. Running three years after terrorists had brought down the Twin Towers in New York City, the ad claimed in its voice over that Kerry would be soft on terrorism, as it showed a young, handsome man, olive skinned and apparently Middle Eastern, turning around and looking furtively. Racism raised its ugly head four years later in false claims that the Democratic black nominee, Barack Obama, had been born in black Africa. The claim was raised again in 2012, when Republican Presidential candidate Mitt Romney said, "Nobody's ever asked to see my birth certificate," which prompted an immediate response from the Obama campaign. (http://www.youtube.com/watch?v=vbStYaQESuw)

In 2008 the Republican Presidential candidate, Sen. John McCain of Arizona attacked his democratic opponent in the ad, "Celebrity," asking "who's the biggest celebrity in the world. It then quickly flashed videos of two long-haired blondes, Britney Spears and Paris before abruptly cutting to Obama's smiling, black face. (http://www.youtube.com/watch?v=KOrmOvHysdU)

Such claims are not merely absurd, they are outright lies. Yet the ads are used, time and again, because they work. Those willing to employ them win, those unable to counter, lose. Thus the legacy of *Choice* and *Daisy* was that the integrity of the electoral process, and yes there was some, became one of the first victims of what was most important: winning, regardless of the cost.

12
MARKETING POLITICS

Murphy and Dolan used greed, spite, jealousy, racial hatred and murder without compunction to further their ends. … The Lincoln County War established nothing and proved nothing. It did not end so much as sputter out in a gradual, almost reluctant disengagement. Nobody won, everybody lost.

Frederick Nolan,
The Lincoln County War[a]

Once created, a political brand has to be sold, which requires marketing. Since those who created the Republican/Libertarian/Tea Party brand are in the real business of selling ExxonMobil's "Tiger in the Tank," a Chevrolet that "Runs Deep," or Burlington Northern's mile-long coal trains as "The cleaner road ahead," it is not surprising that they are very, very good at marketing.

Branding and marketing are the lunch bucket of today's Republican/ Libertarian/Tea Party (RLTP). They identify and motivate voters, educate them, and get them to the polls. Were it not for their finely honed skills, Republican candidates would likely occupy the back benches of Congress and have their noses pressed against the outside glass of the White House, staring inward with envy at the Democratic occupants.

Branding and marketing is, of course, the logical—indeed, inevitable— result of adopting and implementing the Powell Manifesto. The terms and skills are market-developed, like the policies they seek to advance.

What it has produced, however, is a system so cold and calculating, so cynical that Americans should lie awake at night in worry. I cannot, and do not, believe that Thomas Jefferson, John Adams, James Madison, Benjamin Franklin

---

[a] Sunstone Press, 2009.

and the many other Americans who secured our liberty would ever have embraced a system so devoted to greed and self-advancement.

There is no question, however, that market skills are necessities in the political America of the 21st century. That said, hiding behind them are some sentiments that some of us find horrific. That a group of middle-aged Republican men, one of whom is now seeking the Vice Presidency, would model themselves after cold-blooded murderers and rapists, pimply-faced teenagers who shot and killed innocent men, women and children, mercilessly ran their victims to ground then took their lives in cold blood, is beyond comprehension. That they would glorify a group of armed and violent men who terrorized others makes no sense. That they not only choose to do so, but are famously rewarded for it should be, in my judgment, a source of shame for this nation. I am talking about the "Young Guns," which we will examine at greater length later in this chapter.

When most people think of political marketing, television commercials come immediately to mind. And, to be sure, there are plenty of those in most campaigns. But they are not the bread-and-butter of political marketing.

As the *Los Angeles Times* wrote of President George W. Bush's aide, Karl Rove, "using powerful computer systems, modern marketing tools, micro-targeting of supporters and sophisticated get-out-the-vote techniques, he revolutionized the nuts and bolts of campaigning." Some of Rove's skills were acquired while a consultant to tobacco company Philip Morris, even while working for Bush in Texas.[1]

This chapter examines Rove rather closely. First, he is a master of many of the forms of marketing, especially direct mail. Second, he has a long record. Third, he is extraordinarily good. There are very few political aides that can keep their jobs after books have been written about them, instead of the politician they work for. Rove has had several, including *Bush's Brain*, which underestimates the cunning of Bush himself.[2]

Finally, because so much has been written about Rove, his practices are more of an open book than those of most political consultants. As a group, they tend to be secretive and close-mouthed. Marketing a candidate or party is something of a black box and those who are not on the inside can't be certain exactly what goes on in it.

This is complicated by the fact that there are scores of political "consultants." These include people who manage campaigns.

Political marketing is to sell a "product" that consists of its ideological platform and policy proposals; the party leader, candidates and officials; and, party members.

Marketing of political parties and candidates is not all that simple. Yes, there are subliminal messages in commercial advertising, but it sometimes pales in comparison to that of political statements. In a profile of Karl Rove in the *New Yorker* magazine, writer Nicholas Lehman described how this works:

> (S)omething will be aimed simultaneously at both "base" voters, on the right, and "swing" voters, in the middle, like the slogan "compassionate conservatism," which moderates hear as "not all that conservative" and fundamentalists hear as "conservative and dedicated to serving Jesus Christ."[3]

Political marketing starts with research: what do those who will vote want, consciously or subconsciously; how can they be motivated; what issues matter the most. A century ago, candidates relied on their own political intuition. Today, they rely on public opinion polls and focus groups. These will help reveal not only what will or will not appeal to voters, but what specific words and phrases should be used or avoided.

Perhaps the most well known of this art's practitioners is Frank Luntz, a market pollster/political advisor that has developed what one group says is "his own unique way of persuading people."[4] Luntz is a man in love with words and adept at "framing" an issue. He uses them to persuade people to buy a product or policy, but also to determine what specific words work.

Luntz was the pollster whose work led to the Republican Contract with America, and is described as follows:

> He's a pollster with a difference. His real strength is that he polls people to test the effect of words on them! He's a guru to politicians. He guides them as to what words are good to use and what words produce negative emotional responses. Luntz says, "We are a polling firm, yet a majority of our work involves message development. We are a research firm, yet we have written more speeches for more individuals than probably anyone else in Washington."[5]

Luntz uses a room with a two-way mirror and a second, smaller room, in which to view the larger room. There are chairs, of course, and people (the focus group) to sit in them. The groups are relatively small, on the order of 16 or so. There is a television and video player, sheets of words to be tested, helpers to minister to the needs of the group and intensity dials, which participants turn up or down to convey the intensity of their reactions.[6]

Luntz' purpose is to identify the specific words or phrases that should be used, or avoided, in a message.

According to SourceWatch, citing *Salon* magazine[7]

Meeting in November 2011 at the Republican Governors Association, Luntz said he is scared of the Occupy Wall Street movement because protesters are "having an impact on what the American people think of 'capitalism.'" Luntz suggested to soften pro-market rhetoric by—

- Don't talk about "capitalism," instead talk about "economic freedom" or the "free market."

- If you talk about "raising taxes on the rich," the public supports it. But "if you talk about government taking the money from hardworking Americans, the public says 'no.'"

- On advising GOP politicians to tell protesters they are wasting their time—and that they should focus their anger on the Obama administration: "You shouldn't be occupying Wall Street, you should be occupying Washington. You should occupy the White House because it's the policies over the past few years that have created this problem." Be rhetorically empathetic, he advised. Tell occupiers, "I get it," adding, "If that sounds familiar, it's because it's the exact same route President Obama has taken ..."

The purpose of political marketing is not necessarily to sell something successfully, but to appeal to voters. Marketing can also dissemble, thus serving other objectives.

Lehman cites a few examples of Rove's strategies. Proposing eliminating taxation on individuals' dividend income may be unlikely to ever become law, but merely asking for it helps win the hearts of senior citizens, the group most heavily dependent on dividend income, and of the securities industry. Lehman writes that Rove explained to him that "Nearly two-thirds of all voting households own equities," so merely proposing a break on dividends improves a party's chances of capturing votes that might otherwise go to Democrats.

At the time of the interview, Bush had nominated Miguel Angel Estrada Castañeda to a seat on the United States Court of Appeals for the District of Columbia Circuit. Senate Democrats, claiming Estrada was a conservative ideologue with no experience as a judge, and unable to block his nomination in the Senate Judiciary Committee after the Republican Party took control of the Senate in 2002, used a filibuster to prevent his nomination from being given a final confirmation vote by the full Senate on the Senate floor.[8]

Even though the nomination ultimately failed, Rove's view was that it sent a signal to Latinos, a group that Bush was eager to woo. It also consumed the energy and attention of Senate Democrats, so that at the time of the fight over Estrada, an average of six federal Bush judicial nominees were being approved each a month.[9]

There can be no doubt that Rove is one of the most successful Republican marketers. He almost singlehandedly turned Texas—the state that produced Democratic President Lyndon Johnson; former Speaker of the House of Representatives and Franklin Roosevelt's first vice president, John Nance Garner;[10] and President Bill Clinton's Secretary of the Treasury, Lloyd Bentsen—into a Republican state.

When Rove arrived in Texas in January 1977, Republicans held 1 of 30 statewide offices, and the Texas U.S. Senate seat held by John Tower. When he left a quarter of a century later to join Bush in Washington, D.C., Republicans held 29 of 29. Most of them had been Rove clients. When he arrived, there were 21 Republicans out of 181 members in the state legislature. Today there are 107, and Republicans hold substantial majorities in both houses. "It was a stunning transfer of power," wrote the *Texas Monthly*, "and Rove's fingerprints are all over it."[11]

One of Rove's favorite marketing tools (although he was by no means the first to use it) was mailings. These initially were mailings *en masse*. But with the advent of mailing lists and computers, mailings can be targeted. Direct mailers are in the business these days of narrow-casting and targeting, rather than broadcasting.

They also are on a never-ending search for new ways to slice and dice their audiences and undiscovered ways of reaching them. Lehman recounts Rove's suggestion that a client buy the subscription list of *Krugerrand Buyer*, a magazine for investors in the South African gold currency, because they would presumably be good Republican donor prospects. "That's direct-mail thinking," Lehman commented wryly.[12]

Things can be said in a mailing that are read on the privacy of a voter's house, and the message cannot be muddied or refuted by an opponent and shared with the world. In the 2002 Georgia governor's race, for example, Republicans were able to use pro-Confederate flag material with rural voters without the major media markets noticing.

In addition, the widespread collection of information from supermarket purchases to appliance warranty cards means mailing can be finely tuned to a specific audience. For example, a message can be sent only to white Catholic households with two or more children under the age of 15 in Houston, where average income is $60,000. Such a household would be tailor-made for a candidate seeking attention on a proposal to make charter school tuition tax deductible. In direct mail shops, the air is thick with buzzwords like "niche marketing," "micro-modelling," "targeting," and "granular information."[13]

In 1979, Rove took a job with the new Texas governor, Bill Clements, to use direct mail to raise cash to pay off campaign debt. Rove insisted on computers and high-tech ink-jet printers that would allow the Clements campaign to saturate the market. Rove then got his machines, and soon they were spitting out hundreds of thousands of pieces of mail. It was classic Rove: aggressive and totally sure of himself. The committee quickly paid off what Clements owed.[14]

Television gave birth to political consulting as an organized business, and the royalty of political consulting has been made up of people who create television advertising for candidates. Media consultants tend to think in terms of "message"—they look at poll results and decide what note a short television advertisement should strike so as to affect the voting behavior of a large audience made up of people who are only lightly affiliated with politics.

Direct-mail consultants think differently. They are dealing with print, not aural and visual images. They can couple appeals for votes with those for money.

Direct mail also has the advantage of allowing extra length. Instead of a 30-second television commercial, they communicate with long letters, conveying many points. Indeed, when I co-managed the re-election campaign for Sen. Roth in 1976, we would write eight-page, single spaced letters for the elderly in retirement communities. We knew they would be read, because the voters had little else to do.

In contrast, a 30-second spot requires that even the number of syllables be counted. In addition, talent must be hired to make spots, often from New York City or another media center. Direct mail requires only a truly good writer.

One step away from direct mail, but much more selective than television is radio. Not only is it vastly less expensive than television, it can reach much narrower audiences. In Delaware, a television ad required buying the Philadelphia market, even though Roth wanted to reach only Delawareans, which were 5 percent of market. At the time, the state had 17 radio stations, so the state could be blanketed for a small amount of money. In fact, Roth won the 1976 election on radio.

Once the messages have been developed and communicated, there is only one thing left: voting. On election day itself, one of the most important of the marketing tasks is at hand: getting out the vote.

Much as with direct mail, the effort by Republicans will focus on a handful of demographic categories: small-business owners, hunters and sportsmen, pro-life Catholics, evangelicals, and married couples with children. Most of the voter-locating energies will be trained on a dozen swing states that are neither clearly Democratic nor Republican. They are the key to winning a national election.

Often candidates don't try to find their voters until a month or two before an election because it costs so much money. But after the *Citizens United* decision by the U.S. Supreme Court allowing corporations and the rich to pour unlimited amounts of cash into campaigns, that is becoming less and less of a problem. Typically, a campaign will pay telemarketers $270,000 to identify backers.

All of this has described an election as if it were run by a candidate or the party. Today, in the wake of *Citizens United*, campaigns and political marketing are no longer quite so straight-forward. Some developments are outright bizarre, which illustrates the peculiar nature of politics.

Although the addition of Wisconsin Rep. Paul Ryan to the Republican ticket as Mitt Romney's running mate seemed to trigger little attention, the Budget Committee chairman is associated with an effort that seems utterly strange: he is one of three Republican Congressman that have written a book, and created a political action committee, named after the "young guns," a group of murderers and back-shooters that terrorized Lincoln County, New Mexico Territory in 1878.

The Republican/Libertarian/Tea Party young guns are, in addition to Ryan, Eric Cantor of Virginia and Kevin McCarthy of California.

A 1988 film glorified the so-called young guns. As is so often the case, the Hollywood version bore no resemblance to reality. The irony is that the county-wide reign of murder and terror was triggered by the very system that Ryan, Cantor and McCarthy and the RLTP want to shove down the throats of all Americans: unbridled competition and "free" enterprise.

In 1876, Lawrence Murphy and James Dolan had established a monopoly in Lincoln County on blankets, feed, food and other dry goods. An Englishman, John Tunstall, saw the chance to undercut them, and formed a partnership to do this with a local lawyer, Alexander McSween. They sold goods at prices lower than what Murphy charged and would even let customers buy on credit. Not surprisingly, they cut into Murphy's business.

Eventually, both sides had hired murderers. Tunstall was shot in cold blood, through the head, and fell to ground dead. Tunstall's hired guns, who called themselves "the Regulators" and included Billy the Kid, sought revenge. They murdered the sheriff.

What followed were months of back-and-forth revenge killings. Homes were burned until only ashes remained, innocent people murdered and terrorized, and stores looted. Some of this was due to Murphy's men, but much of it was caused by the Regulators.

Finally, the President of the United States intervened and named a new governor. Pat Garret was appointed sheriff. He tracked down and killed the most notorious of the Young Guns, Billy the Kid.[b]

The "Young Guns" nickname for the trio of Representatives was coined not by them, but in 2007 by the *Weekly Standard* newspaper. But Ryan, Cantor and McCarthy quickly embraced it. They started a "fast-on-its-feet campaign outfit to help GOP challengers win House seats," said the *Standard*, adding "Its name was inevitable … Young Guns."[15]

---

[b] An irony is that William Koch, the poorest of the Koch brothers with a net worth of only $3.5 billion, bought a tintype of Billy the Kid in June 2011 for $2.3 million. "I love the Old West," he said. Kirk Mitchell, "Tintype of Billy the Kid fetches $2 million," the *Denver Post*, June 25, 2011, http://www.denverpost.com/breakingnews/ci_18355305#ixzz4uEHbqSYp, accessed Sept. 20, 2012.

The trio acted without hesitation to capitalize on their new found fame:

- They founded the "Young Guns Program" as an organization of House Republicans dedicated to electing open seat and challenger candidates nationwide during the 2007–2008 election cycle. During that cycle, House RLTP challengers won against five incumbent Democrats. Four of those were so-called "Young Guns"—Tom Rooney (FL-16), Bill Cassidy (LA-06), Lynn Jenkins (KS-02), and Pete Olson (TX-22).[16]

- In September 2010, just weeks before the mid-term elections that swept Republicans back into control of the House of Representatives, a book written by the trio, *Young Guns: A New Generation of Conservative Leaders,* was released. Described by Politico.com as a "marketing tool for the men who hope to run the House," the 224-page book featured the three of them prominently on the cover.[17]

- Hard on the heels of the book's publication, Republicans took control of the House in the mid-term elections. Of the more than 90 Young Guns candidates, 62 were elected.[18]

- Then the trio formed three related organizations under the "YG" umbrella—"all of which have nuanced missions and legally separate purposes," according to *Roll Call*, a Capitol Hill newspaper.[19] They are—

  - The super PAC, YG Action Fund;
  - The nonprofit, YG Network; and
  - The wonk shop, YG Policy Center.

Now there are two organizations funneling money to, and attracting publicity for, RLTP candidates: Young Guns and YG Action Fund. The Young Guns program is run by the National Republican Congressional Committee. YG Action Fund is independently managed and independently financially backed.[c] It operates with money collected from millionaires— Republican casino billionaire

---

[c] The largest donors to YG Action Fund are Miriam Adelson, $2,500,000.00; Sheldon Adelson, $2,500,000.00; Bruce Kovner, $125,000.00; Suzanne Kovner, $125,000.00; William Goodwin, $100,000.00; and, Bruce Gottwald, $100,000.00. SunlightFoundation, "YG Action Fund," http://reporting.sunlightfoundation.com/outside-spending/committee/yg-action-fund/C00504 761/#contributors, accessed Sept. 21, 2012.

Sheldon Adelson[d] and his wife Miriam, for example, who gave $5 million—and others. YG has targeted three Democrats and one Republican for defeat; and, two Republicans for election.

Thus, Ryan, Cantor and McCarthy have neatly created both a label—Young Guns—and a marketing mechanism: the Super PAC, the nonprofit and the wonk shop. Republicans are quite frankly much, much better at these market-like efforts than Democrats. That stands to reason, since RLTPs are themselves a product of the so-called market.

Even the thinnest pancake has two sides, however. It's true that one side of Young Guns demonstrates the understanding and mastery by RLTP officials of branding and marketing. But there is another, darker side to the Young Guns saga of today: the complete insensitivity and disregard of the murders, kidnapping, back shootings, arsons and other violence that created the Young Gun notoriety. Is there an evil they would be unwilling to pride themselves on? Apparently not, for instead of condemning these butchers, they implicitly exalt them.

And, finally, they completely ignore the true lesson to be learned from the Lincoln County War. It resulted from and was fueled by an Old West fight between two dry goods merchants for profit and market share: unbridled and unprincipled capitalism, the so-called free market.

---

[d] Adelson spends his money on Republican candidates quite freely. In addition to the $5 million to YG Action Fund, he also reportedly pledged $500,000 to just one House candidate, New Jersey Republican candidate Rabbi Shmuley Boteach. Ian Millhiser, "GOP Casino Baron Sheldon Adelson Pledges $500,000 To Buy A Single House Seat," ThinkProgress.org, http://thinkprogress.org/justice/2012/08/27/750111/gop-casino-baron-sheldon-adelson-pledges-500000-to-buy-a-single-house-seat/ Aug. 27, 2012, accessed Sept. 21, 2012.

13
CORPORATE "NEWS" OUTLETS

American radio is the product of American business! It is just as
much that kind of product as the vacuum cleaner, the washing
machine, the automobile and airplane ... If the legend still persists
that the radio station is some kind of art center, a technical
museum, or a little piece of Hollywood transplanted to your home
town, then the first official act of the second quarter century should
be to list it along with the local dairies, laundries, banks,
restaurants, and filling stations.

J. Harold Ryan
President, National Association of Broadcasters
1945[a]

The American colonies fought a revolution because they were being
governed from 3,000 miles away, with no opportunity to consent, protest or
otherwise be heard. "No taxation without representation" was the rallying cry here,
as was "No legislation without representation."[1] Today it is a demand from tea
partiers[2] (who are, ironically, being financed by the very groups whose dominance
they protest). That remained a governing principle for two centuries—until, that is,
the last 30 years.

In order to be given, consent must be educated, knowing and informed.
People must know what is happening and why. America assured education by
guaranteeing not only freedom of speech, but freedom of the press. As the United
States Supreme Court observed—

(T)he First Amendment does not speak equivocally. It prohibits any
law "abridging the freedom of speech, or of the press." It must be

---

[a] Charles A. Seipmann, *Radio's Second Chance*, p. 25, (Boston, 1947).

taken as a command of the broadest scope that explicit language, read in the context of a liberty-loving society, will allow.[b]

For freedom of speech and press to be effective, however, requires not only that speakers and writers be protected, but also listeners, viewers and readers. To achieve this, the Supreme Court has, in a variety of contexts, referred to a First Amendment right as to "receive information and ideas" writing that—

> It is now well established that the Constitution protects the right to receive information and ideas. This freedom [of speech and press] … necessarily protects the right to receive … *Martin v. City of Struthers*, 319 U. S. 141, 143 (1943) … *Stanley v. Georgia*, 394 U. S. 557, 564 (1969).

Lewis Powell understood the central importance of "the media" in reaching the public. As a lawyer who would be appointed to the U.S. Supreme Court in only a few months, he also knew that the prohibitions in the Constitution extended only to governments or those acting under its authority. If government could not effectively extinguish speech—at least those messages that were disagreeable—corporations could and, Powell said, should.

"Networks should be monitored," counseled Powell, and complaints "should be made promptly and strongly when programs are unfair or inaccurate," with equal time demanded. Corporations owned radio and television stations and newspapers and should employ "every available means" to "challenge and refute unfair attacks, as well as to present the affirmative case through these media."

What Powell proposed, and his readers ultimately implemented, was a privately-financed, counter-revolution that suppresses freedoms of speech and press in America. Corporations, tired of trying to control reporters, simply started buying the outlets and media of those who refused to obey.

The evidence that change in the United States has been systemic is everywhere. It is most visible in the decline of newspapers generally, including the disappearance of entire chains. Knight Ridder, whose papers included the *Miami Herald*, *Detroit News* and *Kansas City Star* to name but a few, was sold to McClatchy in 2006.[3] It was the second-largest newspaper publisher in the United States, with 32 daily newspapers.[4] In the two years that followed the $6.5-billion purchase, McClatchey lost more than eighty percent of its stock value.[5]

---

[b] Bridges v. California, 314 U.S. 252 (1941).

"America's most prized journalistic possessions are suddenly looking like corporate millstones," wrote Eric Alterman in the *New Yorker*. The families that owned the *Los Angeles Times* and the *Wall Street Journal* sold their holdings. The *Washington Post* avoided a similar fate only by rebranding itself as an "education and media company" and clinging to its testing and teaching company, Kaplan, which now brings in at least half the company's revenue.[6]

Newspapers are losing advertisers, readers, market value. Admittedly, some or perhaps even much of this can be attributed to losses to the Internet, Craig's List and other computer-based innovations. However much that might explain the decline of newspapers, it contributes little to knowing why there is explosive growth of television and radio networks, cable television and, especially, the new media, such as Google and Facebook.

The common cause of all these changes has been the gradual, studied, systematic engulfing of all forms of communication by corporations, followed by their conversion into servants of the Republican/Libertarian/Tea Party (RLTP).

The corporate executives and the rich reading Powell's words understood, and they acted. Today in the United States, virtually every word heard, scene seen, and document read is controlled by six giant corporations. There was a time when Richard Nixon plotted to neutralize television and radio networks by threatening them with anti-trust lawsuits filed by his justice department. His adversaries, including the *Washington Post*, were threatened by the loss of their broadcast stations, which supplied the stream of cash required to keep reporters on beats and the presses rolling.

Today, however, corporations and the RLTP have achieved with corporate profits what they could not through government. Protections of citizens, both collective and individuals, to "receive information and ideas" has been effectively and systematically eliminated.

The result is that syndicated "talk show" host Rush Limbaugh is free to attack with impunity a Georgetown University law student, Sandra Fluke, as "a slut" because of her testimony before members of Congress.[7, c] He can proclaim

---

[c] Limbaugh did later apologize for calling Fluke a slut, but in a most peculiar fashion, saying—
A Georgetown coed told Nancy Pelosi's hearing that the women in her law school program are having so much sex they're going broke, so you and I should have to pay for their birth control. So what would you call that? I called it what it is. So, I'm offering a compromise today: I will buy all of the women at Georgetown University as much aspirin to put between

(continued...)

that "If we never elected Democrats again, we would be imminently safer" because safeguards that stood for more than a half-century were withdrawn.[d]

When some criticize Limbaugh, they are attacked by Rush's younger brother, syndicated columnist David, as employing a "Marxist agenda and Stalinist tactics. "They"—in which he included "a number" of "Republican leaders"—"want to destroy the Republican brand."[8] Other RLTP officials, including former Governor of Alaska and Vice Presidential candidate Sarah Palin, say critics are engaged in "hypocrisy."[9]

When Nixon was President, he would dispatch White House aide Chuck Colson to bring pressure to bear on the legendary William S. Paley, founder and owner of the Columbia Broadcasting System, or CBS. Today, there is no need for corporations to voice their complaints, because CBS is now answerable to one of their own. It is controlled by cable network company Viacom and a chain of movie theaters owned by billionaire Sumner Redstone.[10]

A generation ago, National Broadcasting System (NBC) had been overseen from its infancy to maturity by its founder, David Sarnoff, and his son, Robert. Today, NBC is a corporate property, owned 51 percent by cable company Comcast and 49 percent by General Electric. So, too, is the American Broadcasting Company, or ABC. It had been managed for over thirty years, from 1951 to 1986, by Leonard Goldenson. Today ABC is run by the corporation, entertainment giant Walt Disney Enterprises.

These three have at times been overshadowed by Time Warner Inc. (formerly AOL Time Warner). Valued at $26.23 billion, as of mid-2010, it was the world's second largest media and entertainment conglomerate in terms of revenue (behind Disney), as well as the world's largest media conglomerate.[11]

Little known outside its native country of Germany, a corporation there, Bertelsmann AG, is the world's largest publisher of English language books. Worth $19.23 billion (€ 15,253 billion), in 2009 Bertelsmann operated in 63 countries and employed 102,983 workers. Among its some 2,000 subdivisions, subsidiaries, and branches are companies that are household names in the United States: Random House, Knopf, Doubleday and Fodor's Travel.[12]

---

[c] (...continued)
their knees as they want. ... So Miss Fluke and the rest of you feminazis, here's the deal. If we are going to pay for your contraceptives and thus pay for you to have sex, we want something. We want you to post the videos online so we can all watch.

[d] "The Rush Limbaugh Show," May 27, 2003, 12:53 p.m. WMAL, Washington, D.C.

Another network, Fox, has been created since Powell's Manifesto was written. Owned by the multi-national conglomerate News Corp., which is the personal corporation of Australia-born Rupert Murdoch, "Fox has become a central hub of the conservative movement's well-oiled media machine," in the words of the media watchdog Fairness & Accuracy in Reporting (FAIR). It also says that—

> Together with the GOP organization and its satellite think tanks and advocacy groups, this network of fiercely partisan outlets—such as the *Washington Times*, the *Wall Street Journal* editorial page and conservative talk-radio shows like Rush Limbaugh's—forms a highly effective right-wing echo chamber where GOP-friendly news stories can be promoted, repeated and amplified. Fox knows how to play this game better than anyone.[13]

I am a product of American reporting. As a young man, I would boast that ink ran in my veins. But no more. Reporters today wear the same pin stripe suits as their subjects, and think like them, too.

A few years ago, involved in a project to teach Latino and other non-English speaking reporters how air pollution kills and maims, but doesn't have to, I practically fell out of my chair. At a meeting of the International Society of Journalists, an officer described newspapers as "a business."

My mentors include Mark Ethridge, the at-the-time legendary publisher of the *Louisville Courier-Journal*, to the Raleigh, N.C. *News and Observer*'s managing editor Woodrow Price, and Neal Hester, its oldest-in-the-nation wire editor, still hammering out headlines on an battered Underwood manual typewriter, his eyes shielded by a green eyeshade and his shirt sleeves held in place by garters.

Noel Yancey, my first editor at the Associated Press, once scolded me: "if you want the truth, go to a church. We're after facts." He once slashed through my lede for an AP piece on the North Carolina's legislature's annual junket to Wilmington's azalea that began "Millions of azaleas were in bloom." After ripping it off, he scornfully asked "How do you know—did you count them?"

What Lewis Powell sought, and what RLTP has achieved, is the elimination of single-minded, bull headed, fact-driven reporters and editors like these. In their place, the United States today relies on vitriolic "entertainers" like Limbaugh, conclusion-driven columnists like George Will and remote controlled radio stations like those of Clear Channel. It especially deserves attention because Clear Channel is the unequivocal and unapologetic antitheses of reporting—especially on radio and television—as a public service.

If there is only one finger of blame with which to point at the cause of the degradation of American broadcasting, its utter severance from any semblance of morality, the target should be Clear Channel Communications; its founders, and the current owners, which include Bain Capital.

Yes this is the same Bain Capital that Republican nominee for President, Mitt Romney, ran. It is also the same Clear Channel that broadcasts, Rush Limbaugh, Sean Hannity, Glenn Beck and Michael Savage.[14] Do they support Mitt Romney, who was once their boss? You bet.

Consider Rush Limbaugh: "But you know, everybody's talking about Obama and his daily events and so forth. But Romney is kicking butt out there, and Romney is staying on message, and Romney is rapid-firing back."[15] Sean Hannity: the *Washington Post*'s disclosure that Romney and several others had attacked and bullied another student, holding him down and scissoring off his hair was a "ridiculous hit piece."[16] Michael Savage: "Republicans, as you know, leave a lot to the imagination, but we're still going to vote for them to get rid of the Marxist in the White House" and "Obama ate dog meat as a child."[17]

Are such statements truly in the "public interest, convenience or necessity," in the words of the Federal Radio Act and the Federal Communications Act? Thirty years ago, they would not have been. Today, broadcasters do not care. As one of the founders of radio network Clear Channel, said in an interview with *Fortune* magazine, "We're not in the business of providing news and information. We're not in the business of providing well-researched music. We're simply in the business of selling our customers products."[18]

Clear Channel exemplifies the contempt with which broadcasters today treat local listeners.

"Senator Byron Dorgan, Democrat of North Dakota," wrote the *New York Times*, "had a potential disaster in his district when a freight train carrying anhydrous ammonia derailed, releasing a deadly cloud over the city of Minot. When the emergency alert system failed, the police called the town radio stations, six of which are owned by the corporate giant Clear Channel. According to news accounts, no one answered the phone at the stations for more than an hour and a half. Three hundred people were hospitalized, some partially blinded by the ammonia. Pets and livestock were killed."[19]

The airwaves—the ether through which radio and television signals fly—belong to the public, you and me. Yes, acting through the Congress and the federal Communications Commission, we allow those airwaves to be leased, and thus profitized, for a few years at a time. But at the end of every lease period, those airwaves revert to our ownership unless the Federal Communications Commission renews the license.

There have been recent and accelerating attempts by industry to profitize airwaves even further than current law does, relying on outright false statements of law and fact. Most recently, the Federal Communications Commission's former general counsel, Irwin Krasnow, now a Washington, D.C. lawyer, wrote that—

> The concept of public 'ownership' of the airwaves is demonstrably at odds with Congress's intent in enacting the Radio Act of 1927 and the Communications Act of 1934. The spectrum is there whether it is used or not; only when it is enhanced by the use of broadcasters and others does it have any value at all to the public.[20]

That is a not a lie, but a half-truth.[e] Yes, it is a very accurate paraphrase of Ayn Rand 's 1964 statement on the subject, but the Russian-born, libertarian novelist and philosopher was neither a lawyer nor historian.[21] The statement is contained in a document published by The Media Institute, a Washington, D.C.-based free enterprise "charity" whose board of trustees include officers of NBC, Walt Disney, DirectTV, AT&T, News Corp. and Time Warner.[22]

The Radio Act of 1927 made it clear that the government allowed the private owners of radio stations to operate on public airwaves to serve "the public convenience and necessity." This notion of public trusteeship was written into the Communications Act of 1934 and was extended to TV stations when they were granted leases—not ownership—in the form of operating licenses. This is not to say that the government owns the airwaves either.

The architect of the Radio Act of 1927, which created the new Federal Radio Commission was Sen. George Norris of Nebraska. Enacted in the wake of

---

[e] This illustrates the difficulty of chasing and killing a half-truth. Run this quote through a Google search, and many, many instances of its repetition will pop up. Thus, the half-truth acquires a life of its own. Congress knew exactly what it was doing. As one historian explained "broadcasting, like hydroelectric power, was ultimately based on a national resource; the parallel made the use of the air another crucial conservation issue." *See* Erik Barnouw, *A Tower in Babel: A History of Broadcasting in the United States to 1933*, pp. 195–96, (New York, Oxford University Press, 1966).

the Teapot Dome Scandal in which oil belonging to the nation was plundered, Norris viewed the airwaves as comparable to rivers and streams, a resource belonging to "all of us, a source of human happiness." [f] As the U.S. Supreme Court earlier declared "the running water in a great navigable stream is [incapable] of private ownership. ..."[23] So, too, are the airways incapable of private ownership.

Radio's first major venture into elective politics came in late 1933, shortly after the Commission's creation five years earlier. Upton Sinclair, the muck-raking author of *The Jungle* and other exposes of industrial abuse of American workers, won the California Democratic primary for governor besting the Republican nominee's vote count by over 100,000. To beat him, Republicans called on Arthur Lasker, president of the Lord & Thomas advertising firm. His clients included not only food, drug and tobacco firms, but General Electric, RCA, RKO, Cities Service, Commonwealth Edison, Frigidaire and Goodyear.[24]

Sinclair's campaign was founded on his program to End Poverty in California, or EPIC. He wanted to use the state's credit to make idle lands and manufacturing plants available to unemployed workers to grow food and make products. Lasker bombarded voters with messages through radio, movie newsreels and pamphlets. At MGM, each artist received a check already made out to the Republican Party for $150, $200 or another specific amount, accompanied by instructions to sign and date it. Those ignoring instructions promptly received a follow-up telephone call.[25]

Studios filmed fake "newsreels," in which, the *New York Times* reported, "Sinclair supporters are invariably pictured as the riff-raff. Low-paid 'bit' players are said to take the leading roles in most of these 'newsreels' particularly where dialogue is required."[26]

---

[f] As the U.S. Supreme Court explained in *Columbia Broadcasting System, Inc. v. Democratic National Committee*, 412 U.S. 94 (1973), Congress chose a uniquely American approach. "Congress was faced with a fundamental choice between total Government ownership and control of the new medium—the choice of most other countries—or some other alternative. ... The historic aversion to censorship led Congress to enact § 326 of the Act, which explicitly prohibits the Commission from interfering with the exercise of free speech over the broadcast frequencies. Congress pointedly refrained from divesting broadcasters of their control over the selection of voices; § 3 (h) of the Act stands as a firm congressional statement that broadcast licensees are not to be treated as common carriers, obliged to accept whatever is tendered by members of the public. Both these provisions clearly manifest the intention of Congress to maintain a substantial measure of journalistic independence for the broadcast licensee.

Warner Brothers had made a tough and uncompromising film *Wild Boys of the Road* to depict the thousands of young men thrown out of work and forced to live by riding boxcars and living in hobo camps. Termed "one of the darkest, bleakest films of the depression era"[27] and intended to dramatize some of the very ills Sinclair was seeking to end, stills from the movie were circulated as supposed photographs of derelicts drawn to California by the promise of the EPIC program.[28] Describing the election's outcome, one author later wrote—

> When the day came, Sinclair was defeated. Lord & Thomas had
> done its share. There was no doubt now: the advertising agency was
> in politics to stay.[29]

One by one, safeguards that were built into the laws and regulations of broadcasting in the United States have been weakened, repealed or ignored. The 1996 Telecommunications Act allowed corporations to gobble up hundreds of stations, limiting expression over airwaves that are merely licensed to broadcasters but owned by the American public.

Who did this? Republicans. At the behest of corporations and to stifle your ability and mine to listen to truly local stations.

In 1995, Republicans won control of both houses of Congress, the Senate and the House of Representatives, for the first time in nearly a half-century. Vaulted into control by the so-called "Contract with America," Republicans triggered a budget impasse between Congress and the Clinton Administration that resulted in the Federal government shutdowns of 1995 and 1996.[30]

The Telecommunications Act of 1996 was the first major change in U.S. communications law in sixty years. Its goal was to "let anyone enter any communications business—to let any communications business compete in any market against any other." Supposedly, the new law's primary objective was to increase competition by deregulating of the broadcasting market."[31] It had precisely the opposite effect.

There is a maxim in the law that a person intends the natural consequences of his actions. Members of Congress are many things, but they are not fools. Regardless of what they might have said was intended, in truth the 1996 law was yet another step toward implementation of the Powell Manifesto.

As the *New York Times* describes the process, "When a media giant swallows a station, it typically fires the staff and pipes in music along with something that resembles news via satellite. To make the local public think that things have remained the same, the voice track system sometimes includes references to local matters sprinkled into the broadcast."[32]

What happens then is the "ruination of independent radio" in the words of columnist William Saffire. The profitizing of radio and television was begun by Ronald Reagan, but rocketed after the Telecommunications Act of 1996. It increased the number of stations that one entity could own in a single market and permitted companies to buy up as many stations nationally as their deep pockets would allow.[33]

As Common Cause concluded in a 2005 analysis—

Over 10 years, the legislation was supposed to save consumers $550 billion, including $333 billion in lower long-distance rates, $32 billion in lower local phone rates, and $78 billion in lower cable bills. But cable rates have surged by about 50 percent, and local phone rates went up more than 20 percent. Industries supporting the new legislation predicted it would add 1.5 million jobs and boost the economy by $2 trillion. By 2003, however, telecommunications companies' market value had *fallen* by about $2 trillion, and they had shed half a million jobs. (Emphasis in original)[34]

The new law sacrificed variety and local control on the altar of profit, and its sponsors had to have known that would happen. It was the inevitable, absolutely predictable and logical consequence of the law's many weakening provisions. Based on the Common Cause analysis,[35] it is clear that the law had disastrous impacts. Some believe, including me, that this was precisely what was intended.

▸ It lifted the limit on how many radio stations one company could own. The cap had been set at 40 stations. The new law made possible radio giants like Clear Channel, that has more than 1,200 stations, and led to a substantial drop in the number of minority station owners. The music played in Biloxi, Mississippi became the same as that in Portland, Maine or Sacramento, California. Play lists shrank and, in some markets, local news disappeared.

▸ The law lifted from 12, the number of local TV stations any one corporation could own, and expanded the limit on audience reach. One company had been allowed to own stations that reached up to a quarter of U.S. TV households, but the new law raised that national cap to 35 percent.

In the wake of these changes, huge media mergers occurred and media control was concentrated. Viacom, the parent of CBS, Disney, owner of ABC, News Corp, NBC and AOL, owner of Time Warner, controlled 75 percent of all prime-time viewing.

▸ The Act was supposed to lower cable rates by deregulating them. But the reverse happened. Between 1996 and 2003, rates jumped nearly 50 percent.

▸ Recognizing that cable channels might now compete with over-the-air stations, the Act authorized the FCC to ease rules regulation ownership of cable channels by broadcast stations and networks. In theory, competition would increase. In reality, as cable systems increased the number of channels, broadcast networks aggressively expanded their ownership of cable networks with the largest audiences. Within 10 years, 90 percent of the top 50 cable stations were owned by the same corporations as the broadcast networks. Competition, at least in terms of ideas, disappeared, replaced by the strident voices of Rush Limbaugh and others demanding still more changes to boost profits.

As with so much of what is wrong with America today, the beginning of media consolidation and the decline of even-handedness can be traced to Ronald Reagan and his administration. It was Reagan and his appointees that opened the airwaves to the likes of Rush Limbaugh and the Fox Network. If there are among you those who devoutly believe that Limbaugh should be able with impunity to condemn a law student as "a slut," then thank Ronald Reagan, for it was he that removed "fairness" from broadcasting.

The so-called fairness doctrine dates to the earliest years of radio's regulation. The Federal Radio Commission had just been established and its members named, when it issued General Order #32, instructing 164 stations to show cause why they should not be abolished. This was to allow the FRC to start from the ground up, so to speak, to review each of the stations and their merits afresh. On July 9, 1928, of the 164 stations, 110 appeared at a hearing in the Interior Department building.

The FRC counsel, Louis G. Caldwell, later wrote that "We had almost no procedure devised. We had no files. We had affidavits and letters. ... a record that threatened to swamp the commission."[36]

The Commission was confronted with the need to develop a standard by which stations could later be held accountable. It did so by providing the germ of what became in later years the "fairness doctrine." A station, the FRC said, would have to be conducted "with due regard for the opinion of others."[37]

Twenty-one years later, in 1949, the Federal Communications Commission, successor to the FRC, officially introduced the "fairness doctrine." It required broadcasters to both present controversial issues of public importance and to do so in a manner that was, in the Commission's view, honest, equitable and balanced.

The Fairness Doctrine had two basic elements: First, it required broadcasters to discus controversial matters of public interest; and, second, to air contrasting views. These could be in the form of news segments, public affairs shows, or editorials. The doctrine did not require equal time for opposing views but required that contrasting viewpoints be presented.[38]

There were also two corollary rules: the personal attack rule and the "political editorial" rule.

The "personal attack" rule applied whenever a person (or small group) was subject to a personal attack during a broadcast. Stations had to notify such persons (or groups) within a week of the attack, send them transcripts of what was said and offer the opportunity to respond on-the-air.[39]

The "political editorial" rule applied when a station broadcast editorials endorsing or opposing candidates for public office, and stipulated that the unendorsed candidates be notified and allowed a reasonable opportunity to respond.[40]

Taken together, the fairness doctrine and its two corollary rules imposed on radio and television broadcasters, limits on speech what would have been constitutionally intolerable had the government sought to limit newspapers or magazines as such.

It was a full two decades later before the U.S. Supreme Court ruled on the constitutionality of the fairness doctrine.

Fred J. Cook had written a book, *Goldwater: Extremist of the Right*, that was attacked on the daily *Christian Crusade* by Billy James Hargis. It was carried by WGCB in Red Lion, Pennsylvania. Cook demanded time to reply, the station refused and he sued, saying Hargis had engaged in an on-air personal attack. Hargis said the fairness doctrine violated the First Amendment.

In *Red Lion Broadcasting Co. v. FCC*, 395 U.S. 367 (1969), the Court upheld 8–0 the constitutionality of the Fairness Doctrine. Writing for the Court, Justice Byron White said "Licenses to broadcast do not confer ownership of designated frequencies, but only the temporary privilege of using them. Unless renewed, they expire within three years."[41] He continued—

A license permits broadcasting, but the licensee has no constitutional right to be the one who holds the license or to monopolize a radio frequency to the exclusion of his fellow citizens. There is nothing in the First Amendment which prevents the Government from requiring a licensee to share this frequency with others. ... It is the right of the viewers and listeners, not the right of the broadcasters, which is paramount.[42]

But why should broadcasters care? The answer, as is almost invariably the case when corporations are involved, is simple: money. Talk radio is cheap, and the more controversial it becomes, the more cash broadcasters rake in.

In MarketWatch, a daily program on public radio stations, David B. Wilkerson quoted a senior vice president of Premiere, the company that distributes the syndicated talk shows of Rush Limbaugh, Sean Hannity and Glenn Beck. Said Len Klatt of Premiere, "People ask me, 'What happens when Rush says something very controversial about Obama?' They say, 'Well, people are going to tune out,' [but] no, they're not. Because he's talking to his people; they're not going to tune out at all."[43]

Premiere is a subsidiary of Clear Channel. It makes money selling Rush and pals to radios, then still more cash running their programs. Clear Channel won't say exactly how much money it makes—ratings and ad revenue information are "proprietary." But Premiere did reveal that the Limbaugh-Hannity-Beck trio are on pace to see advertising sales increase 10 percent to 40 percent, compared to the year before.[44]

How many listen to Rush? According to the *Washington Post*, the estimates vary wildly, "from 30 million (Pat Buchanan on MSNBC), 20 million (*Time* magazine, ABC News), 19 million (Fox News), 14 million (CNN), or "14.2 million to about 25 million" (*Washington Post*)?"[45]

If the Limbaughs were alone, it would be bad enough, but they're not. The Limbaughs are merely cogs in the wheel of a well organized and funded media machine that includes televisions and radio networks, individual stations as well as groups, newspapers, magazines and a variety of other outlets. They have been intentionally created for the purpose of serving the interests of the Republican Party, and especially the rich and corporations that it serves.

There are "progressive" or "liberal" radio hosts, but according to consultant Holland Cooke "they're not on the biggest stations." The "biggest stations in the most markets," he said. Are owned by Clear Channel. "So the station where you tend to hear Stephanie Miller and Thom Hartmann tends to be a less-traveled place on the radio dial, 1400 AM as opposed to 600 AM. That hurts."[46]

Talk radio also uses that portion of the radio spectrum that is least valuable, the AM band. Frequency modulated signals render sound of a vastly superior quality, which dictates that music stations seek them out. AM stations, by contrast, are under-used and cheaper.

It was apparent in the 1970s that the chief barrier to profitize broadcasting was to jettison the fairness doctrine and its two corollary rules. As is often the case, those who want to make more money can't concede that, so they usually conjure a phony excuse that will pass the laugh test. That's what happened to the Fairness Doctrine.

Ronald Reagan appointed Mark Fowler, a Los Angeles lawyer, who had been a member of the Californian's campaign staff in both 1976 and 1980, to head the FCC. He did and does represent newspapers, book publishers, magazines, broadcasters, cable casters, digital media clients, and advertising agencies.[47] It was Fowler who quickly opened the door to the Doctrine's repeal.

Fowler held television in fairly low regard and once equated it to a "toaster with pictures." Under Fowler, the FCC issued a 1985 "Fairness Report," concluding that the doctrine had a "chilling effect" on public debate and likely violated the First Amendment: "We no longer believe that the Fairness Doctrine, as a matter of policy, serves the public interest."[48]

Two Republican judges, Antonin Scalia and Robert Bork, took note. In 1986, they outvoted a lone dissenter, delivering a 2–1 Court of Appeals' decision that the Fairness Doctrine was not a law passed by Congress and was therefore not binding. It was, they said, merely an agency regulation. That left Fowler's FCC free to abandon the doctrine, and they did. In August 1987 the FCC, with Reagan's support, announced the doctrine was dead and that the agency would no longer enforce it.[49]

Congress sought to revive the doctrine, passing a bill that would have put it back in place. Reagan vetoed the measure. Democrats were unable to override the veto. They tried again in the next Congress, but efforts collapsed under threat of a veto by George H.W. Bush.[50] In October 2000, the U.S. Court of Appeals for the District of Columbia ordered the Federal Communications Commission to repeal the personal attack and political editorial rules, effective immediately.[51]

Not to put too fine a point on this, the Fairness Doctrine was abandoned by a Republican-led Federal Communications Commission. The Doctrine was declared fair game for such abandonment by two Republican judges, one of whom, Antonin Scalia, now serves on the U.S. Supreme Court. The other, Robert Bork sought to serve on the Court. Congress attempted to re-instate the Fairness Doctrine, but the measure passed by both the House and the Senate was vetoed by a Republican President, Ronald Reagan. The two corollary, rules—the prohibitions on the personal attacks and political editorials—were also abandoned.

Broadcasting ownership has become so consolidated that five mammoth corporations now determine what Americans read and hear. Their profits are immense, and increasing. So-called "talk radio," with demagogic slandering personalities, now dominates the radio airwaves. These changes, and others, were made possible by the enactment by a Republican Congress of the first significant changes in sixty years to Federal communications law. These have made it possible for "personalities" to slander with impunity ordinary Americans and to aggressively and unapologetically advance the causes of the RLTP, their party and the issues to which it clings.

It seems unlikely that any of the RLTP-advanced changes will ever be turned back. Limbaugh will remain free to call a young law student "a slut." His brother can continue to condemn those who criticize Limbaugh as Stalinists. Bain Capital will continue to make vast sums of money from its ownership of Clear Channel. Plumbers and furnace repairmen will continue to listen endlessly to the lies and half-truths of talk radio. The decline of print newspapers will continue.

And Americans will be confronted once again with legislation without representation. This time, however, they are more likely to applaud than rebel.

13
APPENDIX I
THE CORPORATE ECHO CHAMBER[a]

NEWSPAPERS

Wall Street Journal - Business and Financial News; Editorial Page
Washington Times (on-line) - Politics, US and World News.
New York Post - Gossip, Sports, Entertainment and More.
Opinion Journal - The Wall Street Journal Editorial Page.
IBD Editorials - Editorials, Political Cartoons, and more from Investor's
    Business Daily.
Pittsburgh *Post Gazette*
Arizona *Republic*
San Diego *Union*
Manchester (N.H.) *Union*
    Clarity Media Group,[1] a Denver-based Publishing Group owned by multi-
    billionaire Philip Anschutz and his wife Nancy. It includes
        San Francisco *Examiner* (purchased in 2004)

---

[a] The phrase "corporate echo chamber" is drawn from the book of the same name by Kathleen Hall Jamieson and Joseph Cappella, two of the nation's foremost experts on politics and communications. Their book is a painstaking analysis of the media establishment created by the rich and corporations. In an examination that ranges from talk radio and Fox News to the editorial page of the *Wall Street Journal*, they show—no surprise here—that in thirty years, the rich have created a self-protective enclave for libertarians and others advancing the cause of the "free market." They attack political opponents, drown out dissent, and forge a form of leadership that has fundamentally altered America and its politics. Unlike others, however, theirs is an academic tome that objectively establishes what others have come to believe based on experience and anecdote. Kathleen Hall Jamieson and Joseph N. Cappella, *Echo Chamber Rush Limbaugh and the Conservative Media Establishment*, Oxford University Press (December 2009).

Washington Examiner, which was spun off from a number of D.C. area
suburban dailies.

Baltimore *Examiner*, which launched in April 2006 and was shut down
in early 2009. (Anschutz has trademarked the name "Examiner" in
more than sixty cities.)

Examiner.com, a hyper-local web portal where citizen journalists write
on local topics, from news to blog-like stories.

Weekly Standard[2] is an American neoconservative opinion magazine
published 48 times per year. Its founding publisher, News
Corporation, debuted the title September 18, 1995. Currently edited
by founder William Kristol and Fred Barnes, the Standard has been
described as a "redoubt of neoconservatism" and as "the neo-con
bible." Since it was founded in 1995, the Weekly Standard has
never been profitable, and has remained in business through
subsidies from wealthy conservative benefactors such as former
owner Rupert Murdoch. Many of the magazine's articles are written
by members of conservative think tanks located in Washington,
D.C.: the American Enterprise Institute, the Ethics and Public
Policy Center, the Foundation for Defense of Democracies, and the
Hudson Institute. Some individuals that have written for the
magazine include Elliott Abrams, Peter Berkowitz, John R. Bolton,
Ellen Bork, Ed Gillespie, Roger Kimball, Harvey Mansfield, Joe
Queenan, Wesley J. Smith, David Brooks and John Yoo. The
magazine's website blog, titled the "Daily Standard," is edited by
John McCormack and Daniel Halper and produces daily articles and
commentary.

STUDENT NEWSPAPERS

Collegiate Network (CN) is a group—really more like a chain—of self-
described "independent" college newspapers, magazines and journals program
administered by the Intercollegiate Studies Institute (ICS). According to the
Foundation Directory on-line, ICS is funded by the collection of foundations
founded by the rich and their corporations. Foundations and the amounts they have
given in the past few years include the Lynde and Harry Bradley Foundation ($1.2
million), Castle Rock ($200,000), DeVos ($3.25 million), Kirby ($2.4 million) and
Murdoch (1.2 million) to name by a few.

CN says member periodicals "serve to focus public awareness on the
politicization of American college and university classrooms, curricula, student life,
and the resulting decline of educational standards."

CN is a vital part of creating and furthering the careers of the "boys and girls from Wichita." These young people are given paid summer internships and postgraduate, year-long fellowships at "prominent media outlets to promising student journalists."

CN periodicals and their names are as follows:[b]

University of California-Irvine - the *Anteater Review*
Binghamton University - the *Binghamton Review*
Brown University - the *Brown Spectator*
University of California-Los Angeles - the *Bruin Standard*
University of California-Berkeley - the *California Patriot*
University of California-San Diego - the *California Review*
Stanford University - the *Cardinal Principle*
University of North Carolina - the *Carolina Review*
Claremont College - the *Claremont Independent*
Cornell University - the *Cornell Review*
Bucknell University - the *Counterweight*
University of Chicago - *Counterpoint*
Seton Hall Law School - the *Cross Examiner*
Dartmouth College - the *Dartmouth Review*
Davidson College - the *Davidson Reader*
Eastern Washington University - the *Eastern Republic*
College of the Holy Cross - the *Fenwick Review*
New York University - the *Filibuster*
Georgetown University - the *Georgetown Academy*; The *Georgetown Federalist*
Gonzaga University - the *Gonzaga Witness*
Duke University - the *Gothic Guardian*
George Washington University - the *GW Patriot*
Harvard University - the *Harvard Ichthus*; The *Harvard Salient*
Hillsdale College - the *Hillsdale Forum*
Indiana University Bloomington - the *Indiana Standard*
University of Notre Dame - the *Irish Rover*
Lehigh University - the *Lehigh Patriot*
Oregon State University - the *Liberty*
Seton Hall University - *Liberty Bell*
Yale University - *Light & Truth*

---

[b] Collegiate Network, http://www.collegiatenetwork.org/papers/, accessed June 18, 2012.

DePaul University - *Lincoln Park Statesman*
University of Michigan - the *Michigan Review*
University of Chicago - the *Midway Review*
University of Minnesota-Morris - the *Morris North Star*
West Virginia University - the *Mountaineer Jeffersonian*
University of Idaho/Washington State University - the *Northwest Alternative*
Northwestern University - the *Northwestern Chronicle*
Boston College - the *Observer at Boston College*
University of Oregon - the *Oregon Commentator*
Wabash College - the *Phoenix*
Portland State University - the *Portland Spectator*
Princeton University - the *Princeton Tory*
Purdue University - the *Purdue Review*
Christendom College - the *Rambler*
Florida State University - the *Seminole Sentinel*
Brigham Young University - *Stance: For the Family*
Stanford University - the *Stanford Review*
University of Maryland - the *Terrapin Times*
Clemson University - the *Tiger Town Observer*
Georgetown University - *Utraque Unum*
Vanderbilt University - the *Vanderbilt Torch*
Villanova University - the *Villanova Times*
University of Virginia - the *Virginia Advocate*
College of William & Mary - the *Virginia Informer*
Wabash College - the *Wabash Commentary*
Marquette University - the *Warrior*
Washington University - the *Washington Witness*
Yale University - *Yale Free Press*

MAGAZINES

The *Weekly Standard* - Important reading for anyone interested in American politics. Edited by Bill Kristol and Fred Barnes.

National Review Online - America's most widely read and influential conservative news magazine and website.

American Spectator - Chronicling the Tragic Comedy of modern liberalism without losing its head, heart, or humor.

Reason Magazine - Free Minds and Free Markets.

Jewish World Review - The intersection of faith, culture and politics.

Capitalism Magazine - Individual Rights are the Moral Basis of Society.

Dartmouth Review - Founded in 1980, its alumni and alumnae include
Dinesh D'Souza, Hugo Restall, James Panero, Laura Ingraham, and
other notable conservative intellectuals.
Human Events

RADIO STATIONS/NETWORKS

Clear Channel Communications, Inc. is an American mass media
company headquartered in San Antonio, Texas. It was founded in 1972 by Lowry
Mays and Red McCombs, and was taken private by Bain Capital LLC and Thomas
H. Lee Partners LP in a leveraged buyout in 2008. Clear Channel specializes in
radio broadcasting, concert promotion and hosting, and fixed advertising in the
United States through its subsidiaries.[3]

Clear Channel is the largest owner of full-power AM, FM, and shortwave
radio stations and twelve radio channels on XM Satellite Radio, and is also the
largest pure-play radio station owner and operator. The group was in the television
business until it sold all of its TV stations to Newport Television in 2008.[4]

In 1992, the U.S. Congress relaxed radio ownership rules slightly, allowing
the company to acquire more than two stations per market. By 1995, Clear Channel
owned 43 radio stations and 16 television stations. In 1996, the
Telecommunications Act of 1996 became law. This act deregulated media
ownership, allowing a company to own more stations than previously. Clear
Channel went on a buying spree, purchasing more than 70 other media companies,
plus individual stations.[5]

With 850 stations, Clear Channel is the largest radio station group owner in
the United States, both by number of stations and by revenue. The 850 stations
reach more than 110 million listeners every week, and 237 million every month.
According to BIA Financial Network, Clear Channel Media & Entertainment
recorded more than $3.5 billion in revenues as of 2005, $1 billion more than the
number-two group owner, CBS Radio.[6]

TELEVISION STATIONS/NETWORKS

FOXNews - Fair and Balanced
Special Report with Bret Baier, Your World with Neil Cavuto,
The O'Reilly Factor with Bill O'Reilly and The Glenn Beck Show.
FOXNews Extras - FOXNews Live Stream | Online Radio | FOX Nation

FOXNews Sunday - From policy debates to political fights, top newsmakers sit down with Chris Wallace. Watch FOX News Sunday on Hulu.com.

Newport Television, LLC is a television station holding company founded by Providence, Equity Partners and Sandy DiPasquale in 2007 to acquire the television stations owned by Clear Channel Communications. In September 2007, Newport agreed to sell KFTY and KVOS-TV to LK Station Group LLC for $26.6 million. The deal was set be completed in March 2008 but eventually collapsed due to LK's lender refusing to provide the funding; KFTY (now KEMO-TV) and KVOS have since been sold to other companies. As of October 10, 2007, Newport has agreed to sell KION-TV, KMUV-LP, K44DN, KKFX-CA, KCOY-TV to Cowles Publishing Company for $41 million. Newport's purchase of the Clear Channel stations and those being resold were granted conditional Federal Communications Commission (FCC) approval, subject to divestitures of media properties owned by other affiliates of Providence Equity Partners in several other markets. The entire deal closed on March 14, 2008 after several stations, in addition to those being divested by Newport, were placed into trust companies. In March 2012, Providence Equity Partners began to explore strategic alternatives for Newport Television, which may lead to a sale of the group.[7]

COLUMNISTS

George Will

COMMENTATORS/BROADCASTERS

Rush Limbaugh
Sean Hannity
Laura Ingraham
Michael Reagan
Glenn Beck

INTERNET & WEB RELATED OUTLETS

Search Engines

Yippy <http://www.yippy.com/>. According to its mission statement, Yippy attempts to be family-friendly and "include only content that is appropriate for all ages." It also promotes "conservative values."

The Conservative Search Engine searches a large number of conservative blogs and conservative websites. As part of the Western Center for

Journalism's mission to equip conservative citizen journalists, we have created this search page to be a research tool for conservative bloggers and other citizen journalists who need the news without all the left-wing propaganda attached.
http://www.westernjournalism.com/blogging-tools/conservative-search-engine

http://pledgeamerica.org/search.html

http://www.conservativeusa.org/search.htm "The web search resource for conservative activists! A project of The Conservative Caucus (Howard Phillips), 450 Maple Avenue East, Vienna, VA 22180 703-938-9626

http://www.search-engine.com/ "Account for domain search-engine.com has been suspended" message provided, May 21, 2012.

Google (Search The Greatest Conservative Resources Online)

RonaldReagan.com proclaims, 'Search the web with confidence and no google spam. The Ronald Reagan Conservative search will give you the most relevant search results. When you need information, search the only conservative search engine!'

OTHER

Billboards

Outdoor Advertising
Billboards at Dundas Square in Toronto, owned by Clear Channel.

Clear Channel Outdoor is an advertising company owned by Clear Channel Communications.[8]

Bought Eller Media, Universal Outdoor, and More Group Plc, giving Clear Channel outdoor advertising space in 25 countries.
Owns part of an Italian street furniture company, Jolly Pubblicita S.p.A.
Owns BBH Exhibits, Yellow Checker Star Cab Displays, Dauphin, Taxi Tops, Donrey Media, and Ackerley Media. Also owns an outdoor advertising company in Switzerland and Poland and a major outdoor advertising firm in Chile.
Has a partnership with APN Outdoor in Australia, which has resulted in a 49% share in Adshel, a street furniture advertising company. APN Outdoor is the majority shareholder (owning 51% of Adshel).[9]
Operates over 500 digital billboards in 32 markets.

13
APPENDIX II
TALK RADIO

SUMMARY, THE STRUCTURAL IMBALANCE OF POLITICAL TALK RADIO
Center for American Progress
By John Halpin, James Heidbreder, Mark Lloyd, Paul Woodhull, Ben Scott,
Josh Silver,
S. Derek Turner; June 20, 2007;
http://www.americanprogress.org/issues/2007/06/talk_radio.html

Despite the dramatic expansion of viewing and listening options for consumers today, traditional radio remains one of the most widely used media formats in America. Arbitron, the national radio ratings company, reports that more than 90 percent of Americans ages 12 or older listen to radio each week, "a higher penetration than television, magazines, newspapers, or the Internet." Although listening hours have declined slightly in recent years, Americans listened on average to 19 hours of radio per week in 2006.

Among radio formats, the combined news/talk format (which includes news/talk/information and talk/personality) leads all others in terms of the total number of stations per format and trails only country music in terms of national audience share. Through more than 1,700 stations across the nation, the combined news/talk format is estimated to reach more than 50 million listeners each week.

As this report will document in detail, conservative talk radio undeniably dominates the format.

Our analysis in the spring of 2007 of the 257 news/talk stations owned by the top five commercial station owners reveals that 91 percent of the total weekday talk radio programming is conservative, and 9 percent is progressive.[1]

Each weekday, 2,570 hours and 15 minutes of conservative talk are broadcast on these stations compared to 254 hours of progressive talk—10 times as much conservative talk as progressive talk.

A separate analysis of all of the news/talk stations in the top 10 radio markets reveals that 76 percent of the programming in these markets is conservative and 24 percent is progressive, although programming is more balanced in markets such as New York and Chicago.

13
APPENDIX III
THE POWER OF GROUP OWNERS

Fox is by no means the first chain of stations to use its muscle to advance a point of view.

During the 1930s and 1940s, so-called "group owners"—people who owned multiple radio stations—rose to power. Unlike the networks, which were constantly in the public spotlight, group owners were able to function in relative anonymity. Many simply wanted to make money, and the best way to do this was to bring a station to health, then sell it at a profit. The gains would be taxed at the low capital gains rate versus the higher rate of profits.

But some group owners, like the Fox Network today, had a private, political agenda. "The Richards stations," three 50,000-watt stations able to blanket almost the entire continent, were based in Cleveland (WGAR), Detroit (WJR) and Hollywood (KMPC). The airwaves were supposed to be public property and stations, therefore, supposedly operated in the public interest. Real life was a different story.

Father Charles Coughlin, "the inventor of hate radio" in the words of *Harper's Magazine*,[1] was like most of the popular broadcasters of the time, loud and simple. At the height of Coughlin's popularity, one-third of the nation tuned into his weekly broadcasts, making him one of the most influential men in America in the early 1930s.[2] His speciality, like those of today successors, was "scapegoating, ridicule, and paranoia."[3] It was at one of the Richards' stations, WGY in Detroit, that Coughlin made his first broadcast.[4]

Coughlin was accused of anti-Semitic overtones, but Richards was the real deal, obsessed with getting "the Jews" out of government. He told his news staffs that Jews were communists, and Communists were Jews. The patriotic mission of his stations was to eliminate them from positions of influence, especially the "Jew-lover" President Franklin Delano Roosevelt.[5] He ordered his staff to use euphemistic nicknames for politicians of the day: Harry Truman was to be called "pipsqueak" by Richards' broadcasters, Vice President Henry Wallace was "tumbleweed," while Richards himself referred to Mrs. Roosevelt as "the old bitch."[6]

LIMBAUGH ON DEMOCRATS

If we never elected Democrats again, we would be imminently safer.

May 27, 2003, 12:53 p.m.
WMAL, Washington, D.C.

Richards was eventually undone by his hatred and called before the Federal Communications Commission, but died before it rendered a judgment.[7, a] Today, Fox News and its commentators, Glenn Beck and Rush Limbaugh, are more powerful than Coughlin and Richards ever were. And, in some ways, while their message is different, it is decidedly more dangerous. They are not overtly anti-Semitic, but they do target certain groups. Because they have tight ties to the RLTP, their messages quickly emerge as partisan political dogma.[8]

---

[a] His widow was allowed to retain control after pledging in 1951 that the stations would not broadcast biased or slanted news. Michigan's Radio & TV Broadcast Guide, "History of Michigan AM Broadcasting," http://www.michiguide.com/history/am.html, accessed May 29, 2012.

13
APPENDIX IV
NEWS CORP. HOLDINGS[a]

NEWSPAPERS

Australia - Published by News Limited
   Australian (Nationwide)
   Community Media Group (16 QLD & NSW suburban/regional titles)
   Cumberland-Courier Newspapers (23 suburban/commuter titles)
   Courier-Mail (Queensland)
   Sunday Mail (Queensland)
   Cairns Post (Cairns, Queensland)
   Gold Coast Bulletin (Gold Coast, Queensland)
   Townsville Bulletin (Townsville, Queensland)
   Daily Telegraph (New South Wales)
   Sunday Telegraph (New South Wales)
   Herald Sun (Victoria)
   Sunday Herald Sun (Victoria)
   Weekly Times (Victoria)
   Leader Newspapers (33 suburban Melbourne, VIC titles)
   MX (Sydney, Melbourne and Brisbane CBD)
   Geelong Advertiser (Geelong, Victoria)
   Advertiser (South Australia)
   Sunday Mail (South Australia)
   Messenger Newspapers (11 suburban Adelaide, SA titles)
   Sunday Times (Western Australia)
   Mercury (Tasmania)
   Quest Newspapers (19 suburban Brisbane, QLD titles)
   Sunday Tasmanian (Tasmania)

---

[a] Based on information provided by Wikipedia.org.

Northern Territory News (Northern Territory)
Sunday Territorian (Northern Territory)
Tablelands Advertiser (Atherton Tablelands and the Far North, Queensland)

Fiji

Fiji Times (National) (10%)
Nai Lalakai (10%)
Shanti Dut (10%)

Papua New Guinea

Papua New Guinea Post-Courier (National) (62.5%)

UK and Ireland Newspapers - Published by Subsidiaries of News International Ltd.

News Group Newspapers Ltd.
Sun (published in Scotland as the *Scottish Sun* and in Ireland as the *Irish Sun*)
Sun on Sunday
Times Newspapers Ltd.
    Sunday Times
    Times
    Times Literary Supplement

U.S. Newspapers and Magazines

New York Post
Community Newspaper Group
    Brooklyn Paper
    Bronx Times-Reporter
    Brooklyn Courier-Life
    TimesLedger Newspapers
Dow Jones & Company
Consumer Media Group
Wall Street Journal
    Wall Street Journal Europe
    Wall Street Journal Asia
    Barron's - weekly financial markets magazine
    Marketwatch -Financial news and information website
    Far Eastern Economic Review
    Enterprise Media Group
Dow Jones Newswires - global, real-time news and information provider.
    Factiva - provides business news and information together with content delivery tools and services.

Dow Jones Indexes - stock market indexes and indicators, including the Dow Jones Industrial Average.

Dow Jones Financial Information Services - produces databases, electronic media, newsletters, conferences, directories, and other information services on specialized markets and industry sectors.

Betten Financial News - leading Dutch language financial and economic news service.

Local Media Group

Ottaway Community Newspapers - 8 daily and 15 weekly regional newspapers.

STOXX (33%) - joint venture with Deutsche Boerse and SWG Group for the development and distribution of Dow Jones STOXX indices.

Vedomosti (33%) - Russia's leading financial newspaper (joint venture with Financial Times and Independent Media).

SmartMoney

The Timesledger Newspapers of Queens, New York:
Bayside Times
Whitestone Times
Flushing Times
Little Neck Ledger
Jamaica Times
Astoria Times
Forest Hills Ledger

The Courier-Life Newspapers in Brooklyn
Brooklyn Paper
Caribbean Life
Flatbush Jewish Journal
Times-Herald Record (Middletown, New York)
The Leader - Corning, NY

MAGAZINES

U.S.A
SmartSource Magazine (weekly Sunday newspaper coupon insert)

Australia
Alpha Magazine
Australian Country Style

Australian Golf Digest
Australian Good Taste
Big League
BCME
Delicious
Donna Hay
Fast Fours
GQ (Australia)
Gardening Australia
InsideOut (Aust)
Lifestyle Pools
Live to Ride
Notebook
Overlander 4WD
Modern Boating
Modern Fishing
Parents
Pure Health
Super Food Ideas
Truck Australia
Truckin' Life
twowheels
twowheels scooter
Vogue (Australia)
Vogue Entertaining & Travel
Vogue Living

United Kingdom
  Inside Out

MUSIC AND RADIO

Fox Film Music Group
Fox News Radio

Russia
  Nashe (50%)
  Best FM (50%)

SPORT

50% of the National Rugby League (Australia and New Zealand)
Majority ownership of the Brisbane Broncos (68.9%) and full ownership of the
    Melbourne Storm rugby league team.
Colorado Rockies (15%)

STUDIOS

Fox Filmed Entertainment: 20th Century Fox's parent company
20th Century Fox: a film production/distribution company
    Fox Searchlight Pictures - specialized films.
    Fox 2000 Pictures - general audience feature films.
20th Century Fox Television - primetime television programming.
20th Television - television distribution (syndication).
Fox 21 - low scripted/budgeted television production company.
Fox Television Studios (productions) - market specific programming, e.g.,
    COPS and network television company.
Fox Television Studios International
Fox World Productions
Fox World Australia
Fox TV Studios France
Fox TV Studios India
Natural History New Zealand - natural world documentaries, non-fiction
programming.
Fox Faith - Promotion and distribution of Christian and related "family
    friendly" movies on DVD and some theatrical release.
Fox Studios Australia, Sydney, New South Wales
Blue Sky Studios - production of CGI films, e.g., Ice Age.
Fox Entertainment Group
New Regency Productions (20%) - general audience feature films.
Regency Enterprises (20%) - parent company of New Regency Productions (50%).
FOX Star Studios New Delhi, India

TELEVISION

On December 22, 2007, News Corp agreed to sell eight of its television
stations to Oak Hill Capital Partners for approximately $1.1 billion. The stations
are US Fox affiliates. These stations, along with those already acquired by Oak Hill
that were formerly owned by The New York Times Company, formed the nucleus
of Oak Hill's Local TV LLC division.

Broadcast

Fox Broadcasting Company (Fox), a U.S. broadcast television network

MyNetworkTV, a U.S. broadcast television network

Fox Television Stations Group, a group of owned and operated Fox television stations

Europe

News Corp Europe

bTV, a broadcast television network in *Bulgaria*, sold to CME in February 2010.

Cielo (100%), a free channel in *Italy*.

LNT (100%), a terrestrial channel in *Latvia*

TV5 Riga (100%), a terrestrial channel in *Latvia*

B1 TV (12.5%), a broadcast television network in *Romania*, in partnership with Ismar International Nvkkkk

Fox Televizija, a broadcast television network in *Serbia* (49%), sold to Antenna Group in January, 2010.

Fox *Turkey*, a Turkish terrestrial channel (56.5%) (formerly TGRT)

Imedi Media Holding (100%), a *Georgia* radio and TV broadcaster.

United Kingdom

ITV plc (7.5%), a British broadcast television network and the UK's largest advertising revenue based broadcaster

Uruguay

Saeta TV Channel 10

Israel

Channel 10 (9%), a terrestrial channel in Israel.

Indonesia

ANTV (20%), a private television station in Indonesia, under the administration and label of STAR TV

New Zealand

Prime Television - commercial TV station, interest held through stake in SKY Network Television

Satellite Television

British Sky Broadcasting, United Kingdom & Ireland (39.1% holding). In practice, a controlling interest.

Sky Network Television, New Zealand (44%)

Sky Italia (100%), Italy's largest pay TV service

Sky Deutschland (49.90%), Germany's largest pay TV provider

Tata Sky (30%), an Indian DirectToHome TeleVision Service Provider (in partnership with Tata Group (70%)).

Foxtel (25%), Australia, a joint venture with Telstra (50%) and Consolidated Media Holdings (25%)

FOX Italy, Italian Broadcast and Production Company (with 2 HDTV)

Star TV Channels (Satellite TeleVision Asian Region), an Asian satellite TV service having 300 million viewers in 53 countries, mainly in India, China & other Asian countries

Phoenix Television (17.6%), satellite TV network with landing rights in Hong Kong, and select provinces on Mainland China.

Cable

Cable TV channels owned (in whole or part) and operated by News Corporation include:

Fox Business Network, a business news channel

Fox Classics, a channel airing classic TV shows & movies

Fox Movie Channel, an all-movie channel that airs commercial-free movies from 20th Century Fox's film library

Fox News Channel, a 24-hour news & opinion channel

Fox Sports Net, a chain of US regional cable news television networks broadcasting local sporting events linked together by national sports news programming. Local channels include Fox Sports Southwest, Fox Sports Detroit, etc. (some affiliates are owned by Cablevision).

SportSouth, a regional sports network in the United States, with its headquarters in Atlanta, Georgia, and affiliate of Fox Sports Net

Sun Sports a regional sports network in the United States, with its headquarters in Miami, Florida, and affiliate of Fox Sports Net

Fox College Sports, a college sports network consisting of three regionally aligned channels, mostly with archived Fox Sports Net programs but also some live and original content

Fox Sports International

Fox Soccer Channel (FSC), a United States digital cable and satellite network specializing mainly in soccer

Fox Soccer Plus, a sister network to FSC, but including coverage of other sports, most notably rugby. Launched in 2010 after News Corporation picked up many of the broadcast rights abandoned by Setanta Sports when it stopped broadcasting in the U.S.

Fox Sports Middle East - English language sports network airing in Middle East countries including Bahrain, Egypt, Jordan, Kuwait, Lebanon, Oman, Qatar, Saudi Arabia, Syria, UAE & Yemen

Fox Pan American Sports (37.9%) - joint venture with Hicks, Muse, and Tate & Furst.

Fox Sports en Español (50%), a Spanish-language North American cable sports network; its sports lineup is tailored to appeal to a Latin American audience.

Fox Sports en Latinoamérica, a Latin American satellite and cable sports network.

FX Networks, a cable network broadcasting reruns of programming previously shown on other channels, but recently creating its own programming, including the Emmy award-winning programs The Shield and Damages.

Speed Channel

FUEL TV

Big Ten Network, cable and satellite channel dedicated to The Big Ten Conference, launched Aug 2007 (49%)

National Geographic Channel (joint venture with National Geographic Society) 67%

National Geographic Channel International 75%

Nat Geo Mundo (joint venture with National Geographic Society)

Nat Geo Wild (joint venture with National Geographic Society)

Fox International Channels, domestic cable channels offering different formats of Fox programming in over thirty countries worldwide.

Fox

Fox Life

Fox Life HD

Fox Crime

FX

Fox Horror

Fox Movies

Fox Sports

Speed Channel

National Geographic Channel

National Geographic Channel HD

National Geographic Wild

National Geographic Adventure

National Geographic Music

National Geographic Junior

Cult

Next:HD
Voyage
Real Estate TV
BabyTV
Fox Toma 1 – Spanish-language television production.
Fox Telecolombia – Spanish-language television production. (51%)
Utarget.Fox – European and Latin American online ad company, plus now handles TV ad sales.
Central & South America
Fox Latin American Channels – channels available in over 17 countries in Latin America
    National Geographic Channel
    National Geographic Channel HD
    National Geographic Wild
    Nat Geo Music
    Universal Channel
    Universal HD
    Fox Channel
    Fox HD
    FX
    Fox Life
    Syfy
    Fox Sports
    Speed Channel
    Baby TV
    Utilisima
Fox One-Stop Media – advertising sales for company owned and third party channels in Latin America
LAPTV (60%) (Latin American Pay Television) operates 8 cable movie channels throughout South America excluding Brazil.
Telecine(12.5%) operates 5 cable movie channels in Brazil.

Australia
Premier Media Group (50%)
Fox Sports 1
Fox Sports 2
Fox Sports 3
SPEED
FoxSportsNews
Fuel TV Australia

Premium Movie Partnership (20%) – movie channels, a joint venture between 20th Century Fox, Sony, NBC Universal, Viacom and Liberty Media

PLATFORMS

India

Hathway Cable & Datacom (22.2%), India's 2nd largest cable network through 7 cities including Bangalore, Chennai, Delhi, Mumbai & Pune

Taiwan

Total TV (20%), Pay TV platform with JV partner KOO's Group majority owner (80%). News Corp also has a 20% interest in the KOO's Group directly

INTERNET

Fox Interactive Media

Foxsports.com – website with sports news, scores, statistics, video and fantasy sports

Hulu (27%) – online video streaming site in partnership with NBC Universal and The Walt Disney Company.

Flektor – provides Web-based tools for photo and video editing and mashups.

IGN Entertainment – Internet entertainment portal (Includes the sites IGN, GameSpy, TeamXbox, 1up.com, and Askmen.com)

Giga.de

Slingshot Labs – web development incubator (Includes the sites DailyFill).

Strategic Data Corp – interactive advertising company which develops technology to deliver targeted internet advertising.

Scout.com

WhatIfSports.com – sports simulation and prediction website. Also provides fantasy-style sports games to play.

Indya.com – 'India's no. 1 Entertainment Portal'

ROO Group Inc (5% increasing to 10% with performance targets)

News Digital Media

News.com.au – Australian-oriented news website

News Lab

CareerOne.com.au (50%) – recruitment advertisement website in partnership with Monster Worldwide.

Carsguide.com.au

in2mobi.com.au

TrueLocal.com.au

Moshtix.com.au – a ticket retailer
Learning Seat
Wego News owns minority stake in Wego.com
Netus (75%) – investment co. in online properties.
REA Group (60.7%)
Realestate.com.au
Casa.it (69.4%), Sky Italia also holds a 30.6% share
atHome group, operator of leading real estate websites in Luxembourg, France,
    Belgium and Germany.
Altowin (51%),provider of office management tools for realestate agents in
Belgium.
Propertyfinder.com (50%), News International holds the remaining 50%
Sherlock Publications, owner of hotproperty.co.uk portal and magazine titles
    'Hot Property', 'Renting' and 'Overseas'
ukpropertyshop.co.uk, most comprehensive UK estate agent directory.
PropertyLook, property websites in Australia and New Zealand.
HomeSite.com.au, home renovation and improvement website.
Square Foot Limited, Hong Kong's largest English Language property magazine
and website
Primedia – Holding co. of Inside DB, a Hong Kong lifestyle magazine.
TadpoleNet Media (10%) Hosts of ArmySailor.com

New Zealand

Fatso – leading online DVD subscription service (ownership through stake
    in Sky Network Television).
Fox Networks – one of the largest international ad networks.
Expedient InfoMedia blog network.

OTHER ASSETS

NDS Group – Conditional access technology and personal digital video
    recorders (PVRs) (49%)
SiVenture
Jungo
CastUP
Broadsystem Ltd (UK) – Telephony provider for media companies, bought in
1991
Broadsystem Australia (Australia)
Broadsystem Ventures (UK) – provider of cheap-rate telephone calls,
    particularly for customers of Sky Television. Bought outright in 1999.
Jamba! – Mobile Entertainment/Mobile Handsets Personalisation/Games.

News Outdoor Group – Largest outdoor advertising company in Eastern Europe with over 70,000 ads including billboards and bus shelters, operating in Bulgaria, Czech Republic, Hungary, India, Israel, Poland, Romania, Russia (96 cities), Turkey & Ukraine.

Maximedia Israel (67%)

Mosgorreklama (50%) – Russia sign and marketing material manufacturer

Kamera Acikhava Reklamclik (?) – leading outdoor advertising company in Turkey

Australian Associated Press (45%) – real time news service.

STATS, Inc. (50%) – worlds leading provider of sporting information and statistical analysis (a JV with Associated Press)

Fox Sports Grill (50%) – Upscale sports bar and restaurant with 7 locations – Scottsdale, Arizona; Irvine, California; Seattle, Washington (U.S. state)|Washington; Plano, Texas; Houston, Texas; San Diego, California; and Atlanta, Georgia (U.S. state)|Georgia.

Fox Sports Skybox (70%) – Sports fan's Bar & Grill at Staples Center and 6 airport restaurants.

News America Marketing (US) – (100%) – nation's leading marketing services company, products include a portfolio of in-store, home-delivered and online media under the SmartSource brand.

Rotana (9%) – Largest Arab entertainment company owned by Saudi Prince Al-Waleed bin Talal

The Daily – iPad only newspaper delivered daily.

Making Fun – social game developer for making games for social networking sites, smartphones, tablets and other devices.

14

YOUR GREAT-, GREAT-, GREAT-GRANDFATHER'S TEA PARTY [THE REAL ONE]

The tea destroyed was contained in three ships, lying near each other at what was called at that time Griffin's wharf, and were surrounded by armed ships of war, the commanders of which had publicly declared that if the rebels, as they were pleased to style the Bostonians, should not withdraw their opposition to the landing of the tea before a certain day, the 17th day of December, 1773, they should on that day force it on shore, under the cover of their cannon's mouth.

"An Eyewitness Account of the Boston Tea Party"
George Hewes[a]

Tea Parties were as abundant in 2009 as daffodils in the Spring or, if you prefer, leaves in the Fall. They seemed to be all the rage. In fact, in Boston, not far from the original Tea Party, there were competing rallies on April 15, 2012.

One rally was held by the Massachusetts Tea Party Coalition, a "Patriots Day Rally" on Boston Common. Starting one hour later, Greater Boston Tea Party held its "Tax Day Rally" at Lincoln Square in Worcester, a Boston suburb.

The Worcester tea partiers urged people to skip the Boston rally. "They're including some social issues that we avoid," said Ken Mandile, a cofounder of the

---

[a] Archiving America, George Hewes, "An Eyewitness Account of the Boston Tea Party," http://www.earlyamerica.com/review/2005_winter_spring/boston_tea_party.htm, accessed Sept. 30, 2012.

Worcester Tea Party. "We stay focused on fiscal responsibility, limited government, and promoting free markets."

According to press reports, Mandile was correct. At Boston Common, banners called for "Freedom Not Socialism," a Texas Congressman attacked "Obamacare" and counter-protestors criticized Rev. Scott Lively, a Springfield, Massachusetts pastor and outspoken critic of homosexuality.[1]

Quite a contrast to the real thing.

To term the transport of thousands of men and women by air conditioned bus to pre-arranged meeting points a "Tea Party" is a cheap and cynical organizing method, an attempt to attract press attention to events that bear no resemblance to what really happened. Those who organized and executed the "the destruction of the tea," a half-century later named the Boston Tea Party, risked their very lives, endured sacrifices and hardships, and later fought for American independence.

To compare the original Boston Tea Party participants to these selfish and short-sighted people that are bused to the meeting points, handed signs to parade and demonstrate, then returned to the security and comfort of their homes, all at the expense of billionaires, is a travesty of the first order, an insult to American democracy and a grave dishonor to those who died to make possible a nation in which men could become rich beyond imagination, yet seek to overthrow the government that made their riches possible.

By the time of the Boston Tea Party, colonists had already died at the hands of British Redcoats. Now known as the Boston Massacre, it was first referred to as "the Bloody Massacre in King Street." Like the Tea Party that was to come later, the Massacre resulted from a change in British tax policy toward American colonists.

Parliament had directly imposed taxes on the American colonies for the first time in the 1760s. A fundamental principle of English law held that taxes could be imposed on citizens only by a body that included their elected representatives. The American colonists, however, were denied representation in Parliament. They insisted, therefore, that a tax on them enacted by Parliament was "taxation without representation."

The tax on tea imported into the colonies was imposed by the Townsend Act of 1767. It served three purposes: (1) to raise money for England generally; (2) to provide a dedicated source of revenue for the salaries of British governors and judges serving in the colonies, thus assuring their loyalty to the crown; and (3) to reduce smuggling. But British officials and many American colonists alike considered the tax of overwhelming symbolic importance.

To the British, the tax represented the right of Parliament, as expressed in the Declaratory Act of 1766, to legislate for the colonies "in all cases whatsoever." To the colonists, it was not just a tax, but one imposed by a legislative body in which they had no voice—"taxation without representation," as it came to be termed.

To enforce the new taxes of the Townsend Act, Britain dispatched its army. The first British troops arrived in Boston in October 1768 and from then onwards there was continuous antagonism between the people of Boston and those trying to enforce the King's rule. The newspapers printed accounts of the 'atrocities' committed by the occupiers.[2]

The Massacre occurred at a confrontation on March 5, 1770 between three to four hundred colonists and British regulars. Exactly what sparked the violence is unknown, but the troops opened fire and five, perhaps six, men were dead of mortal wounds.[b] The first to die was Crispus Attucks, a fugitive slave who had escaped from his master and had worked for twenty years as a merchant seaman. He emerged as the most famous of all the black men to fight in the cause of the Revolution, and become its first martyr. Paul Revere produced a print of the Massacre that flooded the market, spreading word of the violent confrontation well beyond Boston.

For nearly four years tensions remained high in Boston. Then, on December 16, 1773, came yet another event, the Boston Tea Party. Unlike the Massacre, which was the result of a seemingly accidental confrontation, the Tea Party was well organized and executed. It was planned by the Sons of Liberty, a group led by Samuel Adams whose members included John Adams, John Hancock, Paul Revere and the man who is arguably the least well known of the Massachusetts patriots, Dr. Samuel Warren.

---

[b] Most accounts says that five men were killed at the Massacre. Three died on the spot. They were Crispus Attucks, Samuel Gray and James Caldwell. Two others died of their wounds: Samuel Maverick, the next morning and Patrick Carr, two weeks later. A sixth man, Christopher Monk, was severely wounded by a bullet that entered just above his groin and came out of the hip on the opposite side. Permanently and severely disabled, Monk died almost exactly ten years later on April 20, 1780. Boston Massacre Historical Society, "Christopher Monk, the Sixth Victim," http://www.bostonmassacre.net/players/christopher-monk.htm, accessed May 1, 2012.

Although the Tea Party is widely regarded as a protest of the increased price of tea due to taxes imposed by the British, the tea aboard the ships in Boston Harbor would have sold at the lowest price in years. However, the dispute between the American colonists and the British government was so bitter and long-standing that it had taken on a life of its own. While American rage was initially ignited because taxes imposed by Parliament raised the price of tea in the colonies, even as they were refused any representation in the body, it was now much larger than an argument over mere taxes.

Colonists were so enraged, however, that the tea taxes and the policies they represented became identified with one another. Matters concluded with a provocation that Parliament concluded it could not ignore—the destruction of more than $1 million in tea at today's prices. From the colonists' perspective, the British Parliament forced an irrevocable act of defiance by a "detestable measure to distress, enslave and destroy" them. Following "the destruction of the tea," as it was called at the time, each side began preparation for armed conflict.

Great Britain had given the East India Company a monopoly right to bring tea into England. The company paid a duty of about 25 percent, then more taxes were levied when the tea was sold. For export to colonies, after the duty was paid, tea was auctioned to middlemen, who then dealt with merchants in Boston, Philadelphia and other cities. The East India Company exported no tea on its own.

In Holland, however, tea was imported untaxed. It was so much less expensive than English tea, that smuggling grew apace (like bootlegging of whiskey later in history). Sales of East India tea fell in both Great Britain and the American colonies. In Great Britain alone, the East India company was losing £400,000 per year to smuggling. To reduce these losses, Parliament lowered the import duty on tea. Then, to make up for the lost revenue, imposed new taxes in the American colonies, originally to help pay the cost of maintaining an army in North America. Later, the British decided to instead transfer funding for colonial governors and judges from the colonists to Great Britain and use income from the new taxes to pay for them. In a single stroke Great Britain would (1) raise money to pay its war debt; (2) establish the precedent of taxing the colonies; (3) shift the loyalty of judges and governors from the colonies to London; and, (4) reduce—or perhaps even eliminate—the power of the colonies to raise their own revenues.

Opposition to the taxes was slow to begin, but once started it began to accelerate. Boycotts were organized, then the Massachusetts House of Representatives mounted a campaign against the Townshend Acts, enlisting other colonies. The fifty-gun warship *HMS Romney* was sent to Boston, and the troops were dispatched to the colony. John Hancock's sloop *Liberty* was seized. Riots began. Hancock was prosecuted in a highly-publicized trial, defended by his lawyer, John Adams, but the charges were dropped.

As protests mounted, the British Parliament finally repealed most of the taxes, but retained the duty on tea on the grounds that keeping it made clear "the right of taxing the Americans."[3]

Historian Robert Chaffin argued that little had actually changed:

It would be inaccurate to claim that a major part of the Townshend Acts had been repealed. The revenue-producing tea levy, the American Board of Customs and, most important, the principle of making governors and magistrates independent all remained. In fact, the modification of the Townshend Duties Act was scarcely any change at all.[4]

After changes in the tax law, ships loaded with tea were dispatched to New York, Philadelphia, Charleston and Boston. In Charleston, the tea was confiscated by customs officials. In Philadelphia, the ships were turned away and returned to England. In New York, when bad weather delayed the ship, the consignees to whom it was to be delivered resigned, and the ship had no choice but to return home. In Boston, however, three ships successfully made port. The governor, two of whose sons were to receive part of the tea, refused to allow the ships to leave. The *Dartmouth*, *Eleanor* and *Beaver* all remained in port.

More than any other group, the "Sons of Liberty," a group determined to break the American colonies away from England, was responsible for the Tea Party. The Sons had repeatedly incited protests, and were known for tarring and feathering those sympathetic to England. It included men whose names were to later become indelibly associated with the Revolution: Samuel and John Adams, as well as John Hancock, for example. There was one other, however, whose name has passed out of memory but whose contribution to the Revolution was at least as equal as any, and more than most. That was Dr. Samuel Warren.

Incited by the Sons of Liberty, over 5,000 people gathered at the Old South Meeting House, then the largest public building in Boston, at 10:00 a.m. on December 16, 1773, to decide what was to be done about the tea and to plan the Boston Tea Party.[5] Dr. Warren was among them.[6]

A member of the committee appointed by the Boston Town Meeting to request that the British troops be removed from Boston after the Boston Massacre in 1770, Warren also drafted the "Suffolk Resolves," a predecessor to the Declaration of Independence. Although commissioned a major general in the Revolutionary army, Warren chose to fight as a common soldier at the battle of Bunker Hill on June 17, 1775.

Those who participated in the original Boston Tea Party were overwhelmingly young. Two-thirds of those whose ages were known were under 20, including 16 teenagers. Only nine are known to have been 40 years old or older.[7] This is in sharp contrast to the modern tea partiers.

Study the photographs. There is no Crispus Attucks among them, for the faces are uniformly, apparently universally, white. The hair tends to be gray. They are likely seated in lawn chairs or on blankets. They are stirred not to action, but speeches. One veteran reporter, Chip Berlet, described them as follows: "the movement's rank and file tend to be significantly more often white and a little bit wealthier. But what most people in the Tea Party have in common is that they get their information from a very narrow range of sources: Fox News, talk radio, and right-wing publications."[8]

Today, those who object to government have representation, unlike the American colonists. Today, there are no foreign troops. There have been no savage confrontations and deaths. Troops are not hunting men by name. There is no appointed royal governor, but instead one who is elected, as are virtually all other officials with significant authority.

A tea party rally today is likely to have resulted from a billionaire writing a check. The Tea Party of 1773 followed a succession of mass meetings. On November 29, 1773, between 5,000 and 7,000 people attended the mass meeting called by Samuel Adams—so many that it had to be moved from Faneuil Hall to the larger Old South Meeting House. Then, the meeting of "The Body of the People" was spontaneous, and was triggered by the arrival of a ship loaded with tea.[9] Today, a Tea Party rally is likely to have been pre-arranged, with reserved buses and box lunches.[c]

---

[c] At a July 2010 protest of plans to help restore and safeguard the Florida Everglades, sugar producer Florida Crystals fueled the tea party protest by providing participants with free charter bus transportation and box lunches. Andy Reid, *Sun Sentinel*, "Tea party protesters target Crist's Everglades land deal with U.S. Sugar," July 14, 2010. This is the rule, not the exception. See the agenda for another rally, this one sponsored by

(continued...)

The colonists met again on November 30, and still again after that. For almost three weeks, mass meetings at Old South Meeting House tried to find a way to prevent the tea from being unloaded. Today, tea partiers arrive for a Saturday or Sunday afternoon in the sunshine, then return to their homes.

The final meeting of the People was on December 16, 1773. They asked the owner of the *Dartmouth*, Francis Rotch, to make a personal plea to the appointed Acting Royal Governor Hutchinson for permission to leave the harbor without unloading the tea. The colonists were seeking a legal way to refuse the unwanted tea.[10]

Rotch made the long journey to Milton, asked for and was denied permissions to leave Boston Harbor, returned to the Old South Meeting House, where it was near evening so candles had been lighted. When Rotch delivered the news, Samuel Adams declared: "This meeting can do nothing more to save the country!" Many took this to be a signal for the Sons of Liberty to seize the ships and dump their cargo of tea.[11]

There is nothing in the actions of today's tea partiers that even faintly resembles the patience and resolve of those who called for or participated in the Boston Tea Party of 1773.

Those men risked their lives, their freedom and their property. In contrast, today's movement is built on scapegoating, demonization and fear. The Tea Party of 1773 was built on a desire for freedom. Today, many of the tea partiers are also members of "militia," but they bear little resemblance to the Minutemen who were roused from their beds by Paul Revere. They are vigilantes who murder doctors like Dr. George Tiller at his church's entrance, because he provided abortions.

Yet can any different outcome be expected when Republican/Libertarian/ Tea Party (RLTP) politicians put cross hairs on their opponents, as the then-Governor of Alaska Sarah Palin did after the health insurance debate. A commentator on Fox television, she displayed a map of the country targeting specific Congressional districts with cross hairs and the comment "Reload."[12]

---

[c] (...continued)
the billionaire Koch-brothers-funded Americans for Prosperity at
http://gainesvilleteaparty.org/state-fl-info/americans-for-prosperity-tally-rally-latest-info/,
accessed May 1, 2012. A third example was a rally of the Jefferson County (Missouri) Tea Party on March 12, 2012, http://www.jeffcoteaparty.com/2012/03/06/hands-off-my-health-care-afp-rally/, accessed May 2, 2012.

Should it come as a surprise that one of those on Palin's list, was Gabrielle Giffords, the Arizona congresswoman who was shot outside a Tucson Safeway?[13]

The backbone of the Revolution and the events that led up to it were the militia, a term that those who armed themselves today with concealed weapons like to use to describe themselves. In the revolutionary era, militias were formed locally, and called out in times of trouble, such as Indian attacks or war with the French. When the fighting was over, they turned in their muskets, flints and powder and returned home.[14]

Not so today.

When Timothy McVeigh returned home from the Iraq War, he renewed his acquaintance with Terry Nichols. After meeting with Michigan militia, they formed their own small "cell." Calling themselves the "Patriots," they stockpiled several tons of ammonium nitrate explosive. Then on April 19, 1995 McVeigh detonated a 4,800 pound bomb at the Alfred P. Murrah Federal Building in Oklahoma City, Oklahoma, killing 168 people. Many of them were children in the building's day care center.[15] Enraged and not knowing the killers were American, protestors attacked Mosques and Muslims throughout the nation.[16]

Today's tea partiers bask in the reflected glory of revolutionaries who gave their lives. They appropriate for their own selfish and self serving ends the names of Samuel Adams,[17] Ethan Allen,[18] James Madison[19] and scores of others. They draw about themselves the cloak of sacrifice, but of themselves give little. There are no brutal winters, days of starvation and frigid winters with few blankets or little fire.

By 2012, they much more resembled Alice's Tea Party, with participants acting very much like the Mad Hatter and the March Hare. The modern Tea Party factions are products of money from corporations and the rich, especially Charles and David Koch, the oil-rich multi-billionaire brothers from Wichita, Kansas. They employed former House Majority (Republican) Leader Dick Armey from Texas. Using two Washington, D.C.-based front groups, FreedomWorks and American Progress, they created out of whole cloth a movement paid for by the rich, advocating an agenda that favors the rich and publicized by networks and newspapers owned by the rich.

The original Tea Party was also a struggle against history's greatest monopoly, the East India Tea Company's economic interests, to whom the British had granted a monopoly on the export of tea to the American colonies. Today's tea parties are *paid for* by the same sort of economic interests against which the colonists struggled.

Today's Tea Party is, in short, attempting to undo the very interests and philosophies against which America revolted by stealing its heritage. Their premise is that the Revolution and much of America's history since has been marked by tax protests. This is a lie.

Those who organize the tea parties of the 21st century, would have us believe that Americans hate taxes. We even fought a revolution because of them. But is that true?

Not really. Certainly not to the degree that so-called "tea party" protests since 2009 would have us believe. As Reuven S. Avi-Yonah, professor of law at the University of Michigan, wrote in the *New York Times*—

> (T)he remarkable fact is that there were no significant tax protests in the U.S. between the 1790s and the 1970s. In fact, as recently as the 1970s the federal income tax was considered the fairest tax, at a time when the top rate was over 70 percent.[20]

But, one might argue, the folks said to identify with one or more of the "Tea Party" protests surely hate taxes. They're just ordinary Americans, tired of big government, the spending it brings and the taxes that the spending requires. Tea Party protests are spontaneous outbursts by garden variety Americans against taxes and the government spending that leads to their increase. But are they, really? Not according to Avi-Yonah.

In his view, starting with the election of Ronald Reagan, Republicans have sought to vilify the income tax. Polls show this.

Yet Reagan raised taxes twice, once in 1982 and again in 1986. Reagan's vice president, George H.W. Bush, promised "no new taxes" then broke his pledge and lost his re-election bid to Clinton in 1992. But, for sure, it has become difficult for Republicans to raise taxes. Even in the face of two unexpected wars, a huge budget deficit and the worst economic downturn since the Great Depression, Republicans have, in virtual lock-step, opposed tax increases.

In 2011, for example, 238 of 242 House Republicans and 41 out of 47 Senate Republicans signed the Americans for Tax Reform (ATR) "Taxpayer

Protection Pledge."[d] Whether Americans hate no new taxes or not, ATR, headed by Republican activist Grover Norquist, has successfully bullied officials of the Grand Old Party into adopting what former Sen. Alan Simpson (R.WY.), co-chairman of the National Commission on Fiscal Responsibility and Reform, has described as a policy of "[n]o taxes, under any situation, even if your country goes to hell."[e]

The current wave of tax protests are a reflection of this post-1992, Norquist-driven Republican mentality. The tea party "protests" are engineered by political operatives and are far from reflective of general public attitudes toward taxes or toward the government, said Avi-Yonah.

Yet the common, widespread belief today is that objections to taxes caused what is now the United States to revolt against, and win independence from, Great Britain, and that this sentiment has persisted in the United States in the intervening two plus centuries.

Another revolt, called Shays' Rebellion, was supposedly also against taxes. Yes, it caused the Constitution to be written and the nation as we know it to be formed. Thus, it is a useful background against which to judge the Tea Party movement, and other developments of the recent past. What it suggests is that Shays' Rebellion was not as much against taxes as in protest of those who, in 1786, were the counterparts of the contemporary funders of the tea party. In other words, it was the rich then; and it's the rich now.

---

[d] Those taking the pledge promise to "oppose any and all efforts to increase the marginal income tax rate for individuals and business; and to oppose any net reduction or elimination of deductions and credits, unless matched dollar for dollar by further reducing tax rates."

[e] Interviewed on CBS network's "60 Minutes," Simpson said of Norquist—
He may well be the most powerful man in America today. So if that's what he wants, he's got it. You know, he's—megalomaniac, ego maniac, whatever you want to call him. If that's his goal, he's damn near there. He ought to run for president because that will be his platform: 'No taxes, under any situation, even if your country goes to hell.' Simpson also wants to know where Norquist and Americans for Tax Reform, with its multimillion dollar budget gets its money.
Simpson: When you get this powerful, and he is, then it's, 'Where do you get your scratch, Grover?' Is it two people? Is it 10 million people? The American people demand to know where you get your money, Grover babe.
The Pledge: Grover Norquist's hold on the GOP, "60 Minutes," http://www.cbsnews.com/8301-18560_162-57327816/the-pledge-grover-norquists-hold-on-the-gop/?pageNum=4&tag=contentMain;contentBody accessed April 18, 2012

They would have us believe that revolts, especially against taxes, are a huge part of American history, whether it was the "Whiskey Rebellion" against a new U.S. tax on whiskey, which George Washington himself put down, or the "Tea Party" bus rides and rallies of 2009–12. There can be no doubt that the revolts of the past were real. In some of them, Americans lost their lives.

But exactly how real are the newest protests, which are supposedly grass roots outcries, such as the Tea Party Patriot rallies? ("Tea Party Patriots: the Second American Revolution.")[21] Or those of the Tea Party Express ("Propelled by millions of Tea Party supporters across the country, Tea Party Express has become the most aggressive and influential national Tea Party group in the political arena. "We are committed to identifying and supporting conservative candidates and causes that will champion tea party values...")[21] Or the Tea Party of the Patriot Action Network? ("(T)he nation's largest conservative social action network, serving hundreds of thousands of citizens every month.")[22]

The various Tea Parties are paid for by billionaires, such as Charles and David Koch, ranked as the 17th richest people in the world by *Fortune* magazine. The Tea Parties are led by veteran politicians, such as the former House Republican Majority Leader, Dick Armey. Their day-to-day legal work is done by law partners who once worked for the Republican National Committee and the Republican Senatorial Campaign Committee. Yet they profess to speak for ordinary new-to-the-action Americans.

Protests against taxes—whether called the Tea Party, Proposition 13 or Shays' Rebellion—are nothing new in the United States, nor is the Republican Party's opposition to them. Time and again, Republicans (with some exceptions, such as Robert la Follette of Wisconsin) have rushed to the aid of their wealthy patrons to stave off taxes.

In 1909, when Congress began considering approval of a federal income tax, the Republican majority leader and Finance Committee chairman, Nelson W. Aldrich of Rhode Island, pledged that there would be "no income tax, no inheritance tax, no stamp tax, no corporation tax."[23, f] Do any of those strike a familiar chord?

---

[f] Described as tall, aristocratic, self possessed and socially charming, Aldrich "wore his crown of kingship as one who did not feel its weight on his head." His clients included railroads, bankers and industrialists. One newspaper columnists wrote that his job was to "prevent, emasculate or postpone legislation which threatens to interfere with the profits of big business" including postal reforms, employers' liability, conservation, eight-hour legislation, bank depositor security and regulation of corporations.

Current opposition to the inheritance tax is led by Republican anti-tax crusader Grover Norquist, who calls it the "death tax." He compares it to the slaughter of 6 million Jews.[g] A tax is equivalent to slaughtering 6 million men, women and children? It is the equivalent of making lampshades of the skins of some and performing medical experiments on others? Calling a levy on the estates of millionaires a death tax is one thing. Comparing that to the Holocaust is quite another.

But what of the corporate tax, which Sen. Aldrich opposed. According to Fox News, which ran a column by Sen. John Barasso (R.WY.), the highest corporate tax rate in the world is in the United States. "Workers bear most of the burden of high business taxes through lower wages. Consumers pay for some of the cost in the form of higher prices. Senior citizens pay some through lower dividends from the stocks in their retirement account," he counseled.[24]

Perhaps accurate. Definitely misleading.

Corporations pay taxes, not rates. The U.S. tax rate for corporations may be high, but it is easily avoided by simply shifting the corporate headquarters on paper to another country or even a specific city within it. In Zug, Switzerland, for

---

[g] During an interview on the National Public Radio show Fresh Air, Norquist claimed that the estate tax is just as immoral as genocide, because both target only a minority of the population:
Norquist: That's the morality of the Holocaust. "Well, it's only a small percentage," you know. "I mean, it's not you, it's somebody else." [...]
Terry Gross: Excuse me. Excuse me one second. Did you just —
Norquist: Yeah?
Terry Gross: — compare the estate tax with the Holocaust?
Norquist: No, the morality that says it's OK to do something to do a group because they're a small percentage of the population its the morality that says that the Holocaust is OK because they didn't target everybody, just a small percentage. What are you worried about? It's not you. It's not you. It's them. And arguing that it's OK to loot some group because it's them, or kill some group because it's them and because it's a small number, that has no place in a democratic society that treats people equally. [...]
Terry Gross: So you see taxes as being the way they are now terrible discrimination against the wealthy comparable to the kind of discrimination of, say, the Holocaust?
Norquist: Well, what you pick—you can use different rhetoric or different points for different purposes, and I would argue that those who say, 'Don't let this bother you; I'm only doing it—I, the government. The government is only doing it to a small percentage of the population. That is very wrong. And it's immoral. They should treat everybody the same. They shouldn't be shooting anyone, and they shouldn't be taking half of anybody's income or wealth when they die. http://www.nndb.com/people/482/000049335/, accessed April 17, 2012.

example, the corporate tax rate is 15 to 16 percent, less than half of the 35 percent rate in the United States.

The human population of the town of Zug is 26,000; the corporate population is greater, at 30,000 and growing. About 800 corporations a year call Zug their new home, although many are no more than mailboxes.

Texas Democratic Congressman Lloyd Doggett questions whether the recent moves of several companies are legitimate. "A good example is one of my Texas companies that's been in the news lately, Transocean," Rep. Doggett told Lesley Stahl of CBS News "60 minutes" in a segment aired on March 25, 2011.[25]

Transocean owned the drilling rig involved in the giant BP oil spill. It moved to Zug in 2009. Doggett says that Transocean still has about 1,300 employees in its Houston office. "They have 12 or 13 in Switzerland," he added. Another Texas company that moved to Zug is Weatherford, a $10 billion oil field services firm. It still has 2,800 workers in Houston.

In 2004, Congress tried to halt the practice of moving offshore to save taxes by mandating the 35 percent payments. But that didn't stop the exodus. On the contrary, there is now a scramble among nations to lower their corporate tax rates for the purpose of attracting businesses. Japan lowered its rate in April 2012.[26] Across Western Europe, in Asia and in developed countries, governments are following suit in a race to the bottom. And, just as the rats, and later the children, followed the Pied Piper of Hamelin, so, too, are corporations being lured to low tax nations.

The corporate tax rate in Ireland, for example, is 12.5 percent, according to John Chambers, the head of Cisco, the giant high tech company headquartered in San Jose, California. "Almost everybody is in Ireland," said economist Martin Sullivan. "All the pharmaceutical companies, all the high tech companies. You're stupid if you're not in Ireland," he replied. Chambers concurs. Cisco has eight companies there.

Sen. Aldrich pledged in 1909 that there would be no corporate tax, a promise remindful of George H.W. Bush's in New Orleans in 1988 when he accepted the Republican nomination for President:

> "Congress will push me to raise taxes," George Bush told the
> whooping Republican delegates at the party's convention in New
> Orleans (pronounced 'N'awlins' by the natives, and not, as David

Brinkley assured Peter Jennings, 'New Or-le-ans'), "and I'll say no, and they'll push, and I'll say no, and they'll push again, and I'll say to them, 'Read my lips: no new taxes.'"[27]

Republican opposition to taxes, however, depends on who pays them. If it's the ordinary working stiff, taxes are OK. There are few better illustrations of this than "Shays' Rebellion" of 1786–87 in Massachusetts, when the state's merchants and bankers were all too happy to tax the farmers who had survived the hardships of the American Revolution in order to fill the pockets of the many others who had not. Shays' Rebellion was in many ways responsible for the drafting and adoption of the U.S. Constitution and the creation of the United States as we now know it, but at the time it was merely a struggle by farmers to survive in a hostile state.

It all began on an unseasonably cool day in western Massachusetts only ten years and two weeks after the signing of the Declaration of Independence.[h] Those who had fought in the Revolution were paid, but not in money. Instead, they were issued "notes," or promises by the state to pay.

The value of the notes eroded severely. Those issued in April 1778 initially traded at one-quarter of their face value. By 1781, they had plummeted to one-fortieth of their face value. Farmers in western Massachusetts, in the grips of a recession and those who had served in the Revolution left with no pay, had no choice but to sell the notes to speculators at pennies on the dollar. The men needed salt and nails, and had to pay taxes.

In other states, legislatures redeemed the notes at the prices paid for them, not their face value. In Virginia, for example, a note was worth only one-thousandth of its face value.

But in Massachusetts, the legislature was dominated by merchants and bankers. Many of them had bought Massachusetts notes at vastly discounted prices. It decided to redeem the notes at full face value, "a bonanza for speculators." And, to add insult to injury, it added interest at the rate of 6 percent per year.

According to one report, 80 percent of the state debt that resulted from pricing the notes at face value made its way into the hands of speculators who lived

---

[h] This account of Shays' Rebellion is based almost entirely on Leonard L. Richards' masterfully documented and authoritative *Shays's Rebellion: The American Revolution's Final Battle*, University of Pennsylvania Press, Philadelphia, PA (2002).

in or near Boston, and 40 percent went to only 35 men. Of these, all either themselves served in the state legislature, or had relatives who did.

The men who bought the notes were politically powerful. Williams Phillips, for example, was president of the state's only bank. He accumulated £28,000 in state notes.

That, however, was not the end of the story. To pay for the cost of redeeming the notes, special taxes were imposed. One "Old Soldier," as he was identified in the *Massachusetts Gazette* and the *Hampshire Herald*, sold his notes at one-quarter of the face value. Then he was taxed to pay to the holder of the note the three-quarters that he had lost when it was redeemed.

If, in fact, the Old Soldier received 25 percent of the face value, he was fortunate. Most veterans were paid only 10 or 15 percent. Then, they had to pay the five-fold increase in taxes in hard money. Bartered goods—wool or livestock, crops or food—could not be used, only hard cash.

Even worse, the legislature decided to enact two taxes to pay for the cost of redeeming notes. Only 10 percent would be raised by import duties and excise taxes, which would have been levied principally on industrialists and the rich. The remaining 90 percent was to come from a poll tax—that is, a levy for every male aged 16 years or older (sons, for most farmers), and property, especially land. Thus, the legislature took square aim at the very men who had been forced to sell notes at, say, ten cents on the dollar, and taxed them to pay speculators' profits of 900 percent, plus interest.

Taxes imposed by the state were oppressive—many times greater, than those levied by the British on the eve of the American Revolution. Time and again, the towns of western Massachusetts attempted in vain to reverse the laws, but failed. Finally, in frustration, the men of western Massachusetts rose up in a rage and launched Shays' Rebellion.

Reasoning that the most effective way to halt foreclosures and sentences to debtor's prison was to shut the courts that would order them, 1,500 angry farmers converged on August 29, 1786 at the Northampton courthouse and shut it. The judges attempted on September 5th to meet in Worcester, but 300 bayonet wielding farmers blocked their way. In Middlesex, Plymouth and Berkshire Counties more courts were shut, and in late September even the Massachusetts Supreme Court was barred from meeting in Springfield.[28]

Governor James Bowdoin attempted to put down the insurrection by calling out the militia, but in vain. Roughly one-half of the farmers were veterans of the Revolution, and many of the former comrades in arms refused to fight them.

What is most striking about the farmers who rose up in arms was their unity. As historian Leonard Richards wrote—

> Throughout the backcountry, the predilection of family, kin and community generally prevailed. That was especially true in Scots-Irish towns like Colrain and Pelham. They had a long tradition of sticking together. They also had a long tradition of resisting outside authority. For them, assembling a company of warriors was relatively easy. But it also seems to have been relatively easy for tight-knit communities that came out of New England Puritan tradition. What is striking about most of the rebels is that they came out of unified cultures. Class divisions are almost impossible to find. Towns that supported the Regulation (revolt) were not divided, rich versus poor, creditor versus debtor. As a rule, people either moved as one or did not participate.

As 1787 began, Bowdoin had no help from other states or the national government. But he collected enough money from 150 wealthy merchants to raise a private army under the command of Revolutionary War General Benjamin Lincoln to secure "system and order." Lincoln was a stark contrast to the man for whom the rebellion was named, Daniel Shays.

Shays had been an officer in the Revolution, but unlike others he had started in the enlisted ranks, rose to sergeant, then captain. He was so highly regarded that Marquis de Lafayette honored him with a sword. Little else is known of Shays, except that he was a farmer working hard scrabble land.

Shays was by no means the only one of the rebels with a distinguished war record. Some were war heros, known for their bravery not just in Massachusetts, but throughout New England. Captain Adam Wheeler, for example, fought in both the French and Indians War and the Revolution, and had been singled out for conspicuous bravery. He called out for men in his hometown to join in the insurrection. "Liberty," he said "is the prize."

Shays and the other rebel leaders decided to confront Lincoln's force by seizing the federal arsenal in Springfield, which contained several field pieces, 7,000 new muskets with bayonets and 1,300 barrels of powder. The rebels were armed with only, at best, old muskets, some swords or bludgeons. The stores at the arsenal would enable them to fight with newer and better weapons.

Unfortunately for them, their adversary, Major General William Shepherd, anticipated their assault on the federal armory and got there first. The rebels outnumbered Shepherd two-to-one, but communication was complicated because they were divided into three regiments. Moreover, Shepherd had artillery.

A message from one regimental commander attempting to delay the attack by one day was intercepted. Two of the regiments attacked as planned. Shepherd lowered his cannon fire to waist-level, loaded with grapeshot, a mass of slugs loaded into a canvas bag, and fired. Four were killed, and 30 wounded, one mortally. The panicked rebels fled into the snow, continuing their retreat until the early morning of Sunday, February 4th, when they awoke surrounded by Lincoln and his men. They had marched through the night in a blizzard, strung out by drifts into a line five miles long.

With no time to call in other parties or even guards, Shays and the other rebel leaders slipped away, fleeing north across the border into New Hampshire and into Vermont, which was then a wild and dangerous land. Most of the rank-and-file also escaped capture.

The rebels attempted to persuade Ethan Allen, commander of the Green Mountain Boys to take command. Even though he considered the leaders in Massachusetts to be a "pack of Damned Rascals," Allen declined the offer. So did the Canadians and British.

Daniel Shays eventually settled in western New York, where he died in 1825 at the age of 78, having outlived Bowdoin by 32 years and Lincoln by 15.

Shays Rebellion was by no means the last tax revolt in the United States. Colonial officials were so alarmed by Shays' near success that they drafted and adopted a new Constitution, creating a much more powerful central government located in Washington, D.C. Under its first president, George Washington, the government imposed a tax on whiskey, which farmers in western Pennsylvania refused to pay.

One notable historian, William Hoagland, insists that the Whiskey Rebellion was not a revolt against taxes *per se*—

> They wanted taxes to be fair, which to them meant progressive. They
> were not anti-government. They demanded that government invest

not in the finance class but in them, easing their access to credit and economic growth.[29]

"Unlike the so-called 'tea parties' going on now," wrote Hoagland, "it was a revolt not against taxes and government spending but in favor of progressive taxation and government fairness."

The tax was created by Washington's Secretary of the Treasury, Alexander Hamilton. It focused on the one product where small farmers were able to compete against large distillers, whiskey. Its purpose was to use the power of government to drive small operations out of business and restructure the American economy along efficient British lines. Hamilton dedicated the proceeds of the whiskey tax to paying reliable interest to upscale investors in the securitized Revolutionary War debt.

On the face of it, the various tea parties would seem to be merely the latest in the line of tax protests. These have typically been described at grounds-up, grassroots protests, often started by individual citizens.

USA Today, for example, wrote that after the bankruptcy of her husband's business, Jenny Beth Martin and he were cleaning houses in Atlanta to stay afloat when they "heard about a tirade against President Obama's mortgage bailout scheme by a financial news analyst calling for a modern-day Boston Tea Party revolt.

"We had just lost our house and had … moved into the rental house." said Martin. "I didn't want other people paying for my mortgage, and I wanted to prevent that in other places."

She started what is now Tea Party Patriots. Her action and others like it, wrote *USA Today*, "started out as a handful of people blogging about their anger over federal spending—the bailouts, the $787 billion stimulus package and Obama's budget," the paper wrote, "has grown into scores of so-called tea parties across the country."

"The goal is to pressure Congress and states to reject government spending as a way out of the recession and build an anti-spending coalition around regular taxpayers," it concluded.

But is it really that simple?

15
THE "NEW" TEA PARTY GROUPS

Members of the elite agree on the basic outlines of the free enterprise system including profits, private property, the unequal and concentrated distribution of wealth, and the sanctity of private economic power. They take giantism in the world of commerce for granted. More important, they are united in their belief that the primary responsibility of government is to maintain a favorable climate for business. Other governmental responsibilities, such as social welfare and concern for the environment, are secondary to that task.

"The Power Elite,"
University of Delaware[a]

The premise of the Tea Party is that it is a bottoms-up group—a bunch of local organizations, operating in an unconnected, uncoordinated way, a sort of sage brush wildfire of Americans fed up with government (mostly federal, but when it suits them, state or local as well).

In the words of the immortal Colonel Potter of *MASH*, the TV series, "horse hockey."

Exactly when and where the so-called "tea partys" of the 21st century started is unknown. But does it matter? As the saying goes, "Success has many fathers, while failure is an orphan." By almost any measure the tea party seems to have been a resounding success. There is no scarcity of those claiming paternity.

Two years after Democrat Barack Obama was elected President, his party was ignominiously dumped from control of the House of Representatives. In a map of the United States showing Republican gains in red, the country looks like

---

[a] http://www.udel.edu/htr/Psc105/Texts/power.html, accessed Sept. 30, 2012.

somebody butchered a pig. And it wasn't just the breadth of the loss, but the depth: Republicans didn't just win, but won with 70, 80 and 85 percent of the vote.[1]

When and where the tea party began is—except for the lesson that may hold for the future—irrelevant. The important question to ask is "what is it?"

Was it a spontaneous uprising of average citizens? Fox News says so, explaining that people were driven to the streets by "federal spending and intervention that many fear will lead to a crushing tax burden."[2]

Or was it a grassroots movement that was, in the words of the *New York Times*, "more of the Astroturf variety: an occasion largely created by the clamor of cable news and fueled by the financial and political support of current and former Republican leaders."?

Whatever it was—is——there can be no doubt that some very, very rich people or corporations were backing the movement. One of principal groups, Tea Party Patriots, received an anonymous donation of $1 million, which it says was spread around to chapters throughout the country.[3] Even for a multi-millionaire, that's not pocket change, so the giver must have been plenty rich—a billionaire, say.

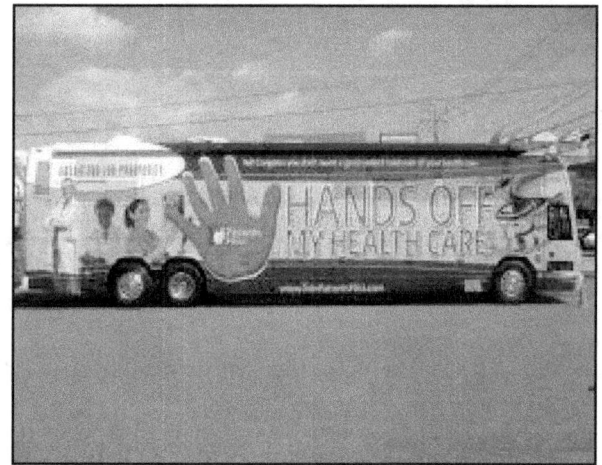

The Americans for Prosperity "Patients First" bus that goes to tea party rallies.

Unquestionably, there are ordinary citizens involved in some of these protests. The *Washington Post* described a 2009 rally in State College, Pennsylvania. Inside, the meeting was calm, and "many attendees were local residents who said they were motivated to turn out not by conservative groups but by personal opposition to Democratic health-care policies," said the *Post*. Outside, however, was an entirely different story.

Hundreds of protesters outside, wrote the *Post*, were "chanting and holding colorful picket signs bearing the logos of various conservative groups. Americans for Prosperity brought a 'Patients First' bus emblazoned with a giant red hand and the slogan: 'Hands Off Our Health Care!'"

Despite these attempts to make the "movement" appear as spontaneous, bottoms-up events, the principal organizers are often Washington, D.C.-based organizations like Americans for Prosperity and FreedomWorks. Heavily staffed and well funded, the two groups provide the logistical and public relations work necessary for planning coast-to-coast protests. For example:

- Freedom Works staffers coordinate conference calls among protesters, contacting conservative activists to give them "sign ideas, sample press releases, and a map of events around the country." It provides how-to guides for delivering a "clear message" to the public and media.

- Americans for Prosperity writes press releases and planed events in New Jersey, Arizona, New Hampshire, Missouri, Kansas, and several other states.[4]

The evidence suggests that, at the very least, big money was applied to nascent protests like a fertilizer to crops, boosting their growth. That money came from some of the richest people in the world—people who have so benefitted from the current and past rules of conduct in America that they have accumulated wealth beyond that of many nations.

We are not talking money for a half-pint of cheap whiskey, but sums that are immense—the size of the Powerball lottery jackpot, for example. Probably more of the money came from giant corporations, but we will never know. Neither giver nor taker is required by law to reveal the gifts, and nobody seems willing to volunteer that information.

The various tea parties all call themselves local, but that is simply untrue. Yes, perhaps a tea party group is located in, say, Cody, Wyoming or Raleigh, North Carolina, but the money to keep the lights on and the doors open comes from some central source. One of these sources—but by no means the only one—is the Koch brothers, Charles and David.

In the words of the *New Yorker* magazine, the "anti-government fervor infusing the 2010 elections represents a political triumph for the Kochs. By giving money to 'educate,' fund, and organize Tea Party protesters, they have helped turn their private agenda into a mass movement."

David and Charles were born into wealth. Each attended the Massachusetts Institute of Technology and was raised at the knee of father Fred, one of the founders of the John Birch Society.

David and Charles took Fred's hundreds of millions, doubled it down, then again, and again until they became richer than many nations. In 2011, *Forbes* ranked them as tied as the fourth richest people in the United States[5] and the twelfth richest in the world.[6] Their combined net worth of $50 billion exceeds the gross domestic product (GDP) of all but 73 of the world's 191 nations.[7] Their company, Koch Industries, see-saws with Cargill as the largest privately- owned company in the United States.[8]

If Koch Industries had been a public company in 2007, it would rank about 16 in the Fortune 500.[9] The list of brand names and products owned by the Kochs is a veritable Who's Who of world goods. They own Brawny paper towels, Angel Soft toilet paper, Mardi Gras napkins and towels, Quilted Northern toilet paper and paper towels, Dixie paper plates, bowls, napkins and cups, Sparkle paper towels, and Vanity Fair paper napkins, bowls, plates and tablecloths. Chances are you have wolfed down a burger made from Koch beef, jogged in Spandex, walked on its Stainmaster carpet, ridden on tires made with its Lycra or even bought a Koch home.

There are many groups through which the Koch brothers peddle influence, but when the subject is the Tea Party, chief among them is Americans for Prosperity, which cannot be examined without looking at another organization, FreedomWorks.

FreedomWorks and its sibling, Americans for Prosperity, were created when two other organizations went their apparently separate ways. The two earlier organizations, Citizens for a Sound Economy (CSE) and Citizens for a Sound Economy Foundation (CSEF), were both founded and funded by the Kochs.

CSE was founded in 1984. Its mission was "to fight for less government, lower taxes, and less regulation."[10] Founded by Charles and David Koch, CSE was for many years home to George H.W. Bush's White House Counsel, C. Boyden Gray, as he organized American corporations to fight strengthening of the Clean Air Act.[11] CSEF was also created in 1984.

In 2004, the two split. CSE became FreedomWorks, while CSEF became Americans for Prosperity. After the split, Richard Armey ran FreedomWorks, while Koch Industries' chief lobbyist Nancy Mitchell Pfotenhauer ran Americans for Prosperity, before leaving to act as Sen. John McCain's spokesperson during the 2008 presidential campaign.

Americans for Prosperity is now headed by Art Pope, a former North Carolina legislator who has been credited with engineering the GOP takeover of the state's General Assembly in 2010 with attack-ad blitzes in a handful of key districts. RLTPs now control both chambers of the legislature for the first time since 1870. This new majority is responsible for the anti-gay Amendment 1, attacks on sea-level science, deep cuts to public education, and a green light for fracking. Pope and David Koch founded AFP.[12]

FreedomWorks has ceased to rely on the Kochs' generosity, but still receives very large contributions from other front-group foundations. For example, in 2007 it received $1 million from the T. Boone Pickens Foundation.[13] In 2008, AFP received a like amount from the David H. Koch Foundation.[14]

FreedomWorks - The prime mover and public face of FreedomWorks is Richard "Dick" Armey, a former Texas Republican Congressman and House Majority Leader. Dana Millbank, writing in the *Washington Post* described him as "the unofficial leader of the anti-Washington 'tea party' movement."[15]

Unlike some others, Armey doesn't hesitate to link the tea party to the Republican Party. In September 2011, FreedomWorks announced that it will create a "Super PAC"—a group that can legally collect and spend unlimited amounts of money with running ads for or against political candidates—with the goal of raising $20 million during the 2012 election cycle.[16]

Armey said FreedomWorks planned to activate over a million Tea Party volunteers during the 2012 cycle. Unlike other PACs, which focus on supporting the candidates of one party or the other, FreedomWorks Super PAC plans to be highly active in Republican primaries, hoping to help fiscally conservative candidates prevail in races in Florida, Arizona and elsewhere. The group is already seeking the defeat of Orrin G. Hatch, the veteran Republican senator from Utah.[17]

"We are not interested in getting Republicans elected," said Matt Kibbe, the group's president. "We're interested in getting fiscal conservatives elected."[18]

[Not everything that Kibbe says can be trusted, however. For example, when he wrote an op-ed posted at Forbes.com, "Organizers planned for 100,000 Tea Party activists to show up on the National Mall, but more than one million turned out."[19] Yet ABC News reported that "approximately 60,000 to 70,000 people flooded Pennsylvania Ave," citing estimates by the Washington D.C. Fire Department.[20] The *New York Times* placed the number of demonstrators at "well into the tens of thousands, though the police declined to estimate the size of the crowd."[21]]

FreedomWorks has been almost spectacularly successful at establishing training programs for tea party activists, but leaves very few, if any, fingerprints.

One of those credited with being a "founder" of the tea party is Keli Carender of Seattle, Washington. She is not exactly what most people think of: Carender has a pierced nose, performs improv on weekends and lives in a neighborhood with more Mexican grocers than coffeehouses.[22]

Carender's first rally drew only 120 people. A week later, she had 300, and six weeks later, 1,200 people gathered for a Tax Day Tea Party. In January 2010, she was one of about 60 tea party leaders flown to Washington to be trained in election activism by FreedomWorks.

One month later, a year to the day of her first protest, Carender stood among a crowd of about 600 on the steps of the Washington State Capitol in Olympia, acknowledging the thanks from a speaker who cited her as the original Tea Party advocate. Around her were the now-familiar signs: "Can you hear us now?" "Is it 2012 yet?" "Tea Party: the party of now."

Ah, money. What wonders it works.

The Tea Party is a revolution against Washington. Is is a protest against government as we know it. People are galvanized by their hatred of faceless bureaucrats. Yet is has all been brought together by two again billionaires, a life-long politician and a bunch of veteran Washington insiders. They all support change.

Let's get serious—two old rich guys, a pol and a bunch of Washington insiders are inciting change? I don't think so.

"There is particular irony,"wrote the *New York Times*, "in Mr. Armey—who has spent three decades in Washington, where he has become one of the city's most enduring insiders—mentoring a movement that wants to hold on to its outsider ethos."[23]

Americans for Prosperity - These groups are coordinated and funded, tied to one another like the hip bone to the thigh bone. Probably some of them genuinely believe that tea parties are spontaneous. But watch the video at http://www.guardian.co.uk/world/2010/oct/13/tea-party-billionaire-koch-brothers, showing the 17th richest person in the world, David Koch, receiving reports from chapters of Americans for Prosperity.

"Five years ago, my brother Charles and I provided the funds to start Americans for Prosperity," he tells the audience. Then the states report.

"We helped organize huge tea parties all throughout the state," brags a young woman from California.. "And on April 15, Tax Day, over 10,000 Californians joined us on the steps of the state capitol and we held one of the largest tea parties in the country."

"Hey, folks, we've held 29 tea parties," adds another with a distinctive southern drawl. Another says "we have the largest tea parties in the state," another "organized dozens of tea parties." "Remarkable—800,000 activists from nothing 5 years ago," says, Koch, beaming. "This is a phenomenal success," he adds, applauding.

Charles Koch, left, and his brother David, tied as the 17th richest persons on earth, according to Forbes magazine. They provide much of the money for tea party events.

The evidence that this is a top-down movement is everywhere, if you just look.

The Tea Party Federation is an umbrella organization that claims to represent 86 Tea Party groups.[24] Its membership rolls are fairly straightforward, including state and local organizations. More interesting are its affiliates,[25] which include a variety of wealthy organizations such as FreedomWorks, also funded by the Kochs, and the National Taxpayers Union.

"One of the most visible groups is Americans for Prosperity," reported the *Washington Post*, "an anti-tax and anti-regulation group known for opposing smoking restrictions and for trying to cast doubt on global warming. The group launched a project called 'Patients First' in June 2009, and has been conducting bus tours around the country to drum up opposition to the health-care legislation."[26]

In 2010, according to the IRS form 990 tax return filed with the Internal Revenue Service, one of the Koch-controlled[b] foundations, the Claude R. Lambe Charitable Foundation, gave $150,000 to Americans for Prosperity.

Americans for Prosperity has also been deeply involved in politics, almost wholly on the side of Republicans.

The Tea Party Express—termed by the *New York Daily News* as "one of the most influential in the conservative movement"—was once headed by California radio host Mark Williams. He left in 2010 to fight proposed construction of a mosque in Lower Manhattan.. According to the *Daily News*, Express raised $2.3 million in 2010, helped elect Sen. Scott Brown in Massachusetts and organized a rally in Nevada that featured a rare Sarah Palin speech.[27]

Tea Party Patriots (TPP) - Perhaps more than any other group, Tea Party Patriots is demonstrably linked to the Republican Party. According to the *Atlanta Journal-Constitution*, "it wants the government to embrace fiscal responsibility, calls for a constitutionally limited government and urges free-market economics". An "umbrella" organization, TPP claims 1,800 chapters with 15 million members.[28]

> One of the most prominent (Tea Party) organizers is FreedomWorks, a Washington-based advocacy group headed by former House majority leader Richard Armey (R-Tex.) that is also pushing to defeat Democratic cte-change legislation. FreedomWorks' major financial backers have included MetLife, Philip Morris and foundations controlled by the archconservative Scaife family, according to tax filings and other records.
>
> *Washington Post*
> Aug. 16, 2009

TPP was co-founded by Jenny Beth Martin and Mark Meckler (who has since resigned).[29] Saying "every revolution needs icons." *Time* magazine named her in 2010 as one of the 100 most influential people in the world.[30]

Describing Martin's venture into national politics that culminated in September 2010 in a march on Washington, *Time* wrote "It was only as she

---

[b] The directors of the Claude Lambe Foundation include Charles G. Koch, Charles C. Koch, Elizabeth R. Koch and Elizabeth B. Koch. Other directors include Richard H. Fink, head of Koch Industries' Washington office; and, Vonda Holliman, also a Koch Industries' employee (http://www.spoke.com/info/pZWiH00/VondaHolliman, accessed May 3, 2012). The Foundation's address is 1515 N Courthouse Rd, Suite 200 in Arlington Virginia, also the location of the Charles Koch Foundation, the Charles Koch Institute and the Koch Foundation Internship Program, according to the search engine Google on May 3, 2012.

watched protesters trickle down Pennsylvania Avenue to promote Tea Party principles, she says, that 'the enormity of the movement hit me.'"[31]

The next words in the *Time* profile say a great deal, but leave even more unsaid: "*The former Republican consultant* is an unlikely beacon. ..." (emphasis added). The connections to the GOP do not stop there.

On October 25, 2010, Mark Meckler, Treasurer, and Jennifer Martin, President of Tea Party Patriots, entered into a contract for MDS Communications to run a telephone fundraising campaign, starting October 8, 2010. MDS was to keep about 70 percent of the money raised. The rest was to be deposited at First Virginia Community Bank at 11325 Random Hills Road in Fairfax, Virginia,[32] which is used by several Republican candidates for offices in states other than Virginia, according to records at the Federal Election Commission.

MDS is a veteran fundraiser for the Republicans, raising more than $3.6 million in 2007–08 alone for the Republican National Committee.[33] It also works for a variety of front groups active in Republican politics, including the Christian Coalition, the Family Research Council, the National Right to Life Committee and the Rutherford Institute.[34]

The law firm listed for TPP is also tightly connected to the Republican Party.[35] The specific lawyer for TPP was "CWEST" of the firm, Holtzman Vogel Josefiak PLLC ,[c] which has offices in Warrenton, Virginia And Washington, D.C. CWEST is presumably Cathleen West.[d, 36]

The firm is heavily Republican. The two senior partners, Alex N. Vogel and Jill Holtzman Vogel, are both veteran GOP operatives. One, Alex Vogel, was chief counsel to Senate Majority Leader, Bill Frist M.D. of Tennessee, after a stint as General Counsel for the National Republican Senatorial Committee and, before that, Deputy Counsel of the Republican National Committee.[37] Jill Holtzman Vogel, the firm's managing partner, was deputy counsel in the Bush Administration's Department of Energy, also deputy counsel and, later, chief

---

[c] HoltzmanVogelJosefiak PLLC provides counseling and compliance services to individuals, corporations, non-profit organizations, trade associations, PACs, Super PACs and candidates who are engaged in influencing the public policy arena in Washington and across the nation. From http://www.hvjlaw.com/about/Default.aspx accessed March 27, 2012.

[d] Cathleen West, Partner http://www.hvjlaw.com/west/, accessed March 27, 2012.

counsel of the Republican National Committee.[38] In November and December of 2000, both worked on the Florida recount for the Bush-Cheney campaign.

In September 2010, TPP announced it had received a $1,000,000 donation from an anonymous donor. The money was to be distributed to its affiliated groups and had to be spent by Election Day on November 2nd, though it could not be used to directly support any candidate.[39]

American Majority - A relatively recent, but rapidly growing addition to the ranks of tea parties is American Majority, a corporate front for training tea party candidates. Established in January 2008, it "trains and equips a national network of leadership committed to individual freedom through limited government and the free market."

American Majority's goal is to train candidates to run for school board, city council or state senate seats in local areas around the U.S., establishing a system of farm teams to groom candidates for still higher offices.

Ned Ryun, one of the group's founders, says "Today's county commissioner, tomorrow's congressman. You've got to feed the system." Founders, Drew and Ned Ryun are the sons of former Kansas Republican Representative Jim Ryun (whose name may be familiar to some readers as the runner who broke the world record in the mile with a time of 3:51.1 in Bakersfield on June 23, 1967).

Drew Ryun was a deputy director at the Republican National Committee, and Ned was a writer in the George W. Bush White House.[40] Eric O'Keefe, who helps lead American Majority, has been a Koch aide and conservative operative who attends and also helps lead Koch strategy meetings.[41]

American Majority helped organize anti-health care "Recess Rallies" in August 2009. It also worked closely with Michelle Malkin, RedState.com, American Liberty Alliance, Smart Girl Politics, Americans for Limited Government, FreedomWorks, the Sam Adams Alliance and other groups to organize opposition to health care reform.[42] In early May 2012, American Majority posted on its website training programs scheduled in Franklin, Wisconsin; Garland, Texas; West Chester, Ohio; McAlester, Oklahoma; Eagle River, Wisconsin; and, Claremore, Oklahoma.[43]

According to a 2010 article in AlterNet, and Ned Ryun himself, over 75 percent of the funding for American Majority comes from the Sam Adams Alliance. In 2008, the year in which American Majority was founded, 88 percent of the alliance's money came from a single donation of $3.7 million.[44]

It is tempting to dismiss what America's billionaires are up to as merely old wine in new bottles. Somehow, however, the explosive growth of the Tea Parties, the transparent way in which they have been funded by the rich, the stubborn refusal of Partiers to recognize that they are being manipulated, the ease with which new groups are created and political rivals eliminated is starkly different than the ham-handed attempts of the American Liberty League to overthrow the government or the John Birch Society to impeach Earl Warren. These are seriously competent, immensely wealthy men and women, single-mindedly pursuing their goal—making America into a safe haven for the rich.

A few years ago I traveled frequently to Thailand. On one trip, I discovered that the American electric utility, Southern California Edison, was planning to construct a new coal-fired power plant about a two-hour drive south of Bangkok at the small community of Bo Nok in the province of Prachuap Khiri Khan on the coast of the Bay of Thailand. SCE had quietly bought up land through intermediaries, telling villagers that a golf resort was to be built. Billboards lined the highway showing locations of streets, tennis courts and other amenities.

SCE planned to build the plant with no air pollution controls, burning coal brought in over a one-mile pier constructed over one of the few coral reefs in Thailand. When word of the project leaked out, local residents protested, 10,000 of them seizing control of the north-south highway. Former U.S. Secretary of State Warren Christopher, paid by Edison, visited the Thai prime minister and warned that further opposition would jeopardize U.S. government aid to Thailand.

The man who led the opposition to the powerplant, Charoen Wat-aksorn, was a tireless and relentless protector of the province. On the evening of June 21, 2004, as darkness was spreading over Prachuap Khiri Khan, Charoen Wat-aksorn climbed off a local bus, moved toward the highway crossing, and he was shot. The bullet entered his side. He tried to run, was shot again, fell and as he lay on the ground was executed, five bullets in his face, head and chest.

I knew the man. Now, as I recall him, he brings to mind the three civil rights workers, murdered and bull dozed into an earthen dam in 1964; and I wonder why America's billionaires, and the political party they own, are so determined to push the nation over cliffs. Is money really that important?

16
TEA PARTY EXPRESS

I know one thing for sure. Doing nothing is the worst thing we could do. This is one of those once-in-a-century kind of crises, and we need to act to prevent it from becoming a once-in-a-century kind of a recession. In Wisconsin, we are already beginning to see the beginning of this. We are already starting to see the job losses. ... I want to know for sure that when the choice was made, I had made the decision to prevent that storm from gathering, to prevent those jobs from being lost, to protect our constituents from losing their retirement funds, from not getting that home loan, that car loan.

Rep. Paul Ryan (R.Wisc.)
Speaking in Favor of TARP[a]
Oct. 3, 2008

On October 3, 2008, 262 members of the U.S. House of Representatives, 171 Democrats and 91 Republicans, lit a fuse. They voted in favor of, and passed, the Troubled Asset Relief Program, or TARP. The taxpayer-backed bailout program rescued the banks and car companies from bankruptcy, but did nothing to help Americans who had lost their jobs, homes or both.

In the angry protests that followed, a new term, "Tea Party," was added to the vernacular within six months. About six months after that, Democrats lost control of the U.S. House of Representatives, some Republicans were voted out of office and the fledgling Presidency of Barack Obama was jeopardized—all because of spontaneous protests in the grand tradition of America.

Or maybe, just maybe, it was a bit more complicated than that. Perhaps those who truly benefitted from the free spending, low tax, fight-a-war policies of

---

[a] Thomas, U.S. Library of Congress, http://thomas.loc.gov/cgi-bin/query/F?r110:3:./temp/~r110u5CLh2:e668040, accessed Sept. 30, 2012.

Ronald Reagan, George H.W. Bush and George W. Bush, seized the opportunity to cut taxes and spending still further, and advance their agenda to its near completion.

By February 2008, the nation was ablaze with protests against the TARP program, with virtually all of the rage directed against Democrats, especially President Barack Obama. April 15, 2009, when the hapless President had been in office less than 90 days, hundreds of "tax day" protests were staged across the nation.

In the months that followed, the heads of politicians rolled, at least figuratively. In Delaware, moderate Republican Mike Castle, a former governor and member of Congress, was denied the GOP nomination for the U.S. Senate in favor of an unknown, who ultimately lost, Christine O'Donnell.

O'Donnell was against sex education, urged that biblical creationism be taught in schools, and professed a belief that homosexuality is a sickness. Four years before her improbable upset victory, O'Donnell told Delaware's largest newspaper, the *Wilmington News-Journal*, that during the 2006 primary she "heard the audible voice of God." Two years later, during another Senate run, she implored voters: "When you go into the voting booth, ask God which candidate will further the kingdom of God."[1]

Although she and the group later split, leading her to file a lawsuit for unlawful gender discrimination, O'Donnell, had previously worked for the Intercollegiate Studies Institute (ISI).[2, b]

She was, in short, the perfect candidate for a new Tea Party group, the Tea Party Express (TPE). In the final weeks before the primary, the California-based TPE gave her more than $250,000, saying it might spend as much as $600,000 backing her.[3, c] O'Donnell cruised to a primary victory with 53 percent of the

---

[b] ISI sponsors the Collegiate Network, which supports over seventy different free market, libertarian or self-styled "conservative" publications on college and university campuses. Publications include the Harvard Salient, Princeton Tory, Stanford Review, Yale Free Press, Duke Review, the Red and Blue at the University of Pennsylvania and the Virginia Advocate at the University of Virginia. The following foundations give money to ISI: Sarah Scaife, Allegheny, Lynde and Harry Bradley, Earhart, JM, John M. Olin , Philip M. McKenna, Claude R. Lambe, Castle Rock and Carthage. People for the American Way, http://www.rightwingwatch.org/content/intercollegiate-studies, accessed May 8, 2012.

[c] O'Donnell was also endorsed by the Tea Party Express, which called her a "strong voice for conservative constitutionalist principles." Other endorsements came from the pro-life Susan B. Anthony List, the Family Research Council, and the National Rifle Association, and conservative commentators Rush Limbaugh, Sean Hannity, and Mark Levin. Wikipedia,

(continued...)

votes.[4] It was the eighth GOP establishment-backed candidate primary upset of 2010, according to ABC News.[5]

Obviously, the TPE was aiming to defeat those Republicans who had strayed from the fold and supported TARP. Right? Wrong.

* * *

Driving, as I had for surely thousands of times, in my suburban neighborhood of McLean, Virginia, I coasted to a stop at the "T" intersection where candidate yard signs were posted for all to see. One catches my eye. It says that Rep. Frank Wolf, my Congressman for nearly 30 years and a stalwart, middle of road, conventional Republican, was endorsed by the TPE. I have followed Wolf for many years, partially because he represented my district, but also because his campaign had been overseen in 1976 by the same consultant who worked for the late Sen. William V. Roth, Jr. of Delaware, whose re-election campaign I was co-managing.

Taking the risk of rear-ending another motorist, I kept my eyes fixed on the sign in bewilderment. Frank Wolf? The consummate Republican insider? Endorsed by Tea Party Express?

Wow.

Wolf, a Republican, was my member of Congress at the time and the senior member of the Virginia Congressional delegation. A senior House Republican, Wolf voted with the Republican leadership and President, "Yes," on House roll call vote number 681, in favor of the "Motion to Concur in Senate Amendments: H R 1424 Emergency Economic Stabilization Act of 2008."[6]

Wolf kept good company that day, at least so far as Republicans are concerned. Others who voted for the proposal by the Republican President, included the House Republican Leader, Rep. John Boehner of Ohio; the man who would become chair of the House Budget Committee when Republicans regained control of the House in 2010, Rep. Paul Ryan of Wisconsin; the Republican Whip and the man who became the GOP's hard right edge in the next Congress, Rep. Eric Cantor of Virginia; and, a veritable Who's Who of the House Republican leadership.

That being the case, how could Wolf have been endorsed by the TPE. Those guys were up in arms over TARP, dead set on throwing every one of the bums out!

---

[c] (...continued)
"Christine O'Donnell," http://en.wikipedia.org/wiki/Christine_O%27Donnell#cite_ref-86, accessed May 8, 2012.

Yet barely two weeks before the election, on October 15, 2010, Wolf was introduced to a meeting of the Northern Virginia Tea Party. As he strode the podium, the room filled with loud and sustained applause, with a few rebel yells. The audience gave him what the hostess termed "a hearty Tea Party Welcome."[7]

Wolf looked good. He was wearing a gray, four-button suit, and seafoam green tie against a sky-blue button-down shirt. All of the roughly 20 listeners that can be seen are white; most are graying; a half-dozen of the men are balding. No non-whites can be seen.

To hear Wolf tell it, the Obama Administration was responsible for virtually all of the evils afflicting America. He was speaking, Wolf said, "not only as a Congressman, but as the father of five children and the grandfather of 15."

"I have never been more concerned for the country. Economically our country is broke. If we were a business we would be filing for bankruptcy." The United States, said Wolf, was carrying a national debt of $13 trillion, and "a trillion-dollar budget deficit for ten years."

"There will be no money for cancer research, Alzheimer's research, Parkinson's, no money for infrastructure." The largest lenders to the United States "America's bankers" Wolf called them "are the Saudis and the Chinese," he continued, and "I think that's fundamentally wrong."

He said everything they wanted to hear, and was rewarded for it by still more applause. Also, he had the support of the "Tea Party Express," just as Christine O'Donnell from Delaware had. This was the same outfit that nearly cost Sen. Lisa Murkowski of Alaska her seat by defeating her in the Republican primary. She struck back with the most successful write-in campaign in history to win the general election, but she barely dodged the bullet fired at her by the TPE.

In Massachusetts, TPE spent nearly $350,000 to back Scott Brown to a surprise victory to claim the Senate seat once held by Ted Kennedy.[8] Although it ultimately failed, TPE spent more than $1 million in an attempt to defeat Senate Democratic Leader Harry Reid. But Kentucky was not a failure. There, Rand Paul won with 56 percent of the vote.[9]

But what, exactly, is the Tea Party Express?

That question was perhaps best answered on May 8, 2012 at a TPE rally in Austin, Texas. One of the speakers was Rand Paul, the libertarian Senator from

Kentucky elected in 2010 with the TPE's help. Another was his father, Ron Paul, a member of the U.S. House of Representatives and a candidate for the Republican nomination for President.

What Ron Paul said to the crowd would have made the late William Simon rise from his grave in hearty applause:

"The revolution is working," the elder Paul said. "We have infiltrated the Republican Party and we will convert the Republican Party into defenders of Liberty." In his book, *A Time for Truth* (ghostwritten by libertarian author Edith Efron),[10] Simon called for seizure of one of the nation's two dominant political parties to form a new libertarian party, the "Liberty Party." For this dubious honor, Simon nominated the Republican Party because it otherwise was doomed to perpetual failure as the "Stupid Party."

What Ron Paul made clear was that Simon's vision, one that has also been nurtured by the influence and vast wealth of the Koch brothers and a scattering of other rich individuals, had been fully realized, and that the instruments of this success were the tea parties.

Further evidence of this was provided on that same day, May 8, 2012, when reporter Alexander Bolton of *The Hill*, a newspaper devoted primarily to covering the politics of the U.S. House and Senate, said that a defeat in that day's primary of veteran Sen. Richard Lugar of Indiana would be a "significant step toward Tea Party takeover of the Senate GOP agenda ."[11]

Much of the responsibility for this shift would belong to the TPE, for after the 2010 elections, it continued the strategy that had produced success then. In 2012, TPE continued its forays into Republican primaries. By May 1, 2012, its independent political action committee, Our Country Deserves Better, had spent—

- In Texas, where former state Solicitor General Ted Cruz was seeking the nomination[12] to succeed retiring Sen. Kay Baily Hutchinson in the U.S. Senate, $28,015 on radio advertising;

- In Nebraska, where Jon C. Bruning[13] was seeking the Republican nomination to succeed retiring Sen. Ben Nelson in the U.S. Senate, $5,395.00 on radio advertising;

- In Missouri, where former State Treasurer Sarah H. Steelman[14] was seeking the Republican nomination against incumbent Sen. Claire McCaskill (D), $19,399.00 on radio advertising; and,

- In Indiana, where Richard Mourdock was seeking the Republican nomination in a primary fight against incumbent Sen. Richard Lugar,[15] $2,540.00 on radio advertising.[16]

The FreedomWorks PAC had also spent over $60,000 in Indiana to defeat incumbent Sen. Richard Lugar.[17]

For its part, the Americans for Prosperity PAC was focusing wholly on defeating Barack Obama, running radio ads against him in eight states, all of which were judged false by PolitiFact.com, which won the Pulitzer Prize for National Reporting for its coverage of the 2008 election.[18] The Kochs were running five ads. PolitiFact judged two to be false, one mostly false and two won the "Pants on Fire!" award for being outrageously false.[19]

THE FALSE, MOSTLY FALSE AND *"PANTS ON FIRE!"* ADS OF THE TEA PARTY AMERICANS FOR PROSPERITY JUDGED BY POLITIFACT.COM

Claim	Truth
The stimulus bill sent tax credits overseas, such as "tens of millions of dollars to build traffic lights in China."	Mostly false: American streetlights, some Chinese parts.
The stimulus bill sent tax credits overseas, such as "half a billion to an electric car company that created hundreds of jobs in Finland."	False: Not tax credits, not stimulus, not to Finland.
"(President Barack Obama gave) half a billion in taxpayer money to help his friends at Solyndra, a business the White House knew was on the path to bankruptcy."	"Subsidized Chinese solar panels got even cheaper (than Solyndra's) as the price of silicon plummeted—along with Solyndra's chances for becoming profitable."

Claim	Truth
The stimulus bill sent tax credits overseas, such as "$1.2 billion to a solar company that's building a plant in Mexico."	"The ad strings together alarming-sounding tidbits about actual stimulus projects to create the impression of something else entirely—in a way that's ultimately ridiculous. And that earns our lowest rating, *Pants on Fire*."
"A government panel that didn't include cancer specialists says women shouldn't receive mammograms until age 50. ... If government takes over health care, recommendations like these could become the law for all kinds of diseases."	The ad contains an "awful lot of misinformation and distortion ... Americans for Prosperity seized on an issue—free mammograms for women between 40 and 50—that was specifically taken care of with not one, but two, Senate amendments. We rule this claim *Pants on Fire*."

For its part the Republican-Liberty Party was continuing to deliver what the rich were demanding.

On April 12, Rep. Paul Ryan—yes, the same Ryan who voted in favor of the Bush-proposed TARP—unveiled the proposed Republican-Liberty Party's budget for the U.S. government.[20]

It would impose trillions of dollars in spending cuts, at least 62 percent of which would come from low-income programs,[21] it would enact new tax cuts that would provide huge windfalls to households at the top of the income scale. New analysis by the Urban-Brookings Tax Policy Center (TPC) found that people earning more than $1 million a year would receive $265,000 apiece in new tax cuts, on average, on top of the $129,000 they would receive from the Ryan budget's extension of President Bush's tax cuts.[22]

The new tax cuts at the top would dwarf those for middle-income families. After-tax incomes would rise by 12.5 percent among millionaires, but just 1.8 percent for middle-income households. Low-income working families would actually be hit with tax increases.

Ryan claimed that the budget would fully offset the cost of proposed tax cuts by closing tax expenditures (tax credits, deductions, and other preferences) for high-income households. But the budget contained no specific proposals to do so, and meeting this goal would be all but impossible, given that the Ryan budget rules out reducing the tax expenditure most heavily tilted to high-income households—the preferential rates for capital gains and dividends.[23]

Samuel and John Adams, Paul Revere, and the many other brave men who stood together, and many of whom died, to form what would eventually become America, would recognize none of this. Today, "tea party" is little more than an electioneering slogan designed to dupe the public into electing men and women to office that will end government as we know it.

The Tea Party of December 16, 1773 was the beginning of American democracy. It seems likely that the election of November 6, 2012 may signal its end.

17
BIG OIL AND BIG TOBACCO: DOUBT IS THEIR PRODUCT

Mankind has a record of reacting *after* a disaster strikes. Dams are built after floods, not before. So far in human history, disasters have not taken place on a global scale. Therefore, we don't really have a tested mechanism for dealing with global threats, such as long-range, worldwide degradation of the environment. If we ignore the present warning signs and wait for an ecological disaster to strike, it will probably be too late. (emphasis in original).

S. Fred Singer,
Science and Environment Policy Project

ExxonMobil learned at the knee of Philip Morris.

To survive the increasingly compelling science showing that tobacco smoke kills and injures, Philip Morris was required to develop some extraordinarily sophisticated techniques. Faced with a similar problem with global warming, ExxonMobil engaged in the highest form of flattery: imitation.

ExxonMobil, the Koch brothers and their allies were doing a more than adequate job at creating doubt and uncertainty about the science of global warming. They recruited members of Congress to their cause and blocked international action with the Byrd-Hagel Amendment. But as the science became more certain and the evidence more compelling, the job got tougher. So, in part because they were guided by the same team of public relations consultants that had engineered the Big Tobacco campaign, Big Oil adopted similar tactics. In fact, Big Oil and Big Tobacco used some of the same scientists.

The alliance between the two industries dates to at least December 1992, when the U.S. Environmental Protection Agency published a 500-page report called Respiratory Health Effects of Passive Smoking. It found that "the widespread exposure to environmental tobacco smoke (ETS) in the United States presents a serious and substantial public health impact. In adults: ETS is a human lung carcinogen, responsible for approximately 3,000 lung cancer deaths annually in U.S. non-smokers."[1]

The findings spelled trouble for the tobacco industry, especially the largest of its companies, Philip Morris, maker of the popular brand of cigarettes, Marlboro. For years, the industry had fended off federal and state regulation with the argument that whether harmful or not, smoking was a voluntary act—people chose to smoke or not, and therefore shouldn't hold the cigarette maker responsible. A finding that innocent bystanders were being poisoned and killed by the product would be a body blow to the industry.

Almost immediately, Philip Morris hired the Washington, D.C. public relations firm APCO Associates, a subsidiary of the giant law firm Arnold & Porter.[2] It, in turn, formed a front group called The Advancement of Sound Science Coalition.[3] The purpose of TAASC, according to a February 1993 APCO memo from senior vice-president Ellen Merlo was "to discredit the EPA report … Concurrently, it is our objective to prevent states and cities, as well as businesses, from passive-smoking bans."

But for the sake of credibility and to create the image of a "grassroots" movement fighting "overregulation," TASSC had to focus on subjects in addition to passive smoking. TASSC was to be "a national coalition intended to educate the media, public officials and the public about the dangers of 'junk science.' Coalition will address credibility of government's scientific studies, risk-assessment techniques and misuse of tax dollars … Upon formation of Coalition, key leaders will begin media outreach, e.g., editorial board tours, opinion articles, and brief elected officials in selected states."

It was important, APCO said, "to ensure that TASSC has a diverse group of contributors;" to "link the tobacco issue with other more 'politically correct' products;" and to associate scientific studies that cast smoking in a bad light with "broader questions about government research and regulations"—such as "global warming," "nuclear waste disposal" and "biotechnology." APCO would engage in the "intensive recruitment of high-profile representatives from business and industry, scientists, public officials, and other individuals interested in promoting the use of sound science."[4]

Voila! Enter global warming, Exxon money and the terms "junk science" and "sound science," which have now become a mantra of big oil, coal, auto, utility and other global warming profiteers. Brown and Williamson, maker of Lucky Strike, Pall Mall, Kool and a number of other cigarette brands stated plainly that the tools used to sell death-dealing tobacco would be used: "Doubt is our product since it is the best means of competing with the 'body of fact' that exists in the mind of the general public. It is also the means of establishing a controversy."

Between 2000 and 2002, TASSC received $30,000 from Exxon that, among other things, helped establish a new website, JunkScience.com, run by Steve Milloy. An on-line columnist for Fox News, Milloy, is but one of that network's voices grinding out pro-Republican, pro-corporate, anti-global warming news. The network is run by Roger Ailes, a veteran—and savvy—Republican campaign consultant.[a] Even after taking over as president of Fox, Ailes continued to advise Republicans, including Bush-the-son, George W. Bush.[5] Tirelessly insisting that media outlets other than Fox are liberals, he has converted the network into a trumpet for pro-corporate, pro-GOP messages, like those from Milloy who is not only in the hire of Fox, but Philip Morris as well.

In 1992, Milloy started working for APCO—Philip Morris's consultants. While there, he set up the JunkScience.com site in 1996, and now boasts on it, that "since April 1, 1996 JunkScience.com has had a discernible impact."[6] In March 1997, the documents show, he was appointed TASSC's executive director. By 1998, as he explained in a memo to TASSC board members, his JunkScience website was being funded by TASSC. Both he and the "coalition" continued to receive money from Philip Morris. An internal document dated February 1998 reveals that TASSC took $200,000 from the tobacco company in 1997. Philip Morris's 2001 budget document records a payment to Steven Milloy of $90,000.

---

[a] In a Jan. 25, 1988 interview with CBS television evening anchor Dan Rather, then-Vice President George H.W. Bush, jump-started his Presidential election campaign. Years earlier Rather had walked off the set in anger because his show had been pre-empted by a sports event. Rather was pressing Bush on the role he might have played in the Iran-contra scandal, when Bush shot back, "It's not fair to judge my whole career by a rehash on Iran," then demanded of Rather, "How would you like it if I judged your career by those seven minutes when you walked off the set in New York?" Widely perceived as Bush spontaneously going on the attack and thus demonstrating his virility, the Vice President was, in fact, reading from cue cards with fist-sized letters. The man holding those cards was Roger Ailes. Craig Crawford, *ATTACK THE MESSENGER: How Politicians Turn You Against the Media*, p. 5, Rowman & Littlefield Publishers, 2006.

Altria, Philip Morris's parent company, admits that Milloy was under contract to the tobacco firm until at least the end of 2005.

During much of this time, Milloy was also a columnist for FoxNews, saying, for example, in 2001 that "anti-smoker propaganda may be killing more smokers than smoking does" and scornfully attacking criticisms of films for showing smoking.[7] On the subject of global warming, he wrote that "enhanced greenhouse warming is still a huge reach" and that "there's no evidence that humanity is *capable* of effecting significant influence on global climate" (emphasis in original) and "Hell - we don't even know if the planet has actually recorded a genuine increase in mean temperature over the last half century."[8]

[Milloy has enjoyed remarkable success in his self-marketing. When the *New York Times* ran a story in 2001 on Consumers Union and its magazine, *Consumer Reports*, the sole critic it quoted was Milloy, but with no mention of his industry funding.[9]]

In 1994, Philip Morris began a nationwide counterattack on second-hand smoke, purchasing full-page advertisements in forty newspapers, including the *New York Times*, the *Washington Post*, the *Los Angeles Times*, the *Chicago Tribune*, and several other daily newspapers. The ads consisted of an article reprinted from Forbes MediaCritic that questioned the notion that second-hand smoke causes cancer in non-smokers, and appeared under the headline, "If We Said It, You Might Not Believe It."

As part of this campaign, APCO recruited spinners of corporate messages, in effect little more than lobbyists. One of these, for example, is Richard Lindzen of the Massachusetts Institute of Technology (MIT), who is a virtual lobbyist. Lindzen is a global warming lobbyist, though he isn't called that.

Like Milloy, Lindzen is one of a handful of scientists who like to refer to themselves as "skeptics" or "contrarians" who are called on by print and electronic reporters to provide "balance" to reporting on global warming. As the nicknames suggest, these are men and women who are out of step with the mainstream scientific community.

Genuine Skeptics or Pay-For-Hire Skeptics?

PASSIVE SMOKING

Steve Milloy
"Anti-smoker propaganda may be killing more smokers than smoking does"[1]

"Secondhand smoke is annoying to many nonsmokers. That is the essence of the controversy and where the debate should lie - the rights of smokers to smoke in public places versus the rights of nonsmokers to be free of tobacco smoke."[2]

Richard Lindzen
The evidence linking passive smoking to cancer is "weak, inconsistent and ambiguous."[3]

S. Fred Singer
"Tobacco smoke when exhaled as secondhand smoke is so diluted that the harmful substances inhaled in the workplace are nearly zero."[4]

"In their anti-smoking zeal the U.S. Environmental Protection Agency had cooked the data on second-hand tobacco smoke claiming 3,000 lung cancer deaths a year."[5]

Michael Crichton
Studies showing 3,000 deaths annually from passive smoking "was openly fraudulent science" (so) "we now have a social policy supported by the grossest of superstitions."[6]

GLOBAL WARMING

Steve Milloy
"Hell—we don't even know if the planet has actually recorded a genuine increase in mean temperature over the last half century."

"It will take all our strength in the coming years to combat global warming alarmism and to keep America from falling into the totalitarian green abyss."[7]

Richard Lindzen
"I think it's [concern about global warming] mainly just like little kids locking themselves in dark closets to see how much they can scare each other and themselves."[8]

ExxonMobil is "the only principled oil and gas company I know in the US" and that "they have a CEO who is not going to be bamboozled by nonsense."[9]

S. Fred Singer
"Are human activities, including the burning of fossil fuel, the primary or even significant cause of the current warming trend? The scientifically appropriate answer—cautious and conforming to the facts—is probably not."[10]

"Contrary to the conventional wisdom and the predictions of computer models, the Earth's climate has not warmed appreciably in the past two decades, and probably not since about 1940."[11]

Michael Crichton
"Nobody believes a weather prediction twelve hours ahead. Now we're asked to believe a prediction that goes out 100 years into the future? And make financial investments based on that prediction? Has everybody lost their minds?"[12]

"Genuine Skeptics" Table Notes:

1. Steve Milloy

2. "Second-Hand Smokescreens," Fox News, June 04, 2001.

3. Richard Lindzen, "Passive Smoking: How Great a Hazard," *Consumers' Research*, July, 1991, http://tobaccodocuments.org/pm/2046323437-3484.html, accessed Kuly 25, 2007.

4. S. Fred Singer; The Week That Was, July 22, 2006, http://www.sepp.org/Archive/weekwas/2006/July%2022.htm

5. Public misled, National PostNovember 22, 2006, http://www.canada.com/nationalpost/financialpost/story.html?id=78f870f0-60ac-460e-860c-33644aa e26f2

6. Michael Crichton; "Aliens Cause Global Warming," California Institute of Technology, Pasadena, CA, January 17, 2003 http://www.michaelcrichton.net/speech-alienscauseglobalwarming.html

7. Climate Confusion FrontPageMagazine.com, January 21, 2009, http://97.74.65.51/readArticle.aspx?ARTID=33775

8. "Could Global Warming Kill Us?", Larry King Live, January 31, 2007.

9. Lesley Curwen, "Science climate conflict warms up," BBC World Service, April 26, 2007.

10. 11/16/2006, Warming Caused by Natural Cycle, Not Humans, http://environment.ncpa.org/news/warming-caused-by-natural-cycle-not-humans

11. Hearing before the Senate Committee on Commerce, Science, and Transportation, Testimony of Prof. S. Fred Singer, July 18, 2000, http://www.nationalcenter.org/KyotoSingerTestimony2000.html

12. "Aliens Cause Global Warming," California Institute of Technology, Pasadena, CA, January 17, 2003 http://www.michaelcrichton.net/speech-alienscauseglobalwarming.html

---

Lindzen is a "scholar" at the Cato Institute, which is widely accepted within the Washington establishment as a "libertarian" think tank. In addition to being a global warming skeptic, he once wrote that the evidence linking passive smoking to cancer was "weak, inconsistent and ambiguous."[10, b] An account on the web of a

---

[b] The author edits and publishes the *Health & Clean Air Newsletter*, which reports on scientific studies as they enter the literature. Although the Newsletter's focus is principally on ambient air pollutants, studies on the impacts of tobacco smoke are also quite relevant. One study, by Vieneis and 26 others examined the association between passive, or environmental tobacco smoke, and the risk of respiratory cancer and chronic obstructive pulmonary disease in former smokers and never smokers in the European Prospective Investigation into Cancer and Nutrition, or EPIC. Examining a cohort of 303,020 people, researchers found an increased risk of lung cancer found in those exposed to ETS at work. Exposure to ETS in childhood was also related to increased risk of lung cancer. BMJ,doi:10 1136/bmj.38327.648472.82 (published 28 January 2005). In a telephone interview with Lindzen some years ago, he told the author that the spread of malaria into regions in which it has hitherto never been found was because global warming was increasing the range in which mosquitos could breed, but rather to the ban on DDT.

(continued...)

presentation made by Lindzen at Washington and Lee University provides some idea of his message:

> (M)y conclusion from Richard's comments is that every scientist, policy-maker, and news media person who claims to believe that we need to limit CO_2 emissions is part of the largest conspiracy ever—Climate Alarmism! (When) I asked him what journals I could read to learn more about climate change. Based on my interpretation of Richard's comments - I can not trust Science or Nature and The Journal of Climate is "o.k." I learned that the petroleum industry has no vested interest in whether or not we have a policy to limit CO_2 emissions ... it is the powerful and well-funded environmental movement that dictates policy decisions. ... I also asked him if every scientist writing that climate change is real and potentially dangerous and thinks we should have limits on CO_2 emissions had abandoned their code of ethics—had every single scientist in the world who thinks this is a real problem sold out for the money—his answer—they never had any ethics.[11]

Other "skeptics" on global warming include Sallie Baliunas, a Harvard University-Smithsonian Institute astrophysicist, who has fellow-like relationships with several industry funded organizations; Patrick Michaels, the state of Virginia's former climatologist and Cato Institute fellow; and S. Fred Singer, head of the Science and Environment Policy Project.

Singer is an interesting study because he wasn't always a skeptic. When he served in the Nixon Administration as Deputy Assistant Secretary of the U.S. Department of the Interior, his views were considerably different.

"Mankind," Singer wrote in January 1970, "has a record of reacting *after* a disaster strikes. Dams are built after floods, not before. So far in human history, disasters have not taken place on a global scale. Therefore, we don't really have a tested mechanism for dealing with global threats, such as long-range, worldwide degradation of the environment. If we ignore the present

---

[b] (...continued)
When asked about contrary conclusions that had been published in *Lancet*, an extremely highly-regarded medical journal, Lindzen said he didn't bother to read such periodicals.

warning signs and wait for an ecological disaster to strike, it will probably be too late. (emphasis in original)."[c]

These days, Singer even denies that chlorofluorocarbons, the industrial chemicals developed by the DuPont Corporation, destroy the stratospeheric ozone layer that shields humanity from the sun's nuclear radiation. But before SEPP started receiving industry money, his views were different, writing in 1970 that "Only within the past year has it been recognized that chlorofluoromethanes used as inert propellants in aerosol spray cans can have far-reaching effects on stratospheric ozone, which in turn would increase levels of biologically harmful ultraviolet radiation at the Earth's surface. And there may be pollution effects extant which we have not yet recognized or whose consequences we cannot yet ascertain."[12]

Now in his 80s, Singer's view is that "Without firm evidence that an appreciable warming will occur as a result of human activities, or that its consequences would be harmful, there can be no justification for bureaucratic remedies or any action beyond a 'no-regrets' policy of energy efficiency and market-based conservation."[13] But when he was a younger scientist, his views were considerably different:

> We can turn to the second question and ask whether changes in climate are necessarily bad. Since throughout history, climate changes have been the rule rather than the exception, and since the biosphere has survived and evolved, one might be tempted to make light of those who decry a warming of the climate, while others worry about keeping back the ice ages. I am persuaded to think that any climate change is bad because of the investments and adaptations that have been made by human beings and all of the things that support human existence on this globe. Even minor fluctuation of climate could change the distribution of fish (the cod has moved further north in the last few decades from Iceland to Central Greenland), upset agriculture (by forcing it onto soils that are not suitable), and inundate coastal cities (by raising sea levels). Such changes could occur at a faster rate perhaps than human society can evolve.[14]

---

[c] *Global Effects of Environmental Pollution: A Symposium Organized by the American Association for the Advancement of Science,* Held in Dallas, Texas, December, 1968, Ed.: S. Fred Singer, p. 206, D. Reidel Publishing (Dordrecht, Holland, 1970)

Today, Singer dismisses concerns over the possibility of hitting the irreversible change triggered by passing a tipping point, saying, "environmentalists talk about 'tipping points' because they are frustrated," adding that "All the climate models that I've seen show only a gradual warming as the level of greenhouse gases increases."

But before he was being funded by the likes of ExxonMobil, Singer had the opposite view: "We do believe, however, that climate changes are generally *triggered*. By this we mean that a small change of a crucial parameter, at the proper time and at the proper place, can cause a large climate change by initiating or triggering an inherent feedback mechanism which exists in our natural environment. This possibility of course must be a source of constant concern. (emphasis in original)[15]

A professor at M.I.T., Lindzen, is also a scholar at the Cato Institute, a Washington, D.C. organization that likes to bill itself as a libertarian think tank. There were virtually none of these organizations when Powell wrote his Manifesto in 1971, but they quickly sprang up. Today, there are at least 400 such groups sustained by upwards of $100 million a year from corporations, the rich and their captive foundations.

The organizations produce "policy studies" (Cato Institute), "backgrounders" (Heritage Foundation) or "issue analysis" (Competitive Enterprise Institute - CEI). Whatever the name, the messages are fundamentally the same. Consider what they have to say about global warming:

Cato: Global warming science is a "constellation of half-truths and misstatements."

CEI: Concerns are based on "scare stories that have been exaggerated by the media and vested interests such as environmental pressure groups."

Heritage: "Virtually all of the alarming rhetoric surrounding global warming is speculative and lies outside the scientific consensus."

They have been extremely effective at exploiting the journalistic demand for "balance" in reporting. James Hansen of the National Atmospheric and Space

Administration's Goddard Space Institute,[d] one the best known and highly regarded climatologists in the world once explained—

> I was about to appear on public television, (when) the producer informed me that the program "must" also include a "contrarian" who would take issue with claims of global warming. Presenting such a view, he told me, was a common practice in commercial television as well as radio and newspapers. Supporters of public TV or advertisers, with their own special interests, require "balance" as a price for their continued financial support.[16]

These supposedly science-based claims enter the Republican/Libertarian/Tea Pary echo chamber, finding their way onto the airwaves, as well as into print and halls of Congress.

Michaels, for example, appeared on CNN's "Capital Gang," where he told millions of viewers that global warming science was the "biggest scandal in the history of environmental sciences" and "our greener friends blame every weather event that they can find on global warming. But when you look at the actual numbers, their claims don't hold up."[17]

Michaels testified before a House of Representatives Committee—chaired by a Republican—saying that global warming "could be benign or even beneficial."[18] Then, he was quoted with approval on the floor of the U.S. Senate, the Chairman of the Committee on Environment and Public Works—again, a Republican—who said that "a new study by Drs. Ross McKitrick and Patrick Michaels that was presented in an article published in the May 25 issue of 'Climate Research'" concluded that "outside the dry/cold regions the measured temperature change is primarily explained by economic and social variables," not global warming.[19]

In the CNN program, the following exchange occurred between Michaels and the interviewer:

O'Beirne: Has there been any climate change in the last century?

---

[d] Millions of Americans have a link to Hansen, but don't know it: his office is a few floors above the New York City restaurant where Jerry Seinfeld, George, Elaine and Cosmo regularly dined in the series.

Michaels: Sure. The temperature of the planet's about 1 degree Fahrenheit warmer than it was 100 years ago. In the last 50 years, there have been changes that look like greenhouse effect changes, meaning the coldest air of the winter has warmed up, Siberia's warmed up from minus 40 to minus 38 in January.

Michaels seemingly blithely accepted global warming as a reality. But in 1986, he was singing a different tune, authoring an article for the *Washington Post* Outlook section headlined "Greenhouse Effect? Then Why is it Cooler?"[20]

Michaels has also misrepresented the conclusions of other scientists. Michaels, for example, charged that in his 1988 testimony before Congress NASA researcher, James Hansen, "overestimated [global warming] by 300 percent" (p. 247). What really happened was that Hansen described three different possible outcomes, depending on how much pollution increased. One of them—the one that Hansen said was most likely—was right on target. Michaels, however, chose the most extreme of the three scenarios to attack, deleting any reference to the other two, then claimed Hansen had been off by 300 percent, proving that computer models can't be trusted.[21]

Another skeptic, this with extraordinarily powerful credentials, is Frederick Seitz, a physicist and former head of the National Academy of Sciences. He is also president emeritus of Rockefeller University and chairman of one of the more outspoken skeptic organizations, the George C. Marshall Institute.[22]

Seitz created a bit of an uproar in 1996 when he wrote an article headlined "A Major Deception on Global Warming" for the *Wall Street Journal*. In it, he charged that when the 1995 assessment of global warming, prepared by the hundreds of scientists for the Intergovernment Panel on Climate Change (IPCC) was done, "key changes were made after the scientists had met and accepted what they thought was the final peer-reviewed version."[23]

Seitz was enraged, saying that "In my more than 60 years as a member of the American scientific community, including service as president of both the National Academy of Sciences and the American Physical Society, I have never witnessed a more disturbing corruption of the peer-review process than the events that led to this IPCC report." Seitz continued that he was "in no position" determine who made the changes, but "Whatever the intent was of those who made these significant changes, their effect is to deceive policy makers and the public into believing that the scientific evidence shows human activities are causing global warming."[24]

Like many of the skeptics, Seitz has a loose connection to the tobacco industry, which developed and utilized many of the techniques employed by ExxonMobil and the global warming skeptics. Indeed, in an interoffice memo of the Phillip Morris Companies dated August 31, 1989—seven years before Seitz wrote the Journal piece—one official, Alexander Holzman, was updating another, Bill Murray, on his attempts to arrange a meeting between Seitz and Murray:

> I spoke to Bill Hobbs about arranging an appointment for you with Dr. Fred Seitz, former head of Rockefeller University and the principal scientific advisor to the R.J. Reynolds medical research program. Bill told me that Dr. Seitz is quite elderly and not sufficiently rational to offer advice.[25]

Industries constantly search for political information, even at the state level. For example, from 1991 to 1996, Karl Rove, later to be George W. Bush's campaign manager and White House aide, was a consultant for Philip Morris. The later conceded that he would share with the tobacco company information acquired working in the political arena, including "political gossip about who was getting ready to run and how they were doing with fund-raising and how they were doing garnering support of key groups, how they were doing with lining up endorsements and so forth," even if he learned this from his involvement in the campaign.[26]

Although executives with tobacco companies have not yet been held legally liable, those cases are muddled considerably by the fact that most of the injured parties voluntarily smoked or allowed themselves to be exposed. In the context of global warming, however, such considerations do not apply. In the judgment of some lawyers, civil and criminal law suits seeking to hold corporate executives and boards of directors criminally or civilly liable are low-hanging fruit simply awaiting an aggressive state attorney general or local district attorney.

Clearly, the case against ExxonMobil executives is damning.

It is clear beyond any credible dispute that some corporations have systemically sought, and with great success, to confuse and misrepresent the science of global warming and, in some instances, attack the scientists themselves. Chief among these is ExxonMobil, though it is by no means alone. Consider the record of ExxonMobil on global warming:

- On September 29, 2000, presidential candidate George W. Bush unveiled an environmental plan that would require power plants to reduce emissions of four main pollutants. If elected, Bush said, he would propose legislation requiring "electric utilities to reduce emissions and significantly improve air quality." Specifically, he promised to "work with Congress, the Environmental Protection Agency, the Department of Energy, consumer and environmental groups, and industry to develop legislation that will establish mandatory reduction targets for emissions of four main pollutants: sulfur dioxide, nitrogen oxide, mercury, and carbon dioxide."[27] Then on March 13, 2001, Bush reneged on his promise and said his administration would not support a mandatory reduction in carbon dioxide emissions from power plants.[28]

Bush offered no explanation for this switch. But briefing papers prepared by Paula Dobriansky, Bush's under-secretary of state, between 2001 and 2004, were revealed later. In them she thanked Exxon executives for the company's "active involvement" in helping to determine climate change policy. Before a meeting with ExxonMobil lobbyist Randy Randol and representatives of the Global Climate Coalition, she wrote that "Potus [president of the United States] rejected Kyoto in part based on input from you."[29] Dobriansky's notes also disclosed that the White House considered Exxon "among the companies most actively and prominently opposed to binding approaches [like Kyoto] to cut greenhouse gas emissions."[30]

- Yet two years after Bush's about-face, Exxon's head of public affairs, Nick Thomas, told a committee of the United Kingdom House of Lords that, "I think we can say categorically we have not campaigned with the United States government or any other government to take any sort of position over Kyoto."[31]

- For years, ExxonMobil's denials, like that of Randol before the House of Lords, were boilerplate responses from the company, saying it was playing no role in the campaign of climate denial in the United States. Yet, according to the a report by the Union of Concerned Scientists, ExxonMobil gave nearly $16 million between 1998 and 2005 to a network of 43 corporate front groups that seek to confuse the public on global warming science.[32]

- Then in September 2006, the Royal Society, Britain's premier scientific academy, took an unprecedented step: it wrote to the oil giant to demand that it withdraw support for dozens of groups that the Society said, had "misrepresented the science of climate change by outright denial of the evidence."[33] The Royal Society cited its own survey, which found that ExxonMobil had in 2005 distributed $2.9 million to 39 groups that the Society said misrepresented the science of climate change. ExxonMobil's own public statements on global warming, said the Society, were "inaccurate and misleading."[34]

- Under pressure in Europe and the United States alike, ExxonMobil said it would halt funding. But two years later, it was revealed that, in violation of that pledge, the company had continued funding corporate fronts.[35] One of recipients of ExxonMobil's largesse, the National Center for Policy Analysis, wrote "NCPA scholars believe that while the causes and consequences of the earth's current warming trend is [sic] still unknown, the cost of actions to substantially reduce CO_2 emissions would be quite high and result in economic decline, accelerated environmental destruction, and do little or nothing to prevent global warming regardless of its cause."

- These are all part of a pattern. After an official in the Administration of George W. Bush, Philip A. Cooney, resigned in the wake of disclosures of hundreds of instances in which he edited government climate reports to play up uncertainty of a human role in global warming or play down evidence of such a role, he was hired by ExxonMobil.[36] Cooney was "lobbying from within," in the words of the *New York Times*.[37]

- In a memo to President George Bush's Council on Environmental Quality (CEQ), ExxonMobil lobbyist Randy Randol denounced esteemed climate scientist Robert Watson, chairman of the IPCC, as someone "handpicked by Al Gore" who is using the media to get "coverage for his views." Thus he asks, "Can Watson be replaced now at the request of the US?" In addition to Watson, Randol names other climate experts who he wants "removed from their positions of influence." A year later, the Bush administration blocked Watson's reelection as IPCC chairman.[38, e]

---

[e] Lobbyists Randy Randol also asked that three others be removed in addition to Watson: Dr. Rosina Bierbaum of the White House Office of Science and Technology Policy; Dr. Michael MacCracken director of the National Assessment Coordination Office of the U.S. Global Change Research Program; and, Jeff Moitke of the U.S. Department of State. They were. The memo can be found at http://www.ucsusa.org/news/press_release/ExxonMobil-GlobalWarming-tobacco.html?wt.rss=rss://www.nrdc.org/media/docs/020403.pdf.

- In 2001, Larisa E. Dobriansky (sister of Paula Dobriansky mentioned above) was appointed deputy assistant secretary for national energy policy at the Department of Energy, to manage the Office of Climate Change Policy. Prior to the appointment, she was an employee of Akin Gump, where she lobbied for ExxonMobil on climate change issues.[39]

- In Congress, the first effort by the Senate to adopt global warming legislation was defeated 43–55 in 2003. The legislation came up the following year. The climate aide to Sen. Richard Lugar (R.Ind.) told *Newsweek* magazine "we were contacted by a lot of lobbyists from API and Exxon-Mobil," says Mark Helmke, "They'd bring up how the science wasn't certain, how there were a lot of skeptics out there." It went down to defeat again.[40]

- The chief executive of ExxonMobil, the world's largest privately owned oil company, is Rex Tillerson. At the company's 2008 annual shareholder's meeting, the *Financial Post* said Tillerson "came out swinging Wednesday against the environmental movement, arguing the science of climate change is far from settled and that his company views it as its 'corporate social responsibility' to continue to supply the world with fossil fuels."[41]

- The directors of ExxonMobil are aware of the company's conduct and its misleading advertisements. On November 23, 2006, just before his departure as head of the National Assessment Coordination Office of the U.S. Global Change Research Program, Dr. Michael MacCracken wrote a letter to then-CEO Lee Raymond and each member of the ExxonMobil board of directors telling them that—

  > ExxonMobil is on the wrong side of the international
  > scientific community, the wrong side of the findings of all
  > the world's leading academies of science, and the wrong side
  > of virtually all of the world's countries as expressed, without
  > dissent, in the IPCC reports ... [42]

Thus, Raymond and the board have not only constructive knowledge of the ExxonMobil employee on the Intergovernmental Panel on Climate Change, but actual knowledge that its statements were directly at odds with the world's premier scientific bodies.

If the shift in public opinion is any indication, ExxonMobil will be able to stay in the fossil fuel business, for public confidence that global warming is occurring and that it is caused by human activity is declining.[f] This is a vindication of the conclusion of U.S. businesses and industries that stand to lose money or perhaps even cease to exist altogether, to support a lavishly funded assault on science.

One of the premier global warming scientific research institutions, the Hadley Center in the United Kingdom, predicts that from 2010 to 2015 at least half the years will be hotter than the current hottest year on record, which is 1998. If scientists at Hadley, together with their American counterparts at the National Aeronautics and Space Administration, are correct, global warming will return with a vengeance in another year or two. (Indeed that may have happened in 2012, judging from the record-breaking droughts and high temperatures.) The world's governments will have lost a decade in which warming could have been slowed, and much of the responsibility for that will belong to those who have knowingly confused and misrepresented science.

In his State of the Union address on January 31, 2006, then-President George Bush offered up a tantalizing suggestion of just how the United States might address global warming: "America," he said, "is addicted to oil." Bush was correct, of course, although his suggested cure, which was to replace 75 percent of the nation's Mideast oil imports by 2025 with ethanol and other energy sources, was off base, since the United States gets less than 20 percent of its oil from the Persian Gulf.

Nevertheless, the use of the term "addiction" was apt, in part because what has happened with respect to global warming—the distortion and confusion of science, the use of supposedly neutral but in fact pay-for-hire front groups, and the deft use of political power to slow and prevent action—is remarkably similar to what happened in the context of America's most powerful conventional addiction, tobacco. This should come as no surprise because many of the very same firms—indeed, some of the same individuals—who engineered and implemented the strategies of Big Tobacco did the same for Big Oil and King Coal.

It may well be that some of the same strategies deployed to combat Big Tobacco might also be appropriate, or even more so, for attacking firms like

---

[f] In a poll of 1,500 adults by the Pew Research Center for the People & the Press, released Oct. 22, 2009, the number of people saying there is strong scientific evidence that the Earth has gotten warmer over the past few decades is down from 71 percent in April of last year and from 77 percent when Pew started asking the question in 2006. The number of people who see the situation as a serious problem also has also declined. GMA News, "Poll: US belief in global warming is cooling," http://www.gmanews.tv/story/175353/poll-us-belief-in-global-warming-is-cooling.

ExxonMobil, Chevron, the Southern Company, Western Fuels and other companies, as well as front groups such as the Cato Institute and the Competitive Enterprise Institute, as well as the senior executives.

There are several avenues that could be pursued, including the following:

- Criminal charges against corporate officers or shareholders.

- Knowing or Reckless Endangerment under media specific statutes.

- Charges under the Racketeer Influenced and Corrupt Organizations Act (RICO) statute.

Despite scholarly criticisms, limited shareholder liability—that is, limiting the loss of a shareholder to the stock owned—is an enduring feature of the economic landscape of the United States. If the sole owner of a business or a partner were to injure others, everything the business owned, as well as the property—home, car, etc.—could be forfeited in a court of law. Not so with corporations, however. Since the early twentieth century, state business corporation statutes have limited the liability of shareholders for corporate obligations to the amount of their investment, except in very rare circumstances.

Yes, charging a corporation with a crime is arguably senseless, for those who ultimately make the decisions are not certificates of stock, but living, breathing humans. But merely because they are officers of a corporation, these individuals make decisions that lead to the deaths and illnesses of others with virtual impunity.

There are statutes that impose criminal liability on officers: for example, a corporate director or officer who intentionally participates in a scheme to defraud someone of money or property and uses mail or interstate wire communications to do so can be imprisoned for up to 20 years and fined up to $250,000.[43] Violations of building codes can result in a criminal conviction.[44] So, too, can failure to pay taxes, as well as violations of trademarks or copyrights, import and export laws, and a wide variety of other statutes.[45]

There can be little doubt that some corporations knowingly and intentionally confused or mis-represented science. Some ran full-page newspaper advertisements or mailed information packets to shareholders. Others made conscious decisions to provide financial support to 501(c)(3) "charities," that used the money to confuse and misrepresent science. Corporate executives knew, or should have known, the science was valid, and that misrepresenting it was exposing the global population to the potentially devastating and irreversible consequences of global warming.

ExxonMobil is a case in point, because its statements and other actions caused the British Royal Society, Britain's premier scientific academy, to demand that the company withdraw support for dozens of groups that had "misrepresented the science of climate change by outright denial of the evidence." The Society also sharply criticized ExxonMobil's "inaccurate and misleading" public statements on global warming.[46] The company pledged to cease such funding, but instead continued it.[g]

> Company records show that ExxonMobil handed over hundreds of thousands of pounds to such lobby groups in 2008. These include the National Center for Policy Analysis (NCPA) in Dallas, Texas, which received $75,000 (£45,500), and the Heritage Foundation in Washington DC, which received $50,000.[h]

For this, ExxonMobil executives and members of its board of directors should, in the view of some, be brought personally to the bar on criminal charges.

THE RACKETEER INFLUENCED AND CORRUPT ORGANIZATIONS ACT (RICO) STATUTE

Enacted in 1970, the object of RICO was to eliminate the influence of the Mafia in America. Through the 1970s, RICO was seldom used outside of that context of the Mafia. Civil claims under RICO were simply not brought.

---

[g] Bob Ward, "Why ExxonMobil must be taken to task over climate denial funding," The *Guardian*, July 1, 2009,
http://www.guardian.co.uk/environment/cif-green/2009/jul/01/bob-ward-exxon-mobil-climate

[h] David Adam, "ExxonMobil continuing to fund climate sceptic groups, records show," The *Guardian*, July 1, 2009,
http://www.guardian.co.uk/environment/2009/jul/01/exxon-mobil-climate-change-sceptics-funding

In the 1980s, however, civil lawyers began exploiting 1964(c)[i] the RICO Act, which allows civil claims to be brought by any person injured in business or property because of a RICO violation. Any person establishing a civil RICO claim automatically receives judgment in the amount of three times actual damages and is awarded costs and attorneys fees. By the late 1980s, according to one expert, "RICO was a (if not the most) commonly asserted claim in federal court. Everyone was trying to depict civil claims, such as common law fraud, product defect, and breach of contract as criminal wrongdoing, which would in turn enable the filing of a civil RICO action."[47]

The father of the RICO, G. Robert Blakey, described the core elements of a RICO suit: "the intentional sale of a defective product that's both addictive and lethal."[48]

ExxonMobil seems particularly vulnerable to these sorts of legal challenges, for several reasons.

First, it has been far and away the most aggressive of all American companies in its efforts to slow or halt action on global warming.

Second, the company's commitment to acceptance of global warming and all that it might bring seems completely unwavering. In June 2012 parts of the U.S. west, including Colorado, were experiencing the worst fire season in its history. The threat was so severe that researchers at Boulder's National Center for Atmospheric Research (NCAR) joined 32,000 other Coloradans in fleeing the fires.

As that was happening, ExxonMobil head Rex Tillerson, told the Council on Foreign Relations in New York City, that the risks of global warming were "manageable." While Tillerson conceded that adaptation would be a "great challenge," he said that "As a species that's why we're all still here: we have spent our entire existence adapting. So we will adapt to this," he said. "It's an engineering problem, and it has engineering solutions."[49]

---

[i] "§ 1964. Civil remedies

"(c) Any person injured in his business or property by reason of a violation of section 1962 of this chapter may sue therefor in any appropriate United States district court and shall recover threefold the damages he sustains and the cost of the suit, including a reasonable attorney's fee, except that no person may rely upon any conduct that would have been actionable as fraud in the purchase or sale of securities to establish a violation of section 1962. The exception contained in the preceding sentence does not apply to an action against any person that is criminally convicted in connection with the fraud, in which case the statute of limitations shall start to run on the date on which the conviction becomes final."

Third, and very importantly, ExxonMobil has actual knowledge of the widespread scientific consensus in support of the proposition that global warming will, without change, occur and the impacts will be devastating. Why? Partially because ExxonMobil holds itself out as a science-based company that employs 14,000 scientists and engineers, and has two employees who are members of the IPCC.[50] They are Dr. Brian P. Flannery and Dr. Haroon S. Kheshgi.[51] In interviews, President Tillerson boasts that ExxonMobil is the only energy company with members on the International Panel of Climate Change.[52, j]

---

[j] Other ExxonMobil mentions of Flannery and Khesghi include the following: "The Intergovernmental Panel on Climate Change (IPCC) prepares periodic climate assessments on science, impacts and adaptation, and mitigation based on the contributions of several hundred expert authors nominated by governments. The majority of experts work in academia and government labs, but a handful work in business, including Haroon Kheshgi and Brian Flannery from ExxonMobil. Over the years, they have contributed to three IPCC assessments and two special reports and have served as review editors for IPCC publications. The valuable contributions of these experts were recognized, when the IPCC received the 2007 Nobel Peace Prize." http://www.exxonmobilcat.com/issues/category/climate_and_emissions, accessed July 17, 2012.

APPENDIX I
THE AMERICAN PETROLEUM
INSTITUTE'S WORK PLAN ON GLOBAL
WARMING[a]

The material below contains a memo by the API from April 1998.

Memo

Joe Walker

To: Global Climate Science Team
Cc: Michelle Ross; Susan Moya
Subject: Draft Global Climate Science Communications plan

*As promised, attached is the draft Global Climate Science Communications Plan
that we developed during our workshop Last Friday. Thanks especially to those of
you who participated in the workshop, and in particular to John Adams for his very
helpful thoughts following up our meeting, and Alan Caudill for turning around the
notes from our workshop so quickly.*

Please review the plan and get back to me with your comments as soon as possible.

*As those of you who were at the workshop know, we have scheduled a follow - up
team meeting to review the plan in person on Friday, April 17, form 1 to 3 p.m. at
the API headquarters. After that, we hope to have a "plan champion" help us move
it forward to potential funding sources, perhaps starting with the global climate
"Coordinating Council." That will be an item for discussion on April 17.*

---

[a] Found at http://www.euronet.nl/users/e_wesker/ew@shell/API-prop.html

Again, thanks for your hard work on this project. Please e-mail me, call or fax me with your comments. Thanks.

Regards,
Joe Walker

Global Climate Science Communications Action Plan

Situation Analysis

In December 1997, the Clinton Administration agreed in Kyoto, Japan, to a treaty to reduce greenhouse gas emissions to prevent what it purports to be changes in the global climate caused by the continuing release of such emissions. The so-called green house gases have many sources. For example, water vapor is a greenhouse gas. But the Clinton Administration's action, if eventually approved by the U.S. Senate, will mainly affect emissions from fossil fuel (gasoline, coal, natural gas, etc.) combustion.

As the climate change debate has evolved, those who oppose action have argued mainly that signing such a treaty will place the U.S. at a competitive disadvantage with most other nations, and will be extremely expensive to implement. Much of the cost will be borne by American consumers who will pay higher prices for most energy and transportation.

The climate change theory being advanced by the treaty supporters is based primarily on forecasting models with a very high degree of uncertainty. In fact, its not known for sure whether (a) climate change actually is occurring, or (b) if it is, whether humans really have any influence on it.

Despite these weaknesses in scientific understanding, those who oppose the treaty have done little to build a case against precipitous action on climate change based on the scientific uncertainty. As a result, the Clinton Administration and environmental groups essentially have had the field to themselves. They have conducted an effective public relations program to convince the American public that the climate is changing, we humans are at fault, and we must do something about it before calamity strikes.

The environmental groups know they have been successful. Commenting after the Kyoto negotiations about recent media coverage of climate change, Tom Wathen, executive vice president of the National Environmental Trust, wrote:

" … As important as the extent of the coverage was the tone and tenor of it. In a change from just six months ago, most media stories no longer presented global warming as just a theory over which reasonable scientists could differ. Most stories described predictions of global warming as the position of the overwhelming number of mainstream scientists. That the environmental community had, to a great extent, settled the scientific issue with the U.S. media is the other great success that began perhaps several months earlier but became apparent during Kyoto."

Because the science underpinning the global climate change theory has not been challenged effectively in the media or through other vehicles reaching the American public, there is widespread ignorance, which works in favor of the Kyoto treaty and against the best interests of the United States. Indeed, the public has been highly receptive to the Clinton Administrations plans. There has been little, if any, public resistance or pressure applied to Congress to reject the treaty, except by those "inside the Beltway" with vested interests.

Moreover, from the political viewpoint, it is difficult for the United States to oppose the treaty solely on economic grounds, valid as the economic issues are. It makes it too easy for others to portray the United States as putting preservation of its own lifestyle above the greater concerns of mankind. This argument, in turn, forces our negotiators to make concessions that have not been well thought through, and in the end may do far more harm than good. This is the process that unfolded at Kyoto, and is very likely to be repeated in Buenos Aires in November 1998.

The advocates of global warming have been successful on the basis of skillfully misrepresenting the science and the extent of agreement on the science, while industry and its partners ceded the science and fought on the economic issues. Yet if we can show that science does not support the Kyoto treaty - which most true climate scientists believe to be the case - this puts the United States in a stronger moral position and frees its negotiators from the need to make concessions as a defense against perceived selfish economic concerns.

Upon this tableau, the Global Climate Science Communications Team (GCSCT) developed an action plan to inform the American public that science does not support the precipitous actions Kyoto would dictate, thereby providing a climate for the right policy decisions to be made. The team considered results from a new public opinion survey in developing the plan.

Charlton Research's survey of 1,100 "informed Americans" suggests that while Americans currently perceive climate change to be a great threat, public opinion is open enough to change on climate science. When informed that "some scientists believe there is not enough evidence to suggest that [what is called global climate change] is a long-term change due to human behavior and activities," 58 percent of those surveyed said they were more likely to oppose the Kyoto treaty. Moreover, half the respondents harbored doubts about climate science.

GCSCT members who contributed to the development of the plan are A. John Adams, John Adams Associates; Candace Crandall, Science and Environmental Policy Project; David Rothbard, Committee For A Constructive Tomorrow; Jeffrey Salmon, The Marshall Institute; Lee Garrigan, environmental issues Council; Lynn Bouchey and Myron Ebell, Frontiers of Freedom; Peter Cleary, Americans for Tax Reform; Randy Randol, Exxon Corp.; Robert Gehri, The Southern Company; Sharon Kneiss, Chevron Corp; Steve Milloy, The Advancement of Sound Science Coalition; and Joseph Walker, American Petroleum Institute.

The action plan is detailed on the following pages.

Global Climate Science Communications Action Plan

Project Goal

A majority of the American public, including industry leadership, recognizes that significant uncertainties exist in climate science, and therefore raises questions among those (e.g. Congress) who chart the future U.S. course on global climate change.

Progress will be measured toward the goal. A measurement of the public's perspective on climate science will be taken before the plan is launched, and the same measurement will be taken at one or more as-yet-to-be-determined intervals as the plan is implemented.

Victory Will Be Achieved When

○ Average citizens "understand" (recognize) uncertainties in climate science; recognition of uncertainties becomes part of the "conventional wisdom"

○   Media "understands" (recognizes) uncertainties in climate science
○   Media coverage reflects balance on climate science and recognition of the validity of viewpoints that challenge the current "conventional wisdom"
○   Industry senior leadership understands uncertainties in climate science, making them stronger ambassadors to those who shape climate policy
○   Those promoting the Kyoto treaty on the basis of extent science appears to be out of touch with reality.

Current Reality

Unless "climate change" becomes a non-issue, meaning that the Kyoto proposal is defeated and there are no further initiatives to thwart the threat of climate change, there may be no moment when we can declare victory for our efforts. It will be necessary to establish measurements for the science effort to track progress toward achieving the goal and strategic success.

Strategies and Tactics

I. National Media Relations Program: Develop and implement a national media relations program to inform the media about uncertainties in climate science; to generate national, regional and local media coverage on the scientific uncertainties, and thereby educate and inform the public, stimulating them to raise questions with policy makers.

Tactics: These tactics will be undertaken between now and the next climate meeting in Buenos Aires/Argentina, in November 1998, and will be continued thereafter, as appropriate. Activities will be launched as soon as the plan is approved, funding obtained, and the necessary resources (e.g., public relations counsel) arranged and deployed. In all cases, tactical implementation will be fully integrated with other elements of this action plan, most especially Strategy II (National Climate Science Data Center).

Identify, recruit and train a team of five independent scientists to participate in media outreach. These will be individuals who do not have a long history of visibility and/or participation in the climate change debate. Rather, this team will consist of new faces who will add their voices to those recognized scientists who already are vocal.

●   Develop a global climate science information kit for media including peer-reviewed papers that undercut the "conventional wisdom" on climate science. This kit also will include understandable communications, including simple fact sheets that present scientific uncertainties in language that the media and public can understand.

- Conduct briefings by media-trained scientists for science writers in the top 20 media markets, using the information kits. Distribute the information kits to daily newspapers nationwide with offer of scientists to brief reporters at each paper. Develop, disseminate radio news releases featuring scientists nationwide, and offer scientists to appear on radio talk shows across the country.

- Produce, distribute a steady stream of climate science information via facsimile and e-mail to science writers around the country.

- Produce, distribute via syndicate and directly to newspapers nationwide a steady stream of op-ed columns and letters to the editor authored by scientists.

- Convince one of the major news national TV journalists (e.g., John Stossel) to produce a report examining the scientific underpinnings of the Kyoto treaty.

- Organize, promote and conduct through grassroots organizations a series of campus/community workshops/debates on climate science in 10 most important states during the period mid-August through October, 1998.

- Consider advertising the scientific uncertainties in select markets to support national, regional and local (e.g., workshops / debates), as appropriate.

National Media Program Budget — $600,000 plus paid advertising

II. Global Climate Science Information Source: Develop and implement a program to inject credible science and scientific accountability into the global climate debate, thereby raising questions about and undercutting the "prevailing scientific wisdom." The strategy will have the added benefit of providing a platform for credible, constructive criticism of the opposition's position on the science.

Tactics: As with the National Media Relations Program, these activities will be undertaken between now and the next climate meeting in Buenos Aires, Argentina, in November 1998, and will continue thereafter. Initiatives will be launched as soon as the plan is approved, funding obtained, and the necessary resources arranged and deployed.

- Establish a Global Climate Science Data Center. The GCSDC will be established in Washington as a non-profit educational foundation with an advisory board of respected climate scientists. It will be staffed initially with professionals on loan from various companies and associations with a major interest in the climate issue. These executives will bring with them knowledge and experience in the following areas.

- Overall history of climate research and the IPCC process;
- Congressional relations and knowledge of where individual Senators stand on the climate issue;
- Knowledge of key climate scientists and where they stand;
- Ability to identify and recruit as many as 20 respected climate scientists to serve on the science advisory board;
- Knowledge and expertise in media relations and with established relationships with science and energy writers, columnists and editorial writers;
- Expertise in grassroots organization; and
- Campaign organization and administration.

The GCSDC will be led by dynamic senior executive with a major personal commitment to the goals of the campaign and easy access to business leaders at the CEO level. The Center will be run on a day-to-day basis by an executive director with responsibility for ensuring targets are met. The Center will be funded at a level that will permit it to succeed, including funding for research contracts that may be deemed appropriate to fill gaps in climate science (e.g., a complete scientific critique of the IPCC research and its conclusions).

- The GCSDC will become a one-stop resource on climate science for members of Congress, the media, industry and all others concerned. It will be in constant contact with the best climate scientists and ensure that their findings and views receive appropriate attention. It will provide them with the logistical and moral support they have been lacking. In short, it will be a sound scientific alternative to the IPCC. Its functions will include:

  - Providing as an easily accessible database (including a website) of all mainstream climate science information.
  - Identifying and establishing cooperative relationships with all major scientists whose research in this field supports our position.
  - Establishing cooperative relationships with other mainstream scientific organizations (e.g., meteorologists, geophysicists) to bring their perspectives to bear on the debate, as appropriate.
  - Developing opportunities to maximize the impact of scientific views consistent with ours with Congress, the media and other key audiences.

  - Monitoring and serving as and early warning system for scientific developments with the potential to impact on the climate science debate, pro and con.
  - Responding to claims from the scientific alarmists and media.

- Providing grants for advocacy on climate science, as deemed appropriate.

Global Climate Science Data Center Budget — $5,000,000 (Spread over two years minimum)

III. National Direct Outreach and Education: Develop and implement a direct outreach program to inform and educate members of Congress, state officials, industry leadership, and school teachers/students about uncertainties in climate science. This strategy will enable Congress, state officials and industry leaders will be able to raise such serious questions about the Kyoto treaty's scientific underpinnings that American policy-makers not only will refuse to endorse it, they will seek to prevent progress toward implementation at the Buenos Aires meeting in November or through other ways. Informing teachers/students about uncertainties in climate science will begin to erect a barrier against further efforts to impose Kyoto-like measures in the future.

Tactics: Informing and educating members of Congress, state officials and industry leaders will be undertaken as soon as the plan is approved, funding is obtained, and the necessary resources are arrayed and will continue through Buenos Aires and for the foreseeable future. The teachers/students outreach program will be developed and launched in early 1999. In all cases, tactical implementation will be fully integrated with other elements of this action plan.

- Develop and conduct through the Global Climate Science Data Center science briefings for Congress, governors, state legislators, and industry leaders by August 1998.

- Develop information kits on climate science targeted specifically at the needs of government officials and industry leaders, to be used in conjunction with and separately from the in-person briefings to further disseminate information on climate science uncertainties and thereby arm these influentials to raise serious questions on the science issue.

- Organize under the GCSDC a "Science Education Task Group" that will serve as the point of outreach to the National Science Teachers Association (NSTA) and other influential science education organizations. Work with NSTA to develop school materials that present a credible, balanced picture of climate science for use in classrooms nationwide.

- Distribute educational materials directly to schools and through grassroots organizations of climate science partners (companies, organizations that participate in this effort).

National Direct Outreach Program Budget — $300,000

IV. Funding/Fund Allocation: Develop and implement program to obtain funding, and to allocate funds to ensure that the program is carried out effectively.

Tactics: This strategy will be implemented as soon as we have the go-ahead to proceed.

- Potential funding sources were identified as American Petroleum Institute (API) and its members; Business Round Table (BRT) and its members, Edison Electric Institute (EEI) and its members; Independent Petroleum Association of America (IPAA) and its members; and the National Mining Association (NMA) and its members.

- Potential fund allocators were identified as the American Legislative Exchange Council (ALEC), Committee For A Constructive Tomorrow (CFACT), Competitive Enterprise Institute , Frontiers of Freedom and The Marshall Institute.

Total Funds Required to Implement Program through November 1998 — $2,000,000 (A significant portion of funding for the GCSDC will be deferred until 1999 and beyond)

Measurements

Various metrics will be used to track progress. These measurements will have to be determined in fleshing out the action plan and may include:

- Baseline public / government official opinion surveys and periodic follow-up surveys on the percentage of Americans and government officials who recognize significant uncertainties in climate science.

- Tracking the percent of media articles that raise questions about climate science.

- Number of Members of Congress exposed to our materials on climate science.

- Number of communications on climate science received by Members of Congress from their constituents.

- Number of radio talk show appearances by scientists questioning the "prevailing wisdom" on climate science.

- Number of school teachers / students reached with our information on climate science.

- Number of science writers briefed and who report upon climate science uncertainties.

- Total audience exposed to newspaper, radio, television coverage of science uncertainties.

APPENDIX II
EXXONMOBIL INFLUENCES ON POLICY

Between 1998 and 2005: ExxonMobil Grants $16 Million to Global Warming Skeptic Organizations[a]

ExxonMobil disperses roughly $16 million to organizations that are challenging the scientific consensus view that greenhouse gases are causing global warming. For many of the organizations, ExxonMobil is their single largest corporate donor, often providing more than 10 percent of their annual budgets. A study by the Union of Concerned Scientists will find that "[v]irtually all of them publish and publicize the work of a nearly identical group of spokespeople, including scientists who misrepresent peer-reviewed climate findings and confuse the public's understanding of global warming. Most of these organizations also include these same individuals as board members or scientific advisers." After the Bush administration withdraws from the Kyoto Protocol (see March 27, 2001), the oil company steps up its support for these organizations. Some of the ExxonMobil-funded groups tell the *New York Times* that the increase is a response to the rising level of public interest in the issue. "Firefighters' budgets go up when fires go up," explains Fred L. Smith, head of the Competitive Enterprise Institute. Explaining ExxonMobil's support for these organizations, company spokesman Tom Cirigliano says: "We want to support organizations that are trying to broaden the debate on an issue that is so important to all of us. There is this whole issue that no one should question the science of global climate change. That is ludicrous. That's the kind of dark-ages thinking that gets you in a lot of trouble." [*New York Times*, 5/28/2003; Union of Concerned Scientists, 2007, pp. 10–11 pdf file]

The following is a list of some of the organizations funded by ExxonMobil:

- American Enterprise Institute (AEI) - AEI receives $1,625,000 from ExxonMobil between and 1998 and 2005. During this period, it plays host

---

[a] http://www.historycommons.org/entity.jsp?entity=heartland_institute_1

to a number of climate contrarians. [Union of Concerned Scientists, 2007, pp. 31 pdf file]

- American Legislative Exchange Council - In 2005, ExxonMobil grants $241,500 to this organization. Its website features a non-peer-reviewed paper by climate contrarian Patrick Michaels. [Union of Concerned Scientists, 2007, pp. 12, 31 pdf file]

- Center for Science and Public Policy - Started at the beginning of 2003, this one-man operation receives $232,000 from ExxonMobil. The organization helps bring scientists to Capitol Hill to testify on global warming and the health effects of mercury. [*New York Times*, 5/28/2003]

- Committee for a Constructive Tomorrow - Between 2004 and 2005, this organization receives $215,000 from ExxonMobil. Its advisory panel includes Sallie Baliunas, Robert Balling, Roger Bate, Sherwood Idso, Patrick Michaels, and Frederick Seitz, all of whom are affiliated with other ExxonMobil-funded organizations. [Union of Concerned Scientists, 2007, pp. 12 pdf file]

- Competitive Enterprise Institute (CEI) - Founded in 1984 to fight government regulation on business, CEI started receiving large grants from ExxonMobil after Myron Ebell moved there from Frontiers of Freedom in 1999. [Union of Concerned Scientists, 2007, pp. 12 pdf file] CEI, along with another ExxonMobil-supported enterprise, the Cooler Heads Coalition, runs the website GlobalWarming.Org, which is part of an effort to "dispel the myths of global warming by exposing flawed economic, scientific, and risk analysis." Between 2000 and 2003, the CEI receives $1,380,000, or 16 percent of the total funds donated by Exxon during that period. [Mother Jones, 5/2005; Mother Jones, 5/2005]

- Frontiers of Freedom - The organization receives $230,000 from Exxon in 2002 and $40,000 in 2001. It has an annual budge of about $700,000. *[New York Times*, 5/28/2003]

- George C. Marshall Institute - The institute is known primarily for its work advocating a "Star Wars" missile defense program. Between 1998 and 2005, Exxon-Mobil grants $630,000 to the Marshall Institute primarily to underwrite the institute's climate change effort. William O'Keefe, the organization's CEO, once worked as the executive vice president and chief operating officer of the American Petroleum Institute. He has also served on the board of directors of the Competitive Enterprise Institute, another global warming skeptic organization, and is chairman emeritus of the Global Climate Coalition. [Union of Concerned Scientists, 2007, pp. 12 pdf file]

- Heartland Institute - In 2005, this organization receives $119,000 from ExxonMobil. Its website offers articles by the same scientists promoted by other ExxonMobil-funded global warming skeptic organizations. [Union of Concerned Scientists, 2007, pp. 12 pdf file]

- Tech Central Station - TCS is a web-based organization that provides news, commentary, and analysis focusing on the societal tensions and strains that are concomitant with historical change. TCS proclaims itself as a strong believer of the "material power of free markets, open societies, and individual human ingenuity to raise living standards and improve lives." Until 2006, the website is operated by a public relations firm called the DCI Group, which is a registered ExxonMobil lobbying firm. In 2003 TCS receives $95,000 from ExxonMobil to be used for "climate change support." TCS contributors on the global warming issue include the same group of people that is promoted by several of the other ExxonMobil-funded global warming skeptic organizations. [Union of Concerned Scientists, 2007, pp. 13 pdf file] In 2006, TCS will pay the public relations firm Medialink Worldwide to produce a video news release that challenges the view that global warming has increased the intensity of hurricanes. The piece is later shown on a Mississippi television station and presented as a regular news report (see June 2006).

1998 and After: ExxonMobil Begins Funding Global Warming Skeptic Organization Frontiers of Freedom[b]

ExxonMobil begins funding the Washington, DC-based organization Frontiers of Freedom. The organization, founded in 1996 by former Senator Malcolm Wallop to promote property rights and critique environmental regulations, will use ExxonMobil's money to participate in an effort (see April 1998) to discredit the scientific consensus that rising global temperatures are being caused by the increase of greenhouse gases. One of the group's staff members is Myron Ebell, an outspoken global warming skeptic. By 2005, ExxonMobil will have provided

---

b

http://www.historycommons.org/context.jsp?item=ExxonMobileFundsFrontiersOfFreedom

$857,000 in funds to Frontiers of Freedom. [Union of Concerned Scientists, 2007, pp. 11 pdf file]

Early 1998: ExxonMobil Helps Form 'Global Climate Science Team'[c]

ExxonMobil helps create the Global Climate Science Team (GCST), a small task force that is charged with discrediting the scientific consensus opinion that greenhouse gases are warming the planet. Members of the task force include ExxonMobil's senior environmental lobbyist, Randy Randol; the American Petroleum Institute's public relations representative, Joe Walker; and Steven Milloy, who heads a nonprofit organization called the Advancement of Sound Science Coalition. [American Petroleum Institute, 4/1998; Union of Concerned Scientists, 2007, pp. 11 pdf file] Milloy's organization had been secretly formed in 1993 by tobacco giant Philip Morris with the goal of creating uncertainty about the health hazards posed by secondhand smoke. [Union of Concerned Scientists, 2007, pp. 11 pdf file]

April 1998: Oil and Gas Industry Representatives Draft Plan to Discredit Prevailing Opinion on Global Warming[d]

The Global Climate Science Team drafts a memo outlining a plan to invest millions of dollars in an effort to undermine support for the Kyoto Protocol and discredit the scientific consensus opinion that greenhouse gases are causing the planet to warm. The draft plan, titled "Global Climate Science Communications Action Plan," concedes that opposition to the protocol is not shared by the public. "There has been little, if any, public resistance or pressure applied to Congress to reject the treaty, except by those 'inside the Beltway' with vested interests," it notes. A key component of the plan would be to "maximize the impact of scientific views consistent with ours on Congress, the media, and other key audiences." To do this, they would "recruit a cadre of scientists who share the industry's views of climate science and to train them in public relations so they can help convince journalists, politicians and the public that the risk of global warming is too uncertain to justify controls on greenhouse gases like carbon dioxide that trap the sun's heat near Earth," the *New York*

---

[c] http://www.historycommons.org/context.jsp?item=GlobalClimateScienceTeam

[d] http://www.historycommons.org/context.jsp?item=global_warming_tmln_1

Times reports. They would look to recruit scientists "who do not have a long history of visibility and/or participation in the climate change debate," the memo says. According to the plan, "Victory will be achieved when … recognition of uncertainty becomes part of the 'conventional wisdom.'" One method the institute would employ to measure the plan's progress would be to count the number of news reports that express uncertainty about the issue of global warming. People involved in devising the strategy included Jeffrey Salmon of the George C. Marshall Institute; Steven Milloy, who later becomes a FoxNews.com columnist; David Rothbard of the Committee for a Constructive Tomorrow, which has received $252,000 from ExxonMobil; Myron Ebell of Frontiers of Freedom, also funded with money ($612,000) from the oil giant; and ExxonMobil lobbyist Randy Randol. Representatives of the Exxon Corporation, the Chevron Corporation, and the Southern Company, were also involved. [American Petroleum Institute, 4/1998; *New York Times*, 4/26/1998; Mother Jones, 5/2005]

February 6, 2001: ExxonMobil Lobbyist Calls on White House to Remove Certain Government Climate Scientists[e]

In a memo to the White House Council on Environmental Quality (CEQ), ExxonMobil lobbyist Randy Randol denounces esteemed climate scientist Robert Watson, chairman of the Intergovernmental Panel on Climate Change (IPCC), as someone "handpicked by Al Gore" who is using the media to get "coverage for his views." Thus he asks, "Can Watson be replaced now at the request of the US?" In addition to Watson, Randol names other climate experts who he wants "removed from their positions of influence." A year later, the Bush administration will block Watson's reelection as IPCC chairman. [Randol, 2/6/2005 pdf file; Mother Jones, 5/2005]

---

e

http://www.historycommons.org/context.jsp?item=RandolCalls4RemovalOfScientists&scale=0#RandolCalls4RemovalOfScientists

(2001): Energy Department Official Says Bush's Withdrawal from Kyoto Based on Input from Oil Industry Representatives[f]

Larisa E. Dobriansky, deputy assistant secretary for national energy policy at the Department of Energy, meets with ExxonMobil lobbyist Randy Randol and the Global Climate Coalition, a group formed to oppose restrictions on greenhouse gases. Members of the coalition include ExxonMobil and the American Petroleum Institute. In the notes she prepared for the meeting, she wrote, "POTUS [President Bush] rejected Kyoto, in part, based on input from you." [Mother Jones, 5/2005]

2002: Center for Science and Public Policy Started with Funds from ExxonMobil[g]

ExxonMobil awards a $232,000 grant to Frontiers of Freedom to help launch a new branch organization called the Center for Science and Public Policy. The one-man operation will help bring scientists to Capitol Hill to testify on global warming and the health effects of mercury. [Union of Concerned Scientists, 2007, pp. 11 pdf file]

April 20, 2002: Indian Engineer and Economist Elected IPCC Chairman[h]

Indian engineer and economist Rajendra K. Pachauri is elected with US backing as chairman of the Intergovernmental Panel on Climate Change. [New York Times, 4/20/2002] US energy industry lobbyists had pressured Washington to block the reelection of Robert T. Watson, whose views about global warming had irked American energy companies (see February 6, 2001 and April 2, 2002).

---

[f]

http://www.historycommons.org/context.jsp?item=the_bush_administration_s_environment al_record_147

[g]

http://www.historycommons.org/entity.jsp?entity=center_for_science_and_public_policy_1

[h]

http://www.historycommons.org/context.jsp?item=the_bush_administration_s_environment al_record_146

June 3, 2002: Email Reveals White House Efforts to Punish EPA Officials For Acknowledging Human Role in Rising Temperatures[i]

Myron Ebell, a director of the Competitive Enterprise Institute (CEI), sends an email to Philip A. Cooney, chief of staff at the White House Council on Environmental Quality, discussing how to respond to a recent EPA report (see May 2002) that acknowledged human activity is contributing to global warming. It was the first time the US government had ever made the admission. In the email, Ebell conveys his plan to discredit the report by suing the agency. He also recommends playing down the report and firing some EPA officials. "It seems to me that the folks at the EPA are the obvious fall guys and we would only hope that the fall guy (or gal) should be as high up as possible," he says in the email. "Perhaps tomorrow we will call for Whitman to be fired. … It seems to me our only leverage to push you in the right direction is to drive a wedge between the president and those in the administration who think that they are serving the president's interests by publishing this rubbish." The organization Ebell represents has received more than $1 million since 1998 from Exxon. Cooney previously worked as a lobbyist for the American Petroleum Institute (see 2001). [Ebell, 6/3/2002; Greenpeace, 9/9/2003; Observer, 9/21/2003]

After January 31, 2003: Scientist Who Wrote Article Skeptical of Global Warming Recruited by ExxonMobil-Funded Organizations[j]

After publishing their heavily criticized article on global warming, Willie Soon and Sallie Baliunas quickly cultivate relationships with at least nine organizations whose climate change work is underwritten by ExxonMobil. Among her other affiliations, Baliunas becomes a board member and senior scientist at the Marshall Institute, a scientific adviser to the Annapolis Center for Science-Based Public Policy, an advisory board member of the Committee for a Constructive Tomorrow, and a contributing scientist to the online forum Tech Central Station. Soon will be the chief scientific researcher for the Center for Science and Public Policy, a senior

---

[i]

http://www.historycommons.org/context.jsp?item=the_bush_administration_s_environment al_record_142

[j]

http://www.historycommons.org/context.jsp?item=BaliunasHooksUpWExxonFundedOrgs

scientist at the George C. Marshall Institute, as well as a contributor to the Heartland Institute. [Union of Concerned Scientists, 2007, pp. 15, 34-35 pdf file]

After November 8, 2004: ExxonMobil-Funded Groups Attack Report on Global Warming[k]

A number of individuals and organizations that have received funding from oil giant ExxonMobil attack the recently released Arctic Climate Impact Assessment (see November 8, 2004), which found that the Arctic is warming "at almost twice the rate as that of the rest of the world." The report said that the unprecedented speed of melting in the Arctic is an indication that the climate is undergoing drastic, possibly irreversible, changes that could result in the extinction of numerous species, cause major changes in regional ecosystems, and undermine the livelihood of circumpolar indigenous populations. One of the first attacks on the report is from FoxNews.com columnist Steven Milloy, an adjunct scholar at the libertarian Cato Institute ($75,000 from ExxonMobil). Milloy operates two ExxonMobil-funded organizations—the Advancement of Sound Science Center ($40,000 from ExxonMobil) and the Free Enterprise Action Institute ($50,000 from ExxonMobil)—both of which are registered to his home address in Potomac, Maryland. In his article, titled "Polar Bear Scare on Thin Ice," he claims that one of the graphs in the study's 149-page overview report contradicts the study's conclusions. Harvard biological oceanographer James McCarthy, a lead author of the report, tells Mother Jones that the conclusions are solid. "In order to take that position, you have to refute what are hundreds of scientific papers that reconstruct various pieces of this climate puzzle," he says. The overview report is a mere summary of a 1,200-plus- page, fully referenced, report, that underwent a rigorous peer-review process before publication. It was based on the work of more than 300 scientists and took four years to complete. Another ExxonMobil-funded group, the George C. Marshall Institute ($310,000 from ExxonMobil), also chimes in, issuing a press release that says the Arctic report was based on "unvalidated climate models and scenarios … that bear little resemblance to reality and how the future is likely to evolve." Then, on the same day the Senate holds a hearing about the report's findings, the Competitive Enterprise Institute (CEI) releases a statement claiming "The Arctic Climate Impact Assessment, despite its recent release, has already generated analysis pointing out numerous flaws and distortions." CEI has received $1,350,000 from ExxonMobil (see May 2005). The Fraser Institute of Vancouver, the recipient of $60,000 from the oil company, claims

---

[k]

http://www.historycommons.org/context.jsp?item=exxonGroupsAttackArcticReport

that "2004 has been one of the cooler years in recent history," a statement that is contradicted a month later by no one less than the United Nations' World Meteorological Organization. It will report that 2004 was "the fourth warmest year in the temperature record since 1861." [Mother Jones, 5/2005]

2005: ExxonMobil Provides $2.9 Million to 39 Groups Involved in Efforts to Misrepresent the Scientific Consensus on Global Warming[l]

According to a study done by Britain's Royal Society, in 2005, ExxonMobil provides $2.9 million in funding to 39 groups that the society says misrepresent climate change. Such groups include the International Policy Network, George C. Marshall Institute, Competitive Enterprise Institute, and Center for the Study of Carbon Dioxide and Global Change. [Guardian, 9/20/2006; New York Times, 9/21/2006]

May 2005: ExxonMobil Funds Efforts to Discredit Scientific Consensus on Global Warming[m]

An investigation by Mother Jones magazine identifies 44 organizations funded by ExxonMobil that are involved in, or associated with, efforts to discredit the scientific consensus view on global warming. Many of these organizations have been on the oil giant's payroll since 1998 (see Between 1998 and 2005). The magazine's investigation finds that the oil company has contributed a total of $8,678,450 to these organizations since 2000 with the single largest donation being given to the Competitive Enterprise Institute (CEI). That organization received $1,380,000, or 16 percent of the total funds donated by Exxon. CEI, along with another Exxon-support enterprise, the Cooler Heads Coalition, runs the website GlobalWarming.Org, which is part of an effort to "dispel the myths of global warming by exposing flawed economic, scientific, and risk analysis." Another large recipient of Exxon's funds is the American Enterprise Institute (AEI), which has received $960,000 from the company. AEI, known for its neoconservatism, has played host to a number of global warming skeptics. [Mother Jones, 5/2005; Mother Jones, 5/2005]

---

[l]

http://www.historycommons.org/context.jsp?item=ExxonMobilFundsGlobalWarmingGroups 2005

[m]

http://www.historycommons.org/context.jsp?item=ExxonFundsGlobalWarmingSkeptics

December 2005: Exxon-Funded Organization Publishes Book on Climate Change[n]

The George C. Marshall Institute publishes a book titled, *Shattered Consensus: The True State of Global Warming*. In its press release announcing the book, the institute says the book "demonstrates the remarkable disparities between so-called 'consensus documents' on global warming ... and climate reality." The book, edited by longtime climate contrarian Patrick Michaels, a meteorologist, features essays contributed by Sallie Baliunas, Robert Balling, Randall S. Cerveny, John Christy, Robert E. Davis, Oliver W. Frauenfeld, Ross McKitrick, Eric S. Posmentier, and Willie Soon. Michaels is affiliated with at least ten organizations that have been funded by ExxonMobil and the Marshall Institute has received some $630,000 from ExxonMobil in support of its climate change program (see Between 1998 and 2005). [George C. Marshall Institute, 12/14/2005; Union of Concerned Scientists, 2007, pp. 12 pdf file]

May 18, 2006–May 28, 2006: Global Warming Skeptic Organization Launches Pro-Greenhouse Gas Advertising Campaign[o]

Following the release of the film, An Inconvenient Truth, the Competitive Enterprise Institute (CEI), a group funded in part by ExxonMobil, launches an advertisement campaign welcoming increased carbon dioxide pollution. "Carbon dioxide: They call it pollution, we call it life," the ad says. [Competitive Enterprise Institute, 5/2006; New York Times, 9/21/2006]

---

[n] http://www.historycommons.org/context.jsp?item=ShatterConsensusBook

[o] http://www.historycommons.org/context.jsp?item=CEIadverts200605

June 2006: Local Mississippi TV Station Airs Piece on Global Warming Paid for by an Organization Partially Funded by ExxonMobil[p]

The broadcast public relations firm Medialink Worldwide produces a video news release (VNR) titled, "Global Warming and Hurricanes: All Hot Air?" Medialink was hired to make the VNR by Tech Central Station, a project of the Republican lobbying and PR firm DCI Group. ExxonMobil, a client of the DCI group, gave Tech Central Science Foundation $95,000 in 2003 and specified that those funds be used for "climate change support." The VNR features meteorologists Dr. William Gray and Dr. James J. O'Brien who deny there's a link between global warming and hurricane intensity. Gray has said in the past that global warming is a "hoax," while O'Brien is listed as an expert at the George C. Marshall Institute, which in 2004 received $170,000 from ExxonMobil. The VNR is aired by WTOK-11 in Meridian, Mississippi on May 31, 2006. The segment is re-voiced by the station anchor, Tom Daniels, who introduces the piece by saying, "Hurricane seasons for the next 20 years could be severe. But don't blame global warming." He does not disclose that the report was produced by a PR firm that was paid by an organization funded by ExxonMobil. [Center for Media and Democracy, 11/14/2006; Democracy Now!, 11/14/2006; San Francisco Chronicle, 11/15/2006]

July 2006: Exxon-Funded Organization Offers to Pay Scientists to Critique 2007 IPCC Report[q]

The American Enterprise Institute (AEI) sends letters to scientists and economists offering to pay them $10,000 each for 500- to 10,000-word essays that provide a "policy critique" of the next report from the UN's Intergovernmental Panel on Climate Change (IPCC), due early next year (see February 2, 2007). The institute, which has received more than $1.6 million in contributions from ExxonMobil (see Between 1998 and 2005), also offers additional payments and travel expense reimbursement. The letters, written by Kenneth Green and Steven Hayward, accuse

---

[p]

http://www.historycommons.org/context.jsp?item=200606AllHotAir&scale=0#200606AllHot
Air

[q]

http://www.historycommons.org/context.jsp?item=AEIGWLettersToScientists&scale=0#AEI
GWLettersToScientists

the UN panel of being "resistant to reasonable criticism and dissent and prone to summary conclusions that are poorly supported by the analytical work." It asks for articles that "thoughtfully explore the limitations of climate model outputs." The letters set a December 15 deadline for the papers, but responses from recipient scientists prompt AEI to cancel the project. The institute had hoped to time the release of the scientists' essays to coincide with that of the IPCC report. David Viner of the Climatic Research Unit at the University of East Anglia describes the AIE effort as a "desperate attempt by an organization who wants to distort science for their own political aims." Similarly, Ben Stewart of Greenpeace remarks: "The AEI is more than just a thinktank, it functions as the Bush administration's intellectual Cosa Nostra. They are White House surrogates in the last throes of their campaign of climate change denial. They lost on the science; they lost on the moral case for action. All they've got left is a suitcase full of cash." Green defends AIE's campaign against the report, saying, "Right now, the whole debate is polarized. One group says that anyone with any doubts whatsoever are deniers and the other group is saying that anyone who wants to take action is alarmist. We don't think that approach has a lot of utility for intelligent policy." [Guardian, 2/2/2007; Reuters, 2/4/2007]

(July 17, 2006): Utility Companies Raise Money for Scientist Who Disputes Consensus Opinion on Global Warming[r]

The Intermountain Rural Electric Association (IREA) of Sedalia, Colorado, gives Patrick Michaels, a climatologist who disputes the consensus opinion that greenhouses gases are responsible for global warming, $100,000 and helps launch a fundraising campaign for him. Michaels had told Western business leaders the year before that he needed more funds to continue his research and writing. In a July 17 letter to 50 other utility companies, Stanley Lewandowski, IREA's general manager, writes, "We cannot allow the discussion to be monopolized by the alarmists." He requests that the other electric cooperatives collaborate on a campaign to discredit "alarmist" scientists and Al Gore's movie An Inconvenient Truth. According to Lewandowski, one company has said it will contribute $50,000 to Michaels, while another plans to give money the following year. [Associated Press, 7/27/2006]

---

[r] http://www.historycommons.org/context.jsp?item=IndustriesFundPatMichaels

April 21, 2007: Ford CEO Acknowledges That Auto Emissions Causing Global Warming[s]

Ford Motor Co. chief executive Alan Mulally acknowledges in a telephone press conference that global warming is happening and is being caused in part by auto emissions. "The vast majority of data indicates that the temperature has increased, and I believe the correlation and the analysis says that is mainly because of the greenhouse gases keeping the heat in. You can just plot it with the Industrial Revolution and the use of all of our resources," he says. [Denver Post, 4/24/2007]

---

[s] http://www.historycommons.org/context.jsp?item=FordCEOAdmitsHumanCause

18

IS YOUR SENATOR A CROOK?

In politics, money is like water against a building's foundation: it will find its way through the tiniest cracks and, in time, a trickle can become a flood. In the theory that money couldn't—and perhaps shouldn't—be stopped entirely, today's campaign finance laws rely on public disclosure. Supposedly, the public and the press can sort through the streams of cash entering a candidate's coffers and trace them back to vested interests, thus exposing politicians to the glare of the public spotlight and, presumably, the wrath of voters.

SEJ Journal
Society of Environmental Journalists
Undated

The internet, Google and other powerful search engines and a multitude of websites have made finding out which corporations are giving money to which politicians quick and easy. It's not a pretty sight.

A case in point is former Republican Sen. Chuck Hagel of Nebraska, who retired in 2009 after two six-year terms and a brief flirtation with a run for the Presidency.[1] His Senate career was fairly ho-hum, except for the first year. That was a doozy, because Hagel managed to almost single-handedly make $1 million for himself, while virtually guaranteeing that the United States would never be a party to international efforts to curb global warming.

Through his efforts during that first year, Hagel's influence continues today. His case illustrates just how easy it is for those who know the ways of Washington to permanently change the course of history. His is a case study in the ease with which money can be raised and, more importantly, the price that the rest of us pay when it is used as a tool by the rich and their corporations.

The irony is that Hagel, a self-made millionaire, had no need for the money that he took, for in 1996, he was the kind of candidate who is every elected politician's worst nightmare: rich.

Running against a
popular Democratic governor,
Ben Nelson, Hagel was initially
given little chance by political
oddsmakers. But he ran a good
campaign, overtook Nelson, and

(T)here is no evidence that the words global warming or anything similar ever crossed Hagel's lips during the campaign.

when things started getting close, Hagel played his trump card: he lent himself
$1 million.

Hagel then won handily, finishing with 56 percent of the vote to Nelson's
42 percent.[a] But he also finished the race with a problem: he was out of pocket the
$1 million he had lent himself.

Hagel's problem—needing to replenish the $1 million missing from his
bank account—was one that those familiar with the ways of Washington know how
to solve. And, although he had not previously held elective office, Hagel was no
stranger to the nation's capital. From 1971 to 1977, he had been chief aide to
Republican Rep. John Y. McCollister, then became a lobbyist for Firestone for
three years, which was followed by a stint in the number two spot at the Veterans'
Administration in the Reagan Administration. It was after this apprenticeship in
Washington politics that Hagel founded Vanguard Cellular Systems and made his
fortune, then returned to Nebraska to lay the foundation for a run for the U.S.
Senate.

Within days of his election, Hagel's coffers began to swell with donations
from special interest groups. Many of those post-election contributions came from
the coal, oil, auto and other industries opposed to action to control global warming,
even though there is no evidence that the words global warming or anything similar
ever crossed Hagel's lips during the campaign. A search of the *Omaha World
Herald* files yielded no mention of the issue by Hagel, campaign newspaper
reporters interviewed by telephone recalled no mention of global warming and
other observers say the subject of global warming never arose. Hagel's office failed
to respond to both written and telephone inquiries on the subject.

Hagel might have been a cipher on global warming before the election, but
he certainly wasn't afterwards. Within months of entering the Senate, Hagel had
become one of the most unflinching allies of the oil, coal, utility and other
industries fighting actions to control global warming. He held hearings, made floor

---

[a] Nelson was elected to Nebraska's other Senate seat in 2000.

statements and speeches and, most importantly, provided the Republican support for the single largest obstacle to a global treaty to deal with climate change, the Byrd-Hagel Resolution. It passed the Senate on June 12, 1997 by a vote of 95–0, with 64 cosponsors. It placed the U.S. Senate, which by Constitutional mandate must approve treaties, on record as opposing any global warming agreement that failed to require "new specific scheduled commitments to limit or reduce greenhouse gas emissions" by China, India, and other developing nations.[b]

The development of the Byrd-Hagel Resolution, and the roles played by coal, railroad and oil corporations, is discussed elsewhere. The purpose of this chapter is to demonstrate the ease with which a relatively modest amount of money can be used to dictate laws.

The Democratic half of the resolution was provided by Sen. Robert C. Byrd of West Virginia. As a young man Byrd had been a coal miner. Ultimately the longest-serving member of the U.S. Senate in history, Byrd was fiercely protective of the state, especially its coal miners and owners. He was a man with a long memory. Those who crossed him eventually paid for it.

His post-election contributors included not only BP Amoco, Chevron, Marathon, Mobil, Occidental, Shell, Tenneco, and Texaco oil companies, but electric utilities in West Virginia, Ohio, the Dakotas, Michigan, California, Pennsylvania, Kansas City, Minnesota, Philadelphia, Georgia, Alabama, Florida, and Tampa, as well as the Big Three car makers of General Motors, Ford and Daimler Chrysler, and several coal companies. Virtually none of these interests had given Hagel even so much as a dollar before the election.

Byrd was determined to prevent the United States from acting against global warming. That would have meant controls on coal, the number one product of West Virginia.

---

[b] The Resolution declared—

That it is the sense of the Senate that—

(1) the United States should not be a signatory to any protocol to, or other agreement regarding, the United Nations Framework Convention on Climate Change of 1992, at negotiations in Kyoto in December 1997, or thereafter, which would—

(A) mandate new commitments to limit or reduce greenhouse gas emissions for the Annex I Parties, unless the protocol or other agreement also mandates new specific scheduled commitments to limit or reduce greenhouse gas emissions for Developing Country Parties within the same compliance period, or

(B) would result in serious harm to the economy of the United States.

But almost every successful legislative initiative is bi-partisan, requiring at least one Democrat and one Republican. Byrd needed a Republican to join him, and Chuck Hagel was just the guy.

While the freshman Senator was busy fighting against an international agreement, his campaign was raising money. During the two years following Hagel's election—with his next election not until 2002—Hagel raised roughly $133,000 from the political action committees of those opposed to action to curb global warming. This was more than five times as much as he raised from these same groups before the election.

His post-election contributors included not only BP Amoco, Chevron, Marathon, Mobil, Occidental, Shell, Tenneco, and Texaco oil companies, but coal-burning electric utilities in West Virginia, Ohio, the Dakotas, Michigan, California, Pennsylvania, Kansas City, Minnesota, Philadelphia, Georgia, Alabama, Florida, and Tampa, as well as the Big Three car makers of General Motors, Ford and Daimler Chrysler, and several coal companies. Virtually none of these interests had given Hagel even so much as a dollar before the election.

These and other contributions did wonders in reducing the debt that Hagel owed himself. Of the $1,099,783 that he collected in 1997–98, he paid $787,000 to himself. In other words, for every $1,000 donated by a coal, oil, utility, auto or other polluting interest, roughly $750 was the equivalent of a direct deposit to his personal bank account. This was, and is, perfectly legal.

It is also perfectly legal to use campaign contributions for all manner of other seemingly unrelated expenses. A candidate can buy a car and repair it, purchase clothing, contribute to other political parties and charities, pay to move relatives and even pay his/her own salary while campaigning. When an incumbent retires, the money tags along and can be used for anything the former office-holder believes to be legitimate.

Finding how much money an office-holder like Hagel raises and from whom is fairly easy. The first step is to determine whether there is (a) a position that logically would attract heavy contributions and (b) a stream of money flowing from vested interests to an office holder.

Step one: check the record. The first stop in this project was to determine what official records there were of Hagel's activities on global warming. This may be the easiest step, especially for those with access to Lexis/Nexis or similar services. To find out what specific legislation a candidate might have sponsored or what words might have been spoken, the best place to look is the website of the Library of Congress, Thomas (http://thomas.loc.gov/home/thomas.php).

Ordinary citizens can also visit Project VoteSmart, http://www.vote-smart.org/, a non-profit institution based in Montana with a branch office in Boston. It bills itself as "a national library of factual

> *Much of what office holders have to provide of value is intangible. They can hold hearings, or not; write letters or otherwise exercise influence in ways that may never be publicly revealed.*

information on over 13,000 elected offices and candidates for public office." The Project is funded by individual contributions as well as the Pew, Carnegie and other foundations. It describes itself as "staffed by both conservatives and liberals of various parties who have volunteered for up to two years." Noting that its members have included Goldwater and McGovern, Carter and Ford, Newt Gingrich and Geraldine Ferraro, the Project says "We will not allow anyone to join our founding board without a political enemy."[2]

VoteSmart's on-site information is too general for a focused inquiry, and Thomas tracks only legislative actions and words. Although these sources can and do show that Hagel quickly became deeply committed and very active in the cause of staving off international action to curb global warming, they can by no means paint a complete picture. Much of what office holders have to provide of value is intangible. They can hold hearings, or not; write letters or otherwise exercise influence in ways that may never be publicly revealed.

Check office-holder's own websites, where they will often boast in their own press releases of their hearing and statements, and don't overlook the obvious—simple searches using engines such as Google, Yahoo, Go, Hotbot or whatever search engine you prefer. Also search local newspapers. Check with political adversaries as well, who often keep close tabs on what their rivals are up to.

Step two: follow the money. Sites that provide information on campaign contributions come and go. Currently, http://www.opensecrets.org/ seems to be the most transparent and easy to use. The Federal Election Commission's official website, http://www.fec.gov/disclosure.shtml, is the most fact-rich, but takes some effort to master.

Another useful site, http://www.publicampaign.org/, is breezy and contains interesting articles. It is "dedicated to sweeping reform that aims to dramatically reduce the role of special interest money in America's elections and the influence of big contributors in American politics." A very accessible and user-friendly site, http://pml.cq.com/, is operated by Political MoneyLine. It describes itself as "the leading source of comprehensive, timely and objective campaign finance and lobbying information." If it isn't, it sure comes close.

For example, a search on August 25, 2012 revealed that multi-billionaire David Koch of Koch Industries had given—

- $1,000,000 to the Republican Governors Association on Feb. 1, 2012;

- $2,500 to the McConnell Senate Committee '14 on Dec. 12, 2011;

- $5,000 to the Koch Industries Inc Political Action Committee (KOCHPAC) on June 230, 2011.

- $1,000,000 to the Republican Governors Association on on April 20, 2011;

- $2,500 to the Hatch Election Committee Inc. On June 28, 2011; and,

- $30,800 to the Republican Senatorial Committee on Jun e 27, 2011.

But an attempt to determine whether the Republican Senatorial Committee had laundered Koch's money, and sent some or all of it on to Hatch (earmarking such gifts is a common practice), triggered the following message "A subscription is required to do this search. Please log in to do this search." Well, it is, after all, a dot com.

That said, it is clear that David Koch can get his telephone calls returned quickly, or the doors opened to visit, virtually any Republican candidate or office-holder.

Further down the page was an article that had nothing to do with campaign contributions, but everything to do with U.S. politics.

The rich and corporations have long since learned that it takes a lot of money to buy hundreds of politicians almost constantly, and the results can be uncertain. With judges, however, the story is different. Their numbers are much smaller, most of them serve for life and the links between what they receive (or own) and their opinions is seldom scrutinized. On the Political Money Line's home page was the following juicy tidbit:

Associate Justice Alito's Free Trips to Hawaii, Italy and Austria
8/25/2012
Associate Justice Samuel Alito was the last on the Supreme Court to
file his personal financial disclosure report for CY2011. He had
received an extension to file. His report indicated he received
transportation, meals and lodging for an eight day trip to Honolulu.
Hawaii to teach at the University of Hawaii. Apparently the January
2011 trip was enough of a benefit since he reported no income from the
trip. Alito also reported a free ten day trip to Rome, Italy, in July 2011,
to teach at the Duquesne University School of Law. Duquesne paid for
the transportation, meals, lodging, and also gave him $15,000. Alito
also reported a free trip to Vienna, Austria in October 2011 to speak at a
conference. The trip was paid for by the Federalist Society. Other non-
investment income in 2011 included $11,955 from Duke Law School
for teaching in September 2011 during a four day trip to Durham, NC.
With investments, Alito did well with one of his largest holdings—
Exxon Mobil Corporation stock—valued at between $100,001 and
$250,000. In 2011, Exxon Mobil's yearly return was 16%.

Do we believe that Justice Alito might have taken part in one or more cases
in which ExxonMobil had interest. Yes. Did ExxonMobil give money to the
Federalist Society and thus indirectly pay Scalia's trip? You bet. It was a
seemingly inconsequential $15,000 for each of the years 2003–06, according to the
fee for service site, Philanthropy Roundtable.com, searched on August 25, 2012.
Chances are good that there was some indirect giving as well, but there are only so
many hours in the day, so the search was suspended.

The principal denier of global warming these days is Republican Sen. James
Inhofe of Oklahoma, author of the book *The Greatest Hoax: How the Global
Warming Conspiracy Threatens Your Future.* Appearing on *Voice of Christian
Youth America* to publicize the book, Inhofe cited the Bible as the source of his
conviction that global warming is a hoax:

> Well actually the Genesis 8:22 that I use in there is that "as long as
> the earth remains there will be springtime and harvest, cold and heat,
> winter and summer, day and night." My point is, God's still up there.
> The arrogance of people to think that we, human beings, would be
> able to change what He is doing in the climate is to me outrageous.[3]

Attempting to track contributions to Inhofe on Political MoneyLine, quickly
triggered the "subscription required," so a move to the FEC's website was required
(http://www.fec.gov/).

Click on the "Campaign Finance Disclosure Portal," then "2012 House and Senate Elections" then "House and Senate Map" then the state of interest (in this case, Oklahoma), then select the election cycle when Inhofe last ran (2007–08), click on "Inhofe," the under "FinalSummary," there is a "Receipts" tab, with selections for "Itemized Individual Contributions" or "Other Committees Contributions." Click on either of these to see who gave to Inhofe.

Political Action Committees (PACs) are the "Other Committees" and they provide fast clues to who is giving dough to Inhofe. Click on it and bingo! Pay dirt. Seventh down is the "ACTION COMM. FOR RURAL ELECTRIFICATION" or ACRE. It always gives to global warming naysayers. They gave Inhofe $5,000 in 2007. ALLEGHENY ENERGY INC FEDERAL PAC, which is a coal-fired electrcity generator in Pennsylavnia, gave him $3,000 in 2008. ARCH COAL donated $4,000. In all, during that election cycle Inhofe raised, said the FEC, $5,267,716. That means that on each and every day of his six-year term from 2003 through 2008, Inhofe had to raise $2,403.15—Saturdays, Sundays, Easter, Christmas and Yom Kippur included.

With so much money spent, it must have been a tight race in 2008. Nope. Inhofe won with 56.7 percent of the vote to 39.2 for his Democratic opponent, a landslide of +17.5 percent for Inhofe.[4]

Do not ignore contributions from individuals. In the aggregate, contributions from individuals to a campaign are roughly the same magnitude as those from political action committees (PACs), so they are important in and of themselves. They can also be a vital clue: finding a $1,000 contribution from an association president or a senior partner in a law firm that represents a major industry is a dead giveaway that money is being directed to a candidate. In Hagel's case, for example, the head of the Global Climate Coalition, William O'Keefe—who was then also a senior vice president of the American Petroleum Association, the trade association of the oil industry—gave $2,000. O'Keefe donated $1,000 on August 1, 1997, and another $1,000 on April 2, 1998.

Look for these $1,000 contributions, which is the most an individual may give under federal law. Contributions of $250 don't count for much in Washington. Second, look for common dates.

In Hagel's case, for example, the head of the Global Climate Coalition, William O'Keefe—who is also a senior vice president of the American Petroleum Association, the trade association of the oil industry—gave $2,000. O'Keefe donated $1,000 on August 1, 1997, and another $1,000 on April 2, 1998.

It's easy to miss contributions when searching individual records. "Bill O'Keefe," for example, is one FEC file while "William O'Keefe" is another, even though the person is the same. Similarly, the O'Keefe who lives in McLean, Virginia is the same O'Keefe who works in Washington, D.C., but, again, the records may be different.

Contributors are supposed to list not only addresses, but employers, so there should be a lot of lawyers. To find out if a lawyer from, say, Van Ness Feldman, might have an interest in global warming or air pollution, return to the PML home page, click on Lobby $ and Lobbyists registrations, select an issue area, then conduct a control-f search for "Van Ness." Up pops a report that the firm represents BP Amoco.

Step three: search for the obvious. A search on Google, for example, for "Koch Industries lobbyists" brought up a lot of sites. One of them, www.desmogblog.com/koch-industries-inc, contained a profile of Koch that revealed it had bankrolled an anti-global warming campaign and one of the most prominent skeptics, Patrick Michaels.

Koch Industries' official position is that it has no stance on global warming. In fact, the company and its owners spend millions, probably more, attempting to destroy the credibility of the sciences and scientists. Desmogblog revealed, for example, the following:

> An Intermountain Rural Electric Association (IREA) memo from 2006 provides the most authoritative information of Koch's position on climate change. The 2006 IREA letter was created in order to drum up support within the coalition against "global warming alarmists."
>
> Within the letter, the IREA states "there are other groups that are interested in the issue of global warming and the concerns about its costs." The letter goes on to say that Koch was working with American Electric Power (AEP) and the Southern Company to produce a film to counteract "An Inconvenient Truth." Even more, the IREA explains that Koch had decided to finance a coalition on the issue. The coalition was to be administered by the National Association of Manufacturers.[c]

---

[c] In fact, the National Association of manufacturers does run a global warming
(continued...)

Finally, the IREA explicitly links Koch to the global warming denialist circle when it declares, "we have met with Koch, CEI and Dr. [Patrick] Michaels, and they meet among themselves periodically to discuss their [global warming] activities."[5]

Step four: look beyond the obvious. One of the first rules of searching for cash-policy connections is to look beyond the obvious. For global warming, for example, the coal, oil, electric utility and auto industries obviously have stakes in the debate. But look for others.

Why do convenience stores care about global warming? Because many, such as ARCO's AM/PM chain and Exxon's Tiger Marts, are owned by oil companies.

Coal, for example, is the number one source of income for U.S. railroads. Moreover, many railroads are themselves coal owners dating from the days when the government gave them land as an inducement to open the West.

The largest single operating expense for many chemical companies is the cost of coal and oil, which are feedstocks for their products. Similarly, steel mills and cement kilns not only consume immense amounts of energy, but also use coal and lime as feedstocks, both of which emit carbon dioxide.

---

[c] (...continued)
program—or more accurately an anti-action-to-control-global-warming program. The NAM's policy is—

"The NAM and our member companies are committed to protecting the environment through greater environmental sustainability, increased energy efficiency and conservation and reducing greenhouse gas emissions believed to be associated with global climate change. We know the U.S. cannot solve the climate change issue alone. The establishment of federal climate change policies to reduce greenhouse gas emissions, whether legislative or regulatory, must be done in a thoughtful, deliberative and transparent process that ensures a competitive level playing field for U.S. companies in the global marketplace.

"Therefore, the NAM opposes any federal or state government actions regarding climate change that could adversely affect the international competitiveness of the U.S. marketplace economy. Any climate change policies should focus on cost-effective reductions, be implemented in concert with all major emitting nations, and take into account all greenhouse sources and sinks. The NAM believes that federal climate policies generally should pre-empt state policies." http://www.nam.org/Issues/Official-Policy-Positions/Energy-and-Resources-Policy/Energy-and-Natural-Resources.aspx#113, accessed Oct. 18, 2012.

Why do convenience stores care about global warming? Because many, such as ARCO's AM/PM chain and Exxon's Tiger Marts, are owned by oil companies.

Step five: look for circumventions. Federal law limits contributions. Individuals are capped at $1,000 per campaign (primary, runoff and general elections each constitute a single campaign, so there is a potential maximum of $3,000. PACs are capped at $5,000. For those who want to give more it's easy to circumvent the rule. Wives can give, and so can children and parents. A company's lawyer, the firm's partners and their wives and children can give. For example, Clayton Yeutter gave Hagel $2,000 in the 1996 campaign cycle, while "homemaker" Christy Bach Yeutter, pitched in another $1,000. Aside from this, there are numerous other ways of skirting the rules.

For example, Netivasion reveals that Hagel received $5,000 from Burlington-Northern (BN) (headquartered in Nebraska, BN also donated $5,000 to Hagel's Democratic opponent, a common practice) and $1,000 from Norfolk Southern. But is that all? Possibly not, for on April 19, 1996, BN gave $2,500 to Keep Our Majority Political Action Committee (KOMPAC), which in turn donated $30,000 on July 2 to the Republican National Committee, which funneled roughly $60,000 to the Nebraska Republican Committee over a period of months, including a payment of $15,312 on July 17. Then on July 20, the Nebraska RC gave $1,000 to Hagel. Was some of BN's April 19 contribution earmarked for Hagel? No way to tell, but earmarks, whether for pork barrel projects or campaign cash, are a part of Washington.

Step six: look for clusters. "Bundles," or gifts collected by a single lobbyist from colleagues, then delivered to the office-holder, are clear signs that a candidate has been adopted by an industry. So are fundraisers. To find these look for donations clustered on or close to the same date.

On April 2, 1998, Hagel collected $15,300 from 19 individuals, almost all from Texas and associated with the oil industry. The three exceptions were Bill O'Keefe of the American Petroleum Industry, Stephen Wood of Reston, Virginia (with Shell Oil) and Washington lawyer Kent Hance. In all likelihood, one or all of these three arranged a fundraiser for Hagel in Texas or they bundled the checks for him.

To do this, scroll to the bottom of Netivasion's page to "Breakout of recipients by date," and press the button. This produces a list of contributions grouped in batches. On April 2, 1998, Hagel collected $15,300 from 19 individuals, almost all from Texas and associated with the oil industry. The three exceptions were Bill O'Keefe of the American Petroleum Industry, Stephen Wood of Reston, Virgina (with Shell Oil) and Washington lawyer Kent Hance. In all likelihood, one or all of these three arranged a fundraiser for Hagel in Texas or they bundled the checks for him. All three are not only Washington veterans, but active in raising and giving money to prevent action against global warming.

O'Keefe was executive vice president of the American Petroleum Institute, the oil industry's trade association. He is also chairman of the Global Climate Coalition, a business confederation founded in 1989 to lobby against actions to curb global warming. O'Keefe has contributed to a half-dozen members of Congress, including Rep. John Dingell of Michigan, a Democrat who is the most outspoken House of Representatives opponent of action to curb global warming.

Wood works for Diefenderfer and Wunder, a Washington lobbying firm that once gave $200,000 to the National Policy Forum, a Republican fundraising arm.[6] The firm's clients include CSX railroad.[7] Other clients include Ashland Oil, Bituminous Coal Operators, the Construction Industry Air Quality Coalition, Industrial Oil Consumers Group, Lonesome Dove Petroleum, Shell Oil, and the Oil Refiners Coalition for Competitive Markets.[8]

Hance, a lawyer and member of Congress from 1979–85, "frequently attends OPEC meetings and is active in the acquisition of international oil & gas drilling rights on behalf of U.S. and international clients," according to his official biography. He also "served on the Finance Committee for U.S. Senator Phil Gramm and U.S. Senator Kay Bailey Hutchison, and on Governor George W. Bush's re-election campaign."

All in all, Hagel did handsomely after his election in 1996. Although his six-year term didn't expire until 2003, he collected $1,099,783 in 1997–98 and another $366,194 in 1999–2000. In 1997–98, more than $600,000 came from PACs, and about $467,000 from individuals. Burlington Northern gave him another $5,000, while Union Pacific kicked in $11,000, starting with a $5,000 gift on January 8, 1997.

Electric utilities, which had given only $4,000 to Hagel in 1995–96 when he was initially running for the Senate, donated 10 times that amount in 1997–98. In 1999–2000, Hagel hit the jackpot in California, especially with Edison Mission Energy (EME) and its related companies. EME is the world's third or fourth largest independent producer of electricity, with plants in 20 or more nations, virtually all of them coal-fired, with no pollution controls—exactly the type of power plants likely to be shut down by a global warming agreement that called for reductions in emissions.

From July 23–August 10, 1999, Hagel received 15 individual contributions from Edison executives totaling $14,500. This was in addition to $10,000 from the firm's political action committee that had been spread over several months.

Also check for in-kind contributions, such as $229.63 paid by the PowerPAC of the Edison Electric Institute to Washington, D.C. caterer Geppetto Catering on April 27, 1999—it's a sure sign that the electricity industry hosted a fundraiser for Hagel on or about that date.

Step seven: look for connections. This is where to find just how much of an investigative reporter you are. Figuratively, grab a piece of string and pull until you unravel something. For example, note that on January 22, 1997 Hagel received $1,000 from the Action Committee for Rural Electrification (ACRE) (as Inhofe did eleven years later), one of the major foes of air pollution regulation in whatever shape or form.

The best site for cross-walking campaign contributions is the FEC's, so head there. Click on the blue-lighted name of ACRE, which brings up its FEC data, showing others to whom it has contributed. Hit control-f, search for 01/22/97, and other names start popping up. Among them: the most outspoken House foe of action to curb global warming, Rep. John Dingell, who also received $1,000 on January 22, 1997. Among the "A" names alone, Hagel and Dingell shared four other contributors related to global warming: Allegheny Energy (an electric utility), AmerEn, Arch Coal (a coal company), and Arnold & Porter (a major Washington law firm with many energy clients).

Step eight: avoid red herrings. There is so much money, from so many different sources that it is dizzying. If ever there were a situation where staying on track is essential this is it. Hagel, for example, received over 2,600 contributions from individuals alone. It is a very common practice for the wealthy to send donations in the names of children, including infants. It is also common practice to ask fund-raisers for names of needy candidates, and in response, to send a sheaf of $1,000 or $500 checks with the names of the payee left blank, so they be filled in later, to the Republican or Democratic party committees. Trying to pin down the connection between a "student" in New York City and a given candidate can be not only be maddening, but a waste of time, because there might be none.

Step nine: examine expenditures. Because all of the sites focus on contributions, not expenditures, this can be tough. But if there's a bureau in Washington or some other way of dispatching a research assistant to the Federal Election Commission, it can be worth it,

> Of the $1,099,783 collected by Hagel in 1997–98, over three-quarters, or $787,000, was used to repay the loan of $1 million made to himself during the campaign. When the Southern Company gave $1,000 on March 11, 1997 and $2,000 on February 2, 1998, it was, in effect, making a direct deposit to Hagel's personal bank account. In 1999–2000, Hagel paid himself another $205,000.

because there is virtually no constraint on how money can be spent. Candidates buy cars (and repairs for them), clothing, dinners and vacations. They give money to the Boy Scouts and the Miss America Pageant, local colleges and universities, state, local and national committees, as well as to other candidates. Washington is awash in vested interest money, some of it spent in the strangest ways. Hagel's cash, however, went mostly to one place: himself.

Of the $1,099,783 collected by Hagel in 1997–98, over three-quarters, or $787,000, was used to repay the loan of $1 million made to himself during the campaign. When the Southern Company gave $1,000 on March 11, 1997 and $2,000 on February 2, 1998, it was, in effect, making a direct deposit to Hagel's personal bank account. In 1999–2000, Hagel paid himself another $205,000.

Step ten: add it up, and trust the facts. Whether Hagel received money because industry liked his views, or whether he adopted those views for the sake of raising money is impossible to say. Indeed, trying to find a brown paper bag stuffed with money trading hands in exchange for a vote may miss the point.

It is a measure of how much America's politicians have changed that in 1952, Richard Nixon was almost forced from the ticket with Dwight Eisenhower because he had accepted and used money for purposes that are today commonplace.[d]

---

[d] In 1952, after it was revealed that then-Senator Richard Nixon of California had a "slush" fund maintained by supporters to pay personal expenses, he was forced to speak on national television to defend himself and secure his place as the nominee for vice president, with former General Dwight Eisenhower at ticket's head. It became known as the "Checkers speech" because, after painting himself as a man of modest means, Nixon said that the family cocker spaniel, Checkers, also had been given to him by a supporter and "Regardless of what they say about it, we're going to keep it." The slush fund was said to be legal, but nevertheless widely viewed as a bribe. The reference to Checkers enthralled voters, who flooded the campaign with demands that Nixon stay on. Today, such slush funds are common.

Perhaps the lesson to be learned from reviewing Chuck Hagel's campaign receipts and expenditures is that a system of corruption that once was conducted at a retail level, one vote at a time, is today done at wholesale. The immense amount of money flowing out of the accounts of big business and into the accounts of politicians does not buy single votes or individual politicians, but rather the entire system, or at least immense chunks of it. Money is applied to fields of Washington in much the same way that fertilizer and pesticides are worked in the soils by a farmer, stunting the growth of plants that are unwanted while bolstering the health of those that are. So, too, are healthy politicians brought to harvest.

Politicians will say they pay no attention to the identities of their contributors, and that there is no connection between what is given to them and what they do. Make your own judgment, but I personally believe that it is simply, and obviously, untrue.

I have personally seen Senators collect $100,000 in campaign contributions from, for example, those that made, sold and used CFCs, better known as "Freons" and soon thereafter offer legislation to keep the chemicals on the market even though they destroy stratospheric ozone. A senator once told me, and to my consternation merely accepted it as reasonable, that another was "not going to be with us" on a floor vote because a lobbyist who had donated $5,000 was demanding his vote (for the record, this involved neither Sen. Stafford nor Sen. Roth).

Admittedly, politicians don't have every contributor in mind every day. When contributors number in the thousands, it's tough to keep track of them all. But one reason companies have lobbyists is to remind forgetful legislators, and they do.

It is human nature, to believe the best. There is a natural inclination to accept expressions of innocence, and dismiss the notion that an official could be bought for $5,000. But look at the money, then the policies. They speak for themselves.

19
KILLING KYOTO

Resolved,

That it is the sense of the Senate that— (1) the United States should not be a signatory to any protocol to, or other agreement regarding, the United Nations Framework Convention on Climate Change of 1992, at negotiations in Kyoto in December 1997, or thereafter, which would—

(A) mandate new commitments to limit or reduce greenhouse gas emissions for the Annex I Parties, unless the protocol or other agreement also mandates new specific scheduled commitments to limit or reduce greenhouse gas emissions for Developing Country Parties within the same compliance period, or

(B) would result in serious harm to the economy of the United States. ...

S. Res. 98,
"The Byrd-Hagel Resolution"[1]

It is Bonn, Germany in 1997. Negotiators from throughout the world are laying the groundwork for another meeting in two months scheduled for Kyoto, Japan where many of the world's governments hope to strike an agreement to combat global warming. In fact, a proposed agreement will emerge from those negotiations, but it will be dead before the details are agreed to, and the man principally responsible is seated here in Bonn, together with his allies from the American corporate community.

There is a certain smugness on the faces of American business lobbyists, for they know that the agreement that will come to be called the Kyoto Protocol after it is negotiated a few months from now, is already dead. Roughly one week before the American lobbyists boarded their flights at Washington 's Dulles Airport, the U.S. Senate had unanimously adopted, by a vote of 95–0, the Byrd-Hagel Resolution, designed to prevent any international agreement to curb global warming.

The resolution said that any agreement that "would result in serious harm to the economy of the United States" was unacceptable and would be rejected by the U.S. Senate, which exercises the Constitutional power to accept or reject treaties with other nations. And, perhaps more importantly, the resolution required that developing nations meet "new specific scheduled commitments to limit or reduce greenhouse gas emissions … within the same compliance period" as rich industrialized nations like the U.S. It is this requirement that is likely to be the deal-buster at international negotiations, because if only a few such nations—or, indeed, just one, if it is important enough—objects to this requirement, talks will be brought to an unbreakable deadlock. The American lobbyists are intending for this to happen.

Roughly one week after the Senate approved Byrd-Hagel, Donald Pearlman, David Finnegan and the other American lobbyists boarded their flights for Bonn. There, the last stake would be driven into the heart of what would later be named the Kyoto Protocol. At the meeting, Pearlman would be seen huddling with a Nigerian delegate, in a mood that was described by an observer as "gleeful."

"We can kill this thing," he was heard to say.[2] They did.

On Friday, December 5, 1997 the "G-77s"[a]— a loose coalition of developing nations, designed to promote its members' collective economic interests— held a press conference. China, supported by Thailand, Saudi Arabia, Iran, Colombia, Malaysia, Nicaragua, Honduras, Syria, Ghana, Togo, Laos, Kuwait, Grenada, Botswana, Bahrain, Mali, Chile, Peru, Trinidad and Tobago, Nigeria, Bangladesh, Kenya, Morocco, Zimbabwe, Indonesia, Uruguay, Central African Republic, Philippines, Venezuela, Costa Rica, Gambia, Argentina, and South Africa on behalf of Southern African Development Community (SADC), said equity and common but differentiated responsibility were the keys to success of the Kyoto Protocol. They noted that the per capita emissions of developing countries were low compared to developed nations.

---

[a] Originally created on June 15, 1964 with 77 members, there are now 132 , even though the name "G-77" has been retained. The Group of 77 at the United Nations, "The Member States of the Group of 77," http://www.g77.org/doc/members.html, accessed Sept. 3, 2012.

The representative of India objected to depriving developing countries of equitable environmental room to grow. The representative of China was to the point, and concluded its statement with one word: "no."[b]

Thus was the Kyoto Protocol killed by Don Pearlman, David Finnegan and other lobbyists for American coal and oil interests.

Nothing to it, really. By 1997, manipulation has been reduced to Betty Crocker chemistry: follow the recipe and the result will be just what you want.

- There must be industry organizations. In this case, there are at least three. Pearlman headed one of them, the Global Climate Council.

- Both the university-based counterintelligensia and the Washington, D.C.-based echo chamber must be engaged and producing documents. They were. Probably about 30 were actively working on global warming as an issue, and several had representatives attending meetings in Kyoto. ExxonMobil had already begun channeling large sums of money to the groups, especially the Competitive Enterprise Institute.

- Members of Congress must have been recruited and involved. They had been. Sen. Robert C. Byrd of West Virginia, the senior Democrat in the Senate was the primary Democratic co-sponsor of the Byrd-Hagel resolution. Because Byrd represents a coal-mining state, was himself once a miner, and was routinely re-elected with only token opposition, very little persuasion would have been required to bring him aboard. To the extent that any was necessary, it was likely provided by the United Mine Workers union, whose president, Rich Trumka, was to be in Kyoto. (Trumka is now president of the AFL-CIO and a speaker at the Democratic National Convention in September 2012.) Byrd's long memory and vindictiveness were so legendary in the Senate none but the most foolhardy were willing to incur his wrath.

- Cash must be flowing to the campaigns of members of Congress. It was. The Republican half of the resolution, Sen. Chuck Hagel of Nebraska, had already received several hundred thousands of dollars in campaign

---

[b] "Highlights from the Third Conference of the Parties to the United Nations Framework Convention on Climate Change," Earth Negotiations Bulletin. Dec. 5, 1997, International Institute for Sustainable Development, http://www.iisd.ca/vol12/enb1272e.html, accessed Dec. 3, 2012.

contributions. Hagel was also in Kyoto. The campaign coffers of key members of both the Senate and House had been filled.

On the opposite side of the Capitol in the House of Representatives, industry water was being carried by a variety of Congressmen. Rep. James Sensenbrenner of Wisconsin, then the Chairman of the House Committee on Science, was raking in the dough as well: $1,000 from Boeing; $500 from Ford; $500 from McDonnell Douglas; $500 from General Electric; $1,000 from Philip Morris; $2,500 from Lockheed-Martin; $500 from Navistar; $750 from Wisconsin Electric; $500 from General Motors; $1,000 from United Parcel Service; $500 from Pfizer; $500 from GTE; $2,000 from AT&T; $2,000 from the National Association of Beverage Retailers Political Action Committee; $3,000 from Dealers Election Action Committee of the National Automobile Dealers Association (NADA); $500 from Allied-Signal; $1,000 from Boeing; $500 from General Electric; $500 from John Deere; and, $500 from General Motors, all in 1997.

The most powerful Democrat fronting for industry in the House was John Dingell, Jr., one of the most widely feared legislators in Congress. Dingell had the power that came from chairing the Committee on Energy and Commerce and wielded it unflinchingly. An avid hunter, Dingell once told a reporter for the *New York Times* that "When I go hunting I take the biggest gun I can carry. When I shoot something I want it to go down. I don't want any cripples walking around."

Due to his bullying tactics, Dingell illustrated not only how corrupt the system had become, but why it needn't be that way.

The Michigan representative, still in Congress in 2012, occupies a seat that was held by his father from 1933 to 1955, when the son was elected. Dingell is always re-elected easily, sometimes with no opposition. Nevertheless, he routinely amasses large amounts of campaign cash. In 1988, for example, when he was unopposed, Dingell still raised $462,180.[18]

The 1997–98 period was no exception. Dingell collected from too many donors to list conveniently, but the gifts included $2,000 from Ford, $1,000 each from Florida Power and Light, Action Committee for Rural Electrification, ICF Kaiser, ARCO, McDermott, Will & Emery, American Crystal Sugar, Elf Atochem, DTE Energy, Houston Industries, and Norfolk Southern—and that was only in January 1997 and just the political action committees.[19]

Committees and subcommittees must be holding hearings and otherwise exerting pressure. They were. October 7, 1997, Sensenbrenner gavelled a hearing by the Science Committee to order, then decried climate science, saying temperatures had been "cooler."

On June 19, 1997, Dingell had testified before the Hagel subcommittee in the Senate, saying that there were five questions to which he had "yet to receive satisfactory answers." He asked whether science had "overreached" and whether there might be an "economic fiasco."[20]

In short, the pieces were in place to kill Kyoto, though the final details were yet to be ironed out. That would happen in Bonn and in the months following.

The gathering in Bonn was a pre-meet to iron out details for the coming session in Kyoto and queue up issues, so policy makers could discuss and resolve them.

At the Beethovenhalle, people mill about talking, smoking, strolling from one group to another, connecting. There is a muffled din of conversation, punctuated by the clinking of cups on saucers. The walnut floored ante-chamber off the ballroom is roughly the size of a basketball court sliced in half lengthwise. Columns of polished black marble support an open upper level where at a dozen small tables people talk over coffee or soft drinks.

On the lower level, where official delegates enter and exit the meeting room, Donald Pearlman is holding court. His black athletic shoes are a striking contrast to his rumpled dark suit and white, shaggy hair. He is seated with a handful of other American lobbyists, at one of a half-dozen groupings of chrome and leather chairs and love seats.

The mix of people seated at the other tables changes regularly, but not at Pearlman's. Delegates from oil rich nations such as Nigeria, Saudi Arabia and Kuwait come to and from the Pearlman table, but he and his American colleagues remain anchored there throughout the day.

An undersecretary at the U.S. Department of Interior during the Reagan Administration, Pearlman heads the Global Climate Council. Its membership is secret because Pearlman exploited a loophole to avoid the requirement of U.N. rules that members of an organization like his be made public. People can only guess who he represents.

In 1997, Pearlman was a lawyer with Patton Boggs, a Washington, D.C.-based firm with over 400 lawyers. It is quite possible—hell, let's admit it, it's virtually certain—that Pearlman's clients included some of the oil-rich nations with which he works closely, because the firm has a long history of representing foreign interests. It now has an office in Doha, Qatar, and once had another in Saudi Arabia.[3] More to the point, Pearlman is a former registered foreign agent for the governments of Abu Dhabi, Oman, Quatar, the United Arab Emirates and other oil rich nations. Whatever the connections between Pearlman and the oil exporters, there is no question that Pearlman serves the delegates of the oil-rich nations as if they were clients, whether or not they are. One person said of a scene he observed in 1990:

> On the first evening in Sundsvaal [August 1990] … Don Pearlman
> was seated in the lobby with five diplomats, all Arab, including the
> head of the Saudi delegation. They had their heads down, copies of
> the draft negotiation text for the IPCC final report open in front of
> them. He looked like a professor holding a tutorial class. As I
> walked passed, I saw him pointing to a particular paragraph and I
> heard him say, quite distinctly, "if we can cut a deal here …"[4]

On another occasion, the Kuwaitis attempted to submit amendments in Pearlman's own handwriting. His tampering with the process—"the shameless way he used the Saudi Arabian delegation as a proxy for his stalling tactics," in the words of one observer—led to so many complaints from the delegates of non-OPEC nations that United Nations officials banned representatives from outside organizations from the meeting room. Even then, Pearlman refused to leave until threatened with being forcibly removed by uniformed guards.[5]

The members of Pearlman's coterie are mostly, like him, fiftyish white American males. There's David "two chair" Finnegan, so named because of his girth, with his belly straining against his shirt buttons. Finnegan worked many years for Rep. John Dingell of Michigan, the chief ally of the auto industry in Congress. Dingell, the longest-serving Democrat in Congress, was then chairman of the House Committee on Energy and Commerce, which has jurisdiction over air pollution generally and global warming specifically.

Now collecting a retirement check from Congress, Finnegan is in Bonn to look after the interests of General Motors, Ford and Chrysler. Finnegan works for a Washington, D.C. law firm that represents the U.S. car makers.

Quick tempered, he is a fierce adversary. At one point later in the meeting, Finnegan's face is inches from mine, flushed with anger as he rages that "America is built on cheap energy, and I've got six children who want their share of the good life."

The lobbyist for the National Coal Association, a middle-aged woman, stands at a younger lobbyist's elbow, as she hitches up her dark skirt and growls something at Pearlman, whose head is tilted to his left resting on the fingertips of his left hand while his eyeglasses are dangling from thumb and forefinger. In his right hand is a cigarette, its smoke curling lazily up through a ficus plant at his shoulder. They talk in sotto voices, and every few minutes one or two will temporarily break away to stroll the walnut stained hardwood floor, pausing for conversation with a delegate.

On Monday, the Clinton Administration's proposal on global warming was released. It proposed what virtually everybody other than officials of his Administration agreed, was no action. The headline of a coal industry newsletter, *World Climate Report*, wryly said it all: "Clinton Secures Place in History, Does Nothing." It added that under the Clinton proposal "atmospheric carbon dioxide levels will continue to rise rapidly, so we'll actually get to see whether those forecasts of big warming are correct or not."[6] (*World Climate Report* is edited by global warming skeptic Patrick Michaels under a contract with Western Fuels Association, a group of coal companies.)

Among delegates in Bonn, there was disappointment in the U.S. announcement, but no surprise. Most had been expecting no better than what Clinton had proposed, which was to wait until the year 2012, then freeze pollution at the levels of 1990.

America's allies were nevertheless sharply critical, as was the European press. "It is simply not good enough," declared Peter Jorgenson, a spokesman for the European Union. Germany's environment minister, Angela Merkel, who would later become Prime Minister, called the proposals "disappointing and insufficient." British deputy prime minister John Prescott said the plan didn't go far enough and urged the U.S. to become "much more ambitious" before final negotiations on the global warming treaty in Kyoto, Japan in early December.[7]

Roughly one of every six persons pre-registered for the Bonn meeting is a U.S. business lobbyist. In all 95 American lobbyists are pre-registered, more than all delegates from South America and Africa combined, and more than any single nation on Earth, save Japan. In contrast, only two American environmental groups, Ozone Action and Climate Action Network-U.S., were signed up.[8]

The American industry groups were hammering home a blend of messages aimed at preventing international agreement, chief among them the rock solid opposition of American business to any reduction whatsoever in global warming pollution. The science supporting global warming is uncertain, they also said, adding that even if temperatures do increase, that will be good. Crops will grow faster in a hotter atmosphere rich with carbon dioxide. Even if that weren't true, the costs of reducing pollution greatly exceed the benefits; a few years delay won't hurt; and, if action must be taken the United States cannot act unilaterally—or even in concert with other developed nations—because pollution growth in fast-growing economies like China and India would overwhelm the efforts of developed nations.

It has been a quarter century since Lewis Powell's Manifesto outlined what has since become a reality. It was 20 years since William Simon filled in the details of the Manifesto and, from the helm of one of the wealthiest foundations in the nation, started implementing his plans to change the Republican Party from the "Stupid Party" to the "Liberty Party," in the millionaire's own words.

By 1997, American corporations have reduced the process of thwarting popular will to a science and, having honed it in the United States, had begun exporting to the international area. They also had ceased to play defense, but had learned, especially in the Reagan Administration, to play offense. No longer content to fend off change that might threaten profit, they now aggressively campaign for benefits, ranging from tax cuts to public subsidies.

There is no complete analogue to the magnificently efficient and remorseless machine that corporations, the rich and the Republicans have constructed. However, the struggle which lies at the core, between wealth and property on the one hand and individual rights and interests at the other, dates to the founding of the nation.

This has been said elsewhere in *Saving Ourselves*, but it bears repeating because it is a truth that has been obscured by nearly a half-century of propaganda from corporations and the rich.

When the Declaration of Independence was drafted, it was modeled on the Virginia Declaration of Rights, which held that all men have certain "inherent rights" including "the enjoyment of life and liberty, with the means of acquiring and possessing property, and pursuing and obtaining happiness and safety."[c] Jefferson

---

[c] The entire first article holds "That all men are by nature equally free and independent, and have certain inherent rights, of which, when they enter into a state of society, they cannot, by any compact, deprive or divest their posterity; namely, the enjoyment of life and liberty, with the means of acquiring and possessing property, and pursuing and obtaining happiness and safety." The Avalon Project at Yale Law School,

(continued...)

and the other drafters eliminated the reference to property, retaining protection of happiness, with slight modification.

Powell, Simon, Reagan, the two Bushs, America's corporations and the rich have succeeded in reversing that 1776 decision, replacing it with a dynamic and complex mechanism with which they have not only taken control of government, but constructed an alternative universe. What is waged is not unlike a war, in which each of the constituent parts play a role to complement other parts. There are generals and privates, infantry divisions and tanks, air wings and artillery. But there is only one fuel: money.

Much of this machine of war is hidden from public view. The visible edges include organizations like the three global warming groups and open advocates like Pearlman and Finnegan and the industry group.

A favorite tactic is to adopt some benign, even inviting, name. For example, as the U.S. Environmental Protection Agency prepared to tighten air pollution standards for soot, which kills upwards of 50,000 Americans per year, and smog, which causes asthma, the energy, transportation and manufacturing companies created the Foundation for Clean Air Progress (FCAP). Its mission: to assure that the public knows that "air quality in the United States has improved dramatically as a result of the combined efforts of government, industry and individuals. Yet, research indicates that the public is largely unaware of this progress and believes that air quality is generally poor and deteriorating."[9]

Often there are several organizations, playing multiple roles.

FCAP operated out of the offices of the public relations firm, Burson-Marsteller, according to the *Post*, which described the effort as a—

> multimillion-dollar campaign to turn back EPA regulations for smog and soot. ... The nerve center behind the attack is a coalition of more than 500 businesses and trade groups that calls itself the Air Quality Standards Coalition. Created specifically to battle the clean air proposals, the coalition operates out of the offices of the National Association of Manufacturers, a Washington-based trade group. Its leadership includes top managers of petroleum, automotive and utility companies as well as longtime

---

[c] (...continued)
"Virginia Declaration of Rights," http://www.yale.edu/lawweb/avalon/virginia.htm, accessed Aug. 1, 2007.

Washington insiders such as C. Boyden Gray, a counsel to former president George Bush.

Typically individual member companies will mount their own efforts to complement the overarching campaign. ExxonMobil, for example, was a member of the coalition, but also sent notices to its credit card customers urging them to oppose the EPA regulations. Other firms helped pay for TV and newspaper ads produced by FCAP.

[While this book focuses on global warming, these techniques are by no means limited to that subject. For example, The Center for Food Integrity (CFI), an industry funded front group aims "to build consumer trust and confidence in the contemporary U.S. food system by sharing accurate, balanced information, correcting misinformation, modeling best practices and engaging stakeholders to address issues that are important to consumers."[10] Its supporters include the American Egg Board, the American Farm Bureau Federation, Monsanto, National Cattlemen's Beef Association, National Chicken Council, National Council of Chain Restaurants, National, Milk Producers Federation, National Pork Board, National Pork Producers Council, National Restaurant Association, National Turkey Federation, Produce Marketing Association, and United Soybean Board.[11]

[The Beverage Institute for Health & Wellness was created by Coca-Cola to counter criticisms of the role of food and beverage companies in the obesity epidemic.[12] Health Care America, funded in part by pharmaceutical and hospital companies, campaigns against national health insurance.[13] The Hygiene Council, funded by the maker of Lysol disinfectant, Easy Off oven cleaner and d-Con rat poison,[14] is to help "improve hygiene standards and overall health."[15, 16]]

Virtually unheard of before 1970, such groups are now routinely created on a regular basis by the high powered lobbyists and public relations firms hired by polluters to fend off new laws, cloud scientific findings, and quell public outcry.

In the context of global warming, one of the most superficially amusing—and alarming—of these groups was first revealed in a full-page newspaper advertisement displaying a donkey sporting ear muffs and a scarf, highlighting a large-typeface question "If the Earth is getting warmer, why is Minnesota getting colder?"

It was a seemingly good question asked by an apparently reputable group, the Information Council on the Environment or "ICE" for short. Trouble is, both the premise behind the question and the group asking it were, once again, little more than fronts for corporate polluters. In this case, the "council" was a public relations and advertising agency operating with coal and electric company money to "reposition global warming as theory (not fact)," in the words of an internal document.

The hook question was based on the spurious claim that Minnesota has cooled. And there was a dip in temperatures from about 1820 to the 1860s. But since then, except for a slight dip in the 1950s, the state has warmed steadily. It's now about 3 degrees Fahrenheit hotter than in 1860, according to researchers at the University of Minnesota.

Such facts notwithstanding, the coal and electric industries flooded the airwaves and saturated the papers of three cities—Bowling Green, Kentucky, Flagstaff, Arizona and Fargo, North Dakota—with variations of the ad to test the effectiveness of their message. Before the ICE campaign had a chance to take hold, however, the group was exposed by articles in both the local papers and the *New York Times* and quickly vanished from view.

Such campaigns cost money. The tab for the three one-week test markets of ICE was put at $500,000 or more. But the evidence suggests they're worth the price from the polluters' perspective. In just the last three years, for example, there was a decline in the apparent level of scientific concern over threats ranging from global warming to dioxin. In virtually every case, a high-powered public relations firm could be found in the background, quietly undermining the credibility of reputable scientists and creating the appearance of scientific disagreement when the dissent within the mainstream of researchers is slim to none.

In the case of ICE, for example, names of three scientists were given to reporters to validate claims of cooling. But when contacted by reporters, two of the three renounced their connections to the ICE campaign.

In the case of global warming, three organizations were initially founded:

- **The Global Climate Council**, headed by Pearlman—as noted earlier, veteran Washington lobbyist, one-time right hand aide to the U.S. Secretary of the Energy and former registered foreign agent for the governments of Abu Dhabi, Oman, Quatar, the United Arab Emirates and other oil rich nations. Pearlman secured official non-governmental organization status for the Climate Council, which at United Nations meetings to hammer out terms of any global agreement to curb warming, gives him access to briefings from the official U.S. delegation[17]—meetings from which the press and public are barred.[18]

- **The Global Climate Coalition** was formed in 1989 and disbanded in 2002. Its members included Amoco, the American Forest & Paper Association, American Petroleum Institute, Chevron, Chrysler, Cyprus AMAX Minerals, Exxon, Ford, General Motors, Shell Oil, Texaco, and the United States Chamber of Commerce. Although theoretically distinct from one another, the differences between The Climate Council and The Global Climate Coalition were in name only. At international meetings, lobbyists for the two organizations clearly collaborated, not only with each other, but with oil exporting nations such as Venezuela, Nigeria and Kuwait. Indeed, at one meeting the comments of an official Kuwait delegate were identical to those of the Dow Chemical Company, which was one of the Coalition members.[19] It was commonplace to see Pearlman or a GCAPSC colleague scratch out a note, send it to a delegate from Saudi Arabia, then see the official stand in the meeting and read verbatim from it.[20]

- **The International Climate Change Partnership**, which holds itself out as more moderate, but nevertheless opposes specific emission limits for various nations and wants action, if any, delayed.[21] Its members include Boeing, Carrier, Dow Chemical, DuPont, General Electric, General Motors, Honeywell, Intel Corporation, Japan Fluorocarbon Manufacturers Association, United Technologies and York International.[22]

With coordinating organizations in place, contributions from the corporate members of such groups began flowing into the accounts of the various front groups, such as the Cato and Competitive Enterprise Institutes. Papers attacking and confusing the science were written by "scholars" such as Patrick Michaels or Richard Lindzen. These are disseminated to and republished by the many front groups such as the Heartland Institute and the Reason Foundation, creating the appearance of a broadbased, grassroots movement.

Michaels is especially prolific, with articles distributed by the Heartland Institute ("Esteemed science journal bows to politics"),[23] the Cato Institute ("Holes in the Greenhouse Effect?"),[24] and Competitive Enterprise Institute ("Greens Oppose Early Credit Bill").[25]

In Boston, Citizens for a Sound Economy sponsored a forum featuring Robert Balling,[26] one of industry's paid skeptics. He told the luncheon audience that records from satellites and airborne balloons indicate that global temperatures had actually decreased over the past decades, a common theme in CSE and oil industry pamphlets.[27] Balling, however, didn't collect the satellite or balloon data. The scientist who did, John Christy, had a different view: he said that these and other measurements show the planet is warming.

Balling is technically correct in saying that there was a slight cooling, but as usual, that's a half truth. The 18-year measurement period started when there was a short-term warming period in the Pacific, then concluded after Mt. Pinatubo, the Philippine volcano that exploded in 1991, blasting a global blanket of soot 20 miles into the air where it circled for five years, reflecting sunlight and cooling Earth—precisely as predicted by the computer models that Balling said were flawed.[28]

The views of Balling and his fellow contrarians were sweeping the libertarian community—and oil-rich nations. Balling's 1992 book, *The Heated Debate*, was published by a conservative think tank, the Pacific Research Institute, one of whose goals is the large scale repeal of environmental regulations. From there, his message circulated to the hundreds of other corporate front groups.

Then, Balling's book was translated into Arabic and distributed to the governments of the OPEC nations. The funding for this edition of the book was provided by the Kuwait Institute for Scientific Research.[29]

Balling's message was also contained in *The True State of the Planet*, published in 1996 by the Competitive Enterprise Institute. Described by one reviewer as "about rhetoric, not scholarship. It aims for hearts, minds and pocketbooks, not truth."[30] *True State* contains a chapter written by Balling.

In none of these writings, nor in his public appearances, did Balling volunteer, nor did his advocates disclose, that over the previous few years he had been paid $311,000 by the oil and coal industries and Kuwait for he, like Pearlman and Finnegan, is a hired gun.[31]

Often these campaigns are overseen and coordinated by professional public relations firms. GCC, for example, hired the Washington office of Rudder & Finn, a New York City-based public relations firm, while the Business Round table signed up Ketchum Public Relations, as well as the public affairs team of Powell and Tate, whose two principals, Jody Powell and Dan Tate, were veterans of the Carter Administration White House. The American Automobile Manufacturers Association also contracted with Ketchum Public Relations,[32] the nation's seventh largest PR agency with $50 million in annual billings.[33] Earlier, in 1993, the American Petroleum Institute (API), just one of fifty-four industry members of the GCC, paid $1.8 million to the public relations firm of Burson-Marsteller.[34]

Charles River Associates, a Boston-based company, drew the task of demonizing actions to curb global warming, producing a study concluding that

20 percent cuts in emissions of carbon dioxide would virtually cripple the global economy, cutting the gross domestic products of developing nations by 50 percent and those of industrialized countries by 3.5 percent.[35] The firm has a history of attacking environmental regulation, saying, for example, on April 30, 1996 that EPA rules for cleaner-burning fuel were responsible for recent price increases because they "almost criminalized the process of producing gasoline."[36] In 1995, Charles River concluded that a federal mandate to increase the gas mileage of cars would actually increase air pollution, while costing the economy $3.8 and 9.9 billion annually.[37]

Not content to argue on the merits, these groups engage in vicious personal attacks, calling their foes "watermelons"—green on the outside, red on the inside. Alternatively, if those who disagree are not communists, then they're unholy: those concerned with global warming are engaged in "a devilish scheme to impose their own vision of a world order," in the words of former Republican Senator Malcolm Wallop of Wyoming, who runs his own front group, the Frontiers of Freedom Institute.[38]

By mid-1997, corporate polluters had, according to the *National Journal*, "assembled an army of lobbyists, grass-roots groups, public relations firms and consultants to press Congress and the Administration to adopt a more pro-business stance" on global warming.[39] Much of the money to fuel this campaign came from the oil, coal and auto industries. The chief spokesman for the GCC was its chairman, William O'Keefe, executive vice president of the American Petroleum Institute. Another outspoken critic was James W. Cicconi, former top official in the Bush Administration White House, partner in the Washington mega-firm of Akin, Gump, Strauss, Hauer & Feld, and the representative of Mobil Oil.

How much money has been pooled by polluters in these three groups is impossible to say. The Coalition alone had an annual budget of $1.2 million,[40] and in the summer of 1997 launched a national radio, television and newspaper campaign with a cost estimated by some to approach $20 million. Radio and television spots blanketed the Washington airwaves throughout the summer and fall of 1997 attacking the possibility of any global accord. The polluter's mantra, "It's not global, and it won't work," echoed throughout Washington, accompanied by claims that gasoline prices would jump 50 cents per gallon.

These same industries claimed in 1970 that meeting auto pollution standards was "not technologically possible," and in 1975 attacked fuel economy standards bitterly, saying they would "outlaw full-size sedans and station wagons," (Chrysler), "require all sub-compact vehicles," (Ford), and "restrict availability of

5 and 6 passenger cars regardless of consumer needs," (General Motors).[41] They claimed in the 1980s that eliminating leaded gasoline, would drive prices up ten cents per gallon, while controlling acid rain would destroy 188,000 jobs.[42] Although, in fact, gasoline prices dropped, and zero jobs were destroyed, the industry claims served to delay elimination of lead for 15 years and control of acid rain for 20. That's why they spend money.

In short order, full-page advertisements on global warming would start appearing in the *Washington Post* and the *New York Times*. The *Post* boasts that "Paid public policy messages also are extremely effective in generating action among Washington leaders with 70 percent stating that they take action in direct response to an advertisement, including discussing the issue or topic, going on the organization's website or sending it to a colleague."[43] Such *Post* ads can cost up to $50,000—a high price for ordinary Americans, but inconsequential to companies like Exxon.

All of this would bear fruit in mid-1997 and beyond, producing what industry wanted: to kill any agreement on global warming. These maneuvers were merely to set the stage for a preemptive strike in favor of profit over protection. It worked—again, because of money.

CORPORATE ANTI-GLOBAL WARMING FRONT GROUPS SUPPORTED BY EXXONMOBIL FOUNDATION 2004

Organization	Amount	Exxon's Statement of Purpose
American Enterprise Institute-Brookings Joint Center for Regulatory Studies[44]	$25,000	climate change
American Enterprise Institute[45]	$225,000	general operating support
Am. Council on Science and Health[46]	$15,000	climate change issue
American Council for Capital Formation[47]	$75,000	GOS
	$90,000	climate change
	$90,000	climate change
American Legislative Exchange Council[48]	$75,000	energy sustainability project (climate change)
	$62,000	energy and climate change
	$30,000	GOS
Atlas Economic Research Foundation[49]	$75,000	project support
Annapolis Center for Science-Based Public Policy[50]	$75,000	project support
Brookings Institution	$75,000	project support
	$50,000	GOS
Center for Defense of Free Enterprise[51]	$60,000	GCC issues
	$70,000	GCC issues
Competitive Enterprise Institute[52]	$90,000	GCC
	$90,000	GCC outreach
Committee for a Constructive Tomorrow[53]	$20,000	climate change issues
	$35,000	
	$20,000	
	$50,000	

Organization	Amount	Exxon's Statement of Purpose
Congress of Racial Equality[54]	$20,000	global climate change issues
	$40,000	global climate change issues
	$75,000	GCC regulation/legislation
Consumer Alert[55]	$10,000	climate change issues (outreach to opinion leaders)
	$15,000	climate change issues (outreach to opinion leaders)
Federalist Society[56]	$15,000	GOS
Frontiers of Freedom Institute[57]	$90,000	climate change outreach
	$40,000	climate change outreach
	$70,000	climate change
	$50,000	climate change
Foundation for Research on Economics and the Environment[58]	$30,000	federal judicial seminars
	$50,000	federal judicial seminars
George C. Marshall Institute[59]	$75,000	climate change
Heartland Institute[60]	$75,000	GOS
MIT Center for Energy and Environmental Policy Research	$90,000	energy policy studies
Media Research Center[61]	$50,000	climate change
National Center for Policy Analysis[62]	$75,000	GOS
	$50,000	GOS
National Center for Policy Research[63]	$50,000	GOS
Pacific Research Institute for Public Policy[64]	$50,000	operating support
	$50,000	climate change

Source: ExxonMobil Foundation year 2000 IRS Form 990, Guidestar.com

OTHER 501(C)(3) ORGANIZATIONS SUPPORTED BY EXXONMOBIL

60/Sixty Plus AssociationAccuracy in
    Academia
Accuracy in Media
Acton Institute for the Study of Religion
    and Liberty
Africa Fighting Malaria
Air Quality Standards Coalition
Alexis de Tocqueville Institution
Alliance for Climate Strategies
American Coal Foundation
American Council for Capital Formation
    Center for Policy Research
American Council on Science and Health
American Enterprise Institute for Public
    Policy Research
American Enterprise Institute-Brookings
Joint Center for Regulatory Studies
American Friends of the Institute for
    Economic Affairs
American Legislative Exchange Council
American Petroleum Institute
American Policy Center
American Recreation Coalition
Americans for Tax Reform
Arizona State University Office of
    Climatology
Aspen Institute
Association of Concerned Taxpayers
Atlantic Legal Foundation
Atlas Economic Research Foundation
Blue Ribbon Coalition
Capital Legal Foundation
Capital Research Center and Greenwatch
Cato Institute
Center for American and International Law
Center for Environmental Education
    Research
Center for Security Policy
Center for Strategic and International
    Studies
Center for the Defense of Free Enterprise
Center for the New West

Center for the Study of Carbon Dioxide and
    Global Change
Centre for the New Europe
Chemical Education Foundation
Citizens for A Sound Economy and CSE
    Educational Foundation
Citizens for the Environment and CFE
    Action Fund
Clean Water Industry Coalition
Committee for a Constructive Tomorrow
Communications Institute
Competitive Enterprise Institute
Congress of Racial Equality
Consumer Alert
Cooler Heads Coalition
Council for Solid Waste Solutions
Defenders of Property Rights
Earthwatch Institute
ECO or Environmental Conservation
    Organization
ExxonMobil Corporation
Federalist Society for Law and Public
    Policy Studies
Foundation for Research on Economics and
    the Environment
Fraser Institute
Free Enterprise Action Institute
Free Enterprise Education Institute
Frontiers of Freedom Institute and
Foundation
George C. Marshall Institute
George Mason University, Law and
Economics Center
Global Climate Coalition
Great Plains Legal Foundation
Greening Earth Society
Harvard Center for Risk Analysis
Heartland Institute
Heritage Foundation
Hoover Institution on War, Revolution and
    Peace, Stanford University
Hudson Institute

Illinois Policy Institute
Independent Commission on Environmental
    Education
Independent Institute
Institute for Biospheric Research
Institute for Energy Research
Institute for Regulatory Science
Institute for the Study of Earth and Man
Institute of Humane Studies, George Mason
    University
International Council for Capital Formation
International Policy Network - North
    America
International Republican Institute
James Madison Institute
Junkscience.com
Landmark Legal FoundationLexington
    Institute
Lindenwood University
Mackinac Center
Manhattan Institute for Policy Research
Media Institute
Media Research Center
Mercatus Center, George Mason University
Mountain States Legal Foundation
National Association of Neighborhoods
National Black Chamber of Commerce
National Center for Policy Analysis
National Center for Public Policy Research
National Council for Environmental
    Balance
National Environmental Policy Institute
National Legal Center for the Public
    Interest
National Policy Forum
National Wetlands Coalition

National Wilderness Institute
New England Legal Foundation
Pacific Legal Foundation
Pacific Research Institute for Public Policy
Property and Environment Research Center,
    formerly Political Economy Research
    Center
Public Interest Watch
Reason Foundation
Reason Public Policy Institute
Science and Environmental Policy Project
Seniors Coalition
Small Business Survival Committee
Southeastern Legal Foundation
Stanford University GCEP
Statistical Assessment Service (STATS)
Tech Central Science Foundation or Tech
    Central Station
Texas Public Policy Foundation
The Advancement of Sound Science
    Center, Inc.
The Advancement of Sound Science
    Coalition
The Annapolis Center for Science-Based
    Public Policy
The Justice Foundation (formerly Texas
    Justice Foundation)
The Locke Institute
United for Jobs
University of Oklahoma Foundation, Inc.
US Russia Business Council
Virginia Institute for Public Policy
Washington Legal Foundation
Weidenbaum Center on the Economy,
Government, and Public Policy
World Climate Report

Corporate Anti-Global Warming Front Groups Supported by General Motors Foundation 2003

Organization	Amount	Representative Quote
Annapolis Center	$25,000	Trumpeting a predicted warming of 11°C may sell lots of magazines, but this was clearly an outlying result, and therefore much less likely to prove accurate in the long run. The truth is much more mundane: most of the warming predictions from these simulations were clustered around the average value for previous climate simulations, about 3.4°C in the next century.[65]
American Enterprise Institute	$100,000	(W)e should consider climate modification. If humanity is powerful enough to disrupt the climate negatively, we might also be able to change it for the better. On a theoretical level, doing so is relatively simple: we need to reduce the earth's absorption of solar radiation. A few scientists have suggested we could accomplish this by using orbiting mirrors to rebalance the amounts of solar radiation different parts of the earth receive.[66]
Heritage Foundation	$25,000	(T)he recent surface warming trend may owe largely to changes in the sun's energy output.[67]
Mercatus Center	$30,000	When it comes time to make the reductions necessary to meet the proposed new level (of fine particles), EPA will order reductions based on a model that underestimates future pollution reductions and fails to recognize the huge improvements in air quality that will result in the coming years as the nation's automobile fleet modernizes.[68] Corporate average fuel economy standards supplant consumer preferences (which) is bound to make consumers worse off.[69]

Organization	Amount	Representative Quote
Heartland Institute	$40,000	The planet is warming at the low end of projections. Antarctica is undoubtedly gaining ice, not losing it. Greenland may be losing a little ice or ... gaining ice dramatically. Clearly, it is going to take quite some time before melting ice can make the oceans rise much, if at all.[70]
George C. Marshall Institute	$10,000	The cold hard realities are that we are where we are, there is no politically viable way of turning the greenhouse clock back, the world is not about to turn away from fossil fuels, and we cannot predict the future as much as we pretend otherwise.[71]
Cato Institute	$25,000	Global warming is vastly overrated as an environmental threat ... largely mythical problem.[72]
Competitive Enterprise Institute	$50,000+ $55,000+ $10,000	There is no "scientific consensus" that global warming will cause damaging climate change. Claims that there is mischaracterize the scientific research.[73]
Reason Foundation	$25,000	Forest sequestration offers a "win-win" approach to global warming. Enhancing sequestration would slow any climate change that might occur due to greenhouse gas emissions, while offering immediate environmental benefits.[74]
American Legislative Exchange Council	$25,000	Absent from the debate (on global warming) is the discussion of human ingenuity and our ability to adapt to our environment; when the temperature increases, we turn on the air conditioner. More people die from cold temperatures than heat, ... "global warming could actually save lives."[75]
Consumer Alert	$25,000	
National Center for Policy Analysis	$25,000	

Organization	Amount	Representative Quote
League of United Latin American Citizens	$70,000+ $30,000	
Harvard Center for Risk Analysis	$50,000	

20

FREEDOM OR BONDAGE

> The direct and intentional taking of innocent human life in abortion, euthanasia, assisted suicide, and embryonic research is rightly understood as murder.

"That They May Have Life,"
First Things, October 2006

One of the great advantages of forging a political alliance with religions is that churches fly under the radar. They collect money, but nobody knows how much. They spend it on a variety of activities, but that, too, is a secret. And, very importantly, their leaders communicate with followers when nobody else is reading, listening or watching. The voice can come from the pulpit, the pastoral letter or a communication from the Bishop. And it can say, with the public none the wiser, that—

> The direct and intentional taking of innocent human life in abortion, euthanasia, assisted suicide, and embryonic research is rightly understood as murder.[1]

That statement is contained in the October 2006 issue of the magazine *First Things*, called by *Newsweek* magazine "the most important vehicle for exploring the tangled web of religion and society in the English-speaking world.."[2] It was signed by 24 of the most well-known religious leaders in America,[a] participants in an effort called Evangelicals and Catholics Together (ECT).[3]

The alliance that Weyrich and others forged with white Christian evangelicals in the 1970s and 1980s was an immensely powerful political weapon, delivering to the Republican/Libertarian/Tea Party a starting base of 30 percent of the votes cast in any election. But to virtually guarantee victory, required one more alliance. The two-century antipathy between Protestants and Catholics had to be broken and the faiths united. In 1994, that happened.

At the urging of former Nixon White House aide Chuck Colson (on whose office wall hung one of his favorite sayings: "When you've got them by the balls their hearts and minds will follow."),[4] a small group of evangelicals and Catholics united to form Evangelicals and Catholics Together.

Convicted of felony for obstruction of justice for his activities in the White House, Colson emerged from prison in 1975 as a born-again Christian. He founded Prison Fellowship, an organization dedicated to assuring that "Jesus Christ's transforming grace and truth be manifested in the lives of prisoners and their families."[5]

Perhaps more importantly, in 1991 Colson also founded the Wilberforce Forum, a conservative Christian political and social self-described "think tank" and action group active in human cloning, stem cell research and related issues. It describes itself as the "Christian worldview thinking, teaching, and advocacy arm

---

[a] Dr. Harold O.J. Brown, Reformed Theological Seminary; Mr. Charles Colson, Prison Fellowship; Dr. Timothy George, Beeson Divinity School; Dr. Kent Hill, Church of the Nazarene; Dr. Frank James, Reformed Theological Seminary; Dr. Cheryl Bridges Johns, Church of God School of Theology; The Rev. T.M. Moore, The Wilberforce Forum, Prison Fellowship; Dr. Thomas Oden, Drew University Emeritus; Dr. James Packer, Regent College; Dr. Sarah Sumner, Azusa Pacific University; Dr. Kevin J. Vanhoozer, Trinity Evangelical Divinity School; Dr. John Woodbridge, Trinity Evangelical Divinity School Roman Catholics; Dr. James J. Buckley, Loyola College in Maryland; Dr. Peter Casarella, Catholic University of America; Dr. Gary Culpepper, Providence College; Avery Cardinal Dulles, S.J., Fordham University; Fr. Thomas Guarino, Seton Hall University; Fr. Arthur Kennedy, University of St. Thomas; Dr. Matthew Levering, Ave Maria University; Fr. Francis Martin, Mother of God Community; Fr. Richard John Neuhaus, Institute on Religion and Public Life; Fr. Edward T. Oakes, S.J., Mundelein Seminary; Mr. George Weigel, Ethics and Public Policy Center; Dr. Robert Louis Wilken, University of Virginia.

of Prison Fellowship."[b] It is named after William Wilberforce a British parliamentarian and leader of the campaign against the slave trade.[6]

In 1994, Colson and Rev. Richard John Neuhaus organized a joint project of the organizations they had founded, Prison Fellowship (founded in 1976, it had a budget of $38 million in 1997) and the Institute on Religion and Public Life (founded in 1989, it had a budget of $1.6 million in 1996). Neuhaus was a theologian who transformed himself from a liberal Lutheran leader of the civil rights and antiwar struggles in the 1960s to a Roman Catholic beacon of the neoconservative movement.[7]

What Colson and Neuhaus created was, in the words of the *New York Times*, "a theological framework for (evangelical Protestants and Catholics) joining forces in the nation's culture wars."[8]

Their work was criticized by some for precisely that reason. One scholar wrote that—

> "Evangelicals and Catholics Together" was an attack on the importance of Christian theology in general and the doctrine of justification by faith alone in particular, in favor of creating a united religious front for political and social action against secular humanism.[9]

But there has also been a conscious effort on the party of conservatives to put aside their differences. Pope Benedict XVI has continued the same outreach to evangelicals that John Paul II started. They have made a firm decision to seek the practical abrogation of what some would consider the most fundamental tenet of American law: separation of church and state.

Some will say that the word "wall" does not appear in the Constitution or that America is indisputably a Christian nation. But, in fact, long before the Constitution was even contemplated, a century before the Revolution, the separation of church and state—and, yes, the word "wall" was used—was the law in some colonies.

---

[b] The Wilberforce Coalition includes the John Templeton Foundation, Wilberforce Central, Wilberforce Forum, Trinity Forum, Gilder-Lehrman Center, Wilberforce House Museum, Set All Free, Walden Media, Wilberforce Institute and Wilberforce University. "Coalition Members, Wilberforce Central, http://www.wilberforcecentral.org/wfc/Coalition/index.htm, accessed Sep. 15, 2012.

The most notable of these was Rhode Island, founded by Roger Williams, a Puritan. He first settled in Massachusetts, where despite having themselves fled religious persecution in England, the settlers declared the colony's official religion to be Puritanism. This was supposedly to prevent what the colonists viewed as "error."

Williams, however, believed that preventing error in religion was impossible, for it required people to interpret God's law, and people would inevitably err. He therefore concluded that government must remove itself from anything that touched upon human beings' relationship with God. A society built on the principles Massachusetts espoused would lead at best to hypocrisy, because forced worship, he wrote, "stinks in God's nostrils." At worst, such a society would lead to a foul corruption—not of the state, which was already corrupt, but of the church.[10]

Fearful of his dangerous views, the Massachusetts colony banished Williams in October, 1665. He survived the winter though barely, due largely to help from Indians. He then traveled south to Narragansett Bay and chose a cove into which two small rivers emptied into a site that "having, of a sense of God's merciful providence unto me in my distress, [I] called the place PROVIDENCE, I desired it might be for a shelter for persons distressed for conscience."[11]

Williams and his fellow colonists believed that mixing church and state corrupted the church. But unable to free themselves of the dangers of the larger and more powerful Massachusetts, Williams returned to England to seek freedom for Rhode Island. On March 14, 1644, the Parliament expressly established Rhode Island as a colony free of any mandated religion whatsoever, a sort of test bed of separation of church and state.[12]

The colonists were given "full Power & Authority to Govern & rule themselves ... by such a form of Civil Government, as by voluntary consent of all, or the greater Part of them shall find most suitable" so long as its laws "be conformable to the Laws of England, so far as the Nature and Constitution of the place will admit."

Most extraordinary, all decisions about religion were left to the "greater Part"—the majority—knowing the majority would keep the state out of matters of worship. Williams had created the freest society in the modern western world.

He then turned to explaining his reasoning, writing *The Bloudy Tenent*, a 400-page book that was initially burned in England, but later reprinted and widely distributed, helping shape other colonies. It, among other things, urged a "hedge or wall of Separation" between church and state. King Charles II confirmed Rhode Island's charter, explicitly stating no one was to be "molested, punished, disquieted, or called in question, for any differences in opinion, in matters of religion." Such language on religious freedom also was written into the concession of land for New Jersey. Similar guarantees appeared in the charter of Carolina, even as that document established the Anglican Church there.

Williams' thoughts largely shaped the debate over religious tolerance in England, influencing John Milton and, particularly, John Locke. They, in turn, were studied closely by Jefferson, James Madison and other architects of the U.S. Constitution. Religious scholar W. K. Jordan, in his classic multivolume study of religious toleration, called Williams' "carefully reasoned argument for the complete dissociation of Church and State ... the most important contribution made during the century in this significant area of political thought."

What evangelical Protestants and Catholics are today seeking to destroy is the wall that was erected, originally by Williams and later by Jefferson and Madison. It is this wall that has protected Americans for 250 years from the bloody conflicts that have bedeviled humanity for thousands of years and resulted in the deaths of millions. America is comparatively free of religious intolerance, but some are seeking to bring this era to an end.

In 1994, American Catholic and Evangelical leaders came together to sign a statement: Evangelicals & Catholics Together: The Christian Mission in the Third Millennium. Its signatories included Chuck Colson, the prominent evangelist and Watergate figure and Pat Robertson, the Christian Broadcast Network founder, as well as Catholics like the late Father Richard John Neuhaus and Cardinal John O'Connor. The document pledged the groups to work together in a common cause on issues like abortion and to not let doctrinal differences or conflicts over recruitment "give comfort to the enemies of Christ."[13]

Although "Evangelicals and Catholics Together" is the most well known of their work products, it is not the most important by any means. That was to come three years later.

The Colson-Neuhaus Group continued its efforts, meeting twice a year and working quietly until November 12, 1997 when a new document,"The Gift of Salvation," was released. Unlike "Evangelicals and Catholics Together," which is filled with expressions of concern about social and political action. "Gift" was designed, in the words of one critic "not to effect a political alliance, but to create a theological, and eventually an ecclesiastical, union."[14]

Also unlike the earlier document, "Gift" was drafted, according to one observer, with the "active involvement, support, and guidance by the Vatican," who said that in a telephone interview, Neuhaus—

> (C)onfirmed that Roman Catholic bishops had indeed attended and been involved in meetings of the Colson-Neuhaus Group, and that Cardinal Edward Cassidy had attended at least two Group meetings in 1996 and 1997, including speaking at the meeting on October 6–7 in New York City at which the latest manifesto, "The Gift of Salvation," was adopted. The substance of the Cardinal's remarks was reprinted in the January 1998 issue of *First Things*, a journal edited by Neuhaus. In addition to Cardinal Cassidy, Dean George reported in a telephone conversation with this writer on January 22 that Archbishop Francis George of Chicago (and) Cardinal John O'Connor of New York have been active participants in the Colson-Neuhaus Group. Archbishop George was recently named a Cardinal.[15]

Thus, in the space of a few years, Colson, Neuhaus and the Catholic Church overcame over two-and-one-half centuries of Protestant-Catholic antipathy to forge a single force. Weyrich had created one political blunt instrument. His was now dwarfed by a larger, more powerful and sophisticated successor. And this one had global ambitions.

The first visible evidence of the new alliance was in the elections of 2004. The Catholic Church became active in support of Republican candidates—George Bush for President and other Republicans for seats in the U.S. Senate—after Bush personally asked Pope John Paul II to provide such assistance.[16]

Then, in 2006, the ECT group formally endorsed the Vatican's "culture of life" program, saying that abortion is "murder."

The Catholic Church had ignored American politics for over two centuries, but since 2004 it hasn't. Why?

Some believe the explanation lies in the Vatican's worldwide agenda to eliminate contraception. One of the strengths of the Roman Catholic Church is that it is an international organization. Despite this, critics tend to try understanding the Church in terms of their own nation, a view that is simply too narrow.

The Catholic Church has been able to maintain the fealty of its parishioners because in poor countries, it is the principal—in many instances, the *only*—source of health care, food, education and other essentials of life. Loyalty to the church is not a matter of choice, but of survival.[c]

This has also been the case in advanced western industrialized nations. In Germany, for example, under the Federal Social Welfare Act and Youth Welfare Act, churches deliver social services with two distinct advantages for organized religions.

First, if a charity desires to deliver services, a "right-of-way law"rule requires government agencies to let it. This allows a charity to cherry pick, choosing to deliver services that make profit, while abandoning those that don't.[17]

Second, the law clearly stipulates the services are to be delivered with tax money from the state.[18] In addition, the Nursing Care Insurance Act[d] expressly requires those requiring care be placed in institutions that takes their religion into account and provide a preference to churches:

> § 2 Self-determination. Those requiring care are to receive in-patient treatment at an institution where they can be ministered to by a cleric of their faith where they have expressed a wish to this effect.

> § 11. Independent [church] charities and private agencies have priority over public agencies.

As a result of these requirements, the number of church employees has exploded. From 1960 through 2003, the employees of the German "Caritas" network of Catholic charities increased 137,496 employees to 499,313, or 263 percent. Its Protestant counterpart, the "Diakonisches Werk," rose from the early 1970s between 175,000 to 452,244 in 2002, an increase of 160 percent. Together, more than 950,000 people are employed by the two church charities.[19]

Such employment provides immense support to the so-called "confessional" organizations. Caritas alone has about 25,000 facilities and offices, some 1.2 million beds and around 5000,000 employees.[20]

---

[c] Respectively, the Bundessozialhilfegesetz/BSHG and the Jugendhilfegesetz, Sozialgesetzbuch VIII.

[d] Pflegeversicherung, Sozialgesetzbuch XI.

Bear in mind, that this is merely one nation of many. If the Catholic Church and its Protestant allies are able to establish a support system that provides even a fraction of the money that will flow through the Affordable Care Act, or "Obamacare," their wealth and influence will increase immensely.

It is unlikely that there is a written agreement between the Republican/ Libertarian/Tea Party (RLTP), but communication does not require writing. Bush, after all, clearly made his desires for support from the Catholic hierarchy plain through a simple and relatively short conversation with Pope John Paul II.

Of the two political parties in the United States, the Republican/ Libertarian/Tea Party is far and away more comfortable to Catholics than the Democrats. The RLTP and the Catholic Church fundamentally agree on abortion and gay marriage, not to mention one other concern of the church: damages from sexual abuse.

The Catholic Church in the United States is under severe financial straits because priests abused young women and, especially, young men. The most effective way to staunch the flow of money from the hundreds of lawsuits is for the Congress to pass a law comparable to that which George Bush demanded as Governor of Texas: tort "reform." And the party that has demonstrated its willingness to pass such a law is the RLTP.

Since 1985, the Catholic Church has been beset by a series of clergy sexual abuse scandals and lawsuits. Those of us in the United States are most familiar with what happened here, but the scandal is by no means uniquely American. What we have seen here, also happened in Ireland, The Netherlands, Germany and Belgium, to name but a few.

According to the *New York Times*, the cases have already cost an estimated $2 billion in settlements. Perhaps more importantly, they have shaken the faith of worshipers, especially in reaction to attempts by church leaders to characterize the cases as attacks on the church.[e]

---

[e] A troubling aspect of the Catholic Church's alliance with the Republican/Libertarian/Tea Party is the manner in which organizations supported by the rich and their foundations have supported echoes of this assertion that claims of rape upheld in court are attacks on the Church. For example, author David F. Pierre, Jr. Of the Media Research Foundation has written *Double Standard: Abuse Scandals and the Attack on the Catholic Church.* One reviewer described it as "a riveting analysis of how money, media, and mayhem transformed a tragedy in the Catholic Church into an attack on the Catholic Church." Another says it "is essential reading for anyone who wants to hear the other side of the clergy

(continued...)

As in society at large, the conflict within the Catholic Church pits traditionalists bent on protecting bishops and priests against those who call for more openness and accountability.[21]

The sexual abuse scandal began in 1985 when Rev. Gilbert Gauthe was convicted and sentenced to 20 years in prison for molesting at least 37 children in Louisiana. Aggrieved parents sued the local diocese, forcing it and its insurance companies to pay $4.2 million to the families of nine children. More than a dozen additional civil suits were filed as more families overcome their hesitance to seek redress from a church that, the words of the *New York Times*, "has been a bedrock of their lives."[22]

When more abuse cases emerged in Dallas, Texas, Santa Fe, New Mexico, Fall River, Massachusetts and Santa Rosa, California, many dioceses adopted the recommendations of the United States Conference of Catholic Bishops. They called for removing priests accused of abuse from service, sending them into treatment and providing victims with counseling and pastoral care.

Victims continued to come forward and church lawyers settled hundreds of lawsuits, paying victims anywhere from a few thousand dollars to millions each. The church also quietly reassigned many of the priests to new parishes.

But the abuse scandal would not go away. It erupted again in Boston in 2002, Ireland in 2009 and Germany in 2010. In Philadelphia, Pennsylvania, a grand jury in 2005 found credible accusations of abuse by 63 priests, whose activities had been covered up by the church. But there were no indictments, mainly because the statute of limitations had expired.

In 2011, after a second Philadelphia grand jury issued its report in February, the district attorney immediately indicted two priests, Charles Engelhardt and James Brennan; a parochial school teacher, Bernard Shero; and a man who had left the priesthood, Edward Avery, on charges of rape or assault. He also indicted Monsignor William Lynn on charges of endangering the welfare of children—the

---

[e] (...continued)
sexual abuse scandal. The side the media hasn't told you. ..." Pierre is with the Media Research Center, headquartered in Alexandria, Virgina, and supported by the following foundations of the rich: Lynde and Harry Bradley, Donner, Communities Foundation of Texas, Inc., Kirby, F. M. Anschutz, DeVos, DeMoss, McCune, Triad, and Armstrong. Other organizations at the same address include the Conservative Victory Committee. MRC is headed by Brent Bozell III, who once said President Obama looks like "a skinny, ghetto crackhead," and is a nephew of the late right wing icon William F. Buckley.

first time a senior church official has been charged with covering up abuse in the sex scandal in the United States. Lynn was convicted of endangering children, after his own lawyer told the jury that "in this trial, you have seen the dark side of the church."[23]

There remains one other possibility: the Catholic Church is becoming active in American politics now because it has concluded that it can without provoking a backlash.

Since the Pilgrims fled the religious persecution in Europe, the Catholic Church has been unpopular in America. Thomas Jefferson wrote in a letter that—

> I do not know that it is a duty to disturb by missionaries the religion and peace of other countries, who may think themselves bound to extinguish by fire and fagot the heresies to which we give the name of conversions, and quote our own example for it. Were the Pope, or his holy allies, to send in mission to us some thousands of Jesuit priests to convert us to their orthodoxy, I suspect that we should deem and treat it as a national aggression on our peace and faith."[f]

This is in part because of the Protestant tradition that has historically prevailed in America. The first of the Protestant Churches, for example, was the Lutheran Church, which specifically provides for separation of church and state. The 28th Article of the Augsburg Confession, on the Power of Bishops, says: "The power of the Church and the civil power must not be confounded. The power of the Church has its own commission, to teach the Gospel and to administer the Sacraments. Let it not break into the office of another; let it not transfer the kingdoms of this world; let it not abrogate the laws of civil rulers; let it not abolish lawful obedience; let it not interfere with judgments concerning civil ordinances or contracts; let it not prescribe laws to civil rulers concerning the form of the commonwealth.[24]

The King James version of the Bible is rife with admonitions to the faithful to distinguish between church and state: As Christ says (John 18:36): "My kingdom is not of this world;" also (Luke 12:14): "Who made me a judge or a divider over you?" Paul also says (Phil. 3:20): "Our citizenship is in heaven." (II Cor.: 10:4):

---

[f] Thomas Jefferson to Michael Megear, 1823. ME 15:434 *The Writings of Thomas Jefferson*, Memorial Edition (Lipscomb and Bergh, editors), 20 Vols., Washington, D.C., 1903–04.

"The weapons of our warfare are not carnal, but mighty through God to the casting down of imaginations." The Bible, in short, commands not only that the faithful discriminate between the duties of church and state, but that both be honored and acknowledged as gifts and blessings of God.[25]

The Catholic Church's view is starkly, diametrically opposed to this.

It has maintained for centuries that all states and governments are subject to it as representing Him who is King of kings and Lord of lords. Pope Gregory VII, who in addressing King Henry IV (December 1076) qualified his "apostolic benediction" with the words : "if he be obedient to the Apostolic See as is becoming in a Christian king," taught that the Pope "has the power to depose emperors;" that "he can be judged by no man;" that "he has the power to absolve the subjects of unjust rulers from their oath of fidelity."[26]

Pope Leo XIII 800 years later proclaimed "The Pope has supreme authority, spiritual and temporal, over all societies; and has the keys of the kingdom of heaven; and has supreme legislative, judicial, and coactive authority in both spheres." Pope Pius X, his successor, likewise said: "The Papacy still maintains and will ever maintain its traditional doctrine of official, political union. The teaching that the Church and State should be separated is a most false and pernicious doctrine."[27]

Some members of the Catholic hierarchy will, for reasons of expediency, proclaim adherence to the American Constitution's principle of separation of Church and State, especially so long as Catholics are in the minority, "yet they unceasingly labor to get control of the State and Federal governments for their own ends" in the words on one Lutheran prelate.[28]

The current Pope is Benedict XVI. Before that he was Prefect of the Congregation for the Doctrine of the Faith, which is the Catholic Church's office of enforcement. He was born in Germany, raised in the Catholic faith, schooled in its traditions, and is said to be "a man of tremendous faith, of great integrity, very great intellect and great dedication."[29]

That said, he is not American, and it is here that the "other Catholicism" prevails. This was described by an American at the *National Catholic Reporter*, John L. Allen, Jr. as follows:

> The brand of Catholicism I picked up—faithful but evolving, open to dissent, engaged with society—was what I assumed was meant by the term "mainstream." This still describes the vast majority of the adult Catholics with whom I work, worship, and

socialize. If it were up to these Catholics, the church tomorrow would probably ordain women and married men, permit birth control, and stop demanding loyalty oaths.[30]

It may be true that there are two brands of Catholicism, Americans and everyplace else. This is not to say, however, that the hierarchy has no influence over its American worshipers. This I can say from first-hand experience.

In 2004, when the RLTP had targeted Sen. Tom Daschle of South Dakota for defeat, I volunteered to go to the state and distribute literature then, on election day itself, "poll watch," which is looking for irregularities. Daschle, then the Democratic Majority Leader in the United States Senate, lost.

It became very clear to me that Tom Daschle lost because of the Catholic Church. The bishop wrote Daschle a supposedly private letter instructing him to cease referring to himself as a Catholic. That supposedly private letter somehow found its way into the hands of the *Times-Argus*, the state's largest newspaper. I became interested in this when one of the Daschle volunteers, a woman who had voted and campaigned for him in every election in which he had been a candidate, said she was not sure that she could vote for Daschle because her Catholic priest had said from the pulpit that to vote for him would be a mortal sin and, if she did, she should find another church.

When I looked into this more, I discovered that at many Catholic churches in South Dakota, there was a red three-ring binder at the church's entrance, summarizing all of Daschle's votes on abortion and gay marriage. What happened to Daschle also happened to Democratic candidates throughout the nation. There were eight toss-up races that year, and the Republicans won seven of them. The margins of victory in those elections, and for George Bush in Ohio, were almost exactly the percentage of Catholics that voted for Bush—or, more accurately, against John Kerry. The sole Democrat to win was a Colorado Hispanic.

It did not happen just in South Dakota and the state that delivered the election to Bush, but throughout the country—to Democrats. I am unaware of comparable campaigns having been mounted in Rhode Island against Lincoln Chafee or in Pennsylvania against Arlen Specter, both Republicans (at the time) who supported "a woman's right to choose." There is no record of Catholics having sought to defeat *Republicans* because of their positions on abortion or gay marriage.

In Alaska, Republican senator Lisa Murkowski was standing for re-election in 2004. An anti-abortion group, the American Life League, included her on a list of pro-abortion Catholic politicians, and called on the church to withhold

Communion. A Mukowski spokeswoman, Kristin Pugh said Murkowski was personally against abortion, but recognized its legality.[31]

But Murkowski was not denied communion. According to press reports, she and Archdiocese of Anchorage Archbishop Roger Schwietz had recently discussed the ad, and "they both strongly disagree with its premise," Pugh said. Rev. Donald Bramble, vicar general of the archdiocese, confirmed Schwietz and Murkowski met privately. He said Schwietz believed Murkowski had considered the issue very carefully.[32]

"We might disagree with her on the particulars, but we see that she's seeking a nuanced approach and we appreciate that," Bramble said.[33]

The difference in the Catholic Church's treatment of Republicans and Democrats with virtually identical positions on abortion and similar issues is stark. So much so, that the *National Catholic Reporter* asked former California Governor Grey Davis—who had just lost a recall election and had been directed not to present himself for communion because of the pro-choice views, "Are the bishops giving Arnold Schwarzenegger, George Pataki and Rudy Giuliani a pass on abortion?" The reporter noted that then-current California governor, Arnold Schwarzenegger. his New York state counterpart, Gov. George Pataki and the former New York Mayor were all pro-choice Catholics and all scheduled to address the 2004 anti-abortion Republican convention.[34, g]

Accompanying abortion and gay marriage at the head of the Church's list of vital issues is funding for stem cell research. It remains adamantly opposed. In Rhode Island, another Republican, Lincoln Chafee was seeking to return to the

---

[g] The Platform of the 2004 Republican Convention provided as follows: "We must keep our pledge to the first guarantee of the Declaration of Independence. That is why we say the unborn child has a fundamental individual right to life which cannot be infringed. We support a human life amendment to the Constitution and we endorse legislation to make it clear that the 14th Amendment's protections apply to unborn children. Our purpose is to have legislative and judicial protection of that right against those who perform abortions. We oppose using public revenues for abortion and will not fund organizations which advocate it. We support the appointment of judges who respect traditional family values and the sanctity of innocent human life.

"We oppose abortion, but our pro-life agenda does not include punitive action against women who have an abortion. We salute those who provide alternatives to abortion and offer adoption services, and we commend Congressional Republicans for expanding assistance to adopting families and for removing racial barriers to adoption."
Source: 2004 Republican Party Platform, p. 86 , Sep 1, 2004, cited by On the Issues, http://www.ontheissues.org/celeb/Republican_Party_Abortion.htm, accessed Sept. 16, 2012.

Senate. During a debate, Chafee was asked if he favored federal subsidies for embryonic stem cell research. His response was—

> CHAFEE: I voted for a bill for federal funding. I believe it could help people with Parkinson's, Alzheimer's, cancer, and spinal cord injury.[35]

Then, he poured salt on the wounds he had just inflicted on the church, saying—

> CHAFEE: I have consistently voted against any federal attempt to ban women's reproductive freedom & choices. If it's left to the states, then only wealthy women will have access to abortions, if they have the resources to travel, whereas poor women would have to resort to the old days of difficult decisions.[36]

Since Chafee is not a Catholic, the church could not deny him communion. But it could to his then-fellow Senator to the north, Susan Collins, who is both Catholic and Republican. Has it? No.

As matters now stand in the United States, the decisions to deny or not deny communion to politicians who vote against the church's policy is supposedly made bishop-by-bishop. As a result, in some states such as South Dakota, communion is not only denied but the church works actively in support of Republicans. In other states, such as Alaska, a politician like Lisa Murkowski may be quietly tolerated.

In fact, the differences in treatment of Republican and Democratic Catholic politicians that the pattern suggests is not bishop-by-bishop differences, but a conscious decision by the Church to exercise its power in favor of one party and against another. In short, I suggest that the Catholic Church, in Rome at least, has decided to join the Republican/Libertarian/Tea Party.

But Americans should be clear: the U.S. Bishops who chose not to deny communion are choosing the American mainstream over the demands of their faith. And, increasingly, their faith is choosing to force its view on Americans who disagree, whether they like it or not.

There is a natural tendency for humans to seek refuge in the certainty and order of religion, for freedom creates fears of chaos, uncertainty and loneliness. And ultimately, that is our choice: freedom or bondage.

21

WILL DEMOCRACY SURVIVE IN AMERICA?

Democratic laws generally tend to promote the welfare of the greatest possible number; for they emanate from the majority of the citizens, who are subject to error, but who cannot have an interest opposed to their own advantage. The laws of an aristocracy tend, on the contrary, to concentrate wealth and power in the hands of the minority; because an aristocracy, by its very nature, constitutes a minority.

Democracy in America
Alexis de Tocqueville, 1835 & 1840

Perhaps it is merely a coincidence that the words "partisan," "political," "polarization," and "purge" all start with the same letter. It is no coincidence, however, that since the mid-1970s, partisan purges have led to political polarization so extreme and widespread that it, in turn, threatens democracy in America.

Some observers say polarization is the result of a philosophical realignment. In the words of one political scientist, "Elite Democrats are almost all liberals, and elite Republicans are almost all conservatives."[1] There is a lot of truth in that statement, though it misstates what today's Republicans are: they are not conservatives, but radicals, men and women bent on establishing as a ruling party one that consistently and scrupulously protects the rich and corporations. Today's Republican/Libertarian/Tea Party (RLTP) does not even faintly resemble the Republican Party of one generation ago.

The reason for this, while cynical, is practical. To make what was once the Republican Party competitive, it has been purged and purified. Where once the Party was heterogenous, it is now homogeneous. Where once one sort of Republican was elected in New Jersey and another in North Dakota, today the candidates are philosophically the same, like cookies shaken out of the same package.

Think of political parties and their candidates as consumer brands, and the need for consistency and homogeneity becomes clear.[2]

If a political party were a soft drink—say, Coca Cola—how would it ever develop a customer base and brand loyalty if a bottle bought on Tuesday tasted different from that purchased on Wednesday, both of which differed from the Thursday version. Or, what if one Apple computer had a 12 inch screen, but the screen of another that initially seemed identical was instead 10 inches? Or, if a shopping experience at Whole Foods one week was fine, but terrible the next?

In modern business, branding is essential. It enables consumers to discriminate between similar products—Coca Cola versus Pepsi Cola, for example. But branding is multipurpose. As one scholar wrote—

> Brands can epitomize the core identity of a company and its products. Brands can also instill personality traits in products; traits with which special segments of consumers can identify. To loyal customers brands can be powerful symbols and complex systems of meaning. Brands can also impact the larger culture by mirroring and shaping mundane aspects of life, even art.[3]

In short, "Political parties offer voters, like brands offer consumers, *bundles of meaning.*" *(Emphasis in original)*.[4]

Until the mid-1970s, political parties were movements and individuals, not brands. Today, there is no overlap at all between the two parties. The most conservative Democrat, Sen. Ben Nelson of Nebraska, is located to the left of the most liberal Republican, Sen. Olympia Snowe of Maine.[5]

What is a Republican today? A conservative who wants to cut taxes and reduce government spending and regulations, while maintaining a strong military. If that is the definition of a Republican, what of a candidate who supports environmental protection, opposes unilateral military intervention and believes spending increases are required for education and Social Security? Could that person possibly be a Republican?

The answer, at least in 1976, was yes. There were conservative Republicans and Democrats, moderates and liberals. Individuals were elected from different states and, hence, had different political qualities, because they were essential to survival. A candidate in Maryland, whether Democrat or Republican, was liberal because voters there simply rejected conservatives. In other states—Arizona, for example—the reverse was true.

Within a state there was room for difference. A politician from Austin, Texas could be liberal, but not one from Houston. Or one from the eastern shore of Maryland could be conservative, but not one from Baltimore.

Today, however, it is different. The Republican Party began branding itself in the 1970s in order to recast itself. In the words of Ford and Nixon's Secretary of the Treasury, William Simon, the Republican Party was being recast by those who took control of it as the "Liberty Party." For this to happen, the party and its candidates must be the same from one state to another, one day to the next, at local, state and federal levels, and whether in the Presidency, Congress or courts. Today, it is the Republican/Libertarian/Tea Party.

There are those who would say that the so-called "liberal" or "moderate" Republicans of the 1970s and before had little in common with their so-called "conservative"colleagues of the same party. If so, New York's liberal Sen. Jacob Javits would never have voted the same way as Sen. John Williams of Delaware, as staunch a conservative as ever strode the floor of the U.S. Congress. But he did.

Both, for example, supported the Civil Rights Act of 1964. One represented a state that abolished slavery in 1827,[6] the other a state where slaves had not only been owned, but continued to be held legally after Lincoln's Emancipation Proclamation.[h]

Of course, they voted differently most of the time. Javits supported Medicare's creation in 1965, while Williams opposed it, for example.[7] The Republican Party was not then peopled solely by conservatives, nor were Democrats all liberal. The result was that the two parties competed and evolved positions that suited the voters.

In the South, Democrats ruled. But they, too, were divided into (relatively) liberal and conservative wings. Balancing the likes of Strom Thurmond, the segregationist Senator from South Carolina and "Dixiecrat" candidate for President in 1948, there was an Al Gore (senior) from Tennessee. If a candidate wanted your

---

[h] The Proclamation applied only to Confederate states, and Delaware was loyal to the Union, so slavery remained legal there. Lincoln issued the Proclamation on January 1, 1863, as the nation approached its third year of bloody civil war. The proclamation declared "that all persons held as slaves" within the rebellious states "are, and henceforward shall be free." National Archives & Records Administration, "The Emancipation Proclamation," http://www.archives.gov/exhibits/featured_documents/emancipation_proclamation/, accessed Sept. 16, 2012.

vote, it required work and you could choose between liberals and conservatives of each party, Republicans and Democrats alike.

Polarization, however, means that all Democrats will be pretty much alike, and so will all Republicans. To the extent that there is an electoral brawl, it is in the primary. But even then, in an RLTP primary contest, one candidate will say "I'm conservative" and the rival will declare "me, too." There is no space left for a candidate who is a mixture of both liberal and conservative.

Office holders who were, at once, liberal on some issues but conservative on others, once existed. Sen. John Chafee of Rhode Island, for example, was a decorated Marine infantry veteran of both World War II and Korea. A former governor of Rhode Island, the nation's most Democratic state, Chafee favored environmental protection, especially of creatures unable to protect themselves. But on matters of defense, he was a hawk—which is what would be expected from a former Republican Secretary of the Navy.[8]

Starting in the 1970s as money from the rich and corporations began flowing into campaign coffers, the Republican Party began purging its more liberal and moderate members.

In 1976, the President was a moderate Republican, Gerald Ford. The Vice Present was a liberal Republican and former Governor of New York, Nelson Rockefeller. There were 37 Republican members of the United States Senate. They included the Minority Leader, Sen. Hugh Scott, a moderate to liberal from Pennsylvania[9] and Assistant Minority Leader Sen. Robert Griffin of Michigan, a moderate who called for President Richard Nixon's resignation in the wake of the Watergate break-in and scandal.[10]

Other Senators included Lowell Weicker, a liberal from Connecticut; William V. Roth, Jr., a Delaware moderate; Charles Percy, an Illinois liberal; Charles "Mac" Mathias, a Maryland liberal; J. Glenn Beall, a Maryland moderate; Edward Brooke, a Massachusetts liberal; Clifford Case, a New Jersey liberal; Jacob Javits, a New York liberal; Mark Hatfield and Robert Packwood, both Oregon liberals; the aforementioned-Scott and liberal Richard Schweicker both of Pennsylvania; John Chafee of Rhode Island; Howard Baker of Tennessee; and, Robert T. Stafford of Vermont, all moderates. I personally worked for two of these men, Roth and Stafford, and with the staffs of all of them. Some of these Senators I knew personally.

Mathias is a textbook example of how the Republican Party sought to purge itself of moderates and liberals. His family had been immersed in Republican politics for generations. Sen. Mathias's great-grandfather served in the Maryland legislature in the 1860s, and his grandfather was a state senator who campaigned with Theodore Roosevelt. When the future senator was a boy, his father took him to the White House to meet presidents Calvin Coolidge and Herbert Hoover.

During his lifetime, Republicans were still often called members of the party of Lincoln. But as the Republican Party increasingly reached out to southern white men for support, as part of the Southern Strategy, Mathias resisted. "We cannot rally a responsible political majority by appealing only to the fears and insecurities of a group that is all white and prematurely aged," he said in 1971.

When Republicans regained control of the U.S. Senate after Reagan's victory in 1980, Mathias should have become chair of the Judiciary Committee by virtue of his seniority. But Strom Thurmond (R-S.C.)—once a segregationist Democrat—led a successful conservative maneuver to seat himself as Judiciary chair instead of Mathias, then abolished a subcommittee that the Marylander chaired.

Mathias was re-elected in 1980 with 66 percent of the vote. Conservative Republicans opposed him, denouncing Mathias as a "communist," "traitor" and "baby killer," and a Republican leader in Baltimore publicly called him "a liberal swine."[11]

Sen. Robert T. Stafford of Vermont took over as chair of the Committee on Environment and Public Works. But not before a group of senior aides to other Republicans warned him that they were monitoring his hiring and Committee legislation. If they were too liberal, they warned, Stafford would be stripped of his chairmanship.

The way in which the Republican Party was gradually purged of moderates and liberals is illustrated by the fate of New Jersey liberal Clifford Case. A New Jersey institution, Case sought a fifth Senate term in 1978. He was opposed by, and lost the Republican primary to, Jeffrey Bell. A Ronald Reagan and anti-tax supporter, Bell had moved to New Jersey expressly to challenge Case.

With a very low turnout in the 1978 primary, Bell defeated Case but went on to lose the general election to Bill Bradley by ten points. Thus, the Republican Party lost a liberal, and the Democrats gained a Senate seat.[12] No Republican has been elected to represent New Jersey in the Senate since Case's last victory in 1972.

In 1982, Stafford barely survived a similar primary challenge in Vermont by former Reagan speech writer and Reagan White House aide John McClaughry. Stafford won the primary, but was damaged, and prevailed in the general election in the closest Senate race in the nation. Had McClaughery won the primary, he would have lost the general election. The Democrats would have gained a Senate seat, and the Republicans lost a moderate vote.[13, i]

In New York, Javits lost a 1980 primary challenge by the comparatively lesser-known Long Island Republican county official Alfonse D'Amato, who went on to win the general election.[14]

Today, only two Republican Senators, both from Maine, are commonly viewed as moderates (although a case can be made that neither is a true moderate, because they seldom vote against their party).[15] Moreover, one of them, Olympia Snowe, is not seeking re-election.

A fundamental premise of democracy is that elections provide an opportunity for voters to control politicians. For this to actually work, however, citizens must know enough about what's happening and why and, most importantly, be willing to shift their votes based on that information. Voters will admittedly decide how to vote based, in part, on some philosophical or other predilections. Some may always vote for blacks, others never; some will tend to prefer a candidate of a certain sex; still others will cast their votes on a single issue. That said, the premise of democracy is choice, driven by knowledge.

If, however, enough voters can be persuaded to reliably deliver their votes to a single candidate in large enough numbers to assure—or even merely increase the likelihood of—a victory regardless of a candidate's stand on the issues or the concerns of voters, then democracy is diminished. Push this far enough, and democracy is destroyed.

This explains why the RLTP has so aggressively courted white evangelicals and white Catholics. It also explains why it has sought the votes of white southern males. And, it explains why it has branded itself as anti-government, anti-tax, and anti-abortion, to name but three.

---

[i] McClaughery now heads the Ethan Allen Institute of Concord, Vermont. It is a so-called "charity" with gross income of $173,781 in 2011, according to the form 990 filed with the Internal Revenue Service. It describes itself on its website as an "independent, nonpartisan, free-market-oriented public policy think tank." McClaughery's campaign manager, Richard Feldman, became a lobbyist for the National Rifle Association (see endnote).

For branding to become an effective strategy for permanently controlling the nation, however, the nature of elections has had to be reshaped. Instead of being driven by local issues, which has been the case since the country's founding, Congressional elections had to be nationalized.

Republicans did this in 1994, using the Contract With America as a tool.[j] Instead of races for the House of Representatives turning on local concerns—a bridge over the Chesapeake and Delaware Canal, the decline in salmon runs in Puget Sound or the construction of a underground subway tunnel through an area rich in natural gas deposits in Los Angeles, for example—the center of attention was on limiting the terms of committee chairs and banning proxy votes. The strategy succeeded, and for the first time in a century, House elections were decided on the basis of national issues, not local concerns.

The impacts of the shift from local issues to those of national concern, has also affected the Senate. The strong influence of national issues on voters has contributed to larger seat swings and more frequent turnover in party control of the Senate. The electoral coalitions supporting Democratic and Republican Senate candidates have become increasingly distinct in terms of race and ideology which has led to increased party loyalty and straight ticket voting.[16]

What is important to bear in mind is that these are changes that have occurred over a generation. It would take that long to restore the previous status quo, even if that were possible. But there's not time, because it seems that one political party—the Republican/Libertarian/Tea Party—will soon be in a position of permanent dominance. Then, it can do as it pleases.

America is now approaching, or may have even passed the point, where democracy ceases to exist. Certainly, that is the direction in which America is

---

[j] On the first day of their majority in the House, the Republicans promised to pass eight major reforms:
- Require all laws that apply to the rest of the country also apply to Congress;
- Select a major, independent auditing firm to conduct a comprehensive audit of Congress for waste, fraud or abuse;
- Cut the number of House committees, and cut committee staff by one-third;
- Limit the terms of all committee chairs;
- Ban the casting of proxy votes in committee;
- Require committee meetings to be open to the public;
- Require three-fifths majority vote to pass a tax increase; and
- Guarantee an honest accounting of the Federal Budget by implementing zero base-line budgeting.

Many of the Contract's policy ideas originated at The Heritage Foundation, the corporate front group founded by Paul Weyrich.

inexorably moving and, barring some change in course, the death of democracy in America is the inevitable result. The hope is that shifts in the electorate will occur before the RLTP can reach a permanent majority.

Because of these changes, politicians and voters alike are "polarized." This means simply that Republicans disagree with Democrats and vice versa. But the disagreement is vehement amongst politicians and voters alike: in 2008, about 90 percent of voters supported their party's candidate.

Increasingly, however, voters are fleeing the two parties to become independents. In North Carolina, for example, Republican registration declined 4 percent, from nearly 35 percent in 2005 to 31 percent in 2010. Democratic registration dropped 2 percent during the same period, while Independent (unaffiliated) identification increased 6 percent from 18 percent in 2005 to almost 24 percent in 2010.[17] This suggests that moderate voters are fleeing both of the parties.

Evidence of the partisan rift is also provided by the decline in "ticket-splitting," when a vote is cast for a presidential candidate of one party, but a Congressional candidate of the other. It seems to be a thing of the past.[18]

In some states (e.g., North Dakota), it has been common for voters to choose one party for the Presidency and the other for the Congressional delegation or the state legislature. In some election years, this happens in more than one third of the states.

For instance, eighteen states chose divided party control between their state house and congressional delegations following the 1990 elections. The prevalence of split partisan majorities peaked again in 1998 and 2000, when fifteen and sixteen states chose split-party delegations, respectively.

Ticket splitting demonstrates that voters are examining specific candidates, and choosing one over the other on a case-by-case basis. It bespeaks an evaluation of each and every candidate and their positions on relevant needs of each office. That is, ticket splitting means voters are not casting ballots based on knee-jerk loyalty.

As party loyalty among voters has increased, rates of split-ticket voting have fallen. Ticket splitting began increasing in the 1950s and peaked around 1980. But during the last twenty years, rates of split-ticket voting have decreased.[19]

Some believe the partisan distinctions that have led to a decline in ticket splitting is good. It shows that voters are being provided with a clear philosophical choice: conservative or liberal.

The purpose of the political structure in the United States, however, is not to provide voters with a clear philosophical choice. It is to provide a mechanism with which to govern the nation. Americans adopted the Constitution, as it declares in the preamble—

> in order to form a more perfect union, establish justice,
> ensure domestic tranquility, provide for the common defense,
> promote the general welfare, and secure the blessings of liberty to
> ourselves and our posterity, do ordain and establish this Constitution
> for the United States of America.

Central to this is the periodic evaluation by voters of specific candidates and specific issues. The evidence suggests, however, that this has ceased to be the case: voters are casting their ballots on the basis of issues that assure an electoral outcome. That is, the RLTP wins.

Elections in a democracy rest on voters evaluating each candidate in every election. Americans clearly once did this. Sadly, the evidence suggests that they have ceased to do so, at least in the past few elections.

Will America survive? Or, more precisely, will democracy in America survive?

22
CONCLUSIONS

Let's admit at the outset that it may not be possible to cure what ails America. Many of those who learn of this book's message may disagree. As far as they are concerned, the nation is functioning quite well. Probably, this is the case with the vast majority of white evangelicals and the white Catholics who heed the dictates of the church hierarchy. Moreover, the many voters who are today's Republicans also very likely disagree with the premise of this book that America is broken.

Together, these three groups may well constitute a majority—in which case, they are by definition correct, and the nation is just fine. Or if not a majority, then a determined enough minority that as a nation we will never reach a consensus.

For everybody's sake, especially that of our children and grandchildren, I hope that we are able to reach a consensus that there is such a thing as global warming, it is caused by humans, can be reversed by humans, and should be. That is the subject of *Cliffs II*, however, so it will be excluded from this discussion.

It seems to me—and these are the views of only one person, albiet one who has devoted the majority of the last twenty years to understanding what has happened to the America of my childhood, youth and young adulthood—that there are several faults that must be remedied. In no particular order, they include the following:

- A way must be found to limit the wealth of American families to a single generation. Almost none of the families, and their foundations, who have stolen America represent the wealth of a single generation. The Kochs, Scaifes, Mellons are all multi-generational rich people who compounded the wealth they inherited, then deployed it as a tool to protect themselves and their money. This must stop. We need a death tax that is confiscatory above a certain level.

- OK, allow some people to inherit millions. When I practiced law, one of my clients owned a ranch in eastern Washington that was larger than one or two states, and most counties. Let people like him keep their money and pass it on, within limits, to their children and grandchildren. Under no circumstances, however, should a person be able to bequeath to another an inheritance greater than the value of many nations.

- Similarly, the concept of allowing unlimited deductions for donations to "charities" such as the Heritage Foundation, the Cato Institute and the Competitive Enterprise Institute is insane. The American Lung Association is a charity, and so is the March of Dimes, the Boy Scouts of America and hundreds of other organizations. The front tanks are not. They exist for the sole purpose of an advancing a philosophy that advances the interests of their donors. Giving money to the Heritage Foundation is not the same thing as dropping some change into the Christmas barrel of the Salvation Army, and never will be.

- Whether churches or religions should be allowed to remain charities is doubtful. If ministers or priests wish to advise from the pulpit that their black worshipers should vote for Democrats or that their white evangelicals and Catholics should vote Republican, it is up to them. But the taxpayers of America should not be subsidizing that choice.

- Corporations are not the same as human Americans. They should not be treated as such. A Supreme Court that chooses to continue the legal nightmare of treating them as such should be either packed with justices that oppose the doctrine or impeached.

It is this last point on which I feel most strongly.

In *Santa Clara County v. Southern Pacific Railroad Company*[k] the U.S. Supreme Court supposedly held that a corporation is a "person." It did not. That is a lie. But it is a lie that has become so firmly established that it is almost universally accepted as the truth—remember Mitt Romney's statement in 2011 at the Iowa State Fair that "Corporations are people, my friend."?[1] Some background:

The *Santa Clara* case was a routine matter brought before the United States Supreme Court, but not decided by it with a formal opinion (e.g., such as that found with *Citizens United* or *Brown v. Board of*

---

[k] 118 U.S. 394 (1886)

Education). Lawyers, professors and judges all universally rely on written opinions to tell them what the law is or what it might become. So do all who might come before a court, any court. The only way to do this is to read an opinion.

Santa Clara was a routine case dealing with taxation of railroad properties, the sort of dispute that the court has resolved thousands of times. In this instance, a report was issued by the Court Reporter, not the Supreme Court itself. The reporter's note claimed that it was the sense of the Court that the Fourteenth Amendment granted equal protection to corporations, as well as humans.[1] That issue had not been raised by either litigant, had not been briefed, had not been argued and there was no decision or written opinion. There is only the word of the Court Reporter.

The nation was founded by human beings to be a republic for human beings. The Constitution was written by human beings to protect human beings. The Fourteenth Amendment was written and adopted to protect human beings—specifically former black slaves. There is not a scintilla of evidence to support the proposition that corporations are to be accorded the same status as humans. They are the creations of humans and exist solely to do our bidding.

How the Reporter's words ever came into being, why they have been so widely, almost universally, accepted can never be completely established. But the results are quite clear. It has led to the mess we are in. Artificial beings are now competing with their creators, the human race, and are winning. To prevail—that is, for humanity to survive—corporations must be brought to heel and, if necessary, eliminated altogether.

It is simply an outrage that such an immense body of law and an attitude that subjugates the interests of human Americans to fictitious creatures such as corporations have come into existence. As then-Justice William Rehnquist wrote "This Court decided at an early date, with neither argument nor discussion, that a

---

[1] The Reporter stated that the Chief Justice opened oral argument on the case by announcing that "The court does not wish to hear argument on the question whether the provision in the Fourteenth Amendment to the Constitution, which forbids a State to deny to any person within its jurisdiction the equal protection of the laws, applies to these corporations. We are all of the opinion that it does."

business corporation is a 'person' entitled to the protection of the Equal Protection Clause of the Fourteenth Amendment."

The decision does not contain such a conclusion, nor did any of the Justices of the Supreme Court of the United States make such a legally binding statement. A report issued by the Court Reporter claimed to state the sense of the Court—without a decision or written opinions published by or of the Court. It is as if the Court Reporter said that the sense of the Court was that strawberry is the favorite ice cream of the United States, and henceforth all courts, legislatures, and restaurants served only strawberry-shortcake, ice cream, pie, fritters, mousse and whatever—just so long as it was strawberry, not blueberry, peach, apple, cherry, maple, chocolate or any other flavor.

Who were these people to make such a decision? Were they on drugs? Why, after nearly one and one-half centuries is the United States adhering to such a manifestly wrong-headed decision?

I cannot go beyond these conclusions at present. The writer is not a repository of wisdom. What I hope is that this book will be read, discussed and point to policy conclusions that will be adopted and solve our problems.

In other words, I hope that Americans can and will fix this themselves, for themselves, not for the rich and their property.

Thank you.

PREVIEW OF *CLIFFS II*

POSITIVE FEEDBACKS AND "TIPPING POINTS" (THINK TWIN TOWERS)

Change in nature is fast, abrupt and usually violent—"stepwise" is the term that scientists like to use. Consider lightening: if change were gradual, it would be a steadily escalating buzz of static electricity. Instead, it announces itself with a thunderous peal after a stepped leader of electricity works its way toward earth to be met by a climbing surge of positive electricity.[1]

Or consider an avalanche, when instead of slowly sliding down a slope, 230,000 cubic meters—enough to cover 20 football fields with snow 10 feet deep—cascades without warning from an unstable snowpack.

Or think of the Twin Towers, which on September 11, 2001, after two Boeing passenger jets crashed into them, they stood, stood, stood. Then, some small point was passed and they collapsed.

These are "tipping points," and humanity is approaching them. We know that there are global warming tipping points, but science is not good enough to predict when a tipping point is passed or, for that matter, where they lie. But this much is certain: they exist, humanity is approaching them and, if one or more is passed, it could be the end of life as we have known it for thousands of years.

But the Republican/Libertarian/Tea Party and those who have been enriched by coal, oil, railroad and many other industries which survive by warming the earth do not care. They do not, after all, laugh or cry, sleep or wake, love or hate. They are mindless and speak only one language: money.

They, in short, do not care that the gravest risks posed by global warming lie not in a gradual rise in temperature over the course of a few decades, but instead in some unpredictable catastrophic event. What might that be? Nobody can predict with certainty because, by definition, we don't know what we don't know. There is compelling evidence that in areas where there are clearly linkages that could trigger runaway global warming, movement in that direction has begun.

The Twin Towers had withstood hurricane-force winds and a terrorist truck bomb. Yet they fell to earth, suddenly, violently and completely.[a] An avalanche on Mont Blanc in July 2012, killed nine climbers. It struck with no warning or sound.[b] Thermonuclear explosions, the

Collapse of the Twin Towers on Sep. 11, 2001 as a tipping point was reached. (Source: University of Sydney http://www.civil.usyd.edu.au/wtc.shtml)

classic examples of passing a tipping point, leveled two Japanese cities, Hiroshima and Nagasaki.

If the earth is not warmer, why are temperatures of air, soil and water increasing? Why are waters of the oceans rising? Why are plants and animals moving up mountains and toward the poles, where it is cooler? If heat is not trapped closer to the earth's surface, why is the stratosphere colder? Why is the United States suffering from the worst drought in a half-century? If it is not hotter,

---

[a] Steven Ashley, "When the Twin Towers Fell," *Scientific American*, Oct. 9, 2001

[b] John Heilprin, "Survivors: Avalanche hit with no warning, no sound," Associated Press, July 13, 2012.

why are thunderstorms and other violent events more frequent and stronger, just as global warming predictions say will happen?

The pieces of change fit together like the parts of a exquisitely complex and well oiled machine. The Arctic and Antarctic are warming and melting, triggering a slowing of the 1,000-year current that warms, cools and feeds the planet. With their supply of nutrient-rich water gone, the tiny plants and animals that form the base of the world's food chain—plankton—are disappearing. Their decline is hastened by the increasing acidity of an ocean in which carbon dioxide is being dissolved, forming carbonic acid.

Permafrost is warming, thawing and rotting, releasing massive amounts of greenhouse gases, which in turn are speeding the warming further, causing still more releases of warming pollutants. In short, what the computer models predict should happen are, in fact, occurring. Humanity is standing at the base of a global Twin Towers, as it collapses on our future.

Every year, the world undergoes such a runaway reaction. In the past it made the evening news and the front pages, but no longer. Now it is relegated to the inside pages and mentioned briefly, if at all, on the nightly news.

In every Antarctic Spring, in the space of five or so days, industrial chemicals—CFCs, better known by their DuPont tradename of "Freons"—utterly destroy stratospheric ozone in the Antarctic to the height of Mt. Everest and over a region the size of North America. The destruction was measured in 1981, but scientists refused to believe the data and ordered a replacement device. It had the same results, and they rejected that too. Three years later, a NASA Nimbus 7 satellite also reported the destruction. Its results also were rejected.

Not until 1985 did the global science community report the destruction. Even then, they couldn't explain why. Industry, especially DuPont, said the destruction was merely "seasonal." After all, it profited immensely from making, selling and using CFCs.

What could explain this? Scientists were baffled. Industry stonewalled. DuPont refused to honor a pledge made years earlier in full-page advertisements in the *Washington Post, New York Times* and other newspapers, and in testimony to the Congress, to stop making CFCs if this happened. The company wanted to keep making and selling CFCs, so it gave prodigious amounts of money to its front group, the Alliance for a Responsible Chlorofluorocarbon Policy. It did what such groups do best: lobby and tell half-truths.

What could industry and scientists alike have possibly overlooked?

Answer: The Antarctic gets cold—really, really cold.

So cold, in fact, that clouds of ice form. Suddenly a "gas phase" reaction that is slow becomes a lightening fast "solid phase"chemical reaction. Ozone destruction in the Antarctic becomes a runaway reaction, the environmental equivalent of a nuclear explosion. Nuclear devices reach a tipping point, a critical mass, then Nagasaki or Hiroshima vanish beneath a mushroom cloud. But they are only two cities. If this happens with global warming, the entire planet and everything on it is at risk, and there can be no return to the environment of the present, ever.

Has it happened in the past? Yes.

Can it happen again? Yes.

Is it happening as you read these words? Probably.

Is there time to save ourselves? Perhaps.

In the case of environmental threats such as global warming, the danger of reaching a tipping point is increased because of the number of changes that can feed on themselves, starting a spiral of heat. When tundra thaws, for example, it begins to decay, releasing both carbon dioxide and methane, which has 20 times the warming power of CO_2 on a molecule-for-molecule basis. They increase the temperature, which triggers still more releases of greenhouse gases, which, in turn, further boosts warming. Thus the hotter it gets, the hotter it will get.

For myself, I believe that humanity has five or at most 10 years to reverse the warming trend. My political experience leads me to believe that corporations, especially the oil, coal, electricity and auto companies, have such a firm grip on political decision-making in the United States that action will be taken either too late or not at all. Though it saddens me to write this, I believe my children and billions of others, will fail to live out their natural lives.

There are at least ten possible tipping points and positive feedbacks that have been identified, and movement is occurring in each. It would be bad enough for one of them to tip, but the catastrophic threat is that when one tips, it will trigger changes that will precipitate a tip in all ten, and probably others that haven't yet been identified. It is simply impossible to quantify the risk of reaching one or more tipping points, so ultimately the determination is both personal and subjective. For myself, I believe that humanity has five or at most 10 years to reverse the warming trend. My political experience leads me to believe that corporations, especially the oil, coal, electricity and auto companies, have such a firm grip on political decision making in the United States that action will be taken either too late or not at all.

Though it saddens me to write this, I believe my children and billions of others, will fail to live out their natural lives.

ARCTIC WARMING AND MELTING

The danger of melting in the Arctic—or, for that matter, any area covered by snow and ice—is that as dark soils or waters are exposed they will absorb more sunlight, thus increasing warming that will melt more ice and snow, exposing still more dark surfaces. This has almost certainly begun in the Arctic—and the implications extend much further.

The Arctic has been warming for quite some time, but the insulating effect of the snow and ice, combined with the extremely long time frame required to change ocean temperatures, have masked some of the changes. Once movement starts, however, scientists say a feedback will be

The effects of an ice-free Arctic will not stop there. It will likely extend to the entire planet, possibly triggering a series of feedbacks that would leave the Earth irrevocably altered and hostile to life as we know it. (Source: freewebs.com)

kicked in leading to, in the words of two snow and ice specialists, "a substantial increase" in Arctic Ocean air temperatures.[2] Recent studies show that melting has now begun, and is happening at two to three times the rates predicted by computer models.

A study published in 2007 in the journal *Geophysical Research Letters*, found that the actual rate at which summer sea ice had shrunk per decade during the past 50 years was more than three times faster than an average of 18 of the most highly regarded climate simulations. Arctic sea ice is now melting at a rate far quicker than predicted by climate change computer models and could disappear completely before the middle of the century.

Retreating Arctic ice is a key indicator of the pace of global warming, and one that could have devastating repercussions for the wider climate, including warmer oceans and rising sea levels.[3] The extent of summer sea-ice has decreased by nearly 40 percent compared to the 1979–2000 average. The ice is thinning and 2008 is even worse.

The year started with Arctic ice covering a larger area than at the beginning of 2007, according to data from the U.S. National Snow and Ice Data Center (NSIDC). But by the beginning of the summer, ice levels had shrunk beyond those of June 2007, a summer that broke records for sea ice loss.[4] Preliminary data showed that the vast expanse of ice at the top of the world was some 55,800 square miles smaller than it was on the same date in 2007.[5] Scientists on the project said much of the ice was so thin it melted easily, and that Arctic seas might be ice-free in the summer within five to ten years.[6]

The consequences, however, extend far beyond the Arctic—indeed to the entire planet. Melting, especially if reinforced by a five- to ten-year period of sudden, deep sea-ice meltbacks could be 3.5 times higher than climate models typically project, according to a study published in June 2008 issue of *Geophysical Research Letters*.[7] It predicts that added warmth will extend 900 miles into the North American and Eurasian continents, thawing vast stretches of tundra and permafrost, setting off a second positive feedback. Again, as noted earlier, as these soils thaw, they decay, releasing the greenhouse gases carbon dioxide and methane. Those will accelerate warming further, causing more methane and carbon dioxide to enter the air and trap heat (see the discussion of tundra thawing below).

The reaction of the global community, however, has not been to undertake immediate action to halt or at least slow melting, but instead to squabble over the spoils. For example, as milder temperatures made exploration of the Arctic sea floor possible for the first time, Russia's biggest-ever research expedition to the region steamed in to explore the seabed in a search for oil and gas.[8]

ANTARCTIC MELTING

The Antarctic Ice Sheet is vast, about 2,000 miles (3,000 kilometers) wide and up to 3 miles (4.5 kilometers) thick. It holds 90 percent of the world's ice, and the disappearance of even its smaller West Antarctic ice sheet would raise worldwide sea levels by an estimated 20 feet. If the entire Antarctic melted completely, sea levels would rise by about 210 feet (70 meters) worldwide, destroying virtually all of the world's coastal cities. Most scientists think such a large change is unlikely except over thousands of years. However, a loss of even 5 percent would radically transform Earth's coastal regions.

Warmer temperatures and disappearing sea ice in the Southern Ocean appear to be causing food shortages that could threaten Antarctic whales, seals and penguins. The vanishing ice in the winter has resulted in an 80 percent drop in the number of Antarctic krill, a shrimp-like crustacean that is a major source of food for animals in the region. (Source: www.msnbc.msn.com/id/6398305/)

Scientists seeking to determine how the Antarctic ice sheet has changed in recent years, have concluded that it is losing as much as 36 cubic miles of ice a year in a trend that they link to global warming, according to a new paper that provides the first evidence that the sheet's total mass is shrinking significantly.[9]

The new findings, using data from two NASA satellites called the Gravity Recovery and Climate Experiment (GRACE), suggest that global sea levels could rise substantially. They also concluded that the amount of water pouring annually from the ice sheet into the ocean, which is roughly equivalent to the amount that the United States uses in three months, is raising global sea levels by 0.4 millimeters a year.

TUNDRA THAWING

Time is ticking on a climate time bomb throughout Alaska, Canada, Siberia and other frozen regions as tundra, permafrost—permanently frozen ground—and other places where carbon has been stored for centuries begin to thaw. The evidence for this, whether anecdotal or scientific, is compelling.

In addition to northern Alaska, the permafrost zone includes most other Arctic land, such as northern Canada and much of Siberia, as well as the higher reaches of mountainous regions such as the Alps and Tibet. All report permafrost thaw. To track these changes, the Global Terrestrial Network for Permafrost (GTNP) was created, and it shows a warming trend throughout the permafrost zone.

This huge expanse of western Siberia is thawing for the first time since its formation, 11,000 years ago. The area, which is the size of France and Germany combined, will release methane and carbon dioxide, both greenhouse gases, as it thaws, thus further accelerating warming. (Source: BBC.)

Some of these frozen soils are much richer in carbon than ordinary earth. They contain large amounts of grass roots, animal bones, and other materials resulting in average carbon contents of 2 to 5 percent—roughly 10 to 30 times that in deep, non-permafrost mineral soils.[10]

Carbon, which has been stored in these soils for tens of thousands of years, is being released by rising temperatures, accelerating global warming. A study of so-called "thaw" lakes in Siberia, for example, estimated that methane emissions rose 58 percent from 1974 to 2000.[11] In Manitoba, Canada, a researcher reported that permafrost thaw had accelerated significantly since 1950,[12] as temperatures rose 1.32° C. A 1999 study found general warming in Alaska from the late 1980s to 1996 ranging from 0.5° to 1.5°C, with an annual warming rate of 0.05° to 0.2°C.[13] Boreholes in Svalbard, Norway indicate that ground temperatures rose 0.4°C from 1994 to 2004, four times faster than they did in the previous century.[14]

Thawing permafrost can cause buildings and roads to collapse, pipelines to crack, landslides to increase in the soil-based permafrost of Canada, and destabilize in mountainous regions (e.g., the Alps), causing slope failures such as in the Alps.[15]

CHERSKY, Russia — Sergei Zimov waded through knee-deep snow to reach a frozen lake where so much methane belches out of the melting permafrost that it spews from the ice like small geysers.

In the frigid twilight, the Russian scientist struck a match to make a jet of the greenhouse gas visible. The sudden plume of fire threw him backward. Zimov stood up, brushed the snow off his parka and beamed.

"Sometimes a big explosion happens, because the gas comes out like a bomb," Zimov said. "There are a million lakes like this in northern Siberia."

INTERRUPTION OF ATLANTIC CONVEYER BELT

The world is warmed and cooled—in short, made liveable for humans—by a conveyor belt of ocean waters that travel tens of thousands of miles over a thousand years, shifting energy from the torrid Pacific and Indian Oceans to the frigid waters of the North Atlantic. If it stops, and there is persuasive evidence that it is at least slowing, the world as we know it will cease to exist.

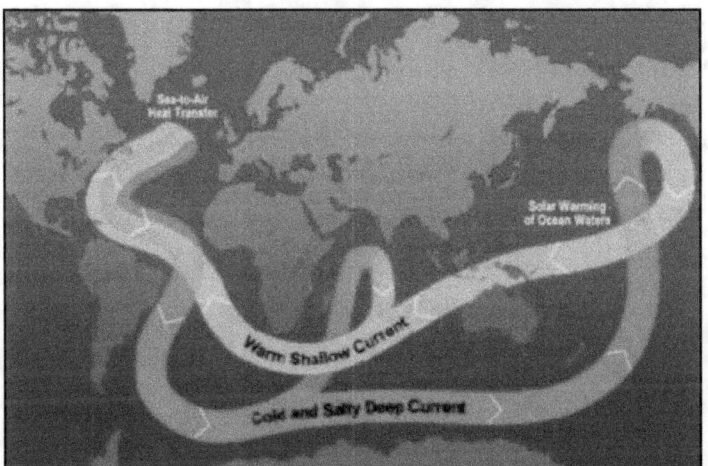

The Gulf Stream brings warm tropical waters north, boosting the temperatures of Europe by about 18°F (10°C) in the winter. As it cools to freezing, the water sinks to the ocean floor, flows through the Atlantic Basin around South Africa, into the Indian Ocean past Australia into the Pacific Ocean Basin, where it rises to be rewarmed. The entire journey takes 1,000–1,200 years, and makes Europe habitable. If the current fails to sink because it is too warm or the salt level is lowered by melting fresh water from the Arctic ice and glaciers, Europe will likely enter a new Ice Age. (Sources: NASA and NOAA.)

The conveyor belt travels to the east of North America, where it is called the Gulf Stream, to the east of Greenland. There winds blowing over its surface extract water and energy, forming clouds that travel across western Europe to roughly Moscow, Russia, dropping energy-rich rain and snow in their wake. Now heavier because it is saltier and cooler, the current drops to the ocean to begin its return journey.

But this powerful ocean current bathing Britain and northern Europe in warm waters from the tropics has weakened dramatically in recent years, a consequence of global warming. And that could, regardless of what intuition might suggest, trigger more severe winters and cooler summers across the region—even a little ice age, like the one that caused temperatures in Europe to plummet about 12 centuries ago.

As the belt rises to the surface, it carries with it the nutrients that feed plankton, that are the base of the world's food chain. If the belt slows, plankton levels fall as they, in effect, are starved—and plankton levels have dropped sharply (see plankton decline, below).

Researchers on a scientific expedition in the Atlantic Ocean measured the strength of the current between Africa and the east coast of America and found that circulation has slowed by 30 percent since an expedition 12 years earlier. Previous expeditions to check the current flow in 1957, 1981 and 1992 found only minor changes in its strength, although a slowing was picked up in 1998.

As winds pass over the current, they drain its heat energy—the equivalent of about one teaspoon of sugar in every cubic centimeter—boosting European temperatures by 10°C in some regions. The researchers found that the circulation has dropped by 6 million tons of water per second.

Scientists believe that if the current remains in its weakened state, temperatures in Britain are likely to drop by an average of 1°C. Harry Bryden at the National Oceanography Centre in Southampton who led the study said that "Models show that if it shuts down completely, 20 years later, the temperature is 4° to 6°C cooler over the UK and north-western Europe."[16]

PLANKTON DECLINE

The base of the global food chain is formed by trillions of tiny plants and animals, or plankton, most so small as to be barely visible to the human eye. If plankton die, so do the fish, whales and other sea creatures that feed on them. Satellite surveys have detected a sharp decline in plankton in several of the world's oceans—a situation that could threaten the marine food chain and undercut one of the world's natural buffers to global warming.

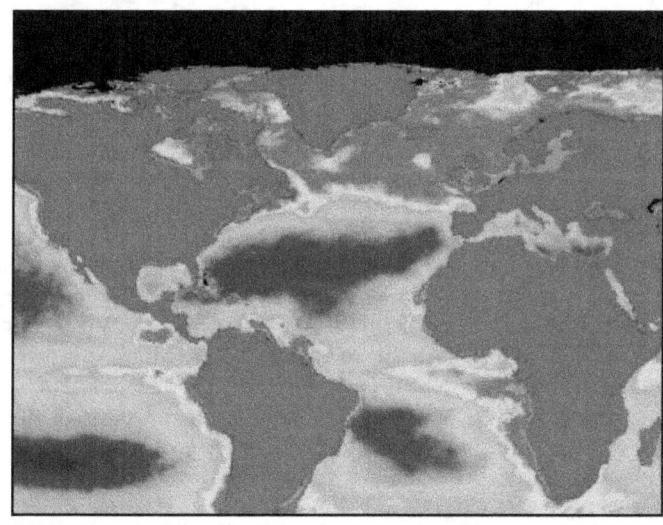

A check up of the Earth's planetary health reveals that the lowest rung in the ocean food chain is shrinking. For the past 20 years (early 1980s to present), phytoplankton concentrations declined as much as 30 percent in northern oceans. Scientists from NASA and the National Oceanic and Atmospheric Administration (NOAA) say warmer ocean temperatures and low winds may be depriving the tiny ocean plants of necessary nutrients. However, they still do not know if the loss of phytoplankton is a long-term trend or a climate oscillation.

Plankton include organisms such as diatoms,[17] dinoflagellates,[18] and krill,[19] as well as as the microscopic larva of crabs, sea urchins, and fish. Plankton also include tiny photosynthetic organisms that are so numerous and productive that they are responsible for generating more oxygen than all the other plants on Earth combined.

The decline in these free-floating, microscopic organisms—the plants are called phytoplankton and the animals zooplankton—varies from ocean to ocean. The greatest decline is in the Northern Pacific Ocean, where summer levels have dropped by more than 30 percent since the 1980s.[20] The data was collected in the summers (July–September) from 1979–2000.

In the North Atlantic, phytoplankton concentrations dropped by 14 percent since the 1980s. Like the North Pacific, as shown in Figure 6, there is a lot of red representing a slight increase in phytoplankton but it does not make up for the large decreases shown in blue.

These declines are consistent with computer models of what will happen if the oceanic conveyor belt is interrupted (see above). In the computer simulations, a disruption of the belt leads to a collapse of the North Atlantic plankton stocks to less than half of their initial levels because the organisms are, in effect, starved when the nutrients in the deep oceans are no longer being brought to the surface by the conveyor.[21]

Observed and projected decline in global ocean pH, 1750–2100. Photo by Rhett A. Butler (Source: news.mongabay.com/2008/0522-oceans.html)

OCEAN ACIDIFICATION

In nature, there is no free lunch. Change has consequences, even when it appears that the change may be beneficial. One change triggers another, and it causes yet a third, and so it goes like a string of dominos, all falling because the one in front fell.

For many years, for example, scientists have been grateful that oceans absorb much of the carbon dioxide created by burning coal and oil. But the chemical doesn't disappear. It merely changes its identity: dissolved in ocean waters, carbon dioxide forms carbonic acid—a weak acid admittedly, but an acid nonetheless. It has increased the acidity of oceans by about 30 percent. This, in turn, reduces the amount of calcium carbonate required for coral, plankton and other creatures with shells to make them. Indeed, in studies mimicking future ocean acidification, the shells of aquatic animals began dissolving within a matter of two days.[22]

Deep ocean waters normally are more acidic and have higher CO_2 levels than shallow waters because decomposing organic matter sinks and makes the deep water acidic, and deep water contains CO_2 which was absorbed when the water last circulated to the surface. However, changing temperature and circulation pulls deep waters to the surface, flushing it onto the continental shelves. When researchers with the National Oceanic and Atmospheric Administration's Pacific Marine Environmental Laboratory sampled waters along 13 survey lines extending from British Columbia, Canada to Baja California, Mexico in the spring of 2007, they not only found that the water was more acidic than expected close to shore and near the surface, but that the entire water column was undersaturated in shell-forming carbonate down to 50 meters in places.[23] Researchers attributed this to continually rising levels of human-emitted CO_2.

This was the first time acidified ocean water has been found on the continental shelf of western North America, and it happened 100 years before computer models predicted it would. The lead scientist in the study termed the finding "truly astonishing." Another commented that it was one more "example where what's happening in the natural world seems to be happening much faster than what our climate models predict."[24]

The acidified water was last exposed to the atmosphere about 50 years ago, when carbon-dioxide levels were much lower. Water rising from the depths over the coming decades will have absorbed more carbon dioxide, and will be even more acidic. Models suggest this could reduce levels of carbonate by 50 percent.

CORAL BLEACHING

Humans die in heat, and so do sea creatures. Among the hardest hit are the world's corals. Global warming has reduced many reefs to rubble, a collapse that has deprived fish of food and shelter, causing fish diversity to fall by half in some areas, according to the first long-term study of the effects of warming-caused bleaching on coral reefs and fish.

Small but prolonged rises in sea temperature force coral colonies to expel the algae that lend them their color but, most importantly, provide food. The relationship between the corals and their algae is one of nature's most delicate and complex. Thriving coral are powerful enough to build the largest living organism on the planet, the Great Barrier Reef. Their health underpins the economies and living standards of many tropical nations and societies who harvest their food from the reefs or have developing tourism industries. When stressed, however, coral will expel their algae in a process known as bleaching that turns dying reefs ghostly white. Some reefs can recover from such events, but many do not.

Warmer waters kill the tiny algae that lend coral their colors and, most importantly, provide food. (Source: Photo by Ray Berkelmans, AIMS.)

In 1998, heat triggered a global bleaching and die off of coral, killing over 16 percent of the world's reefs in one year. The reefs near Africa's Seychelles islands, north of Madagascar, were particularly hard hit, so researchers returned eight years later to gauge the extent of the recovery. What they found were coral reefs still unable to recover.[25]

"The outlook for recovery is quite bleak for the Seychelles," said lead study author Nicholas Graham, a tropical marine biologist at England's University of Newcastle Upon Tyne.[26]

In the long term, heat-induced coral bleaching will almost certainly impact fisheries production. Some species are likely to die and go extinct, disrupting the food chain that sustains much of life on Earth. This, combined with the increasing acidification, may have devastating effects on fishery stocks.[27]

FOREST DIEBACK/FIRES

Forest fires in the western United States have been increasing "suddenly and dramatically," according to a 2006 study that examined a database of 1,166 forest wildfires from 1970 to 2003.[28] These fires representative another powerful feedback mechanism. They release not only prodigious amounts of carbon dioxide and methane, but also black carbon (BC). The fires are thought to account for

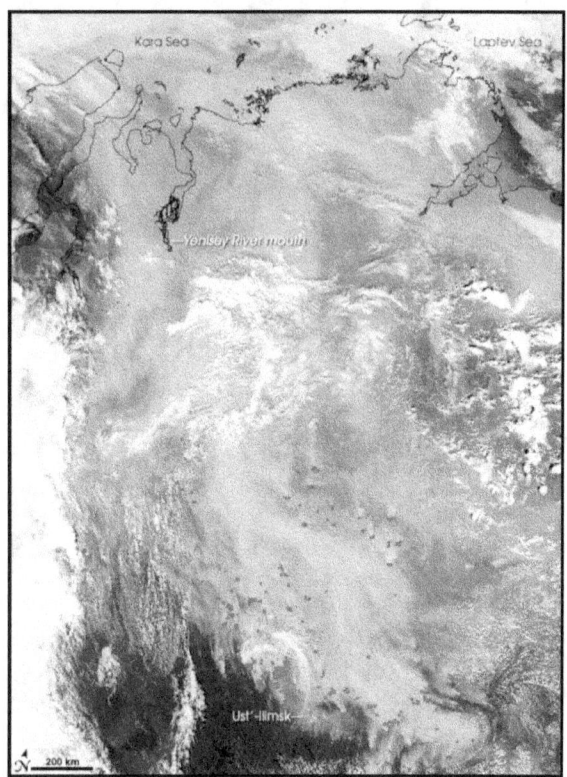

In 2006, forest fires were burning across a broad swath of the Central Siberian Plateau, pictured here from a NASA satellite, with actively burning fires marked in red. The shroud of smoke spreads over thousands of square miles, and is a major source of black carbon that is causing warming and melting in the Arctic. If this were imposed on a map of the United States, it would stretch east to west from California to the New Mexico-Texas state line, and north to south more than a hundred miles beyond the Mexico and Canadian borders. (Source: NASA.)

roughly 40 percent of global releases of BC, and much of it falls in the areas where it can do the most harm—the snow covered Arctic and the mountain regions, where they darken surfaces, thus increasing absorption of heat from sunlight.[29, c] By one estimate, the warming caused by black carbon is placed at roughly 40 percent of that from burning coal, oil and other fossil fuels.[30] Increased warming brought on by the fires dries trees and underbrush even further, making them even more susceptible to fire, thus producing more warming.

There is no doubt that the number and intensity of fires has increased. In the mid 1980s there was a jump of four times the average number of wildfires in the West compared with the early 1980s and 1970s. The total area burned was six-and-a-half times greater in the mid 1980s than the earlier years examined. The wildfire season has also extended by 78 days in the more recent period of 1987 to 2003 compared to 1970 through 1986.

---

[c] The Arctic is especially susceptible to the impact of human-generated particles and other pollution. In recent years the Arctic has significantly warmed, and sea-ice cover and glacial snow have diminished. Likely causes for these trends include changing weather patterns and the effects of pollution. Black carbon has been implicated as playing a major role in melting ice and snow. When soot falls on ice, it darkens the surface and accelerates melting by increasing absorbed sunlight. Airborne soot also warms the air and affects weather patterns and clouds. See Flanner, M.G. et. al. Present-day climate forcing and response from black carbon in snow JGR, V. 112, D11202, doi:10.1029/2006JD008003, 2007.

The researchers also found that 56 percent of the wildfires and 72 percent of the total burnt area occurred during the years when the snow melted early. When the snowmelt season occurred later than average, only 11 percent of wildfires occurred.[31]

Forest fires have been on the rise in Alaska as well.

This trend will almost certainly accelerate. As part of the 4th Assessment of the Intergovernmental Panel on Climate Change (IPCC), seven general circulation models were used to predict future temperatures, and all projected June to August temperature increases of 2° to 5°C by 2040 to 2069 for western North America.[32] The models also project a decline in rain and snow of up to 15 percent. That is a June to August temperature increase of 3°C, or roughly triple the rise that has already caused the devastating wildfires of the past two decades.

These new sources of global warming pollutants will certainly accelerate the buildup of greenhouse gases and create a positive feedback, or as it is called by some, a "feed-forward" acceleration of global warming.[33]

The United States is by no means the only place fires are on the rise. Wildfire burn areas in Canada are expected to increase by 74 to 118 percent, in the next century.[34] Devastating forest fires in Siberia that send a pall of smoke worldwide are happening more frequently because of climate change and in turn accelerating the pace of global warming.[35]

In Central Siberia alone fires destroyed 15,000 square miles in 2003, triggering plumes which were linked with air pollution measured as far away as America. The forest fires send as much greenhouse gas into the atmosphere as the total EU reduction commitment under the Kyoto protocol. An international team, led by Professor Heiko Balzter of the Department of Geography at the University of Leicester, concluded that Siberian fires are being influenced by climate change.[36]

Balzter said "Last century a typical forest in Siberia had about 100 years after a fire to recover before it burned again. But new observations by Russian scientist Dr. Vyacheslav Kharuk have shown that fire now returns more frequently,

The formation of ozone, or smog, increases in lock step with temperature, so global concentrations will increase with global warming. Highly toxic to plants and humans alike, ozone causes forest decline and death, which in turn reduces the ability of trees and other plants to remove carbon dioxide and other pollutants from the air, leading to still higher temperatures. (Source: www.lexi-tv.de/lexikon/thema.as)

about every 65 years. At the same time annual temperatures in Siberia have risen by almost 2°C, about twice as fast as the global average. And since 1990 the warming of Siberia has become even faster than before."[37]

TROPOSPHERIC OZONE OR "SMOG" FORMATION

In Los Angeles, the smog capital of America, there has never been a violation of the health standards for smog when the temperature was below 70°F—but there's never not been a violation when it's 90°F or more. That's because ozone is formed in lock step with heat, with both rising in a straight line, which means that as the Earth's temperature rises, so too may concentrations of ozone, which already hover at levels toxic to plants throughout much of the world.[38]

There are several ways in which ozone might trigger a feedback.

First, because ozone is itself a greenhouse gas, higher temperatures could boost its formation, which might in turn accelerate warming. Although not subject to the Kyoto Protocol, ozone is a powerful cause of global warming, roughly equal to methane and black carbon.[39]

Ozone is formed when oxides of nitrogen, which is chiefly from vehicles and powerplants, reacts with unburnt gasoline fumes and other volatile organic compounds. The higher the temperature, the faster ozone is formed. One analysis of the effect of higher temperatures due to global warming concluded that ozone would increase 3 to 10 percent in various regions of California, and even with aggressive reduction if emissions of ozone precursors might be ineffective at bringing smog levels down in some regions, especially San Francisco.[40]

In addition, ozone poisons plants and suppresses photosynthesis. That, in turn, reduces their ability to absorb carbon dioxide from the atmosphere and sequester it in their tissues, especially in trees.[41]

Third, ozone's warming effects are especially strong in the Arctic, where it is thought to account for one-third to one-half of the observed warming during winter and spring.[42]

Whether due to global warming or some other cause, background levels of ozone are increasing in widely separated regions of the world. At Mace Head on the west coast of Ireland, concentrations rose about 0.5 parts per billion per year between 1987 and 2003.[43] In the United States, the results of one model depicting higher temperatures "show that the severity and duration of summertime regional pollution episodes in the midwestern and northeastern United States increase significantly relative to the present," predicting that concentration will rise 5 to 10 percent and duration increase from 2 to 3 to 4 days.[44] The researchers observed that their results "imply that it may be equally important to consider the effects of a changing climate when planning for the future attainment of regional-scale air quality standard."[45]

DESERTIFICATION

In the sun-baked province of Murcia, Spain, lush fields of lettuce and hothouses of tomatoes line the roads and the landscape is dotted with plush pastel vacation homes that give way to wide sandy beaches. In a place where existence has been hardscrabble for centuries, prosperity has come calling—but the stay may be temporary.[46]

Murcia, like many areas of the world, is running out of water, and as supplies dwindle the land becomes that most inhospitable of places, a

With higher temperatures, water evaporates from soils, leading to the formation and expansion of deserts. As the land in arid, semi-dry areas becomes degraded, soil loses its productivity and vegetation thins, causing prolonged droughts and floods. One major study predicts that over one-half of the world's land will be subject to drought by century's end. (Source: www.worldrevolution.org/)

desert. The feedback in desertification is fairly straightforward. As hotter air born of global warming sucks more and more moisture from the soils or shifts rainfall away from the lands and into oceans, a vicious cycle is set off. Huge swaths of land cease to grow plants, losing their ability to remove carbon dioxide from the air and store it in their tissues. With their growth suppressed, plants drop less and less litter, leaving the soil increasingly vulnerable to drying.[47] When rain does fall, the soils are unable to hold it, so floods are triggered.

As the land produces less and less food, pressure builds to farm and graze it more intensively, hastening its further decline. As desert shrubs invade, the barren areas between them lose soil fertility, so the soil is lost to erosion. Land that was once productive becomes instead a barren wasteland.[48]

Desertification directly triggers warming, increasing temperatures in one study by 0.7°C per decade.[49] One comprehensive analysis, the first of its kind, predicts that global warming is likely to push soils that are already weakened over the edge, triggering an increase in the area affected by the most extreme drought from 3 to 30 percent and areas of severe drought up from 8 to 40 percent of total land area. It predicts that up to half of the earth's surface would be affected by moderate drought at any one time.[50]

ENDNOTES

CHAPTER 2

1. John F. Kennedy (October 3, 1963). "Remarks in Heber Springs, Arkansas, at the Dedication of Greers Ferry Dam." The American Presidency Project.

2. Bruce Bartlett, "Are Taxes in the U.S. High or Low?" *New York Times*, May 31, 2011.

3. Bruce Bartlett, "Are Taxes in the U.S. High or Low?" *New York Times*, May 31, 2011.

4. Bruce Bartlett, "Are Taxes in the U.S. High or Low?" *New York Times*, May 31, 2011.

5. Anthony B. Anderson, Thomas Piketty and Immanuel Saiz, "Top Incomes in the Long Run of History," Figures 13–16, NBER 15408, Oct., 2009, *NBER Working Papers*, National Bureau for Economic Research, Boston, Mass.

6. Christina Rexrode and Bernard Condon, "Typical CEO made $9.6M last year, AP study finds," the Associated Press, May 25, 2012.

7. Christina Rexrode and Bernard Condon, "Typical CEO made $9.6M last year, AP study finds," the Associated Press, May 25, 2012.

8. Christina Rexrode and Bernard Condon, "Typical CEO made $9.6M last year, AP study finds," the Associated Press, May 25, 2012.

9. Michael Sivey, "Our Net Worth Is Down 39%. How Worried Should We Be?" *Time, June 20, 2012.*

10. Michael Sivey, "Our Net Worth Is Down 39%. How Worried Should We Be?" *Time, June 20, 2012.*

11. Timothy Noah, "The United States of Inequality,"*Slate*, Sept. 14, 2010, http://www.slate.com/articles/news_and_politics/the_great_divergence/features/2010/the_u nited_states_of_inequality/the_stinking_rich_and_the_great_divergence.html, accessed Aug. 7, 2012.

12. Timothy Noah, "The United States of Inequality,"*Slate*, Sept. 14, 2010, http://www.slate.com/articles/news_and_politics/the_great_divergence/features/2010/the_u nited_states_of_inequality/the_stinking_rich_and_the_great_divergence.html, accessed Aug. 7, 2012.

13. Timothy Noah, "The United States of Inequality,"*Slate*, Sept. 14, 2010, http://www.slate.com/articles/news_and_politics/the_great_divergence/features/2010/the_u nited_states_of_inequality/the_stinking_rich_and_the_great_divergence.html, accessed Aug. 7, 2012.

14. Timothy Noah, "The United States of Inequality,"*Slate*, Sept. 14, 2010, http://www.slate.com/articles/news_and_politics/the_great_divergence/features/2010/the_u nited_states_of_inequality/the_stinking_rich_and_the_great_divergence.html, accessed Aug. 7, 2012.

15. Timothy Noah, "The United States of Inequality,"*Slate*, Sept. 14, 2010, http://www.slate.com/articles/news_and_politics/the_great_divergence/features/2010/the_u nited_states_of_inequality/the_stinking_rich_and_the_great_divergence.html, accessed Aug. 7, 2012.

16. Peter Edelman, "Poverty in America: Why Can't We End It?" *New York Times*, July 28, 2012.

17. Michael McAuliff, "House GOP Budget: Paul Ryan Plan Adds Food Stamps, Welfare Cuts To Medicare-Slashing Plan," *Huffington Post*, March 20, 2012, http://www.huffingtonpost.com/2012/03/20/house-gop-budget-plan_n_1366455.html, accessed Aug. 7, 2012.

18. "Study Shows Mitt Romney-Paul Ryan Budget Is Real Class Warfare," *U.S. News & World Report*, June 20, 2012.

19. Congressional Budget Office, *The Long-Term Budgetary Impact of Paths for Federal Revenues and Spending Specified by Chairman Ryan*, U.S. Congress, March, 2012.

20. Congressional Budget Office, *The Long-Term Budgetary Impact of Paths for Federal Revenues and Spending Specified by Chairman Ryan*, U.S. Congress, March, 2012.

21. James Surowiecki, "Call That a Budget?" *New Yorker*, April 9, 2012.

22. Ezra Klein, "The unrealistic assumptions behind Paul Ryan's budget numbers, *Washington Post*, March 20,2012, http://www.washingtonpost.com/blogs/ezra-klein/post/the-unrealistic-assumptions-behind-paul-ryans-budget-numbers/2011/08/25/gIQAEZrePS_blog.html, accessed August 7, 2012.

23. Jeremy Herb, "GOP budget boosts defense spending," DEFCON Hill, The Hill, March 3, 2012, http://thehill.com/blogs/defcon-hill/budget-appropriations/216925-gop-budget-boosts-defense-spending, accessed Aug. 7, 2012.

24. Jeremy Herb, "GOP budget boosts defense spending," DEFCON Hill, The Hill, March 3, 2012, http://thehill.com/blogs/defcon-hill/budget-appropriations/216925-gop-budget-boosts-defense-spending, accessed Aug. 7, 2012.

25. Benjamin M. Friedman, "Minding the Gap," *New York Times*, May 25, 2012.

CHAPTER 3

1. The National Archives, "Declaration of Independence - a History," http://www.archives.gov/exhibits/charters/declaration_history.html, accessed May 10, 2012.

2. The National Archives, "Declaration of Independence - a History," http://www.archives.gov/exhibits/charters/declaration_history.html, accessed May 10, 2012.

3. The National Archives, "Declaration of Independence - a History," http://www.archives.gov/exhibits/charters/declaration_history.html, accessed May 10, 2012.

4. University of Virginia, Founders Early Access, "Thomas Jefferson to James Madison, 30 Aug. 1823," http://rotunda.upress.virginia.edu/founders/default.xqy?keys=FOEA-print-02-02-02-0027, accessed May 10, 2012.

5. The Virginia Declaration was largely the work of George Mason, one of Virginia's wealthiest planters, a neighbor and friend of Washington. "The Virginia Declaration of Rights," http://www.constitution.org/bcp/virg_dor.htm#001, accessed May 14, 2012. It seems likely that his favorable treatment of property accounts for the appropriation of his name and image by many libertarians.

6. The U.S. National Archives, "The Bill of Rights - The Virginia Declaration of Rights," http://www.archives.gov/exhibits/charters/virginia_declaration_of_rights.html, accessed May 12, 2012.

7. This is thought by some to have been based on John Locke's trilogy of rights, "life liberty and property." David M. Post, "Jeffersonian Revisions of Locke: Education, Property-Rights, and Liberty," *Journal of the History of Ideas*, Vol. 47, No. 1 (Jan.–Mar. 1986), pp. 147–157.

8. The Virginia Declaration of Rights, http://www.constitution.org/bcp/virg_dor.htm.

9. The Declaration of Independence, http://www.ushistory.org/declaration/document/index.htm.

10. The White House, "The Constitution," http://www.whitehouse.gov/our-government/the-constitution, accessed May 15, 2012.

11. University of Missouri at Kansas City, "The Bill of Rights: Its History and Significance," http://law2.umkc.edu/faculty/projects/ftrials/conlaw/billofrightsintro.html, accessed May 15, 2012.

12. James Madison, The Federalist Papers: Federalist No. 43, "The Same Subject Continued: The Powers Conferred by the Constitution Further Considered," Library of Congress, http://thomas.loc.gov/home/histdox/fed_43.html, accessed July 2, 2012.

13. James Madison, The Federalist Papers: Federalist No. 43, "The Same Subject Continued: The Powers Conferred by the Constitution Further Considered," Library of Congress, http://thomas.loc.gov/home/histdox/fed_43.html, accessed July 2, 2012.

14. James Madison, The Federalist Papers: Federalist No. 43, "The Same Subject Continued: The Powers Conferred by the Constitution Further Considered," Library of Congress, http://thomas.loc.gov/home/histdox/fed_43.html, accessed July 2, 2012.

15. James Madison, The Federalist Papers: Federalist No. 43, "The Same Subject Continued: The Powers Conferred by the Constitution Further Considered," Library of Congress, http://thomas.loc.gov/home/histdox/fed_43.html, accessed July 2, 2012.

16. Paul T. Mero, "The Citadel of Private Property," The Sutherland Institute, April, 2007, http://sutherlandinstitute.org/uploaded_files/sdmc/citadelprivateproperty.pdf, accessed July 2, 2012.

17. Library of Congress, *The Federalist Papers,* "10, The Same Subject Continued: The Union as a Safeguard Against Domestic Faction and Insurrection," http://thomas.loc.gov/home/histdox/fedpapers.html, accessed July 2, 2012.

18. National Archives and Records Administration, "Washington's Inaugural Address of 1789," http://www.archives.gov/exhibits/american_originals/inaugtxt.html, accessed July 2, 2012.

19. "The Migration or Importation of such Persons as any of the States now existing shall think proper to admit, shall not be prohibited by the Congress prior to the Year one thousand eight hundred and eight, but a tax or duty may be imposed on such Importation, not exceeding ten dollars for each Person." U.S. Constitution - Article 1 Section 9.

20. "Representatives and direct Taxes shall be apportioned among the several States which may be included within this Union, according to their respective Numbers, which shall be determined by adding to the whole Number of free Persons, including those bound to Service for a Term of Years, and excluding Indians not taxed, three fifths of all other Persons." U.S. Constitution - Article 1 Section 2 (modified by the 14th Amendment).

21. "No Person held to Service or Labour in one State, under the Laws thereof, escaping into another, shall, in Consequence of any Law or Regulation therein, be discharged from such Service or Labour, but shall be delivered up on Claim of the Party to whom such Service or Labour may be due." U.S. Constitution - Article 4 Section 2 (The clause in parentheses is superseded by the 13th Amendment.).

22. Thomas H. O'Connor, *Lords of the Loom: the Cotton Whigs and the Coming of the Civil War.* Charles Scribner's Sons (New York, 1968).

23. Cotton Whigs differed considerably on their rationale for supporting the institution of slavery, with some, such as Daniel Webster, believing that if it were merely not allowed to spread, it would wither and die. Junius P. Rodriguez, *Slavery in the United States: A Social, Political, and Historical Encyclopedia, V. 2*, ABC-CLIO (2007), p. 514.

24. Political Debates Between Abraham Lincoln and Stephen A. Douglas in the Celebrated Campaign of 1858 in Illinois: Including the Preceding Speeches of Each at Chicago, Springfield, Etc., Also the Two Great Speeches of Abraham Lincoln in Ohio in 1859 By Abraham Lincoln, Stephen Arnold Douglas, Published by Burrows Bros. Co., 1894.

25. Dred Scott was the slave of an army physician who had lived in the Wisconsin Territory, where slavery was illegal. Upon returning to Missouri, Scott sued for his freedom on the grounds that he had once lived in a free territory.

26. Library of Congress, Primary Documents in American History, Abraham Lincoln's Second Inaugural Address, http://www.loc.gov/rr/program/bib/ourdocs/Lincoln2nd.html, accessed May 15, 2012.

27. Wikipedia, "List of incidents of civil unrest in the United States," http://en.wikipedia.org/wiki/List_of_incidents_of_civil_unrest_in_the_United_States#1900.E2.80.931950s, accessed May 15, 2012.

28. Wikipedia, "List of incidents of civil unrest in the United States," http://en.wikipedia.org/wiki/List_of_incidents_of_civil_unrest_in_the_United_States#1900.E2.80.931950s, accessed May 15, 2012.

29. *New York Times*, "League is Formed to Scan New Deal, 'Protect Rights,'" August 23, 1934, accessed May 15, 2012.

30. Gerard Colby, *Du Pont Dynasty: Behind the Nylon Curtain*, Carol Publishing Group (1984).

31. Gerard Colby, *Du Pont Dynasty: Behind the Nylon Curtain*, Carol Publishing Group (1984).

32. Gerard Colby, *Du Pont Dynasty: Behind the Nylon Curtain*, Carol Publishing Group (1984).

33. Richard Sanders, "Andrew W. Mellon (1855–1937)," *Press for Conversion!*, http://coat.ncf.ca/our_magazine/links/53/mellon.html, accessed May 16, 2012.

34. Jules Archer, *The Plot to Seize the White House*, Skyhorse Publishing, 2007.

35. Franklin D. Roosevelt, "1936 State of the Union Address," http://www.janda.org/politxts/State%20of%20Union%20Addresses/1934-1945%20Roosevelt/FDR36.html, accessed May 10, 2012.

36. Erik Barnouw, *A History of Broadcasting in the United States: Volume 2: The Golden Web*, 1933 to 1953, Oxford University Press (1968), pp. 14–15.

37. Gerard Colby, *Du Pont Dynasty: Behind the Nylon Curtain*, Carol Publishing Group (1984).

38. Library of Congress, "Brown at Fifty," http://www.loc.gov/exhibits/brown/brown-brown.html, accessed May 16, 2012.

39. Political Research Associates, "Searching the Right for Progressive Changemakers," http://www.publiceye.org/tooclose/jbs.html, accessed May 16, 2012.

40. John Birch Society, "Fred Koch," http://www.jbs.org/fred-koch, accessed May 16, 2012.

41. Political Research Associates, "Searching the Right for Progressive Changemakers," http://www.publiceye.org/tooclose/jbs.html, accessed May 16, 2012.

42. Political Research Associates, "Searching the Right for Progressive Changemakers," http://www.publiceye.org/tooclose/jbs.html, accessed May 16, 2012.

43. Political Research Associates, "Searching the Right for Progressive Changemakers," http://www.publiceye.org/tooclose/jbs.html, accessed May 16, 2012.

44. Political Research Associates, "Searching the Right for Progressive Changemakers," http://www.publiceye.org/tooclose/jbs.html, accessed May 16, 2012.

45. Political Research Associates, "Searching the Right for Progressive Changemakers," http://www.publiceye.org/tooclose/jbs.html, accessed May 16, 2012.

46. Political Research Associates, "Searching the Right for Progressive Changemakers," http://www.publiceye.org/tooclose/jbs.html, accessed May 16, 2012.

47. John Birch Society, "Freedom's Forefront," http://www.jbs.org/news/freedom-s-forefront, accessed May 16, 2012.

48. Library of Congress, "Primary Documents in American History - Nullification Proclamation," http://www.loc.gov/rr/program/bib/ourdocs/Nullification.html, accessed May 16, 2012.

49. Library of Congress, "Primary Documents in American History - Nullification Proclamation," http://www.loc.gov/rr/program/bib/ourdocs/Nullification.html, accessed May 16, 2012.

50. *Jules Archer, The Plot to Seize the White House*, Hawthorne Books (New York, 1973), p. 201.

51. Adele M. Stan, "Billionaire Who Denies Connection to Tea Parties Bankrolls Tea-Partying Glenn Beck Fans," AlterNet, Aug. 29, 2010, accessed ???? http://www.alternet.org/teaparty/148014/billionaire_who_denies_connection_to_tea_parties_bankrolls_tea-partying_glenn_beck_fans/.

52. "Right Now - Dick Armey: Please, Koch, keep distancing yourself from me," *Washington Post*, June 28, 2010, http://voices.washingtonpost.com/right-now/2010/04/dick_armey_please_koch_keep_di.html, accessed May 11, 2012.

53. Foundation Directory Online, a fee-for-subscription service, http://fconline.foundationcenter.org/fdo_grant_search.php, accessed May 11, 2012.

CHAPTER 4

1. "BORAH FOR STATE RIGHTS; Opposes Anti-Lynching Bill as Unconstitutional," *New York Times*, June 12, 1922.

2. The Associated Press "Would 'Veto' Anti-Lynching Bill.; BORAH WILL START CAMPAIGN ON RADIO," *New York Times*, Nov. 24, 1935.

3. "CLOSURE IS BEATEN AGAIN IN SENATE; Anti-Lynching Bill Sponsors Gain Four Votes but Lose on Roll-Call, 46 to 42 FILIBUSTER 6 WEEKS OLD," *New York Times*, Feb. 17, 1938.

4. "One Man's Stand," *Time*, June 26, 1964.

5. Statement of Sen. Barry Goldwater, *Congressional Record*, June 18, 1964.

6. Ted Gittinger and Allen Fisher, "LBJ Champions the Civil Rights Act of 1964, Part 2," *Prologue Magazine*, National Archives, accessed July 10, 2007, http://www.archives.gov/publications/prologue/2004/summer/civil-rights-act-2.html. Also, CQ Encylopedia of American Government, accessed July 10, 2007 http://www.cqpress.com/incontext/SupremeCourt/filibuster.htm

7. Indeed, the decisive 67th vote was provided by Delaware Republican John Williams, one of the Senate's most conservative member and the representative of the last state in the Union to maintain slavery, because Lincoln's Emancipation Proclamation abolished the practice only in Confederate states and Delaware was part of the Union.

8. Kinder, Donald R. and Sanders, Lynn M.; *Divided By Color: Racial Politics and Democratic Ideals*; The University of Chicago Press; 1996; Chap. 8 - The Electoral Temptations of Race; p. 209.

9. Kinder, Donald R. and Sanders, Lynn M.; *Divided By Color: Racial Politics and Democratic Ideals*; The University of Chicago Press; 1996; Chap. 8 - The Electoral Temptations of Race; p. 208.

10. "Nixon, Richard Milhous (1913–1994)," *King Encyclopedia*, Stanford University, http://www.stanford.edu/group/King/about_king/encyclopedia/nixon_richard.html.

11. Donald R. Kinder and Lynn M. Sanders, *Divided by Color: Racial Politics and Democratic Ideals*, pp. 206–7, University of Chicago Press (Chicago, 1996).

12. Kinder, Donald R. and Sanders, Lynn M.; *Divided By Color: Racial Politics and Democratic Ideals*; The University of Chicago Press; 1996; Chap. 8 - The Electoral Temptations of Race; p. 201.

13. Clifton White and William Gill, *Suite 3505: The Story of the Draft Goldwater Movement*, pp. 404–5, Ashbrook Press (Ashbrook, Ohio, 1992).

14. Ibid. Goldwater's tally in the southern states presaged his November victory. Of the five Deep South states that he carried in November, he received the following votes for the nomination: Alabama, 20 of 20; Georgia, 22 of 24 Louisiana 20 of 20; Mississippi, 13 of 13; and, South Carolina, 16 of 16.

15. Harry S. Dent, *The Prodigal South Returns to Power*, p. 64, John S. Wiley & Sons (1978).

16. Kinder, Donald R. and Sanders, Lynn M.; *Divided By Color: Racial Politics and Democratic Ideals*; The University of Chicago Press; 1996; Chap. 8 - The Electoral Temptations of Race; p. 202 *citing* Quoted in Kelley 1966, pp. 52–53. The Republican platform conceded nothing to the moderates; indeed, it repudiated past Republican policies. Amendments to the platform, including one that would endorse and continue the party's moderately progressive position on civil rights, were crushed.

17. The National Archives, William E. Miller, "Speech to Pennsylvania Union League Club," Oct. 13, 1964, box 5, W Series, GP.

18. Marilyn W. Thompson and Jack Bass, *Strom: The Complicated Personal and Political Life of Strom Thurmond*, p. 183 (Public Affairs, 2005). Also, "Mr. McCain's Message on Race," *New York Times*, April 21, 2000.

19. John F. Kennedy, Radio and Television Report to the American People on Civil Rights, The White House, June 11, 1963, John F. Kennedy Presidential Library & Museum, http://www.jfklibrary.org/Historical+Resources/Archives/Reference+Desk/Speeches/JFK/00 3POF03CivilRights06111963.htm

20. Kinder, Donald R. and Sanders, Lynn M.; *Divided By Color: Racial Politics and Democratic Ideals*; The University of Chicago Press; 1996; Chap. 8 - The Electoral Temptations of Race; pp. 203–4 *citing* Black and Black 1992, p. 153.

21. Grantham, Dewey W.; *The South in Modern America*; New York, NY: HarperCollins Publishers, Inc.; 1994; Chapter 9 - The Second Reconstruction; p. 247 *citing* Heleniak, "Lyndon Johnson in New Orleans," p. 269.

22. Grantham, Dewey W.; *The South in Modern America*; New York, NY: HarperCollins Publishers, Inc.; 1994; Chapter 9 - The Second Reconstruction; p. 245 *citing* Quoted in Goldfield, *Black, White and Southern,* p. 196.

23. Grantham, Dewey W.; *The South in Modern America*; New York, NY: HarperCollins Publishers, Inc.; 1994; Chapter 9 - The Second Reconstruction; p. 247 *citing* Quoted in Black and Black, *The Vital South*, p. 151.

24. Grantham, Dewey W.; *The South in Modern America*; New York, NY: HarperCollins Publishers, Inc.; 1994; Chapter 9 - The Second Reconstruction; p. 247 *citing* Quoted in Black and Black, *The Vital South*, pp. 147–58, 199–210.

25. Grantham, Dewey W.; *The South in Modern America*; New York, NY: HarperCollins Publishers, Inc.; 1994; Chapter 9 - The Second Reconstruction; p. 247 *citing* Cosman, *Five States for Goldwater*, p. 55.

26. Theodore H. White, *The Making of the President 1964*, p. 332, Atheneum Publishers, New York, 1965.

27. Donald R. Kinder and Lynn M. Sanders, *Divided by Color: Racial Politics and Democratic Ideals*, p. 206, University of Chicago Press (Chicago, 1996).

28. "Lyndon's Full House," *Time*, Nov. 4, 1964.

29. Harry S. Dent, *The Prodigal South Returns to Power*, p. 69, John S. Wiley & Sons (1978).

30. "Lyndon's Full House," *Time*, Nov. 4, 1964.

31. Gerald C. Wright, Leroy N. Rieselbach, Lawrence C. Dodd, *Congress and policy change*, Algora Publishing, 1986, p. 84.

32. Harry S. Dent, *The Prodigal South Returns to Power*, p. 67, John Wiley & Sons (1978).

33. Philip A. Klinkner, *The Losing Parties: Out-Party National Committees, 1956-1993*, p. 59, Yale University Press. 1994, Yale University Press.

34. Philip A. Klinkner, *The Losing Parties: Out-Party National Committees, 1956-1993*, p. 60, Yale University Press. 1994, Yale University Press.

35. Kinder, Donald R. and Sanders, Lynn M.; *Divided By Color: Racial Politics and Democratic Ideals*; The University of Chicago Press; 1996; Chap. 5 - Subtle Prejudice for Modern Times; p. 92.

36. Kinder, Donald R. and Sanders, Lynn M.; *Divided By Color: Racial Politics and Democratic Ideals*; The University of Chicago Press; 1996; Chap. 5 - Subtle Prejudice for Modern Times; p. 92 **citing** See, e.g., Feagin and Sikes 1994; Jaynes and Williams 1989; Kirschenman and Neckerman 1991; Yinger 1986; Sigelman and Welch 1991.

37. Kinder, Donald R. and Sanders, Lynn M.; *Divided By Color: Racial Politics and Democratic Ideals*; The University of Chicago Press; 1996; Chap. 8 - The Electoral Temptations of Race; p. 223.

38. Kinder, Donald R. and Sanders, Lynn M.; *Divided By Color: Racial Politics and Democratic Ideals*; The University of Chicago Press; 1996; Chap. 5 - Subtle Prejudice for Modern Times; p. 105.

39. Kinder, Donald R. and Sanders, Lynn M.; *Divided By Color: Racial Politics and Democratic Ideals*; The University of Chicago Press; 1996; Chap. 5 - Subtle Prejudice for Modern Times; pp. 105–6.

40. Bob Herbert, "Impossible, Ridiculous, Repugnant," *New York Times*, Oct. 6, 2005.

41. Nadine Cohodas, *Strom Thurmond & the Politics of Southern Change*, pp. 177–78, Mercer University Press, 1994.

42. Nadine Cohodas, *Strom Thurmond & the Politics of Southern Change*, pp. 177–78, Mercer University Press, 1994.

43. "1948 Presidential General Election Results," http://uselectionatlas.org/RESULTS/national.php?year=1948&f=0.

44. Tim Craig and Michael D. Shear, "Allen Quip Provokes Outrage, Apology," *Washington Post*, Aug. 15, 2006.

45. Tim Craig and Michael D. Shear, "Allen Quip Provokes Outrage, Apology," *Washington Post*, Aug. 15, 2006.

46. Michael D. Shear and Tim Craig, "After 2 Decades in Ascent, A Stunning Breakdown," *Washington Post*, Nov. 10, 2006.

47. Dana Milbank, "The Senator's Gentile Rebuke," *Washington Post*, Sep. 19, 2006.

48. Kate Zernike, "Buzzwords; Macaca," *New York Times*, Dec. 24, 2006.

49. E.J. Kessler, "Alleged Slur Casts Spotlight On Senator's (Jewish?) Roots," *Forward*, Aug 25, 2006.

50. Dana Milbank, "The Senator's Gentile Rebuke, *Washington Post*, Sep. 19, 2006.

51. Dana Milbank, "The Senator's Gentile Rebuke, *Washington Post*, Sep. 19, 2006.

52. Marc Fisher, "Whose Words Are These?" *Washington Post*, Sep. 28, 2006.

53. CNN, U.S. SENATE / VIRGINIA / EXIT POLL, http://www.cnn.com/ELECTION/2006/pages/results/states/VA/S/01/epolls.0.html.

54. The Ostroy Report, "Corker Campaign Imploding, Putting Tennessee Senate Seat Closer in Democratic Hands Than Ever," Sep. 30, 2006, http://ostroyreport.blogspot.com/2006/09/corker-campaign-imploding-putting.html.

55. Peter Wallsten, "GOP attack ad draws heat for racial overtones," *Los Angeles Times*, Oct. 24, 2006.

56. Peter Wallsten, "GOP attack ad draws heat for racial overtones," *Los Angeles Times*, Oct. 24, 2006.

57. The Goldman School of Public Policy and The Chief Justice Earl Warren Institute on Race, Ethnicity & Diversity, UC Berkeley Law School, University of California, Berkeley, "Race-Bait '08: Lessons Learned from the Political Dirty Dozen" http://www.law.berkeley.edu/files/RaceCardReportFinalJan7.2008.FINAL.pdf, accessed Sept. 14, 2012.

CHAPTER 5

1. "The Architect of the New Conservatism - Paul M. Weyrich, 1942 - 2008," http://www.snetcentral.com/WEYRICH.pdf, accessed July 11, 2010.

2. Sandra Day O'Connor, *The Majesty of the Law*, Random House, 2004.

3. David Grann, "Robespierre of the Right: What I ate at the revolution," The New Republic,
October 27, 1997.

4. Tevi Troy, "Devaluing the Think Tank," *National Affairs*, Winter 2012.

5. Tevi Troy, "Devaluing the Think Tank," *National Affairs*, Winter 2012.

6. Bruce Weber, "Paul Weyrich, 66, a Conservative Strategist, Dies," *New York Times*, Dec. 18, 2008.

7. Bruce Weber, "Paul Weyrich, 66, a Conservative Strategist, Dies," *New York Times*, Dec. 18, 2008.

8. Bruce Weber, "Paul Weyrich, 66, a Conservative Strategist, Dies," *New York Times*, Dec. 18, 2008.

9. Tevi Troy, "Devaluing the Think Tank," *National Affairs*, Winter 2012.

10. *Washington Post* stated in its October 26, 2007 publication.

11. Simon Papers, "Biographical Sketch ," Layfayette University, http://academicmuseum.lafayette.edu/special/simon/bio.html, accessed July 7, 2012.

12. L. J. Davis, "William Simon's Facific Overtures," *New York Times Magazine*, Dec. 27, 1987.

13. L. J. Davis, "William Simon's Facific Overtures," *New York Times Magazine*, Dec. 27, 1987.

14. L. J. Davis, "William Simon's Facific Overtures," *New York Times Magazine*, Dec. 27, 1987.

15. "Simon Says: The former Treasury Secretary on service, donor intent, and Bill Gates," *Philanthropy Magazine*, January/February, 2000, http://www.philanthropyroundtable.org/topic/excellence_in_philanthropy/simon_says, accessed July 12, 2012.

16. "Simon Says: The former Treasury Secretary on service, donor intent, and Bill Gates," *Philanthropy Magazine*, January/February, 2000, http://www.philanthropyroundtable.org/topic/excellence_in_philanthropy/simon_says, accessed July 12, 2012.

17. "Simon Says: The former Treasury Secretary on service, donor intent, and Bill Gates," *Philanthropy Magazine*, January/February, 2000, http://www.philanthropyroundtable.org/topic/excellence_in_philanthropy/simon_says, accessed July 12, 2012.

CHAPTER 6

1. Matea Gold, "Supreme Court strengthens Citizens United decision with Montana ruling," *Los Angeles Times*, June 25, 2012.

2. *American Tradition Partnership, Inc., Fka Western Tradition Partnership, Inc., et al. v. Steve Bullock, Attorney General of Montana, et al.*, 567 U.S. 2012.

3. Mike Sacks, "Supreme Court Reverses Anti-Citizens United Ruling From Montana," *Huffington Post*, http://www.huffingtonpost.com/2012/06/25/supreme-court-reversed-citzens-united-montana n_1605355.html, accessed July 12, 2012.

4. Brief of the Chamber of Commerce of the United States of America as *Amicus Curiae* in Support of Petitioners, http://sblog.s3.amazonaws.com/wp-content/uploads/ 2012/05/11-1179-Chamber-of-Commerce-C ert-Amicus.pdf, accessed July 12, 2012. See also Jeffrey D. Clements and Bill Moyers, *Corporations Are Not People: Why They Have More Rights Than You Do and What You Can Do About It*, p. 191 (Google eBook, 2012).

5. *First National Bank of Boston et al. v. Bellotti,* 435 U.S. 765 (1978).

6. Linda Greenhouse, "The Legacy of Lewis F. Powell Jr.," *New York Times*, Dec. 4, 2002.

7. A.C. Pritchard, *Justice Lewis F. Powell, Jr., and the Counterrevolution in the Federal Securities Laws*, 52 Duke L J. 841, 844, 946–47 (2003).

8. A.C. Pritchard, *Justice Lewis F. Powell, Jr., and the Counterrevolution in the Federal Securities Laws*, 52 Duke L J. 841, 844, 946–47 (2003).

9. Powell was a member of the Board of Directors of Philip Morris, http://tobaccodocuments.org/ti/TIMN0439926-9962.html, accessed July 7, 2012.

10. Robert L. Kerr, "The 'Attack' Memorandum and the First Amendment," *Journal of Media Law & Ethics, Volume 2, Numbers 3/4* (Summer/Fall 2010).

11. Craig Evan Klafter, *Justice Lewis F. Powell, Jr.: A Pragmatic Realist*, 8 B.U. PUB. INT. L.J. 1, 8 (1998).

12. Lewis F. Powell, Jr., "A Strategy for Campus Peace," .American Association of Colleges and Universities, Washington, D.C., Nov. 11, 1968, http://www.eric.ed.gov/PDFS/ED025991.pdf, accessed July 12, 2012.

13. Lewis F. Powell, Jr., "A Strategy for Campus Peace," American Association of Colleges and Universities, Washington, D.C., Nov. 11, 1968, http://www.eric.ed.gov/PDFS/ED025991.pdf, accessed July 12, 2012.

14. Lewis F. Powell, Jr., "A Strategy for Campus Peace," American Association of Colleges and Universities, Washington, D.C., Nov. 11, 1968, http://www.eric.ed.gov/PDFS/ED025991.pdf, accessed July 12, 2012.

15. Lewis F. Powell, Jr., "A Strategy for Campus Pace," .American Association of Colleges and Universities, Washington, D.C., Nov. 11, 1968, http://www.eric.ed.gov/PDFS/ED025991.pdf, accessed July 12, 2012.

16. Lewis F. Powell, Jr., "A Lawyer Looks at Civil Disobedience," *Washington and Lee Law Review*, Fall, 1966.

17. Lewis F. Powell, Jr., "A Lawyer Looks at Civil Disobedience," *Washington and Lee Law Review*, Fall, 1966.

18. Jeffrey D. Clements and Bill Moyers, *Corporations Are Not People: Why They Have More Rights Than You Do and What You Can Do About It*, (Google eBook, 2012).

19. Jeffrey D. Clements and Bill Moyers, *Corporations Are Not People: Why They Have More Rights Than You Do and What You Can Do About It*, (Google eBook, 2012).

20. *First National Bank of Boston et al. v. Bellotti,* 435 U.S. 765 (1978).

21. *First National Bank of Boston et al. v. Bellotti,* 435 U.S. 765 (1978).

22. Robert L. Kerr, "The 'Attack' Memorandum and the First Amendment," *Journal of Media Law & Ethics, Volume 2, Numbers 3/4* (Summer/Fall 2010).

23. Robert L. Kerr, "The 'Attack' Memorandum and the First Amendment," *Journal of Media Law & Ethics, Volume 2, Numbers 3/4* (Summer/Fall 2010).

24. Robert L. Kerr, "The 'Attack' Memorandum and the First Amendment," *Journal of Media Law & Ethics, Volume 2, Numbers 3/4* (Summer/Fall 2010).

25. Robert L. Kerr, "The 'Attack' Memorandum and the First Amendment," *Journal of Media Law & Ethics, Volume 2, Numbers 3/4* (Summer/Fall 2010).

26. Robert L. Kerr, "The 'Attack' Memorandum and the First Amendment," *Journal of Media Law & Ethics, Volume 2, Numbers 3/4* (Summer/Fall 2010).

27. Robert L. Kerr, "The 'Attack' Memorandum and the First Amendment," *Journal of Media Law & Ethics, Volume 2, Numbers 3/4* (Summer/Fall 2010).

28. *First National Bank of Boston et al. v. Bellotti*, 435 U.S. 765, 822 (1978).

29. *Bellotti*, 435 U.S. at 809 (White, J., dissenting).

30. *Bellotti*, 435 U.S. at 809 (White, J., dissenting).

31. Morton Mintz, "Corporate Campaign Finance Elephant," http://www.populist.com/07.11.mintz.html, accessed April 23, 2012.

32. Morton Mintz, "Corporate Campaign Finance Elephant," http://www.populist.com/07.11.mintz.html, accessed April 23, 2012.

33. Morton Mintz, "Corporate Campaign Finance Elephant," http://www.populist.com/07.11.mintz.html, accessed April 23, 2012.

34. Robert L. Kerr, "The 'Attack' Memorandum and the First Amendment," *Journal of Media Law & Ethics, Volume 2, Numbers 3/4* (Summer/Fall 2010).

35. Linda Greenhouse "Over the Cliff," *New York Times,* Aug. 24, 2011.

CHAPTER 6, APPENDIX

1. Variously called: the "free enterprise system," "capitalism," and the "profit system." The American political system of democracy under the rule of law is also under attack, often by the same individuals and organizations who seek to undermine the enterprise system.

2. *Richmond News Leader*, June 8, 1970. Column of William F. Buckley, Jr.

3. *N.Y. Times Service* article, reprinted *Richmond Times-Dis*patch, May 17, 1971.

4. Stewart Alsop, Yale and the Deadly Danger, *Newsweek*, May 18. 1970.

5. Editorial, Richmond Times-Dispatch, July 7, 1971.

6. Dr. Milton Friedman, Prof. of Economics, U. of Chicago, writing a foreword to Dr. Arthur A. Shenfield's Rockford College lectures entitled "The Ideological War Against Western Society," copyrighted 1970 by Rockford College.

7. *Fortune*; May 1971, p. 145. This Fortune analysis of the Nader influence includes a reference to Nader's visit to a college where he was paid a lecture fee of $2,500 for "denouncing America's big corporations in venomous language ... bringing (rousing and spontaneous) bursts of applause" when he was asked when he planned to run for President.

8. *Washington Post*, Column of William Raspberry, June 28, 1971.

9. Jeffrey St. John, *Wall Street Journal*, May 21, 1971.

10. Barron's National Business and Financial Weekly, "The Total Break with America, The Fifth Annual Conference of Socialist Scholars," Sept. 15, 1969.

11. On many campuses freedom of speech has been denied to all who express moderate or conservative viewpoints.

12. It has been estimated that the evening half-hour news programs of the networks reach daily some 50,000,000 Americans.

13. One illustration of the type of article which should not go unanswered appeared in the popular *New York Times* of July 19, 1971. This was entitled "A Populist Manifesto" by ultra liberal Jack Newfield—who argued that "the root need in our country is 'to redistribute wealth.'"

14. The recent "freeze" of prices and wages may well be justified by the current inflationary crisis. But if imposed as a permanent measure the enterprise system will have sustained a near fatal blow.

CHAPTER 7

1. John S. Saloma, *Ominous Politics: The New Conservative Labyrinth*, Hill and Wang, 1984.

2. Paul Weyrich, "A Conservative Lament," *Washington Post*, March 3, 1987.

3. L. J. Davis, "William Simon's Facific Overtures," *New York Times Magazine*, Dec. 27, 1987.

4. L. J. Davis, "William Simon's Facific Overtures," *New York Times Magazine*, Dec. 27, 1987.

5. William Simon, *A Time for Truth*, p. 232, Reader's Digest Press (1978).

6. Martin Weil, "William Simon Dies; Treasury Secretary, Financier," *Washington Post*, June 4, 2000.

7. Richard W. Stevenson, "Bill Simon's Audacious S. & L. Gamble," *New York Times*, Feb. 11, 1990.

8. Kathryn Jean Lopez, "Freedom's Mr. Moneybags: John J. Miller on the John M. Olin Foundation," National Review Online, November 10, 2005, http://www.nationalreview.com/interrogatory/miller200511100823.asp.

9. Stephen Beale "Brown Hires Radical Professor," Oct 9, 2009, http://www.nas.org/articles/Brown_Hires_Radical_Professor1, accessed July 2, 2012.

10. Ashley Thorne, "The Radical Roots of Campus Protests," April 9, 2010, http://www.nas.org/articles/The_Radical_Roots_of_Campus_Protests, accessed July 2, 2012.

11. "Radical Professors Indoctrinate Students," June 20, 2012, http://blog.eagleforum.org/2012/06/radical-professors-indoctrinate.html, accessed July 2, 2012.

12. Carol Iannone, ""Either Feminism or Humanity," ("Radical feminists are impatient with the Bill of Rights.") http://www.springerlink.com/content/bjn9da7409vjfjr9/, accessed July 2, 2012.

13. Political Debates Between Abraham Lincoln and Stephen A. Douglas in the Celebrated Campaign of 1858 in Illinois: Including the Preceding Speeches of Each at Chicago, Springfield, etc. Also the Two Great Speeches of Abraham Lincoln in Ohio in 1859. By Abraham Lincoln, Stephen Arnold Douglas, Published by Burrows Bros. Co., 1894.

14. William Simon, *A Time for Truth*, p. 234, Reader's Digest Press (1978).

15. William Simon, *A Time for Truth*, p. 219, Reader's Digest Press (1978).

16. William Simon, *A Time for Truth*, p. 229, Reader's Digest Press (1978).

17. William Simon, *A Time for Truth*, p. 233, Reader's Digest Press (1978).

18. John J. Miller, Foundation's End: The last days of John M. Olin's conservative fortune," *National Review Online*, April 06, 2005, http://www.nationalreview.com/miller/miller200504060758.asp.

19. "Philanthropy Roundtable," *Chemistry Daily,* http://www.chemistrydaily.com/chemistry/Philanthropy_Roundtable; also, "Philanthropy Roundtable," *SourceWatch,* http://www.sourcewatch.org/index.php?title=Philanthropy_Roundtable.

20. "History," http://www.philanthropyroundtable.org/content.asp?pl=406&contentid=432.

21. With $706 million in assets (2005), the Lynde and Harry Bradley Foundation of Milwaukee, Wisconsin is the country's largest and most influential right-wing foundation. As of the end of 2005, it was giving away more than $34 million a year [Bradley Foundation 2005 IRS 99-PF]. Media Transparaency, http://www.mediatransparency.org/funderprofile.php?funderID=1
The following grants were reported in 2007:

* $3,000,000 to Charter School Growth Fund, Broomfield, CO. For general operating support, payable over 1 year.
* $1,550,000 to American Civil Rights Institute, Sacramento, CA. For public education about race-preferential governmental policies and practices, payable over 1 year.
* $1,000,000 to Encounter for Culture and Education, Milwaukee, WI. For general operations, payable over 1 year.
* $1,000,000 to Marquette University, Milwaukee, WI. For construction of new law school, payable over 1 year.
* $425,000 to American Enterprise Institute for Public Policy Research, Washington, DC. For Foreign and Defense Policy Studies, work of Karlyn Bowman, Bradley Lectures, and conference on utopian ideologies and political violence, payable over 1 year.
* $400,000 to National Strategy Information Center, Washington, DC. For general operations, payable over 1 year.
* $300,000 to Intercollegiate Studies Institute, Wilmington, DE. For Civic Literacy Project and University Reform Program, payable over 1 year.
* $50,000 to American Symphony Orchestra League, New York, NY. For Learning and Leadership Development seminars, payable over 1 year.
* $50,000 to Heritage Foundation, Washington, DC. For First Principles Project, payable over 1 year.
* $50,000 to University of Arkansas, Fayetteville, AR. For evaluation of Milwaukee Parental Choice Program, payable over 1 year.

22. SourceWatch, http://www.sourcewatch.org/index.php?title=Smith_Richardson_Foundation. According to the Foundation, most projects funded are initiated by the foundation. The staff does not meet with applicants. Application form not required. According to SourceWatch, the Foundation has given approximately $99,686,911 to a total of 266 grantees. Conservative and centrist think tanks that received substantial sums were:

*   Center for Strategic and International Studies - $3,135,061
*   American Enterprise Institute - $2,942,532
*   Paul H. Nitze School of Advanced International Studies (SAIS) at John Hopkins - $2,680,334

* Brookings Institute - $2,629,870
* RAND Corporation - $1,854,061
* Hudson Institute - $1,595,510
* National Institute for Public Policy - $1,534,334
* Urban Institute - $1,492,624
* Freedom House, Inc. - $1,109,500
* Council on Foreign Relations - $883,023

The Foundation funded the early 'supply-side' books of Jude Wanniski and George Gilder. It is also listed in the acknowledgments for Dennis King's study of the LaRouche movement, Lyndon LaRouche and the New American Fascism (1989).

23. John Pitman with Cristina von Zeppelin, Chandrani Ghosh and David Armstrong, "The World's Billionaires: The Dynasties, *Forbes*, Feb. 28, 2002. Scaife reported the following grants in 2006:

* $800,000 to Heritage Foundation, Washington, DC. For general operating support, payable over 1 year.
* $625,000 to Social Philosophy and Policy Foundation, Bowling Green, OH, payable over 1 year.
* $484,000 to Maldon Institute, Baltimore, MD. For general operating support, payable over 1 year.
* $450,000 to Institute for Foreign Policy Analysis, Cambridge, MA. For general operating support, payable over 1 year.
* $385,000 to Center for Strategic and International Studies, Washington, DC. For Senior Advisor Post and project support, payable over 1 year.
* $300,000 to Tufts University, Medford, MA, payable over 1 year.
* $150,000 to Competitive Enterprise Institute, Washington, DC. For general operating support, payable over 1 year.
* $150,000 to Southwest Missouri State University Foundation, Springfield, MO, payable over 1 year.
* $140,000 to Collegiate Network, Wilmington, DE. For general operating support, payable over 1 year.
* $130,000 to American Bar Association Fund for Justice and Education, Chicago, IL. For Standing Committee on Law and National Security, payable over 1 year.

Carthage reported the following grants in 2006:

* $475,000 to Free Congress Research and Education Foundation, Washington, DC. For general operating and program support, payable over 1 year.
* $300,000 to Federation for American Immigration Reform, Washington, DC. For general operating and project support, payable over 1 year.
* $250,000 to Counterterrorism and Security Educational Research Foundation, Washington, DC. For Investigative Project, payable over 1 year.
* $250,000 to Landmark Legal Foundation, Kansas City, MO. For general operating support, payable over 1 year.
* $200,000 to Committee for a Constructive Tomorrow, Washington, DC. For general operating support, payable over 1 year.
* $175,000 to Pacific Legal Foundation, Sacramento, CA. For general operating support, payable over 1 year.
* $150,000 to American Foreign Policy Council, Washington, DC. For general operating support, payable over 1 year.

- $120,000 to American Jewish Committee, New York, NY. For publication support, payable over 1 year.
- $100,000 to Americas Survival, Owings, MD. For program support, payable over 1 year.
- $100,000 to Defenders of Property Rights, Washington, DC. For general operating support, payable over 1 year.

24. Kennametal, http://www.kennametal.com/en/corporate/index.jhtml.
The following grants were reported in 2005:

- $105,000 to Intercollegiate Studies Institute, Wilmington, DE, payable over 1 year.
- $95,000 to Commonwealth Foundation for Public Policy Alternatives, Harrisburg, PA, payable over 1 year.
- $65,000 to Heritage Foundation, Washington, DC, payable over 1 year.
- $60,000 to Intercollegiate Studies Institute, Wilmington, DE, payable over 1 year.
- $50,000 to Claremont Institute for the Study of Statesmanship and Political Philosophy, Claremont, CA, payable over 1 year.
- $40,000 to Pacific Research Institute for Public Policy, San Francisco, CA, payable over 1 year.
- $29,275 to Foundation for Free Enterprise Education, Erie, PA, payable over 1 year.
- $25,000 to Capital Research Center, Washington, DC, payable over 1 year.
- $25,000 to Federalist Society for Law and Public Policy Studies, Washington, DC, payable over 1 year.
- $22,000 to Pennsylvanians for Effective Government Education Committee, Harrisburg, PA, payable over 1 year.
- $20,000 to George Mason University Foundation, Arlington, VA, payable over 1 year.

25. Wikipedia, http://en.wikipedia.org/wiki/John_M._Olin_Foundation
Because the Foundation has dissolved, information is no longer available from the Foundation Directory. However, SourceWatch reported the following: In 2001, the Foundation expended $20,482,961 to fund right-wing think tanks including the American Enterprise Institute (AEI), the Brookings Institution, the Center for Strategic and International Studies (CSIS), the Claremont Institute for the Study of Statesmanship and Political Philosophy, the Council on Foreign Relations (CFR), the Heritage Foundation, the Hoover Institution on War, Revolution and Peace, the Hudson Institute, the Independent Women's Forum, the Paul H. Nitze School of Advanced International Studies (SAIS) at Johns Hopkins University, the Manhattan Institute for Public Policy Research, and the Project for the New American Century (PNAC). "The Foundation also gives large sums of money to promote conservative programs in the country's most prestigious colleges and universities."

26. "Henry Salvatori," Society of Exploration Geophysicists,
http://www.mssu.edu/seg-vm/bio_henry_salvatori.html
Inexplicably, detailed information on the Foundation's gifts could not be found. Anecdotally, however, it is known that it has supported Heritage Foundation, the Claremont Institute and George Mason University.

27. Right Web, http://rightweb.irc-online.org/profile/511.html.
The following grants were reported in 2006:

- $225,000 to Social Philosophy and Policy Foundation, Bowling Green, OH. For Scholars in Social Philosophy and Policy programs, payable over 1 year.
- $150,000 to Intercollegiate Studies Institute, Wilmington, DE. For Richard M. Weaver Fellowship program during academic year, payable over 1 year.
- $128,267 to Institute of World Politics, Washington, DC. For professor, payable over 1 year.
- $75,000 to Social Philosophy and Policy Foundation, Bowling Green, OH. For six visiting scholars in Visiting Scholars program, payable over 1 year.
- $73,000 to George Mason University, Arlington, VA. For Humane Studies Fellows Research Colloquium and Career Development Seminar, payable over 1 year.
- $53,000 to University of Pittsburgh, Pittsburgh, PA. For graduate fellowship in philosophy, payable over 1 year.
- $30,368 to University of Dallas, Irving, TX. For graduate fellowship in political philosophy, payable over 1 year.
- $30,000 to Atlas Economic Research Foundation, Arlington, VA. For graduate fellowship in economics at George Mason University, payable over 1 year.
- $30,000 to George Mason University, Arlington, VA. To provide general support for Institute's Advanced Academic programs, payable over 1 year.
- $30,000 to Tax Foundation, Washington, DC. For research staff, payable over 1 year.

28. JM Foundation, http://www.dkosopedia.com/wiki/JM_Foundation
According to Media Transparency between 1995 and 2004 the Foundation contributed $ 9,285,243 to the following groups (with those that received most at the top of the list).

Some of the more notable groups include:

*   Hoover Institution on War, Revolution and Peace
*   Intercollegiate Studies Institute, Inc.
*   Independent Women's Forum
*   Heritage Foundation, The
*   Heartland Institute
*   Goldwater Institute
*   Hudson Institute, Inc.
*   Cato Institute
*   Center for Security Policy
*   Competitive Enterprise Institute
*   American Enterprise Institute for Public Policy Research
*   Institute for Humane Studies
*   Cascade Policy Institute
*   Institute of World Politics
*   Freedom House, Inc.
*   Layalina Productions
*   Wildlife Conservation Society
*   Ronald Reagan Presidential Foundation, The
*   Center for Media and Public Affairs, Inc.
*   Empowerment Network Foundation, The
*   American Studies Center, The
*   Mountain States Legal Foundation

29. John J. Miller, "Foundation's End: The last days of John M. Olin's conservative fortune," *National Review Online*, April 06, 2005, http://www.nationalreview.com/miller/miller200504060758.asp.

30. John M. Olin Institute for Strategic Studies, http://www.wcfia.harvard.edu/olin/index.htm.

31. Debra Cassens Weiss, "Justices Help Federalist Society Celebrate 25 Years," *ABA Journal*, http://www.abajournal.com/news/justices_help_federalist_society_celebrate_25_years/.

32. Federalist Society, http://www.fed-soc.org/Chapters/ChaptersList_ByType.asp?type=2.

33. Charles Lane, "Roberts Listed in Federalist Society '97-98 Directory: Court Nominee Said He Has No Memory of Membership, July 25, 2005.

34. Jerry Landay, "The Conservative Cabal That's Transforming American Law.," *Washington Monthly*, March 2000.

35. Debra Cassens Weiss, "Justices Help Federalist Society Celebrate 25 Years," ABA Journal, http://www.abajournal.com/news/justices_help_federalist_society_celebrate_25_years/.

36. Jerry Landay, "The Conservative Cabal That's Transforming American Law.," *Washington Monthly*, March 2000.

37. Carrie Johnson, "Internal Justice Dept. Report Cites Illegal Hiring Practices," *Washington Post*, July 29, 2008.

38. "Justice Department Tracked Federalist Society Influence On U.S. Attorneys," ThinkProgress, http://thinkprogress.org/2007/04/13/federalist-attorneys/.

39. Thomas G. West, "Allan Bloom and America," The Claremont Institute, http://www.claremont.org/publications/pubid.664/pub_detail.asp.

40. John J. Miller, "Foundation's End: The last days of John M. Olin's conservative fortune," April 6, 2005, The National Review Online, http://www.nationalreview.com/miller/miller200504060758.asp.

41. Fox Butterfield, "The Uproar at Dartmouth: How a Conservative Weekly Inflamed a Campus," *New York Times*, Oct. 7, 1990.

42. Fox Butterfield, "The Uproar at Dartmouth: How a Conservative Weekly Inflamed a Campus," *New York Times*, Oct. 7, 1990.

43. Kyle Crichton, "Departing President: William G. Bowen; the Economist Who Taught Princeton Basic Economics," *New York Times*, May 10, 1987.

44. "Judge Alito, in His Own Words," *New York Times*, Jan. 12, 2006.

45. "Critical Monthly Rouses Princeton," *New York Times*, April 29, 1984.

46. "Advertise," *National Review Online*, http://www.nationalreview.com/mediakit/.

47. Philip Longman, "Reagan's Disappearing Bureaucrats," *New York Times*, Feb. 14, 1988.

48. Philip Longman, "Reagan's Disappearing Bureaucrats," *New York Times*, Feb. 14, 1988.

49. Dinesh D'Souza, *The End of Racism: Principles for a Multiracial Society*, Free Press, 1995.

50. Dinesh D'Souza, "The End of Racism: The White Man's Burden," *Washington Post*, http://www.washingtonpost.com/wp-srv/style/longterm/books/chap1/endofrac.htm.

51. Dinesh D'Souza, *The Enemy at Home: The Cultural Left and Its Responsibility For 9/11*, Random House Digital, Inc., Feb 12, 2008.

52. "Interview with Ralph K. Winter: Role changes for Judicial Conduct," *Daily Record*, July 26, 2007.

53. About Laura Ingram, http://www.lauraingraham.com/pg/jsp/general/aboutlaura.jsp.

54. About Laura Ingram, http://www.lauraingraham.com/pg/jsp/general/aboutlaura.jsp.

55. http://www.amvalues.org/issues.php.

56. Lawrence C. Soley, *Leasing the Ivory Tower: the Corporate Takeover of Academia*, p.109, South End Press (Boston, 1995)

57. Lawrence C. Soley, *Leasing the Ivory Tower: the Corporate Takeover of Academia*, p.109, South End Press (Boston, 1995)

58. Lawrence C. Soley, *Leasing the Ivory Tower: the Corporate Takeover of Academia*, p.109, South End Press (Boston, 1995)

59. "Fellows by Name," The Hoover Institution, http://www.hoover.org/bios?sortBy=name&c=y.

60. Exxon Education Foundation Dimensions reports, Worldwide Giving Reports and IRS forms 990.

61. Tom Bethel, "ENVIRONMENT: The Politics behind Global Warming, http://www.hoover.org/publications/digest/3532036.html.

62. Bruce Berkowitz , "ENVIRONMENT: The Pseudoscience of Global Warming,"http://www.hoover.org/publications/digest/3460191.html.

63. Richard A. Epstein, "Why Care Reform May Be Bad for Your Health," http://www.hoover.org/publications/digest/3484076.html.

64. David R. Henderson, "ECONOMICS: The Right Minimum Wage? Zero," http://www.hoover.org/publications/digest/5854446.html.

65. "RECIPIENT GRANTS, Hoover Institution on War, Revolution and Peace,"
MediaTransparency,
http://www.mediatransparency.org/recipientgrants.php?recipientID=157.

66. Edgard on-line,
http://sec.edgar-online.com/2000/05/18/15/0001095811-00-001549/Section5.asp.

67. Timken, http://www.timken.com/EN-US/PRODUCTS/BEARINGS/Pages/default.aspx.

68. Thomas J. Tierney,
http://www.baruch.cuny.edu/spa/researchcenters/nonprofitstrategy/documents/ThomasJTie
rneybio.pdf.

69. Lawrence C. Soley, *Leasing the Ivory Tower: the Corporate Takeover of Academia*,
p.119–16, South End Press (Boston, 1995)

70. Foundation Center Online (paid subscription required),
http://fconline.foundationcenter.org/fdo_grant_search.php.

71. "Social Philosophy and Policy Foundation," MediaTransparency,
http://www.mediatransparency.org/recipientgrants.php?recipientID=305.

72. Washington University,
http://www.mediatransparency.org/recipientgrants.php?recipientID=350.

73. David Warner, "How do federal rules affect you?" *Nation's Business*, May, 1992.

74. Ed Rubenstein, "Regulation redux - increase in government regulation of business,"
National Review, March 18, 1988.

75. Edward H. Crane, David Boaz, *An American vision: policies for the '90s*, Cato Institute,
1989.

CHAPTER 8

1. Curtis Moore, "Rethinking the Think Tanks—How industry-funded 'experts' twist the
environmental debate." *Sierra*, July/August, 2002.

2. "The Principled Entrepreneur,"*The American*, July–August 2007, accessed Oct. 2, 2012.

3. "Our annual ranking of America's largest corporations," *FORTUNE*,
http://money.cnn.com/magazines/fortune/fortune500/2007/, accessed Oct. 2, 2012.

4. Lizette Alvarez, G.O.P. Aims to Remake Florida Supreme Court," *New York Times*,
Oct. 2, 2012.

5. Lizette Alvarez, G.O.P. Aims to Remake Florida Supreme Court," *New York Times*,
Oct. 2, 2012.

6. John Romano, "Republican lawmakers, but only a few, speak out against politicizing justice retention vote," *Tampa Bay Times*, Oct. 16, 2012.

7. John Romano, "Republican lawmakers, but only a few, speak out against politicizing justice retention vote," *Tampa Bay Times*, Oct. 16, 2012.

8. Curtis A. Moore, "Paying with our Money and our Future: The Hidden Costs of the Keystone XL Pipeline," Americas Program of the Center for International Policy, http://www.cipamericas.org/archives/6530, accessed Oct. 2, 2012.

CHAPTER 9

1. Dan Cox, "Young White Evangelicals: Less Republican, Still Conservative," Pew Research Center for the People & the Press Sept. 28, 2007, http://www.pewforum.org/Politics-and-Elections/Young-White-Evangelicals-Less-Republican-Still-Conservative.aspx, accessed Aug. 8, 2012.

2. David Brody, "Mitt Romney and the Teavangelicals," June 18, 2012, http://www.huffingtonpost.com/david-brody/mitt-romney-and-the-teava_b_1605726.html, accessed Aug. 14, 2012.

3. David Brody, "Mitt Romney and the Teavangelicals," June 18, 2012, http://www.huffingtonpost.com/david-brody/mitt-romney-and-the-teava_b_1605726.html, accessed Aug. 14, 2012.

4. David Brody, "Mitt Romney and the Teavangelicals," June 18, 2012, http://www.huffingtonpost.com/david-brody/mitt-romney-and-the-teava_b_1605726.html, accessed Aug. 14, 2012.

5. Martin, William; *With God On Our Side*; New York, NY: Broadway Books; 1996; Chapter 3 - A Man on Horseback; p. 97.

6. Martin, William; *With God On Our Side*; New York, NY: Broadway Books; 1996; Chapter 3 - A Man on Horseback; p. 97.

7. Martin, William; *With God On Our Side*; New York, NY: Broadway Books; 1996; Chapter 3 - A Man on Horseback; p. 98.

8. Martin, William; *With God On Our Side*; New York, NY: Broadway Books; 1996; Chapter 3 - A Man on Horseback; p. 99.

9. Martin, William; *With God On Our Side*; New York, NY: Broadway Books; 1996; Chapter 3 - A Man on Horseback; p. 99.

10. "White Evangelicals Turn Out Big, Vote Republican," Nov. 5, 2010, http://www.newsmax.com/Politics/white-evangelical-Christians-Reed/2010/11/05/id/376191, accessed Aug. 8, 2012.

11. Phil Hirschkorn and Jennifer De Pinto, "White Evangelicals are half of GOP primary voters," CBS News, March 15, 2012.

12. Henry J. Reske, "Poll: Evangelicals Flock to Support Romney," May 10, 2012, http://www.newsmax.com/Newsfront/evangelicals-Romney-flock-poll/2012/05/10/id/438683, accessed Aug. 8, 2012.

13. Brad Knickerbocker, "Sen. Orrin Hatch survives tea party primary challenge: how he did it," *Christian Science Monitor*, June 27, 2012.

14. Patrik Johnson, "Missouri primary: Tea party win sets up battle for control of Senate," *Christian Science Monitor*, Aug. 8, 2012.

15. "As it happened: Super Tuesday," BBC News, http://www.bbc.co.uk/news/world-us-canada-17277353?oo=14213, accessed Aug. 8, 2012.

16. Barma Group, "Election 2012 Priorities: How the Faith of Likely Voters Affects the Issues They Care About," http://www.barna.org/faith-spirituality/563-election-2012-priorities-how-the-faith-of-likely-voters-affects-the-issues-they-care-about, accessed Aug. 7, 2012.

17. Barma Group, "Election 2012 Priorities: How the Faith of Likely Voters Affects the Issues They Care About," http://www.barna.org/faith-spirituality/563-election-2012-priorities-how-the-faith-of-likely-voters-affects-the-issues-they-care-about, accessed Aug. 7, 2012.

18. Barma Group, "Election 2012 Priorities: How the Faith of Likely Voters Affects the Issues They Care About," http://www.barna.org/faith-spirituality/563-election-2012-priorities-how-the-faith-of-likely-voters-affects-the-issues-they-care-about, accessed Aug. 7, 2012.

19. Barma Group, "Election 2012 Priorities: How the Faith of Likely Voters Affects the Issues They Care About," http://www.barna.org/faith-spirituality/563-election-2012-priorities-how-the-faith-of-likely-voters-affects-the-issues-they-care-about, accessed Aug. 7, 2012.

20. Curtis Moore and Alan Miller, *Green Gold: Japan, Germany, the United States, and the Race for Environmental Technology*, Beacon Press (Boston, 1994).

21. Paul Stanley, "What Do Evangelical Leaders Think Is the Nation's Top Issue?" *Christian Post*, Jan. 12, 2012, http://www.christianpost.com/news/what-do-evangelical-leaders-think-is-the-nations-top-issue-68370/, accessed July 23, 2012.

22. Curtis Moore, "Paying with our Money and our Future: The Hidden Costs of the Keystone XL Pipeline," America's Program, March 8, 2012, http://www.cipamericas.org/archives/6530.

23. "Bloomberg to Candidates: Get Serious on Immigration Reform," Fox News, August 15, 2012, http://latino.foxnews.com/latino/politics/2012/08/15/bloomberg-to-candidates-get-serious-on-immigration-reform/#ixzz23ewLK300, accessed August 15, 2012.

24. Trip Gabriel, "Vouchers Unspoken, Romney Hails School Choice," *New York Times*, June 11, 2012.

25. Dwight T. Barrett, *School vouchers and religion: An examination on attitudes of evangelical parochial leaders in Southern California*, a dissertation, http://udini.proquest.com/view/school-vouchers-and-religion-an-goid:746479450/, accessed Aug. 15, 2012.

26. "The House's Immigrant Betrayal With New Violence Against Women Act," The Daily Beast, May 17, 2012, http://www.thedailybeast.com/articles/2012/05/17/the-house-s-immigrant-betrayal-with-new-violence-against-women-act.html, accessed Aug. 15, 2012.

CHAPTER 10

1. Gretchen Morgenson, "The Curtain Opens on 401(k) Fees," *New York Times*, June 2, 2012.

2. According to the Internal Revenue Service, "A CODA is an arrangement that allows eligible employees to make a cash or deferred election with respect to contributions to, or accruals or benefits under, a plan intended to satisfy the requirements of section 401(a). A cash or deferred election is any direct or indirect election by an employee (or modification of an earlier election) to have the employer either: (1) provide an amount to the employee in the form of cash or some other taxable benefit that is not currently available; or (2) contribute an amount to a trust, or provide an accrual or other benefit, under a plan deferring the receipt of compensation. The election must be made before the taxable benefit is 'currently available' to the participant." *Internal Revenue Manual*, Part 4. Examining Process, Ch. 72, Sec. 2. Cash or Deferred Arrangements.

3. Employee Benefit Research Institute, "History of 401(k) Plans: An Update," February, 2005, http://www.ebri.org/pdf/publications/facts/0205fact.a.pdf, accessed Aug. 23, 2012.

4. Investment Company Institute, "401(k) Plans: A 25-Year Retrospective," http://www.ici.org/pdf/per12-02.pdf, accessed Aug. 20, 2012.

5. Investment Company Institute, "401(k) Plans: A 25-Year Retrospective," http://www.ici.org/pdf/per12-02.pdf, accessed Aug. 20, 2012.

6. Stephane Fitch, "Wal-Mart 401(k) Pays Retail," *Forbes Magazine*, Jan. 18, 2010.

7. Kelly Services, "Benefits and Perks," http://www.kellyservices.us/US/Careers/Corporate-Branch-Benefits-and-Perks/, accessed Aug. 23, 2012.

8. McDonald's, "Benefits," http://www.mcdonalds.com/us/en/careers/benefits.html, accessed Aug. 23, 2012.

9. "Teamsters-UPS 401(k) Plan," https://www.retirement.prudential.com/cws/teamsterups/, accessed Aug. 23, 2012.

10. IBM, "2012 Benefitws Summary,"
http://www-01.ibm.com/employment/us/benefits/2012_Benefits_Brochure.pdf, accessed
Aug. 23, 2012.

11. Investment Company Institute, "401(k) Plans: A 25-Year Retrospective,"
http://www.ici.org/pdf/per12-02.pdf, accessed Aug. 20, 2012.

12. Bullfax.com, "The 401(k) Disaster," http://www.bullfax.com/?q=node-401k-disaster,
accessed Aug. 23, 2012.

13. Leigh Strope, "Retirement plans take hit in economic downturn, increasing worries for
many aging workers," The Associated Press, July 30, 2001.

14. Leigh Strope, "Retirement plans take hit in economic downturn, increasing worries for
many aging workers," The Associated Press, July 30, 2001.

15. Leigh Stropes, "Coping with cracks in our nest eggs," The Associated Press, Aug. 6,
2001.

16. Jon Healey, "GOP platform presents Medicare as a 401(k) plan," *Los Angeles Times*,
Aug. 21, 2012.

17. Timothy Curry and Lynn Shibut "The Cost of the Savings and Loan Crisis: Truth and
Consequences," *FDIC Banking Review*, December, 2000,
http://www.fdic.gov/bank/analytical/banking/2000dec/brv13n2_2.pdf, accessed Aug. 19,
2012.

18. Kitty Calavita, Henry N. Pontell and Robert H. Tillman, *Big Money Crime: Fraud and
Politics in the Savings and Loan Crisis*, University of California Press, Ltd., London,
England, 1997, p. 91.

19. Kitty Calavita, Henry N. Pontell and Robert H. Tillman, *Big Money Crime: Fraud and
Politics in the Savings and Loan Crisis*, University of California Press, Ltd., London,
England, 1997, p. 91.

20. Federal Deposit Insurance Corporation, "The S&L Crisis: A Chrono-Bibliography,"
http://www.fdic.gov/bank/historical/s&l/index.html, accessed Aug. 19, 2012.

21. Federal Deposit Insurance Corporation, "The S&L Crisis: A Chrono-Bibliography,"
http://www.fdic.gov/bank/historical/s&l/index.html, accessed Aug. 19, 2012.

22. Federal Deposit Insurance Corporation, "The S&L Crisis: A Chrono-Bibliography,"
http://www.fdic.gov/bank/historical/s&l/index.html, accessed Aug. 19, 2012.

23. Federal Deposit Insurance Corporation, "The S&L Crisis: A Chrono-Bibliography,"
http://www.fdic.gov/bank/historical/s&l/index.html, accessed Aug. 19, 2012.

24. Federal Deposit Insurance Corporation, "The S&L Crisis: A Chrono-Bibliography,"
http://www.fdic.gov/bank/historical/s&l/index.html, accessed Aug. 19, 2012.

25. Federal Deposit Insurance Corporation, "The S&L Crisis: A Chrono-Bibliography," http://www.fdic.gov/bank/historical/s&l/index.html, accessed Aug. 19, 2012.

26. Federal Deposit Insurance Corporation, "The S&L Crisis: A Chrono-Bibliography," http://www.fdic.gov/bank/historical/s&l/index.html, accessed Aug. 19, 2012.

27. Timothy Curry and Lynn Shibut "The Cost of the Savings and Loan Crisis: Truth and Consequences," *FDIC Banking Review*, December, 2000, http://www.fdic.gov/bank/analytical/banking/2000dec/brv13n2_2.pdf, accessed Aug. 19, 2012.

28. Eric Lipton and Andrew Martin, "For Banks, Wads of Cash and Loads of Trouble [brokered deposits and risky loans]," *New York Times*, July 4, 2009.

29. Nathaniel C. Nash, "Washington Talk: Q&A: Edwin J. Gray; Four Years of Overseeing the Troubled Thrifts," *New York Times*, July 15, 1987.

30. Nathaniel C. Nash, "Washington Talk: Q&A: Edwin J. Gray; Four Years of Overseeing the Troubled Thrifts," *New York Times*, July 15, 1987.

31. Gretchen Morgenson and Louise Story, "In Financial Crisis, No Prosecutions of Top Figures," *New York Times*, April 14, 2011.

32. Federal Deposit Insurance Corporation, "The S&L Crisis: A Chrono-Bibliography," http://www.fdic.gov/bank/historical/s&l/index.html, accessed Aug. 19, 2012.

33. This account is based largely on Mike Rowan, "Great Stock Market Crashes: Black Monday In 1987," http://www.dailymarkets.com/economy/2009/08/20/great-stock-market-crashes-black-monday-in-1987/, accessed Aug. 19, 2012. Updated by Mike Rowan August 21, 2009.

34. This account is based largely on Mike Rowan, "Great Stock Market Crashes: Black Monday In 1987," http://www.dailymarkets.com/economy/2009/08/20/great-stock-market-crashes-black-monday-in-1987/, accessed Aug. 19, 2012. Updated by Mike Rowan August 21, 2009

35. Matthew Bandyk, "The Lessons of 'Black Monday'- The 1987 crash seemed catastrophic at the time but didn't derail the long-term investor," *U.S. News & World Report*, Oct. 19, 2007.

36. Matthew Bandyk, "The Lessons of 'Black Monday'- The 1987 crash seemed catastrophic at the time but didn't derail the long-term investor," *U.S. News & World Report*, Oct. 19, 2007.

37. Walter Hamilton, "Black Monday: Never again?" *Los Angeles Times,* Oct. 18, 2007.

38. Dana Anspach, "Black Monday And The Bear Market of 2002," About.com, http://moneyover55.about.com/od/howtoinvest/ss/blackmonday_2.htm, accessed Aug. 20, 2012.

39. Conservable Economist, "Why Didn't Dot-Com Crash Hurt Like Housing Crash Did?" http://conversableeconomist.blogspot.com/2011/10/why-didnt-dot-com-crash-hurt-like.html, accessed Aug. 23, 2012 *citing* Table B.100 of the Federal Reserves Flow of Funds Accounts in September 2003.

40. About.com, "Dot.com Collapse Heads Stories from 2000," http://stocks.about.com/od/marketnews/a/112309decade-1.htm, accessed Aug. 23, 2012.

41. PBS NewsHour, "Making Sen$e of Bailouts: Why the U.S. Government Bought 'Troubled Assets'," Aug. 2, 2012, http://www.pbs.org/newshour/bb/business/july-dec12/makingsense_08-02.html, accessed Aug. 23, 2012.

42. PBS NewsHour, "Making Sen$e of Bailouts: Why the U.S. Government Bought 'Troubled Assets'," Aug. 2, 2012, http://www.pbs.org/newshour/bb/business/july-dec12/makingsense_08-02.html, accessed Aug. 23, 2012.

43. PBS NewsHour, "Making Sen$e of Bailouts: Why the U.S. Government Bought 'Troubled Assets'," Aug. 2, 2012, http://www.pbs.org/newshour/bb/business/july-dec12/makingsense_08-02.html, accessed Aug. 23, 2012.

44. PBS NewsHour, "Making Sen$e of Bailouts: Why the U.S. Government Bought 'Troubled Assets'," Aug. 2, 2012, http://www.pbs.org/newshour/bb/business/july-dec12/makingsense_08-02.html, accessed Aug. 23, 2012.

45. PBS NewsHour, "Making Sen$e of Bailouts: Why the U.S. Government Bought 'Troubled Assets'," Aug. 2, 2012, http://www.pbs.org/newshour/bb/business/july-dec12/makingsense_08-02.html, accessed Aug. 23, 2012.

CHAPTER 11

1. Will Storey, "Revisiting the Daisy Ad Revolution," *New York Times*, Oct. 20, 2011, http://thecaucus.blogs.nytimes.com/2011/10/24/revisiting-the-daisy-ad-revolution/, accessed Aug. 19, 2012.

2. Will Storey, "Revisiting the Daisy Ad Revolution," *New York Times*, Oct. 20, 2011, http://thecaucus.blogs.nytimes.com/2011/10/24/revisiting-the-daisy-ad-revolution/, accessed Aug. 19, 2012.

3. Samuel G. Freedman, "The First Days of the Loaded Political Image," *New York Times,* Sep 1, 1996.

4. Theodore H. White, The Making of the President 1964 (New York: Atheneum Publishers, 1964), p. 322.

5. Tony Schwartz, The Responsive Chord (New York: Anchor Press / Doubleday, 1973), p. 93.

6. Denis Higgins, *The Art of Writing Advertising* (Chicago: Advertising Publications, 1965), p. 24, cited in Daisy: the Complete History of an Infamous and Iconic Ad - Part Three, http://www.conelrad.com/daisy/daisy3.php#123.

7. Samuel G. Freedman, "The First Days of the Loaded Political Image," *New York Times*, Sep. 1, 1996.

8. Samuel G. Freedman, "The First Days of the Loaded Political Image," *New York Times*, Sep. 1, 1996.

9. Samuel G. Freedman, "The First Days of the Loaded Political Image," *New York Times*, Sep. 1, 1996.

10. Paul Krugman, "Republicans and Race," *New York Times*, Nov. 19, 2007.

11. Paul Krugman, "Republicans and Race," *New York Times*, Nov. 19, 2007.

CHAPTER 12

1. The account of Rove's deposition, found at http://legacy.library.ucsf.edu/tid/voq07a00, in a tobacco case is as follows:
"The witness, a consultant for Philip Morris, was deposed by the plaintiffs. He summarized his personal and professional background, including his work for the Republican party in a number of political campaigns. He indicated that he attended five different universities but did not graduate from any of them. He characterized the news that Mike Gunn was resigning from the Mississippi Senate to join the Tobacco Institute as "a sad commentary on the Tobacco Institute and a vast improvement for the Mississippi Senate." He reported that he was first approached by Philip Morris to begin working for them in 1991. He said that his association with Philip Morris ended by mutual agreement in 1996, in part because he began to feel uncomfortable working in the political arena and then sharing that information with Philip Morris. He said that he felt it was inappropriate for him to tell Philip Morris about polling information that he had access to as a result of his role in George W. Bush's gubernatorial campaign. However, he did share "political gossip about who was getting ready to run and how they were doing with fund-raising and how they were doing garnering support of key groups, how they were doing with lining up endorsements and so forth," even if he learned this from his involvement in the campaign. He said that George W. Bush was aware of his work for Philip Morris and told him not to discuss tobacco issues with him, including product liability. He reported that the only topics that were considered off-limits for advice were tobacco issues and "issues on which I didn't have any expertise, and which had no political implications." However the witness acknowledged that they did discuss tort reform. He indicated that there was a distinction between the two but did not elaborate. He agreed that tobacco is "broadly" part of the subject matter of tort reform and product liability. He maintained that he never saw a conflict between his consulting work for Philip Morris and his consulting work for Governor Bush. He declared that there are "too many lawsuits and too many frivolous claims filed by people against other people ... the legal system is jury-rigged. And it's rigged in a certain way."

2. James Moore and Wayne Slater, *Bush's Brain*, John Wiley & Sons, Hoboken, N.J., 2003.

3. Nicholas Lemann, "The Controller: Karl Rove is working to get George Bush reelected, but he has bigger plans," *New Yorker*, May 12, 2003.

4. SlideShare, "The Frank Luntz Method,"
http://www.slideshare.net/jessestarmer/the-frank-luntz-method, accessed Sep. 20, 2012.

5. Katherine Yurica, "Frank Luntz, the Propagandist of the Century," Yurica Report,
http://www.yuricareport.com/Dominionism/LuntzPropagandistOfCentury.html, accessed Sept. 20, 2012.

6. SlideShare, "The Frank Luntz Method,"
http://www.slideshare.net/jessestarmer/the-frank-luntz-method, accessed Sep. 20, 2012.

7. Justin Elliott, "GOP Message Man 'Frightened to Death' of Occupy," *Salon*, December 1, 2011

8. Wikipedia, "Miguel Estrada," http://en.wikipedia.org/wiki/Miguel_Estrada, accessed Sept. 20, 2012.

9. Nicholas Lemann, "The Controller: Karl Rove is working to get George Bush reelected, but he has bigger plans," *New Yorker*, May 12, 2003.

10. Wikipedia, John Nance Garner," http://en.wikipedia.org/wiki/John_Nance_Garner, accessed Sept. 20, 2012.

11. "Genius," *Texas Monthly*, March, 2003.

12. Nicholas Lemann, "The Controller: Karl Rove is working to get George Bush reelected, but he has bigger plans," *New Yorker*, May 12, 2003.

13. Nicholas Lemann, "The Controller: Karl Rove is working to get George Bush reelected, but he has bigger plans," *New Yorker*, May 12, 2003.

14. "Genius," *Texas Monthly*, March, 2003.

15. "Young Guns II," The Weekly Standard, Sept. 4, 2010,
http://www.weeklystandard.com/blogs/young-guns-ii, accessed Sept. 21, 2012.

16. Wikipedia,
http://en.wikipedia.org/wiki/National_Republican_Congressional_Committee#cite_note-gop youngguns-2, *citing* About young guns (n.d.). Retrieved from http://www.gopyoungguns.com/about.

17. "'Young Guns' offers GOP blueprint," Politico.com,
http://www.politico.com/news/stories/0810/41606.html, accessed Sept. 21, 2012.
http://www.politico.com/news/stories/0810/41606.html#ixzz4u9OoE7xH

18. "About" Young Guns, National Republican Congressional Committee, http://gopyoungguns.com/about/, accessed Sept. 21, 2012.

19. Shira Toeplitz, "Dissecting Tactics of Young Guns," *Roll Call*, July 16, 2012.

CHAPTER 13

1. Jack P. Greene, *Understanding the American Revolution: Issues and Actors*, p. 76, University of Virginia Press (1995).

2. See, e.g., *Patriot Post*, "Obama Care Architect: Premiums to Soar," http://patriotpost.us/opinion/12592/comments/new?parent_id=242493, accessed June 15, 2012.

3. Wikipedia, "Knight Ridder," http://en.wikipedia.org/wiki/Knight_Ridder#List_of_newspapers, accessed June 14, 2012.

4. Daily newspapers owned by Knight Ridder and its predecessors included:
        American News (Aberdeen, South Dakota), 1928–2006
        Akron Beacon Journal (Akron, Ohio), 1903–2006
        Belleville News-Democrat (Belleville, Illinois), 1997–2006
        The *Bellingham Herald* (Bellingham, Washington), 2005–2006
        Sun Herald (Biloxi, Mississippi), 1986–2006
        Boca Raton News (Boca Raton, Florida), 1969–1997
        The *Daily Camera* (Boulder, Colorado), 1969–1997
        The *Herald* (Bradenton) (Bradenton, Florida), 1973–2006
        The *Idaho Statesman* (Boise, Idaho), 2005–2006
        Chicago Daily News (Chicago, Illinois), 1944–1959
        The *Charlotte Observer* (Charlotte, North Carolina), 1955–2006
        The *State* (Columbia, South Carolina), 1986–2006
        Columbus Ledger-Enquirer (Columbus, Georgia), 1973–2006
        Contra Costa Times (Walnut Creek, California), 1995–2006
        Detroit Free Press (Detroit, Michigan), 1940–2005
        Duluth News Tribune (Duluth, Minnesota), 1936–2006
        Fort Worth Star-Telegram (Fort Worth, Texas), 1997–2006
        The *Post-Tribune* (Gary, Indiana), 1966–1998
        Grand Forks Herald (Grand Forks, North Dakota), 1929–2006
        The *Kansas City Star* (Kansas City, Missouri), 1997–2006
        Lexington Herald-Leader (Lexington, Kentucky), 1973–2006
        Long Beach Press-Telegram (Long Beach, California), 1952–1997
        The *Telegraph* (Macon, Georgia), 1969–2006
        The *Miami Herald* (Miami, Florida), 1937–2006
        El Nuevo Herald (Miami, Florida), 1977–2006
        Monterey County Herald (Monterey, California), 1997–2006
        The *Sun News* (Myrtle Beach, South Carolina), 1986–2006
        The *News-Sentinel* (Fort Wayne, Indiana), 1980–2006
        The *Olathe News* (Olathe, Kansas), 2000–2006
        The *Olympian* (Olympia, Washington), 2005–2006
        Palo Alto Daily News (Palo Alto, California), 2005–2006
        Pasadena Star-News (Pasadena, California), 1956–1989

Philadelphia Daily News (Philadelphia, Pennsylvania), 1969–2006
The *Philadelphia Inquirer* (Philadelphia, Pennsylvania), 1969–2006
Saint Paul Pioneer Press (St. Paul, Minnesota), 1927–2006
San Jose Mercury News (San Jose, California), 1952–2006
The *Tribune* (San Luis Obispo, California), 1997–2006
Starkville Daily News (Starkville, Mississippi), 1986–1987
Centre Daily Times (State College, Pennsylvania), 1979–2006
Tallahassee Democrat (Tallahassee, Florida), 1965–2005
The *Daily Times-Leader* (West Point, Mississippi), 1986–1987
The *Wichita Eagle* (Wichita, Kansas), 1973–2006
The *Times Leader* (Wilkes-Barre, Pennsylvania), 1997–2006

5. Eric Alterman, "Out of Print - The death and life of the American newspaper," *New Yorker*, March 31, 2008.

6. Eric Alterman, "Out of Print - The death and life of the American newspaper," *New Yorker*, March 31, 2008.

7. About.com, "Rush Limbaugh Quotes - The Dumbest Things Rush Limbaugh Has Ever Said," http://politicalhumor.about.com/od/rushlimbaugh/a/limbaughquotes.htm, accessed May 29, 2012.

8. David Limbaugh, "This Is Way Bigger Than Rush," TownHall.com, http://townhall.com/columnists/davidlimbaugh/2009/03/03/this_is_way_bigger_than_rush/page/full/, accessed June 8, 2012.

9. M.J. Lee, "Sarah Palin defends Rush Limbaugh, cites 'hypocrisy'," Politico.com, http://www.politico.com/news/stories/0312/73706.html, accessed June 10, 2012.

10. Sumner Redstone," *Forbes*, http://www.forbes.com/profile/sumner-redstone/, accessed June 13, 2012.

11. Wikipedia, "Time Warner," http://en.wikipedia.org/wiki/Time_Warner, accessed June 5, 2012.

12. Wikipedia, "Random House," http://en.wikipedia.org/wiki/Random_House, accessed June 5, 2012. According to Wikipedia, Bertelsmann is majority owned (77.4%) by the Bertelsmann Foundation, a non-profit organization and political think tank founded by the Mohn family. The Mohn family owns the remaining 22.6% of the company.

Bertelsmann is currently organized into the following four divisions:
• RTL Group, Europe's biggest broadcaster of radio and television, which is also the umbrella division for Bertelsmann's movie and TV production enterprises;
• Gruner + Jahr, the biggest magazine publisher in Europe;
• Random House, the world's largest trade book publisher—Random House is the world's largest publisher of English language books; and,
• Arvato, an international media and communications service provider.

Random House, Inc. is the largest general-interest trade book publisher in the world. It has been owned since 1998 by Bertelsmann and has become the umbrella brand for Bertelsmann book publishing. Random House is considered one of the "Big Six" publishing companies, along with Hachette, Macmillan, Penguin, HarperCollins and Simon & Schuster.

13. Seth Ackerman, "The Most Biased Name in News—Fox News Channel's extraordinary right-wing tilt," Fairness & Accuracy in Reporting, July/August 2001, http://www.fair.org/index.php?page=1067, accessed June 13, 2012.

14. Michael Snyder, "Bain Capital Owns Clear Channel (Romney Supported by Talk Show sphere)," InfoWars.com, January 13, 2012 http://www.infowars.com/bain-capital-owns-clear-channel-romney-supported-by-talk-show-sphere/, accessed June 15, 2012. See also Wikipedia, "Bain Capital," http://en.wikipedia.org/wiki/Bain_Capital, accessed June 5, 2012.

15. Rush Limbaugh, "Mitt is Kicking Butt Out There," May 25, 2012, http://www.rushlimbaugh.com/daily/2012/05/25/mitt_is_kicking_butt_out_there, accessed June 15, 2012.

16. YouTube, "Sean Hannity Contrasts Barack Obama's and Mitt Romney's Past Wrongs (5/10/12)," http://www.youtube.com/watch?v=HloM5A7bzE4, accessed June 15, 2012.

17. YouTube, "Michael Savage - Obama Ate Dog, Romney Bites Back - (4/18/12)," http://www.youtube.com/watch?v=V8mHdHAtFNs, accessed June 15, 2012.

18. Wikipedia.org, "Lowry May," http://en.wikipedia.org/wiki/Lowry_Mays, accessed June 13, 2012.

19. Brent Staples, "Editorial Observer; The Trouble With Corporate Radio: The Day the Protest Music Died," New York Times, Feb. 20, 2003.

20. Erwin G. Krasnow, "Speaking Freely: Latest in essay series examines 'The First Amendment and the Fallacy of the Public's Airwaves,'" The Thomas Jefferson Center, http://www.tjcenter.org/2011/05/02/speaking-freely-latest-in-essay-series-examines-the-first-amendment-and-the-fallacy-of-the-publics-airwaves/, accessed June 12, 2012.

21. Ayn Rand, "Check Your Premises - The Property Status of Airwaves," The Objectivist Newsletter, V.. 3, No. 4 April, 1964, http://www.criminalgovernment.com/docs/aynrand.html, accessed June 14, 2012.

22. "Board of Trustees," The Media Institute, http://www.mediainstitute.org/BoardofTrustees.php, accessed June 15, 2012.

23. United States v. Chandler-Dunbar Co., 229 U. S. 53, at 69 (1913).

24. Erik Barnouw, The Golden Web: A History of Broadcasting in the United States, Vol. II—1933 to 1953, pp. 14–16, Oxford University Press, New York, 1968.

25. Erik Barnouw, The Golden Web: A History of Broadcasting in the United States, Vol. II—1933 to 1953, pp. 14–16, Oxford University Press, New York, 1968.

26. "Hollywood Masses the Full Power of Her Resources to Fight Sinclair," *New York Times*, Nov. 4, 1934.

27. "Wild Boys of the Road (1933)," http://twentyfourframes.wordpress.com/2009/04/06/wild-boys-of-the-road-1933-william-wellman/, accessed May 29, 2012.

28. Erik Barnouw, *The Golden Web: A History of Broadcasting in the United States, Vol. II—1933 to 1953*, pp. 14–16, Oxford University Press, New York, 1968.

29. Erik Barnouw, *The Golden Web: A History of Broadcasting in the United States, Vol. II–1933 to 1953*, pp. 14–16, Oxford University Press, New York, 1968.

30. Wikipedia, "104th United States Congress," http://en.wikipedia.org/wiki/104th_United_States_Congress, accessed June 15, 2012.

31. Wikipedia, "Telecommunications Act of 1996," LINK "http://en.wikipedia.org/wiki/Telecommunications_Act_of_1996," accessed June 15, 2012.

32. Brent Staples, "Editorial Observer; The Trouble With Corporate Radio: The Day the Protest Music Died," *New York Times*, Feb. 20, 2003.

33. Brent Staples, "Editorial Observer; The Trouble With Corporate Radio: The Day the Protest Music Died," *New York Times*, Feb. 20, 2003.

34. Common Cause, *The Fallout from the Telecommunications Act of 1996: Unintended Consequences and Lessons Learned*, May 0, 2005, http://www.commoncause.org/atf/cf/%7BFB3C17E2-CDD1-4DF6-92BE-BD4429893665%7D/FALLOUT_FROM_THE_TELECOMM_ACT_5-9-05.PDF, accessed June 15, 2012.

35. Common Cause, *The Fallout from the Telecommunications Act of 1996: Unintended Consequences and Lessons Learned*, May 9, 2005, http://www.commoncause.org/atf/cf/%7BFB3C17E2-CDD1-4DF6-92BE-BD4429893665%7D/FALLOUT_FROM_THE_TELECOMM_ACT_5-9-05.PDF, accessed June 15, 2012.

36. Erik Barnouw, *A Tower in Babel: A History of Broadcasting in the United States to 1933*, pp. 215–16, (New York, Oxford University Press, 1966).

37. Erik Barnouw, *A Tower in Babel: A History of Broadcasting in the United States to 1933*, pp. 216–17, (New York, Oxford University Press, 1966).

38. Steve Rendall, "The Fairness Doctrine: How We Lost it, and Why We Need it Back." Common Dreams, Feb. 12, 2005, Fairness and Accuracy In Reporting, http://www.commondreams.org/views05/0212-03.htm, accessed June 15, 2012.

39. Wikipedia.org, "Fairness Doctrine," http://en.wikipedia.org/wiki/Fairness_Doctrine#Corollary_rules, accessed June 15, 2012.

40. Wikipedia.org, "Fairness Doctrine,"
http://en.wikipedia.org/wiki/Fairness_Doctrine#Corollary_rules, accessed June 15, 2012.

41. *Red Lion Broadcasting Co., Inc., et al. v. Federal Communications Commission et al.*
395 U.S. 367, 394 (1969).

42. *Red Lion Broadcasting Co., Inc., et al. v. Federal Communications Commission et al.*
395 U.S. 367, 390 (1969).

43. "Nasty politics cause talk radio profits, says clear channel," Blatherwatch, Sept. 23,
2010, http://blatherwatch.blogs.com/talk_radio/2010/09/nasty-politics-cause-talk-radio-
profits-says-clear-channel.html, accessed June 15, 2012.

44. "Nasty politics cause talk radio profits, says clear channel," Blatherwatch, Sept. 23,
2010, http://blatherwatch.blogs.com/talk_radio/2010/09/nasty-politics-cause-talk-radio-
profits-says-clear-channel.html, accessed June 15, 2012.

45. Paul Farhi, "Limbaugh's Audience Size? It's Largely Up in the Air," *Washington Post*,
March 7, 2009

46. "Nasty politics cause talk radio profits, says clear channel," Blatherwatch, Sept. 23,
2010, http://blatherwatch.blogs.com/talk_radio/2010/09/nasty-politics-cause-talk-radio-
profits-says-clear-channel.html, accessed June 15, 2012.

47. "Mark Fowler," Satterlee Stephens Burke & Burke LLP,
http://www.ssbb.com/index.php/attorneys/entry/41, accessed June 15, 2012.

48. Eric Boehlert, "Fair and balanced?," *Salon*, Feb 1, 2005,
http://www.salon.com/2005/02/01/fairness_6/, accessed June 15, 2012.

49. Eric Boehlert, "Fair and balanced?," *Salon*, Feb 1, 2005,
http://www.salon.com/2005/02/01/fairness_6/, accessed June 15, 2012.

50. Eric Boehlert, "Fair and balanced?," *Salon*, Feb 1, 2005,
http://www.salon.com/2005/02/01/fairness_6/, accessed June 15, 2012.

51. "News Release: Court Repeals Personal Attack and Political Editorial Rules,"
Oct. 11, 2000, Radio and Television Digital News Association,
http://www.rtdna.org/pages/media_items/news-release-court-repeals-personal-attack-and-
political-editorial-rules422.php, accessed June 15, 2012.

CHAPTER 13, APPENDIX I

1. Wikipedia, "Philip Anschutz, http://en.wikipedia.org/wiki/Philip_Anschutz, accessed June
18, 2012.

2. Wikipedia, "The Weekly Standard," http://en.wikipedia.org/wiki/Weekly_Standard,
accessed June 18, 2012.

3. Wikipedia, "Clear Channel Communications," http://en.wikipedia.org/wiki/Clear_Channel_Communications, accessed May 21, 2012.

4. Wikipedia, "Clear Channel Communications," http://en.wikipedia.org/wiki/Clear_Channel_Communications, accessed May 21, 2012.

5. Wikipedia, "Clear Channel Communications," http://en.wikipedia.org/wiki/Clear_Channel_Communications, accessed May 21, 2012.

6. Wikipedia, "Clear Channel Communications," http://en.wikipedia.org/wiki/Clear_Channel_Communications, accessed May 21, 2012.

7. Wikipedia, "Newport Television," http://en.wikipedia.org/wiki/Newport_Television, accessed May 21, 2012.

8. Wikipedia, "Clear Channel Communications," http://en.wikipedia.org/wiki/Clear_Channel_Communications, accessed May 21, 2012.

9. Wikipedia, "Clear Channel Communications," http://en.wikipedia.org/wiki/Clear_Channel_Communications, accessed May 21, 2012.

CHAPTER 13, APPENDIX II

1. Center for American Progress, John Halpin, James Heidbreder, Mark Lloyd, Paul Woodhull, Ben Scott, Josh Silver, S. Derek Turner, *The Structural Imbalance of Political Talk Radio,*June 20, 2007, http://www.americanprogress.org/issues/2007/06/talk_radio.html, accessed June 15, 2012.

CHAPTER 13, APPENDIX III

1. Scott Horton, "The Heirs of Father Coughlin," *Harper's Magazine*, March 17, 2009.

2. Social Security History, "Father Charles E. Coughlin," http://www.ssa.gov/history/cough.html, accessed May 29, 2012.

3. Scott Horton, "The Heirs of Father Coughlin," *Harper's Magazine*, March 17, 2009.

4. Erik Barnouw, *The Golden Web: A History of Broadcasting in the United States, Vol. II—1933 to 1953*, pp. 14–16, Oxford University Press, New York, 1968.

5. Erik Barnouw, *The Golden Web: A History of Broadcasting in the United States, Vol. II—1933 to 1953*, pp. 14–16, Oxford University Press, New York, 1968.

6. Erik Barnouw, *The Golden Web: A History of Broadcasting in the United States, Vol. II—1933 to 1953*, pp. 14–16, Oxford University Press, New York, 1968.

7. Erik Barnouw, *The Golden Web: A History of Broadcasting in the United States, Vol. II—1933 to 1953*, pp. 14–16, Oxford University Press, New York, 1968.

8. Scott Horton, "The Heirs of Father Coughlin," *Harper's Magazine*, March 17, 2009.

CHAPTER 14

1. Travis Andersen and Emily Sweeney, "Dual rallies highlight fracture in Mass. Tea Party," *Boston Globe*, April 16, 2012.

2. Boston Massacre Historical Society, http://www.bostonmassacre.net/, accessed May 1, 2012.

3. Bernhard Knollenberg, *Growth of the American Revolution, 1766–1775.* New York: Free Press, 1975.

4. Robert J. Chaffin, "The Townshend Acts crisis, 1767–1770." *The Blackwell Encyclopedia of the American Revolution*. Jack P. Greene, and J.R. Pole, eds. Malden, Massachusetts: Blackwell, 1991; reprint 1999.

5. The Tea Party Museum, Tea Party Leaders, INK"http://www.bostonteapartyship.com/boston-tea-party-facts,"http://www.bostonteapartyship.com/boston-tea-party-facts, accessed April 25, 2012.

6. How the Boston Tea Party Began," http://www.oldsouthmeetinghouse.org/osmh_123456789files/BostonTeaPartyBegan.aspx, accessed May 1, 2012.

7. Boston Tea Party Historical Society, http://www.boston-tea-party.org/participants/participants.html, accessed May 1, 2012.

8. David Barsamian, "Chip Berlet On The Tea Party And The Rise Of Right-Wing Populism," November 2010, http://www.thesunmagazine.org/issues/419/brewing_up_trouble, accessed Oct. 24, 2011.

9. Old South Meeting House, "How the Boston Tea Party Began," http://www.oldsouthmeetinghouse.org/osmh_123456789files/BostonTeaPartyBegan.aspx, accessed May 1, 2012.

10. Old South Meeting House, "How the Boston Tea Party Began," http://www.oldsouthmeetinghouse.org/osmh_123456789files/BostonTeaPartyBegan.aspx, accessed May 1, 2012.

11. Old South Meeting House, "How the Boston Tea Party Began," http://www.oldsouthmeetinghouse.org/osmh_123456789files/BostonTeaPartyBegan.aspx, accessed May 1, 2012.

12. "The Top 10 political quotes of 2010," *Christian Science Monitor*, http://www.csmonitor.com/USA/Politics/2010/1229/The-Top-10-political-quotes-of-2010/Sarah-Palin-reload, accessed May 1, 2012.

13. John Nichols, "Palin Put a Gun Target on Giffords's District; Now a Colleague Says: 'Palin Needs to Look at Her Own Behavior,'" The *Nation*, Jan. 9, 2011.

14. Minutemen, http://www.ushistory.org/people/minutemen.htm, accessed May 2, 2012.

15. US Domestic Terrorism - Michigan Militia, History Commons, http://www.historycommons.org/timeline.jsp?timeline=us_domestic_terrorism_tmln&haitian_elite_2021_organizations=haitian_elite_2021_michigan_militia, accessed May 1, 2012.

16. Ballard C. Campbell, *Disasters, Accidents, and Crises in American History*, Facts on File, Inc., New York 2008.

17. Sam Adams Alliance, http://samadamsalliance.org/about, accessed April 28, 2012.

18. Ethan Allen Institute, http://www.ethanallen.org/, accessed April 30, 2012.

19. The James Madison Institute, http://www.jamesmadison.org/, accessed May 2, 2012.

20. Reuven S. Avi-Yonah, Irwin I. Cohn professor of law at the University of Michigan, "From the 1790s to 'No New Taxes,'" writing in "Tax Revolts: Some Succeed, Most Don't," *New York Times*, April 15, 2009.

21. http://www.teapartypatriots.org/, accessed April17, 2012.

21. http://www.teapartyexpress.org/mission, accessed April 17, 2012.

22. http://www.patriotactionnetwork.com/, accessed April 17, 2012.

23. Roy Gillispie Blakey and Gladys C. Blakey, *The Federal Income Tax,* p. 28, The Lawbook Exchange, Ltd., Clark, N.J. (2006).

24. http://www.foxnews.com/opinion/2012/03/30/no-joke-obama-corporate-tax-rates-are-worst-in-world/ #ixzz1sLLVmqAA, accessed April 17, 2012.

25. CBS News, 60 Minutes, March 25, 2011, http://www.cbsnews.com/2100-18560_162-20046867.html, accessed April 18, 2012.

26. Daniel J. Mitchell, "With Washington Now Imposing the World's Highest Corporate Tax Rate, Every Day is April Fool's Day for American Companies," *Forbes*, April 1, 2012, http://www.forbes.com/sites/danielmitchell/2012/04/01/with-washington-now-imposing-the-worlds-highest-corporate-tax-rate-every-day-is-april-fools-day-for-american-companies/, accessed April 18, 2012.

27. William Safire, "On Language: Read My Lips," *New York Times*, Sept. 04, 1988.

28. Tony Williams, *America's Beginnings: the Dramatic Events that Shaped a Nation's Character*, pp.153–56, Rowman & Littlefield Publishers, Inc., Lanham, Maryland (2010).

29. William Hogeland, author of "The Whiskey Rebellion: George Washington, Alexander Hamilton, and the Frontier Rebels Who Challenged America's Newfound Sovereignty," writing in "Tax Revolts: Some Succeed, Most Don't," *New York Times*, April 15, 2009.

CHAPTER 15

1. "Election Results 2010," *New York Times*, http://elections.nytimes.com/2010/results/senate, accessed May 3, 2012.

2. Judson Berger, "First 100 Days: Modern-Day Tea Parties Give Taxpayers Chance to Scream for Better Representation, *Fox News,* April 9, 2009, http://www.foxnews.com/politics/2009/04/09/modern-day-tea-parties-taxpayers-chance-scream-better-representation, accessed April 17, 2012.

3. Kristin Jensen, "Tea Party Patriots to Hand Out $1 Million for November Election Spending By Kristin Jensen," *Bloomberg News*, Sep 21, 2010.

4. Lee Fang, "Spontaneous Uprising? Corporate Lobbyists Helping To Orchestrate Radical Anti-Obama Tea Party Protests," April 9, 2009 http://thinkprogress.org/politics/2009/04/09/37433/lobbyists-planning-teaparties/, accessed May 4, 2012.

5. "The Forbes 400: The 400 Richest People in America," http://www.forbes.com/forbes-400/, accessed May 3, 2012.

6. "The World's Billionaires," http://www.forbes.com/billionaires/list/, accessed May 3, 2012.

7. Wikipedia, "List of Countries by GDP (nominal)," http://en.wikipedia.org/wiki/List_of_countries_by_GDP_%28nominal%29, accessed May 3, 2012.

8. Leslie Wayne, "Pulling the Wraps Off Koch Industries," *New York Times*, Nov. 20, 1994.

9. "The Principled Entrepreneur, *The American*. July–August 2007, http://www.american.com/archive/2007/july-august-magazine-contents/the-principled-entrepreneur, accessed May 4, 2012.

10. Wikipedia, Citizens for a Sound Economy," http://en.wikipedia.org/wiki/Citizens_for_a_Sound_Economy, accessed May 4, 2012.

11. SourceWatch, "C. Boyden Gray," http://www.sourcewatch.org/index.php?title=C._Boyden_Gray, accessed May 2, 2012.

12. Julie Bykowicz, "Koch Group to Honor Koch During Republican Convention," *Bloomberg*, Aug. 22, 2012, http://go.bloomberg.com/political-capital/2012-08-22/koch-group-to-honor-koch-during-republican-convention/, accessed Sept. 30, 2012.

13. Foundation Directory on-line, a subscription service, http://fconline.foundationcenter.org/fdo_grant_search.php, accessed May 4, 2012.

14. Foundation Directory on-line, a subscription service, http://fconline.foundationcenter.org/fdo_grant_search.php, accessed May 4, 2012.

15. Dana Milbank, "Dick Armey's 'tea party' history is a strange brew," *Washington Post*, March 16, 2010.
http://www.washingtonpost.com/wp-dyn/content/article/2010/03/15/AR2010031503730.html accessed March 27, 2012.

16. Nicholas Confessore, "Tea Party Group to Form Super PAC," *New York Times*, Sept. 23, 2011,
http://thecaucus.blogs.nytimes.com/2011/09/23/tea-party-group-to-form-a-super-pac/?ref=dickarmey, accessed May 4, 2012.

17. Nicholas Confessore, "Tea Party Group to Form Super PAC," *New York Times*, Sept. 23, 2011,
http://thecaucus.blogs.nytimes.com/2011/09/23/tea-party-group-to-form-a-super-pac/?ref=dickarmey, accessed May 4, 2012.

18. Nicholas Confessore, "Tea Party Group to Form Super PAC," *New York Times*, Sept. 23, 2011,
http://thecaucus.blogs.nytimes.com/2011/09/23/tea-party-group-to-form-a-super-pac/?ref=dickarmey, accessed May 4, 2012.

19.
http://www.forbes.com/sites/mattkibbe/2011/10/19/occupy-wall-street-is-certainly-no-tea-party/#comments

20.
http://abcnews.go.com/Politics/tea-party-protesters-march-washington/story?id=8557120

21. http://www.nytimes.com/2009/09/13/us/politics/13protestweb.html

22. Kate Zernike, "Unlikely Activist Who Got to the Tea Party Early," *New York Times*, Feb. 27, 2010.

23. "Dick Armey," *New York Times*,
http://topics.nytimes.com/topics/reference/timestopics/people/a/dick_armey/index.html, accessed March 27, 2012.

24. Helen Kennedy, "Tea Party Express leader Mark Williams kicked out over 'Colored People' letter," *New York Daily News*, July 18, 2010.

25. The list of affiliates includes several well-funded organizations, such as the following: 60 Plus, Americans for Prosperity, Americans for Tax Reform, Bannon Strategic Advisors, Citizens Against Government Waste, Citizens United, Constitutional Sovereignty Alliance, Contract From America, Doctor Patient Medical Association, Family Research Council, FreedomWorks, Heartland Institute, Institute for Liberty, Let Freedom Ring, Moms for America, National Taxpayers Union, Ronald Reagan Institute for, Conservative Leadership, Richard Viguerie, Tea Party Patriots Live!, Victory Media Group Affiliate Relationships, National Tea Party Federation,
http://www.thenationalteapartyfederation.com/Membership_List.html, accessed May 1, 2012.

26. Dan Eggen and Philip Rucker, "Conservative Mainstays and Fledgling Advocacy Groups Drive Health-Reform Opposition," *Washington Post*, August 16, 2009.

27. Helen Kennedy, "Tea Party Express leader Mark Williams kicked out over 'Colored People' letter," *New York Daily News*, July 18, 2010.

28. Mark Davis "Jenny Beth Martin: The head Tea Party Patriot," http://www.ajc.com/news/georgia-politics-elections/jenny-beth-martin-the-522344.html, accessed March 27, 2012.

29. Meckler resigned Feb. 23, 2012, saying in an e-mail that he had lost "influence in the leadership of the organization, and it has been that way for quite some time." "Exclusive: Co-founder Mark Meckler resigns from Tea Party Patriots," The *Daily Caller,* http://dailycaller.com/2012/02/24/exclusive-co-founder-mark-meckler-resigns-from-tea-party-patriots/#ixzz1qLJ3gaSf, accessed March 27, 2012.

30. Alex Altman, "Jenny Beth Martin - The 2010 TIME 100," *Time*, April 29, 2010, http://www.time.com/time/specials/packages/article/0,28804,1984685_1984864_1985462,00.html #ixzz1tuXbfCMl, accessed March 27, 2012.

31. Alex Altman, "Jenny Beth Martin - The 2010 TIME 100," *Time*, April 29, 2010, http://www.time.com/time/specials/packages/article/0,28804,1984685_1984864_1985462,00.html #ixzz1tuXbfCMl, accessed March 27, 2012.

32. http://www.sos.state.co.us/ccsa/ViewReports.do?ceId=3627&evId=3627&evEntityType=SN, accessed March 27, 2012.

33. Open Secrets, http://www.opensecrets.org/parties/expenddetail.php?cmte=RNC&cycle=2008&txt=MDS%20COMMUNICATIONS, accessed March 27, 2012.

34. New Hampshire Attorney General, http://128.121.25.104:8080/awweb/pdfopener?md=1&did=22179, accessed March 27, 2012.

35. According to its website, the firm offers the following services: Our attorneys offer highly specialized guidance on federal law, including the Federal Election Campaign Act, the Ethics in Government Act, the Lobbying Disclosure Act, and the Internal Revenue Code, as well as analogous state law and Congressional rules.

The legal and regulatory environment has become increasingly complex and more individuals and advocacy groups find themselves under aggressive scrutiny. Having served in national political party committees, presidential campaigns, Congress and the Executive Branch, our attorneys are uniquely qualified to assure clients that their activities will withstand the most intense review.

PRACTICE AREAS

Election Law
PACs, Super PACs candidate committees and election administration are now subject to extensive and constantly increasing federal and state regulation. We provide counsel on all campaign finance and election law matters, including organization of state and federal PACs, Super PACs and candidate committees. We assist with reporting, ongoing compliance, and defending against enforcement actions, administrative complaint and audit matters.

Lobbying and Government Ethics
Our firm counsels clients on the gift rules and other federal, state, and local lobbying registration and disclosure laws. We provide comprehensive, 50-state analysis of direct and grassroots lobbying rules. This includes state and federal rules applicable to television, mail, internet and phone programs.

Tax-Exempt Organizations
Tax-exempt organizations play an increasingly significant role in educating the public and influencing public policy. We counsel tax-exempt entities including public charities, social welfare organizations, trade associations, 527s and other political committees. All are subject to extensive federal, state and local regulation. We advise clients on all such matters, including formation of tax-exempt entities, application for recognition of tax-exempt status, corporate governance, and compliance with IRS, FEC and lobbying rules. Additionally, we provide state charities bureau registration and compliance services to charities, fundraising counsel and professional solicitors.

36. Cathleen West, Partner http://www.hvjlaw.com/west/, accessed March 27, 2012, provides the following information:

Contact
Cathleen West has extensive experience counseling clients in the areas of lobbying and ethics, and issue advocacy tax-exempt organizations. She also provides counsel in the areas of campaign finance and election law. Cathleen is a principal advisor to major corporations, governmental affairs firms, trade associations, and non-profit organizations. She is also a speaker on the topics of lobbying and ethics compliance, and tax-exempt organizations, and she has devoted her time pro bono to organizations and causes.

Prior to joining the firm in 2004, Cathleen served as a fellow on the U.S. Senate Finance Committee under Chairman Senator Charles Grassley, in the areas of tax and employee benefits law. Previously, she was a staff attorney for the American Bar Association in Washington, D.C., where she directed special projects for an ABA Commission, and was a contributor to an ABA publication.

37. http://www.hvjlaw.com/vogel/, accessed March 27, 2012.

38. http://www.hvjlaw.com/holtzman/, accessed March 27, 2012.

39. "Tea Party Patriots Receives $1,000,000 Donation," COTO Report, http://coto2.wordpress.com/2010/09/22/tea-party-patriots-receives-1000000-donation/, accessed May 4, 2012.

40. Alex Pappas, "American Majority Wants to Infuse New Tea Party Blood in System," The *Daily Caller*, Dec. 21, 2010, http://dailycaller.com/2010/12/20/american-majority-wants-to-infuse-new-tea-party-blood-in-system/

41. "Proud American," (The 9-12 Project) A Recap of the American Majority Post-Party Summit in Kansas City, accessed May 4, 2012. Also, Lee Fang, "Koch Industries Slashed WI Jobs, Helped Elect Scott Walker, Now Orchestrating Pro-Walker Protest," ThinkProgress.org, accessed May 4, 2012.

42. American Majority, American Majority Web Site, accessed August 15, 2009.

43. "Get Trained," http://americanmajority.org/, accessed May 4, 2012.

44. George Monbiot, "Are Right-Wing Libertarian Internet Trolls Getting Paid to Dumb Down Online Conversations?" AlterNet, http://www.alternet.org/media/149197/are_right-wing_libertarian_internet_trolls_getting_paid_to_dumb_down_online_conversations, accessed May 4, 2012. Also, Alex Pappas, "American Majority Wants to Infuse New Tea Party Blood in System," The Daily Caller, December 21, 2010.

CHAPTER 16

1. Ginger Gibson, "Delaware politics: From middle-class New Jersey, moral activist Christine O'Donnell knew 'God was calling,'" *Wilmington News-Journal*, Oct. 10, 2010.

2. John McCormack (2010-09-02). "Citing 'Mental Anguish,' Christine O'Donnell Sought $6.95 Million in Gender Discrimination Lawsuit Against Conservative Group." *Weekly Standard*, Sept. 2, 2010, http://www.weeklystandard.com/blogs/citing-mental-anguish-christine-odonnell-sought-69-million-gender-discrimination-lawsuit-again, accessed May 8, 2012.

3. Jonathan Weisman, (2010-08-30). "Tea Party Backs O'Donnell in Delaware." *Wall Street Journal*, Aug. 30, 2010, http://www.webcitation.org/5u8rtEaNf, accessed May 8, 2012.

4. Jessica Yellin, "Christine O'Donnell wins Delaware GOP Senate primary," Cable Network News, Sept. 15, 2010, http://www.cnn.com/2010/POLITICS/09/14/delaware.senate.primary/index.html, accessed May 8, 2012.

5. Devin Dwyer, "Christine O'Donnell, Tea Party Shock GOP Establishment in Delaware," ABC News, Sep. 14, 2010, http://abcnews.go.com/blogs/politics/2010/09/christine-odonnell-tea-party-shock-gop-establishment-in-delaware/, accessed May 8, 2012.

6. http://www.opencongress.org/roll_call/sublist/5099?party=Republican&vote=Aye, accessed May 7, 2012.

7. "Frank Wolf intro at NoVA Tea Party Luncheon," You Tube, http://www.youtube.com/watch?v=2RWEZkxnXZY, accessed May 7, 2012.

8. Janie Lorber and Eric Lipton, "G.O.P. Insider Fuels Tea Party and Suspicion," *New York Times*, Sep. 18, 2010.

9. Roger Alford and Bruce Schreiner, "Kentucky Election Results: Rand Paul Defeats Jack Conway In 2010 Senate Race," *The Huffington Post*, Nov. 2, 2010, http://www.huffingtonpost.com/2010/11/02/kentucky-election-results_n_765986.html, accessed May 8, 2012.

10. Wikipedia, William E. Simon, http://en.wikipedia.org/wiki/William_E._Simon, accessed May 8, 2012.

11. Alexander Bolton, "Tea Party sees gains in Senate," The *Hill*, May 8, 2012.

12. Ted Cruz for Senate, http://www.tedcruz.org/bio/, accessed May 8, 2012.

13. Jon C. Bruning for Senate, http://www.jonbruning.com/home/, accessed May 8, 2012.

14. OpenSecrets, http://www.opensecrets.org/races/summary.php?id=MOS2&cycle=2012, accessed May 8, 2012.

15. Politico.com, "Richard Mourdock has aura of victory vs. Richard Lugar," http://www.politico.com/news/stories/0512/76028.html, accessed May 8, 2012.

16. Federal Election Commission, http://query.nictusa.com/cgi-bin/dcdev/indexp/, accessed May 8, 2012.

17. Federal Election Commission, http://query.nictusa.com/cgi-bin/dcdev/indexp/, accessed May 8, 2012.

18. PolitiFact, "Americans for Prosperity's file," http://www.politifact.com/personalities/americans-prosperity/, accessed May 8, 2012.

19. PolitiFact, "Americans for Prosperity's file," http://www.politifact.com/personalities/americans-prosperity/, accessed May 8, 2012.

20. Chuck Marr, "New Tax Cuts in Ryan Budget Would Give Millionaires $265,000 on Top of Bush Tax Cuts," April 12, 2012, http://www.cbpp.org/cms/index.cfm?fa=view&id=3728, accessed May 8, 2012.

21. Kelsey Merrick and Jim Horney, "Chairman Ryan Gets 62 Percent of His Huge Budget Cuts from Programs for Lower-Income Americans," Center on Budget and Policy Priorities, March 23, 2012, http://www.cbpp.org/cms/index.cfm?fa=view&id=3723.

22. Tables T12-0126 and T10-0132, Tax Policy Center.

23. Chuck Marr, "Ryan Budget's Claim to Finance Its Tax Cuts for the Wealthy by Curbing Their Tax Breaks Does Not Withstand Scrutiny," Center on Budget and Policy Priorities, March 22, 2012, http://www.cbpp.org/cms/index.cfm?fa=view&id=3722.

CHAPTER 17

1. U.S. Environmental Protection Agency, "Fact Sheet: Respiratory Health Effects of Passive Smoking," Office of Research and Development and Office of Air and Radiation, Jan. 1993.

2. APCO specializes in coalition building, grassroots advocacy, media relations, online communication, opinion research, positioning and strategic counsel. Its roster of D.C. heavy hitters include former Senate Majority Leader Bob Dole (R-Kan.) and former Secretary of State Henry Kissinger. Clients of the D.C. office have included Pfizer, Dow Corning, the American Tort Reform Association, Alaska Airlines, World Wrestling Entertainment and the government of Turkey. The Hill Staff, "Message-makers: Washington's public affairs, public relations firms," May 11, 2005, http://thehill.com/business--lobby/message-makers-washingtons-public-affairs-public-relations-firms-2005-05-11.html, accessed July 26, 2007.

3. George Monbiot, "The Denial Industry," *The Guardian*, Sep. 19, 2006, http://environment.guardian.co.uk/climatechange/story/0,,1875762,00.html, accessed July 26, 2007.

4. George Monbiot, "The denial industry," The *Guardian*, Sep. 19, 2006.

5. Bill and Jim Rutenberg, "Fox News Head Sent a Policy Note to Bush," *New York Times*, Nov. 19, 2002. Also, "The Fox News Presidential Adviser," *New York Times*, Nov. 21, 2002.

6. http://www.junkscience.com/Junkman.html, accessed July 25, 2007.

7. "Kite flying of the day:"and "Ban fails to stop smoking ads," http://junkscience.com/jan01.htm, accessed July 26, 2007.

8. "Coral studies and El Niños" and "Societal collapse driven by abrupt climate change, not social, economic and political forces" and "Societal collapse driven by abrupt climate change, not social, economic and political forces," http://junkscience.com/jan01.htm, accessed July 26, 2007.

9. Robert Worth, "IN BUSINESS; Testing Toasters, Boots and S.U.V.'s," *New York Times*, April 8, 2001.

10. Richard Lindzen, "Passive Smoking: How Great a Hazard," *Consumers' Research*, July, 1991, http://tobaccodocuments.org/pm/2046323437-3484.html, accessed Kuly 25, 2007.

11. The General, "Richard Lindzen: Climate skeptic or Conspiracy theorist?" http://www.env-econ.net/2006/05/richard_lindzen.html, accessed July 26, 2007.

12. Fred S. Singer, Ed., *The Changing Global Environment*, p. vi, Reidel Publishing (Dordrecht, The Netherlands, 1975).

13. http://www.sepp.org/keyissue.html

14. Fred S. Singer, Ed., *The Changing Global Environment*, p. 5, Reidel Publishing (Dordrecht, The Netherlands, 1975).

15. Fred S. Singer, Ed., *The Changing Global Environment*, p. 4, Reidel Publishing (Dordrecht, The Netherlands, 1975).

16. James Hansen, "Review: The Threat to the Planet," *New York Review of Books*, July 13, 2006.

17. Cable Network News, "Capital Gang," Aug. 19, 2002, http://www.cato.org/research/articles/michaels-020819.html, accessed July 20, 2007.

18. Statement of Patrick J. Michaels, before the Committee on Small Business, United States House of Representatives, July 29, 1998.

19. Statement of Sen. James Inhofe, *Congressional Record*, p. S11293, Oct. 11, 2004.

20. Patrick Michaels, "Greenhouse Effect? Then Why is it Cooler?" *Washington Post*, June 15, 1986.

21. Real Climate: Climate Science From Climate Scientists, "Michael Crichton's State of Confusion," http://www.realclimate.org/index.php?p=74, accessed July 21, 2007.

22. Frederick Seitz, "A Major Deception on Global Warming," *Wall Street Journal*, June 2, 1996.

23. Frederick Seitz, "A Major Doooption on Global Warming," *Wall Street Journal*, June 12, 1996.

24. Frederick Seitz, "A Major Deception on Global Warming," *Wall Street Journal*, June 12, 1996.

25. Alexander Holzman, "PHILIP MORRIS COMPANIES INC., INTER-OFFICE CORRESPONDENCE, 120 PARK AVENUE, NEW YORK, NY 10017, Aug. 31, 1989, http://tobaccodocuments.org/pm/2023266534.html, access July 25, 2007.

26. Legacy Tobacco Documents Library, "Deposition of KARL CHRISTIAN ROVE, August 26, 1997," http://legacy.library.ucsf.edu/tid/voq07a00, accessed July 17, 2012.

27. George W. Bush, "A Comprehensive National Energy Policy," Saginaw, Michigan, Sep. 29, 2000, http://web.archive.org/web/20010111035000/http://www.georgebush.com/News/speeches/092900_energy.html.

28. Seth Borenstein, "Bush Changes Pledge on Emissions," *Philadelphia Inquirer*, March 14, 2001.

29. Clara Jeffery and Monika Bauerlein, "Let Them Eat CO2," *Huffington Post*, Nov. 1, 2006,
http://www.huffingtonpost.com/clara-jeffery-and-monika-bauerlein/let-them-eat-co2_b_3303
8.html

30. Rep. Jim McDermott, "Gratitude For the Free Press In England," U.S. House of Representatives, Extension of Remarks , June 8, 2005,
http://www.house.gov/mcdermott/sp050608a.shtml

31. Rep. Jim McDermott, "Gratitude For the Free Press In England," U.S. House of Representatives, Extension of Remarks, June 8, 2005.

32. Union of Concerned Scientists, "Oil Company Spent Nearly $16 Million to Fund Skeptic Groups, Create Confusion, Jan. 3, 2007
http://www.ucsusa.org/news/press_release/ExxonMobil-GlobalWarming-tobacco.html?wt.rs
s=rss

33. David Adam, "Royal Society tells Exxon: stop funding climate change denial," The *Guardian*, Sep. 20, 2006. One example is contained in statements of the chairman of a group called the Science and Environmental Policy Project, Frederick Seitz. Seitz, now dead, was a physicist who in the 1960s was president of the U.S. National Academy of Sciences. In 1998, he wrote a document, known as the Oregon Petition, which has been cited by almost every journalist who claims that climate change is a myth.

The document reads as follows: "We urge the United States government to reject the global warming agreement that was written in Kyoto, Japan, in December 1997, and any other similar proposals. The proposed limits on greenhouse gases would harm the environment, hinder the advance of science and technology, and damage the health and welfare of mankind. There is no convincing scientific evidence that human release of carbon dioxide, methane, or other greenhouse gases is causing or will, in the foreseeable future, cause catastrophic heating of the Earth's atmosphere and disruption of the Earth's climate. Moreover, there is substantial scientific evidence that increases in atmospheric carbon dioxide produce many beneficial effects upon the natural plant and animal environments of the Earth."

Below is a letter from Bob Ward, Senior Manager, Policy Communication to Nick Thomas, Director, Corporate Affairs, ExxonMobil.

THE ROYAL SOCIETY

Nick Thomas
Director, Corporate Affairs
Esso UK Limited
UK Public Affairs
ExxonMobil House, Mailpoint 8
Ermyn Bay
Leatherhead
Surrey
KT22 8UX

6-9 Carlton House Terrace
London SW1Y 5AG
tel +44 020 7451 2516
fax +44 020 7451 2615
mob +44 07811 320346

www.royalsoc.ac.uk

4 September 2006
Our ref: BW/NT/CC

Dear Nick

Thank-you for your recent letter and accompanying copies of the 2005 ExxonMobil 'Corporate Citizenship Report' and the 'UK and Ireland Corporate Citizenship' brochure. I have read both with interest, but I am writing to express my disappointment at the inaccurate and misleading view of the science of climate change that these documents present.

In particular, I was very surprised to read the following passage from the section on Environmental performance under the sub-heading of 'Uncertainty and risk' (p.23) in the 'Corporate Citizenship Report':

"While assessments such as those of the IPCC have expressed growing confidence that recent warming can be attributed to increases in greenhouse gases, these conclusions rely on expert judgment rather than objective, reproducible statistical methods. Taken together, gaps in the scientific basis for theoretical climate models and the interplay of significant natural variability make it very difficult to determine objectively the extent to which recent climate changes might be the result of human actions."

These statements also appear, of course, in the ExxonMobil document on 'Tomorrow's Energy', which was published in February. As I mentioned during our meeting in July, these statements are very misleading. The "expert judgment" of the Intergovernmental Panel on Climate Change was actually based on objective and quantitative analyses and methods, including advanced statistical appraisals, which carefully accounted for the interplay of natural variability, and which have been independently reproduced.

Furthermore, these statements in your documents are not consistent with the scientific literature that has been published on this issue. For instance, Chapter 12 of the contribution of IPCC working group 1 to the Third Assessment Report provided an overview of scientific papers relating to the 'Detection of climate change and attribution of causes' that had been published up to the end of 2000. The chapter concluded: "In the light of new evidence and taking into account the remaining uncertainties, most of the observed warming over the last 50 years is likely to have been due to the increase in greenhouse gas

President Lord Rees of Ludlow
Executive Secretary Stephen Cox CVO

Founded in 1660, the Royal Society
is the independent scientific academy
of the UK, dedicated to promoting
excellence in science

Registered Charity No 207043

concentrations". The chapter gives a detailed overview of the evidence, citing 167 references, and points out that "The warming over the last 50 years due to anthropogenic greenhouse gases can be identified despite uncertainties in forcing due to anthropogenic sulphate aerosol and natural factors (volcanoes and solar irradiance)".

What is even more surprising about your documents' lack of consistency with the IPCC's assessment is that one of ExxonMobil's employees, Haroon Kheshgi, was one of the contributing authors on Chapter 12.

Since the publication of the IPCC Third Assessment Report in 2001, many other papers have been published which record new evidence about the causes of climate change. For instance, a major review article by the International Ad Hoc Detection and Attribution Group ('Detecting and attributing external influences on the climate system: a review of recent advances', published in the 1 May 2005 issue of the *Journal of Climate* – copy enclosed) concluded that "the recent research supports and strengthens the IPCC Third Assessment Report conclusion that 'most of the global warming over the past 50 years is likely due to the increase in greenhouse gases'". This review paper cites 147 references.

The IPCC's conclusions have been endorsed by the world's other leading scientific organisations. For example, the science academies of the G8 nations plus Brazil, China and India, in June 2005 published a joint statement on 'Global response to climate change'. This statement pointed out that "it is likely that most of the warming in recent decades can be attributed to human activities".

It is very disappointing that the ExxonMobil 2005 Corporate Citizenship Report, like 'Tomorrow's Energy', leaves readers with such an inaccurate and misleading impression of the evidence on the causes of climate change that is documented in the scientific literature. It is very difficult to reconcile the misrepresentations of climate change science in these documents with ExxonMobil's claim to be an industry leader.

At our meeting in July, I also told you of my concerns about the support that ExxonMobil has been giving to organisations that have been misinforming the public about the science of climate change. You indicated that ExxonMobil would not be providing any further funding to these organisations. I would be grateful if you could let me know when ExxonMobil plans to carry out this pledge, and if you could provide me with a list of which organisations will no longer be receiving funding.

I have carried out an ad hoc survey on the websites of organisations that are listed in the ExxonMobil 2005 Worldwide Giving Report for 'public information and policy research', which is published on your website. Of those organisations whose websites feature information about climate change, I found that 25 offered views that are consistent with the scientific literature. However, some 39 organisations were featuring information on their websites that misrepresented the science of climate change, by outright denial of the evidence that greenhouse gases are driving climate change, or by overstating the amount and significance of uncertainty in knowledge, or by conveying a misleading impression of the potential impacts of anthropogenic climate change. My analysis indicates that ExxonMobil last year provided more than $2.9 million to organisations in the United States which misinformed the public about climate change through their websites.

As you know, the Worldwide Giving Report only lists organisations in the United States which have received support from ExxonMobil. I would be grateful if you could let me know which organisations in the UK and other European countries have been receiving funding from ExxonMobil so that I can work out which of these have been similarly providing inaccurate and misleading information to the public.

I appreciate that I have raised some substantial issues in this letter, but I would be grateful to receive a prompt response from you – I have shared the contents of your documents with some climate researchers who are Fellows of the Royal Society and it would be useful to update them about whether ExxonMobil will be continuing to express views that are inconsistent with the findings of their work.

Yours sincerely

Bob Ward
Senior Manager, Policy Communication
email bob.ward@royalsoc.ac.uk

34. David Adam, "Royal Society tells Exxon: stop funding climate change denial," The *Guardian*, Sep. 20, 2006

35. Company records show that ExxonMobil handed over hundreds of thousands of pounds to such lobby groups in 2008. These include the National Center for Policy Analysis (NCPA) in Dallas, Texas, which received $75,000 and the Heritage Foundation in Washington, D.C., which received $50,000. David Adam, "ExxonMobil continuing to fund climate sceptic groups, records show," The *Guardian*, July 1, 2009.

36. Andrew C. Revkin and Matthew L. Wald, "Material Shows Weakening Of Climate Change Reports," *New York Times*, March 20, 2007.

37. "Lobbying From Within," *New York Times*, June 17, 2005.

38. Chris Mooney, "Some Like It Hot," *Mother Jones*, May/June 2005.

39. Chris Mooney, "Some Like it Hot," *Mother Jones*, May/June, 2005.

40. Sharon Begley, "The Truth About Denial," *Newsweek*, Aug. 13, 2007.

41. Claudia Cattaneo, "Exxon Mobil CEO takes aim at environmentalists," *Financial Post*, May 29, 2008 http://www.financialpost.com/story.html?id=547068.

42. The full text of Dr. Michael MacCracken's letter to ExxonMobil Chairman and CEO Lee Raymond can be found at http://www.climatesciencewatch.org/index.php/csw/details/maccracken-exxon-letter/ and is pasted below. Individually addressed copies of the letter were also sent to all other members of the ExxonMobil board of directors.

Office of the U.S. Global Change Research Program
September 26, 2002

Lee R. Raymond
Chairman and Chief Executive
ExxonMobil Corp.
5959 Las Colinas Blvd.
Irving, TX 75039

RE: With regard to the ExxonMobil facsimile on February 6, 2001 from Dr. A. G. Randol to Mr. John Howard of the Council on Environmental Quality

Dear Mr. Raymond:

As former director of the National Assessment Coordination Office of the US Global Change Research Program, I am writing to you in order to provide a response to the critical comments from ExxonMobil about the US National Assessment of the Potential Consequences of Climate Variability and Change. In that the National Assessment report provided the basis for the US National Communication released in June, I feel it important to clarify the issues and specifically address a number of the criticisms.

On August 10, 2000, ExxonMobil ran an advertisement in the Washington Post entitled "Political cart before a scientific horse" that was severely critical of the draft synthesis report[1]. In partial fulfillment of a Congressional call for periodic assessments in the Global Change Research Act of 1990, the preparation of this report had, at this point, been in progress for several years under the leadership of a federal advisory committee.

Without having participated in the Federal Register review process that had led up to the draft report being made available for public comment (after two rounds of technical review), nor having participated in the public meetings discussing the draft report and its contents until the very end, the ExxonMobil proceeded to make a number of charges in the advertisement, generally based on rather poor understanding of what was being done and why the National Assessment was being undertaken.

With respect to general tone of the advertisement, ExxonMobil charged that the report was a "political document" and "not objective." Actual examination of the report would have shown that this report was prepared by a panel of experts having no political connections and that the report had been very carefully reviewed by technical experts to ensure objectivity. The federal advisory committee, officially named the National Assessment Synthesis Team (NAST), was composed of widely recognized scientific and economic experts from universities, industry, NGO, and government centers and institutions. The NAST was in turn overseen by a review panel under the auspices of the President's National Science and Technology Council, and included two Nobel prize winners, among other leading figures.

In that the report neither recommended any policies nor specifically concerned the Kyoto Protocol that was being discussed by the Presidential candidates, it is not at all obvious how the document was a case of "the administration [seeking] to gain support for its own policies, which could damage the economy and employment" As a reading of the report would have made evident, the whole intent of the report was to provide information to facilitate adaptation to the emerging and projected changes so as to reduce potential damages and limit damage to the economy. [I should add that, as for others, it will be important for ExxonMobil to be taking account of the changing climate to ensure early preparation and effective adaptation to avoid the most severe consequences.]

As a general conclusion, the ExxonMobil advertisement advocated more research while saying it would be too expensive to deal with the problem. The National Assessment did indeed recommend more research, but at the same time indicated that there is sufficient knowledge to justify consideration of steps to adapt to the changes in climate now underway and that are inevitable as a result of the world's present commitment to use of fossil fuels for energy. In my earlier experience, arguing for study of adaptation had been a position of industry[2], but now when this was attempted, ExxonMobil argued this was premature. Roughly, this is equivalent to turning your back on the future and putting your head in the sand—with this position, it is no wonder ExxonMobil is the target of environmental and shareholder critics.

In addition to offering general criticisms, the ExxonMobil advertisement made several specific comments about the state of the science. The criticisms are quoted below, accompanied by a response:

1. Advertisement: Climate models "are not yet capable of predicting Earths global climate." Response: A reading of both the national assessment report and the reports of the Intergovernmental Panel on Climate Change (IPCC[3]) makes clear that scientists are not claiming to make predictions—it is widely agreed that models cannot predict ahead exactly what will happen over the coming century. Instead, the scientific community is using models to construct projections; that is, plausible what-if estimations of what the future might look like. Based on their ability to represent the major features of the climate's behavior, these models are quite capable of doing this. I rather imagine that each of you constructs what-if scenarios all the time—what if the price of oil goes over $30 per barrel; what if there is a war in the Middle East, etc.? As the National Assessment report made clear: "Scenarios are plausible alternative futureseach an example of what might happen under particular assumptions. Scenarios are not specific predictions or forecasts. Rather scenarios provide a starting point for examining questions about an uncertain future and can help us visualize alternative futures in concrete and human terms. The military and industry frequently use these powerful tools for future planning in high-stakes situations. Using scenarios helps to identify vulnerabilities and plan for contingencies" (page 4).
2. Advertisement: "Today's global models simply dont work at the regional level. For example, one of the report models says the Great Lakes' water level will be five feet lower; the other says it will be one foot higher (italics in original)."
Response: Studies reported in the IPCC report indicate that climate models generally give quite similar results when evaluated at the subcontinental level. Indeed, there are shortcomings in the capabilities of climate models for representing the details of prospective changes at the regional level (where a region is roughly the size of one to a few states), but the types of shortcomings mainly concern whether the change is likely to be a bit larger or smaller than the mean change for that continent or that area of the subcontinen—u(not at all whether there will be no change or a significant change. Thus, while the models may not give reliable indications of whether the temperature rise in Detroit will be larger or smaller than in Atlanta, both will be warming substantially. With respect to the specific example for the Great Lakes that is mentioned in the advertisement, a bit of reading would have shown that this study actually used the results from 9 models (the use of 2 was the minimum encouraged for all the activities in the National Assessment) and 8 of the 9 gave a substantial decrease in Great Lakes levels. That we included results from models with differing results in our analysis is exactly what one is supposed to do in a scenario analysis—consider the range of possible outcomes so as to not too narrowly

constrain the consideration of vulnerabilities. Does ExxonMobil only consider scenarios that foresee a single future possibility, and only when it knows exactly what the future will bring? When ExxonMobil prepares to develop an oil field, do your experts know exactly how much each well will produce, or do they convey a sense of things to you and consider various possibilities?

3. Advertisement: "The overview report was released even though most of the underlying reports and analyses are not yet available for scientific peer review or public comment." Response: In that assessment and analysis is really an ongoing process and not something that will or should ever end, the report of the NAST was a snapshot of what was known at the time, taken after many of the underlying assessment activities had prepared their findings and, although only some had been published, many had also been reported in journal publications and in other traditional ways. In addition, the Foundation report of 600 pages prepared by the NAST provided all the detailed backup information to substantiate the summary provided in the Overview report of 150 pages. The chapters of the Foundation report, which were not even mentioned in the advertisement, are full, peer-reviewed articles with extensive references for all the findings. These full scientific papers were prepared in close association with the various regional and sectoral assessment teams (you can go to our Web site http://www.usgcrp.gov and under Assessments gain access to all the materials). This Foundation report had simultaneously been released for public comment, and so everything in the Overview report was fully documented and reviewed both technically and as part of the public review process. Quite clearly, in contradiction to the ExxonMobil charge, all the information that would have been needed for review of the Overview document was readily available (and, in any case, ExxonMobil never even asked for such materials or participated in the review).

I could go on, but I hope this suffices to make clear that more thorough consideration and investigation should have been given by ExxonMobil to the content and process of the National Assessment.

The National Assessment report was delivered to Congress in November 2000 at the conclusion of NAST's term, which had been extended from earlier in the year in order to provide time to fulfill the many review requirements that were called for and completed. The report was later published by Cambridge University Press. So that you can personally consider the appropriateness of the National Assessment's findings, I am including a copy of the final report and a copy of the advertisement for your consideration.

The next step in the attack on the National Assessment came in February 2001, when Dr. A. G. Randol of ExxonMobil sent a facsimile to the new Administration urging the termination of the involvement of four individuals involved in climate change activities (see http://www.nrdc.org/media/docs/020403.pdf as it was the NRDC that made this communication available). ExxonMobil has already been criticized publicly for urging that Dr. Robert Watson, who had become chief scientist at the World Bank after a career in NASA and the White House Office of Science and Technology Policy (OSTP), not be supported by the US in the IPCC elections. For those interested in keeping the IPCC focus on science and uncertainties about climate change, it did seem strange that an economist was ultimately supported by the US and elected in the spring of 2002. Of the other three named in Randol's communication, Dr. Rosina Bierbaum's appointment at OSTP was, not surprisingly, not renewed (she is now dean of the Department of Natural Resources at the University of Michigan); and Mr. Jeffrey Miotke, who was a career foreign service officer simply representing our country's official position, was essentially harassed out of that position (rather a harsh penalty for a very capable public servant carrying out his instructions). And I am the fourth, named presumably as a representative of all those who participated in the US National Assessment.

Although the Administration had originally distanced itself somewhat from the National Assessment, discussions held as part of my on-going participation in the preparation of the

Impacts and Adaptation chapter of the recent US Climate Action Report 2002 , led the Administration to come to accept the National Assessment findings as the basis of that chapter in the report (the report can be viewed at http://www.epa.gov/globalwarming/publications/car/index.html). While release of the report by the Administration in late May was accompanied by a bit of a media stir, the results of the National Assessment that were presented had been carefully reviewed and approved by all the agencies and by the key personnel in the Executive Office. I would particularly urge you to also read Chapter 6 in order to see how carefully the National Assessment and the Climate Action Report present the state of knowledge and uncertainties and then offer a range of insights about the types of changes and impacts that those of us in the US are likely to experience. ExxonMobil can choose to ignore such information (e.g., how conditions in Alaska are rather rapidly changing and the implications this will have), but it will be doing so at its economic peril for it is very clear that the climate in coming decades will be different, perhaps substantially different than in the past.

As an example of how various groups are responding to the findings of the National Assessment, the US Department of Transportation (DOT) is convening a workshop on October 1-2 to consider the vulnerability to climate variations and change of the US transportation infrastructure and operations. As just a few examples of the types of issues that are expected to be considered, DOT has recognized that many airports, rail lines, roads, and port facilities are located in low-lying coastal areas exposed to rising sea level and increasing storm surge heights, that an increased incidence of heavy rains (a trend already evident during the 20th century) may increase the scour below bridges, that the lower levels of the Great Lakes and some river systems are likely to cause problems for barge and ship traffic, and so forth. The objective of the workshop is to identify potential threats and then figure out what more information and what types of approaches could help to alleviate potential damages and ensure effective investment of transportation resources. Having the details of exactly when and how the changes will occur is not necessary for consideration of potential vulnerabilities and possible approaches to amelioration, and those participating are coming not to argue about uncertainties, but to figure out how even uncertain knowledge can be considered in their planning.

With the conclusion of the overall assessment activities, my assignment with the USGCRP will be ending at the end of September; at that point, the last of the "ExxonMobil Four" will be out of the Administration. For your information, my undergraduate degree is in engineering from Princeton, my Ph.D. is in Applied Science from the University of California, and I have been employed by the University of California's Lawrence Livermore National Laboratory for 34 years, leading work in my research areas of air quality and climate modeling for 25 years prior to coming to Washington to assist the US Global Change Research Program starting in 1993. For the National Assessment, which began in 1997, my role as executive director of the National Assessment Coordination Office was as a facilitator, helping to coordinate the work of the synthesis panel referred to above and more than a score of regional and sectoral assessments that were also underway.

While my departure may be satisfying to ExxonMobil, I can assure you that this will not make the scientific challenge of climate change and its impacts go away. That 150 countries unanimously agree about the science of this issue is not because of some "green" conspiracy, but because of the solid scientific underpinning for this issue. Certainly, there are uncertainties, but decisions are made under uncertainty all the time—that is what executives are well paid to do. In this case, ExxonMobil is on the wrong side of the international scientific community, the wrong side of the findings of all the world's leading academies of science, and the wrong side of virtually all of the world's countries as expressed, without dissent, in the IPCC reports. As well, ExxonMobil may well find itself having to comply with the Kyoto Protocol in its international operations even if it has discouraged movement on the issue here in the US. To call ExxonMobil's position out of the mainstream is thus a gross understatement. There can be all kinds of perspectives about what one might or might not do to start to limit the extent of the change[4], but to be in opposition to the key scientific findings is rather appalling for such an established and scientific organization.

I offer this advice to you in remembrance of my great grandfather, Samuel Calvin Tate Dodd, who a century ago was legal counsel to John D. Rockefeller (notably, he took no stock to ensure his opinions would not be tainted by the economic implications of his advice). What I rather imagine he would say is that you are on the wrong side of history, and you need to find a way to change your position. The Bishops of the Catholic Church have put out a very thoughtful statement that I commend to your attention (copy included) about what the basis for your consideration should be. I would be pleased to help arrange suitable speakers if ExxonMobil changes its mind and looks forward responsibly into the future and the impacts likely to affect not only ExxonMobil and society, but your children and grandchildren.

Sincerely yours,

Michael MacCracken, retiring Senior Scientist
Office of the U. S. Global Change Research Program
(on assignment from the Lawrence Livermore National Laboratory)
Enclosures:
National Assessment Overview Report
Copy of ExxonMobil Advertisement of August 10, 2000
IPCC Synthesis Report (including Summary for Policymakers and Technical Summary reports of the three IPCC Working Groups
"Global Climate Change: a plea for dialogue, prudence and the common good," a statement of the U.S. Catholic Bishops

[1] This was actually not the first involvement of ExxonMobil regarding the National Assessment; a few years ago an executive in Exxon's Gulf Coast region reportedly tried actively to halt the participation of the EPA's Gulf Coast laboratory in the EPA's support for the Gulf Coast assessment led by Southern University on behalf of four Historically Black Colleges and Universities. EPA headquarters ensured the effort proceeded.

[2] Indeed, Dr. Brian Flannery of ExxonMobil asked for a study to "augment and contribute to the IPCC" (just as the US National Assessment was designed to do) in his June 20, 2001 letter to Dr. Ralph Cicerone concerning the June 2001 National Academy of Sciences (NAS) study. The National Assessment was just such a study, which was why its findings were endorsed in the NAS report, which is clearly evident if, as the Flannery letter urged, "interested people will read the full report."

[3] IPCC brings together the scientific expertise of about 150 countries, producing consensus assessments on a periodic basis. A copy of the most recent IPCC Synthesis Report is included for your information.

[4] While a range of positions is possible, it seems particularly strange that ExxonMobil takes the position that it does in that future global warming will be caused most by emissions from use of coal rather than by emissions from use of petroleum or natural gas.

A note on sources referenced in the letter:
LINK to the U.S. National Assessment of the Potential Consequences of Climate Variability and Change

LINK to ExxonMobil operative Randy Randol's February 6, 2001, memo to the White House Council on Environmental Quality, is posted on the Natural Resources Defense Council Web site.

The EPA global warming Web site, recently reactivated and revamped after 4 years of inactivity (see our October 20 entry on this), no longer features the U.S. Climate Action Report 2002 document at the link cited in MacCracken's letter. The report can be accessed via a LINK to the archived former EPA global warming site.

The U.S. Climate Action Report 2002 is also available on CD from the Global Change Research Information Office online catalog.

43. Sec. 1343. Fraud by wire, radio, or television

> Whoever, having devised or intending to devise any scheme or artifice to defraud, or for obtaining money or property by means of false or fraudulent pretenses, representations, or promises, transmits or causes to be transmitted by means of wire, radio, or television communication in interstate or foreign commerce, any writings, signs, signals, pictures, or sounds for the purpose of executing such scheme or artifice, shall be fined under this title or imprisoned not more than 20 years, or both. If the violation occurs in relation to, or involving any benefit authorized, transported, transmitted, transferred, disbursed, or paid in connection with, a presidentially declared major disaster or emergency (as those terms are defined in section 102 of the Robert T. Stafford Disaster Relief and Emergency Assistance Act (42 U.S.C. 5122)), or affects a financial institution, such person shall be fined not more than $1,000,000 or imprisoned not more than 30 years, or both.

44. Kristin L. Smith Poppenberg, "Corporate Officers May Face Personal Criminal Liability for Building Code Violations," http://library.findlaw.com/2004/Mar/10/133333.html.

45. See, e.g., Margaret P. Spencer and Ronald R. Sims, *Eds., Corporate misconduct: the legal, societal, and management issues*, Quorum Books, Westport, Conn. (1995).

46. See endnote 33 for the text of the letter.

47. Jeffrey Ernest Grell, author of *Grell on RICO*, http://www.ricoact.com/

48. FrontLine online "Inside the Tobacco Deal," http://www.pbs.org/wgbh/pages/frontline/shows/settlement/interviews/blakey.html

49. Rebecca Leber,"As Exxon CEO Calls Global Warming's Impacts 'Manageable', Colorado Wildfires Shutter Climate Lab," Climate Progress / News Report, June 28, 2012, http://www.nationofchange.org/exxon-ceo-calls-global-warming-s-impacts-manageable-colorado-wildfires-shutter-climate-lab-134089452, accessed July 17, 2012.

50. Intergovernmental Panel on Climate Change. IPCC Expert Meeting On Industrial Technology Development, Transfer And Diffusion. Bilthoven, Netherlands. UNT Digital Library. http://digital.library.unt.edu/ark:/67531/metadc29369/. Accessed July 17, 2012.

51. Intergovernmental Panel on Climate Change. IPCC Expert Meeting On Industrial Technology Development, Transfer And Diffusion. Bilthoven, Netherlands. UNT Digital Library. http://digital.library.unt.edu/ark:/67531/metadc29369/. Accessed July 17, 2012.

52. Thomas Stilson, "ExxonMobil CEO Rex Tillerson Discusses the Future of Energy and Environmental Issues to Stanford Community," *Stanford Review*, Feb. 28, 2009, http://stanfordreview.org/article/exxonmobil-ceo-rex-tillerson-discusses-future-ener

CHAPTER 18

1. Josh Kraushaar, "Chuck Hagel to call it quits," Politico.com, Sept. 9, 2007, http://www.politico.com/news/stories/0907/5715.html, accessed Aug. 25, 2012.

2. http://www.vote-smart.org

3. Brad Johnson, " Inhofe: God Says Global Warming Is A Hoax," ThinkProgress, March 9, 2012, http://thinkprogress.org/climate/2012/03/09/441515/inhofe-god-says-global-warming-is-a-hoax/, accessed Aug. 25, 2012.

4. RealClearPolitics, "Oklahoma Senate," http://www.realclearpolitics.com/epolls/2008/senate/ok/oklahoma_senate-921.html, accessed Aug. 25, 2012.

5. Profile: Koch Industries, Inc., http://www.desmogblog.com/koch-industries-inc, accessed Aug. 25, 2012.

6. "WEPCO Listed Among Big donors to GOP's Policy Issues'Forum,'" Madison, Wi., *Capital Times*, July 31, 1997, p 1A.

7. "Tri-state-area lobbyists," Gannett News Service, July 1, 1997.

8. Jeffrey St. Clair, "U.S.-Environment: Energy Companies Blow Off Smog Rules," Inter Press Service English News Wire, Jan. 28, 1997.

CHAPTER 19

1. Bill Summary & Status, 105th Congress (1997 - 1998). S.RES.98, http://thomas.loc.gov/cgi-bin/bdquery/z?d105:S.RES.98:, accessed Sept. 30, 2012

2. Newell, P., *Climate for change: non-state actors and the global politics of the greenhouse*. Cambridge University Press (2000).

3. Hoover's Profile, "Patton Boggs LLP," Answers.com, http://www.answers.com/topic/patton-boggs-llp?cat=biz-fin, accessed Aug. 10, 2007.

4. Jeremy Leggett, *The Carbon War: dispatches from the end of the oil century*, Peguin Press (1999).

5. Jeremy Leggett, *The Carbon War: dispatches from the end of the oil century*, Peguin Press (1999).

6. "Clinton Secures Place in History, Does Nothing," *World Climate Report*, p. 1, Nov. 10, 1997.

7. William Drozdiak, "Allies Scorn U.S. Plan To Cut Gas Emissions," *International Herald Tribune*, A1, Oct. 24, 1997

8. United Nations Framework Convention on Climate Change, Provisional List of Participants, Oct. 17, 1997.

9. http://www.cleanairprogress.org/about/index.asp, accessed Sep. 27, 2007.

10. The Center for Food Integrity, "Our Mission," http://www.foodintegrity.org/index.html, accessed Aug. 2, 2007.

11. The Center for Food Integrity, "Our Supporters," http://www.foodintegrity.org/index.html, accessed Aug. 2, 2007.

12. According to Coke, the role of the institute is to support nutrition research, education, and outreach. According to PR Week, the institute will also "communicate with health professionals and consumers about nutrition, physical activity, and health maintenance issues." Betsy McKay, "Defensive Coke Backs Research That Asks: Is Sugar All Bad?" *Wall Street Journal*, Oct. 22, 2004.

13. Among other things, it placed an advertisement in a Capitol Hill newspaper claiming that "In America, you wait in line to see a movie. In government-run health care systems, you wait to see a doctor." Kevin Sack, "For Filmmaker, 'Sicko' Is a Jumping-Off Point for Health Care Change," *New York Times*, June 24, 2007.

14. Reckitt Benckiser, http://www.homesolutionsnews.us/, accessed Aug. 2, 2007.

15. CNW Group, "Media Advisory - International health experts to reveal good and bad world hygiene habits," Aug. 29, 2006, http://www.newswire.ca/en/releases/archive/August2006/29/c9189.html, accessed Aug. 2, 2007.

16. The hundreds of other sham organizations that purport to represent "citizens" or constitute "alliances," such as—
- *The Marine Preservation Association,* a non-profit organization created and funded by about fifteen major oil companies ranging from Exxon to Texaco, that funnels money into efforts to repeal oil spill liability laws in states from Maine to California. MPA sounds as if it's dedicated to protecting the environment, but its articles of incorporation say MPA is "organized exclusively to promote the welfare and interests of the petroleum and energy industries."
- *The National Wetlands Coalition,* a group that sports an eco-sensitive logo of a waterbird in flight over cattails and marsh grasses, but is "at the forefront of an aggressive effort to rein in federal wetlands rules," according to the *Washington Post*. With an annual budget of $400,000 and a membership list that includes Exxon, Shell, Texaco and a wide range of real estate interests, the coalition is seeking multi-billion dollar buyouts from Federal taxpayers as the price of allowing swamplands and marshes to remain undeveloped.
- *Responsible Industry for a Safe Environment (RISE),* a half-million dollar per year lobbying group supported by pesticide manufacturers that is "aiming to kill" proposals

that lawn care companies be required to post warnings after spraying chemicals that can cause cancer and nervous system damage.

- *The Safe Buildings Alliance,* a group of three former manufacturers of asbestos, peddles the feel-good message that "you have more of a chance of being hit by lightning than dying from asbestos," in the words of its, vice president, Jeff Taylor. Never mind that some experts put the numbers of Americans killed by exposure to the cancer-causing mineral at 100,000 over the last several decades.

17. Ross Gelbspan, *The Heat is On: the high stakes battle over Earth's threatened climate,* p. 119, Addison Wesley (Reading MA, 1997).

18. Pearlman operates out of Patton, Boggs and Blow, one of Washington's premier law/lobbying firms. He refuses to reveal his clients, but they must include the Southern Company, a major coal-burning electric utility, because Pearlman is almost invariably accompanied by one of its officials on his numerous foreign trips. According to its IRS charter, the Council's purpose is to represent U.S.-based energy companies "whose business could be adversely affected by laws related to potential global climate change."

19. Daniel Lashof, Natural Resources Defense Council.

20. Personal observations.

21. "Global Climate Coalition," *Corporate Watch*.

22. International Climate Change Partnership, "ICCP Core Beliefs," and "ICCP Membership Information," http://www.iccp.net/membership.html, accessed Aug. 2, 2007.

23. http://www.heartland.org/Article.cfm?artId=9557, accessed Aug. 2, 2007.

24. http://www.cato.org/dailys/6-30-97.html, and more recently, "Is the Sky Really Falling? A Review of Recent Global Warming Scare Stories," Policy Analysis no. 576, August 23, 2006, http://www.cato.org/people/michaels.html, both accessed Aug. 2, 2006.

25. http://www.cei.org/gencon/014,02849.cfm, accessed Aug. 2, 2007.

26. The firm's chief executive officer, David Finn, said in a March 24, 1994 advertisement in the *New York Times* that "In my family, being Jewish has always meant devotion to study and ethical behavior." (Myra Peabody Gossens, founder of her own firm, which she "guided from formation to merger with Rudder Finn," was honored with a Skirts in Power Award. "D.C. Chamber Honors Six Business women," *Washington Afro-American*, May 28, 1994.)

27. "CSE Criticizes Clinton's reliance on 'Junk Science'," U.S. Newswire, June 27, 1997.

28. Fred Pearce, "Greenhouse Wars," *New Scientist* p. 38, July 19, 1997.

29. Ross Gelbspan, *The Heat is On: the high stakes battle over Earth's threatened climate,* p. 45, Addison Wesley (Reading MA, 1997).

30. John Braden, "The True State of the Planet (Book Reviews)," *American Journal of Agricultural Economics*, p. 472, May 1, 1996.

31. Gary Lee, "Industry Funds Global-Warming Skeptics; Scientists Dispute Charges That Oil and Coal Money Biased Their Work," *Washington Post*, p. A8, March 21, 1996.

32. The firm's chief executive officer, David Finn, said in a March 24, 1994 advertisement in the *New York Times* that "In my family, being Jewish has always meant devotion to study and ethical behavior." (Myra Peabody Gossens, founder of her own firm, which she "guided from formation to merger with Rudder Finn," was honored with a Skirts in Power Award. "D.C. Chamber Honors Six Business women," *Washington Afro-American*, May 28, 1994.)

33. Octavio Emilio Nuiry, "Spin Doctors," *Hispanic*, July 31, 1994.

34. Ross Gelbspan, *The Heat is On: the high stakes battle over Earth's threatened climate*, p. 56, Addison Wesley (Reading MA, 1997).

35. Inter Press Service English Newswire, "Environment: U.N. Climate Conference Opens, Some Nations Backtrack," July 9, 1996.

36. John Ydstie, "Oil Industry Says Market Forces Cause High Cost of Gas," *All Things Considered*, National Public Radio, April 30, 1996.

37. Alexander Miles, "Higher Fuel Economy Costly to Cut Fuel Use," Reuters, Aug. 3, 1995.

38. Greenwire, Aug. 8, 1997, citing *The Journal of Commerce*, June 23, 1997.

39. The firm's chief executive officer, David Finn, said in a March 24, 1994 advertisement in the *New York Times* that "In my family, being Jewish has always meant devotion to study and ethical behavior." (Myra Peabody Gossens, founder of her own firm, which she "guided from formation to merger with Rudder Finn," was honored with a Skirts in Power Award. "D.C. Chamber Honors Six Business women," *Washington Afro-American*, May 28, 1994.)

40. Peter Stone, "The Heat's On," *National Journal*, p. 1505, July 26, 1997.

41. Curtis A. Moore and Alan S. Miller *Green Gold: Japan, Germany, the United States, and the Race for Environmental Technology*, p. 133, Beacon Press (Boston, 1994).

42. Testimony of Chris Farrand, Peabody Coal, Committee on Environment and Public Works, U.S. Senate, Oct. 29, 1981, Washington, D.C.

43. *Washington Post*, "Washington Post Media," **citing** 2005 Washington Leadership Study, QSA Research & Strategy, http://www.washingtonpostads.com/adsite/contact/international/page1952.html, accessed Aug. 1, 2007.

44. Find "Climate of Fear" by Richard Lindzen. Policy Matters 06-10. (April 2006) at the website.

45. 29 April, 2004
"Take global climate policy, long a favorite bludgeon for the enviro-lobby. Environmental activists and foreign leaders have metaphorically all but shot, buried, exhumed, drawn, quartered, and cast to the four winds the Bush administration for 'abandoning' the Kyoto global warming treaty. Last year, however, proved to be a watershed in global climate policy and science that may vindicate the President's decision. For starters, the Kyoto treaty was politically doomed when Russia finally rejected it. Their reason? Putin's economic minister Andrei Illarionov told reporters the treaty would place 'significant limitations on the economic growth of Russia.' This was an especially serious setback for Kyoto backers, as the treaty's emissions-trading provisions already granted Russia a sweetheart economic deal."
Source: "Where Are the Weapons of Mass Environmental Destruction?" AEOnline 4/29/04

1 September, 2001
"The key features of the climate change debate are large degrees of uncertainty and a long time horizon. Although it is fairly well-established that the Earth's atmosphere has warmed somewhat (one degree Fahrenheit) during the past century, it's not clear why this happened. The warming may have been due to human impositions (the burning of fossil fuels and other incidents of industrial growth), or to natural solar or climate variations, or to some of each. Whatever the causes, we don't know if future warming trends will be large or small, or whether the net environmental and economic consequences (including both beneficial and harmful effects) may be large or small."
Source: "The Kyoto Treaty Deserved to Die" AEOnline, 9/1/01

46. 14 October, 1997
"[I]f global climate change occurs as gradually as the Intergovernmental Panel on Climate Change has predicted, policymakers can safely take several decades to plan a response, and scientists will have enough time to develop cost-effective and anti-climate-change strategies. Implementation of current proposals for mitigation measures—measures to stabilize the concentration of greenhouse gases in the atmosphere—would be both costly and ineffective."
Source: "Global Climate Change and Human Health," ACSH 10/97

47. "Given the severe macroeconomic impacts the Kyoto Protocol would impose on the United States, including reducing U.S. GDP by 1–4 percent, slowing wage growth significantly, worsening the distribution of income, and reducing growth in living standards, Dr. Thorning called for a new approach. Voluntary measures to reduce CO_2 emissions should include modifications to U.S. tax policy that reduce the cost of capital for energy-efficient investments." Source: ACCF website 3/04

48. 1 January, 2004
"Carbon dioxide, the inescapable by-product of burning fossil fuels, is beneficial to plant and human life alike. The effort to regulate it as a greenhouse gas is an attempt to tax energy."
Source: SONS-OF-KYOTO™ LEGISLATION, ALEC press release, 1/21/04

49. 2 August, 2002
Wrote to President Bush, discouraging him from attending the UN Summit on Sustainable Development. Bush did not attend.Source: "Corporate-funded Lobbyists Aimed to Sabotage Johannesburg Summit," Africa News, 8/19/2002

50. The Annapolis Center actively argues against the idea that global warming is the result of burning fossil fuels. They also advocate increased logging for better forest health and question rising mercury levels among other things. The Annapolis Center is funded primarily by the National Association of Manufacturers. The Center's founder and COO, Richard Seibert was a former National Association of Manufacturers Vice President.

51. "We are sick to death of environmentalism and so we will destroy it. We will not allow our right to own property and use nature's resources for the benefit of mankind to be stripped from us by a bunch of eco-facists."—Ron Arnold
Source: "New, militant antienvironmentalists fight to return nature to a back seat." Boston Globe, January 13, 1992

52. "Although global warming has been described as the greatest threat facing mankind, the policies designed to address global warming actually pose a greater threat. The Kyoto Protocol and similar domestic schemes to ration carbon-based energy use would do little to slow carbon dioxide emissions, but would have enormous costs. These costs would eventually fall most heavily on the poorest nations in the world. Luckily, predictions of the extent of future warming are based on implausible scientific and economic assumptions, and the negative impacts of predicted warming have been vastly exaggerated. In the unlikely event that global warming turns out to be a problem, the correct approach is not energy rationing, but rather long-term technological transformation and building resiliency in societies by increasing wealth. CEI has been a leader in the fight against the global warming scare."
Source: CEI website - global warming

53. 7 April, 2004
"President Bush, of course, deserves even more credit for showing leadership in putting the breaks on this misguided treaty. When he first refused to go along with the Kyoto Protocol, howls of protest went up from those decrying his insensitivity to addressing this 'pressing' problem. Since then, however, nations such as Japan, Australia, Russia, and now Germany have likewise backpeddled on Kyoto compliance. One can't help but think, now in this baseball season, that maybe this President, a former owner of the Texas Rangers, knows when, and when not, to play ball."
Source: Committee for a Constructive Tomorrow CFACT Website 5/03

54. 22 April, 2004
Spokesman Niger Innis spoke at a Capitol Hill briefing called "Eco-Imperialism: Reflections on Earth Day." Other speakers at the briefing included climate change skeptics Sallie Baliunas, Roger Bate, and Paul Driessen.
Source: "Eco-Imperialism: Reflections on Earth Day" PR Newswire, 4/22/04

55. 7 June, 2002
Executive Director Frances Smith signed a letter to President Bush, asking him to withdraw the "Climate Action Report 2002" and demand that it be rewritten based on "sound science." The letter also recommends that Bush "dismiss or re-assign all administration

employees who are not pursuing your agenda, just as you have done in several similar instances."
Source: Joint Letter To President Bush On The EPA's Climate Action Report 6/7/02

56. "FACTSHEET: Federalist Society for Law and Public Policy Studies,"
http://www.exxonsecrets.org/html/orgfactsheet.php?id=33, accessed Aug. 12, 2012. See also Exxon Mobil Corporation, "2011 Worldwide Contributions and Community Investments Public Information and Policy Research,"
http://www.exxonmobil.com/Corporate/Files/gcr_contributions_pubpolicy11.pdf, accessed Aug. 12, 2012.

57. 2 February, 2004
"Climate has always varied, often with large swings … These dramatic climatic ebbs and flows are naturally occurring events. A more appropriate response to potential climate change is the production and employment of resources toward meaningful adaptation strategies."
Source: Frontiers of Freedom, "Science Hill Watch" 2/2/04

58. 13 November, 2002
"Given the uncertainty around warming, and the fact that some models predict that temperature increases of up to 4.5 degrees Fahrenheit would have beneficial effects, increasing our adaptability to change may be more important than cutting emissions. The best way to do this, particularly for the developing world, is through economic growth. The wealthier a nation, the easier to adapt to changed conditions. Richer countries have greater resources to deal with environmental problems."
Source: "Resiliency Is the Key to Climate Change" 11/13/02

59. "Wise, effective climate policy flows from a sound scientific foundation and a clear understanding of what science does and does not tell us about human influence and about courses of action to manage risk. Many of the temperature data and computer models used to predict climate change are themselves uncertain. Reducing these many uncertainties requires a significant shift in the way climate change research is carried out in the U.S. and elsewhere."
Source: George Marshall Institute website 4/04

60. "Some environmentalists call for a "save-the-day" strategy to 'stop global warming,' saying it is better to be safe than sorry. Such a position seems logical until we stop to think: Immediate action wouldn't make us any safer, but it would surely make us poorer. And being poorer would make us less safe."
Source: Heartland Institute "Instant Expert Guide: Global Warming"

61. "There is a lot of misinformation about climate change flowing through the establishment media. It's the result of junk science that environmental extremists use to paint a distorted picture." Source: Media Research Center "MRC Releases Primer for Reporters Covering Climate Change."

62. "NCPA scholars believe that while the causes and consequences of the earth's current warming trend is still unknown, the cost of actions to substantially reduce CO_2 emissions would be quite high and result in economic decline, accelerated environmental destruction, and do little or nothing to prevent global warming regardless of its cause."
Source: NCPA website 4/04

63. "There is no serious evidence that man-made global warming is taking place."
Source: NCPPR website 4/04

64. 4 February, 2001
"This winter's big chill has given global warming enthusiasts some explaining to do.
Whether global warming, if it occurs at all, would be a good or bad thing, is another debate entirely."
Source: "Global Warming Suffers a Chilling Effect," SF Examiner, 2/4/01

65. "Selling Climate Calamity,"
http://www.indepundit.com/archive2/annapctr/2005/01/selling_climate_1.html#more

66. "How to Think Sensibly about Global Warming,"
http://www.aei.org/publications/pubID.24545,filter.all/pub_detail.asp

67. "Warming Up to the Truth: The Real Story About Climate Change,"
http://www.heritage.org/Research/EnergyandEnvironment/HL758.cfm

68. "The Environmental Protection Agency's Proposed Rule For National Ambient Air Quality Standards For Particulate Matter,"
http://www.mercatus.org/Publications/pubID.2243,cfilter.0/pub_detail.asp

69. "Fuel Economy Standards for Light Trucks,"
http://www.mercatus.org/Publications/pubID.1331,cfilter.0/pub_detail.asp

70. "Warming Likely to Have Modest Effect on Sea Level, If Any,"
http://www.heartland.org/Article.cfm?artId=18250

71. "Climate Policy: A Reality Check," http://www.marshall.org/article.php?id=341

72. "The Satanic Gases: Clearing the Air about Global Warming,"
http://www.catostore.org/index.asp?fa=ProductDetails&method=cats&scid=17&pid=144919

73. "Global Warming FAQ: What Every Citizen Needs to Know About Global Warming,"
http://www.cei.org/utils/printer.cfm?AID=5331

74. "Q&A About Forests and Global Climate Change,"
http://www.reason.org/qa_forests.pdf

75. "ALEC RELEASES NEW REPORT ON GLOBAL WARMING AND KYOTO PROTOCOL,"
http://www.alec.org/news/press-releases/press-releases-2002/april/on-earth-day-alec-releases-new-report-on-global-warming-and-kyoto-protocol.html

CHAPTER 20

1. "That They May Have Life," *First Things*, October, 2006.

2. "Richard John Neuhaus, 1936–2009," *Newsweek*, Jan. 10, 2009.

3. The declaration was accompanied by the following explanatory statement: "From its beginnings in 1992, Evangelicals and Catholics Together (ECT) has been very deliberately an unofficial project composed of a continuing working group of participants who speak from and to their several ecclesial communities. There is an acknowledged difference between Catholic and evangelical participation, in that Catholic participants are bound by and determined to be faithful to the central teaching authority, or Magisterium, of the Catholic Church. In the communities that comprise contemporary evangelicalism, doctrinal and theological leadership is exercised by individuals and institutions that have earned the confidence of Christians within their various spheres of influence. We are pleased to note that the following evangelical leaders are among those who have endorsed the most recent statement, 'That They May Have Life.'"

4. There are many variants on this quotation—'em instead of them, for example—but its essence remains the same in all of them. Peter Roff, "Charles Colson's Sin—and Salvation," *U.S. News & World Report*, April 23, 2012.

5. Peter Roff, "Charles Colson's Sin—and Salvation," *U.S. News & World Report*, April 23, 2012.

6. Wilberforce Central, http://www.wilberforcecentral.org/wfc/Coalition/index.htm, accessed Sept. 15, 2012.

7. Laurie Goodstein, "Rev. R. J. Neuhaus, Political Theologian, Dies at 72," *New York Times*, Jan. 8, 2009.

8. Laurie Goodstein, "Rev. R. J. Neuhaus, Political Theologian, Dies at 72," *New York Times*, Jan. 8, 2009.

9. John W. Robbins, "Healing the Mortal Wound," The Trinity Foundation, http://www.trinityfoundation.org/journal.php?id=146, accessed Sept. 15, 2012.

10. John M. Barry "God, Government and Roger Williams' Big Idea," Smithsonian,com, http://www.smithsonianmag.com/history-archaeology/God-Government-and-Roger-Williams-Big-Idea.html#ixzz4udTgvG7d *and* http://www.smithsonianmag.com/history-archaeology/God-Government-and-Roger-Williams-Big-Idea.html#ixzz4udUjh9eP, accessed Sept. 10, 2012.

11. John M. Barry "God, Government and Roger Williams' Big Idea," Smithsonian,com, http://www.smithsonianmag.com/history-archaeology/God-Government-and-Roger-Williams-Big-Idea.html#ixzz4udTgvG7d *and* http://www.smithsonianmag.com/history-archaeology/God-Government-and-Roger-Williams-Big-Idea.html#ixzz4udUjh9eP, accessed Sept. 10, 2012.

12. John M. Barry "God, Government and Roger Williams' Big Idea," Smithsonian,com, http://www.smithsonianmag.com/history-archaeology/God-Government-and-Roger-Williams-Big-Idea.html#ixzz4udTgvG7d *and* http://www.smithsonianmag.com/history-archaeology/God-Government-and-Roger-Williams-Big-Idea.html#ixzz4udUjh9eP, accessed Sept. 10, 2012.

13. Matthew Cooper, "Santorum and the Catholic-Evangelical Alliance," *National Journal*, Jan. 3, 2012.

14. John W. Robbins, "Healing the Mortal Wound," The Trinity Foundation, http://www.trinityfoundation.org/journal.php?id=146, accessed Sept. 15, 2012.

15. John W. Robbins, "Healing the Mortal Wound," The Trinity Foundation, http://www.trinityfoundation.org/journal.php?id=146, accessed Sept. 15, 2012.

16. "Vatican wants United States to stay in Iraq," MSNBC, Jan. 12, 2005.

17. Carsten Frerk, "German taxpayers subsidise over 90% of faith-based social services," Concordat Watch, http://www.concordatwatch.eu/showtopic.php?org_id=858&kb_header_id=32561, accessed Sept. 15, 2012.

18. Carsten Frerk, "German taxpayers subsidise over 90% of faith-based social services," Concordat Watch, http://www.concordatwatch.eu/showtopic.php?org_id=858&kb_header_id=32561, accessed Sept. 15, 2012.

19. Carsten Frerk, "German taxpayers subsidise over 90% of faith-based social services," Concordat Watch, http://www.concordatwatch.eu/showtopic.php?org_id=858&kb_header_id=32561, accessed Sept. 15, 2012.

20. Carsten Frerk, "German taxpayers subsidise over 90% of faith-based social services," Concordat Watch, http://www.concordatwatch.eu/showtopic.php?org_id=858&kb_header_id=32561, accessed Sept. 15, 2012.

21. It is remarkable that since its founding in 1976, the principal organization devoted to what it describes as "continuing education to a network of foundations and donors supporting Catholic-sponsored programs and institutions" seems to have not once focused on the child abuse scandals. A review of publications and symposia of the nonprofit Foundations and Donors Interested in Catholic Activities (FADICA), which is to "strengthen and promote Catholic philanthropy" shows not one mention of this.

22. Jon Nordheimer, "Sex Charges Against Priest Embroil Louisiana Parents," *New York Times*, June 20, 1985.

23. Jon Hurdle and Erik Eckholm, "Cardinal's Aide Is Found Guilty in Abuse Case," *New York Times*, June 22, 2012

24. "The Augsburg Confession, The Confession of Faith which was submitted to His Imperial Majesty Charles V at the Diet of Augsburg in the year 1530 by certain princes and cities," http://bookofconcord.org/augsburgconfession.php, accessed Sept. 16, 2012.

25. George O. Lillegard ,"The Principle of the Separation of Church and State Applied to Our Times," Presented to the 23rd regular convention of the Norwegian Synod of the American Lutheran Church held at Fairview Luth. Church, Minn. MN, June 13–19, 1940, www.wlsessays.net/files/LillegardChurch.rtf, accessed Sept. 10, 2012.

26. George O. Lillegard ,"The Principle of the Separation of Church and State Applied to Our Times," Presented to the 23rd regular convention of the Norwegian Synod of the American Lutheran Church held at Fairview Luth. Church, Minn. MN, June 13–19, 1940, www.wlsessays.net/files/LillegardChurch.rtf, accessed Sept. 10, 2012.

27. George O. Lillegard ,"The Principle of the Separation of Church and State Applied to Our Times," Presented to the 23rd regular convention of the Norwegian Synod of the American Lutheran Church held at Fairview Luth. Church, Minn. MN, June 13–19, 1940, www.wlsessays.net/files/LillegardChurch.rtf, accessed Sept. 10, 2012.

28. George O. Lillegard ,"The Principle of the Separation of Church and State Applied to Our Times," Presented to the 23rd regular convention of the Norwegian Synod of the American Lutheran Church held at Fairview Luth. Church, Minn. MN, June 13–19, 1940, www.wlsessays.net/files/LillegardChurch.rtf, accessed Sept. 10, 2012.

29. John L. Allem, Jr., *Cardinal Ratzinger*, p. xi, Continuum International Publishing Group, 2000, London.

30. John L. Allem, Jr., *Cardinal Ratzinger*, p. ix, Continuum International Publishing Group, 2000, London.

31. "Group: Deny communion to senator for her views," the Associated Press, Sept. 3, 2004.

32. "Group: Deny communion to senator for her views," the Associated Press, Sept. 3, 2004.

33. "Group: Deny communion to senator for her views," the Associated Press, Sept. 3, 2004.

34. Joe Feuerherd, "Catholic League Targets Kerry Outreach; Former Governor Davis on Consistency; Poll Results; What Would Clinton Do?," National Catholic Reporter, Aug. 11, 2004.

35. "Lincoln Chafee on Abortion," Former Republican Senator (RI, 1999–2007) http://www.ontheissues.org/social/Lincoln_Chafee_Abortion.htm, accessed Sept. 10, 2012.

36. "Lincoln Chafee on Abortion," Former Republican Senator (RI, 1999–2007) http://www.ontheissues.org/social/Lincoln_Chafee_Abortion.htm, accessed Sept. 10, 2012.

CHAPTER 21

1. Matthew Levendusky, *The Partisan Sort: How Liberals Became Democrats and Conservatives Became Republicans*, p. 2, University of Chicago Press, Chicago, 2009.

2. Gracieli Scremin, *Political Parties as Brands: Developing and Testing a Conceptual Framework*, Proquest Information and Learning Company, 2007. This is an insightful and helpful discussion of the importance of branding as a political strategy.

3. Gracieli Scremin, *Political Parties as Brands: Developing and Testing a Conceptual Framework*, Proquest Information and Learning Company, 2007. This is an insightful and helpful discussion of the importance of branding as a political strategy.

4. Gracieli Scremin, *Political Parties as Brands: Developing and Testing a Conceptual Framework*, Proquest Information and Learning Company, 2007. This is an insightful and helpful discussion of the importance of branding as a political strategy.

5. Alan I. Abramowitz, "U.S. Senate Elections in a Polarized Era," Conference on Legislative Elections, Process and Policy: The Influence of Bicameralism, Vanderbilt University, Oct. 22–24, 2009, http://www.vanderbilt.edu/csdi/archived/Bicameralism%20papers/abromowitz3.pdf, accessed Sept. 18, 2012.

6. New York Historical Society, "Slavery in New York," http://www.slaveryinnewyork.org/about_exhibit.htm, accessed Sept. 17, 2012.

7. "Medicare and Medicaid Votes in 1965," http://www.scribd.com/doc/30907302/Votes-Medicare-1965, accessed Sept. 18, 2012.

8. "CHAFEE, John Hubbard, (1922–1999)," Biographical Directory of the United States Congress, http://bioguide.congress.gov/scripts/biodisplay.pl?index=c000269, accessed Sep. 18, 2012.

9. "Hugh Scott," Wikipedia, http://en.wikipedia.org/wiki/Hugh_Scott, accessed Sep. 18, 2012.

10. George Weeks, "Michigan Politics," *St. Ignace News*, http://www.stignacenews.com/news/2012-02-02/Columns/Michigan_Politics.html, accessed Sept. 18, 2012.

11. Matt Schudel, "Former U.S. Sen. Charles McC. Mathias Jr. of Maryland dies at 87," *Washington Post*, Jan. 26, 2010.

12. "Brief Biography of Clifford P. Case II, Loyal Son, Scholar, Statesman," Rutgers University, http://njdh.scc-net.rutgers.edu/enj/lessons/questioning_executive_power/pdf/case_biography.pdf, accessed Sept. 18, 2012.

13. Richard Feldman, *Ricochet: Confessions of a Gun Lobbyist*, John Wiley & Sons, Hoboken, N.J. 2008.

14. "Jacob K. Javits," Wikipedia, http://en.wikipedia.org/wiki/Jacob_K._Javits, accessed Sept. 18, 2012.

15. "Dems prevail as Collins, Snowe reject Senate tax-cut plan for middle class," The Associated Press, July 25, 2012.

16. Alan I. Abramowitz, "U.S. Senate Elections in a Polarized Era," Conference on Legislative Elections, Process and Policy: The Influence of Bicameralism, Vanderbilt University, Oct. 22–24, 2009,

http://www.vanderbilt.edu/csdi/archived/Bicameralism%20papers/abromowitz3.pdf,
accessed Sept. 18, 2012.

17. McKenzie Young, "Partisanship and Ideological Changes in an Evolving Southern State," Prepared for Presentation at the 2011 Southern Political Science Association Conference New Orleans, LA, Jan. 8th, 2011,
http://www.elon.edu/docs/e-web/administration/president/lumenprize/paperFall10.pdf,
accessed Sept. 17, 2012.

18. David C. Kimball and Cassie A. Gross, "The Growing Polarization of American Voters," Presented at *The State of the Parties: 2004 and Beyond* conference, Akron, OH, October 6, 2005.

19. Bradford H. Bishop and Rebecca S. Hatch, "Ticket Splitting in a Complex Federal System," 83rd Annual Meeting of the Southern Political Science Association, New Orleans, LA, January 12–14, 2012, http://www.duke.edu/~bhb11/ticket%20splitting.pdf, accessed Sept. 18, 2012.

1. Philip Rucker, "Mitt Romney says 'corporations are people' at Iowa State Fair," *Washington Post*, Aug. 11, 2011

PREVIEW, CLIFFS II

1. "Lightening," *National Geographic*,
http://environment.nationalgeographic.com/environment/natural-disasters/lightning-profile/,
accessed Sept. 5, 2012.

2. Mark C. Serreze, M.C. & Francis, J.A. The Arctic Amplification Debate, J. Climatic Change. June, 2006. DOI10.1007/s10584-005-9017-y, p. 241–264.
Rises in surface air temperature (SAT) in response to increasing concentrations of greenhouse gases (GHGs) are expected to be amplified in northern high latitudes, with warming most pronounced over the Arctic Ocean owing to the loss of sea ice. Observations document recent warming, but an enhanced Arctic Ocean signal is not readily evident. This disparity, combined with varying model projections of SAT change, and large variability in observed SAT over the 20th century, may lead one to question the concept of Arctic amplification. Disparity is greatly reduced, however, if one compares observed trajectories to near-future simulations (2010–2029), rather than to the doubled-CO_2 or late 21st century conditions that are typically cited. These near-future simulations document a preconditioning phase of Arctic amplification, characterized by the initial retreat and thinning of sea ice, with imprints of low-frequency variability. Observations show these same basic features, but with SATs over the Arctic Ocean still largely constrained by the insulating effects of the ice cover and thermal inertia of the upper ocean. Given the general consistency with model projections, we are likely near the threshold when absorption of solar radiation during summer limits ice growth the following autumn and winter, initiating a feedback leading to a substantial increase in Arctic Ocean SATs.

3. http://www.cnn.com/2007/TECH/science/05/02/arctic.ice/.

4. Richard Black, "Arctic sea ice melt 'even faster'," BBC News, June 18, 2008, http://news.bbc.co.uk/1/hi/sci/tech/7461707.stm

5. Peter N. Spotts, "Arctic sea ice melting faster than expected," Christian Science Monitor, June 12, 2008,
http://features.csmonitor.com/environment/2008/06/12/arctic-sea-ice-melting-faster-than-expected/

6. Richard Black, "Arctic sea ice melt 'even faster'," BBC News, June 18, 2008,
http://news.bbc.co.uk/1/hi/sci/tech/7461707.stm

7. Peter N. Spotts, "Arctic sea ice melting faster than expected," *Christian Science Monitor*, June 12, 2008,
http://features.csmonitor.com/environment/2008/06/12/arctic-sea-ice-melting-faster-than-expected/

8. Fred Weir, "As icecaps melt, Russia races for Arctic's resources," *Christian Science Monitor*, July 31, 2007 http://www.csmonitor.com/2007/0731/p01s01-woeu.html.

9. Juliet Eilperin, "Antarctic Ice Sheet Is Melting Rapidly - New Study Warns Of Rising Sea Levels," *Washington Post*, March 3, 2006, p. A1

10. Zimov, S.A., Schuur, E. A. G. & Chapin, F. S. III. Permafrost and the Global Carbon Budget. Science, June 16, 2006: Vol. 312. no. 5780, pp. 1612–1613, DOI:10.1126/science.1128908.
Climate warming will thaw permafrost, releasing trapped carbon from this high-latitude reservoir and further exacerbating global warming.

11. K. M. Walte et. al. Methane bubbling from Siberian thaw lakes as a positive feedback to climate warming. Nature 443, 71–75, 7 September 2006. | doi:10.1038.
Large uncertainties in the budget of atmospheric methane, an important greenhouse gas, limit the accuracy of climate change projections. Thaw lakes in North Siberia are known to emit methane, but the magnitude of these emissions remains uncertain because most methane is released through ebullition (bubbling), which is spatially and temporally variable. Here we report a new method of measuring ebullition and use it to quantify methane emissions from two thaw lakes in North Siberia. We show that ebullition accounts for 95 percent of methane emissions from these lakes, and that methane flux from thaw lakes in our study region may be five times higher than previously estimated. Extrapolation of these fluxes indicates that thaw lakes in North Siberia emit 3.8 teragrams of methane per year, which increases present estimates of methane emissions from northern wetlands (< 6–40 teragrams per year) by between 10 and 63 percent. We find that thawing permafrost along lake margins accounts for most of the methane released from the lakes, and estimate that an expansion of thaw lakes between 1974 and 2000, which was concurrent with regional warming, increased methane emissions in our study region by 58 percent. Furthermore, the Pleistocene age (35,260–42,900 years) of methane emitted from hotspots along thawing lake margins indicates that this positive feedback to climate warming has led to the release of old carbon stocks previously stored in permafrost.

12. Camill, P. Permafrost Thaw Accelerates in Boreal Peatlands During Late-20th Century Climate Warming. Climatic Change, Volume 68, Numbers 1–2 , DOI 10.1007/s10584-005-4785-y, pp. 135–52, January, 2005.
Permafrost covers 25% of the land surface in the northern hemisphere, where mean annual ground temperature is less than 0°C. A 1.4–5.8 °C warming by 2100 will likely change the sign of mean annual air and ground temperatures over much of the zones of sporadic and discontinuous permafrost in the northern hemisphere, causing widespread

permafrost thaw. In this study, I examined rates of discontinuous permafrost thaw in the boreal peatlands of northern Manitoba, Canada, using a combination of tree-ring analyses to document thaw rates from 1941–1991 and direct measurements of permanent benchmarks established in 1995 and resurveyed in 2002. I used instrumented records of mean annual and seasonal air temperatures, mean winter snow depth, and duration of continuous snow pack from climate stations across northern Manitoba to analyze temporal and spatial trends in these variables and their potential impacts on thaw. Permafrost thaw in central Canadian peatlands has accelerated significantly since 1950, concurrent with a significant, late-20th-century average climate warming of +1.32°C in this region. There were strong seasonal differences in warming in northern Manitoba, with highest rates of warming during winter (+1.39°C to +1.66°C) and spring (+0.56°C to +0.78°C) at southern climate stations where permafrost thaw was most rapid. Projecting current warming trends to year 2100, I show that trends for north-central Canada are in good agreement with general circulation models, which suggest a 4–8°C warming at high latitudes. This magnitude of warming will begin to eliminate most of the present range of sporadic and discontinuous permafrost in central Canada by 2100.

13. Osterkamp, T. E. & Romanovsky,V. E. Evidence for warming and thawing of discontinuous permafrost in Alaska. Permafrost and Periglacial Processes, V. 10 Issue 1, pages 17–37, May 18, 1999.
Data show that permafrost temperatures along a north-south transect of Alaska from Old Man to Gulkana and at Healy generally warmed in the late 1980s to 1996. This trend was not followed at Eagle, about 330 km east of the transect. Estimates of the magnitude of the warming at the permafrost table ranged from 0.5°C to 1.5°C. Warming rates near the permafrost table were about 0.05 to 0.2°C a-1. No reliable trends in the depth of the base of ice-bearing permafrost or in the depth of the 0°C isotherm could be detected. Thermal offset allowed mean annual temperatures at the permafrost table to remain below 0°C with ground surface temperatures up to 2.5°C for a period of 8 years. The observed warming has probably caused discontinuous permafrost in marginal areas to begin thawing. Thawing permafrost and thermokarst have been observed at several sites. Thawing rates at the permafrost table at two sites were about 0.1 m a-1, indicating time scales of the order of a century to thaw the top 10 metres of ice-rich permafrost. Calculated thawing rates at the permafrost base are an order of magnitude smaller. Calibrated numerical models indicate that the permafrost warmed in the late 1960s and early 1970s in response to changes in air temperatures and snow covers. Additional warming in the late 1970s was caused by an increase in air temperatures beginning in 1977. Permafrost temperatures were nearly stable during the 1980s and then warmed again from the late 1980s to 1996, primarily in response to increased snow depths. This interpretation appears to be valid for all the sites in the region of the transect and at Healy.

14. Molly Bentley, "Earth's permafrost starts to squelch," BBC News, Dec. 29, 2004, http://news.bbc.co.uk/2/hi/science/nature/4120755.stm.

15. A colorful account of thawing in Siberia follows:

By| Tribune correspondent
   12:38 AM CDT, May 5, 2008

CHERSKY, Russia — Sergei Zimov waded through knee-deep snow to reach a frozen lake where so much methane belches out of the melting permafrost that it spews from the ice like small geysers.

In the frigid twilight, the Russian scientist struck a match to make a jet of the greenhouse gas visible. The sudden plume of fire threw him backward. Zimov stood up, brushed the snow off his parka and beamed.

"Sometimes a big explosion happens, because the gas comes out like a bomb," Zimov said. "There are a million lakes like this in northern Siberia."

In a country where many scientists scoff at the existence of global warming, Zimov has been waging a lonely campaign to warn the world about Russia's melting permafrost and its nexus with climate change. His laboratory is the vast expanse of tundra and larch forest along the East Siberian Sea, an icy corner of the world that Zimov has scrutinized almost entirely on his own for 28 years.

Far from the archetypal scientist, the beefy, 53-year-old Russian with a mound of gray-brown hair and piercing blue eyes reigns over his patch of Siberia not with pipette and beaker, but with the swagger of a Cossack and an encyclopedic knowledge of his surroundings.

Alex Rodriguez , "Freezing to show warming trend - Though dismissed in Russia, scientist's climate research in remote Siberia is heating up discussions in the West," May 5, 2008. http://www.chicagotribune.com/news/nationworld/chi-siberia-loner_rodriguezmay05,0,7326792.story

16. Ian Sample, "Alarm over dramatic weakening of Gulf Stream," *The Guardian*, Dec. 1, 2005 http://www.guardian.co.uk/environment/2005/dec/01/science.climatechange

17.
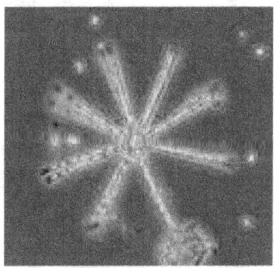

18.
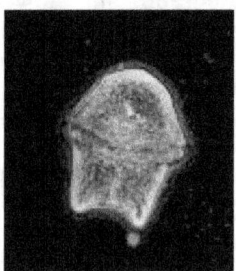

19.

20. Mike Toner, "Plankton Declining in Oceans, Study Finds," *Atlanta Journal-Constitution* Aug. 20, 2002. See also Goddard Space Flight Center, National Oceanic and Atmospheric Administration, "Phytoplankton in Northern Oceans Have Declined from 1980s Levels," Aug. 08, 2002, http://www.gsfc.nasa.gov/topstory/20020801plankton.html.

21. Schmittner, A. Decline of the marine ecosystem caused by a reduction in the Atlantic overturning circulation. *Nature* 434, 628–633, 31 March 2005, | doi:10.1038/nature03476. Reorganizations of the Atlantic meridional overturning circulation were associated with large and abrupt climatic changes in the North Atlantic region during the last glacial period. Projections with climate models suggest that similar reorganizations may also occur in response to anthropogenic global warming. Here I use ensemble simulations with a coupled climate-ecosytem model of intermediate complexity to investigate the possible consequences of such disturbances to the marine ecosystem. In the simulations, a disruption of the Atlantic meridional overturning circulation leads to a collapse of the North Atlantic plankton stocks to less than half of their initial biomass, owing to rapid shoaling of winter mixed layers and their associated separation from the deep ocean nutrient reservoir. Globally integrated export production declines by more than 20 percent owing to reduced upwelling of nutrient-rich deep water and gradual depletion of upper ocean nutrient concentrations. These model results are consistent with the available high-resolution palaeorecord, and suggest that global ocean productivity is sensitive to changes in the Atlantic meridional overturning circulation.

22. James C. Orr, J.T. et. al. Anthropogenic ocean acidification over the twenty-first century and its impact on calcifying organisms. Nature 437, 681–686, Sep. 29, 2005, doi:10.1038/nature04095.

Today's surface ocean is saturated with respect to calcium carbonate, but increasing atmospheric carbon dioxide concentrations are reducing ocean pH and carbonate ion concentrations, and thus the level of calcium carbonate saturation. Experimental evidence suggests that if these trends continue, key marine organisms—such as corals and some plankton—will have difficulty maintaining their external calcium carbonate skeletons. Here we use 13 models of the ocean-carbon cycle to assess calcium carbonate saturation under the IS92a 'business-as-usual' scenario for future emissions of anthropogenic carbon dioxide. In our projections, Southern Ocean surface waters will begin to become undersaturated with respect to aragonite, a metastable form of calcium carbonate, by the year 2050. By 2100, this undersaturation could extend throughout the entire Southern Ocean and into the subarctic Pacific Ocean. When live pteropods were exposed to our predicted level of undersaturation during a two-day shipboard experiment, their aragonite shells showed notable dissolution. Our findings indicate that conditions detrimental to high-latitude ecosystems could develop within decades, not centuries as suggested previously.

23. Richard A. Feely, R.A. et. al. Evidence for Upwelling of Corrosive "Acidified" Water onto the Continental Shelf. *Science,* June 13, 2008: Vol. 320. no. 5882, pp. 1490–1492, DOI: 10.1126/science.1155676.
The absorption of atmospheric carbon dioxide (CO_2) into the ocean lowers the pH of the waters. This so-called ocean acidification could have important consequences for marine ecosystems. To better understand the extent of this ocean acidification in coastal waters, we conducted hydrographic surveys along the continental shelf of western North America from central Canada to northern Mexico. We observed seawater that is undersaturated with respect to aragonite upwelling onto large portions of the continental shelf, reaching depths of ~40 to 120 meters along most transect lines and all the way to the surface on one

transect off northern California. Although seasonal upwelling of the undersaturated waters onto the shelf is a natural phenomenon in this region, the ocean uptake of anthropogenic CO_2 has increased the areal extent of the affected area.

24. Sandi Doughton, "Acidified ocean water rising up nearly 100 years earlier than scientists predicted," *Seattle Times*, May 22, 2008.

25. Nicholas A. J. Graham , N.A.J. et. al. Dynamic fragility of oceanic coral reef ecosystems. Proceedings of the National Academy of Sciences, Washington, D.C., May 18, 2006.
As one of the most diverse and productive ecosystems known, and one of the first ecosystems to exhibit major climate-warming impacts (coral bleaching), coral reefs have drawn much scientific attention to what may prove to be their Achilles heel, the thermal sensitivity of reef-building corals. Here we show that climate change-driven loss of live coral, and ultimately structural complexity, in the Seychelles results in local extinctions, substantial reductions in species richness, reduced taxonomic distinctness, and a loss of species within key functional groups of reef fish. The importance of deteriorating physical structure to these patterns demonstrates the longer-term impacts of bleaching on reefs and raises questions over the potential for recovery. We suggest that isolated reef systems may be more susceptible to climate change, despite escaping many of the stressors impacting continental reefs.

26. Sean Markey, "Global Warming Has Devastating Effect on Coral Reefs, Study Shows," National Geographic News, May 16, 2006
http://news.nationalgeographic.com/news/2006/05/warming-coral.html.

27. K. M. Brander, K.M. Global fish production and climate change. Proceedings of the National Academy of Sciences, Dec. 11, 2007, vol. 104,| no. 50, 19709–19714.
Current global fisheries production of {approx}160 million tons is rising as a result of increases in aquaculture production. A number of climate-related threats to both capture fisheries and aquaculture are identified, but we have low confidence in predictions of future fisheries production because of uncertainty over future global aquatic net primary production and the transfer of this production through the food chain to human consumption. Recent changes in the distribution and productivity of a number of fish species can be ascribed with high confidence to regional climate variability, such as the El Niño-Southern Oscillation. Future production may increase in some high-latitude regions because of warming and decreased ice cover, but the dynamics in low-latitude regions are governed by different processes, and production may decline as a result of reduced vertical mixing of the water column and, hence, reduced recycling of nutrients. There are strong interactions between the effects of fishing and the effects of climate because fishing reduces the age, size, and geographic diversity of populations and the biodiversity of marine ecosystems, making both more sensitive to additional stresses such as climate change. Inland fisheries are additionally threatened by changes in precipitation and water management. The frequency and intensity of extreme climate events is likely to have a major impact on future fisheries production in both inland and marine systems. Reducing fishing mortality in the majority of fisheries, which are currently fully exploited or overexploited, is the principal feasible means of reducing the impacts of climate change.

28. Westerling, A.L. Warming and Earlier Spring Increases Western U.S. Forest Wildfire Activity. *Science*, Aug. 18, 2006: Vol. 313. no. 5789, pp. 940–943, DOI: 10.1126/science.1128834
Western United States forest wildfire activity is widely thought to have increased in recent

decades, but surprisingly, the extent of recent changes has never been systematically documented. Nor has it been established to what degree climate may be driving regional changes in wildfire. Much of the public and scientific discussion of changes in western United States wildfire has focused rather on the effects of 19th and 20th century land-use history. We compiled a comprehensive database of large wildfires in western United States forests since 1970 and compared it to hydro-climatic and land-surface data. Here, we show that large wildfire activity increased suddenly and dramatically in the mid-1980s, with higher large-wildfire frequency, longer wildfire durations, and longer wildfire seasons. The greatest increases occurred in mid-elevation, Northern Rockies forests, where land-use histories have relatively little effect on fire risks, and are strongly associated with increased spring and summer temperatures and an earlier spring snowmelt.

29. Flanner, M.G. et. al. Present-day climate forcing and response from black carbon in snow JGR, V. 112, D11202, doi:10.1029/2006JD008003, 2007.
We apply our Snow, Ice, and Aerosol Radiative (SNICAR) model, coupled to a general circulation model with prognostic carbon aerosol transport, to improve understanding of climate forcing and response from black carbon (BC) in snow. Building on two previous studies, we account for interannually varying biomass burning BC emissions, snow aging, and aerosol scavenging by snow meltwater. We assess uncertainty in forcing estimates from these factors, as well as BC optical properties and snow cover fraction. BC emissions are the largest source of uncertainty, followed by snow aging. The rate of snow aging determines snowpack effective radius (r_e), which directly controls snow reflectance and the magnitude of albedo change caused by BC. For a reasonable r_e range, reflectance reduction from BC varies threefold. Inefficient meltwater scavenging keeps hydrophobic impurities near the surface during melt and enhances forcing. Applying biomass burning BC emission inventories for a strong (1998) and weak (2001) boreal fire year, we estimate global annual mean BC/snow surface radiative forcing from all sources (fossil fuel, biofuel, and biomass burning) of +0.054 (0.007–0.13) and +0.049 (0.007–0.12) W m-2, respectively. Snow forcing from only fossil fuel + biofuel sources is +0.043 W m-2 (forcing from only fossil fuels is +0.033 W m-2), suggesting that the anthropogenic contribution to total forcing is at least 80%. The 1998 global land and sea-ice snowpack absorbed 0.60 and 0.23 W m-2, respectively, because of direct BC/snow forcing. The forcing is maximum coincidentally with snowmelt onset, triggering strong snow-albedo feedback in local springtime. Consequently, the "efficacy" of BC/snow forcing is more than three times greater than forcing by CO_2. The 1998 and 2001 land snowmelt rates north of 50°N are 28% and 19% greater in the month preceding maximum melt of control simulations without BC in snow. With climate feedbacks, global annual mean 2-meter air temperature warms 0.15 and 0.10°C, when BC is included in snow, whereas annual arctic warming is 1.61 and 0.50°C. Stronger high-latitude climate response in 1998 than 2001 is at least partially caused by boreal fires, which account for nearly all of the 35% biomass burning contribution to 1998 arctic forcing. Efficacy was anomalously large in this experiment, however, and more research is required to elucidate the role of boreal fires, which we suggest have maximum arctic BC/snow forcing potential during April–June. Model BC concentrations in snow agree reasonably well (r = 0.78) with a set of 23 observations from various locations, spanning nearly 4 orders of magnitude. We predict concentrations in excess of 1000 ng g-1 for snow in northeast China, enough to lower snow albedo by more than 0.13. The greatest instantaneous forcing is over the Tibetan Plateau, exceeding 20 W m-2 in some places during spring. These results indicate that snow darkening is an important component of carbon aerosol climate forcing.

30. van der Werf, G.R. et. al. Continental-Scale Partitioning of Fire Emissions During the 1997 to 2001 El Niño/La Niña Period. *Science* 2 January 2004:Vol. 303. no. 5654, pp. 73–76
DOI: 10.1126/science.1090753.
During the 1997 to 1998 El Niño, drought conditions triggered widespread increases in fire activity, releasing CH_4 and CO_2 to the atmosphere. We evaluated the contribution of fires from different continents to variability in these greenhouse gases from 1997 to 2001, using satellite-based estimates of fire activity, biogeochemical modeling, and an inverse analysis of atmospheric CO anomalies. During the 1997 to 1998 El Niño, the fire emissions anomaly was 2.1 ± 0.8 petagrams of carbon, or 66 ± 24% of the CO_2 growth rate anomaly. The main contributors were Southeast Asia (60%), Central and South America (30%), and boreal regions of Eurasia and North America (10%).

31. Westerling, A.L. Warming and Earlier Spring Increases Western U.S. Forest Wildfire Activity. *Science*, Aug. 18, 2006: Vol. 313. no. 5789, pp. 940–943, DOI: 10.1126/science.1128834
Western United States forest wildfire activity is widely thought to have increased in recent decades, but surprisingly, the extent of recent changes has never been systematically documented. Nor has it been established to what degree climate may be driving regional changes in wildfire. Much of the public and scientific discussion of changes in western United States wildfire has focused rather on the effects of 19th and 20th century land-use history. We compiled a comprehensive database of large wildfires in western United States forests since 1970 and compared it to hydro-climatic and land-surface data. Here, we show that large wildfire activity increased suddenly and dramatically in the mid-1980s, with higher large-wildfire frequency, longer wildfire durations, and longer wildfire seasons. The greatest increases occurred in mid-elevation, Northern Rockies forests, where land-use histories have relatively little effect on fire risks, and are strongly associated with increased spring and summer temperatures and an earlier spring snowmelt.

32. Intergovernmental Panel on Climate Change (IPCC) - Working Group 2,
http://www.ipcc.ch/ipccreports/ar4-wg2.htm.

33. Steven W. Running, S.W. Is Global Warming Causing More, Larger Wildfires? *Science*, Aug. 18, 2006: Vol. 313. no. 5789, pp. 927–928 DOI: 10.1126/science.1130370.

34. Flannigan, M.D., et. al. Future Area Burned in Canada. Climatic Change. V 72, N 1-2 / September, 2005.
Historical relationships between weather, the Canadian fire weather index (FWI) system components and area burned in Canadian ecozones were analysed on a monthly basis in tandem with output from the Canadian and the Hadley Centre GCMs to project future area burned. Temperature and fuel moisture were the variables best related to historical monthly area burned with 36–64% of the variance explained depending on ecozone. Our results suggest significant increases in future area burned although there are large regional variations in fire activity. This was especially true for the Canadian GCM where some ecozones show little change in area burned, however area burned was not projected to decrease in any of the ecozones modelled. On average, area burned in Canada is projected to increase by 74–118% by the end of this century in a 3 × CO_2 scenario. These estimates do not explicitly take into account any changes in vegetation, ignitions, fire season length, and human activity (fire management and land use activities) that may influence area burned. However, the estimated increases in area burned would have significant ecological, economic and social impacts for Canada.

35. Roger Highfield, "Siberian forest fires due to climate change," Jan. 1, 2007, *London Telegraph*,
http://www.telegraph.co.uk/earth/main.jhtml?xml=/earth/2007/08/01/scisiberia101.xml

36. Balzter, H., Gerard, F., Weedon, G., Grey, W., Combal, B., Bartholome, E., Bartalev, S. and Los, S., 2007, Coupling of vegetation growing season anomalies with hemispheric and regional scale climate patterns in Central and East Siberia, Journal of Climate 20:15, 3713–3729, doi: 10.1175/JCLI4226

37. Roger Highfield, "Siberian forest fires due to climate change," Jan. 1, 2007, *London Telegraph*,
http://www.telegraph.co.uk/earth/main.jhtml?xml=/earth/2007/08/01/scisiberia101.xml

38. Hopkin, M. Carbon sinks threatened by increasing ozone. Nature 448, 396–397 (26 July 2007) | doi:10.1038/448396b; Published online 25 July 2007.
Pollutant poisons plants and hampers photosynthesis.

Rising levels of ozone pollution over the coming century will erode the ability of plants to absorb carbon dioxide from the atmosphere, a new climate-modelling study predicts. Ozone is already known to be a minor greenhouse gas, but the new calculations highlight another, indirect way in which it is likely to influence global warming by 2100.

39. National Oceanic and Atmospheric Administration, Greenhouse Gases, Frequently Asked Questions, http://www.ncdc.noaa.gov/oa/climate/gases.html#oz.

40. Steiner, A.L. Influence of future climate and emissions on regional air quality in California. JG R, V. 111, D18303, doi:10.1029/2005JD006935, 2006
http://www.agu.org/pubs/crossref/2006/2005JD006935.shtml.
Using a chemical transport model simulating ozone concentrations in central California, we evaluate the effects of variables associated with future changes in climate and ozone precursor emissions, including (1) increasing temperature; (2) increasing atmospheric water vapor; (3) increasing biogenic VOC emissions due to temperature; (4) projected decreases in anthropogenic NO_x, VOC, and CO emissions in California for 2050; and (5) the influence of changing ozone, CO, and methane at the western boundary. Climatic changes expected for temperature, atmospheric water vapor, and biogenic VOC emissions each individually cause a 1–5% increase in the daily peak ozone. Projected reductions in anthropogenic emissions of 10–50% in NO_x and 50–70% in VOCs and CO have the greatest single effect, reducing ozone by 8–15% in urban areas. Changes to the chemical boundary conditions lead to ozone increases of 6% in the San Francisco Bay area and along the west coast but only 1–2% inland. Simulations combining climate effects predict that ozone will increase 3–10% in various regions of California. This increase is partly offset by projected future emissions reductions, and a combined climate and emissions simulation yields ozone reductions of 3–9% in the Central Valley and almost no net change in the San Francisco Bay area. We find that different portions of the model domain have widely varying sensitivity to climate parameters. In particular, the San Francisco Bay region is more strongly influenced by temperature changes than inland regions, indicating that air quality in this region may worsen under future climate regimes.

41. Hopkin, M. Carbon sinks threatened by increasing ozone. Nature 448, 396–397 (26 July 2007) | doi:10.1038/448396b; July 25, 2007.
Pollutant poisons plants and hampers photosynthesis.

Rising levels of ozone pollution over the coming century will erode the ability of plants to absorb carbon dioxide from the atmosphere, a new climate-modelling study predicts. Ozone is already known to be a minor greenhouse gas, but the new calculations highlight another, indirect way in which it is likely to influence global warming by 2100.

42. NASA News Stories Archive, "NASA STUDY LINKS "SMOG" TO ARCTIC WARMING," March 15, 2006,
http://earthobservatory.nasa.gov/Newsroom/NasaNews/2006/2006031521918.html

43. P. G. Simmonds, P.G. Significant growth in surface ozone at Mace Head, Ireland, 1987–2003. Atmos. Env. V. 38, Issue 28, Sep. 2004, pp. 4769–4778, doi:10.1016/j.atmosenv.2004.04.036
Background ozone O_3 observations at Mace Head on the west coast of Ireland since 1987 show a significant positive trend of 0.49±0.19 ppb year-1 through to 2003. Increasing trends are observed for all seasons, with the largest trends during the winter season, 0.63±0.31 ppb year-1 and the smallest trends during the summer, 0.39±0.25 ppb year-1. However, this growth rate has not been consistent over time with a major anomaly evident in 1998–1999. This major O_3 perturbation is correlated with variations of CO_2, CO, CH_4, H_2 and CH_3Cl, which are likely due to large-scale biomass burning events in tropical and boreal regions during 1997–1999 coupled with an intense El Niño event.

44. Mickley, L.J. et. al. Effects of future climate change on regional air pollution episodes in the United States. Geophys. Res. Lett. Vol. 31, no. 24, [np]. Dec
We examine the impact of future climate change on regional air pollution meteorology in the United States by conducting a transient climate change (1950–2052) simulation in a general circulation model (GCM) of the Goddard Institute of Space Studies (GISS). We include in the GCM two tracers of anthropogenic pollution, combustion carbon monoxide (COt) and black carbon (BCt). Sources of both tracers and the loss frequency of COt are held constant in time, while wet deposition of BCt responds to the changing climate. Results show that the severity and duration of summertime regional pollution episodes in the midwestern and northeastern United States increase significantly relative to present. Pollutant concentrations during these episodes increase by 5–10% and the mean episode duration increases from 2 to 3–4 days. These increases appear to be driven by a decline in the frequency of mid-latitude cyclones tracking across southern Canada. The cold fronts associated with these cyclones are known to provide the main mechanism for ventilation of the midwestern and northeastern United States. Mid-latitude cyclone frequency is expected to decrease in a warmer climate; such a decrease is already apparent in long-term observations. Mixing depths over the midwest and northeast increase by 100–240 m in our future-climate simulation, not enough to compensate for the increased stagnation resulting from reduced cyclone frequency.

45. C. Hogrefe, et. al. Simulating changes in regional air pollution over the eastern United States due to changes in global and regional climate and emissions JGR, VOL. 109, D22301, doi:10.1029/2004JD004690, 2004.
To simulate ozone (O_3) air quality in future decades over the eastern United States, a modeling system consisting of the NASA Goddard Institute for Space Studies Atmosphere-Ocean Global Climate Model, the Pennsylvania State University/National Center for Atmospheric Research mesoscale regional climate model (MM5), and the Community Multiscale Air Quality model has been applied. Estimates of future emissions of greenhouse gases and ozone precursors are based on the A2 scenario developed by the Intergovernmental Panel on Climate Change (IPCC), one of the scenarios with the highest growth of CO_2 among all IPCC scenarios. Simulation results for five summers in the 2020s,

2050s, and 2080s indicate that summertime average daily maximum 8-hour O_3 concentrations increase by 2.7, 4.2, and 5.0 ppb, respectively, as a result of regional climate change alone with respect to five summers in the 1990s. Through additional sensitivity simulations for the five summers in the 2050s the relative impact of changes in regional climate, anthropogenic emissions within the modeling domain, and changed boundary conditions approximating possible changes of global atmospheric composition was investigated. Changed boundary conditions are found to be the largest contributor to changes in predicted summertime average daily maximum 8-hour O_3 concentrations (5.0 ppb), followed by the effects of regional climate change (4.2 ppb) and the effects of increased anthropogenic emissions (1.3 ppb). However, when changes in the fourth highest summertime 8-hour O_3 concentration are considered, changes in regional climate are the most important contributor to simulated concentration changes (7.6 ppb), followed by the effect of increased anthropogenic emissions (3.9 ppb) and increased boundary conditions (2.8 ppb). Thus, while previous studies have pointed out the potentially important contribution of growing global emissions and intercontinental transport to O_3 air quality in the United States for future decades, the results presented here imply that it may be equally important to consider the effects of a changing climate when planning for the future attainment of regional-scale air quality standards such as the U.S. national ambient air quality standard that is based on the fourth highest annual daily maximum 8-hour O_3 concentration.

46. Elisabeth Rosenthal, "In Spain, Water Is a New Battleground," *New York Times*, June 3, 2008, http://www.nytimes.com/2008/06/03/world/europe/03dry.html?scp=1&sq=global+warming+Desertification&st=nyt.

47. "Desertification Alters Regional Ecosystem Climate Interactions," *ScienceDaily*, Jan. 27, 2005, http://www.sciencedaily.com/releases/2005/01/050125091447.htm.

48. William H. Schlesinger, W.H. et. al. Biological Feedbacks in Global Desertification. *Science*, March 2, 1990: Vol. 247. no. 4946, pp. 1043–1048, DOI: 10.1126/science.247.4946.1043.
Studies of ecosystem processes on the Jornada Experimental Range in southern New Mexico suggest that longterm grazing of semiarid grasslands leads to an increase in the spatial and temporal heterogeneity of water, nitrogen, and other soil resources. Heterogeneity of soil resources promotes invasion by desert shrubs, which leads to a further localization of soil resources under shrub canopies. In the barren area between shrubs, soil fertility is lost by erosion and gaseous emissions. This positive feedback leads to the desertification of formerly productive land in southern New Mexico and in other regions, such as the Sahel. Future desertification is likely to be exacerbated by global climate warming and to cause significant changes in global biogeochemical cycles.

49. Nasrallah, H.A. & Balling Jr., R.C. Impact of desertification on temperature trends in the Middle East. Environmental Monitoring and Assessment, Volume 37, Numbers 1-3, pp 265–271 Jan. 1995, DOI 10.1007/BF00546894.
The intense interest in desertification and climate change has stimulated detailed studies of temperature records in many areas of the world. In this investigation, the temperature records from the Middle East region are analyzed over the period 1950–1990. Results reveal a linear, statistically significant temperature increase of 0.07 °C/decade over the 41-year period. An analysis of spatial controls on these temperature changes reveals a warming effect associated with both overgrazing and the degree of human-induced desertification. The results of this study are consistent with theoretical and empirical studies

predicting and demonstrating a warming signal associated with these land surface changes in the world's dryland areas.

50. Burke, E. J., Brown, S. J., and Christidis, N., 2006: Modeling the recent evolution of global drought and projections for the 21st century with the Hadley Centre climate model. J Hydrometeorol, 7, 1,113–1,125. doi: 10.1175/JHM544.1.

INDEX